The Church O...
Presidin...

Bishop Charles E. Blake, Sr.

Christ's Extreme Sacrifice Calls For Our Extreme Commitment

"For the love of Christ constraineth us; because we thus judge, that if one died for all, then were all dead: And that he died for all, that they which live should not henceforth live unto themselves, but unto him which died for them, and rose again."
- 2 Corinthians 5:14-15 (KJV)

Order materials today from the Power for Living Series:

Church Of God In Christ Publishing House
2500 Lamar Avenue, Memphis, Tennessee 38114
P.O. Box 140636, Memphis, Tennessee 38114
Toll Free: 1-877-746-8578 | Fax: (901) 743-1555
Website: www.cogicpublishinghouse.net
Email: sales@cogicpublishinghouse.net

CHURCH OF GOD IN CHRIST, INC.
ANNUAL SUNDAY SCHOOL LESSON COMMENTARY 2015–2016
INTERNATIONAL SUNDAY SCHOOL LESSONS

Mark A. Ellis

Chairman, Publishing Board

Copyright © 2015 by Urban Ministries, Inc.

Bible art: Aaron and Alan Hicks

TABLE OF CONTENTS

Winter Quarter 2015-2016

Fall Quarter 2015

TABLE OF CONTENTS

TABLE OF CONTENTS

FROM THE PRESIDING BISHOP'S DESK

To all Students and Teachers of Sunday School,

I want to express my heartfelt gratitude to all of those who have consistently purchased our Annual Commentary for the past four years. Your continued dedication to the Church Of God In Christ's literature has helped to enrich the lives of those you have come in contact with in our local, district, and jurisdictional Sunday School Departments. I also want to say welcome and thank you to all of those who are first-time buyers of our Annual Commentary; I pray that this book will richly enhance your lives for the betterment of your families and also your very own spiritual life.

This year is going to be a year of not only receiving spiritual growth from seeds which have been previously sown, but I also believe it will be a year of dedication, fasting, prayer, and extreme spiritual growth and commitment.

The theme for this year has been "Christ's Extreme Sacrifice Calls For Our Extreme Commitment." Therefore, I have agreed to include, for the first time ever, a copy of the message God gave me to preach during our 2015 Leadership Conference.

I pray this message will enrich your lives as it has enriched mine. Please feel free to use it any way God places in your Spirit. My hope is many sermons, homilies, and teaching excerpts will be extracted from it. I am truly humbled by the God-inspired messages which may be gleamed from this, because that is how God works.

Let me thank UMI and the Church Of God In Christ's Publishing Board and Publishing House for their hard work and dedication in supporting churches across the country who support what we believe, not only as a church but as a people. I would like to also say thank you to Bishop Alton Gatlin and his entire Sunday School Department Team for their hard work as well. Lastly but not least, thank you members of the Church Of God In Christ, thank you every Pastor, First Lady, Elder, Missionary, Teacher, and Student who have purchased our literature. Because of your support, our church will not only go forward but be a better ministry for future generations.

Bishop Charles Edward Blake Sr.
Presiding Bishop of the Church Of God In Christ Inc.
Seventh in Succession

FROM THE DESK OF CHAIRMAN MARK ELLIS

To God be the glory for all of the many wonderful things he has done,

What a blessing and joy it is to write another heartfelt letter for our own Sunday School Annual Commentary. Since undertaking this wonderful project with UMI, it has been a blessing to the body of the Church Of God In Christ.

Hebrews 9:22 says, **"And almost all things are by the law purged with blood; and without shedding of blood is no remission,"** which means that without sacrifice of life, the condemnation of sin would constantly mark us for hell. The use of blood sacrifices in the Bible is important, because in order for man to continue to live under the almighty power of God, the purest substance which causes man to live must be shed. So God instituted the blood sacrifice by using the purest of animals to cover the stains of sin caused by the fall of Adam. Yet those sacrifices were not enough, because an animal's blood was not human blood; therefore it could only go so far to cover, not erase, the black mark of sin.

Therefore, in order for man to have a total attainment for his sins, a man who was pure of sin had to be sacrificed in order for the contamination of sin to be completely erased. It was impossible to use the descendants of Adam, because their blood was no longer pure due to the corruptive nature of sin. God put His plan in motion and in Genesis 3:15 says, **"And I will put enmity between thee and the woman, and between thy seed and her seed; it shall bruise thy head, and thou shalt bruise his heel."** The plan from the beginning of the fall was to have Jesus come down in flesh and pay for the sins of the entire human race, by undergoing the most extreme sacrifice a man can give—through death, as stated by John 15:13: **"Greater love hath no man than this, that a man lay down his life for his friends.'"**

Jesus laid down His life for His friends, those who walked with Him daily, who listened to His wisdom, and who believed in Him as the Son of God. In addition, because Jesus was divine was able to see the millions of followers who would do just like His disciples.

Christ's Extreme Sacrifice Calls For Our Extreme Commitment; **"For the love of Christ constraineth us; because we thus judge, that if one died for all then were all dead: And that he died for all, that they which live should not henceforth live unto themselves, but unto him which died for them, and rose again"** (2 Corinthians 5:14–15). We are indebted to Jesus because of His sacrifice, and indebted to the Father because He is the Father and provided the sacrifice. People of God, now is the time for us to show forth our dedication to the faith which we hold so dear. Now is the time for us to sustain holiness and righteousness; now is the time for us to stand against the kingdom of Satan because of the Extreme Sacrifice that Jesus gave for us.

Just like Jesus descended into hell and snatched the keys of death from the devil, we too must descend into the battlefield and fight for the Kingdom of God. For every injustice we must stand, for every attack against Christianity we must stand, and for every discrimination against the children of God we must stand. Just as Christ hung on the Cross bleeding for our sins, we must lift up our Christ through our commitment. **"And I, if I be lifted up from the Earth, will draw all men unto me"** (John 12:32).

Superintendent Mark A. Ellis
Chairman of the Publishing Board
Church Of God In Christ, Inc.

FROM THE CHAIRMAN OF MARKETING

To all Believers and Workers of Christ everywhere,

Do you remember the day you received Jesus Christ as your personal Savior? Can you recall the time of day that the stain of sin was erased from your life? Can you openly reflect on how empowered you became in your dedication to God? Can you boldly tell of how your personal commitment to the Kingdom of God increased? Have you talked about the still small voice speaking to your soul encouraging you to continue pushing in the midst of a dark situation?

If you can recall all of these things that happened on that great day, then surely we can renew the fight for holiness and peace with all men and women. We are living in a period in which people are constantly battling with mental, physical, and spiritual issues, yet it appears as if the voice of Christ has been silenced by His own people. How can men and women of different nationalities and religions have the same day of change that we had when our commitment to God the Father has waned? What would we be if Christ's commitment on the Cross waned? What would we have become if Christ did not fight for all of God's creation to be accepted into the baptism of His own blood?

Christ's Extreme Sacrifice Calls for Our Extreme Commitment! His personal sacrifice calls for us to not only be committed when it comes to personal salvation, but to drive our commitment within our churches, communities, schools, and government. As Starbucks CEO Howard Schultz said, "When you're surrounded by people who share a passionate commitment around a common purpose, anything is possible."

As children of God, we must become passionate about the sacrifice of Christ Jesus, and tell of how His saving grace allowed us to have a new chance at life. We owe God more than just words of adoration and hand claps of praise, more than just dancing and singing because He brought us out of the jaws of death; what God has done for us will never come close to paying off our indebtedness to Him. We are slaves to Him! We are shackled and chained to a ministry, a path, a way of life that calls for us to moan and cry commitment. Romans 12:1 declares, "I beseech you therefore, brethren, by the mercies of God, that ye present you bodies a living sacrifice, holy acceptable unto God, which is your reasonable service." Holiness is our reasonable service to God; sanctification is our reasonable service to God; attending church and working in a ministry are our reasonable service to God, but talking about Jesus, winning a soul to Christ, and showing compassion for your enemies and those who have wronged you; you then must go beyond your reasonable service.

Many thanks to the Saints of God, the Church Of God In Christ Publishing Board/ House, and their continued dedication to the Word and work of the Lord. To all of the departments and churches across the country for their loyal support of the Church Of God In Christ's literature. As always, let me personally thank each of you for your continued support and encouragement by purchasing the curriculums. Remember, without you, this dream wouldn't have become a reality, and a church without its people is just an empty shell.

Yours for service,

Evangelist Sandra Smith Jones
Chairman of Marketing/Sales
Church Of God In Christ Publishing Board

FROM THE SENIOR ADVISOR TO THE PUBLISHING HOUSE

Dear Sunday School Scholar,

The Church Of God In Christ Publishing Board is providing this excellent curriculum for your use and edification. I know you will enjoy the time spent preparing yourself to teach and be taught the meaning and purpose for the Word of God in everyday living. The devil has attempted to thwart the religious and practical agenda for the Word in our daily lives, but the Sunday School and the Power For Living curriculum are major tactics against that objective. This letter is my attempt to convince you to maintain your commitment and faithfulness to Sunday School and especially use of our COGIC curriculum. Remember Galatians 6:6–7: "Let him that is taught in the word communicate unto him that teacheth in all good things. Be not deceived; God is not mocked: for whatsoever a man soweth, that shall he also reap." Therefore, we are committed to sowing the Word of God through our Power For Living curriculum and our churches, families, and life experiences will do better!

There is no greater goal than entire families weekly attending Sunday School and receiving a fresh and anointed Word during class. Each teacher has the opportunity of using the hour to nourish the student with Word, purpose, and spirit that enables him or her to encounter the coming week's circumstances. The goal of educating is truly powerful and is the means of providing a systematic righteous method to instill principles and establish well-developed points of reference and guidance to successful living.

Now laid before you is a year's worth of Scripture and commentary leading to personal communication that will enable you to nourish and sustain the Sunday School student. Weekly, I teach a class of young men that I developed from the surrounding community. This time is a very positive time to establish a line of evidence that church is yet a viable source for life. The lesson is presented each Sunday, and if they stay for worship, I will stand to preach to members and visitors more ready to hear a fresh and anointed Word. Conversely, those who don't attend Sunday School are usually less prepared to hear, understand, and be led by the Word. The Bible is correct: "So then faith cometh by hearing, and hearing by the word of God" (Romans 10:17). Take every opportunity to create stronger disciples and use the Power For Living curriculum for training believers to make a better community.

Bless You,

Bishop David Allen Hall Sr.

FROM THE INTERNATIONAL SUNDAY SCHOOL PRESIDENT

Greetings Saints of God,

What a joy it is to greet you in the Name of the Lord! We are so grateful for the opportunity to again partner with the COGIC Publishing Board in producing what we believe is a thorough, concise, and most helpful Annual Sunday School Commentary.

Our Presiding Bishop has challenged us to consider how Christ's Extreme Sacrifice Calls for Our Extreme Commitment (2 Corinthians 5:14–15). As Sunday School leaders and workers, we must ask ourselves on a weekly basis: are we making the extreme commitment necessary for our students and Sunday Schools to flourish and grow?

As a sanctified church, it is critical that we maintain our witness and make a commitment to holy living. One of the ways this is accomplished is through the systematic study of God's Word in Sunday School, the biblical foundation for every believer.

How are we going to attract those not attending Sunday School? How are we going to reach the lost in our church communities? How are we going to impact our city? These questions should come to mind as we seek the Lord for a radical vision for our Sunday Schools within the walls of our church and in the community and city beyond our church's walls.

The Quarterly Commentaries and Teacher Tips offered this year were written by some of our church's finest scholars and theologians. These tools are purposed to aid you in making that extreme commitment to your class and/or Sunday School.

It's time for us to prepare for the great harvest of souls that is upon us! Join me in seeking the King for a radical vision to accomplish His bidding upon the earth through the ministry of Sunday School!

In His Service,
Bishop Alton E. Gatlin

FROM THE COGIC-UMI
SUNDAY SCHOOL LIAISON

Dear Sunday School Student,

Welcome to what will be twelve months of Bible Study of some of the most important themes in the Word of God. The Presiding Bishop's theme, "Christ's Extreme Sacrifice Calls for Our Extreme Commitment," is perfect for the Sunday School Curriculum planned for 2015–2016.

The lessons for the first three months are designed to help us achieve true spiritual growth as we study the work of the Holy Spirit in the book of Acts. Just like praying, sharing, being in unity, witnessing, and having courage was vital to the growth of the early church, it is equally important today. There will always be opposition to the truth. Therefore it becomes the believer's duty to never allow the enemies of the faith to cause them to waver. The Spirit is not for sale. The believer, also, should not be biased or prejudiced; he or she should want everyone, in spite of any racial or cultural differences, to be saved. The reading for this quarter seeks to accomplish this in each of us.

The lessons in the winter quarter will focus on worship. They will show how the most important evidence of true sacrifice is obedience to God's Word. Even though certain days are set aside to celebrate certain aspects of service and praise, the most important evidence of true worship is in how we love and treat our brother. The quarter will also lift the importance of Christian marriage and a strong family to the building of God's Kingdom.

The spring quarter might be one of the most important quarters of the year. The indispensable foundation to the spiritual growth of any believer is the strength of his faith: "...without faith it is impossible to please him" (Hebrews 11:6). The lessons on powerful faith, simple faith, struggling faith, Resurrection faith, renewed faith, increased faith, etc., will inspire your commitment to God to go to an higher level.

And finally, the summer quarter focuses on the Believer becoming a new creation. This lesson centers on repentance and obedience to God being a vital part of the new birth. This quarter also raises and attempts to answer the question, why people do things they know are wrong? You will take a close look at how and why the world has gone wrong and what God is doing to repair it.

The 2015-2016 Annual Commentary for this coming year is excellent and fits perfectly with the Presiding Bishop's theme. The weapons of the saints are not like those in the world. No matter how great the opposition, we must continue to be steadfast in love and faith. If you study carefully all the lessons in this commentary, your ability to be "steadfast and unmovable" will always abound.

Bishop J. L. Whitehead Jr., B.A., M.Div.

Review Team:
Pastor Charles Hawthorne, Ph.D., Elder Herman W. Hullum, B.A., M.A., D.Min., Evangelist Iretha Sanford, Th.D. (candidate), Elder Avery Brown, B.A., M.A., M.Div.

COGIC PUBLISHING BOARD
2015-2016

Mark Ellis
Chairman of the Board

Uleses Henderson
1st Vice Chairman
(Incumbent)

Sandra S. Jones
Vice Chairman
(Incumbent)

Dr. Joe Chase Jr.
Secretary
(Incumbent)

Bishop E. Charles
Connor
(Incumbent)

Bishop David Hall Sr.

Bishop Welton
Lawrence
(Incumbent)

Bishop O.L. Meadows
(Incumbent)

Stephen Savage
COGIC Photographer
(Incumbent)

Reggie Witherspoon
(Incumbent)

Superintendent
Tony Campbell

Dr. Sabrina Ellis

Supervisor
Gracie Davis Harris

Administrative
Assistant
Dr. Philip Jackson

The team who works diligently every day to bring the best in scriptural discipleship publications to you and your Church.

Vickie Burse
Chief Operations Officer

Veronica Johnson
Executive Admin Assistant

LaTrina Smith
Accounting Manager

Margaret Hinton
Accounting Lead

Dorothy Driver
Accounting Clerk

Delores Johnson
Receptionist

Barachias Irons
Manuscript Supervisor

Darius Willis
Special Projects Coordinator

Anissa Everett
Design Artist

Erica Wilkins
Proofreader

Myers Jimerson
Proofreader

Phyllis Dearing
Proofreader

James Ross
Picker, Packer, Shipper

Samantha Martin
Operations Supervisor

Willie Simms
Picker, Packer, Shipper

John Davis
Auditor

Cebron Lee
Picker

Joseph Davis IV
Picker

LaQuanta Reed
Auditor

Tiffany Douglas
Auditor

Sherri Elrod
Auditor

Gloria Lee
CSR

Judy Booth
CSR

Damonic David
CSR

Tephanie Calvin
CSR

Edward Broen
CSR

LaTonya Rogers
CSR

LaTonya Richardson
CSR

The Publishing House Team Customer Service Department
They process credit card payments for phone orders
Handle all email and mail-in orders with an up-to-date tracking system

Warehouse/Shipping Department
Utilize state-of-the-art inventory control and order picking technology

Production/Pre-press Department
One six-pocket Muller Martini Saddle Stitcher

Manuscript Department
Responsible for all reading, proofing, editing, and editorial enhancing of all literature

HISTORIC EXECUTIVE COMMISSION OF BISHOP MASON

The Church Of God In Christ celebrates its historic 107–108th year as a primary classical Holiness-Pentecostal body and global voice of holiness. These men of God took their mandates seriously and set the standards we all enjoy today. They believed as a collective body in holiness, evangelizing the world and edifying believers through our faith, worship, and commitment to biblically based tenets. *"Their legacy and hard work continues today."*

(Seated, left to right): Bishop Barker; Bishop O.M. Kelly; Bishop J.O. Patterson Sr.; Bishop U.E. Miller; Bishop J.S. Bailey; Bishop C.H. Mason *(Centered)*; Bishop A.B. McEwen; Bishop O.T. Jones Sr.; Bishop S.E. Crouch; Bishop W. Wells; Bishop F.D. Washington.

(Standing, left to right): Bishop L.H. Ford; Bishop C.L. Anderson; Bishop J. White; Bishop C.E. Bennett; Bishop R.E. Ranger; Bishop F.L. Haynes; Bishop B. Lyles; Bishop C.D. Love; Bishop Coy Brown; Bishop T.D. Iglehart; Bishop A.M. Cohen.

This was the Executive Board of Bishop C.H. Mason, men of power and influence, men who helped begin the process in the life of the Church Of God In Christ.

THE MESSAGE FOR
THE CHURCH OF GOD IN CHRIST

by Presiding Bishop Charles E. Blake, Sr.

Christ's Extreme Sacrifice
Calls For Our Extreme Commitment

"For the love of Christ constraineth us; because we thus judge, that if one died for all, then were all dead: And that he died for all, that they which live should not henceforth live unto themselves, but unto him which died for them, and rose again" (2 Corinthians 5:14–15).

Individuals who have made extreme sacrifices, extreme commitments, and radical departures from the norm have transformed the world. Extreme people have brought about extreme changes. There are a host of highly motivated entities and groups in our world today. They exert and exercise tremendous influence on the attitudes and behavior of people. The impact of their actions and mentality has had and continues to have a transformational effect on the nature and quality of life.

Osama bin Laden was born in 1957. His father was a billionaire who had gained his wealth through massive construction projects. Osama inherited over 20 million dollars and received an allowance of an additional seven million dollars per year.

He was raised to be a devout Sunni Muslim. He strongly hated the materialism and moral practices of the U.S. He strongly hated Jewish people, Christians, and Shia Muslims. He dedicated his life and fortune to developing an army of militant terrorist soldiers who would fight against these enemies.

Though he was wealthy, he lived like a nomad: sleeping in caves and tents, being ejected from one nation after another, that he might pursue his cause and accomplish his objectives.

On September 11, 2001, nineteen of his men undertook a suicide mission and boarded four separate airplanes: two of them crashed into the World Trade Center towers, one into the Pentagon, and the final plane crashed en route to Washington, D.C., to impact the White House or another critical target. About three thousand people died that day, and over the years, hundreds of thousands more died in other missions and conflicts in which he was involved. One evil, deranged, highly motivated man had a devastating impact on the world. He died for his cause on May 2, 2011. To this day, groups like ISIS, al Qaeda, and the Taliban continue his evil legacy, placing fear in the hearts of millions. One man changed the way we travel, the American way of life, and the lives of millions.

Bill Gates makes one hundred dollars per second. His net worth is 80 billion dollars—eighty thousand million dollars. He dropped out of Harvard to start Microsoft at the age of 20. The year of his 23rd birthday, Microsoft made 2.5 million dollars.

A short time later, he created the software MS-DOS and licensed IBM to use the software in each of its computers, and also sold licenses to other computer manufacturers. Microsoft west public in 1986 at $21 dollars a share, and one year later stock sold at $90 dollars per share. He became a billionaire at 38 years of age.

I would say that he is an extremely high-motivated individual who has had a significant impact on the world. He changed the way we work and the way we live.

Martin Luther King Jr. was a highly motivated and extremely committed individual. He was physically assaulted and ultimately assassinated because of his commitment to freedom and justice. An annual national holiday is proclaimed in his honor, celebrated the third Monday of January. He was a champion for freedom and justice and his life made a difference.

Bishop C.H. Mason, founder of the Church Of God In Christ, was a highly motivated and extremely committed individual. Because of his stand against war and the bearing of arms, he came under the scrutiny of the FBI. Because of his preaching crusades, he sometimes faced jail in towns where they did not want him to preach. The Church Of God In Christ stands as a beacon light proclaiming the significance of his ministry.

Individuals who made extreme sacrifices, extreme commitments, and radical departures from the norm have transformed the world. The Apostle Paul was a radical servant of the Lord. He was well qualified to talk about effective and productive service, for he was a tireless evangelist, ready to endure hardness as a good soldier of Jesus Christ.

When other so-called religious leaders tried to diminish and minimize his ministry, he responded: "I say again, let no one think me a fool. If otherwise, at least receive me as a fool, that I also may boast a little. Are they Hebrews? So am I. Are they Israelites? So am I. Are they the seed of Abraham? So am I. Are they ministers of Christ?—I speak as a fool—I am more: in labors more abundant, in stripes above measure, in prisons more frequently, in deaths often. From the Jews five times I received forty stripes minus one. Three times I was beaten with rods; once I was stoned; three times I was shipwrecked; a night and a day I have been in the deep; in journeys often, in perils of waters, in perils of robbers, in perils of my own countrymen, in perils of the Gentiles, in perils in the city, in perils in the wilderness, in perils in the sea, in perils among false brethren; in weariness and toil, in sleeplessness often, in hunger and thirst, in fastings often, in cold and nakedness—besides the other things, what comes upon me daily: my deep concern for all the churches" (2 Corinthians 11:16, 22–28, NKJV).

His letters comprise a significant portion of the New Testament. Ultimately, he was executed because of his faith. Paul was a person of extreme commitment.

In one of his letters, Paul gives us insights into the why of his commitment: "Therefore, since we have this ministry, as we have received mercy, we do not lose heart. But we have renounced the hidden things of shame, not walking in craftiness nor handling the word of God deceitfully, but by manifestation of the truth commending ourselves to every man's conscience in the sight of God" (2 Corinthians 4:1–2, NKJV).

We must remember that God has honored us by calling us into the ministry. In this passage is the sense of God's grace and mercy in giving frail humans a part in God's ministry. Paul indicates that he is determined to walk in integrity to be genuine. He says, since God picked us out for this, we are convinced that when God gives the assignment, He gives the ability. So we can step out and be extreme; "being confident of this very thing, that He who has begun a good work in you will complete it until the day of Jesus Christ" (Philippians 1:6, NKJV).

And then in 2 Corinthians 4:7–9, Paul says, "But we have this treasure in earthen vessels, that the excellence of the power may be of God and not of us. We are hard-pressed on every side, yet not crushed; we are perplexed, but not in despair; persecuted, but not forsaken; struck down, but not destroyed" (NKJV).

It's not the package; it's the medicine in the package. The medicine is the Gospel given to Paul. The package was his human body. Give men the medicine and God will do the rest. Understand that it is not you, it's the God in you. You always have something left. You are never crushed, in despair, forsaken or destroyed. God gives you strength to endure. You can make the extreme commitment.

"Therefore we do not lose heart. Even though our outward man is perishing, yet the inward man is being renewed day by day. For our light affliction, which is but for a moment, is working for us a far more exceeding and eternal weight of glory, while we do not look at the things which are seen, but at the things which are not seen. For the things which are seen are temporary, but the things which are not seen are eternal" (2 Corinthians 4:16–18, NKJV).

So Paul says the next step towards extreme commitment is to look at what you cannot see. Look at what God can do and is doing in and for the inward man, not at your problems or your circumstances. Don't look at temporary stuff. If is not about this world that we see and touch, we are reaching toward the eternal. It's a light affliction, but it's working for us.

"For we know that if our earthly house, this tent, is destroyed, we have a building from God, a house not made with hands, eternal in the heavens" (2 Corinthians 5:1, NKJV).

Paul knows he can be extreme here because this is not the main event. When it's over down here, he's going up there.

"Now He who has prepared us for this very thing is God, who also has given us the Spirit as a guarantee. So we are always confident, knowing that while we are at home in the body we are absent from the Lord. For we walk by faith, not by sight. We are confident, yes, well pleased rather to be absent from the body and to be present with the Lord" (2 Corinthians 5–8, NKJV).

The Spirit resides with us to let us know that God is going to keep His promises. People who are not going to keep their promise usually get scarce when the due date is near. Whatever you are going through, let the Holy Ghost fill you and minister to you. Sometimes the Holy Ghost shows up just to let you know that everything is all right. To be absent from the body is to be present with the Lord. When our loved ones who are believers die, we stand around the physical body and feel sorry for them and for ourselves, but their spirits are already in the sweet presence of the Lord.

"For the love of Christ compels us, because we judge thus: that if One died for all, then all died; and He died for all, that those who live should live no longer for themselves, but for Him who died for them and rose again" (2 Corinthians 5:14–15, NKJV).

Time and time again, the Bible proclaims that those who don't know Jesus Christ are spiritually dead.

"For to be carnally minded is death, but to be spiritually minded is life and peace" (Romans 8:6, NKJV).

Paul would remember when he had no clue regarding the work and the will of God. He had actually fought the church, and participated in the murder of Stephen, a deacon.

A spiritually dead person is unresponsive to God. He or she is doomed in this world and the world to come. He or she is sentenced to death and waiting to be executed.

Paul says that without Christ, we were all dead.

"And you He made alive, who were dead in trespasses and sins, in which you once walked according to the course of this world, according to the prince of the power of the air, the spirit who now works in the sons of disobedience, among whom also we all once conducted ourselves in the lusts of our flesh, fulfilling the desires of the flesh and of the mind, and were by nature children of wrath, just as the others" (Ephesians 2:1–3, NKJV).

"This is a faithful saying and worthy of all acceptance, that Christ Jesus came into the world to save sinners, of whom I am chief" (1 Timothy 1:15, NKJV).

"For I am the least of the apostles, who am not worthy to be called an apostle, because I persecuted the church of God. But by the grace of God I am what I am" (from 1 Corinthians 15:9–10, NKJV).

"Greater love has no one than this, than to lay down one's life for his friends" (John 15:13, NKJV).

There are no words that one can speak—no level of eloquence, no action that one can initiate, no gesture, no gift—as forceful than laying down one's life for another. Militants die for their god. Our God became man and died for us.

He was our substitute—innocent, worthy, related.

It was not an impulsive rash action; it was planned from the foundation of the world. His excellence for our pitifulness.

It was as if a man wanted to help dogs—He became a dog, lived as a dog, was treated like a dog, died like a dog. That condescension would not be a great as what Jesus has done.

"And the Word became flesh and dwelt among us, and we beheld His glory, the glory as of the only begotten of the Father, full of grace and truth" (John 1:14, NKJV).

"Let this mind be in you which was also in Christ Jesus, who, being in the form of God, did not consider it robbery to be equal with God, but made Himself of no reputation, taking the form of a bondservant, and coming in the likeness of men. And being found in appearance as a man, He humbled Himself and became obedient to the point of death, even the death of the cross. Therefore God also has highly exalted Him and given Him the name which is above every name, that at the name of Jesus every knee should bow, of those in heaven, and of those on earth, and of those under the earth, and that every tongue should confess that Jesus Christ is Lord, to the glory of God the Father" (Philippians 2:5–11, NKJV).

He arose from the dead. He is both Lord and King. His Resurrection assures that that His sacrifice is accepted by God the Father.

His love constrains us, compels us. To constrain is to secure as if by bonds, to hold back by force. To compel is to drive forcefully or irresistibly. It is to impose overwhelming pressure.

We should not therefore live for ourselves, but Him who died for us and rose again. What do you do for someone who dies for you and rises from the dead?

He made the extreme sacrifice for us; we should make the extreme commitment to Him.

We should make an extreme commitment to His Kingdom agenda. He is King of kings and Lord of lords.

He needs some radical servants.

"But seek first the kingdom of God and His righteousness, and all these things shall be added to you" (Matthew 6:33, NKJV).

We need to make an extreme commitment to faith. We need to make up our minds that we are just going to believe God. The Church Of God In Christ was a faith church before there was a faith church. Our God is still able to raise the dead and heal incurable diseases. He still calls those things that be not as though they were. With God, nothing is impossible. You name it, God can do it. God is still a miracle worker.

"Most assuredly, I say to you, he who believes in Me, the works that I do he will do also; and greater works than these he will do, because I go to My Father. And whatever you ask in my name, that I will do, that the Father may be glorified in the Son. If you ask anything in my name, I will do it" (John 14:12–14, NKJV).

We need to make an extreme commitment to holy living. We still believe Hebrews 12:14: "Pursue peace with all people, and holiness, without which no one will see the Lord" (NKJV).

"Because it is written, 'Be holy, for I am holy'" (1 Peter 1:16, NKJV).

How can we transform the world for Jesus Christ if we are held captive by the same sins that captivate the world?

If a terrorist can die for his faith, then at least we should be willing to live holy for Jesus Christ.

"I beseech you therefore, brethren, by the mercies of God, that you present your bodies a living sacrifice, holy, acceptable to God, which is your reasonable service" (Romans 12:1, NKJV).

We need to make an extreme commitment to radical vision.

"Enlarge the place of your tent, And let them stretch out the curtains of your dwellings; Do not spare; Lengthen your cords, And strengthen your stakes. For you shall expand to the right and to the left, And your descendants will inherit the nations, And make the desolate cities inhabited" (Isaiah 54:2–3, NKJV).

"Ask of Me, and I will give You The nations for Your inheritance, And the ends of the earth for Your possession" (Psalm 2:8, NKJV).

"'Call to Me, and I will answer you, and show you great and mighty things, which you do not know'" (Jeremiah 33:3, NKJV).

Make a radical commitment to be filled with the Holy Ghost.

"But you shall receive power when the Holy Spirit has come upon you; and you shall be witnesses to Me in Jerusalem, and in all Judea and Samaria, and to the end of the earth" (Acts 1:8, NKJV).

"Behold, I give you the authority to trample on serpents and scorpions, and over all the power of the enemy, and nothing shall by any means hurt you" (Luke 10:19, NKJV).

We should make an extreme commitment to holiness.

"Therefore, having these promises, beloved, let us cleanse ourselves from all filthiness of the flesh and spirit, perfecting holiness in the fear of God" (2 Corinthians 7:1, NKJV).

We should make a real commitment to love God and love one another.

"By this we know love, because He laid down His life for us. And we also ought to lay down our lives for the brethren" (1 John 3:16, NKJV).

"Beloved, let us love one another, for love is of God; and everyone who loves is born of God and knows God. He who does not love does not know God, for God is love. In this the love of God was manifested toward us, that God has sent His only begotten Son into the world, that we might live through Him. In this is love, not that we loved God, but that He loved us and sent His Son to be the propitiation for our sins. Beloved, if God so loved us, we also ought to love one another" (1 John 4:7–11, NKJV).

Too few who say that they believe are willing to make an extreme commitment.

"Brethren, I do not count myself to have apprehended; but one thing I do, forgetting those things which are behind and reaching forward to those things which are ahead, I press toward the goal for the prize of the upward call of God in Christ Jesus" (Philippians 3:13–14, NKJV).

"Who shall separate us from the love of Christ? Shall tribulation, or distress, or persecution, or famine, or nakedness, or peril, or sword? ... Yet in all these things we are more than conquerors through Him who loved us. For I am persuaded that neither death nor life, nor angels nor principalities nor powers, nor things present nor things to come, nor height nor depth, nor any other created thing, shall be able to separate us from the love of God which is in Christ Jesus our Lord" (Romans 8:35, 37–39, NKJV).

God said to the church at Ephesus, "You have left your first love." "You don't love Me like you once did."

He said to the church at Laodicea, "I wish that you were either hot or cold, but you are lukewarm."

God is looking for somebody who will be radical for Him.

There is a promotion on the other side of your commitment.

Daniel went through the lion's den, then "So this Daniel prospered in the reign of Darius and in the reign of Cyrus the Persian" (Daniel 6:28, NKJV).

Shadrach, Meshach, and Abed-Nego endured the fiery furnace, "Then the king promoted

Shadrach, Meshach, and Abed-Nego in the province of Babylon" (Daniel 3:30, NKJV).

Abraham was commanded by God to sacrifice his son Isaac, "Then the Angel of the LORD called to Abraham a second time out of heaven, and said: "By Myself I have sworn, says the LORD, because you have done this thing, and have not withheld your son, your only son— blessing I will bless you, and multiplying I will multiply your descendants as the stars of the heaven and as the sand which is on the seashore; and your descendants shall possess the gate of their enemies. In your seed all the nations of the earth shall be blessed, because you have obeyed My voice" (Genesis 22:15–18, NKJV).

"Those who go down to the sea in ships, Who do business on great waters, They see the works of the LORD, And His wonders in the deep" (Psalm 107:23–24, NKJV).

"When He had stopped speaking, He said to Simon, 'Launch out into the deep and let down your nets for a catch.' But Simon answered and said to Him, 'Master, we have toiled all night and caught nothing; nevertheless at Your word I will let down the net'" (Luke 5:4–5, NKJV).

DEPARTMENT OF WOMEN CHURCH OF GOD IN CHRIST 2015-2016

Mother Willie Mae Rivers

We recognize the Department of Women of the Church Of God In Christ in this edition of the 2015-2016 Annual Commentary. As the Church Of God In Christ Publishing House, we want to recognize the women of the Church because they helped bring organization, scriptural knowledge, soul winning, prayer, doctrinal study of the Bible, and overall curriculum structure to the Church which we all enjoy today.

CHURCH OF GOD IN CHRIST, INC. DEPARTMENT OF WOMEN GENERAL SUPERVISOR
(Ex Officio-All Boards)

Mother Willie Mae Rivers

PRESIDENT OF WOMEN'S INTERNATIONAL CONVENTION, ASSISTANT GENERAL SUPERVISOR & CHAIRPERSON OF EXECUTIVE BUSINESS AFFAIRS

Dr. Barbara McCoo Lewis

EXECUTIVES:

Mother Olive L. Brown
*Executive Secretary &
Executive Financial Officer*

Mother Dianne M. Bogan
Assistant Executive Secretary

Mother Stella M. Watson
Assistant Executive Financial Officer

Mother Edith L. McGrew
Vice Chairperson, Executive Board

Mother Artaska King
Chairperson, Advisory Board

Mother (Dr.) Barbara McCoo Lewis
International Marshal

Dr. Juliet White
Assistant Marshal

Mother Dianne M. Bogan
Adjutant Sister to the General Supervisor

Mother Annie P. Moody
Personal Aide to the General Supervisor

History of the Department of Women (Condensed)

Mother
Lizzie Robinson

During the infancy of the Church Of God In Christ in the early 1900s, the work among the women had been started, but lacked organization. They began searching for a woman capable of directing a Women's Department. The name Lizzie Woods—a matron at the Baptist Academy—was continuously brought to Elder Mason's attention. After inquiring, he formed an acquaintance with her. She was introduced to the Church Of God In Christ through the preaching of Elder D.W. Delk. In May 1911, while General Overseer Mason was holding a meeting in the Academy, she received the baptism of the Holy Ghost.

Bishop Charles Mason, with the keen insight God had given him, saw that Lizzie Woods (who later became Lizzie Woods Robinson) would be an organizer able to inspire and direct.

In 1911 at the General Convocation in Memphis, Tennessee, she was appointed Overseer of the Women's Work by Bishop Mason to organize and create such work as would be beneficial to the Church. Mother Robinson began by admonishing the women according to Jeremiah 9:17–20, "Thus saith the LORD of hosts, Consider ye, and call for the mourning women, that they may come; and send for the cunning women, that they may come; and let them make haste, and take up a wailing for us, that our eyes may run down with tears, and our eyelids gush out with waters. For a voice of wailing is heard out of Zion, How are we spoiled! We are greatly confounded, because we have forsaken the land, because our dwellings have cast us out. Yet hear the word of the LORD, O ye women, and let your ear receive the word of his mouth, and teach your daughters wailing, and every one her neighbor lamentation."

Observing a group of women praying and another group reading and studying the Bible, Mother Robinson began her organization by combining the two groups, forming the Prayer and Bible Band. This band was designated to educate others in scriptural knowledge for the purpose of soul winning. Today this band serves as a doctrinal study of the Bible.

This was the beginning of the organizational structure of the Department of Women as we know it.

The Department of Women

The Department of Women shall be under the supervision and direction of a National Supervisor, appointed by the Presiding Bishop with the approval of the General Board. She is the chief administrator of the Department of Women. Her duties are tremendous and varied. The total operation of the Department is her responsibility. If she is to succeed, she must have impeccable character, maintain a consistent prayer life, and have compassion and love for all. With God's wisdom and the guidance of the Holy Spirit, she will be able to fulfill the task assigned to her.

With the consent of the Presiding Bishop and the General Leaders of our Church, the General Supervisor is empowered to:

1. Appoint all Presidents or Chairpersons of the National Boards of the Department of Women.

2. Issue all Certificated of Appointment for these appointees to National Offices, and Certificates of Appointment for National Staff members, as well.

3. Approve all Board, Auxiliaries, Units, Committees, and Personnel that are a part of the Department of Women.

4. Issue all Licenses for women, through the Jurisdictional Supervisor, on a State or Jurisdictional level.

All recommended appointees must have the endorsement of the local Pastor, Jurisdictional Bishop, and the Jurisdictional Supervisor.

The General Supervisor shall review the work of every Jurisdictional Supervisor and National Auxiliary and Unit Leader. She is to keep them informed and give them directions as to the total women's work.

In addition to her administrative duties, she must be an encourager in spiritual matters, a counselor, a judge, an arbitrator, and an advisor. Above all, she is to be an example to the flock and a "Mother" to all.

Jurisdictional Supervisor

In each State/Jurisdiction there is a Supervisor/State Mother who is the leader of the Department of Women. This Supervisor is a liaison between the Women's Department and the Jurisdictional Bishop and General Supervisor. She must be a strong supporter of the Bishop and his vision for the work. She must also be a strong supporter of the General Supervisor, for her direction for the Women's work will come from the General Supervisor. She must be a participant in and a supporter of the Bishop's programs for the Jurisdiction. She must use her influence to encourage the women to do the same. It is appropriate that the Bishop may assign responsibilities to the Supervisor and Women's Department. When this is done, the Supervisor should carry out those duties to the best of her ability.

The Jurisdictional Supervisor, under the direction of her Bishop, is then empowered to:

1. Appoint her official staff and personnel to assist her in carrying out the program for the women's ministry as given to her by the Jurisdictional Bishop and General Supervisor.

2. Examine and appoint all women eligible for credentials in her jurisdiction and obtain license certificates of appointment from the National Department of Women.

3. Issue these license and or certificates of appointment to women who have met all qualifications required on the district, jurisdictional, or national level.

4. Advise of financial obligations in support of ministry of the Department of Women on the jurisdictional and national level. She or her designee will report all finance from the auxiliaries, units, and credential women.

5. A full financial accounting of all income and expenditures should be submitted to the Jurisdictional Bishop.

One of the prime objectives is to work in harmony and agreement with the Jurisdictional Bishop and organize the department of women in the jurisdiction. A strong, well-organized women's department is an asset to the local church, district, and jurisdiction to offer training of women to implement programs in the local church that will help to build the Kingdom of God. Her works should also carry this same program into the districts. When the local and district work is strong, the national and international work will be strengthened. The Supervisor's activity in the jurisdiction must be reviewed and approved by the Jurisdictional Bishop.

The Supervisor's greatest concern should be the up building of the Kingdom of God. She must visit the churches in the jurisdiction. Her focus should be on instructing women to build ministries through prayer and evangelism. The total ministry should include credential holders as well as non-credential holding women. She must not neglect her local church while covering the jurisdictional women's work.

JURISDICTIONAL SUPERVISORS:

Mother Willie Mae Rivers *General Supervisor - South Carolina*	Supv. Agnes Yaba Agyeman *The Republic of Ghana*	Supv. Claudine T. Austin *Virginia Third*
Supv. Barbara McCoo Lewis *Assistant General Supervisor*	Supv. Clara M. Allen *New Hampshire-Greater Eccl.*	Supv. Alberta M. Baker *Florida-Southwestern*
Barbara McCoo Lewis *California-Southern First*	Supv. Katie Allen *Pennsylvania-Commonwealth*	Supv. Margarett L. Baker *Hawaii*
Supv. Corene Wade-Adams *Michigan-North Central*	Supv. Carolyn Anderson *Indiana Second*	Supv. (Dr.) Diana C. Banks *Maryland-Central*
Supv. Doris Ade' *Maine*	Supv. Linda Ashley *Pakistan*	Supv. Mary E. Barnes *Texas Northwest*

Supv. Fanneree Baymon
Massachusetts First

Supv. Wilma S. Beauford, Ph.D.
Pennsylvania Western First

Supv. Lenora C. Beets
Iowa 2nd

Supv. Donya M. Bell
Kentucky-Second

Supv. Hattie K. Bell
Alabama-Third

Supv. Gwendolyn Bell Badon
Louisiana-Eastern, Third

Supv. (Open)
Republic of Rwanda, East Africa

Supv. Dianne M. Bogan
Michigan-Great Lakes, First

Supv. Theresa E. Bolden
Missouri-Eastern, First

Supv. Verna M. Bonner
Tennessee-Eastern Second

Supv. Marjorie Y. Booker
Puerto Rico Commonwealth

Supv. Emma Jane Bowen
Arizona

Supv. Carol T. Brown
West Africa – Ivory Coast

Supv. D. Ann Brown
*South Africa Seventh
Ecclesiastical*

Supv. Olive L. Brown
New Jersey First

Supv. Barbara Bryant
California Southern Evangelistic

Supv. Norma L. Burrell
Michigan Northeast

Supv. Beverly Bush
Indiana North Third

Supv. (Dr.) Joyce Thomas
Campbell
Texas-Southeast Second

Supv. Darlene Carter
EDO COGIC, Nigeria

Supv. Althea Chaplin
New York Western First

Supv. Cecille Ruth Collins
Florida-Southern 3rd

Supv. Armizetta H. Conner
West Virginia

Supv. Annie M. Cooper
Texas-Southwest

Supv. Elizabeth Copeland
Philippines

Supv. Patricia A. Crisp
Oklahoma-Southeast

Supv. Marilyn Cross
Illinois-Third

Supv. Angie Dell Cullins
Illinois-Sixth

Supv. Frances S. Curtis
Michigan-Southwest Second

Supv. Dianne Custis
Delaware

Supv. Plumie Dancey
*California-Northern
Metropolitan*

Supv. Alberta W. Davis
Kansas-Central

Supv. Curlie Davis
Washington State

Supv. Grace Davis-Harris
Wisconsin-Northwest

Supv. Desig. Donna Dawkins
Republic of Panama

Supv. Johnnie S.
Dawson-Harrison
Bahamas

Supv. Hazel B. DeLoney
Arkansas-First

Actg. Supv.
Ann Dickerson-Bragg
*Actg. California Southern
Evangelistic & India*

Supv. Anita Dunn
Ohio Southern

Supv. Claudette Duncan
Malawi Central Africa

Supv. Lendora Early
Arkansas-Third 4

Supv. Ruby M. Earven
Canada COGIC/Michigan

Supv. Mildred Loman Eason
Florida-Central Second

Supv. Mary Ella Eaton
Mississippi-Southern Second

Supv. Regina Edwards
Michigan-Southwest First

Supv. Amy L. Engram
Georgia-Southern Second

Supv. Terrie B. Estes
Connecticut-First

Supv. Ophelia Evans
Texas-Northeast Third

Supv. Valerie J. Fields
Nova Scotia Maritimes

Supv. Bernadette Felder
Nova Scotia Maritimes

Supv. Bertha Fitts
Georgia-Northern Second

Supv. Betty Fort
California-Southern Metro

Supv. Girtha M. Foster
Idaho

Supv. Annie Franklin
Missouri-Western Second

Supv. Gloria Green Fraser
Connecticut-Second

Supv. Sarah Ann Gaston
Mississippi-Northern

Supv. Mabel Gibbons
Alaska

Supv. Thelma Giles-Butts
Ohio-North First

Supv. Barbara
Gillespie-Washington
Illinois-Central 5

Supv. Beulah LaRonce Gordon
Georgia-Southeast

Supv. Lillian E. Gray
Vermont

Supv. Barbara Green
New Jersey-Garden State

Supv. Betty Jean Green
Oregon-Northwest

Supv. Trena Green
Oregon First

Supv. Cloretta Grice
Delaware (Fellowship)

Supv. Gina Hardwick-Johnson
Illinois Seventh

Supv. Frances E. Harris
Montana

Supv. Marcelle Harris
New York-Eastern First

Supv. Shirley M. Harris
Wyoming

Supv. Patricia Ann Hayes
Minnesota

Supv. Pia Haynes Williams
Texas Northeast First

Supv. Valor Herring
California-Western

Supv. JoAnn G. Hill
Florida-Eastern

Supv. Minnie Hill
Haiti

Supv. Perrella Hines
Georgia-Western

Supv. Mary F. Hodge
California- Southern Third

Supv. Anita L. Hollis
Michigan Great Lakes Second 6

Supv. Jacquelin G. Holmes
Virginia-Second

Supv. Martha J. Holmes
Nebraska Eastern

Supv. JoAnne Hooks
California-Southern Fourth

Supv. Corine Huffman
Oklahoma-Northwest

Supv. Shirley Ann Hughes
Illinois First

Supv. Wilma Jean Hughey,
Ph.D.
New York-Western Second

Supv. Richardine L. Hunt
California-Northern First

Supv. Barbara A. Jackson
Ohio Central West

Supv. Annette James
Trinidad & Tobago

Supv. Diane L. Jenkins
Georgia-Northern First

Supv. (Dr.) Sheary D. Johnson
Virginia Fourth

Supv. Blondean Jones
Ohio Northwest

Supv. Princeola H. Jones
New York Central

Supv. Freddie Mae Joy
Maryland Greater First

Supv. Beatrice Ilene Kendell
Michigan Southeast

Supv. Mary Beth Kennedy
Africa-Democratic Republic of Congo

Supv. Harrizene L. Keyes
North Carolina-Greater

Supv. Mary T. Kincaid
Illinois-Fifth East 7

Supv. Artaska King
Wisconsin-Third

Supv. Daisy Leonora King
Jamaica, West Indies

Supv. Sideary M. King
India Fourth

Supv. Deborah R. Kitchen
New Jersey-South

Supv. Lula M. Kitchen
New Mexico

Supv. Maritza Knight
Rhode Island

Supv. Farine Lee
California-North Central

Supv. Peggy Lee
Texas-South Central

Supv. Edna P. Lewis
New York Eastern Third

Supv. Patricia R. Lewis
Brazil

Supv. Mildred Linzy
Korea

Supv. Ernestine R. Lipford
Tennessee-Fifth

Supv. ViCurtis E. Little
Washington, District of Columbia

Supv. Gladys Lockett-Ross
Texas Central Metropolitan

Supv. Patricia D. Lofton
North Carolina-Second

Supv. Gloria J. Lynch
California-Southern Second

Supv. Elizabeth Makopo
South Africa

Supv. Sharon Manning
Connecticut Southern New England

Supv. Martina Martin
Philippines 8

Supv. Vineda Martin
Pennsylvania-Western Second Eccl.

Supv. Willie Mae Martin
Louisiana Eastern Second

Supv. Mattie J. Mayes
Ohio Central East

Supv. (Dr.) Lena Jones McClain
Texas-Southeast First

Supv. Rubeinstein McClure
New York-Southeast

Supv. Alma Faye McDonnell
Nevada First Ecclesiastical

Supv. Blanche D. McGee
California-Valley

Supv. Edith L. McGrew
Georgia Southern Central

Supv. Geraldine E. Miller
Tennessee-Headquarters

Supv. F. Gene Mitchell
Nigeria, Edo State

Supv. Monica Mngadi
South Africa

Supv. Ruthell Monk
Arkansas-Fourth

Supv. Roxalana Moore
Illinois-Southeast

Supv. Betty J. Owens Morrison
Kansas East

Supv. Artie M. Morrow
Texas-Northeast Second

Supv. Bertha Mae Mullins
Nevada Northern First

Supv. Frankie Davis Murray
Mississippi-Southern First

Supv. Dian M. Myler
California-Northeast

Supv. Emily Myrick
Pennsylvania-Koinonia 9

Supv. Sarah L. Newton
Missouri Western First

Supv. Martha Nichols
Michigan-Western

Supv. Maddaline Ann Norfleet
Ethiopia Ecclesiastical

Supv. Geneva Lee Odems
Arkansas Fourth

Supv. Martha Ann Parker
Nebraska

Supv. Emma W. Person
California-Greater Northern II

Supv. Lula Mae Pope
Texas-East

Supv. Katherine Arnett Porter
Montana

Supv. Ida M. Porter
Tennessee-Central

Supv. Dorothy J. Pulliam
Alabama-Second

Supv. Virgie Mae Pulliam
Missouri-Southeast Third

Supv. Evonia L. Purkett
Illinois-Southern Ecclesiastical

Supv. Dollie Simmons Reed
Florida Northwest

Supv. – Open (Reynolds)
Ohio-Northeast

Supv. J.V. Reynolds
UK (United Kingdom)

Supv. Dorothy Richardson
Louisiana Eastern First

Supv. D. Lynnette Riddick
Texas-Western

Supv. Juanita Robinson
Pennsylvania-Eastern

Supv. Gloria Rodgers
Africa-Nigeria 10

Supv. Cheryl J. Rountree
North Dakota

Supv. Nannie Doris Rule
Illinois-Northern

Supv. Herldleen Russell
*Republic of Uganda,
East Africa*

Supv. - Open
Maryland Greater First

Supv. Emma R. Sanders
Indiana North Central/

West Africa Liberia

Supv. Lucy M. Sanders
Georgia-Southern First

Supv. Nancy F. Sanford
*Michigan Northwestern
Harvest*

Supv. – Open (Wagoner)
California Evangel

Supv. Jerrine M. Simmons
St. Lucia Eastern Caribbean

Supv. Christine C. Simpson
Columbia-South America

Supv. Valerie E. D. Sims
Belize, Central America

Supv. Carolyn L. Singleton
New York Eastern Fourth

Supv. Carolyn Smith
Utah

Supv. Doris Smith
Barbados, West Indies

Supv. Rosa Marie Smith
Illinois-Fifth West

Supv. Willie Mae Smith
Barbados & Caribbean

Supv. Clararetha Spencer
Turks and Caicos Islands

Supv. Romanetha Stallworth
Kentucky First

Supv. Dixie Stokes
Canada Western 11

Supv. Darlene B. Stone
Indiana First

Supv. Earlie M.
Strozier-Peppers
Michigan-Southwest Third

Supv. Corine Swindell
Texas-Lone Star

Supv. Marlene D. Talley
Pennsylvania-Keystone

Supv. Mattie B. Taylor
Alabama-First

Supv. Vicki Taylor
Kansas-Southwest

Supv. (Dr.) Wilma H. Taylor
*Republic of Guyana-South
America*

Supv. Billie Jo Thomas
Wisconsin-Southeast First

Supv. Refina Santana Garcia
de Tolentino
Dominican Republic

Supv. Nellie M. Townes
Virginia First

Supv. Charlease Trueblood
Pennsylvania Central

Supv. Mary B. Tucker
*Georgia Northern Central /
Bermuda*

Supv. Lee E. Van Zandt
Maryland-Eastern Shore/
Chile, South America

Supv. Marion V. Vickers
New York-Eastern Second

Supv. LaWanna M. Viers
Good News Eccl. Ikeja Lagos
Nigeria, West Africa

Supv. Joan Walker
California-Southwest

Supv. Mary Jane Walton
Michigan-Southwest Fourth

Supv. Dorothy Ware
Tennessee Eastern First 12

Supv. Bertha A. Washington
Colorado

Supv. Joyce L. Washington
Texas-Southeast Third

Supv. Jeanette A. Watkins
Arkansas Second

Supv. Eulah D. Watson
Mexico

Supv. Stella M. Watson
Germany

Supv. Rosetta Watts
Missouri-Eastern Second

Supv. Ethel Weatherly
Pennsylvania, Penn State
Jurisdiction

Supv. (Dr.) Mary M. Welch
California-Northwest

Supv. DeOla Wells-Johnson
Tennessee Fourth

Supv. Vivian M. Wesson
Tennessee Southwest

Supv. Loretta L. Whitsett
Michigan Southwest Agape

Supv. LuVonia Whittley
Illinois-Midwest

Supv. Helen V. Williams
Guatemala

Supv. Ruby D. Williams
Florida-Western

Supv. Ruby Lois Williams
Georgia Metro

Supv. – Open (Willis)
South Dakota

Supv. Velma Wilson-Slack
Louisiana-Greater New
Orleans

Supv. Vanessa Winbush
Gatlin
Louisiana-First

Supv. Vivian B. Wooden
New Jersey-Third

Supv. Robin L. Wright
Japan 13

Supv. (Open) King
Vancouver, British Columbia

Supv. – (Open) Young

Contact:
Dist. Missy Gwendolyn
Townsend
15250 32nd Avenue So.,
#69795
Seatac, WA 98168
206-588-6910

OVERVIEW SCRIPTURE MEMORIZATION
Levite Ministry

Tony Simmons
Church Of God
In Christ

The Levite Ministry (concept of Scripture Memorization) is a new initiative of the International Sunday School Department of the Church Of God In Christ led by Bishop Alton Gatlin. It is a comprehensive memorization ministry to train the entire church from ages 3 to 100. Since the program is promoted through the Sunday School Department, it gives the Sunday School teacher the opportunity, along with studying the Word of God weekly, to incorporate Scripture memorization for development of daily personal devotion, increase Bible knowledge, and increase understanding of life application. Through the implementation of Sunday School, students learn to love God's Word and memorize it daily, which will benefit all churches and bless the Kingdom of God, as we have a better understanding of what it means to live a holy life that pleases God by memorizing His Word. The Bible declares in Psalm 119:11: "Thy word have I hid in mine heart, that I might not sin against thee."

SCRIPTURE LEVITE MINISTRY IN SUNDAY SCHOOL
Scripture Memorization

Deuteronomy 31:8	Job 13:15	Matthew 18:20
Psalm 9:10	2 Corinthians 5:17	Matthew 4:19
Psalm 23:4	Romans 12:1	Galatians 2:20
Psalm 55:22	2 Timothy 3:16	John 14:21
Matthew 11:28–29	John 15:7	Joshua 1:8
John 14:27	Isaiah 41:10	Philippians 4:6–7
John 16:33	Philippians 4:13	Hebrews 10:24–25
Romans 8:6	Isaiah 26:3	Romans 1:16
Philippian 4:6–7	Lamentations 3:22–23	Romans 3:23
Colossians 3:15	1 Peter 5:7	Romans 6:23
Deuteronomy 7:9	Psalm 119:11	Ephesians 2:8–9
Psalm 32:8	Matthew 6:33	John 1:12
2 Timothy 3:16–17	Luke 9:23	Isaiah 53:6
1 John 5:14	Mark 10:45	Hebrews 9:27
Numbers 23:19	2 Corinthians 4:5	1 Peter 3:18

Revelation 3:20

John 5:24

1 Corinthians 3:16

1 Corinthians 2:12

Ezra 7:10

Revelation 4:11

Jeremiah 31:17

Jeremiah 10:12

Exodus 15:11

Ephesians 1:11

1 John 4:10

John 1:14

John 1:1

Hebrews 13:8

Acts 2:24

Acts 2:36

1 Peter 5:8

Galatians 5:16

Ephesians 4:30

James 4:10

Jeremiah 29:11

Psalm 121:1

Proverbs 3:6

Acts 1:8

Isaiah 65:24

Psalm 34:8

Psalm 20:7

Mark 11:24

Matthew 7:7

Proverbs 18:10

Jeremiah 32:27

Psalm 30:15

Psalm 63:1–2

Psalm 85:6

John 14:14

Philippians 4:8

Jeremiah 9:23–24

Isaiah 9:6

John 1:3

1 John 1:9

Romans 10:9

Matthew 11:29

Micah 6:8

Romans 10:17

Psalm 37:4

Matthew 16:26

Matthew 21:22

Psalm 30:5

2 Timothy 1:7

Psalm 16:11

Proverbs 22:6

John 10:10

Genesis 1:27

Matthew 5:44

1 Chronicles 16:11

John 11:25

Joshua 24:15

Deuteronomy 6:5

James 2:17

Matthews 17:20

Hebrews 10:38

1 Peter 1:9

Romans 5:2

Luke 17:6

2 Corinthian 5:6

1 John 5:4

James 1:12

Colossians 2:7

James 1:6

Exodus 20:12

Proverbs 15:20

Psalm 107:9

Hebrews 13:7

2 Chronicles 32:7

Ephesians 2:14

Proverbs 16:3

Psalm 19:14

James 3:18

Psalm 107:1

Deuteronomy 7:9

Job 36:11

Psalm 103:12

Proverbs 18:24

Proverbs 17:7

Proverbs 27:6

Proverbs 8:32–33

1 Corinthians 11:1

1 Peter 2:21–22

Ecclesiastes 4:9–10

Ecclesiastes 4:12

Romans 15:5

Psalm 150:6

Matthews 26:41

Jeremiah 1:4

Deuteronomy 5:16

Psalm 133

CHURCH OF GOD IN CHRIST
2015-2016 ANNUAL COMMENTARY
SUNDAY SCHOOL OVERVIEW

The Demonstration of the Power of Prayer

Our current theme, "Christ's Extreme Sacrifice Calls for Our Extreme Commitment," reminds us that we should endeavor to honor His sacrifice by developing the character of Christ. In an effort to do so, we are about to embark on a journey through the birth of the New Testament church. These lessons allow us insight into the believers' relationship with God and one another. We will learn how a group of ordinary people were endowed with power by the Holy Spirit to do extraordinary things. They referred to the believers of the day as those of "the way," and it was said of them that they had come to turn the world upside down and they did. Although there was no Christian church as we know it now, the believers of the early church were united. The Scripture reminds us that the evidence of their unity is that they had all things in common, and there was no lack among them. Believers were persecuted by authorities to stop the growth of the church. This had the unintended effect of causing them to disperse to the surrounding communities and spread the Gospel in the region and eventually throughout the world. We will also take a closer look at the strength of the early church in the demonstration of power of prayer.

As instructors, we want to assist our students with the practical application of the lessons by establishing goals and developing the strategies to achieve them. So in keeping with our theme, in this unit we might discuss ways in which we can solidify our commitment to our local assembly through our service of giving and prayer. We want to discuss unity in the assembly as we provoke each other to good works, and one of the good works of the church in this unit is evangelism. We can challenge your students to go boldly into all the world with the Gospel.

It is said that in order to know who you are, you must also know where you are from. Our study of the Hebrew customs and traditions allows us better to understand the foundations of our Christian traditions. It is important to the preservation of family and faith to distinguish celebrations and customs even as we commiserate in times of sorrow. These customs are often the glue that unites the family and ultimately the society.

These lessons reminds us of the value of family traditions and marking the remembrance of events with distinction and celebration.

To highlight our theme in this unit, we can examine ways in which Jesus honored the Hebrew traditions. We also want to emphasize our commitment to family and spiritual heritage. We might suggest ways in which we can help restore and better relate to those who are closest to us.

It is the power of faith that framed the worlds, and in our next lessons, the power of faith is discussed through the life and ministry of Jesus. We will take a closer look at the Author and Finisher of our faith as we see Him in the Gospels. This segment will prompt us to examine the evidence of our life to be certain that we are in the faith. The exploration of faith will reignite our fervor for the things of God, as we study and stir the measure of faith He has imparted to each of us.

Once again in keeping with our theme "Christ's Extreme Sacrifice Calls for our Extreme Commitment," we should commit to our faith as Christ commands. The Scripture admonishes us to hold on to our faith, and keep it until the Lord's return. As instructors, we can discuss what it means to have faith in God as well as having His faith for our circumstances.

Finally, the last segment of lessons takes us back to the inception of this body of believers whom we now call the church, as we look through the lens of the Old Testament and the consequences of sin and the subsequent judgment of God. We are made privy to the Israelites' sinful nature and the effects of an encounter of an unholy people with a holy God. We follow the progression of a nation from sin to salvation as they repent and receive God's mercy. Our human inability to achieve righteousness through our efforts is apparent in this segment, as we receive the revelation of the gift of Christ to the world through the miraculous grace and mercy of God.

Consequently, with all we have studied to this point, we come full circle in this unit, as we acknowledge that Christ's extreme sacrifice required Him to humble Himself. In order to accept the gift of grace bestowed on man by God, we too must make a commitment to remain humble.

Supertindent Steve Hawkins
El Shaddai Church Of God In Christ

Administrative Assistant, Superintendent Steve A. Hawkins was born in Waco, Texas, the third child of Elder Lewis Hawkins Sr. and Missionary Lester Pearl (Robinson) Hawkins. He is the grandson of Elder Steve Robinson, a Texas pioneer of the Church Of God In Christ.

Supt. Hawkins followed the footsteps of his father and attended Saints Academy and received an Associate Arts Degree from Saints Junior College (Church Of God In Christ), Lexington, Mississippi. While in attendance at Saints Junior College in 1967, he accepted Christ as his personal savior through the Word of God delivered by his former classmate, the late Bishop Walter E. Bogan. Supt. Hawkins later attended William Tyndale College - Farmington Hills, Michigan and received his Bachelor of Arts Degree (major - Theology and minor - Business Administration). He is an Administrative Assistant in Michigan Southeast Ecclesiastical Jurisdiction, under Bishop Roger L. Jones Sr., Chairman of the Pastors and Elders Council in the Jurisdiction and a faithful member and supporter of the National Pastors and Elders Council Church Of God In Christ.

With the blessings of his pastor, he accepted the call of God and founded the El Shaddai Ministries COGIC on June 15, 1997. Administrative Assistant Hawkins is married to Doris McGee Hawkins, whom he met while attending Saints Academy Junior College in Lexington, Mississippi, and he is the father of three children. His vision is simply to love the people, win souls, help to set the captive free, and to feed and encourage the body of Christ through preaching and teaching the unadulterated Word of God. He has a tremendous desire to share the Gospel with the incarcerated, the addicted, the abused, the abuser, and those who have never attended church. His vision also includes providing safe and affordable housing, a food pantry, and an educational and recreational center in the community in which he serves. His motto: "It's All About Souls."

INTERNATIONAL SUNDAY SCHOOL DEPARTMENT CHURCH OF GOD IN CHRIST

Greetings Sunday School Family!

It is with great excitement that we again join in partnership with the Publishing Board of the Church Of God In Christ to bring you the 2015-16 Annual COGIC Sunday School Commentary. It is our collective purpose and desire to provide current, insightful, and relevant tools to aid local Sunday School departments and their students in digging deeply into God's Word to find its relevance for their lives.

We are not only concerned about the study of God's Word, but also motivated to provide teaching tips and tools for instruction, study, and growth of local Sunday School classes.

This year, we have four of our church's leading Sunday School theologians introducing each quarter's theme with a Quarterly Commentary.

FALL QUARTER	Dr. William C. McCoy – Wisconsin First Jurisdiction
WINTER QUARTER	Dr. Rodney L. Atkins – Texas Northeast Second Jurisdiction
SPRING QUARTER	Dr. Jeannette H. Donald – Louisiana East First Jurisdiction
SUMMER QUARTER	Elder Oscar Owens – Southern California First Jurisdiction

At the beginning of each quarter's lessons, you will find teaching tips written by another group of talented Sunday School teachers and leaders sharing what the Lord has given them to grow and excel the ministry of Sunday School.

Let's get serious about the ministry of Sunday School! In order to win against the devices of Satan, we must prepare the troops for battle by arming them with the Word of God!

We release blessings and growth upon every local Sunday School. Be strong in the Lord and in the power of His might!

In His Service,

Vice President Althea Sims
ISSD Associate Editor

THE CHRISTIAN COMMUNITY
MATURATION OF THE SPIRITUAL COMMUNITY
By Dr. William C. McCoy

It is exciting to see both physical and psychological growth in the life of a child. Parents around the world utilize closet doors and doorframes alike to record periodic growth spurts of their children—keeping a running history of the physical maturation process. Equally important but harder to overtly measure is the psychological growth that occurs. It is particularly in the toddler stages that we observe phenomenal and rapid advancements in speech, reasoning, and reflection. All of this is a natural part of the maturation process of a child. As it is in the natural, so it is in the spiritual.

The Birth: The Christian church underwent a maturation process akin to that of a child. The birth or beginning of the church demonstrates a fledgling community dedicated to embracing and strengthening their fellow believer. They became strengthened primarily by prayer (Lesson 1), which provided the conduit necessary for a fresh touch of the Holy Spirit, which provided a sense of renewal and refreshing. In addition to prayer, their lives were enhanced even more when they touched the lives of others in a very tangible way (Lesson 2) by giving of all earthly possessions to aid the newly-established ministry. However, God demonstrated that He would not tolerate trickery or deceit, and ended the lives of Ananias and Sapphira in an instant. Teaching and healing continued to manifest itself by the work of the Holy Spirit through the disciples, but they were met with resistance by those devoid of understanding God's love, and they found it vital to stand on the foundation of truth (Lesson 3) given to us through the Gospel of Jesus Christ. Such a stand alienated the early Christians among peers and acquaintances, but they held fast to the faithfulness of God (Lesson 4), as evidenced by the anointed testimony of Stephen, designed to pierce the heart and soul of believers and non-believers alike.

Internal Growth: The pain associated with growth can at times seem unbearable. As we occasionally glance in the mirror of yesteryear, we can observe the many incidences in our lives that marked a period of growth and self-reflection. The same can be said of the early church, which endured a series of incidences that stood as challenges to the very core of its vitality and foundation. The apostle Peter found it necessary to assert that God's power was only available by genuine repentance of sins and through the acceptance of His salvation (Lesson 5), not in the exchange of money, as Simon the sorcerer thought. The conversion of Saul to Paul was demonstration enough of this fact, but even Paul had to prove his conversion among the people (Lesson 6) due to the rigidity of his past. Peter's personal revelation of feigned partiality toward the Gentiles (Lesson 7) reminds us that spiritual growth is an intricate part of our Christian walk, and that God has unique ways of revealing to us what is right and wrong. Thanks be to God that He does not leave us in a state of darkness and self-righteousness! It is God's Spirit that opens the pathways of truth (Lesson 8) in every situation necessary to prepare us for whatever assignment He has for us. Such was the case in Peter's recounting of God's divine revelation of salvation for the Gentiles. Despite this revelation, persecution continued, and Peter landed in jail, but through prayer and supplication (Lesson 9), his deliverance was nothing short of miraculous and an affirming display of God's power. Such displays of God's power lead to faith that is necessary to buoy the Christian through the turbulent waters of present doubt and future denial. By navigating the waters of spiritual challenges, God was able to orchestrate the internal growth of the early church, and it was through persecution that He orchestrated external growth as well.

External Growth: When we can intentionally affect the lives around us in a positive and meaningful way, we transcend from growth focused on the internal to the external. Similarly, as the church successfully dealt with internal issues, it began to transcend to a higher calling: the Great Commission. It was an intentional growth, but one fueled by a response to persecution and the saints fleeing for safer locales. In fulfilling the commission, God had to assure His people that He made no distinctions (Lesson 10) between the Jews and the Gentiles; salvation was for all, regardless of individual customs. This was an important concept, for it brought insightful congruence between the Law of Moses and God's New Testament revelations. Armed with the opportunity to "go into all the world," Paul took the Gospel on the road. These trips included Derbe, Macedonia, and Philippi (Lesson 11); Thessalonica, Berea, and Athens (Lesson 12); and continued into Corinth, Syria, Ephesus, and beyond (Lesson 13). As the very essence of external growth in the new church, the Gospel began to change the face of the community by reaching the people through the preaching of the Gospel and the teaching of God's Word.

Dr. William C. McCoy serves as the Sunday School Superintendent for Wisconsin 1st Jurisdiction under the leadership of Bishop Sedgwick Daniels, general board member. He also serves as the Co-Pastor of Greater New Unity COGIC in Rockford, Illinois. Dr. McCoy works professionally as the Director of Ethics for Northern Illinois University's College of Business. His dissertation centered on "Teaching the Adult Sunday School Teacher How to Teach Better".

OUR AIM: TRANSFORMATION
by Evangelist Betty J. Byrd

The following information is designed to support and aid both the COGIC Commentary series and Sunday School leaders by providing innovative teaching suggestions, proven growth strategies, and thoughtful learning opportunities, thus exciting, benefiting, and enhancing the user.

"I beseech you therefore, brethren, by the mercies of God, that ye present your bodies a living sacrifice, holy, acceptable unto God, which is your reasonable service. And be not conformed to this world: but be ye transformed by the renewing of your mind, that ye may prove what is that good, and acceptable, and perfect, will of God" (Romans 12:1–2, KJV).

Introduction/Overview: *Transformed means "a radical change in form, appearance or character." In 1984, a new action figure toy debuted in America: Transformers. This toy was able to change from one form into another (robots to vehicles and vice versa). Their theme song was "Transformers, more than meets the eye, robots in disguise." These robots could disguise themselves so well, their enemies couldn't recognize them. Wow—transformation!*

When we receive Christ in our lives, we are called to a change—our mind, our body, and our service.

We must avoid conformity. Conforming is going along to get along, behaving in a way that is acceptable to most people, living according to the standards of the day. We must not allow the world to become the model or blueprint for our lives!

God is calling us to non-conformity and change by the renewing of our minds; if you follow Jesus Christ as His disciple (servant), your life will never be the same.

As teachers, we must allow a total transformation to transfigure our lives and behavior and we must also teach our students that a total transformation must take place in their lives to conform to the will of God. It is now inherent on the teachers to help the students understand, and to guide them through the process to achieve this radical change of life.

We Present and Teach Bodily Transformation

In Romans 12:1, Paul calls the disciples to action: to offer a living sacrifice, which is our body. Paul is encouraging us to offer our bodies (our entire beings) in the task of service. The fact that it is a living sacrifice (as opposed to the Old Testament animal sacrifices) tells us that it is really about living the new life that we have received from Jesus (Matthew 16:25–26; 1 Corinthians 6:19–20; 1 Peter 4:3–4; James 1:27; Titus 2:7–8). Our bodies belong to God for His use and service, and it is incumbent upon teachers to make it a reachable and obtainable goal for every student by living the life before them.

Students Must Understand Transformation and Non-Conformity

We must teach the concept "and make plain" the difference between transformation and non-conformity talked about in Romans 12:2, so that we make God's Word the blueprint for our lives. In verse 2, Paul shows us how we live out the call in verse 1 for transformation. As disciples of God, His will for our lives has to set the pace. Our new life is not about what the world expects, but what God expects and has done for us in His mercy. There is a challenge for us in the renewal of our minds, but God is able to help us, and He is the source of our strength (1 John 2:15–17; Colossians 3:1–2).

Paul gets practical in describing the transformation that takes place. He encourages us to live the lives that we have been set free to live, a life marked by serving.

Transformation—Renewing of Mind

Proverbs 23:7a states "for as he thinketh in his heart, so is he." We act out what we first think. To experience transformation into the image of Christ, there must be a change of mind "to do according to all that is written" in the Word of God (Joshua 1:8). Thoughts are powerful, and according to the writer of the book of Proverbs, they have creative ability.

Joyce Meyer said, "You cannot have a positive life and a negative mind." Your life will not change until your thinking does.

Transformation—Will of God

God has a good and acceptable and perfect will for each of us. Man exists to glorify God. Paul says in Romans 12:2, "Do not be conformed to this world, but be transformed by the renewal of your mind, that by testing you may discern what is the will of God, what is good and acceptable and perfect" (ESV). God is forming people who will prove the value of His way by conscious choices and deliberate obedience.

Transformed to Serve

Transformation has no age limit, and for Christian living and witnessing, it is essential for both young and old. The work of renewing our mind in the image of Christ is a lifelong effort and experience. We must constantly continue to be transformed into the likeness of Christ by God through the renewing of our minds and attitudes. The requirement for being used by Christ simply calls for obedience to His leading and His Word, and to be available to serve His people. "Then he said to his disciples, The harvest is plentiful but the workers are few. Ask the Lord of the harvest, therefore, to send out workers into his harvest field" (Matthew 9:37–38). Jesus did not say "young or old workers"—just workers. The requirement for being used by Christ is simply being available and being obedient to His leading. Pray today and ask the Lord to reveal to you how you can serve Him.

In every age, the greatest threat to the people of God was and is conforming to the time they lived in. As workers of God, we must be able to change and convey change by living a transformed, godly life. We must use the Word of God as the tool to measure our conformity to Him, not what the world dictates. We must know that God is calling for the young and old to transform and prove His good and perfect will.

Our job as a Sunday School leader is to make sure that each person knows that God wants to use them in His work—no age limit, young or seasoned. God is waiting for the transformed worker.

Evangelist Betty J. Byrd
Adult Sunday School Teacher
Fairfield First COGIC, Elder James Brinkley, Jr., Pastor
Alabama First Jurisdiction
Jurisdictional Young Women's Christian Council (YWCC) President
Mother Mattie B. Taylor, Jurisdictional Supervisor
Bishop O. L. Meadows, Jurisdictional Prelate

SPIRITUAL FITNESS TEST

by Jurisdictional Field Representative Sandra Daniel

The following information is designed to support and aid both the COGIC Commentary series and Sunday School leaders by providing innovative teaching suggestions, proven growth strategies, and thoughtful learning opportunities, thus exciting, benefiting, and enhancing the user.

What is the purpose of exercise?

_____

_____

_____

What are results from a lack of exercise?

_____

_____

_____

Can the results be reversed?

_____

_____

_____

What happens if we wait too long?

_____

_____

_____

What do you do to build up your spiritual stamina? List it here.

_____

_____

_____

_____

_____

_____

In 1 Corinthians 9:24–27, Paul writes about athletes who trained hard. The athletes didn't just want to be fit—they wanted to win! Our ultimate goal is to win the race that is set before us. Have you found yourself too fatigued to run? What do you do to build up your spiritual stamina? Is it working? Where have you fallen short?

_____

_____

_____

_____

We must put on our armor and be fit to fight victoriously

Work on these five spiritual fitness steps to train yourself to become spiritually fit. Keep a weekly chart to record your progress.

Are you winning the race?

	Read your Bible and meditate on the Word	Pray every day	Pray for others	Perform a random act of kindness daily	Work toward pleasing God in all that you do
SUNDAY					
MONDAY					
TUESDAY					
WEDNESDAY					
THURSDAY					
FRIDAY					
SATURDAY					

Jurisdictional Field Representative Sandra Daniel
Evangelist Sandra Daniel serves as the Jurisdictional Field Representative for Southern California First Jurisdiction under the leadership of Bishop Joe L. Ealy and General Assistant Supervisor/ Jurisdictional Supervisor, Mother Barbara McCoo Lewis. She is the Assistant Director of Leadership Ministry for the International Sunday School Department.

GOT STRATEGIES?
ENGAGING STUDENTS IN YOUR SUNDAY SCHOOL CLASS
by Evangelist Yvonne Atkins

The following information is designed to support and aid both the COGIC Commentary series and Sunday School leaders by providing innovative teaching suggestions, proven growth strategies, and thoughtful learning opportunities, thus exciting, benefiting, and enhancing the user.

In Sunday School classrooms, we want students of all ages to be engaged, active, and interested. When students arrive to class, we want them to want to be in class, eager to read their lesson, and ready to be engaged.

Explore

When students enter the Sunday School classroom, have a focus—something to get them interested in the lesson.

- Brainstorm (tell students the topic and let them tell what they think the lesson is going to talk about), discuss (give students a question relating to the lesson; make the question one without a yes or no answer)

- Biblical pictures, maps (students can find where the area is located on a map or globe, show biblical pictures of places, people, clothes, artifacts)

- Items relating to the lesson (if you have pictures or items that can engage students' five senses, this will help make the lesson relevant)

- Magazines, newspapers (current events that relate to the lesson)

Explain

Help students understand what they are learning in today's lesson

- Explain Scriptures

- Give students some background information to help them better understand the lesson

- Define, discuss vocabulary

Engage/Elaborate

Make the lesson relevant for students

- Movement (especially younger students—jumping, skipping, hand movements, etc.)

- Music

- Storytelling and re-telling (have students retell the lesson)

- Reader's Theater (give students a specific part of the lesson; let students practice and then read their parts)

- I Have/Who Has (for Scripture Reading)—This is a great way to get students to read the Scripture. The first Scripture will have (Begin) so that the students will know who starts.

I Have: Ephesians 6:10 "Finally, my brethren, be strong in the Lord, and in the power of his might." Who Has: Ephesians 6:11 (whoever has this card will read 6:11 and at the end you will write "Who Has...") This continues until every card is read.

- Charades (act out Scriptures, scenes in the Bible relating to the lesson)

- Group presentations (students write what the Scriptures and lesson mean—draw, make a song, poem, etc.)

- Gallery Walk (students display what they have produced, walk around viewing each other's work). Teachers can play music and give students posted notes to leave positive affirmations.

Evaluate

Make sure the students have time to reflect on what was learned.

- Exit Tickets (see illustrations below)

- Talk to a partner

- Tell or write two things you learned today

- Give students a Scripture Card with the memory verse for the next lesson

EXIT TICKET

The Most Important Thing I Learned Today......

EXIT TICKET

Rate Your Understanding of Today's Lesson
(1–10, 10 meaning you totally understand).
Explain your answer.

EXIT TICKET

One Question I Have About What I Learned Today...

Victory Temple Church of God in Christ

LEVITE MINISTRY SCRIPTURE CARD

Ephesians 6:11 Memory Verse

"Put on the full armour of God, that ye may be able
to stand against the wiles of the devil."

Research says that your attention span is about as long as your age. So remember, 5-year-olds can focus for about 5 minutes, 10-year-olds 10 minutes, and the maximum amount of attention time is about 15–20 minutes. Movement is very important. Get students moving!

First Lady Yvonne Atkins
Adult Women Sunday School Teacher (Ages 40-50)
Victory Temple Church of God in Christ
Texas Northeast Jurisdiction #2
Prelate, Bishop Dr. David R. Houston
Supervisor of Women Mother Artie Morrow

QUARTERLY QUIZ

The questions on this page may be used in several ways: as a pretest at the beginning of the quarter; as a review at the end of the quarter; or as a review after each lesson. The questions are based on the Scripture text of each lesson (King James Version).

LESSON 1

1. Why did the disciples ask God to perform signs and wonders (**Acts 4:29**)?

_____

_____

2. What sign did the Lord give that showed the disciples' prayer was honored (**v. 31**)?

_____

_____

LESSON 2

1. Define the word *lacked* in verse 34 and *consolation* in verse 36 (**Acts 4:34, 36**).

_____

_____

2. Name one reason some Christians do not share what they need to help others.

_____

_____

LESSON 3

1. How did Peter explain the apostles' disregard for the Sanhedrin's orders (**Acts 5:29**)?

_____

_____

2. Name the two men that Gamaliel gives as examples to the council for not touching the apostles (**vv. 36–37**).

_____

_____

LESSON 4

1. Stephen is described as what type of Jew in the Light on the Word section?

_____

_____

2. David wanted to build God a house of worship. Who did the Lord allow to build a temple (**Acts 7:47**)?

_____

_____

LESSON 5

1. What prompted the Apostles Peter and John to visit Samaria (**Acts 9:14**)?

_____

_____

2. Which apostle preached about the Kingdom of God and Christ in **verse 12**?

_____

_____

QUARTERLY QUIZ

LESSON 6

1. Did the Christian Jews initially believe or doubt Saul's testimony (**Acts 9:21**)?

_____

_____

2. Saul increased in strength, but in what city did he "confound" the Jews (**v. 22**)?

_____

_____

LESSON 7

1. Despite how this would appear to Jewish leaders, why did Peter agree to go to Cornelius' home (**Acts 10:28–29**)?

_____

_____

2. Who is Simon Peter staying with when he is summoned to visit Cornelius? Whose message is Cornelius waiting to hear (**vv. 32, 34**)?

_____

_____

LESSON 8

1. What is the significance of Peter refusing the Lord's direction three times during his vision (**Acts 11:10**)?

_____

_____

2. Why do you think Peter chose six other men to travel with him to Caesarea? Why do you think he was careful to point this out (**v. 12**)?

_____

_____

LESSON 9

1. How many squads and soldiers guarded Peter (**v. 6**)?

_____

_____

2. The church responded to Peter's imprisonment by doing what (**v. 5**)?

_____

_____

LESSON 10

1. "And God, which knoweth the _____, bare them witness, giving them the Holy Ghost, even as he did unto us; And put no _____ between us and them, purifying their hearts by _____" (**Acts 15:8–9, KJV**).

_____

_____

2. Why was there great joy among the believers (**v. 3**)?

_____

_____

QUARTERLY QUIZ

LESSON 11

1. Where was the prayer meeting held (**Acts 16:13**)?

_____

_____

2. Why do think that Lydia needed to insist so strongly that Paul and his men stay at her home (**v. 15**)?

_____

_____

LESSON 12

1. Describe Paul and Silas' audience and who believed their truth of God's Word (**Acts 17:4**).

_____

_____

2. How did the Bereans respond to Paul's message (**vv. 11–12**)?

_____

_____

LESSON 13

1. Explain what *pressed* means in **Acts 18:5**.

_____

_____

2. Why did Paul shave his head in Cenchrea (**v. 18**)?

_____

_____

Answers to Quarterly Quiz can be found on page 508

PRAYING FOR ONE ANOTHER

BIBLE BASIS: ACTS 4:23–31

BIBLE TRUTH: Prayer is a powerful weapon that God has given His people.

MEMORY VERSE: "And when they had prayed, the place was shaken where they were assembled together; and they were all filled with the Holy Ghost, and they spake the word of God with boldness" (Acts 4:31).

LESSON AIM: By the end of the lesson, we will: REVIEW the apostles' prayer for strength to speak with boldness and to continue Jesus' ministry while under political duress; GAIN insights into prayer as a means through which Christians can remain strong voices for change and effective ministries in their communities today; and ASK God in bold prayers to empower their mission and ministry.

TEACHER PREPARATION

MATERIALS NEEDED: Quarterly Commentary/Teacher Manual, Adult Quarterly, Adult resources—charts, worksheets, and other teaching tools, paper, pens, pencils, Bibles (several different versions)

OTHER MATERIALS NEEDED / TEACHER'S NOTES:

_____

_____

LIFE NEED FOR TODAY'S LESSON
People share their various gifts and talents in various ways.

BIBLE LEARNING
The Holy Spirit filled believers and they spoke God's Word with boldness.

BIBLE APPLICATION
Followers of Christ draw strength from Him as they seek God in prayer.

STUDENTS' RESPONSES
Believers will take comfort in knowing that God answers prayer.

LESSON SCRIPTURE

ACTS 4:23–31, KJV

23 And being let go, they went to their own company, and reported all that the chief priests and elders had said unto them.

24 And when they heard that, they lifted up their voice to God with one accord, and said, Lord, thou art God, which hast made

ACTS 4:23–31, NIV

23 On their release, Peter and John went back to their own people and reported all that the chief priests and the elders had said to them.

24 When they heard this, they raised their voices together in prayer to God. "Sovereign

heaven, and earth, and the sea, and all that in them is:

25 Who by the mouth of thy servant David hast said, Why did the heathen rage, and the people imagine vain things?

26 The kings of the earth stood up, and the rulers were gathered together against the Lord, and against his Christ.

27 For of a truth against thy holy child Jesus, whom thou hast anointed, both Herod, and Pontius Pilate, with the Gentiles, and the people of Israel, were gathered together,

28 For to do whatsoever thy hand and thy counsel determined before to be done.

29 And now, Lord, behold their threatenings: and grant unto thy servants, that with all boldness they may speak thy word,

30 By stretching forth thine hand to heal; and that signs and wonders may be done by the name of thy holy child Jesus.

31 And when they had prayed, the place was shaken where they were assembled together; and they were all filled with the Holy Ghost, and they spake the word of God with boldness.

Lord," they said, "you made the heavens and the earth and the sea, and everything in them.

25 You spoke by the Holy Spirit through the mouth of your servant, our father David: "'Why do the nations rage and the peoples plot in vain?

26 The kings of the earth rise up and the rulers band together against the Lord and against his anointed one.'

27 Indeed Herod and Pontius Pilate met together with the Gentiles and the people of Israel in this city to conspire against your holy servant Jesus, whom you anointed.

28 They did what your power and will had decided beforehand should happen.

29 Now, Lord, consider their threats and enable your servants to speak your word with great boldness.

30 Stretch out your hand to heal and perform signs and wonders through the name of your holy servant Jesus."

31 After they prayed, the place where they were meeting was shaken. And they were all filled with the Holy Spirit and spoke the word of God boldly.

LIGHT ON THE WORD

Sadducees. The Sadducees were a sectarian party within the Jewish priesthood comprised mostly of aristocrats. They tended to be conservative and were more interested in maintaining power than in the religious purity of Israel. They were frequently in conflict with the Pharisees, rejecting the Oral Torah and teachings on angels and demons, along with the notion of resurrection. Because of their associations with the Temple, they disappeared after its destruction in 70 AD.

Sanhedrin. The Sanhedrin was the highest Jewish tribunal during the Greco-Roman period. They were a council that consisted of 70 aristocratic elders who were led by a hereditary high priest. According to **Matthew 16:21 and 27:41**, the Sanhedrin consisted of the chief priests, the scribes, and the elders. Its decisions were final in matters concerning Mosaic Law.

TEACHING THE BIBLE LESSON

LIFE NEED FOR TODAY'S LESSON

AIM: Students will discuss how they share their various gifts and talents in various ways.

INTRODUCTION

The Power of God's Word

In Chapter 3, God uses Peter to heal a crippled man who sat at the temple gate daily begging for help. Once the man was healed, he began to dance and praise God to the amazement of those around him. Peter and John used this moment as an opportunity to share the Gospel of Jesus Christ and explain how faith in Christ made the man whole. The priests, temple guard, and Sadducees were disturbed by Peter and John teaching the people about Jesus and His Resurrection, and threw them both in jail. As a result of Peter and John's message, the church added five thousand believers. The council was afraid of the people's reaction if they were to harm Peter and John, so they decided to bring them before the council and question them.

The Holy Spirit gave Peter the courage to speak and the words to say to the council. The council was amazed by the boldness and skillful use of Scripture by these ordinary men. Since they were not able to deny the miracle that had been performed, the council decided to try to stop the Gospel's spread by demanding that Peter and John stop preaching about Jesus and threatening them.

BIBLE LEARNING

AIM: Students will know that the Holy Spirit will fill them to speak God's Word with boldness.

I. PREPARED FOR OPPOSITION (Acts 4:23)

In **verse 23**, Peter and John return to the believers and share all that the council did and said to them. Jesus had warned His followers of this very situation (**Luke 12:11–12**). Peter and John had experienced opposition because of their commitment to the Gospel. They had healed a crippled beggar in the name of Jesus. This had confused the council members of the Sanhedrin because Peter and John were not religious teachers, but men of Galilee who healed in the name of Jesus of Nazareth, a man the council had condemned to death.

Peter and John reported to the fledgling church what the Sanhedrin told them. They were officially told to not speak or preach in the name of Jesus. It wasn't the healing that was so bad in the eyes of the Jewish leaders, but the Gospel message and the name of Jesus. The two apostles were beaten as an act of discipline to ensure the Sanhedrin's orders were followed. This beating was also probably used as an example to instill fear in their followers. Ultimately Peter and John rejoiced in their suffering, since they were suffering for Christ. It was the treasure of the Gospel message that inspired the prayers of the new church, and it should inspire our prayers as well.

Acts 4:23–31

23 And being let go, they went to their own company, and reported all that the chief priests and elders had said unto them.

The expression "their own company" (Gk. *idios*, **I-dee-os**), or "their own circle," denotes the Christian community. It suggests that after their release, Peter and John returned to "headquarters," perhaps the Upper Room of **Acts 1:13**, where members of the new community had no doubt been engaged in intercessory prayer for them. They reported their experience with the council. This report must have caused the early company fear. The persecution of leaders is a tactic that is often used to silence their followers.

II. GOD PREVAILS OVER OPPOSITION (vv. 24–28)

This portion of the lesson begins what is sometimes called the Believer's Prayer. These early believers quote **Psalm 2** in their prayer. This psalm, most likely a coronation psalm, is attributed to David. It describes the hostility that accompanied the installation of a king. The king, God's servant, is a consecrated worshiper and the recipient of hostility from the Gentile nations. As the nations attempt to oppose or dethrone the king God has anointed, they are told it is all for nothing; their efforts will fail. These nations are not just opposing an earthly king, but God Himself.

The believers go on to describe the hostility that Jesus faced at the hands of these same leaders and how their treatment of Jesus did not derail God's divine plan. The Jewish leaders and Roman authorities had attempted to silence Jesus in death, but in vain—He rose from the dead. Now Jesus is crowned Lord of the universe due to His Resurrection and ascension to heaven. The believers trust in the resurrected King who is sovereign over the authorities of this earth. Any attempt at opposing the spread of the Gospel message is a vain attempt. Just like the Gentile kings of **Psalm 2**, the Jewish leaders' opposition is in vain.

24 And when they heard that, they lifted up their voice to God with one accord, and said, Lord, thou art God, which hast made heaven, and earth, and the sea, and all that in them is.

With one accord, they turned to God in prayer. The Greek word for "one accord" or "together" is *homothumadon* (**ho-mo-thoo-ma-DON**), which indicates that they were like one person in prayer. It is a combination of two Greek words meaning "together" and "passion." The disciples were all praying together with the same passion and ardor. It does not mean they all simultaneously said the same words. One of the leaders may have prayed accompanied by a responsive "amen" from the rest. It was more like an orchestra with the Holy Spirit as the conductor. There is power in a gathering of believers when they are in "one accord" (see **vv. 24–31**).

They addressed God as "Lord" or "Master" (Gk. *despotes*, **des-POE-tace**), a term denoting the sovereignty of God and His absolute control over all creation. The term is also used for a slave owner or a ruler with unchallengeable power. In the disciples' prayer, the term certainly points to the fact that the authority of the council was subject to a higher authority still, and that the law of men cannot overturn the decrees of God (cf. **vv. 19–20**). The disciples filled their minds with thoughts of the sovereignty of God before stating their petition. The sovereign God is the God of creation. He made the heaven, the earth, the sea, and everything in them (cf. **17:24, 26**; see also **Nehemiah 9:6; Psalm 146:6**).

25 Who by the mouth of thy servant David hast said, Why did the heathen rage, and the people imagine vain things? 26 The kings of the earth stood up, and the rulers

were gathered together against the Lord, and against his Christ. 27 For of a truth against thy holy child Jesus, whom thou hast anointed, both Herod, and Pontius Pilate, with the Gentiles, and the people of Israel, were gathered together. 28 For to do whatsoever thy hand and thy counsel determined before to be done.

The sovereign Lord is the God of revelation. He had revealed to His servant David the opposition Christ would face from various groups. "Why did the heathen rage" is quoted from **Psalm 2:1–2**. **Psalm 2** originally referred to the accession of a Davidic king, the Lord's Anointed, and the revolt of His vassals. It was interpreted by the Jews and the early Christian church as a Messianic psalm (cf. **Acts 13:33; Hebrews 5:5**). In the psalm, the "heathen" (Gk. **ETH-nos**, people other than the Israelites) is paired with the "people" (Gk. **lah-OSE**, Israelites, the people of God). In other words, both God's people and those from outside resisted God's chosen leader. Here the community references the psalm to reveal the extent of Jesus' rejection as the Messiah. Once again, it is only a few from among God's people and from the Gentiles who accept God's chosen Messiah.

"The kings of the earth" (and "the rulers", who stood up against the Lord and His Christ, were represented by Herod Antipas, the Tetrarch of Galilee and Peraea (**Luke 23:7**), Pontius Pilate, and even Herod the Great, who attempted to kill Jesus at the start of His time on earth. This shows that the sovereign Lord is the God of history. The Greek conjunction *gar* (**GAR**), which indicates a cause or reason proves the truth of the preceding prophecy by pointing to its historical fulfillment. Herod, Pontius Pilate, the Gentiles, and the people of Israel are clearly identified with the kings, the rulers, the nations, and the people of **Psalm 2:1–2** as quoted in **Acts 4:25**.

The expression "thy holy child Jesus" explicitly identifies Jesus with the royal Son of God addressed in **Psalm 2:7**. Jesus is both the obedient Son and the One whom God anointed or made Messiah. Jesus, "whom thou hast anointed," refers to the Holy Spirit's identification of Him as Messiah at His baptism. The Holy Spirit's resting on Jesus signaled His anointing or empowerment and the inaugaration of His earthly ministry (cf. **10:38; Luke 3:21–22; 4:18–21; Isaiah 61:1**).

SEARCH THE SCRIPTURES

QUESTION 1
The Holy Spirit gave Peter the ability to do what?

Speak with courage and the words to say to the Council.

QUESTION 2
Who are the "kings of the earth"?

Herod Antipas, the Tetrarch of Galilee and Peraea, Pontius Pilate, and Herod the Great.

LIGHT ON THE WORD

God's Power and Guidance
God causes even His enemies to do what He has determined beforehand. The purposes of the rulers and the people were overruled by the sovereign Lord for the accomplishment of His will. Herod and Pilate simply carried out the foreordained counsel of God that His Messiah would suffer (cf. **Acts 2:23, 3:18**). The word "hand" (*cheir*, **KHAIR**) refers to God's action, His controlling power as well as his guidance (cf. **11:21; 13:11; Exodus 3:20; Jeremiah 15:6; Ezekiel 6:14**).

III. EMPOWERED FOR OPPOSITION (vv. 29–31)

At the end of the prayer, the believers appeal to God to give them greater boldness and empower them to perform greater works in Jesus' name. They accept and embrace the fact that they will face opposition. David faced it. Jesus faced it. Their request is not for God to alleviate it or make a way for them to escape it. They are not concerned about themselves, but focused on the Gospel being heard, and they understand that the plan of God has a history of hostility from those who feel threatened by it. They seek God and ask to be empowered and strengthened so that they can continue to serve Him with boldness.

God responds to their request with a physical sign: the entire place shakes. This must have confirmed and strengthened their faith. The disciples are then empowered with boldness to preach the name of Jesus. It is important to note that the power the apostles sought was so they could better serve God and others, while the power that the council sought was strictly for their own benefit. As we seek God for power, we need to have a proper understanding of what power is for. God empowers us to serve others and not ourselves.

29 And now, Lord, behold their threatenings: and grant unto thy servants, that will all boldness they may speak thy word. 30 By stretching forth thine hand to heal; and that signs and wonders may be done by the name of thy holy child Jesus. 31 And when they had prayed, the place of shaken where they assembled together; and they were all filled with the Holy Ghost, and they spake the word of God with boldness.

The council's threats were not a cause for fear and silence, but bolder speech. The apostles therefore prayed that they might have courage to proclaim the Word of God "with all boldness." The Greek word for "boldness" (*parresia*, **pah-reh-SEE-a**) in this context refers to freedom in speaking and unreservedness of utterance. The disciples wanted to speak the message of the Gospel without fear. The word "servants" comes from the Greek word *doulos* (**DOO-las**), which means slave and contrasts with the majesty of "Lord" from **verse 24**.

The disciples' next request is that God would place the seal of His public approval on their witness by granting further mighty works of healing and similar signs and wonders through the same name that had cured the lame man—the name of Jesus.

The term "hand," most frequently used to refer to God's act of punishment, here denotes His action in bringing blessing (cf. **Luke 5:13**). It was of course the apostles' hands that were stretched out to heal, but, as in **Acts 3:16**, they attributed their power to God working through them as they restored men to wholeness in the name of Jesus.

The account here is reminiscent of the description of what happened on the Day of Pentecost, both in the external signs of the Spirit's coming and in the disciples' prayerful attitude when He comes. In answer to the disciples' united and earnest prayers, the place was shaken, they were all filled with the Holy Spirit, and they proclaimed the Word of God boldly. They were encouraged to continue to proclaim the faith despite the council's threats.

The shaking (Gk. *saleuo*, **sal-EW-oh**) of the place where the disciples were symbolizes the presence of God (cf. **Exodus 19:18; Isaiah 6:4**). The assurance of divine favor and help came even as they prayed. An earthquake might be a cause for fear to some, but to those who see it as an answer to prayer, it is an encouragement. The verb "filled" followed by the verb "spake" indicates the immediate and continuous action of the disciples. They were continuously proclaiming the Word of God with boldness.

SEARCH THE SCRIPTURES

QUESTION 3

In **verse 24**, what is the Greek word for boldness, and define what it means in this context.

The Greek word for boldness is *parresia.* **Boldness refers to freedom in speaking and unreservedness of utterance.**

LIGHT ON THE WORD

Prayer and Power

Christians must come together to prayer for strength and boldness to serve others. As the church faces many challenges, bold prayer is needed from believers to empower the mission and ministry that God has given believers.

BIBLE APPLICATION

AIM: Students will know that followers of Christ will draw strength from Him as they seek God in prayer.

Many circumstances in life can challenge our faith and hinder our relationship with God. This is why we must stay ready and willing to pray for one another. In order for Christians to witness boldly, we must have uncompromising trust in God's plan in spite of opposition.

STUDENT'S RESPONSES

AIM: Believers will take comfort in knowing that God answers prayer.

Our ability to effect change is directly related to our prayer life, personal worship, and relationship with God. This is where we start. The church in Acts began with prayer, but their prayer empowered them to go out into the community and do works for the benefit of others. Brainstorm some areas in which your community needs change. Pray as a class for God to empower you to serve. Ask God for boldness to step out and serve the community and watch Him move.

PRAYER

Dear Lord, we pray for boldness to speak Your Word and live Your Word as we share the Christian faith with others. In the Name of Jesus we pray, amen.

HOW TO SAY IT

Sanhedrin.   san-**HEED**-rin.

Sadducees.   sa-dyu-**SEES**.

PREPARE FOR NEXT SUNDAY

Read **Acts 4:34–5:10** and "Sharing All Things."

DAILY HOME BIBLE READINGS

MONDAY
Prayer of Humility
(Matthew 6:9–15)

TUESDAY
Prayer of Gratitude
(2 Chronicles 6:1–15)

WEDNESDAY
Open-Hearted Life
(2 Corinthians 6:1–13)

THURSDAY
Greater Things Through Prayer
(John 14:11–13)

FRIDAY
No One Else
(Acts 4:1–12)

SATURDAY
No Other Authority
(Acts 4:13–22)

SUNDAY
Praying With Boldness
(Acts 4:23–31)

Sources:
Carson, D.A., France, R.T., Motyer, J.A., Wenham, J.G. *New Bible Commentary*. Downers Grove, IL: Intervarsity Press, 1993.
Keener, Craig S. *IVP Bible Background Commentary*. Downers Grove, IL: Intervarsity, Press, 1993.
Polhill, John B. Acts. *New American Commentary: An Exegetical and Theological Exposition of Holy Scripture*. Nashville: B&H Publishing, 1992.

COMMENTS / NOTES:

SHARING ALL THINGS

BIBLE BASIS: ACTS 4:34–5:10

BIBLE TRUTH: The early followers of Jesus shared everything with one another, so there was not a needy person among them.

MEMORY VERSE: "Neither was there any among them that lacked: for as many as were possessors of lands or houses sold them, and brought the prices of the things that were sold"

(Acts 4:34).

LESSON AIM: By the end of the lesson, we will: UNDERSTAND the sacrifices and rewards of the early Christians' willingness to share their possessions with others; EXAMINE our motivation for making sacrificial offerings; and DRAFT a list of statements that would motivate others to contribute freely to a community project.

TEACHER PREPARATION

MATERIALS NEEDED: Quarterly Commentary/Teacher Manual, Adult Quarterly, Adult resources—charts, worksheets, and other teaching tools, paper, pens, pencils, Bibles (several different versions)

OTHER MATERIALS NEEDED / TEACHER'S NOTES:

_____

_____

LESSON OVERVIEW

LIFE NEED FOR TODAY'S LESSON
Although there are exceptions, most people are glad to share what they have with those in need.

BIBLE LEARNING
Some believers did not share with those in need and were punished.

BIBLE APPLICATION
Believers in Christ have the responsibility to care for others.

STUDENTS' RESPONSES
Believers should have the right intentions as they provide for those in need.

LESSON SCRIPTURE

ACTS 4:34–5:10, KJV

34 Neither was there any among them that lacked: for as many as were possessors of lands or houses sold them, and brought the prices of the things that were sold,

ACTS 4:34–5:10, NIV

34 that there were no needy persons among them. For from time to time those who owned land or houses sold them, brought the money from the sales

35 And laid them down at the apostles' feet: and distribution was made unto every man according as he had need.

36 And Joses, who by the apostles was surnamed Barnabas, (which is, being interpreted, The son of consolation,) a Levite, and of the country of Cyprus,

37 Having land, sold it, and brought the money, and laid it at the apostles' feet.

5:1 But a certain man named Ananias, with Sapphira his wife, sold a possession,

2 And kept back part of the price, his wife also being privy to it, and brought a certain part, and laid it at the apostles' feet.

3 But Peter said, Ananias, why hath Satan filled thine heart to lie to the Holy Ghost, and to keep back part of the price of the land?

4 Whiles it remained, was it not thine own? and after it was sold, was it not in thine own power? why hast thou conceived this thing in thine heart? thou hast not lied unto men, but unto God.

5 And Ananias hearing these words fell down, and gave up the ghost: and great fear came on all them that heard these things.

6 And the young men arose, wound him up, and carried him out, and buried him.

7 And it was about the space of three hours after, when his wife, not knowing what was done, came in.

8 And Peter answered unto her, Tell me whether ye sold the land for so much? And she said, Yea, for so much.

9 Then Peter said unto her, How is it that ye have agreed together to tempt the Spirit of the Lord? behold, the feet of them which

35 and put it at the apostles' feet, and it was distributed to anyone who had need.

36 Joseph, a Levite from Cyprus, whom the apostles called Barnabas (which means "son of encouragement"),

37 sold a field he owned and brought the money and put it at the apostles' feet.

5:1 Now a man named Ananias, together with his wife Sapphira, also sold a piece of property.

2 With his wife's full knowledge he kept back part of the money for himself, but brought the rest and put it at the apostles' feet.

3 Then Peter said, "Ananias, how is it that Satan has so filled your heart that you have lied to the Holy Spirit and have kept for yourself some of the money you received for the land?

4 Didn't it belong to you before it was sold? And after it was sold, wasn't the money at your disposal? What made you think of doing such a thing? You have not lied just to human beings but to God."

5 When Ananias heard this, he fell down and died. And great fear seized all who heard what had happened.

6 Then some young men came forward, wrapped up his body, and carried him out and buried him.

7 About three hours later his wife came in, not knowing what had happened.

8 Peter asked her, "Tell me, is this the price you and Ananias got for the land?" "Yes," she said, "that is the price."

9 Peter said to her, "How could you conspire to test the Spirit of the Lord? Listen! The feet of the men who buried your husband are at

have buried thy husband are at the door, and shall carry thee out.

10 Then fell she down straightway at his feet, and yielded up the ghost: and the young men came in, and found her dead, and, carrying her forth, buried her by her husband.

the door, and they will carry you out also."

10 At that moment she fell down at his feet and died. Then the young men came in and, finding her dead, carried her out and buried her beside her husband.

LIGHT ON THE WORD

Barnabas. Barnabas means "son of encouragement" in Aramaic. This was the name given by the Apostles to Joses, a Levite from Cyprus. Barnabas was an early convert to Christianity. His character and faith soon brought him into a position of leadership in the church. When Paul was first converted, many of the believers were afraid to accept him. Barnabas eased their fears by speaking to the church on behalf of the apostles. Barnabas was one of Paul's companions during the early part of his ministry.

Levite. The Levites were the priestly tribe of Israel. All of Israel's priests are descended from this tribe. However, there is a fundamental difference between priests and Levites. All priests come from the tribe of Levi; however, not all Levites can become priests, who must be descendants of Aaron. Priests are consecrated and were the only ones that could minster at the altar and enter into the holy places. Levites were purified and were set aside to help the priests in performing their duties.

TEACHING THE BIBLE LESSON

LIFE NEED FOR TODAY'S LESSON

AIM: Students will appreciate that although there are exceptions, most people are glad to share what they have with those in need.

INTRODUCTION

The Spirit of Generosity

The generosity described in this lesson is a continuation of the giving described in Acts 2:44–45: "And all that believed were together, and had all things common; and sold their possessions and goods, and parted them to all men, as every man had need." The Gospel message of Jesus' extravagant love had a significant impact on the early church. The reality of Jesus' tremendous sacrifice inspired them to sacrifice for the benefit of others. They were not comfortable seeing their brothers and sisters in Christ go without. This conviction led them to do more than just pray for their brothers and sisters; it prompted them to take personal action. In this lesson, we see that the spirit of generosity is still needed in the church.

BIBLE LEARNING

AIM: Students will learn that some believers in the early church did not share with those in need and were punished.

I. UNRESERVED GENEROSITY
(Acts 4:34–37)

In the Old Testament, we see that God is consistently concerned with the plight of those less fortunate. Israel was chastised many times because they had failed to take care of those unable to take care of themselves: widows, orphans, and the poor. God makes clear that Israel is responsible for taking care of one another (**Deuteronomy 15:4**). He also commands Israel to bring all the tithes and offerings to the house of God so that there would be provision there (**Malachi 3:10**). This was so the poor would know that they could come to the temple and find food.

As a response to the generosity Jesus showed them, the early church provided for all so that no one "lacked." Their possessions and goods were shared in common and given to anyone who was in need. This was remarkable in first century Palestine, as most of the population lived in poverty. The early church provided the context to live out Jesus' command to "sell your possessions and give to the poor" (**Matthew 19:21, Luke 12:33, NIV**). The community of the new covenant shared everything.

Acts 4:35–5:10

34 Neither was there any among them that lacked: for as many as were possessors of lands or houses sold them, and brought the prices of the things that were sold, 35 And laid them down at the apostles' feet: and distribution was made unto every man according as he had need. 36 And Joses, who by the apostles was surnamed Barnabas, (which is, being interpreted, The son of consolation,) a Levite, and of the country of Cyprus, 37 Having land, sold it, and brought the money, and laid it at the apostles' feet.

The first phrase in this verse echoes the words of **Deuteronomy 15:4**: "There shall be no poor among you." In this way, Luke (who wrote Acts to follow his Gospel) paints a picture of the early church as a new Israel. This would have appealed to those in the Jewish community, as they could see the church fulfilling the role of the ideal community in the age to come. This community was attractive to those Jews living in poverty at this time.

What is striking about the Christians' sharing all their goods in common is that it was a voluntary practice. The iterative imperfect tense is used in **34b–35**. This tense indicates that the community members used to sell their property and share the wealth as a regular practice. There is evidence that the Qumran communities near the Dead Sea around the time of Christ practiced the surrender of property. There is a similar generosity of spirit and on-going commitment to communal needs here in Acts.

Laying the money at the apostles' feet was an act of submission—not to the apostles as mere men, but to Christ. The twelve represented Christ on earth. The act of the believers laying the money at their feet was symbolic of submitting their wealth to Christ. This was not worship of the apostles but a symbolic statement. The apostles actually turned over the responsibility of distributing the proceeds to the seven deacons once this duty distracted them from their main task of prayer and preaching the Word (**Acts 6:1–7**).

Barnabas' given name was Joses or Joseph. The apostles who spoke Aramaic nicknamed Joses "Barnabas," meaning "son of prophecy," from the Aramaic *bar* meaning "son of" and *nabu* meaning "prophecy." Some have given the nickname a slightly different meaning, translating it as "son of refreshment." Based on his intimate knowledge of the man, Luke translated the Aramaic into Greek as *huios parakleseos*, which is translated variously as "son of consolation/exhortation/encouragement." Parakleseos comes from the same root as the word Jesus used in His promise to send the Holy Spirit: "And I will pray to the Father and He will give you another Comforter [*parakletos*], that He may abide with you forever" (**John 14:16**). Luke uses these exact words to indicate that the Holy Spirit had distinguished Himself in Barnabas. It is interesting to note that the main function of prophecy (from which we get part of the compound of Barnabas' name) is to build up, encourage, and comfort (**1 Corinthians 14:3**). Whenever we see Barnabas in the pages of the New Testament, he is building up, encouraging, and comforting others to be their best for Jesus.

SEARCH THE SCRIPTURES

QUESTION 1

What was Barnabas' birth name?

Joses.

LIGHT ON THE WORD

The Giving Apostle

Although Barnabas is a well-known apostle in the New Testament, nothing is known of his life before he makes his initial appearance in Acts. The great missionary came from a Jewish-Cypriot family, but he had family in Jerusalem, including the Apostle John Mark (**Colossians 4:10**). In our scriptural introduction to Barnabas, he has sold some property and given all the proceeds to the apostles to distribute to the church as they saw fit.

II. Consequences of Deception (5:1–10)

The story of Ananias and Sapphira is puzzling. The generosity displayed by the early church was completely spontaneous. No one was commanded to sell their property and give the money to the apostles. People chose to do it because it was their heart's desire to make sure their brothers and sisters in Christ were well cared for. The field was Ananias and Sapphira's to do with as they pleased. It would stand to reason that if they decided to give the apostles part of the money and keep part of the money for themselves, that would have been perfectly acceptable.

What prompted them to lie to the apostles? Maybe they wanted to appear generous so they could become leaders in the church. Maybe they wanted to be seen giving a lot of money like the rich people in **Mark 12:41–43**. Whatever their reason, what happened to them serves as a strong reminder that the façade we put up to impress others is not able to stand in the presence of the Holy Spirit. God is a discerner of the heart, thoughts, and intents of people. It is impossible to lie to Him; He knows us and whether what we do is sincere or for show and appearance. God will reward us according to our intentions, so make sure that all that you do is done with a pure heart and not a hidden agenda.

5:1 But a certain man named Ananias, with Sapphira his wife, sold a possession, 2 And kept back part of the price, his wife also being privy to it, and brought a certain part, and laid it at the apostles' feet. 3 But Peter said, Ananias, why hath Satan filled thine heart to lie to the Holy Ghost, and to keep back part of the price of the land? 4 Whiles it remained, was it not thine own? and after it was sold, was it not in thine own power? why hast thou conceived this thing in thine heart? thou hast not lied unto men, but unto God. 5 And Ananias hearing these words fell down, and gave up the ghost: and great fear came on all them that heard these things. 6 And the young men arose, wound him up, and carried him out, and buried him. 7 And it was about the space of three hours after, when his wife, not knowing what was done, came in. 8 And Peter answered unto her, Tell me whether ye sold the land for so much? And she said, Yea, for so much. 9 Then Peter said unto her, How is it that ye have agreed together to tempt the Spirit of the Lord? behold, the feet of them which have buried thy husband are at the door, and shall carry thee out. 10 Then fell she down straightway at his feet, and yielded up the ghost: and the young men came in, and found her dead, and, carrying her forth, buried her by her husband. 11 And great fear came upon the whole church and upon all who heard of these things.

Nothing is known about Ananias and his wife Sapphira outside of their sin. It is a sad reminder that sometimes we may be known for all the bad we have done and not the good. The name Ananias means "one whom God has graciously given" and it stands in stark contrast to the stinginess of his actions in this narrative. His actions also stand in stark contrast to the actions of Barnabas, who gave all of the money from the sale of his land to the church. This was in direct contradiction of the work of faith being done in the hearts of those early believers. They truly believed everything was to be shared by all; apparently Ananias and his wife Sapphira did not.

Sapphira was named as an accomplice in this act of selfishness and dishonesty. The Bible does not say that she actually sold the land or kept back the proceeds. It does say that she had knowledge of what Ananias did. She is guilty because she knowingly went along with it. The word in the King James is "privy" (Gk. *sunorao*, **soon-ah-RAH-oh**). It is a compound verb using the Greek words for "together with" and "to see or know." She was not an innocent party but knew what was going on and considered it in her best interest to keep some of the money as well.

Peter as one of the apostles confronts Ananias. The Holy Spirit revealed Ananias' sin to him. Two things come to mind as we look at Peter's words of confrontation. First he says that Satan, not the Holy Spirit, had filled Ananias' heart. The direct influence of Satan himself prompted Ananias to keep some of the money and lie to the apostles and the rest of the church.

Peter then goes right to the heart of the matter. The land was Ananias' property before it was sold. The money was his when he sold the land. It made no sense to lie to the church. Ultimately Ananias did not lie to the church, but to God. He had broken the trust of the community through his selfish and deceptive act. The word for "kept back" can also mean "to pilfer or embezzle." Once Ananias pledged to give the proceeds to the church, it was the Lord's property; to keep some was embezzlement. His act was a sin not just against the community but against God. The

word for "conceived" (Gk. *tithemi*, **TI-thay-mee**) also means "set" or "appointed" and indicates the premeditation on the part of Ananias. This was not a knee-jerk reaction, but a planned scheme to deceive the church.

Immediately Ananias is judged, convicted, and executed. We do not know what caused Ananias' death. One thing we know for sure is that this judgment was God's judgment. Immediately the result is that "great fear came upon all who heard it"—not an ordinary fear but a "great fear." Here we see the effect of Ananias' death and the possible reason for Luke including this incident in the narrative. Luke wanted to show the hand of God in forming the community and protecting its purity.

For the young men to immediately wrap him up and carry him out without ceremony showed that this was divine judgment. In first century Palestine, only the burials of criminals and those who committed suicide were done with this much urgency. The young men were back within a matter of three hours.

Next, Peter confronts Sapphira. She had walked in not knowing what had happened. Luke does not state where this meeting took place and who was present. All he wants the reader to focus on is the seriousness of the couple's deception. Peter questions her on the price of the sale. It doesn't state how much it was and whether it was for good reason—any amount was enough to warrant the judgment of the Lord. Peter in his question gives Sapphira a chance to repent of her wrongdoing. To her demise, she does not repent but continues with the lie.

Peter's reaction is similar to what he said to Ananias: It was not to men that she had lied, but to God. Ananias and Sapphira had both agreed (Gk. *sumphoneo*, **sum-foe-NEH-oh**), which literally means to "sound together" indicating they both were on one accord, indicating their planning to lie to the community. This was not a mere reaction, but a formulated, well thought out plan to deceive the community. Peter then lets Sapphira know she will meet the same fate as her husband.

Sapphira fell down dead in the same way her husband did. The same young men who had carried Ananias out to be buried also carried her out. They were together in their sin, and now they lay together in death. It is interesting to note that Luke mentions the sin and fate of Sapphira as well as her husband. Throughout the books of Luke and Acts, women are given an equal amount of attention as men. It is the same in this case, although Sapphira's actions are far from praiseworthy. Still, it shows Luke's focus on the value of women as equal agents and recipients in God's economy.

Again we hear that "a great fear" comes on not only the whole church but also everyone who heard about these things. Here we see Luke writing not only from a spiritual perspective, but also as an apologist for the church. He is showing his audience that the early church community was the real thing. It was in fact God's community empowered by the Spirit and tasked to continue the ministry of the crucified and resurrected Messiah.

SEARCH THE SCRIPTURES

QUESTION 2
Was Ananias free to do what he wanted to do with the money after selling his land?

Yes.

LIGHT ON THE WORD

Knowing Our Hearts
God is a discerner of the heart, thoughts, and intents of people. It is impossible to lie to Him; He knows us and whether what we do is sincere or for show and appearance. God will reward us according to our intentions, so make sure that all that you do is done with a pure heart and not a hidden agenda.

BIBLE APPLICATION

AIM: Students will know that believers in Christ are responsible to care for others.

Today it seems like people are quick to cast the church and Christians in a negative light. Pastors of large congregations are criticized for their congregations being too large. Pastors of small congregations are criticized for their congregations not growing. This is all the more reason for us to make sure that we are sincere in all that we do. Engaging in pointless arguments will not do anything to advance the cause of Christianity. However, displays of sincere compassion, generosity, and concern will silence any critic.

STUDENT'S RESPONSES

AIM: Students will understand that believers should have the right intentions when caring for those in need.

We at times get stuck thinking that making periodic contributions to the "Benevolence Fund" is all that we need to do in terms of helping others. While making contributions is a great thing, this lesson emphasizes the whole community's responsibility to care for all those in need. Together with the class, plan a project in which you can pool your resources together to sacrificially help someone in need.

PRAYER

Dear Jesus, help us to be honest with You, ourselves, and others. Let us not create stories and lies that cause pain, problems, and even death. As we accept the purity of Your love and goodness, we will create hearts that are acceptable unto You. In the Name of Jesus we pray, amen.

HOW TO SAY IT

Privy   PRI-vee.

Cyprus   SAI-pris.

PREPARE FOR NEXT SUNDAY

Read **Acts 5:27–29, 33–42** and "Witnessing to the Truth."

DAILY HOME BIBLE READINGS

MONDAY
Rescuing the Weak
(Psalm 82)

TUESDAY
Living Blamelessly
(Psalm 26)

WEDNESDAY
Sharing Generously
(1 Timothy 5:11–19)

THURSDAY
Sharing with All
(Isaiah 1:15–18)

FRIDAY
Sharing Troubles
(Philippians 4:1–14)

SATURDAY
Sharing Out of Abundance
(Luke 3:10–16)

SUNDAY
Sharing All Things
(Acts 4:34–5:10)

Sources:

Carson, D.A., France, R.T., Motyer, J.A., Wenham, J.G. *New Bible Commentary.* Downers Grove, IL: Intervarsity Press, 1993.

Keener, Craig S. *IVP Bible Background Commentary.* Downers Grove, IL: Intervarsity Press, 1993.

Polhill, John B. Acts. *New American Commentary: An Exegetical and Theological Exposition of Holy Scripture.* Nashville: B&H Publishing, 1992.

COMMENTS / NOTES:

_____

_____

_____

_____

_____

_____

_____

_____

_____

_____

_____

_____

_____

_____

_____

_____

_____

_____

_____

_____

_____

_____

_____

_____

_____

_____

_____

_____

_____

_____

_____

_____

_____

_____

_____

_____

_____

WITNESSING TO THE TRUTH

BIBLE BASIS: ACTS 5:27–29, 33–42

BIBLE TRUTH: The apostles knew that they were obeying God's calling, even when the authorities tried to stop them.

MEMORY VERSE: "Then Peter and the other apostles answered and said, We ought to obey God rather than men" (Acts 5:29).

LESSON AIM: By the end of this lesson we will: EXAMINE the apostles' proclamation of Jesus as the Messiah despite being ordered not to do so by the Sanhedrin; ASSESS our commitment to witnessing and proclaiming the name of Jesus; and IDENTIFY and overcome barriers to evangelism efforts within and without the church community.

TEACHER PREPARATION

MATERIALS NEEDED: Quarterly Commentary/Teacher Manual, Adult Quarterly, Adult resources—charts, worksheets, and other teaching tools, paper, pens, pencils, Bibles (several different versions)

OTHER MATERIALS NEEDED / TEACHER'S NOTES:

_____

_____

LESSON OVERVIEW

LIFE NEED FOR TODAY'S LESSON
Sometime people are so dedicated to a cause that they will go to any lengths, even enduring pain and suffering to achieving their goals.

BIBLE LEARNING
The apostles believed their commitment to Christ was greater than the authority of others.

BIBLE APPLICATION
Christians can develop a stronger commitment to God and a willingness to follow Christ.

STUDENTS' RESPONSES
Believers learn that in spite of difficult times, they can depend on the Lord.

LESSON SCRIPTURE

ACTS 5:27–29, 33–42, KJV

27 And when they had brought them, they set them before the council: and the high priest asked them,

28 Saying, Did not we straitly command you that ye should not teach in this name? and, behold, ye have filled Jerusalem with

ACTS 5:27–29, 33–42, NIV

27 The apostles were brought in and made to appear before the Sanhedrin to be questioned by the high priest.

28 "We gave you strict orders not to teach in this name," he said. "Yet you have filled Jerusalem with your teaching and are

your doctrine, and intend to bring this man's blood upon us.

29 Then Peter and the other apostles answered and said, We ought to obey God rather than men.

33 When they heard that, they were cut to the heart, and took counsel to slay them.

34 Then stood there up one in the council, a Pharisee, named Gamaliel, a doctor of the law, had in reputation among all the people, and commanded to put the apostles forth a little space;

35 And said unto them, Ye men of Israel, take heed to yourselves what ye intend to do as touching these men.

36 For before these days rose up Theudas, boasting himself to be somebody; to whom a number of men, about four hundred, joined themselves: who was slain; and all, as many as obeyed him, were scattered, and brought to nought.

37 After this man rose up Judas of Galilee in the days of the taxing, and drew away much people after him: he also perished; and all, even as many as obeyed him, were dispersed.

38 And now I say unto you, Refrain from these men, and let them alone: for if this counsel or this work be of men, it will come to nought:

39 But if it be of God, ye cannot overthrow it; lest haply ye be found even to fight against God.

40 And to him they agreed: and when they had called the apostles, and beaten them, they commanded that they should not speak in the name of Jesus, and let them go.

41 And they departed from the presence of

determined to make us guilty of this man's blood."

29 Peter and the other apostles replied: "We must obey God rather than human beings!

33 When they heard this, they were furious and wanted to put them to death.

34 But a Pharisee named Gamaliel, a teacher of the law, who was honored by all the people, stood up in the Sanhedrin and ordered that the men be put outside for a little while.

35 Then he addressed the Sanhedrin: "Men of Israel, consider carefully what you intend to do to these men.

36 Some time ago Theudas appeared, claiming to be somebody, and about four hundred men rallied to him. He was killed, all his followers were dispersed, and it all came to nothing.

37 After him, Judas the Galilean appeared in the days of the census and led a band of people in revolt. He too was killed, and all his followers were scattered.

38 Therefore, in the present case I advise you: Leave these men alone! Let them go! For if their purpose or activity is of human origin, it will fail.

39 But if it is from God, you will not be able to stop these men; you will only find yourselves fighting against God."

40 His speech persuaded them. They called the apostles in and had them flogged. Then they ordered them not to speak in the name of Jesus, and let them go.

41 The apostles left the Sanhedrin, rejoicing because they had been counted worthy of suffering disgrace for the Name.

the council, rejoicing that they were counted worthy to suffer shame for his name.

42 And daily in the temple, and in every house, they ceased not to teach and preach Jesus Christ.

42 Day after day, in the temple courts and from house to house, they never stopped teaching and proclaiming the good news that Jesus is the Messiah.

LIGHT ON THE WORD

The council. This refers to the Sanhedrin, the highest Jewish council. Comprised of the high priest, elders, scribes, and members of prominent families, the Sanhedrin presided over civil, criminal, and religious matters. Both Pharisees and Sadducees were represented in the council.

Apostles. This word comes from the Greek *apostolos*, which means "sent ones." These were the twelve men that Jesus chose from among His wider group of disciples to be with Him and to teach. This title was conferred upon them by Jesus Himself in **Luke 6:13**. Paul is also considered an apostle, though he was not one of the Twelve. He was personally commissioned by Jesus to be an apostle.

TEACHING THE BIBLE LESSON

LIFE NEED FOR TODAY'S LESSON

AIM: Students will know that some people are so dedicated to a cause that they will go to any lengths, even enduring pain and suffering, to achieve their goals.

INTRODUCTION

Teaching in Difficult Times
The fifth chapter of Acts gives an account of the powerful ministry of the apostles.

The apostles had been commissioned by Jesus Himself to teach and be witnesses in **Matthew 28:19–20**. Following the outpouring of the Holy Spirit, the apostles taught powerfully, and their teaching was accompanied by signs and wonders. The high priest and the Sadducees were filled with jealousy and had Peter and John arrested. However, an angel appeared to them during the night, freed them, and instructed them to teach the Word of Life, the words of salvation and eternal life. At this time, Christianity was called "The Way" and "The Life" (**Acts 9:2**).

BIBLE LEARNING

AIM: Students will learn that believers can develop a stronger commitment to God and a willingness to follow Christ.

I. CHOOSING TO OBEY GOD (Acts 5:27–29)

The Sanhedrin forbid Peter and John from teaching in the name of Jesus (**Acts 4:18**). However, Jesus had given them a mandate to teach. An angel had further instructed them the previous night. Knowing that it could result in persecution, the apostles continue to "fill Jerusalem" with their teaching and perform signs and wonders. The apostles have already been imprisoned and seen the treatment Jesus received for going against the religious establishment. The apostles are very aware of the danger of spreading their message. Staring into the face of persecution and possibly death, the apostles consciously choose to obey God, even at personal cost to themselves.

Acts 5:27–29, 33–42

27 And when they had brought them, they set them before the council: and the high priest asked them, 28 Saying, Did not we straitly command you that ye should not teach in this name? and, behold, ye have filled Jerusalem with your doctrine, and intend to bring this man's blood upon us. 29 Then Peter and the other apostles answered and said, We ought to obey God rather than men.

The disciples had been arrested and imprisoned the night before. They were now apprehended again in the morning. Having placed the disciples before the Sanhedrin, the high priest brings a threefold charge against them.

First, the apostles are accused of violating the previous injunction given to them not to preach in the name of Jesus. The phrase translated here as "straitly command" in Greek is *paraggelia paraggello* (**pah-ron-ghe-LEE-ah pah-ron-GHEL-loh**) or "to command a command." Use of a verb with its cognate dative like this can emphasize the idea of the verb. So rather than just being "commanded," they were "straitly commanded." The apostles were violating the authority of the high priest, who was the de facto ruler over the Jewish nation.

Second, it is a grievous accusation that the apostles had "filled" (Gk. *pleroo*, **play-ROW-oh**) Jerusalem with their doctrine. This word means to fill up to the full or completely. The apostles had filled Jerusalem with the teaching of Christ's death and resurrection. In just

a short time, all Jerusalem knew of Christ's resurrection.

Lastly, the Sanhedrin claims the apostles mean to blame the council for Jesus' death. The Sanhedrin might say this intending to insinuate the disciples were inciting the populace to sedition, but more clearly they are revealing their own guilty consciences.

SEARCH THE SCRIPTURES

QUESTION 1
What is the name of the council that Peter and the other apostles had to appear before? How many charges were brought against them?

The Sanhedrin and 3.

LIGHT ON THE WORD

Obedience to God
The disciples refuse to be intimidated. Without any denial or hesitation, Peter provides a powerful rejoinder that obedience to God takes priority over the conflicting orders of the Sanhedrin. The word for "obey" (Gk. *peitharcheo*, **pay-thar-KHEH-oh**) here specifically means to obey a ruler or superior. For Peter, obedience to God is non-negotiable and takes precedence over the commandments of men.

II. WORDS OF CAUTION (vv. 33–39)

The Sanhedrin is in a difficult situation. On one hand, they are furious with the apostles for teaching and healing in Jesus' name and even more so for defying their orders. On the other hand, they fear the people and do not want to upset them. The Sanhedrin wants to kill the apostles, but Gamaliel, the most prominent rabbi of their time, cautions them not to act on their wishes (**vv. 34–36**).

Gamaliel urges the council to proceed with caution. Theudas and Judas had come and caused the people to revolt, but when they were killed, their followers scattered. Unfortunately, Gamaliel put Jesus in the same category as the impostors. He felt that, given enough time, Jesus' followers would also disband. Gamaliel also acknowledges the possibility that the apostles were sent from God. He understands that if, indeed, the apostles are from God, the Sanhedrin will not be able to stop them.

33 When they heard that, they were cut to the heart, and took counsel to slay them. 34 Then stood there up one in the council, a Pharisee, named Gamaliel, a doctor of the law, had in reputation among all the people, and commanded to put the apostles forth a little space; 35 And said unto them, Ye men of Israel, take heed to yourselves what ye intend to do as touching these men. 36 For before these days rose up Theudas, boasting himself to be somebody; to whom a number of men, about four hundred, joined themselves: who was slain; and all, as many as obeyed him, were scattered, and brought to nought. 37 After this man rose up Judas of Galilee in the days of the taxing, and drew away much people after him: he also perished; and all, even as many as obeyed him, were dispersed. 38 And now I say unto you, Refrain from these men, and let them alone: for if this counsel or this work be of men, it will come to nought: 39 But if it be of God, ye cannot overthrow it; lest haply ye be found even to fight against God.

When the members of the Sanhedrin hear Peter's response (**vv. 29–32**), they are cut to the heart or "enraged" (RSV). The Greek verb *diaprio* (**dee-ah-PREE-oh**) translated here as "cut to the heart" has the root meaning of being "sawn through." It is found only here and in **verse 7:54**. It means that they were violently enraged, indicating a state of very

sharp vexation resulting in inward rage. It is a situation where personal rage dethrones reason. Like wounded and cornered beasts, the only recourse is to destroy their pursuers. So they resolve to kill the disciples.

When the Sanhedrin seemed likely to resort to violent measures against the apostles, Gamaliel, a Pharisee among them, intervenes. He was a kindly man who was loved and respected, and, obviously, was more tolerant than his fellows. Had the Sanhedrin not been restrained by Gamaliel's cool and wise advice, they probably would have ordered the stoning of the disciples as they later did Stephen. Three important things are to be noted of Gamaliel: he was a Pharisee, a doctor of the law, and had a reputation among all the people. Hence he was best qualified and suited to defend the apostles. He was the teacher of Saul, who became Paul the apostle (**Acts 22:3**), and he was the grandson of Hillel, and the most influential rabbi of his time. Ancient Jewish scholars wrote of him that, "Since Rabban Gamaliel the elder died there has been no more reverence for the law; and purity and abstinence died out at the same time." Like his grandfather Hillel, he was noted for his liberal attitude.

SEARCH THE SCRIPTURES

QUESTION 2
Describe who was Gamaliel and his relationship to Peter and John.

Gamaliel was a Pharisee, a doctor of the law, and had a reputation among all the people. He defended the apostles.

LIGHT ON THE WORD

Gamaliel, the Defender
Gamaliel's advice is to stand away from these men and let them alone. He warns the court to exercise caution lest they find themselves

going against God. If the counsel or work is of men—literally "out of men," that is "of human origin"—it would come to nothing and be overthrown. To bolster his argument, he cites two examples that were probably well known to the members of the court. First he cites Theudas. In those days Palestine had a quick succession of firebrand leaders who set themselves up as the deliverers of their country and sometimes even as the Messiah. Among them was a man named Theudas, who led a band of people out to the Jordan with the promise that he could divide the waters and that they would walk over in dry land, and whose rising was swiftly dealt with. Gamaliel's second example is Judas. He had rebelled at the time of the census taken by the governor Quirinius in A.D. 6 in order to arrange taxation. Judas took up the position that God was the King of Israel, and to Him alone tribute was due; all other taxation was impious and to pay it was a blasphemy. He attempted to raise a revolution but failed.

III. PERSECUTION AND JOY (vv. 40–42)

Bearing Gamaliel's warning in mind, the Sanhedrin calls the apostles in once again. They repeat their orders not to teach in the name of Jesus. Because they disobeyed the Sanhedrin's initial orders, the apostles are punished according to Jewish law, which called for thirty-nine lashes on bare skin with a leather whip. The beating not only gave vent to the Sanhedrin's fury but was intended to deter and shame the apostles. By bringing shame on the apostles, they hoped to also bring shame on those listening to their teaching.

Rather than being frightened or embittered, the apostles go away rejoicing. They are honored to suffer disgrace for the name of Jesus. Christ had warned them that persecution would come: "God blesses you when people mock you and persecute you and lie about you and say all sorts of evil things against you because you are my followers. Be happy about it! Be very glad! For a great reward awaits you in heaven. And remember, the ancient prophets were persecuted in the same way" (**Matthew 5:11–12, NLT**). Not only do the apostles rejoice, they redouble their efforts. Every day they teach about Jesus (**v. 42**), whether in the temple or in people's homes. The apostles joyfully follow Jesus' instructions knowing that they put themselves in danger by doing so.

40 And to him they agreed: and when they had called the apostles, and beaten them, they commanded that they should not speak in the name of Jesus, and let them go. 41 And they departed from the presence of the council, rejoicing that they were counted worthy to suffer shame for his name. 42 And daily in the temple, and in every house, they ceased not to teach and preach Jesus Christ.

The Sanhedrin listens to Gamaliel and once again, after threatening the apostles, lets them go, but this time with a flogging. The exact word for "beaten" (Gk. *dero*, **DEH-ro**) was originally used for flaying and skinning. It is also a general word for violent whipping. In other words, the apostles received a beating that left wounds on the skin. Flogging was the customary punishment used as a warning not to persist in an offense. It consisted of thirty-nine lashes, often referred to as the forty less one (cf. **2 Corinthians 11:24**), based on **Deuteronomy 25:3**. It was still a cruel punishment. With bared chest and in a kneeling position, one was beaten with a tripled strap of calf hide across both chest and back, two on the back for each stripe across the chest. Men were known to have died from the ordeal. As before, the apostles are warned not to continue their witness in Jesus' name.

This time the warning is reinforced with somewhat stronger persuasion.

The apostles remain undeterred. They are determined to face whatever dangers threaten. They are not cowed by the council's threats and commands. The apostles continue to obey God rather than men. In fact, they rejoice at having suffered for Jesus' name. This word "suffer shame" (Gk. *atimazo*, **ah-ti-MAHD-zo**) means to suffer dishonor and disgrace. This psychological suffering serves as a counterpoint to the physical beating they received. And the witness to the name continues—publicly in the temple and privately in Christians' homes. They rejoice in persecution for two reasons. First, it is an opportunity to demonstrate their loyalty to Christ. Second, it is a real opportunity to share in the experience of Christ. Those who share in the cross-bearing will share in the crown-wearing.

SEARCH THE SCRIPTURES

QUESTION 3
Why did the apostles rejoice?

The apostles rejoiced because they were counted worthy to suffer for the Gospel.

LIGHT ON THE WORD

Proclaiming the Gospel
The apostles' witness, their proclamation of the Gospel, is their primary task and occupation. Spence-Jones sums up these verses beautifully:

"The spirit and conduct of the apostles here recorded is a precious example to their successors. To glory in the cross, to count shame endured for Christ's sake the highest for Christ's sake the highest honor, and to be unwearied and undaunted in teaching and preaching Jesus Christ through good report and through evil report, is the true character

and work of every bishop of souls."

BIBLE APPLICATION

AIM: Students will understand the importance of developing a stronger commitment to God and a willingness to follow Christ.

Many Christians in the United States are not willing to sacrifice their comfort, let alone their lives, for God. Around the world, Christians are persecuted, tortured, and killed for preaching Jesus. Christians are persecuted in over fifty countries, including imprisonment, torture, and martyrdom. The five counties that have the most severe persecution are North Korea, Somalia, Syria, Iraq, and Afghanistan. Still, the church is growing in these hostile nations. They follow the example of the apostles, most of whom paid for their obedience with their lives. The apostles were willing to do whatever it took to obey God. Are you?

STUDENT'S RESPONSES

AIM: Students will learn that in spite of difficult times, they can depend on the Lord.

Like the apostles, we are to continue to proclaim the name of Jesus even in difficult circumstances. They never stopped proclaiming the Good News of Christ even in the face of imprisonment and beatings. Even amid persecution, the apostles rejoiced because they valued their obedience to Jesus more than their safety or lives. They were determined to make Christ known even at great personal cost, and felt privileged to suffer for the name of Christ.

While we have relative freedom to share the Gospel in the United States, many do not have the same opportunity. Research different organizations that aid those in other countries who are persecuted, such as Voice of the

Martyrs (http://www.persecution.com) or Open Doors USA (http://www.opendoorsusa.org). Look for opportunities to write to those who are suffering persecution for their faith in other countries.

PRAYER

Dear Jesus, bless us to stand up with courage and conviction for knowing and believing in You and Your Word. Our determination to witness to others about who You are, is a reflection of Your strength and live. In the Name of Jesus, we pray. Amen.

HOW TO SAY IT

Gamaliel.	gah-**mah**-**LEE**-ale.
Quirinius.	kwih-**RIN**-ee-uhs.
Rabban.	**RAH**-ban.
Theudas.	**THOO**-duhs.

PREPARE FOR NEXT SUNDAY

Read **Acts 7:2–4, 8–10, 17, 33–34, 45–47, 53** and "Remembering God's Faithfulness."

DAILY HOME BIBLE READINGS

MONDAY
The Cause of Truth
(Psalm 45:1–4, 6–7)

TUESDAY
The Life of Truth
(Proverbs 14:22–29)

WEDNESDAY
The Power of Truth
(Luke 4:14–19)

THURSDAY
Avoid Foolishness; Live Truthfully
(2 Timothy 2:14–16, 22–26)

FRIDAY
Trustworthy and Truth
(Revelation 22:1–7)

SATURDAY
Prevailing Truth
(Acts 4:5–12)

SUNDAY
Witnessing the Truth
(Acts 5:27–29, 33–42)

Sources:

Alexander, Joseph A. *Commentary on Acts of the Apostles.* Grand Rapids: Zondervan Publishing House, 1956 (reprint).

Bruce, F. F. *The Book of the Acts.* The New International Commentary on the New Testament. Grand Rapids, Mich.: William B. Eerdmans Publishing Co., 1988.

Carter, Charles W. and Ralph Earle. *The Acts of the Apostles.* Salem, Ohio: Schmul Publishing Co., 1959.

Dockery, David S., ed. *Holman Concise Bible Commentary.* Nashville, TN: Broadman & Holman Publishers, 1998.

Henry, Matthew. *Matthew Henry's Commentary on the Whole Bible: Complete and Unabridged in One Volume.* Peabody: Hendrickson, 1994.

Johnson, Luke Timothy. *The Acts of the Apostles.* Sacra Pagina Series. Vol. 5, Collegeville, Minn.: Liturgical Press, 1992.

Marshall, I Howard. *The Acts of the Apostles: An Introduction and Commentary.* The Tyndale New Testament Commentaries. Grand Rapids, Mich.: W.B. Eerdmans Pub. Co., 1980.

Polhill, John B. Acts, vol. 26, *The New American Commentary.* Nashville: Broadman & Holman Publishers, 1995.

Schuerer, Emil. *A History of The Jewish People in the Time of Jesus Christ.* Edinburgh: T & T Clark, 1885.

Spence-Jones, H. D. M., ed. *Acts of the Apostles, The Pulpit Commentary, Vol. 1.* London; New York: Funk & Wagnalls Company, 1909.

The Holy Bible: English Standard Version. Wheaton: Standard Bible Society, 2001.

Utley, Robert James. *Luke the Historian: The Book of Acts. Vol. 3B.* Study Guide Commentary Series. Marshall, TX: Bible Lessons International, 2003.

Wiersbe, Warren W. *The Bible Exposition Commentary.* Wheaton, IL: Victor Books, 1996.

COMMENTS / NOTES:

_____

_____

_____

_____

_____

_____

_____

_____

_____

_____

_____

REMEMBERING GOD'S FAITHFULNESS

BIBLE BASIS: ACTS 7:2–4, 8–10, 17, 33–34, 45–47, 53

BIBLE TRUTH: Stephen spoke to the council on the history of God's faithfulness.

MEMORY VERSE: "But he, being full of the Holy Ghost, looked up stedfastly into heaven, and saw the glory of God, and Jesus standing on the right hand of God" (Acts 7:55).

LESSON AIM: By the end of this lesson we will: STUDY Stephen's proclamation before the council in which he reminded the Jews of God's faithfulness through the ages and their disregard of God's law; REFLECT on the meaning of beliefs and a willingness to stand firm in life-threatening circumstances; and COMMIT to stand for beliefs about God in all circumstances.

TEACHER PREPARATION

MATERIALS NEEDED: Quarterly Commentary/Teacher Manual, Adult Quarterly, Adult resources—charts, worksheets, and other teaching tools, paper, pens, pencils, Bibles (several different versions)

OTHER MATERIALS NEEDED / TEACHER'S NOTES:

_____

_____

LESSON OVERVIEW

LIFE NEED FOR TODAY'S LESSON
People will defend against all criticism of their beliefs.

BIBLE APPLICATION
Followers of Christ experience the faithfulness of God and share their experiences with others.

BIBLE LEARNING
Stephen spoke critically and directly to his accusers, the Sanhedrin council.

STUDENTS' RESPONSES
Christians should commit and live out their commitment for Christ at all times.

LESSON SCRIPTURE

ACTS 7:2–4, 8–10, 17, 33–34, 45–47, 53, KJV

2 And he said, Men, brethren, and fathers, hearken; The God of glory appeared unto our father Abraham, when he was in Mesopotamia, before he dwelt in Charran,

3 And said unto him, Get thee out of thy

ACTS 7:2–4, 8–10, 17, 33–34, 45–47, 53, NIV

2 To this he replied: "Brothers and fathers, listen to me! The God of glory appeared to our father Abraham while he was still in Mesopotamia, before he lived in Harran.

3 'Leave your country and your people,' God

country, and from thy kindred, and come into the land which I shall shew thee.

4 Then came he out of the land of the Chaldaeans, and dwelt in Charran: and from thence, when his father was dead, he removed him into this land, wherein ye now dwell.

8 And he gave him the covenant of circumcision: and so Abraham begat Isaac, and circumcised him the eighth day; and Isaac begat Jacob; and Jacob begat the twelve patriarchs.

9 And the patriarchs, moved with envy, sold Joseph into Egypt: but God was with him,

10 And delivered him out of all his afflictions, and gave him favour and wisdom in the sight of Pharaoh king of Egypt; and he made him governor over Egypt and all his house.

17 But when the time of the promise drew nigh, which God had sworn to Abraham, the people grew and multiplied in Egypt,

33 Then said the Lord to him [Moses], Put off thy shoes from thy feet: for the place where thou standest is holy ground.

34 I have seen, I have seen the affliction of my people which is in Egypt, and I have heard their groaning, and am come down to deliver them. And now come, I will send thee into Egypt.

45 Which also our fathers that came after brought in with Jesus into the possession of the Gentiles, whom God drave out before the face of our fathers, unto the days of David;

46 Who found favour before God, and desired to find a tabernacle for the God of Jacob.

said, 'and go to the land I will show you.'

4 "So he left the land of the Chaldeans and settled in Harran. After the death of his father, God sent him to this land where you are now living.

8 Then he gave Abraham the covenant of circumcision. And Abraham became the father of Isaac and circumcised him eight days after his birth. Later Isaac became the father of Jacob, and Jacob became the father of the twelve patriarchs.

9 "Because the patriarchs were jealous of Joseph, they sold him as a slave into Egypt. But God was with him

10 and rescued him from all his troubles. He gave Joseph wisdom and enabled him to gain the goodwill of Pharaoh king of Egypt. So Pharaoh made him ruler over Egypt and all his palace.

17 "As the time drew near for God to fulfill his promise to Abraham, the number of our people in Egypt had greatly increased.

33 "Then the Lord said to him, 'Take off your sandals, for the place where you are standing is holy ground.

34 I have indeed seen the oppression of my people in Egypt. I have heard their groaning and have come down to set them free. Now come, I will send you back to Egypt.'

45 After receiving the tabernacle, our ancestors under Joshua brought it with them when they took the land from the nations God drove out before them. It remained in the land until the time of David,

46 who enjoyed God's favor and asked that he might provide a dwelling place for the God of Jacob.

47 But it was Solomon who built a house for

79

47 But Solomon built him an house.

53 Who have received the law by the disposition of angels, and have not kept it.

him.

53 you who have received the law that was given through angels but have not obeyed it."

LIGHT ON THE WORD

Stephen. Stephen was one of the seven men chosen to serve the church as the first deacons. Because the Scriptures he uses in his defense are from the Septuagint (i.e., from the Greek translation of the Old Testament, rather than the original Hebrew), Stephen was most likely a Hellenist Jew. He preached Christ with wisdom and power, which angered the religious establishment. As a result, Stephen became the church's first martyr.

TEACHING THE BIBLE LESSON

LIFE NEED FOR TODAY'S LESSON

AIM: Students will learn that people will defend against all criticism of their beliefs, even if their life is in danger.

INTRODUCTION

Stephen's Irritating Speech

Following the release of the apostles in Acts 5, the message of Christ continued to spread with power. The apostles chose seven men to serve, including Stephen, who were filled with the Spirit and wisdom. Today's lesson highlights some of Stephen's speech to the Sanhedrin after his arrest. He was charged with speaking blasphemy against God, His temple, and Moses. Stephen's response does not directly answer the Sanhedrin's charges; rather, he turns their charges against them

and explains how they have rejected God. In addition to being full of the Spirit, Stephen was well acquainted with the Scriptures and the history of Israel. This made a powerful combination as he spoke before the Sanhedrin.

BIBLE LEARNING

AIM: Students will learn how Stephen spoke critically and directly to his accusers, the Sanhedrin council.

I. THE LORD'S PROMISES TO ABRAHAM (Acts 7:2–4, 8)

While Stephen is accused of being a blasphemer and an apostate from the Jewish faith, he refers to Abraham as "our father Abraham," counting himself among the faithful. Stephen begins his discourse with the call of Abraham, the father of the Jewish faith. God calls Abraham out of Mesopotamia, which was filled with idol worship. Abraham's initial move was to Haran, where he remained until his father died five years later. From there, he moved to Canaan. He was promised a son and given a covenant which was sealed with circumcision. When Isaac was born, he was circumcised on the eighth day. Isaac became the father of Jacob, who was the father of the patriarchs of the twelve tribes of Israel. God was faithful to the promise he made to Abraham that he would have a multitude of descendants.

Acts 7:2–4, 8–10, 17, 33–34, 45–47, 53

2 And he said, Men, brethren, and fathers, hearken; The God of glory appeared unto our father Abraham, when he was in Mesopotamia, before he dwelt in Charran, 3 And said unto him, Get thee out of thy country, and from thy kindred, and come into the land which I shall shew thee. 4 Then came he out of the land of the Chaldaeans, and dwelt in Charran: and from thence, when his father was dead, he removed him into this land, wherein ye now dwell.

Stephen has been falsely accused of blasphemy (6:13). The high priest, acting as the leader of the Sanhedrin, demanded to know whether the accusations were true or not (7:1). What follows in the rest of **Chapter 7** is Stephen's response. Although Stephen's speech in **Acts 7** has often been referred to as his speech before the Sanhedrin, it is more than that—it is his restatement of the teachings that have caused much irritation and resentment. It is notable that although Stephen would disagree with his audience, he began his speech with great deference to his hearers. He started by reminding them that they were his Jewish "brothers" and showed respect to the members of the Sanhedrin by referring to them as "fathers." The elders of Israel were thought of as fathers who ruled the nation. The opening words, "the God of glory" (Gk. *theos tes doxes*, **the-AHS tays DOK-says**), or the God who revealed Himself, are an implied answer to the accusation of blaspheming God. It is no accident that Stephen describes God as such, for His glory is seen in His self-manifestation, which was usually connected to the temple. Alexander gives an excellent explanation of the phrase as: "The God of glory, not merely the glorious [wonderful] God, or

the God worthy to be glorified (**Psalm 29:1; Revelation 4:11**), but more specifically, that God who sensibly revealed himself of old, which is a standing sense of glory… in the Old Testament." It is the God of Glory who appeared (Gk. *optanomai*, **op-TAH-no-my**) or caused Himself to be seen. Thus Stephen identifies himself with the religious faith of his audience.

He then quickly moves into his survey of patriarchal history by quoting **Genesis 12:1**, God's call to Abraham to leave land and relatives and travel to a land to which He would direct him. God revealed Himself to Abraham in His full glory, even in a pagan land. Although **Genesis 12:1** is set in the context of Abraham's residency in Haran, Stephen placed the call in an earlier context when Abraham lived in Ur before ever leaving for Haran (**Genesis 11:32**), a conclusion one could draw from **Genesis 15:7**. By thus stressing that the call came to Abraham at the very beginning, Stephen implicitly made the point that God was in control of Abraham's entire movement. Stephen must have understood that the words of God to Terah in **Genesis 11:32** were similar to those in **Genesis 12:1**. In obedience to God, Abraham with his father Terah left the land of Chaldea (the same as Mesopotamia) and resided in Haran. Abraham promptly and cheerfully obeyed God. He did not know where he was going (**Hebrews 11:8**), but at the call of God he set forth promptly and willingly. We ought to learn a lesson from Abraham. When God distinctly speaks to us, whatever He may bid us do, at whatever cost we may be required to obey, it is only fitting for us to comply instantly and cheerfully. From Haran, God called Abraham into "this land where you are now living" (**v. 4**).

8 And he gave him the covenant of circumcision: and so Abraham begat Isaac, and

circumcised him the eighth day; and Isaac begat Jacob; and Jacob begat the twelve patriarchs.

Verse 8 is a transition verse, showing the beginnings of the fulfillment of God's promises to Abraham and leading into the history of the patriarchs. The covenant of circumcision (Genesis 17:10–14) implies the begetting (Gk. gennao, geh-NAH-oh) or fathering of children, and the circumcision of Isaac confirms that God kept His promise to give descendants to Abraham (Genesis 21:4). Stephen moved quickly through the patriarchal history using the motif of circumcision, from Isaac to Jacob to the twelve patriarchs. The stage was now set for the next step in Stephen's promise-fulfillment pattern: the story of Joseph.

II. THE LORD'S DELIVERANCE THROUGH JOSEPH (vv. 9–10)

As he continues the history of God's work in Israel, Stephen then describes the story of Joseph. Joseph's brothers sold him into slavery in Egypt. However, God accomplishes His purposes in spite of them.

God was with Joseph and delivered him from his troubles. He found favor in the Pharaoh's sight and was placed in a position of authority. In turn, God used Joseph's position to deliver the patriarchs in a time of famine. The patriarchs sojourned in Egypt, which was a fulfillment of God's proclamation that they would be sojourners in a land that was not their own (vv. 6–7). God was faithful to every word He had spoken.

9 And the patriarchs, moved with envy, sold Joseph into Egypt: but God was with him, 10 And delivered him out of all his afflictions, and gave him favour and wisdom in the sight of Pharaoh king of Egypt; and he made him governor over Egypt and all his house.

Stephen recounts the story of Joseph—Joseph's being sold into Egypt out of envy (Gk. zeloo, zay-LOH-oh) or boiling hatred and anger by his brothers, his deliverance from affliction and rise to power in Egypt, the two visits of his brothers in the time of famine, and finally the descent of Jacob's whole clan into Egypt (vv. 9–15). Although Joseph suffered much in Egypt, God was with him (v. 9) even in his afflictions (Gk. thlipsis, THLEEP-sees). The word for "afflictions" means pressure or being pressed together, and metaphorically oppression, distress, and anything which causes one to feel pressured. Stephen's story of Joseph shows that God could not be limited to the temple. He was rejected and cast aside by his brothers, but God revealed himself to Joseph, even in Egypt. Although the Genesis narrative has much to say about Joseph's suffering, Stephen chooses not to dwell on this, instead stressing God's presence with Joseph. God fulfilled His promises through Joseph, delivering Israel from famine by his hand and granting him "favour and wisdom." This word "favour" (Gk. charis, KHA-rees) is also translated "grace" in other places in the New Testament (Luke 2:40; Ephesians 2:8). It is God's unmerited favor, which was given to Joseph in the court of Pharaoh. Though Joseph was characterized by wisdom and favor, his brothers were marked by jealousy, which led them to sell Joseph into Egypt (v. 9). Significantly, Stephen did not identify them as Joseph's "brothers" but rather as "the patriarchs," the fathers of Israel.

SEARCH THE SCRIPTURES

QUESTION 1
Stephen calls Joseph's brothers by their names or patriarchs?

Patriarchs

QUESTION 2
Joseph was granted what by God?

Favor and wisdom

LIGHT ON THE WORD

God's Favor

Wisdom is a particular sign of God's favor to His faithful disciples and would characterize Moses as well later in Stephen's speech (7:22). God gave Joseph favor with people, which allowed him to rise in the eyes of Pharaoh, who established him as ruler over Egypt and the royal household (**v. 10**).

III. THE LORD'S DELIVERANCE THROUGH MOSES (vv. 17, 33–34, 45–47)

Stephen then touches on the story of Moses, who fulfilled God's promise to deliver Israel. The Exodus and the establishment of the tabernacle were major points in Jewish history. Stephen describes the way that Moses was commissioned and that his coming was the fulfillment of promise. Again, God intervened in Israel's history to show His kindness and faithfulness. The Israelites were delivered from bondage in Egypt, sustained in the wilderness, and given the Law; yet they rejected God by rejecting Moses (e.g., **Exodus 12:1–2, 16:3**).

After the Exodus, the Lord established the tabernacle with Israel. The Jews accused Stephen of speaking against the temple because they equated the temple with the presence of God. However, Stephen demonstrates that the presence of God was with His people long before the temple was built.

17 But when the time of the promise drew nigh, which God had sworn to Abraham, the people grew and multiplied in Egypt. 33 Then said the Lord to him, Put off thy shoes from thy feet: for the place where thou standest is holy ground. 34 I have seen, I have seen the affliction of my people which is in Egypt, and I have heard their groaning, and am come down to deliver them. And now come, I will send thee into Egypt.

God never fails to act on time. The descendants of Jacob continued to live in Egypt and multiply until the time was near for the fulfillment of God's promise to Abraham. It was not the divine plan that Israel remain in Egypt surrounded by paganism, so God permitted the Israelites to be enslaved and maltreated until they would be ready and glad to leave Egypt. Eighty years before their departure, their deliverer Moses was born. Preserved from death in infancy, God later prepared him for the momentous and monumental task with forty years of royal training in leadership in Pharaoh's palace. It was followed by forty years of learning patience and submission in the wilderness. As the time of promise was drawing near, God was at work. This was the promise of Abraham that Stephen already quoted.

Stephen recounts Moses' encounter with God in **Exodus 3:1–10**. God commanded Moses to remove his sandals because he was standing on holy ground (**v. 33, Exodus 3:5**). Stephen's inclusion of this detail may have been a subtle reminder to his hearers that there was holy ground elsewhere, far from the temple in Jerusalem. God's self-revelation was and is not confined to Jewish soil in particular or anywhere in general. In other words, no place on earth is innately holy. The message Moses received was that of God's faithfulness to His promise to the patriarchs and His awareness of the distress of their descendants in Egypt. God was about to deliver them through the hand of Moses.

45 Which also our father that came after brought in with Jesus into the possession of

the Gentiles, whom God drave out before the face of our fathers, unto the days of David; 46 Who found favour before God, and desired to find a tabernacle for the God of Jacob. 47 But Solomon built him an house.

Stephen replies to the charges of blasphemy against the temple by showing that the Israelites worshiped God in the wilderness in the tabernacle, which was God's pattern for the temple (a later construction of Solomon's). God gave the guidelines and pattern to Moses. It remained the place of worship after the conquest under Jesus (Gk. *Iesous*, ee-ye-SOOS). This name means "God is salvation." While in the New Testament it is used most often for Christ, it is also a Greek transliteration of Joshua, the captain of the Israelites who brought the nation into the Promised Land. From his time onwards, the tabernacle remained in the land, passed down from generation to generation until the time of David. The word for tabernacle is *skenoma* (Gk. SKAY-no-mah), which is a pitched tent or booth. By highlighting its mobile nature, Stephen clearly implies that the true spiritual worship of God is not confined to allocation or material buildings, and that in the same way that God was worshiped in the wilderness before there was a temple, so He may be worshiped now without a temple.

SEARCH THE SCRIPTURES

QUESTION 3
Stephen was charged with _____.

blasphemy

LIGHT ON THE WORD

House of Worship
David desired to build a temple, but God was perfectly satisfied with the tabernacle; He did not want David to build Him a house. Instead, He would raise up a successor to David who would build such a house (Gk. *oikos*, OY-kose), which is a fixed residence or permanent dwelling. Solomon was that successor who built "a house" for God (v. 47).

IV. ISRAEL'S REJECTION (v. 53)

In his discourse, Stephen shows the Sanhedrin that they have been resisting God from the beginning. The Jews were quick to identify themselves as children of Abraham, but they failed to demonstrate the faith of Abraham. They felt that their biological ties to Abraham took precedence over their personal faith in his God.

The Jewish council was guilty of the same sin their forefathers committed: rejecting those sent by God. Stephen turns the council's own charges against them. They were the sons of the murderers of the prophets and they were following in their father's footsteps by killing Jesus.

53 Who have received the law by the disposition of angels, and have not kept it.

The whole purpose of Stephen's speech now becomes clear. He ends with a declaration of Israel's rebellion. By rejecting Christ, the Jewish leaders had filled up the measure of their fathers. Stephen's historical narrative had illustrated Israel's constant rejection of God's chosen leaders that climaxed in their treatment of Jesus. In its earliest days as a nation, Israel disobeyed the law of God, although it had received the law by the disposition (Gk. *diatage*, dee-ah-tah-GAY) or ordinance of angels. This is nowhere mentioned in the biblical text but is found in rabbinical sources. Moses, Joseph, and the prophets are all types of and pointers to Christ in that they were sent by God and rejected by their own people. Stephen pointed out to his hearers that they had already rejected and killed Christ and they needed to repent.

SEARCH THE SCRIPTURES

QUESTION 4
Stephen accused the leaders of deliberately _____ God's law "that was given through _____" (NIV, v. 53).

Disobeying, angels.

LIGHT ON THE WORD

Resisting God
Though the Jewish council had received the Law and had the presence of God with them, they continued to resist God and those He sent. This was the ultimate example of the nation's unfaithfulness in spite of God's faithfulness to them.

BIBLE APPLICATION

AIM: Students will experience the faithfulness of God and share their experiences with others.

The people of Israel had been rejecting God throughout the years despite His faithfulness to them. Rather than seeing the Law as a beginning, the Jews refused to accept anything new. They had become so entrenched in religious traditions that the Jews did not recognize the Truth when He came to them.

As Christians filled with the Holy Spirit, we recognize that God does not reside in buildings. His Spirit is boundless. We have received the truth of God's Word in Jesus Christ. Like Stephen, we are to proclaim the truth of Christ in all circumstances. Stephen became the Church's first martyr because he witnessed to the truth. Like Stephen, let us remember God's faithfulness to His people throughout history, embrace the truth of Christ, and proclaim the truth boldly.

STUDENT'S RESPONSES

AIM: Students will discover that Christians should commitment and live out their commitment for Christ at all times.

Like Stephen, we should study the Scriptures and learn about the faithfulness of God. We should respect customs and traditions but not idolize them, nor should we become so fixated on them that we miss what God is doing today. Compare and contrast what it would mean to insist on traditions or being stubborn versus taking a legitimate stand for what is right because of a biblical principle.

PRAYER

Dear God, we pray for those who stand up for their beliefs in You. Thank You for Your protection and care for believers who are able to share the "Good News" of Christ. In the Name of Jesus we pray. Amen.

HOW TO SAY IT

Chaldea.	kal-**DEE**-uh.
Charran.	**KAIR**-uhn.
Mesopotamia	me-soh-puh-**TAY**-mee-uh.
Sanhedrin.	san-**HEE**-drihn.
Tabernacle.	**TAB**-uhr-na-kul.

PREPARE FOR NEXT SUNDAY

Read **Acts 5:27–29, 33–42** and "Witnessing to the Truth."

DAILY HOME BIBLE READINGS

MONDAY
Remembering God's Commands
(Deuteronomy 7:1–11)

TUESDAY
Remembering God's Love
(Psalm 31:1–5, 19–24)

WEDNESDAY
Remembering God's Word
(Psalm 119:89–94)

THURSDAY
Remembering God's Grace
(1 Corinthians 1:1–9)

FRIDAY
Remembering God's Will
(1 Thessalonians 5:16–25)

SATURDAY
Responding to God's Faithfulness
(Acts 6:7–15)

SUNDAY
Remembering God's Faithfulness
(Acts 7:2–4, 8–10, 17, 33–34, 45–47, 53)

Sources:

Alexander, Joseph A. *Commentary on Acts of the Apostles*. Grand Rapids, MI: Zondervan, 1956.

Arrington, French L. *The Acts of the Apostles: An Introduction and Commentary*. Peabody, MA: Hendrickson, 1988.

Bruce, F. F. *The Book of the Acts. The New International Commentary on the New Testament*. Grand Rapids, MI: William B. Eerdmans Publishing Co., 1988.

Henry, Matthew. *Matthew Henry's Commentary on the Whole Bible: Complete and Unabridged in One Volume*. Peabody, MA: Hendrickson, 1994.

Jamieson, Robert, A. R. Fausset, and David Brown. *Commentary Critical and Explanatory on the Whole Bible*. Oak Harbor, WA: Logos Research Systems, Inc., 1997.

Johnson, Luke Timothy. *The Acts of the Apostles*. Sacra Pagina Series. Vol. 5. Collegeville, MN: Liturgical Press, 1992.

Marshall, I Howard. *The Acts of the Apostles: An Introduction and Commentary*. The Tyndale New Testament Commentaries. Grand Rapids, MI: William B. Eerdmans Publishing Co., 1980.

Polhill, John B. *Acts*. The New American Commentary, vol. 26. Nashville, TN: Broadman & Holman Publishers, 1995.

Wiersbe, Warren W. *The Bible Exposition Commentary*. Wheaton, IL: Victor Books, 1996.

COMMENTS / NOTES:

THE SPIRIT IS NOT FOR SALE

BIBLE BASIS: Acts 8:9–24

BIBLE TRUTH: Peter claims that inspiring speakers have spiritual power when one's heart is right before God.

MEMORY VERSE: "Then answered Simon, and said, Pray ye to the LORD for me, that none of these things which ye have spoken come upon me" (Acts 8:24).

LESSON AIM: By the end of this lesson we will: RECALL the proclamation of the good news of Jesus Christ and to reveal the power of the Holy Spirit; AFFIRM the necessity of being right with God in order to receive spiritual power from God; and DECIDE and act on witnessing to others about the power of the Holy Spirit.

TEACHER PREPARATION

MATERIALS NEEDED: Quarterly Commentary/Teacher Manual, Adult Quarterly, Adult resources—charts, worksheets, and other teaching tools, paper, pens, pencils, Bibles (several different versions)

OTHER MATERIALS NEEDED / TEACHER'S NOTES:

_____

_____

LESSON OVERVIEW

LIFE NEED FOR TODAY'S LESSON
People gather to hear inspiring speakers.

BIBLE LEARNING
Peter proclaims inspiring speakers are those whose hearts are right before God.

BIBLE APPLICATION
The main source of power in being a witness for Christ is the Holy Spirit.

STUDENTS' RESPONSES
Christians learn how to have the right attitude in regards to spiritual power from God.

LESSON SCRIPTURE

ACTS 8:9–24, KJV

9 But there was a certain man, called Simon, which beforetime in the same city used sorcery, and bewitched the people of Samaria, giving out that himself was some great one:

10 To whom they all gave heed, from the least to the greatest, saying, This man is the great power of God.

ACTS 8:9–24, NIV

9 Now for some time a man named Simon had practiced sorcery in the city and amazed all the people of Samaria. He boasted that he was someone great,

10 and all the people, both high and low, gave him their attention and exclaimed, "This man is rightly called the Great Power

11 And to him they had regard, because that of long time he had bewitched them with sorceries.

12 But when they believed Philip preaching the things concerning the kingdom of God, and the name of Jesus Christ, they were baptized, both men and women.

13 Then Simon himself believed also: and when he was baptized, he continued with Philip, and wondered, beholding the miracles and signs which were done.

14 Now when the apostles which were at Jerusalem heard that Samaria had received the word of God, they sent unto them Peter and John:

15 Who, when they were come down, prayed for them, that they might receive the Holy Ghost:

16 (For as yet he was fallen upon none of them: only they were baptized in the name of the Lord Jesus.)

17 Then laid they their hands on them, and they received the Holy Ghost.

18 And when Simon saw that through laying on of the apostles' hands the Holy Ghost was given, he offered them money,

19 Saying, Give me also this power, that on whomsoever I lay hands, he may receive the Holy Ghost.

20 But Peter said unto him, Thy money perish with thee, because thou hast thought that the gift of God may be purchased with money.

21 Thou hast neither part nor lot in this matter: for thy heart is not right in the sight of God.

22 Repent therefore of this thy wickedness,

of God."

11 They followed him because he had amazed them for a long time with his sorcery.

12 But when they believed Philip as he proclaimed the good news of the kingdom of God and the name of Jesus Christ, they were baptized, both men and women.

13 Simon himself believed and was baptized. And he followed Philip everywhere, astonished by the great signs and miracles he saw.

14 When the apostles in Jerusalem heard that Samaria had accepted the word of God, they sent Peter and John to Samaria.

15 When they arrived, they prayed for the new believers there that they might receive the Holy Spirit,

16 because the Holy Spirit had not yet come on any of them; they had simply been baptized in the name of the Lord Jesus.

17 Then Peter and John placed their hands on them, and they received the Holy Spirit.

18 When Simon saw that the Spirit was given at the laying on of the apostles' hands, he offered them money

19 and said, "Give me also this ability so that everyone on whom I lay my hands may receive the Holy Spirit."

20 Peter answered: "May your money perish with you, because you thought you could buy the gift of God with money!

21 You have no part or share in this ministry, because your heart is not right before God.

22 Repent of this wickedness and pray to the Lord in the hope that he may forgive you for having such a thought in your heart.

and pray God, if perhaps the thought of thine heart may be forgiven thee.

23 For I perceive that thou art in the gall of bitterness, and in the bond of iniquity.

24 Then answered Simon, and said, Pray ye to the LORD for me, that none of these things which ye have spoken come upon me.

23 For I see that you are full of bitterness and captive to sin."

24 Then Simon answered, "Pray to the Lord for me so that nothing you have said may happen to me."

LIGHT ON THE WORD

Philip. Philip is a Hellenistic Jew and one of the seven men chosen by the church in Jerusalem to oversee the day-to-day ministry of support to the underprivileged widows of the Christian community. Whether he is technically regarded as a deacon is not absolutely clear; however, the work accomplished by this group of men has been generally accepted as the origin of the order of the Diaconate (**Acts 6:1–7**). Of the seven, Stephen and Philip are the only ones of whom biblical scholars have a further record in the New Testament. They are described as men of good repute, full of the Spirit and wisdom (**Acts 6:3**).

Samaria. The capital of the Northern Kingdom of Israel. The people of Samaria were classified as a controversial group from the Jews. The group resided north of Judea and south of Galilee in unfriendly tension with its Jewish neighbors. It is not clear when the group known as Samaritans began to populate Samaria, but it could have been as early as the Assyrian destruction of the Northern Kingdom. Because the Samaritans did not consider Jerusalem their primary center of worship, choosing instead to establish various worship sites, especially Mt. Gerizim in the Greco-Roman period, Jews often treated them as Gentiles. All marriages between the groups were forbidden and social relations were greatly restricted. Jesus' attitude toward this detested group drastically contrasted with existing sentiment. It is difficult to determine precisely when the Samaritan sect arose and when the final break with Judaism occurred. Old Testament Scriptures suggest the Samaritan sect originated from repopulated foreign peoples whose worship of God was only a covering for underlying idolatry. In the great commission given prior to His ascension, Jesus told His disciples to take the Gospel to Samaria (**Acts 1:8**). The missionary activity of the early church did indeed include this region.

TEACHING THE BIBLE LESSON

LIFE NEED FOR TODAY'S LESSON

AIM: Students will better understand why people gather to hear inspiring speakers.

INTRODUCTION

Spreading the Good News

The book of Acts begins with the outpouring of the promised Holy Spirit and the commencement of the proclamation of the

Gospel of Jesus Christ. The book of Acts provides an eye witness account of the birth and spread of the church. The Gospel first went to the Jews; but some of them, rejected it. A remnant of the Jews, of course, gladly received the Good News. Although the early disciples experienced resistance from Jews in many places, they also encountered many who believed the gospel and converted, and it is because of the work of primarily Jewish disciples that the gospel was spread to the Gentiles as well. God's plan was to spread the gospel from Jerusalem to Judea, Samaria, and the ends of the earth (**Acts 1:8**). One strong proponent for spreading the Good News was Philip, who became known as "the Evangelist." The designation is well deserved, for when the Jerusalem Christians were scattered by the persecution led by Saul of Tarsus, Philip went to the city of Samaria and proclaimed the gospel with such power that a great number of people joyfully turned to Christ (**Acts 8:1–8**).

BIBLE LEARNING

AIM: Students will discover that Peter believes that inspiring speakers are those whose hearts are right before God.

I. CONNED BY THE POWER OF DECEPTION (vv. 9–13)

Many people in the first century were influenced by enchanters and magicians. The so-called miracle workers were empowered by the enemy, Satan, and performed acts of exorcisms and healings (**Matthew 24:24; 2 Thessalonians 2:9**). These sorcerers used trickery and magic to deceive their audiences. Most acts were preformed for financial gain. Unfortunately, much of this same kind of dishonesty operates in modern-day churches and pulls overwhelming audience participation. Some Christians are still looking for

"quick fixes" and are naïve when it comes to the power of God. They cannot discern when someone is functioning from authentic spiritual power that originates only through Jesus Christ, and are blind by the power of deception and fall victims to financial fraud. The power that comes from Christ is genuine, loving, and sincere and should not be commercialized for profit.

9 But there was a certain man, called Simon, which beforetime in the same city used sorcery, and bewitched the people of Samaria, giving out that himself was some great one: 10 To whom they all gave heed, from the least to the greatest, saying, This man is the great power of God. 11 And to him they had regard, because that of long time he had bewitched them with sorceries. 12 But when they believed Philip preaching the things concerning the kingdom of God, and the name of Jesus Christ, they were baptized, both men and women. 13 Then Simon himself believed also: and when he was baptized, he continued with Philip, and wondered, beholding the miracles and signs, which were done.

For some time before Philip arrived in Samaria, the town had been "bewitched" (Gk. *existemi*, **ex-IS-tay-mee**) by a man named Simon. The word "existemi" means to throw out of place. In this context it meant that the people of Samaria were amazed, astonished, and thrown into wonderment. He practiced witchcraft or "sorcery" (Gk. *mageuo*, **mah-GEW-oh**). Simon used his magical skills to persuade the people of Samaria that he was somebody great (cf. **5:36**). According to church tradition, Simon was said to have traveled to Rome and begun a Gnostic sect called the Simonians. This group was said to have erected a statue in his honor and worshiped him as a god, as well as his consort Helena as a goddess. Although we cannot confirm whether Simonians are directly connected to Simon Magus, this tradition supports the claim of Acts that he made himself to be "some great one."

Luke adds that as a result of the Samaritans' bewitchment they all gave heed (*prosecho*, **pro-SEH-kho**). This word literally means to bring or be with. In this context it means to turn the mind or attention to. Through his signs and wonders, Simon gained a following all over Samaria. We do not know whether at this time Simon had a particular doctrine, but we can see he had a significant influence over the population. Everyone, "the least" (Gk. *mikros*, **mi-KROS**) and "the greatest" (Gk. *megas*, **MEH-gas**), crowded around him, saying that Simon was in some way the special channel of the power of God or the supreme emanation of God Himself. This type of thought was totally antithetical to the Christian message, that Christ was shown to the be the power of God through His resurrection. In this environment, Philip was sent to preach and show people the genuine power of God in the Gospel message of Jesus Christ. For a long time the people "had regard," the same word used in **verse 10** for "they all gave heed." Here Luke underscores the influence Simon had by using the same word but attaching it to duration of time versus the wide range of people. They were devoted to Simon because he had used witchcraft to bewitch them.

Philip did not preach about himself. Philip was preaching (Gk. *euaggelizo*, **ew-ang-ghe-LEED-zo**) "the things concerning the kingdom of God, and the name of Jesus Christ." Here we see the early Christian message, about the kingdom of God and the name of Jesus Christ. In other words, the kingdom and the King. The Samaritans "believed" (Gk. *pisteuo*, **peest-EW-oh**) and "were baptized" (Gk. *baptizo*, **bap-TEED-zo**). In this way, they responded completely to the message of the Good News. They believed and showed it through baptsim.

It says that even Simon believed and was baptized. He followed Philip everywhere, amazed by the great signs and miracles he saw. After having amazed others with his magic practice he himself was amazed. In view of what is said later in **verse 21**, we do not know whether Simon really believed. The Bible language does not always make a distcintion between believing and professing to believe (cf. **James 2:19**). He may have been more amazed by Philip's healing power than by his message.

SEARCH THE SCRIPTURES

QUESTION 1
Describe Simon and what people said about his power.

Simon practiced witchcraft or sorcery. Through his magical powers, he was able to persuade the people of Samaria that he was great and a special channel of power to God, or even God Himself.

LIGHT ON THE WORD

Philip Reaches Out
Unlike most of the other Jews, Philip, one of the deacons in charge of food distribution, spread the Gospel with such power that a great number of people joyfully turned to Christ (**Acts 8:1–8**). He did not limit his audience to other Jews. He went directly to Samaria, the last place many Jews would go, due to age-old prejudice. The Samaritans responded in large numbers. When word got back to Jerusalem, Peter and John were sent to evaluate Philip's ministry. After seeing firsthand God's acceptance of those who previously were considered unacceptable, they quickly became involved in the ministry.

II. CONVERTED BY THE POWER OF THE HOLY SPIRIT (vv. 14–17)

Jewish believers still had doubt that Gentiles (non-Jews) and half-Jews were eligible candidates for the Holy Spirit. The apostles sent Peter and John to investigate this new group of Samaritan believers. They had to keep this new group of believers from becoming disconnected from other disciples. It was necessary not only for the Samaritans' sake but also for the apostles to witness the amazing power of the Holy Spirit. Some biblical scholars believe this dramatic filling of the Spirit validated the importance of powerful and effective preaching of believers. The prevailing pride of some of the Jews was such that they despised the Samaritans and regarded the Gentiles as ceremonially unclean. Philip's preaching and the laying of hands by the Apostles reflected the way the Gospel penetrated social barriers and dissolved racial prejudices. This event also demonstrated that the grace of God in Christ Jesus is freely available to all.

14 Now when the apostles which were at Jersualem heard that Samaria had received the word of God, they sent unto them Peter and John: 15 Who, when they were come down, prayed for them, that they might receive the Holy Ghost: 16 (For as yet he was fallen upon none of them: only they were baptized in the name of the Lord Jesus.) 17 Then laid they their hands on them, and they received the Holy Ghost.

When the "apostles" (Gk. *apostolos*, ah-POS-toe-los) heard that Samaria had received (Gk. dechomai, **DEH-kho-my**) the Word of God, they "sent" (Gk. *apostello*, **ah-po-STEL-lo**; the Greek words for sent and apostle have the same root meaning, literally "the delegated, delegated") Peter and John, to investigate. . On one occasion, James and John had wanted to call fire down from heaven to consume a Samaritan city (cf. **Luke 9:51–56**). It was fitting that one of them should be a part of the delegation that now went to welcome the people of Samaria into the church.

When they arrived, they discovered that although the Samaritans had believed and had been baptized into the name of Jesus, they had not yet received the Holy Ghost. So they prayed for them that they might receive (Gk. *lambano*, **lam-BA-no**) the Holy Ghost. This verb for receive, "lambano" is used in two diferrent ways. Usually in the narrative sense, it means to take or to grasp. The other sesne is to passively receive and this is used quite often in the more theologicallysignificant verses. Although this passage in Acts is a narrative, the second sense is in mind here as they are receiving something from God, not taking or grasping it. Here we see the Holy Spirit as something divinely given. This stands in contrast to Simon's later thinking that he could own the power of the Spirit and use this power for his own purposes.

The Holy Ghost had not yet come upon (Gk. *epipipto*, **eh-pee-PEEP-to**) any of the Samaritans. The word here means to literally "fall on with force." They had simply been baptized into the name of the Lord Jesus. This statement raises some questions that have caused much perplexity and division: How did the apostles know that the Samaritans had not received the Holy Ghost? In the light of **Acts 2:38**, how could the Samaritans have believed and been baptized and not received the Spirit? The Samaritan Christians' experience is the typical experience of Christian life. Becoming a Christian is a process consisting first of conversion and water baptism. Repentance is the initial part of the conversion. Notice how John the Baptist said that one must bring fruit mete for repentance in order to be a candidate for water baptism. The next part is sanctification, which prepares one to receive the gift, or baptism of the Holy Spirit.

In addition to praying for them, the apostles laid (Gk. *epitethemi*, **eh-pee-TEE-thay-mee**) their hands, thus identifying the people for whom they prayed with the rest of the church, particularly the mother church in Jerusalem. In answer to their prayers, the believers received the Holy Ghost.

III. CORRECTED BY THE POWER OF FORGIVENESS (vv. 18-24)

Our society values materialism. So it is no surprise that just about anything has a "price." The lesson of Simon the magician is instructive to those of any age who would presume to barter God's spiritual gifts in hope of personal gain. Simon practiced the art of deception because that is all he knew. His success in trickery prompted great courage. He thought money had the power to buy anything he wanted. When he offered Peter and John money in exchange for the gift of the Holy Spirit it provoked Peter's unequivocal rebuke. The Holy Spirit is not for sale. No amount of money can purchase salvation. To receive the gift of the Holy Spirit, one has to repent, turn from sin and ask God to come into his or her life. God's precious power is only achieved through repentance and belief in Jesus Christ. Simon's response to Peter's reprimand also shows his willingness to receive correction. He admitted his error and sought forgiveness. He recognized the authority given to Peter and John, and more importantly, he acknowledged the power behind the prayers of the righteous.

18 Now when Simon saw that the Spirit was given through the laying on of the apostles' hands, he offered them money, 19 saying, "Give me this power also, so that anyone on whom I lay my hands may receive the Holy Spirit." 20 But Peter said to him, "May your silver perish with you, because you thought you could obtain the gift of God with money!

21 You have neither part nor lot in this matter, for your heart is not right before God. 22 Repent, therefore, of this wickedness of yours, and pray to the Lord that, if possible, the intent of your heart may be forgiven you. 23 For I see that you are in the gall of bitterness and in the bond of iniquity." 24 And Simon answered, "Pray for me to the Lord, that nothing of what you have said may come upon me."

Simon mistook the power of the Holy Spirit as something that could be purchased with money. He misunderstood the Holy Spirit's purpose; it was not another magician's trick to manipulate and gather followers. Simon asks the apostles to give him the same "power" (*exousia*, **ek-zoo-SEE-ah**) or authority; in this context, the power of one who has sway over others. It is not clear whether Simon believed the power he would have would help him t control others or of the Holy Spirit. Either way; he was mistaken, the Holy Spirit is God and cannot be controlled and manipulated out of personal self-interest.

Peter gives Simon a scathing rebuke not a curse, but more like a prediction. He explains that Simon could not buy the Spirit of God; it is a gift (*dorea*, **do-re-AH**). The word in the New Testament, always denotes a supernatural or spiritual gift from God. Simon thought it could be bought the same way you could buy anything else. Peter perceives Simon's spiritual dullness and lets him know he had no part (*meris*, **meh-REES**) or assigned share in the experience of the Holy Spirit. He also says Simon has no lot (*kleros*, **KLAY-ros**), which was the determining a person's share, as of an inheritance, through casting of lots. This was sometimes done by writing the names of individuals on broken pieces of wood or pottery, then placing them into a vase or garment and shaking them. The first one to fall out would be the person chosen for an assignment or to receive a share of wealth, land, etc. This was not done by chance. Peter uses both meris and kleros to make his point: Simon has no part by design or chance in the Holy Spirit through buying it.

Peter tells Simon to repent (Gk. *metanoeo*, **me-tuh-nah-EH-oh**), which is a command to change his mind. It is not enough to feel sorry for what he has done. He also has to come to a new understanding regarding supernatural powers and how the Holy Spirit is obtained. Peter uses two words related to intellect here. The first is repent and the second is intent (Gk. *epinoia*, **eh-pee-NOY-ah**), which is an idea or thought process. Simon must not only realize that what he has done is wrong and pray to God, he must also change his understanding and way of thinking so that such ideas no longer influence his mind or his actions. Peter's mention of the gall of bitterness may be a reference to **Deuteronomy 29:18**, which associates idolatry with bitterness and poison. Peter puts this gall in parallel with the bond of iniquity, suggesting that the two are one and the same. It is Simon's misunderstanding of the Holy Spirit that has ensnared him in a bitter pitfall of sin.

Simon's answer to Peter may have come from remorse and an attempt to avoid the condemnation Peter spoke about not a genuine desire to repent. He mentions nothing about his sin or believing in Christ; his main concern seems to be avoiding punishment. He also asks Peter to pray in his stead as opposed to trusting in Christ and seeking God in prayer himself.

SEARCH THE SCRIPTURES

QUESTION 2
How did Simon think he could "acquire" the Holy Spirit?

Simon thought that he could buy the Holy Spirit.

QUESTION 3
Peter tells Simon that he has to _____ for asking to buy the Holy Spirit.

Repent

LIGHT ON THE WORD
Peter Reprimands Simon
God's precious power is only achieved through repentance and belief in Jesus Christ. Simon's response to Peter's reprimand also shows his willingness to receive correction. He admitted his error and sought forgiveness. He recognized the authority given to Peter and John and more importantly, he acknowledged the power behind the prayers of the righteous.

BIBLE APPLICATION

AIM: Students will know that the main source of power in being a witness for Christ is the Holy Spirit.

Religious charlatans have been around since ancient times. Many people fall prey to an assortment of scams. Christians are no exception. Some are victimized by charismatic individuals who pervert the gospel for profit. True Christian leadership draws others by the power of the Holy Spirit, not by false pretense. They are messengers of God who exalt the person of Jesus Christ.

STUDENT'S RESPONSES

AIM: Students will see that Christians learn how to have the right attitude in regards to spiritual power from God.

Often we are missing something in our spiritual life. It may be a sense of dryness or emptiness. This may be due to the absence of the Holy Spirit's ministry in our lives. Whether you are a new Christian or someone who is mature in the faith you are always in need of spiritual renewal. Pray for the Holy Spirit to fill and empower you to minister to others. Next share your experience with someone else and pray that they would receive the ministry of the Holy Spirit.

PRAYER

Sweet Holy Spirit! Sweet Holy Spirit! You presence in our lives is amazing. We rejoice that You guide us and protect us each and every day. Although the world rejects God's presence and grace, we stand with the right attitude to serve You and worship. In the Name of Jesus we pray. Amen.

HOW TO SAY IT

Diaconate.   DEE-ah-ko-nayt.

Samaria   suh-ME-ree-uh.

PREPARE FOR NEXT SUNDAY

Read **Acts 9:19b–31** and "Saul Earns Credibility."

DAILY HOME BIBLE READINGS

MONDAY
Never Moved
(Psalm 15)

TUESDAY
Be Content
(Hebrews 13:5–10)

WEDNESDAY
Stand Firm
(Ephesians 6:14–18)

THURSDAY
Stand Boldly
(Acts 13:52—14:3)

FRIDAY
Stand Regardless
(Acts 8:1–8)

SATURDAY
Stand Ready
(Acts 8:26–40)

SUNDAY
The Spirit is Not For Sale
(Acts 8:9–24)

Sources:
Keener, Craig S. IVP Bible Background Commentary. Downers Grove, IL: Intervarsity, Press, 1993.
Carson, D.A., France, R.T., Motyer, J.A., Wenham, J.G., New Bible Commentary. Downers Grove, IL: Intervarsity Press, 1993.
Polhill, John B. Acts. New American Commentary: An Exegetical and Theological Exposition of Holy Scripture. Nashville: B&H Publishing, 1992.

COMMENTS / NOTES:

_____
_____
_____
_____
_____
_____
_____
_____
_____
_____
_____
_____
_____
_____
_____
_____
_____
_____
_____
_____
_____

SAUL EARNS CREDIBILITY

BIBLE BASIS: ACTS 9:19b–31

BIBLE TRUTH: Saul's bold and powerful preaching caused the numbers of the church to increase.

MEMORY VERSE: "And straightway he preached Christ in the synagogues, that he is the Son of God" (Acts 9:20).

LESSON AIM: By the end of this lesson we will:

RECALL Saul's acceptance as a Christian and the reward of his zeal in preaching about Jesus; EXAMINE the church's willingness to accept and meaningfully include in the body of Christ those whose background is perceived as being suspect and encourage their bold witness about the change in their lives; and CELEBRATE those whose lives were transformed by Jesus Christ and then became bold witnesses for His cause.

TEACHER PREPARATION

MATERIALS NEEDED: Quarterly Commentary/Teacher Manual, Adult Quarterly, Adult resources—charts, worksheets, and other teaching tools, paper, pens, pencils, Bibles (several different versions)

OTHER MATERIALS NEEDED / TEACHER'S NOTES:

_____

_____

LESSON OVERVIEW

LIFE NEED FOR TODAY'S LESSON
People who are effective advocates boldly tell others about their deepest convictions.

BIBLE LEARNING
Saul earned credibility among many of the believers.

BIBLE APPLICATION
Christians are able to have a bold and strong impact on the lives of others.

STUDENTS' RESPONSES
Christians should not judge others by their past and neglect to see the power of the Holy Spirit in the lives of others.

LESSON SCRIPTURE

ACTS 9:19b–31, KJV

19b Then was Saul certain days with the disciples which were at Damascus.

20 And straightway he preached Christ in the synagogues, that he is the Son of God.

ACTS 9:19b–31, NIV

19b Saul spent several days with the disciples in Damascus.

20 At once he began to preach in the synagogues that Jesus is the Son of God.

21 But all that heard him were amazed, and said; Is not this he that destroyed them which called on this name in Jerusalem, and came hither for that intent, that he might bring them bound unto the chief priests?

22 But Saul increased the more in strength, and confounded the Jews which dwelt at Damascus, proving that this is very Christ.

23 And after that many days were fulfilled, the Jews took counsel to kill him:

24 But their laying await was known of Saul. And they watched the gates day and night to kill him.

25 Then the disciples took him by night, and let him down by the wall in a basket.

26 And when Saul was come to Jerusalem, he assayed to join himself to the disciples: but they were all afraid of him, and believed not that he was a disciple.

27 But Barnabas took him, and brought him to the apostles, and declared unto them how he had seen the Lord in the way, and that he had spoken to him, and how he had preached boldly at Damascus in the name of Jesus.

28 And he was with them coming in and going out at Jerusalem.

29 And he spake boldly in the name of the Lord Jesus, and disputed against the Grecians: but they went about to slay him.

30 Which when the brethren knew, they brought him down to Caesarea, and sent him forth to Tarsus.

31 Then had the churches rest throughout all Judaea and Galilee and Samaria, and were edified; and walking in the fear of the Lord, and in the comfort of the Holy Ghost, were multiplied.

21 All those who heard him were astonished and asked, "Isn't he the man who raised havoc in Jerusalem among those who call on this name? And hasn't he come here to take them as prisoners to the chief priests?"

22 Yet Saul grew more and more powerful and baffled the Jews living in Damascus by proving that Jesus is the Messiah.

23 After many days had gone by, there was a conspiracy among the Jews to kill him,

24 but Saul learned of their plan. Day and night they kept close watch on the city gates in order to kill him.

25 But his followers took him by night and lowered him in a basket through an opening in the wall.

26 When he came to Jerusalem, he tried to join the disciples, but they were all afraid of him, not believing that he really was a disciple.

27 But Barnabas took him and brought him to the apostles. He told them how Saul on his journey had seen the Lord and that the Lord had spoken to him, and how in Damascus he had preached fearlessly in the name of Jesus.

28 So Saul stayed with them and moved about freely in Jerusalem, speaking boldly in the name of the Lord.

29 He talked and debated with the Hellenistic Jews, but they tried to kill him.

30 When the believers learned of this, they took him down to Caesarea and sent him off to Tarsus.

31 Then the church throughout Judea, Galilee and Samaria enjoyed a time of peace and was strengthened. Living in the fear of

the Lord and encouraged by the Holy Spirit, it increased in numbers.

LIGHT ON THE WORD

Saul. Before Paul's conversion to the great apostle and prominent leader of the first-century church, he was Saul the persecutor of Christians. He attained letters from Jerusalem's high priest authorizing him to arrest believers and bring them to Jerusalem for trial (**Acts 9:1–2**). Saul traveled to Damascus for this purpose. Then, on the outskirts of the city came the event that transformed this persecutor of Jesus Christ and destroyer of the infant church into the chief propagator of the Gospel of grace and master builder of the church (**1 Corinthians 3:10; 1 Timothy 1:13**).

Damascus. A Syrian oasis city protected on three sides by mountains and situated on trade routes about 160 miles northeast of Jerusalem. The name Damascus can also refer to the surrounding area in the southwestern part of the modern nation of Syria. Many crops in this area grow well because the land is watered by two rivers: Abana, "the Cool" (modern Nahr Barada), which runs from the northwest mountains through a deep ravine to the city; and Pharpar, "the Crooked" (modern Nahr-el-A-waj), which flows west to east.

TEACHING THE BIBLE LESSON

LIFE NEED FOR TODAY'S LESSON

AIM: Students will learn that people who are effective advocates boldly tell others about their deepest convictions.

INTRODUCTION

Paul Saw the Light

Before Saul's great conversion, he witness ed the stoning of the first Christian martyr, Stephen. Stephen's death commenced the events that would culminate in Saul's conversion and commission as the Apostle to the Gentiles. This transformation had lasting significance in Saul's life; meticulous accounts of it are given in the book of Acts (**9:1–19, 22:1–21, 26:1–23**) and referenced in his own writings (**1 Corinthians 15:9; Galatians 1:13–17**). But as an oppressor of the church, Saul breathed threats and murder against the disciples of the Lord. He tried to abolish the church, imprisoning both male and female Christians. While traveling toward Damascus, a light from heaven shone around Saul and his traveling companions and they fell to the ground (**Acts 9:1–19**). Temporarily blinded, Saul was led into Damascus. There, the disciple Ananias and the Christian community forgave Saul, baptized him, and helped him through the bewildering event of his conversion.

BIBLE LEARNING

AIM: Students will discover how Saul earned credibility among many of the believers.

I. TESTIFYING POWER OF GOD'S LOVE (Acts 9:19b–25)

The sincerity of a speaker makes his or her testimony powerful, believable, and influential. A testimony has greater credibility when the listener can attest to the enormous change in the speaker's life, and this is evidenced in Saul's life. The voice of Saul echoed in the ears of those who were once viewed as prey to his persecution. Now, the man who despised Christians has become one! The man who persecuted the church is a member of it! The one who denied the existence of the truth is teaching others to accept the same. His experience with Jesus was authentic. It is difficult to convince others to believe in something we do not believe ourselves. When we have an encounter with God, one that radically changes our lives, it is difficult to keep the Good News to ourselves. Paul spent time studying Jesus and wasted no time in sharing the Gospel with others. Too often we want to wait until we feel thoroughly grounded in our faith before we speak to anyone about Jesus' goodness. It is essential that we, the Lord's disciples, spread the Good News and become advocates for the Lord. God has done a marvelous thing in our lives; He saved and redeemed us! Salvation alone is justification enough to testify of the Lord's unmerited grace and mercy.

Saul was a brilliant scholar and could masterfully articulate a convincing argument. However, what convinced his listener was the evidence of God operating in his life. Our testimony should be backed up by a changed life.

Acts 9:19b–31

19b Then was Saul certain days with the disciples which were at Damascus. 20 And straightway he preached Christ in the synagogues, that he is the Son of God. 21 But all that heard him were amazed, and said; Is not this he that destroyed them which called on this name in Jerusalem, and came hither for that intent, that he might bring them bound unto the chief priests? 22 But Saul increased the more in strength, and confounded the Jews which dwelt at Damascus, proving that this is very Christ.

This passage discusses the account of Saul's conversion experience and his stay in Damascus with the disciples for several days after his baptism. Although he had an extensive knowledge of the Old Testament, Saul was still a new convert and needed further instructions concerning the teachings about Christ prior to his stepping out to reach others for Christ. Evidently he was soon ready, because we find him straightway (Gk. *eutheos*, **ew-THEH-ose**) or "at once" preaching in the Jewish synagogues that Jesus is the Son of God. Many attempts have been made to explain Saul's conversion vision, often in the form of rationalistic explanations, such as a thunderstorm outside Damascus, an epileptic seizure, or psychogenic blindness as the result of repressed guilt. All such ideas are merely speculative. What the accounts in **Galatians 1:15–17, 1 Corinthians 15:8–9**, and **Acts 9** picture is a radical conversion experience. Saul the persecutor was stopped dead in his tracks on the Damascus road. The crucified and risen Jesus showed Himself to Saul, who was completely transformed from persecutor to witness. The one who would be the captor of Christians became a captive of Christ. For Saul and for Luke (the author of Acts), a totally different man emerged from that vision of the risen Lord, and that is conversion. There is only one word with which one can describe Paul's experience—a miracle, the result of direct divine action. When all is said and done, both Saul and the book of Acts give strikingly similar pictures of his conversion.

Immediately following his conversion, Saul not only identifies himself with the disciples who resided in Damascus but also starts proclaiming Christ as the living "Son of God," a phrase which occurs in Acts only here, but which nevertheless became a central concept for Saul and his apostolic ministry (cf. **Romans 1:1–4**). The extent of the astonishment or amazement of his Jewish listeners in the synagogue is seen in the Greek word *existemi* (Gk., **ek-SEES-tay-mee**), which includes the root meaning of standing out of oneself. As it was in the case of Ananias (**vv. 13–14**), they simply could not believe that the former persecutor who sought to destroy (Gk. *portheo*, **por-THEH-oh**, to ravage or sack) the church had made such a radical about-face. Luke described him as "proving" (Gk. *sumbibazo*, **soom-bee-BAD-zo**) that Jesus is the Christ. The word, used only in Acts and Saul's letters, means to join or put together, demonstrate, or deduce, and seems to picture his joining Old Testament prophecies with their fulfillment in Christ, thus demonstrating that Jesus was the Christ, the Messiah promised by God to Israel. The result was that Saul's Jewish listeners were confounded and unable to respond to Paul's skillful interpretations of the Scriptures.

23 And after that many days were fulfilled, the Jews took counsel to kill him: 24 But their laying await was known of Saul. And they watched the gates day and night to kill him. 25 Then the disciples took him by night, and let him down by the wall in a basket.

According to Paul's account in **Galatians 1:18**, in the third year after his conversion he went to Jerusalem. The "many days" here corresponds to that account. The expression "after three years" is probably an inclusive reckoning (**Galatians 1:18**). In Jewish reckoning, any part of a year was considered a year. "Three years" would thus refer to two full years and any portion of the third, from its beginning to its end, or even one full year and any portion of two others. It was during this period that Paul visited Arabia before returning to Damascus. Unable to refute Saul, the exasperated Jews in Damascus finally took counsel, that is, conspired to kill him. The Greek word *anaireo* (**ah-neye-REH-oh**) translated here as "kill" used here literally means to take away or to do away with. When Saul and the disciples learned of the plot, plans were made for assuring his escape from the Jews. Since the Jewish plotters must have been carefully watching the city gates for Saul, the disciples chose another route for his escape. He was lowered in a basket through the window of a house built along the city wall. Paul also referred to this event in **2 Corinthians 11:32–33**.

2. TRANSFORMING POWER OF GOD'S LOVE (VV. 26–31)

Saul had a horrible reputation with fellow Christians. Many did not trust him and doubted the legitimacy of his transformation. Despite the naysayers, Saul continued to preach the Word of God with power and conviction. Saul's advocate, Barnabas, came alongside him and vouched for his authenticity. He journeyed with Saul and introduced him to the Apostles and other believers, who welcomed him into the community. Like Barnabas, it is essential that we rally behind new Christians who have tarnished reputations. Encouragement is essential to the growth of new believers. Reassurance stifles the pessimistic darts thrown by other followers who doubt their conversion. No matter how one has lived in the past, we must be willing to accept and welcome all of God's children into the family of faith. God has already accepted us and others into the fold, so who are we to deny membership to anyone? Saul's transforming life is an excellent example of the tremendous, incomprehensible, and unfailing love God has for humanity. God can change anyone; His grace and love do not discriminate. The person our society thinks is less deserving of forgiveness and transformation is a prime candidate to become an instrument for the Lord's divine purpose. Saul's zealous and bold proclamation of the Good News of Jesus Christ drew many to God; lives and communities were empowered. The church flourished and grew stronger as many decided to give their lives to Christ and live in fear of the Lord.

26 And when Saul was come to Jerusalem, he assayed to join himself to the disciples: but they were all afraid of him, and believed not that he was a disciple. 27 But Barnabas took him, and brought him to the apostles,

and declared unto them how he had seen the Lord in the way, and that he had spoken to him, and how he had preached boldly at Damascus in the name of Jesus. 28 And he was with them coming in and going out at Jerusalem. 29 And he spake boldly in the name of the Lord Jesus, and disputed against the Grecians: but they went about to slay him. 30 Which when the brethren knew, they brought him down to Caesarea, and sent him forth to Tarsus. 31 Then had the churches rest throughout all Judaea and Galilee and Samaria, and were edified; and walking in the fear of the Lord, and in the comfort of the Holy Ghost, were multiplied.

On arriving in Jerusalem, Saul attempted to join up with the Christian community there but was at first rejected. Like Ananias, they knew his reputation as a persecutor and were not convinced that so vehement an enemy could now be a Christian brother. In character with what we learn of him in Acts, Barnabas enters the picture as mediator and facilitates the acceptance of Paul by taking him to the apostles and testifying to his conversion. Barnabas' testimony would fully rehabilitate Saul in the minds of the apostles. Thus he secured Saul's acceptance in the apostolic circle. Saul was now "with them coming in and going out among them" in Jerusalem (v. 28). The expression is reminiscent of Acts 1:21, where it refers to the circle of apostles. That meaning may well be intended here. Saul was fully accepted into the apostolic circle. He too was a "witness" for Christ. As he had previously done in Damascus, Saul testified in the synagogues and was resisted. This time Saul debated with his fellow "Grecians," or Greek-speaking Jews. One is reminded of Stephen, and it may have been in the same synagogue that Saul gave his testimony for Christ (cf. 6:9-10). Earlier they had succeeded in having Stephen killed; now they determined to do the same to Saul. Again the plot to kill Saul leaked, and the Christians hastened Saul off to the port of Caesarea and from there to his hometown of Tarsus.

Verse 31 concludes the story of Saul's conversion and the end of the persecution that broke out after Stephen's death (8:1). The persecution was now ended with the conversion of its most ardent advocate into a witness for Christ. The church throughout all of Judea, Galilee, and Samaria was at peace. Although the Jerusalem church was now decentralized, it was still regarded as unified. The "peace" (NLT) of the church is described in terms of edification (the building up of the believers), walking in the fear of the Lord (reverence and worship), the "comfort" (KJV) or "encouragement" (NLT) of the Spirit, and multiplication and growth, terms reminiscent of the earlier summaries in Acts (cf. 2:43–47). It is a familiar pattern. The Lord brings His people through a time of crisis. Through His deliverance, the church finds peace and continues to flourish (cf. 5:42).

SEARCH THE SCRIPTURES

QUESTION 1
What happened when Paul attempted connect with apostles and the Christan community?

They were afraid of him.

QUESTION 2
How does Barnabas help others accept and feel more comfortable with Paul?

Barnabas served as a mediator and introduced him to others.

LIGHT ON THE WORD

Preparing for Ministry
The Jews threatened Paul with death because of his radical preaching of Jesus as Messiah, but he was protected by the believers and delivered from his pursuers. The preparation of Paul's ministry lasted approximately thirteen years. While in the Arabian desert, Saul had time to pray and reflect on Stephen's death, the implication of his conversion, the vision from Jesus, and all its meaning in light of Jewish

theology. This lasted approximately three years. Subsequently, Saul returned to Damascus and visited Peter in Jerusalem for fifteen days. The final phase of Saul's preparation came when Barnabas went to Tarsus to look for him and bring him to Antioch. There he stayed for approximately ten years.

BIBLE APPLICATION

AIM: Students will learn that Christians are able to have a bold and strong impact on the lives of others.

All kinds of people go to the hospital: the educated and illiterate, poor and privileged, thieves and stellar citizens gather in one facility seeking medical assistance. The church is similar to a hospital. Regardless of a person's lifestyle or background, anyone in need of God's attention is invited to join. All are welcome to receive the gift of life through accepting Christ Jesus as Lord and Savior. Believers should welcome new brothers and sisters into the family of faith.

STUDENT'S RESPONSES

AIM: Students will acknowledge that Christians should not judge others by their past and neglect to see the power of the Holy Spirit in the lives of others.

As ambassadors of Christ Jesus, we should declare boldly the life-changing experience we have in Him. People around us should know we are Christians. Our lives should reflect what we preach and inspire others to seek Christ. One of the ways we grow in our passion for telling others about our experience with Christ is to review the story of how we came to know Him. As a class, write out your individual testimonies of how you came to become a follower of Christ. Share your stories with the other class members.

PRAYER

Lord, we are ambassadors of Your Holy Word. Guide our tongues and allow us to hear and see what we need to do as we share Your Word. Bless us and keep us. In the Name of Jesus, we pray. Amen.

HOW TO SAY IT

Ananias.   a-nuh-NEE-uhs.

Barnabas.   BAHR-nuh-buhs.

PREPARE FOR NEXT SUNDAY

Read **Acts 10:24–38** and "Peter Takes a Risk."

DAILY HOME BIBLE READINGS

MONDAY
God's Perfect Way
(Psalm 18:20–30)

TUESDAY
God's Trustworthy Way
(Psalm 112:1–2, 6–9)

WEDNESDAY
God's Holy Way
(1 Peter 1:16–19)

THURSDAY
God's Generous Way
(Luke 11:32–36)

FRIDAY
God's Surprising Way
(Acts 9:1–9)

SATURDAY
God's Unconventional Way
(Acts 9:10–19)

SUNDAY
Saul Earns Credibility
(Acts 9:20–31)

Sources:
Carson, D.A., France, R.T., Motyer, J.A., Wenham, J.G. *New Bible Commentary.* Downers Grove, IL: Intervarsity Press, 1993.
Keener, Craig S. *IVP Bible Background Commentary.* Downers Grove, IL: Intervarsity Press, 1993.
Polhill, John B. Acts. *New American Commentary: An Exegetical and Theological Exposition of Holy Scripture.* Nashville: B&H Publishing, 1992.

PETER TAKES A RISK

BIBLE BASIS: ACTS 10:24–38

BIBLE TRUTH: Peter's recognition that God shows no partiality allowed him to tell the Good News to the Gentiles.

MEMORY VERSE: "Then Peter opened his mouth, and said, Of a truth I perceive that God is no respecter of persons: But in every nation he that feareth him, and worketh righteousness, is accepted with him" (Acts 10:34–35).

LESSON AIM: By the end of the lesson, we will: BECOME aware that Peter told the Gentiles about the message of God's love; CELEBRATE that God loves all people; and FIND ways to communicate God's love to those who do not know Jesus Christ as Savior.

TEACHER PREPARATION

MATERIALS NEEDED: Quarterly Commentary/Teacher Manual, Adult Quarterly, Adult resources—charts, worksheets, and other teaching tools, paper, pens, pencils, Bibles (several different versions)

OTHER MATERIALS NEEDED / TEACHER'S NOTES:

_____

_____

_____

LESSON OVERVIEW

LIFE NEED FOR TODAY'S LESSON
People often show partiality to some and not others.

BIBLE LEARNING
Peter took risks and shared the Good News of Christ outside of the Jewish community.

BIBLE APPLICATION
Believers understand that sharing the Gospel is challenging.

STUDENTS' RESPONSES
God expects believers to extend a welcome to all.

LESSON SCRIPTURE

ACTS 10:24–38, KJV

24 And the morrow after they entered into Cæsarea. And Cornelius waited for them, and had called together his kinsmen and near friends.

25 And as Peter was coming in, Cornelius met him, and fell down at his feet, and worshipped him.

ACTS 10:24–38, NIV

24 The following day he arrived in Caesarea. Cornelius was expecting them and had called together his relatives and close friends.

25 As Peter entered the house, Cornelius met him and fell at his feet in reverence.

26 But Peter made him get up. "Stand up,"

26 But Peter took him up, saying, Stand up; I myself also am a man.

27 And as he talked with him, he went in, and found many that were come together.

28 And he said unto them, Ye know how that it is an unlawful thing for a man that is a Jew to keep company, or come unto one of another nation; but God hath shewed me that I should not call any man common or unclean.

29 Therefore came I unto you without gainsaying, as soon as I was sent for: I ask therefore for what intent ye have sent for me?

30 And Cornelius said, Four days ago I was fasting until this hour; and at the ninth hour I prayed in my house, and, behold, a man stood before me in bright clothing,

31 And said, Cornelius, thy prayer is heard, and thine alms are had in remembrance in the sight of God.

32 Send therefore to Joppa, and call hither Simon, whose surname is Peter; he is lodged in the house of one Simon a tanner by the sea side: who, when he cometh, shall speak unto thee.

33 Immediately therefore I sent to thee; and thou hast well done that thou art come. Now therefore are we all here present before God, to hear all things that are commanded thee of God.

34 Then Peter opened his mouth, and said, Of a truth I perceive that God is no respecter of persons:

35 But in every nation he that feareth him, and worketh righteousness, is accepted with him.

36 The word which God sent unto the children of Israel, preaching peace by Jesus

he said, "I am only a man myself."

27 While talking with him, Peter went inside and found a large gathering of people.

28 He said to them: "You are well aware that it is against our law for a Jew to associate with or visit a Gentile. But God has shown me that I should not call anyone impure or unclean.

29 So when I was sent for, I came without raising any objection. May I ask why you sent for me?"

30 Cornelius answered: "Three days ago I was in my house praying at this hour, at three in the afternoon. Suddenly a man in shining clothes stood before me

31 and said, 'Cornelius, God has heard your prayer and remembered your gifts to the poor.

32 Send to Joppa for Simon who is called Peter. He is a guest in the home of Simon the tanner, who lives by the sea.'

33 So I sent for you immediately, and it was good of you to come. Now we are all here in the presence of God to listen to everything the Lord has commanded you to tell us."

34 Then Peter began to speak: "I now realize how true it is that God does not show favoritism

35 but accepts from every nation the one who fears him and does what is right.

36 You know the message God sent to the people of Israel, announcing the good news of peace through Jesus Christ, who is Lord of all.

37 You know what has happened throughout the province of Judea, beginning in Galilee after the baptism that John

Christ: (he is Lord of all:)

37 That word, I say, ye know, which was published throughout all Judæa, and began from Galilee, after the baptism which John preached;

38 How God anointed Jesus of Nazareth with the Holy Ghost and with power: who went about doing good, and healing all that were oppressed of the devil; for God was with him.

preached—

38 how God anointed Jesus of Nazareth with the Holy Spirit and power, and how he went around doing good and healing all who were under the power of the devil, because God was with him.

LIGHT ON THE WORD

Caesarea. Caesarea, also known as Caesarea Maritima ("of the sea") or Caesarea Augusta, (named after its founder Caesar Augustus) was a port city located 25 miles north of modern-day Tel Aviv. The city was built by Herod the Great sometime between 22 and 10 B.C. Caesarea, known for being a very beautiful city, contained many marbled structures. It was also known to contain a large hippodrome, a theater, a sewer system, and a sheltered harbor. There were five main roads leading into the city which, in addition to the harbor, made transporting people and goods easy.

Tanner. A tanner's job was to clean and prepare animal hides to be used as leather. They employed a process that stripped the remaining hair, fat, and flesh from the animal skins. As one might imagine, it was considered an undesirable job due to the sights and smells it entailed. Furthermore, tanners were considered ceremonially unclean by Jews, because they were in constant contact with dead animals. Tanneries were often required to operate outside of city walls or along sea shores in order to keep away the odors they created.

TEACHING THE BIBLE LESSON

LIFE NEED FOR TODAY'S LESSON

AIM: Students will discuss how people often show partiality to some and not others.

INTRODUCTION

Tension in the Jewish Community

Jewish law was very specific about what Jews were to eat and how they were to conduct themselves. The dietary laws that Peter references are found in **Leviticus 11:1–47**. In their original form, these rules were meant to protect the people of Israel and set them apart as God's people. These laws and covenant agreements made it possible for sinful humanity to commune with God. However, through Christ's sacrifice, God had removed the barrier of sin between Himself and His people. Humanity could now commune with God through the acceptance of His Son Jesus Christ (**Romans 3:21–26**). This transition from law to grace through Christ created friction between Jewish Christians who still held to their Jewish culture and the new Gentile believers who hadn't converted to Judaism. Some Jewish believers expected that non-Jewish believers would fully convert to Judaism, taking on all Jewish customs and practices, including circumcision. This tension not only threatened the spread of the Gospel to Gentiles, but also the unity and potency of the Christian church.

Philip's encounter with an Ethiopian eunuch is recorded earlier in **Acts 8:26–38**. Similarly, salvation is given to the Ethiopian man based on his acceptance of Christ, not his cultural background. While this instance occurred in relative isolation, Peter's later interactions with Cornelius would be publicly known. This would represent a deep challenge to the beliefs of Jewish Christians, but it would also be an opportunity for them to finally understand God's will for the Gentiles.

BIBLE LEARNING

AIM: Students will learn that Peter took risks and shared the Good News of Christ outside of the Jewish community.

I. PETER MEETS CORNELIUS
(Acts 10:24–26)

Peter, being obedient to the prompting of the Lord, has agreed to travel with Cornelius' men to Caesarea. Cornelius, apparently certain of Peter's arrival, has gathered friends and family to hear what Peter will share with them once he arrives. Cornelius' actions are indicative of his trust and belief in what God has instructed him to do. Not only does Cornelius do what he is instructed by sending men to find Peter, he expectantly looks forward to what God will do when Peter arrives.

Cornelius' response to Peter's arrival is to worship him. Peter quickly asks Cornelius to stop worshiping him and stand. Peter was already taking a risk by entering into the home of a Gentile, something forbidden by Jewish culture. It was important for Jews to avoid any appearance of idolatry, which included entering into the home of idolaters. Cornelius' worship of Peter would

have been of immediate concern because it might have appeared to others that Peter was engaging in idolatry.

Acts 10:24–38

24 And the morrow after they entered into Caesarea. And Cornelius waited for them, and he had called together his kinsmen and near friends. 25 And as Peter was coming in, Cornelius met him, and fell down at his feet, and worshipped him. 26 But Peter took him up, saying, Stand up; I myself also am a man.

Peter enters into Caesarea after Cornelius dispatches a group to request Peter's presence in their home. Peter was accompanied by some disciples from Joppa on this journey. This would prove valuable as they would be eyewitnesses to what happened during Peter's preaching. Cornelius, seeing the gravity and importance of the occasion, invites his kinsmen and his close friends into his house.

Cornelius is struck with awe at Peter's visit. From this, we can infer that Cornelius believed Peter to be a servant of Jesus thinking that Peter is able to impart salvation. As a Greek Gentile who was steeped in paganism, the centurion offers him the required obeisance as a semidivine son of God who had supernatural powers. Cornelius' reaction is ingrained and reflexive. Peter refuses this worship and tells him to stand up because he was not a god, but a man.

II. PETER SPEAKS TO CORNELIUS' GUESTS (vv. 27–29)

Upon entering Cornelius' home, Peter becomes aware that Cornelius has invited his friends and household to hear Peter. He explains his decision to accept Cornelius' invitation despite potential purity issues for entering a Gentile's home. He alludes to the vision he saw (**Acts 10:11–16**), sharing that he now understands that he is to no longer consider Gentiles unclean or impure.

Consider how it must have felt for Cornelius and his friends to hear Peter, a devout Jew, tell them that he would no longer consider them impure because they are not Jewish like him. Furthermore, it was the God whom he serves that had shown him this truth.

27 And as he talked with him, he went in, and found many that were come together. 28 And he said unto them, Ye know how that it is an unlawful thing for a man that is a Jew to keep company, or come unto one of another nation; but God hath shewed me that I should not call any man common or unclean. 29 Therefore came I unto you without gainsaying, as soon as I was sent for: I ask therefore for what intent ye have sent for me?

Peter talks to Cornelius as they walk into the home. When he sees all the people gathered together, he sees an opportunity to express what God has revealed to him. He reminds them of how his presence there is unlawful (Gk. *athemitos*, **ah-THEH-mee-tos**), or contrary to accepted morality or social convention. In the Jewish context, it means forbidden and disgusting. Peter states that it is contrary to Jewish law for him to "keep company" with (Gk. *kollao*, **ko-LAH-oh**) or join together with a Gentile or enter a Gentile's home. Such practices were not prohibited by Jewish law. Instead, Peter is echoing a common Gentile perception at the time which developed out of table fellowship issues which caused some Jews to avoid eating with Gentiles because certain foods were prohibited in the Mosaic laws. Cornelius and his Gentile associates would have been surprised that Peter was willing to come into his home, and Peter explains that not only is it possible for them to fellowship together, but God has even told Peter that he should no longer think of anyone or anything as unclean (i.e., unacceptable to God without ritual purification). Peter says God has "shewed" (Gk. *deiknumi*, **DAKE-noo-mee**) him that he should not call any man common or unclean. The word for

shewed means to establish the validity of something with an explanation or example. Here the explanation or example is the vision Peter receives on the rooftop of Simon the tanner (**Acts 10:9–16**). This vision is the basis for Peter's going to Cornelius' house without gainsaying (Gk. *anantirretos*, **ah-nahn-TEE-ray-tose**), or without objection.

QUESTION 1

The apostles traveled to _____ and were greeted by Cornelius.

Caesarea.

QUESTION 2

John states that people who fear and do what is right before God, are accepted by God. True or False?

False; it was Peter who said this.

III. CORNELIUS' STORY (vv. 30–33)

It is now Cornelius' turn to explain why he has called for Peter. He describes the visit he received from the angel. Earlier in the chapter, Cornelius is described as being a "devout man" who "feared God" (**vv. 1–2**). The fact that he was fasting and praying when the Lord sent him the message is proof of this. His generosity to the poor has been noticed by God as well. Rather than explaining God's acceptance of Gentiles to Cornelius directly, the angel directs him to find Peter. In his obedience, Cornelius is used by God to help orchestrate His will for his family and Peter. God intends to minister to both parties in this experience. Cornelius now explains that they have been waiting expectantly for what God wishes to speak to them through Peter.

30 And Cornelius said, Four days ago I was fasting until this hour; and at the ninth hour I prayed in my house, and, behold, a man stood before me in bright clothing, 31 And said, Cornelius, thy prayer is heard, and thine alms are had in remembrance in the sight of God. 32

Send therefore to Joppa, and call hither Simon, whose surname is Peter; he is lodged in the house of one Simon a tanner by the sea side: who, when he cometh, shall speak unto thee. 33 Immediately therefore I sent to thee; and thou hast well done that thou art come. Now therefore are we all here present before God, to hear all things that are commanded thee of God.

Cornelius was a Roman centurion, or a captain in the army. Although the root word in centurion means "a hundred," a Roman centurion of this time would command eighty men. The Bible says he was a "devout man," which means he tried to be godly in his ways and gave God due reverence, evident by the fact that he positively influenced all those in his house, and he gave money to the poor while praying to God "alway" (**Acts 10:1–2**).

Cornelius recounted to Peter how God had given him a vision to send for Peter. It was around "the ninth hour," or 3 p.m., when Cornelius had a supernatural encounter. This mention of the ninth hour indicates Cornelius' adherence to the Jewish times of prayer, which corresponded with the morning and evening offerings in the temple. As a result of this Gentile man's efforts to know God, he was blessed with the vision, which would start a series of events leading to his salvation. The man who wore "bright clothing" was identified as an angel in the actual vision (**v. 3**). It is interesting that God spoke to both Peter and Cornelius in visions leading up to this fateful event.

The angel in the vision let Cornelius know that God had heard his prayer and his alms (Gk. *eleemosune*, **eh-leh-ay-moh-SOO-neigh**) were remembered (Gk. *mnaomai*, **muh-NAH-oh-my**), or God was mindful of them. The word for alms is literally compassion or pity. For some Jews in the Roman period, almsgiving was considered compatible with righteousness. Luke clearly intends to show that

Cornelius was a righteous man and that God was answering the prayer of this righteous God-fearer. These God-fearers were Gentiles who were sympathetic to the Jewish religion. These were not full converts who were circumcised, but those who contributed to the synagogue and demonstrated piety.

Cornelius recounted his vision to Peter to explain why he had sent for him. The angel had instructed him, and therefore God had instructed him to do so. The omniscient God knew exactly where Peter was, just as He knows where all of our blessings are. The blessing that God had for Cornelius was that Peter would speak the gift of the Gospel message to him.

Peter was lodging with Simon the tanner (Gk. *burseus*, **bur-seh-OOS**). A tanner was a laborer who created leather from hides and skins by treating them with mineral lime and juices and leaves from various other plants. This leather was often used for making tents. The tabernacle coverings were made from the skins of rams or goats and were more than likely created by tanners (**Exodus 25:5, 26:14, 35:7, 23, 36:19**). Tanners were despised in Jewish culture. They were not allowed to go to the temple during pilgrimage season, and had their own synagogues because of the bad odor created by the animal hides. Even in Levirate marriage, the Mishnah or oral law allowed for the wife of the deceased brother of a tanner to remain a widow by saying "I could endure your brother, but I cannot endure you." Due to the odors, tanners were required to do their work outside the gates of the city or by the coast.

Cornelius thanked Peter for coming, but what he did not know was that God gave Peter a vision just before Cornelius's messengers arrived. In Peter's vision, God dealt with his feelings of prejudice toward Gentiles, while telling him to go with Cornelius' messengers

(Acts 10:9–20). The mighty providence of God works everything out. God can weave a tapestry of people and events in our lives which appear to be unrelated or are totally unknown to us. Then, when the time is right, God will pull all the pieces together so that we are blessed with something He has been preparing for us for some time. Cornelius showed his love for his household by having everyone gathered to hear Peter's words. His example shows that we should not be selfish with God's Word of salvation. We should see that all of our relatives and friends get to hear it, whether from us or someone else. We owe it to those we love to give them a chance to hear the Gospel and receive the gift of salvation through Jesus Christ our Lord.

IV. PETER DELIVERS THE GOSPEL (vv. 34–38)

At this point, it all becomes clear to Peter what God was doing and what he was to preach to Cornelius' people. Gentile uncleanness would no longer be a barrier to fellowship between Gentile and Jewish believers. God does not view Gentiles as unclean nor withhold fellowship from Gentiles on account of their racial and religious heritage, and neither should the Jewish people. They only need fear God and do what is right. Again, consider the impact of hearing Peter speak these words to the Gentile audience in Cornelius' home.

34 Then Peter opened his mouth, and said, Of a truth I perceive that God is no respecter of persons. 35 But in every nation he that feareth him, and worketh righteousness, is accepted with him. 36 The word which God sent unto the children of Israel, preaching peace by Jesus Christ: (he is Lord of all:) 37 That word, I say, ye know, which was published throughout all Judea, and began from Galilee, after the baptism which John preached; 38 How God anointed Jesus of Nazareth with the Holy Ghost and with power: who went about doing good, and healing all that were oppressed of the devil; for God was with Him.

Peter knew why he was there, so he went right to work. He began by acknowledging the truth that God had shown him in his own vision: "God is no respecter of persons." The phrase "respecter of persons" (Gk. *prosopolemptes*, **pro-so-po-LAYMP-tase**) is actually a single compound word in Greek that can mean "accepter of people." In this context it can be translated as "one who discriminates." Peter lays out the foundation of his message: God is not one who discriminates.

In the event at Cornelius' house, God was using a formerly prejudiced Peter to initiate opening up the invitation of the Gospel to Gentiles everywhere. No matter what nationality, God accepts the one who "feareth" (Gk. *phobeo*, **fo-BEH-oh**) Him, which means showing Him deference and reverence. He also accepts the one who "worketh" (Gk. *ergazomai*, **er-GOD-zo-my**) righteousness, which is to "produce" righteousness. This is an appropriate description of Cornelius as a God-fearer who prayed and gave alms regularly.

Peter began to lay out the chronological progression of the Gospel. He told his audience that God started by sending His Word to the Children of Israel. This Word was the preaching of peace (Gk. *eirene*, **ay-RAY-nay**) by Jesus Christ. Peter shows how the Gospel was first given to Israel and was expected, according to Old Testament prophecy, to bring peace (Isaiah 52:7). Later in Isaiah, peace would be proclaimed to everyone far and near which includes Gentiles as well as the Jews (Isaiah 57:19). Peter also says that Jesus is "Lord of all," reinforcing the truth of God being "no respecter of persons" (v. 34).

Peter encouraged them by saying that they already knew about some aspects of the message, which had spread to areas beyond

Jerusalem. The word for published (Gk. *gino-mai*, **GIH-no-my**) here is not in the sense of a publishing a book, but can mean to arise in history or come on the stage (cf. John 1:4). Judea was usually the name of the southern region of Palestine. In this case, it is a term for the whole of the Roman province of Judea. He indicated that the ministry of Jesus began in Galilee after His baptism by John the Baptist. John preached a message of water baptism and repentance from sin (**Mark 1:4**).

Peter then told his audience about the earthly ministry of Jesus. He said that Jesus was "anointed with the Holy Ghost and with power" (**Matthew 3:16**). Then Jesus did good and miraculous works, such as healing people with all sorts of ailments (cf. **Matthew 8:2–3, 9:20–22, 12:10–13; John 11:43–44**). The word for "doing good" can mean more than just being a "do-gooder"; it can specifically refer to rulers and deities who benefit their subjects. By using the phrase "God was with him," Peter connects Jesus to Old Testament figures such as Joseph, David, and Nehemiah (**Genesis 39:3, 23, 1 Samuel 18:12; Nehemiah 1:8**). These figures enjoyed the approval of God and His blessing on their endeavors. God Himself expressed that He was with Jesus, saying, "This is my beloved Son, in whom I am well pleased; hear ye him" (**Matthew 17:5**). Through this description, Peter establishes the uniqueness of Jesus' life and ministry and how the God who accepts all endorsed His ministry.

SEARCH THE SCRIPTURES

QUESTION 1

Why was it considered against Jewish law for Peter to go into the house of Cornelius (**NIV, v. 28**)?

QUESTION 2

What caused Peter to realize that God does not show favoritism (**NIV, v. 34**)?

LIGHT ON THE WORD

Gentile Believers

Peter acknowledges that his audience has most likely heard of Jesus' ministry and the Good News preached to the Jewish people. However, he now preaches the Gospel message to Gentile believers who have been informed of their full acceptance by God. They now know that their Christian faith and identity is considered the same as Jewish believers.

BIBLE APPLICATION

AIM: Students will understand that sharing the Gospel is challenging.

Jewish and Gentile believers were learning that salvation was based on their acceptance of Christ, not cultural heritage or outward actions. Today, despite having freely received the acceptance and love of God through Jesus Christ, it is easy for us to slip into thinking that we have somehow done (or can continue doing) things that warrant God's approval. This quickly results in judging others based on how well they live up to a human standard of righteousness. However, when we remember that we are only accepted by God's grace through Jesus Christ, we can extend grace, love, and acceptance to those around us (**Romans 5:15–17**).

STUDENT'S RESPONSES

AIM: Students will know that God expects believers to extend a welcome to all.

Peter took a risk by going to Cornelius' home and ministering to his household. Are there any ways in which God is asking you to take a risk to reach out to someone? Prayerfully consider stepping out and allowing the Holy Spirit to guide you in ministering to that person.

PRAYER

Dear Gracious God, Your love is gracious and everlasting. Your Word is loving and encouraging for us even when others speak against You. Bless us and keep us in Your perfect care. In the Name of Jesus, we pray. Amen.

HOW TO SAY IT

Caesarea.   SEE-se-ree-uh.

Joppa.   JAH-puh.

PREPARE FOR NEXT SUNDAY

Read **Acts 11:1–18** and "Trusting the Spirit."

Sources:

Alexander, David, and Pat Alexander. *Zondervan Handbook to the Bible*. Grand Rapids, MI: Zondervan, 1999. 649.

Barker, Kenneth L. and Kohlenberger III, John R., eds. *The Expositor's Bible Commentary—Abridged Edition: New Testament*. Grand Rapids, MI: Zondervan, 1994. 441.

Burge, Gary M. and Hill, Andrew E. eds. *Baker Illustrated Bible Commentary*. Grand Rapids, MI: Baker Books, 2012. 1187.

Carson, D. A., R. T. France, J. A. Motyer, G. J. Wenham, Eds. *New Bible Commentary*. Downer's Grove, IL: Intervarsity Press, 1994. 1082.

Elwell, Walter A. ed. *Baker Commentary on the Bible*. Grand Rapids, MI: Baker Books, 1989. 898-899.

Elwell, Walter A. and Yarbrough, Robert W. *Encountering the New Testament: A Historical and Theological Survey*. Grand Rapids, MI: Baker Books, 1998. 227.

Kaiser, Walter C. Jr., and Garrett, Duane. *NIV Archaeological Study Bible*. Grand Rapids, MI: Zondervan, 2005. 1784, 1786.

Keener, Craig S. *The IVP Bible Background Commentary: New Testament*. Downers Grove, IL: InterVarsity Press, 1993. 352-353.

Orr, James, ed. "Tanner." *International Standard Bible Encyclopedia*. Electronic Edition. Omaha, NE: Quickverse, 1998.

Richards, Lawrence O. ed. "Tanning." *Richards Complete Bible Dictionary*. Iowa Falls, IA: World Bible Publishers, 2002.

Thayer, Joseph. "anantirrhetos." *Thayer's Greek Definitions*. 3rd ed. Electronic Edition, Quickverse. El Cajon, CA: Institute for Creation Research, 1999.

Thayer, Joseph. "prosopoleptes." *Thayer's Greek Definitions*. 3rd ed. Electronic Edition, Quickverse. El Cajon, CA: Institute for Creation Research, 1999.

DAILY HOME BIBLE READINGS

MONDAY
God's Love Prevails
(Romans 8:31–39)

TUESDAY
Peter Takes a Risk
(Matthew 14:22–33)

WEDNESDAY
Lord of the Sabbath
(Matthew 12:1–8)

THURSDAY
Peter is Stretched
(Acts 10:1–16)

FRIDAY
Peter Follows Through
(Acts 10:17–23)

SATURDAY
God is For All
(Acts 10:39–48)

SUNDAY
Peter Takes Another Risk
(Acts 10:24–38)

COMMENTS / NOTES:

TRUSTING THE SPIRIT

BIBLE BASIS: ACTS 11:1–18

BIBLE TRUTH: Peter's testimony to the power of the Holy Spirit converting Gentiles increased the Jerusalem's church support of Peter.

MEMORY VERSE: "Forasmuch then as God gave them the like gift as he did unto us, who believed on the Lord Jesus Christ; what was I, that I could withstand God?" (Acts 11:17).

LESSON AIM: By the end of the lesson, we will LEARN that Peter's preaching to the Gentiles was affirmed by the believers in Jerusalem; FEEL comfortable with reaching out to different peoples; IDENTIFY Christian Scriptures that include all in the Body of Christ.

TEACHER PREPARATION

MATERIALS NEEDED: Quarterly Commentary/Teacher Manual, Adult Quarterly, Adult resources—charts, worksheets, and other teaching tools, paper, pens, pencils, Bibles (several different versions)

OTHER MATERIALS NEEDED / TEACHER'S NOTES:

_____

_____

LESSON OVERVIEW

LIFE NEED FOR TODAY'S LESSON
People who act outside of the norm are required to justify their actions.

BIBLE LEARNING
The church in Jerusalem supported Peter's preaching and conversions of the Gentiles.

BIBLE APPLICATION
God desires that believers would communicate His love toward others regardless of their cultural or religious backgrounds.

STUDENTS' RESPONSES
Christians should trust the Holy Spirit to guide them as they witness to others about Christ.

LESSON SCRIPTURE

ACTS 11:1–18, KJV

1 And the apostles and brethren that were in Judaea heard that the Gentiles had also received the word of God.

2 And when Peter was come up to Jerusalem, they that were of the circumcision contended with him,

ACTS 11:1–18, NIV

1 The apostles and the believers throughout Judea heard that the Gentiles also had received the word of God.

2 So when Peter went up to Jerusalem, the circumcised believers criticized him

3 and said, "You went into the house of

3 Saying, Thou wentest in to men uncircumcised, and didst eat with them.

4 But Peter rehearsed the matter from the beginning, and expounded it by order unto them, saying,

5 I was in the city of Joppa praying: and in a trance I saw a vision, A certain vessel descend, as it had been a great sheet, let down from heaven by four corners; and it came even to me:

6 Upon the which when I had fastened mine eyes, I considered, and saw fourfooted beasts of the earth, and wild beasts, and creeping things, and fowls of the air.

7 And I heard a voice saying unto me, Arise, Peter; slay and eat.

8 But I said, Not so, Lord: for nothing common or unclean hath at any time entered into my mouth.

9 But the voice answered me again from heaven, What God hath cleansed, that call not thou common.

10 And this was done three times: and all were drawn up again into heaven.

11 And, behold, immediately there were three men already come unto the house where I was, sent from Caesarea unto me.

12 And the Spirit bade me go with them, nothing doubting. Moreover these six brethren accompanied me, and we entered into the man's house:

13 And he shewed us how he had seen an angel in his house, which stood and said unto him, Send men to Joppa, and call for Simon, whose surname is Peter;

14 Who shall tell thee words, whereby thou and all thy house shall be saved.

uncircumcised men and ate with them."

4 Starting from the beginning, Peter told them the whole story:

5 "I was in the city of Joppa praying, and in a trance I saw a vision. I saw something like a large sheet being let down from heaven by its four corners, and it came down to where I was.

6 I looked into it and saw four-footed animals of the earth, wild beasts, reptiles and birds.

7 Then I heard a voice telling me, 'Get up, Peter. Kill and eat.'

8 "I replied, 'Surely not, Lord! Nothing impure or unclean has ever entered my mouth.'

9 "The voice spoke from heaven a second time, 'Do not call anything impure that God has made clean.'

10 This happened three times, and then it was all pulled up to heaven again.

11 "Right then three men who had been sent to me from Caesarea stopped at the house where I was staying.

12 The Spirit told me to have no hesitation about going with them. These six brothers also went with me, and we entered the man's house.

13 He told us how he had seen an angel appear in his house and say, 'Send to Joppa for Simon who is called Peter.

14 He will bring you a message through which you and all your household will be saved.'

15 "As I began to speak, the Holy Spirit came on them as he had come on us at the beginning.

15 And as I began to speak, the Holy Ghost fell on them, as on us at the beginning.

16 Then remembered I the word of the Lord, how that he said, John indeed baptized with water; but ye shall be baptized with the Holy Ghost.

17 Forasmuch then as God gave them the like gift as he did unto us, who believed on the Lord Jesus Christ; what was I, that I could withstand God?

18 When they heard these things, they held their peace, and glorified God, saying, Then hath God also to the Gentiles granted repentance unto life.

16 Then I remembered what the Lord had said: 'John baptized with water, but you will be baptized with the Holy Spirit.'

17 So if God gave them the same gift he gave us who believed in the Lord Jesus Christ, who was I to think that I could stand in God's way?"

18 When they heard this, they had no further objections and praised God, saying, "So then, even to Gentiles God has granted repentance that leads to life."

LIGHT ON THE WORD

Joppa. The ancient city of Joppa was situated south of Caesarea, on the Mediterranean Sea. History records that the city contained beautiful gardens and was known for being home to craftsmen who worked with wood, metal, and leather. The city dates back to 1650 B.C. and was originally located on a small rocky hill. Joppa contained a natural harbor, with a rocky reef that runs along its coast. It served as the main port city to Jerusalem, which was approximately 30 miles inland, and to the south. Joppa is often remembered as the city that Jonah fled from just before his encounter with the large fish. The modern city of Jaffa exists in its location today.

Judea. Judea is the Roman name for the imperial province in the location of former Judah. Judea was a mountainous, desert region that included Joppa, Samaria, Jerusalem, and Caesarea. It wasn't as fertile as the region of Galilee to the north, but its inhabitants still raised sheep and grew olives and grapes. They also mined salt from the Dead Sea, located along the eastern border. The economy of the region relied heavily upon the city of Jerusalem. Taxes and payment for goods were collected from the travelers who frequented the city. During the first century, roughly half of all inhabitants in the region lived in or around Jerusalem.

TEACHING THE BIBLE LESSON

LIFE NEED FOR TODAY'S LESSON

AIM: Students will see how people who act outside of the norm are required to justify their actions.

INTRODUCTION

God Speaks to Peter

Jesus gave the early church a commission to expand beyond Jerusalem and Judea in preaching the Gospel (**Acts 1:8**). We do not know whether the disciples understood this as a commission to preach specifically to the Gentiles or only to the Jews of the Diaspora. Up until the time of the first persecution following the martyrdom of Stephen, the Gospel was restricted to the Jewish people.

The persecution scattered the believers and many of the Greek-speaking Jews began to preach the Gospel everywhere they went (**Acts 8:4**). Philipp began to preach in Samaria and this was the first significant advance of the Gospel into non-Jewish territory (**Acts 8:5–12**). After the conversion of Saul, the churches enjoyed a relative peace (**Acts 9:31**).

BIBLE LEARNING

AIM: Students will explore how the church in Jerusalem supported Peter's preaching and conversions of the Gentiles.

I. PETER IS CHALLENGED
(Acts 11:1–3)

Peter most likely knew that he would be expected to account for his actions in Caesarea. By the time he returns to Jerusalem, word has already spread of his encounter with Cornelius and his family. The believers referred to as "of the circumcision" in **verse 2** are Christian Jews who strongly identified with their Jewish heritage. It was disturbing to them that Peter had seemingly set aside his Jewish piety. Peter had eaten with Gentiles, clearly violating Kosher law. From the perspective of first century Jews, this placed Peter in the company of idolaters and people considered unclean because they did not adhere to Jewish dietary restrictions. Furthermore, sharing a meal was a sign of intimate fellowship and acceptance in the Jewish culture. God calls us to accept people not just in our heads but to show our acceptance and connect with them on a personal level.

Acts 11:1–18

1 And the apostles and brethren that were in Judaea heard that the Gentiles had also received the word of God. 2 And when Peter was come up to Jerusalem, they that were
of the circumcision contended with him, 3 Saying, Thou wentest in to men uncircumcised, and didst eat with them.**

The news concerning the reception of the Gentiles into the Christian fellowship, marked by the conversion of Cornelius, has reached Jerusalem. The conversion of Cornelius was a landmark in the history of the Gospel's advance from its strictly Jewish beginnings to its saturation of the Roman Empire. It was a proof that the sovereign God was not confined to the traditional forms of Judaism and could bring a Gentile directly into relationship with Himself through Jesus Christ apart from any prior commitment to distinctive Jewish beliefs or lifestyle. However, Peter's actions were an affront to the traditions and prejudices of the Jewish Christians. The Jerusalem council summoned him to give an account of all that had transpired. He needed to provide answers to those who might have been unsettled by the episode, probably thinking that he had taken a liberal attitude toward the law. It says that those who were "of the circumcision" (Gk. *peritome*, **peh-ree-toh-MAY**), or circumcised Jews, contended (Gk. *diakrino*, **dee-ah-KREE-no**) or disputed with Peter. He was attacked not for preaching to the "uncircumcised" Gentiles or their being baptized, but for his social relations with them. Peter's eating with the Gentiles showed his acceptance of them as fellow Christians, and they were still uncircumcised (**v. 3**). Peter defends his actions by narrating how God led him to Cornelius and how the Spirit fell on Cornelius and his household.

II. PETER SHARES HIS VISION (vv. 4–10)

Peter responds to his critics by first citing his experience in Joppa. While in a trance, he had received the unsettling directive that he should kill and eat animals that Jews are clearly forbidden to eat. The foods that Peter refers to as "common or unclean" (**Acts 11:8**) are described at length in **Leviticus 11**. Among these restrictions are very specific rules related to these animals. Only certain animals that walked on all fours were allowed to be eaten. Specific birds and insects, like the locust, were allowed, while most others were off limits. Peter's response to the Lord indicates that he is very aware of these restrictions. He explains that he has never once violated them and refuses to do so. Peter's protest is met with the correction that he is to no longer consider something unclean if God has declared it otherwise. Upon waking, Peter must have been somewhat confused by what he saw and heard. But he would eventually understand it completely. We can only understand God fully if we continue obeying His revelation.

4 But Peter rehearsed the matter from the beginning, and expounded it by order unto them, saying, 5 I was in the city of Joppa praying: and in a trance I saw a vision, A certain vessel descend, as it had been a great sheet, let down from heaven by four corners; and it came even to me: 6 Upon the which when I had fastened mine eyes, I considered, and saw fourfooted beasts of the earth, and wild beasts, and creeping things, and fowls of the air 7 And I heard a voice saying unto me, Arise, Peter; slay and eat. 8 But I said, Not so, Lord: for nothing common or unclean hath at any time entered into my mouth. 9 But the voice answered me again from heaven, What God hath cleansed, that call not thou common. 10 And this was done three times: and all were drawn up again into heaven.

Peter relates his vision by quickly leading them to the main issue—God's acceptance of the Gentiles. Peter begins with his own vision in **11:5–10**, which is a detailed retelling of **10:9–16**. In fact, that is the most extensive repetition in his report to Jerusalem. For Peter, it was the heart of the matter—there are no unclean people, and God accepts the Gentiles.

It all began with Peter on a rooftop in Joppa. This is where he experienced a vision (Gk. *horama*, **HO-rah-mah**), which is a sight divinely granted in a trance (Gk. *ekstasis*, **EK-sta-sees**) or ecstasy. A trance can be defined as a throwing of the mind out of its normal state. Although the person is awake, the mind is closed off from surrounding physical objects and fixed on the divine forms and things within a particular vision. When Peter was in the trance, he observed a sheet coming down out of heaven filled with all kinds of animals forbidden for Jews to eat, because they were not kosher. As the sheet was let down from heaven, a voice said, "Arise, Peter; slay and eat." Peter's response was that he had never eaten anything common (Gk. *koinos*, **koy-NOS**) or unclean (Gk. *akathartos*, **ah-KA-thar-tose**). *Koinos* is the term the Jews of that day used for anything common or eaten by anybody, i.e., the Gentiles. The word for unclean is also a general word for uncleansed and specifically for things that are Levitically unclean. In using both words, we see Peter explicitly stating his case: He has never eaten these animals and never intended to.

Next the voice says, "What God hath cleansed, that call not thou common." In other words, what was considered unclean, God has now cleansed. This was done three times. In Scripture when something happens three times, it is usually an indication of the thing being established by God, as in the case of Jonah being three days in the belly of the whale or the angels crying out "Holy, Holy, Holy" to God on the throne. This was significant, as Peter was being asked to do something that was in violation of everything he knew as a Jew. His core identity was being challenged in this vision and would be again further in the narrative.

SEARCH THE SCRIPTURES

QUESTION 1
In what city was Peter when God shared a vision with Peter (**v. 5**)?

Joppa

QUESTION 2

Describe the beasts that Peter saw in the vision (v. 6).

The beasts were four-footed and wild beasts.

LIGHT ON THE WORD

Entering a Gentile Home

Peter receives a revelation from God concerning the Gentiles' inclusion into His people and the blessings of the Gospel. This results in his preaching to Cornelius the centurion and all of his household turning to Christ. After this, Peter returns to Jerusalem to give an account of his entering a Gentile home and preaching the Good News. As Peter tells this narrative, he highlights the theological and experiential evidence to convince the church leaders of the rightness of his actions.

III. PETER'S JOURNEY TO CAESAREA (vv. 11–14)

Peter immediately has the opportunity to begin acting on his new information. He obediently agrees to travel to Caesarea, but is still not fully aware of the significance of the Lord's message. His reservations about traveling with the Gentile men might have kept him in Joppa if it weren't for the Holy Spirit's reassurance (v. 12). Note that God's guidance factors heavily in Peter's retelling of the experience. His decision to travel to Caesarea wasn't based solely on his own desire; he was being obedient to God's direction.

The story moves ahead to Cornelius' retelling of his own experience in Caesarea. Again, Peter gives God the credit for orchestrating all these events. As Peter retells it, Cornelius is promised that based on the message that Peter would share, he and his entire household would be saved.

11 And, behold, immediately there were three men already come unto the house where I was, sent from Caesarea unto me. 12 And the spirit bade me go with them, nothing doubting. Moreover these six brethren accompanied me, and we entered into the man's house: 13 And he shewed us how he had seen an angel in his house, which stood and said unto him, Send men to Joppa, and call for Simon, whose surname is Peter; 14 Who shall tell thee words, whereby thou and all thy house shall be saved. 15 And as I began to speak, the Holy Ghost fell on them, as on us at the beginning. 16 Then remembered I the word of the Lord, how that he said, John indeed baptized with water; but ye shall be baptized with the Holy Ghost. 17 Forasmuch then as God gave them the like gift as he did unto us, who believed on the Lord Jesus Christ; what was I, that I could withstand God? 18 When they heard these things, they held their peace, and glorified God, saying, Then hath God also to the Gentiles granted repentance unto life.

Verses 11–12 summarize the narrative of **10:17–25**, relating the arrival of the three messengers from Cornelius and Peter's accompanying them to Caesarea. The most significant difference from the earlier account is Peter's mention of six brothers from Joppa who accompanied him to Caesarea (**v. 12**). "These six" whom Peter brought to Jerusalem served as witnesses to what transpired in Cornelius's home (cf. **10:45**).

Verses 13–14 summarize Cornelius' vision, how the angel instructed him to send to Joppa for Peter. **Verse 14** is more specific than any of the accounts of Cornelius' vision in Acts 10. Peter was to bring a message to Cornelius "through which [he] and all [his] household [would] be saved." This expansion elucidates Cornelius' eager anticipation of Peter's message in **10:33**. There is no need for Peter to summarize the sermon he gave Cornelius before the Jerusalem Christians, so he quickly moves to the coming of the Spirit on the Gentiles at the house (**v. 15**). Peter notes how the event interrupted his sermon and adds that the Spirit came upon them just "as on us at the beginning." This compares the episode at Cornelius' house to that on the day of Pentecost. Peter makes explicit here what was implicit in **10:46**. He continues to draw the comparison in **v. 16**, which harkens back to **Acts 1:5** and Jesus' prediction of a baptism with the Holy Spirit. Jesus' prediction was fulfilled for the apostles at Pentecost; for Cornelius and his fellow Gentiles, it was fulfilled with the coming of the Spirit at Cornelius's house. Certainly for Peter, it was a Gentile Pentecost. He could hardly make more explicit comparisons!

Peter concludes his report in Jerusalem (**vv. 17–18**) by reminding his hearers once again that God gave the gift of the Spirit to the Gentiles and added, "What was I, that I could withstand God," that is, "Who am I to think that I can oppose God?" Peter uses the same verb *koluo* (Gk. **ko-LOO-oh**) that he previously used in **10:47** to express the same idea of opposing God, to question whether it was appropriate for anyone to forbid or oppose the baptism of the Gentiles. For anyone to do so would be tantamount to opposing God, for His leading of Peter and Cornelius was beyond doubt. God intended to include the Gentiles in His people; He was clearly behind it.

The Jerusalem leaders quietly listened as Peter told his story. There is no sign that they interrupted him or distrusted his words. As they listened, they realized that they had been wrong. They seemed to be more eager to grasp truth than to defend their own positions, a timely lesson for any Christian, particularly leaders today. When Peter clearly showed that God was bigger than their opinions, they let their prejudices go. After Peter finished, the conservative Jerusalem group had no further objections (**v. 18**). In the face of the evidence that Peter provided, his critics had nothing more to say. They accepted what had happened, concluding that God had granted even the Gentiles repentance, reaching out to those to whom they would not have reached out and in a manner they never would have approved. Silence quickly gave way to praise of God in His triumphant advance of the Gospel. God had granted "repentance unto life" to the Gentiles. They rejoiced in the results of Peter's action, which previously they had criticized.

IV. PETER'S CHALLENGERS ARE CONVINCED (vv. 15–18)

The circumcised believers that Peter is speaking to were about to hear something that would take them all by surprise. Peter shares the Gospel with Cornelius and his household, and at that point, the Holy Spirit fell on everyone there. Peter draws the connection between this event at Cornelius' home and the event they had all experienced on the Day of Pentecost (**Acts 2:1–13**). In pouring out the Holy Spirit on these Gentile believers just as He had on the apostles, God has shown that He views them in the same way. Despite their cultural differences, the gift of the Holy Spirit was an experience that they shared in common. Furthermore, Peter points out the words of Christ regarding baptism with the Holy Spirit: "John indeed baptized with water; but ye shall be baptized with the Holy Ghost" (**Acts 11:16**). Along with circumcision, ritual cleansing was also used as an indication of conversion to Judaism. By referring to the Gentile experience as a baptism with the Holy Spirit, Peter indicates that God now sees them as converted.

Peter completes his argument by once again explaining that God's will was at work in all of these events. To oppose the course of events that played out would have been to oppose God.

SEARCH THE SCRIPTURES

QUESTION 3
How did the Holy Spirit interact with the Gentiles (v. 15)?

The Holy Spirit fell on them as to this happened to Peter and other believers.

QUESTION 4
Peter challenged the conservative Jerusalem

group to answer what question?

"...who was I to stand in God's way?" (v. 17).

LIGHT ON THE WORD

Salvation and the Gentiles

Peter's challengers have heard enough to come to the same conclusion. God had chosen to extend salvation to the Gentiles, through Jesus Christ, regardless of their non-Jewish heritage.

BIBLE APPLICATION

AIM: Students will learn that God desires that believers would communicate His love toward others regardless of their cultural or religious backgrounds.

Peter and the Jewish Christians had to overcome biases that developed out of their initial desire to do what was right. What were initially legitimate convictions about how to please God had turned into shows of favoritism and bigotry. This same dynamic plays itself out in today's Christian church. Often, one group's differing religious views become a reason they are mistrusted or mistreated by other believers. Regardless of our differing views, we are all one body in Christ (**1 Corinthians 12:12–13**).

STUDENT'S RESPONSES

AIM: Students will learn that they should trust the Holy Spirit to guide them as they witness to others about Christ.

Do you see yourself as someone who is welcoming to others despite significant outward differences? If so, how might you be able to encourage your friends to see people the way God sees them?

Do you sometimes feel pressure to treat people differently because they don't share your beliefs or background? We can ask God to give us the strength and guidance of the Holy Spirit to help us accept others and show Christ's love.

PRAYER

Lord, we adore You and worship You. The Holy Spirit comforts us and allows us to share the joy of Jesus with family, friends, and those we do not know. Your gentle care is refreshing and good news for us all. In the Name of Jesus, we pray. Amen.

HOW TO SAY IT

Judaea.   joo-DEE-uh.

Expounded.   eks-POWN-ded.

PREPARE FOR NEXT SUNDAY

Read **Acts 12:1–11** and "Prayer Works!"

DAILY HOME BIBLE READINGS

MONDAY
A Light to the Nations
(Acts 10:24–38)

TUESDAY
Water for Everyone
(John 4:3–14)

WEDNESDAY
Your Gentle Defense
(1 Peter 3:13–18)

THURSDAY
Strangers Become Heaven's Citizens
(Ephesians 2:11–22)

FRIDAY
Good News to Great Joy
(Acts 8:4–8)

SATURDAY
Called Christians
(Acts 10:19–26)

SUNDAY
Trusting the Spirit
(Acts 11:1–18)

Sources:

Arrington, French L. The Acts of the Apostles: An Introduction and Commentary. Peabody, Mass.: Hendrickson, 1988.

Barker, Kenneth L. and Kohlenberger III, John R., eds. *The Expositor's Bible Commentary– Abridged Edition: New Testament.* Grand Rapids, MI: Zondervan, 1994. 442-443.

Keener, Craig S. *The IVP Bible Background Commentary: New Testament.* Downers Grove, IL: InterVarsity Press, 1993. 354.

Longenecker, Richard N. "Acts," in *The Expositor's Bible Commentary: Luke–Acts (Revised Edition),* ed. Tremper Longman III and David E. Garland, vol. 10 (Grand Rapids, MI: Zondervan, 2007), 884.

Marshall, I Howard. *The Acts of the Apostles: An Introduction and Commentary.* The Tyndale New Testament Commentaries. Grand Rapids, Mich.: W.B. Eerdmans Pub. Co., 1980.

Polhill, John B. Acts, vol. 26, The New American Commentary (Nashville: Broadman & Holman Publishers, 1995.

COMMENTS / NOTES:

PRAYER WORKS!

BIBLE BASIS: ACTS 12:1–11

BIBLE TRUTH: The fervent prayer of the church in Acts and the work of an angel provided Peter's deliverance.

MEMORY VERSE: "Peter therefore was kept in prison: but prayer was made without ceasing of the church unto God for him" (Acts 12:5).

LESSON AIM: By the end of the lesson, we will: EXPLORE the story of Peter's deliverance from prison; RECOGNIZE and appreciate the power of prayer in difficult circumstances; and COMMIT to praying for those whose witness puts them in life-threatening or difficult situations.

TEACHER PREPARATION

MATERIALS NEEDED: Quarterly Commentary/Teacher Manual, Adult Quarterly, Adult resources—charts, worksheets, and other teaching tools, paper, pens, pencils, Bibles (several different versions)

OTHER MATERIALS NEEDED / TEACHER'S NOTES:

_____

_____

LESSON OVERVIEW

LIFE NEED FOR TODAY'S LESSON
In the midst of perilous life situations, deliverance sometimes appears to come through miraculous means.

BIBLE LEARNING
God's power is greater than any situation.

BIBLE APPLICATION
Believers should prayer together and expect God to answer.

STUDENTS' RESPONSES
Christians learn that God can rescue people from dangerous circumstances.

LESSON SCRIPTURE

ACTS 12:1–11, KJV

1 Now about that time Herod the king stretched forth his hands to vex certain of the church.

2 And he killed James the brother of John with the sword.

3 And because he saw it pleased the Jews, he proceeded further to take Peter also.

ACTS 12:1–11, NIV

1 It was about this time that King Herod arrested some who belonged to the church, intending to persecute them.

2 He had James, the brother of John, put to death with the sword.

3 When he saw that this met with approval among the Jews, he proceeded to seize

(Then were the days of unleavened bread.)

4 And when he had apprehended him, he put him in prison, and delivered him to four quaternions of soldiers to keep him; intending after Easter to bring him forth to the people.

5 Peter therefore was kept in prison: but prayer was made without ceasing of the church unto God for him.

6 And when Herod would have brought him forth, the same night Peter was sleeping between two soldiers, bound with two chains: and the keepers before the door kept the prison.

7 And, behold, the angel of the Lord came upon him, and a light shined in the prison: and he smote Peter on the side, and raised him up, saying, Arise up quickly. And his chains fell off from his hands.

8 And the angel said unto him, Gird thyself, and bind on thy sandals. And so he did. And he saith unto him, Cast thy garment about thee, and follow me.

9 And he went out, and followed him; and wist not that it was true which was done by the angel; but thought he saw a vision.

10 When they were past the first and the second ward, they came unto the iron gate that leadeth unto the city; which opened to them of his own accord: and they went out, and passed on through one street; and forthwith the angel departed from him.

11 And when Peter was come to himself, he said, Now I know of a surety, that the Lord hath sent his angel, and hath delivered me out of the hand of Herod, and from all the expectation of the people of the Jews.

Peter also. This happened during the Festival of Unleavened Bread.

4 After arresting him, he put him in prison, handing him over to be guarded by four squads of four soldiers each. Herod intended to bring him out for public trial after the Passover.

5 So Peter was kept in prison, but the church was earnestly praying to God for him.

6 The night before Herod was to bring him to trial, Peter was sleeping between two soldiers, bound with two chains, and sentries stood guard at the entrance.

7 Suddenly an angel of the Lord appeared and a light shone in the cell. He struck Peter on the side and woke him up. "Quick, get up!" he said, and the chains fell off Peter's wrists.

8 Then the angel said to him, "Put on your clothes and sandals." And Peter did so. "Wrap your cloak around you and follow me," the angel told him.

9 Peter followed him out of the prison, but he had no idea that what the angel was doing was really happening; he thought he was seeing a vision.

10 They passed the first and second guards and came to the iron gate leading to the city. It opened for them by itself, and they went through it. When they had walked the length of one street, suddenly the angel left him.

11 Then Peter came to himself and said, "Now I know without a doubt that the Lord has sent his angel and rescued me from Herod's clutches and from everything the Jewish people were hoping would happen."

LIGHT ON THE WORD

Herod the King. It is understood that "Herod the King" is Herod Agrippa, who was appointed by the Roman emperor Claudius to rule over Judea. He is not the same King Herod mentioned in the Gospels in the accounts of Jesus' life. However, he continues the negative legacy that the name Herod carried against Jesus and now His followers. The political scene surrounding the early church was marked by conflicts between the various Roman rulers, Jewish hierarchy, and the growing separation between Jewish traditionalists and the new sect of believers in Christ, "Christians," which included both Jews and Gentiles.

James. James was the brother of John and one of the twelve disciples who walked the earth with Jesus. Jesus called him, along with his brother John, "Boanerges" or "Sons of Thunder" for their strong fiery tempers (**Mark 3:17**). We know nothing about James' ministry after the ascension of Christ except that he was beheaded by King Herod Agrippa in AD 44. Thus he was the first apostle to die as a martyr.

TEACHING THE BIBLE LESSON

LIFE NEED FOR TODAY'S LESSON

AIM: Students are reminded that in the midst of perilous life situations, deliverance sometimes appears to come through miraculous means.

INTRODUCTION

God's People and Church Persecuted

God's people have always been persecuted or hunted down throughout the centuries. During the time of the Old Testament, this persecution was directed toward many of the Old Testament prophets. Elijah was an enemy of the state during the wicked reign of Ahab (**1 Kings 19:1–3**). Jeremiah was thrown in prison by King Zedekiah (**Jeremiah 32:1–5**). Rabbinical sources state that Isaiah was sawed in half during the reign of King Manasseh. Regardless of whether they escaped or lost their lives, these prophets depended on and trusted in God.

The early church faced waves of persecution. This began with the martydom of Stephen and was led by Saul the Pharisee. Once Saul was converted to Christ, the churches had rest from persecution and gained a short season of peace. Soon, during a time of famine, the church was targeted by King Herod Agrippa, who was pro-Pharisee and beloved by the Jewish establishment.

BIBLE LEARNING

AIM: Students will know that believers should prayer together and expect God to answer.

I. PUNISHED FOR PREACHING (Acts 12:1–3)

Peter seems to have been made for tough times, considering the various challenges he experienced during and since his days walking with Jesus. He was once personally vexed by the crowing rooster when he realized he had denied Jesus just before the crucifixion (**John 18:15–27**). Now, Peter finds himself the victim of a vengeful and jealous king seeking to kill him as an example to deter believers in Christ. The persecution of the early church came largely from two forces: the imperial Roman government and the established Jewish leadership (cf. **Acts 9:1–2**). Referred to as "Herod," the king is Herod Agrippa, who like many similar rulers was known for his violent acts toward his enemies. Killing James "with the sword" is generally understood to be a beheading (**v. 2**). This was also intended to be Peter's fate. Beheading is a severe and immediate form of capital punishment, symbolizing silencing of offender. Herod's desire to "vex" or torment the church by punishing its leaders was a ploy to keep followers in line by brutish example.

Acts 12:1–11

1 Now about that time Herod the king stretched forth his hands to vex certain of the church. 2 And he killed James the brother of John with the sword. 3 And because he saw it pleased the Jews, he proceeded further to take Peter also. (Then were the days of unleavened bread.)

The "time" referred to is during a famine in Judea (**Acts 11:28**). This is now the third of four Herods to enter the Luke-Acts narrative. The first was Herod the Great, who reigned during the priesthood of Zacharias (**Luke 1:5**). The second was Herod Antipas, who shadowed Jesus' ministry, death, and resurrection (**Luke 9:7–9; 23:7–15**). This "Herod the king" in **Acts 12:1** is Herod Agrippa I, the grandson of Herod the Great and the father of Herod Agrippa II (**Acts 25:13–26**). Herod Agrippa I had been brought up in Rome, where he made many influential friends—among whom were Gaius Caligula and Claudius. When Caligula became emperor (AD 37–41), he granted Herod the tetrarchies ruled by Philip and Lysanius (**Luke 3:1**). Later he added the tetrarchy of Herod Antipas to Herod Agrippa's possessions. After Caligula's assassination, Herod helped Claudius receive confirmation from the Roman senate as emperor. The new emperor added Judea and Samaria to Herod's kingdom. So from AD 41 to the time of his death in AD 44, Herod Agrippa I ruled over a reassembled kingdom the same size as his grandfather, Herod the Great. He was as loved by the Jewish establishment as his grandfather was hated.

Herod Agrippa was committed to maintaining a peace favorable to Rome—a policy called "Pax Romana." Therefore, he supported the religious establishment and was hostile toward all who saw things differently. Because he saw Jewish Christians as disruptive, he sought to suppress them. To this end, he arrested some of Jesus' followers and had James executed. This James was one of the first followers of Jesus (**Luke 5:10**) and was one of the Twelve (**Luke 6:14–16**). He, along with his brother John (son of Zebedee) and Peter were close friends with Jesus (**Luke 8:51, 9:28**). He was often called James the Great to distinguish him from James the son of Alphaeus (**Acts 1:13**). He was also not to be confused with James, the half-brother of Jesus (**Galatians 1:19**). The death of James signaled the end of the short period of tranquility enjoyed by the Jerusalem leadership after Saul's conversion (**Acts 9:31**).

Upon seeing that his action pleased the Jews, Herod Agrippa I had Peter arrested to preserve the status quo. The reason "it pleased the Jews" may also lie in the means of James' execution. In the Talmud, the rabbis considered beheading the most shameful of all deaths, reserved for those who had no share in the world to come. The execution of James was therefore a gesture of solidarity on Herod's part with the Jewish majority, a statement that he regarded Jesus' followers as apostates and agitators. Luke parenthetically told his readers that these "were the days of unleavened bread." Although the celebration of the feast began with the Passover meal on 14 Nisan (the first month of the Jewish calendar), the "days of unleavened bread" continued for seven days more (**Exodus 12:3–20, 23:15, 34:18**). The reader is expected to make the connection between this arrest and that of Jesus, which also occurred at Passover.

SEARCH THE SCRIPTURES

QUESTION 1
James was a significant church leader. How was James killed?

A sword.

LIGHT ON THE WORD

Herod Terrorizes the Church

To appease the Jewish leaders and redirect them from the critical issue of famine, Herod chose to terrorize the church. In this situation, the church needed to depend on God in the same way as the Old Testament prophets.

II. BOXED IN (vv. 4–6)

Peter's crime of preaching could not have been so severe as to warrant the intensity of his imprisonment, yet he is held like one sentenced for a capital crime. He is guarded by a group of four soldiers who completely surround Peter at all times. Two are on watch and the other two are chained to him (**v. 6**). In essence, being surrounded on four sides, Peter was boxed in. Not only was he relegated to the enclosed box of the prison cell, but with round-the-clock guards, and two of them physically bound to him, there was absolutely no way to escape.

In light of the lesson's theme, Peter's circumstances are clearly at such a critical point that only prayer—and a divine intervention—could bring about a change. Prayer is described as offering, or an address to God. That the church prayed "without ceasing" underscores the importance of communicating with God even more fervently when other resources are not available. Addressing the king through political appeal is not mentioned. A rescue or demand for a proper trial is not attempted. There is only the church instituting constant and fervent prayer, a concept that remains today (**1 Thessalonians 5:17**). If indeed a believer is found to be in an impossible situation, there is no other remedy than to call upon the King of Kings.

4 And when he had apprehended him, he put him in prison, and delivered him to four quaternions of soldiers to keep him; intending after Easter to bring him forth to the people. 5 Peter therefore was kept in prison: but prayer was made without ceasing of the church unto God for him. 6 And when Herod would have brought him forth, the same night Peter was sleeping between two soldiers, bound with two chains: and the keepers before the door kept the prison.

The delay functions in the narrative to build tension and allows the reader to see the activity of the church working against that of Herod. Overall, the action stands in contrast to the summary execution of James by "the sword" in **verse 2**. We can see the importance of this trial in the eyes of Herod as Peter is guarded by four quaternions, or sixteen soldiers.

While Peter was in prison, the believers were continually praying to God for him. Throughout Acts, the church is portrayed as a praying community (**Acts 1:14, 24; 2:42; 4:24–30; 13:3**). The adverbial phrase "without ceasing" (Gk. *ektenes*, ek-teh-OSE) denotes eagerness and earnestness. It is from a verb that means to stretch out the hand, implying an attitude of not relaxing until a thing is accomplished. The community's prayer is contrasted with Peter's powerlessness to escape.

Herod may have heard of Peter and John's earlier escape and decided to fortify security measures (**Acts 5:17–20**). Luke takes time to break down the duties of one quaternion. The custom with such squads was to have four men on duty at a time, in four revolving watches. Here two slept next to Peter and one was at each of the two guard posts (**v. 10**). These elaborate security measures heighten the wonder of the escape.

III. DIVINE DELIVERANCE (vv. 7–10)

It is difficult to imagine how Peter could possibly sleep (**v. 6**) or get any rest. As he faces his death sentence, as well as being physically chained to two guards, he is as tightly confined as possible. Yet God uses sleep as a method of veiling His actions while enforcing His will. Peter has no time to ask questions or to confirm the angel's identity or purpose; he is only able to follow instructions to end the present dilemma (**v. 8**). Whether through a vision or an angel or ghost, God hears the prayers of His people and delivers them out of their trials.

7 And, behold, the angel of the Lord came upon him, and a light shined in the prison: and he smote Peter on the side, and raised him up, saying, Arise up quickly. And his chains fell off from his hands. 8 And the angel said unto him, Gird thyself, and bind on thy sandals. And so he did. And he saith unto him, Cast thy garment about thee, and follow me. 9 And he went out, and followed him; and wist not that it was true which was done by the angel; but thought he saw a vision. 10 When they were past the first and the second ward, they came unto the iron gate that leadeth unto the city; which opened to them of his own accord: and they went out, and passed on through one street; and forthwith the angel departed from him.

The angel appears to Peter and instructs him to get up. These messengers from God played an important role through substantial portions of the books of Luke and Acts (**Luke 1:11, 26; 2:9, 13; Acts 8:26; 27:23**). Together, the use of the words "behold" (Gk. *idou*, **ee-DOO**) and "came upon" (Gk. *ephistemi*, **eh-FEES-tay-me**) gives the sense of a sudden and startling appearance (cf. Luke 2:9). As with the appearance to Saul, "light" (Gk. *phos*, **FOCE**) was a sign of heavenly presence (**Acts 9:3; 22:6, 9–11**).

Peter followed the instructions of the angel, although he believed it was a vision. It is important to note that Peter gets fully dressed. He puts on his shoes and belt as well as his outer garment or coat. This indicates it was not a swift escape made with human effort, but the work of God. The verb "thought" (Gk. *dokeo*, **doh-keh-OH**) is

in the imperfect active tense, which means that while the escape was taking place, he kept on thinking and being confused about whether he was in a vision. It is only after the angel departs that Peter realizes the escape is real.

IV. THE DOORS OF THE CHURCH ARE OPEN (vv. 11–12)

Peter "came to himself." He collected his thoughts, or gathered his head; his physical head was literally saved in those moments. King Herod had threatened Peter with beheading, thus silencing the spread of God's Word, but now after the miraculous rescue by the angel, Peter can think clearly. He says he is absolutely sure the Lord has delivered him. Prayer will be effective as it will invoke God's presence and action. Peter realizes he had not been dreaming; it had to be the activity of God that set him free.

Once Peter regains full consciousness, he quickly finds his way to the church. There the believers prayed for Peter, not knowing how God would answer, but knowing for "surety," truth above all, that He would answer. Although Peter was very much a believer and no doubt prayed for his own escape, the church needed to see for themselves how God heard them. Peter could not introduce the church to the angel, nor invite it in to explain how a blow to the side could both awaken him and removed his chains. All he had was his physical body as proof not only that he had escaped, but that God indeed answers prayer.

11 And when Peter was come to himself, he said, Now I know of a surety, that the Lord hath sent his angel, and hath delivered me out of the hand of Herod, and from all the expectation of the people of the Jews.

The withdrawal of the angel of the Lord corresponds to Peter's "coming to himself." The Greek phrase (*en heauto ginomai*; **en he-ow-TOE**

GHEE-no-my) indicates that Peter's state of being changed. He was no longer sleeping but in waking consciousness. In this state, he is able to understand what has happened to him and that it was not simply a dream.

The phrase "now I know of a surety, that the Lord hath sent his angel" is a declaration that Peter is aware this whole ordeal was not a dream, but orchestrated by God. The word "surety" (Gk. *alethos*, **ah-ley-THOS**) means simply truth or reality. As in **Acts 12:3**, Luke joins the power of Herod to the hostile expectation of the Jews. Here the adverbial use of the term "expectation" (Gk. *prosdokia*, **pros-doe-KEE-ah**) is used. In the New Testament it is only used here and in **Luke 21:26**. The word can be used for positive or negative expectation. It is in the negative sense here, as Peter realizes that he has been rescued from the persecution of Herod and the vocal Jewish leadership who influenced him.

SEARCH THE SCRIPTURES

QUESTION 2
What three commands did the angel give Peter (vv. 7–8)?

Quickly get up, "put on your clothes and sandals; wrap your cloak around you; and follow me."

QUESTION 3
Peter thought that he was _____ ____ _____.

seeing a vision

LIGHT ON THE WORD

God's Angel
The angel of the Lord provides some contrast to popular images of these celestial beings. With more boisterous action than the singing, fluttering angels of popular culture, this angel "smote" or hit Peter in the side.

BIBLE APPLICATION

AIM: Students will learn that believers should prayer together and expect God to answer.

The church is depicted in this lesson as a place of refuge and mutual support. Unfortunately, today the church seems to be the last place considered for those needs. It is very important that believers remember how unity is a common thread which God uses not only to build His kingdom, but also protect and love His people. Is the church today anything like the church that prayed for Paul?

STUDENT'S RESPONSES

AIM: Students will learn that God can rescue people from dangerous circumstances.

Often we pray without considering whether our prayers are heard. Instead of praying as an empty ritual, we can practice praying in faith that God will answer. Encourage the class to discuss and select an issue or current event for which they will pray over a period of time. Select someone in the class to monitor the situation and give a report of their prayers at work.

PRAYER

Our Provider and our Deliverer, we are so grateful that You take care of us and provide a way out of no way. We worship and adore You for showing us Your mercy each and every day. In the Name of Jesus we pray. Amen.

HOW TO SAY IT

Quaternions.   kwa-ter-**NEE**-yins.

Surety.   **SHER**-eh-tee.

PREPARE FOR NEXT SUNDAY

Read **Acts 15:1–12** and "God Makes No Distinction."

DAILY HOME BIBLE READINGS

MONDAY
The Rock That Saves
(Psalm 18:1–9)

TUESDAY
The Shepherd Who Restores
(Psalm 80:1–3, 7, 17–19)

WEDNESDAY
God Saves Daniel
(Daniel 6:19–23)

THURSDAY
The Faithful God
(Daniel 6:25–28)

FRIDAY
God Saves Paul
(Acts 27:14–25)

SATURDAY
The Freeing God
(Acts 12:12–18)

SUNDAY
God Rescues Peter
(Acts 12:1–11)

Sources:
Carson, D.A., France, R.T., Motyer, J.A., Wenham, J.G. New Bible Commentary. Downers Grove, IL: InterVarsity Press, 1993.
Keener, Craig S. IVP Bible Background Commentary. Downers Grove, IL: InterVarsity Press, 1993.
Polhill, John B. Acts. New American Commentary: An Exegetical and Theological Exposition of Holy Scripture. Nashville: B&H Publishing, 1992.

COMMENTS / NOTES:

GOD MAKES NO DISTINCTION

BIBLE BASIS: ACTS 15:1–12

BIBLE TRUTH: Luke claimed that the Jerusalem council had power to change the Law of Moses in order to make it congruent to God's action.

MEMORY VERSE: "And God, which knoweth the hearts, bare them witness, giving them the Holy Ghost, even as he did unto us; And put no difference between us and them, purifying their hearts by faith" (Acts 15:8–9).

LESSON AIM: By the end of this lesson, we will: REVIEW the story of how the Jerusalem council listened to Paul and Barnabas as they told of the signs and wonders God did among the Gentiles; REFLECT on how difficult it can be to reconcile law and God's action; and INITIATE a process of discernment of God's will when the law and God's actions appear to conflict.

TEACHER PREPARATION

MATERIALS NEEDED: Quarterly Commentary/Teacher Manual, Adult Quarterly, Adult resources—charts, worksheets, and other teaching tools, paper, pens, pencils, Bibles (several different versions)

OTHER MATERIALS NEEDED / TEACHER'S NOTES:

_____

_____

LESSON OVERVIEW

LIFE NEED FOR TODAY'S LESSON
Laws are an integral part of civilized society and some laws change as society changes. However, no law will negate or supersede the Word of God.

BIBLE LEARNING
Paul and Barnabas shared the power of God's mighty acts in the Gentile community.

BIBLE APPLICATION
Christians should remember that it is important to know that God gives everyone an equal opportunity.

STUDENTS' RESPONSES
Christians understand that it can be difficult to choose between God's laws and society's laws.

LESSON SCRIPTURE

ACTS 15:1–12, KJV

1 And certain men which came down from Judaea taught the brethren, and said, Except ye be circumcised after the manner of Moses, ye cannot be saved.

ACTS 15:1–12, NIV

1 Certain people came down from Judea to Antioch and were teaching the believers: "Unless you are circumcised, according to the custom taught by Moses, you cannot be saved."

2 When therefore Paul and Barnabas had no small dissension and disputation with them, they determined that Paul and Barnabas, and certain other of them, should go up to Jerusalem unto the apostles and elders about this question.

3 And being brought on their way by the church, they passed through Phenice and Samaria, declaring the conversion of the Gentiles: and they caused great joy unto all the brethren.

4 And when they were come to Jerusalem, they were received of the church, and of the apostles and elders, and they declared all things that God had done with them.

5 But there rose up certain of the sect of the Pharisees which believed, saying, That it was needful to circumcise them, and to command them to keep the law of Moses.

6 And the apostles and elders came together for to consider of this matter.

7 And when there had been much disputing, Peter rose up, and said unto them, Men and brethren, ye know how that a good while ago God made choice among us, that the Gentiles by my mouth should hear the word of the gospel, and believe.

8 And God, which knoweth the hearts, bare them witness, giving them the Holy Ghost, even as he did unto us;

9 And put no difference between us and them, purifying their hearts by faith.

10 Now therefore why tempt ye God, to put a yoke upon the neck of the disciples, which neither our fathers nor we were able to bear?

11 But we believe that through the grace of the Lord Jesus Christ we shall be saved, even as they.

2 This brought Paul and Barnabas into sharp dispute and debate with them. So Paul and Barnabas were appointed, along with some other believers, to go up to Jerusalem to see the apostles and elders about this question.

3 The church sent them on their way, and as they traveled through Phoenicia and Samaria, they told how the Gentiles had been converted. This news made all the believers very glad.

4 When they came to Jerusalem, they were welcomed by the church and the apostles and elders, to whom they reported everything God had done through them.

5 Then some of the believers who belonged to the party of the Pharisees stood up and said, "The Gentiles must be circumcised and required to keep the law of Moses."

6 The apostles and elders met to consider this question.

7 After much discussion, Peter got up and addressed them: "Brothers, you know that some time ago God made a choice among you that the Gentiles might hear from my lips the message of the gospel and believe.

8 God, who knows the heart, showed that he accepted them by giving the Holy Spirit to them, just as he did to us.

9 He did not discriminate between us and them, for he purified their hearts by faith.

10 Now then, why do you try to test God by putting on the necks of Gentiles a yoke that neither we nor our ancestors have been able to bear?

11 No! We believe it is through the grace of our Lord Jesus that we are saved, just as they are."

12 The whole assembly became silent as

12 Then all the multitude kept silence, and gave audience to Barnabas and Paul, declaring what miracles and wonders God had wrought among the Gentiles by them.

they listened to Barnabas and Paul telling about the signs and wonders God had done among the Gentiles through them.

LIGHT ON THE WORD

Phenice. The country on the eastern Mediterranean coast situated just north of Palestine. This land lay at the foot of the Lebanon mountains and was located within the Syrian coastal plain. The cities of this region were world-renowned ports where trade flourished. Phenice was also one of the places Christian refugees fled to during Saul's persecution (**Acts 11:19**). It is here where Paul and Barnabas visited to encourage the disciples.

Samaria. Samaria was a province north of Judea and south of Galilee. It contained a population descended from a mixed ancestry of Jews and other Gentile nations. These populations worshiped similar to the Jews, except they did not worship at Jerusalem, but Mt. Gerizim. This caused hostility between the Jews and the people of Samaria which continued until Jesus' day. Philip, one of the Seven, journeyed to Samaria and preached the Gospel there. Many believed in his preaching and became the first Samaritan converts (**Acts 8:4–12**).

TEACHING THE BIBLE LESSON

LIFE NEED FOR TODAY'S LESSON

AIM: Students will see how laws are an integral part of civilized society, and that some laws must change as society changes. However, no law will negate or supersede God.

INTRODUCTION

The Radical Movement

The events recorded in the book of Acts reflect a period marked by political and social upheaval. While the ancient world was no stranger to religious debates, the absolutely radical movement incited by Jesus and His disciples was continuing to make waves. As the early church was developing, it was still very much a sect of Judaism, since Jesus and His disciples were committed to their Hebrew roots. Nevertheless, just as Jesus had to stand against the rulers, high priests, and Pharisees, so now would His disciples, both original and newly converted, have to contend with those who attempted to straddle the line between grace and the law. The central debate in this passage centers on the Jews' historical separation from Gentiles. The conversion of Cornelius and his household in Acts 10–11 sparked a controversy that epitomized the explosive birth and growth of the Christian church.

BIBLE LEARNING

AIM: Students will discover that Paul and Barnabas shared the power of God's mighty acts in the Gentile community.

I. GOD'S WILL DEBATED (Acts 15:1–3)

The "certain men" who initiated the circumcision controversy in the early church are known as Judaizers. Their desire to navigate the demands of God's Law and His grace would not be the first or last such attempt in the life of the church. While it is difficult to imagine a modern debate of this type, it is not unlike the various divisions that have created the many different denominations of the Christian faith. It is true that circumcision was indeed God's command, initially given to Abraham in **Genesis 17:10**.

Notably, Paul and Barnabas were chosen to discuss the case against physical circumcision on their journey. Paul, especially, was no stranger to Jewish tradition and law, at times recalling the depth of his religious pedigree (**Philippians 3:4–6**). Additionally, Paul had the unique position of being both the chief persecutor of the church (**Acts 9:1–5**) as well as one of its most prolific champions. In preparation for the debate ahead, it is important to note that they stopped to report the effect of the Gospel message on the Gentiles along the way. Their emphasis on the salvation of Gentiles is important as it helped to verify the authenticity of the Gospel's power among those not born Jews. Of course the result of their report is the "great joy" experienced by the brethren. The Christian message is ultimately joy that comes individually to those who accept eternal life, and collectively as more are added to the body of Christ.

Acts 15:1–12

15:1 And certain men which came down from Judaea taught the brethren, and said, Except ye be circumcised after the manner of Moses, ye cannot be saved. 2 When therefore Paul and Barnabas had no small dissension and disputation with them, they determined that Paul and Barnabas, and certain other of them, should go up to Jerusalem unto the apostles and elders about this question. 3 And being brought on their way by the church, they passed through Phenice and Samaria, declaring the conversion of the

Gentiles: and they caused great joy unto all the brethren.

Some say these "certain men" were (1) proselytes to the Jewish religion, (2) the Pharisees, or (3) priests who were obedient to the Jewish faith. Whoever they were, they were recent Jewish converts to Christianity. The men arrived in Antioch from Judea. They came to Antioch, the headquarters of those who preached to the Gentiles, preaching a doctrine different from what Paul, Barnabas, and the other leaders of Christianity taught. Their message to the Gentile Christians was that they would now have to submit to circumcision and the Jewish ceremonial law. They taught that unless people were circumcised after the manner (Gk. *ethos*, **EE-thoce**) or customs prescribed by the law, they were not saved. Although many of the Jews embraced Christianity, they did not want to release their Jewish heritage and customs. Not only did they continue to observe Jewish rituals and laws, some also wanted to impose these requirements on the Gentile Christians.

Many Jews at this time believed that Gentiles would be saved by keeping the seven Noahide laws (**Genesis 9:1–7**). These were the laws the Jews believed were binding for all people because they were given to Noah, the ancestor of all the people to repopulate the earth after the Flood. Other Jews believed Gentiles could only be right with God by observing the whole Torah, including the ceremonial laws. For men this meant circumcision, and for both genders it meant observance of dietary laws. This debate about what was required for Gentiles spilled over into the open argument in **Acts 15**.

Paul, Barnabas, and the other leaders of the Gentile Christians would not see the truth betrayed or distorted. They taught: (1) Christ came to free us from the yoke of ceremonial law, (2) Jews and Gentiles were united in

Christ, and (3) salvation comes by belief in Jesus Christ. Baptism and the Lord's Supper were the two ritual instructions given to the church. Paul and the other leaders could not bear to hear of circumcising the Gentile converts because God had already affirmed the acceptance of Gentiles by filling them with the Holy Spirit. Those Judaizers who came with this doctrine claimed they came at the directions of the apostles and elders at Jerusalem. Therefore, the church at Antioch appointed Paul and Barnabas to go to Jerusalem to present this case to the apostles and elders. Since the apostles and elders established Christianity in Jerusalem, their opinion in this matter was very crucial. It was necessary to hear what they had to say in order to put an end to the controversy, and to silence these teachers and false apostles.

Paul and Barnabas traveled or passed through Phenice or Phoenicia and Samaria declaring (*ekdiegeomai*, **ek-dee-ay-GEH-oh-my**) which means to narrate in full or wholly the conversion of the Gentiles. The word for conversion (*epistrophe*, **eh-pee-stroh-FAY**) means a turning about or turning around. Their report resulted in joy for all the church.

II. GOD'S WILL CONSIDERED (vv. 4–6)

Some would discourage debate among believers, seeing it as a sign of division. Yet, God encourages His children to seek His will actively and engage each other with Scripture, prayer, and a desire for unity. This quest for unity seems to be the missing element to the discussion initiated by the Judaizers. As a result, Paul and Barnabas must engage in what amounts to a trial to plead the case for grace against the position of the law, which mandated circumcision. This trial pointed toward the definition of what true belief would come to mean.

Today's debates rarely involve physical alteration of the body; however, many religious rites and activities must be carefully considered not only for their historical significance, but also their spiritual relevance. The apostles and elders coming together to discuss a difficult situation presents a great role model for the contemporary church to follow. While there were legitimate foundations to both sides of the debate, it was certainly worth discussing, rather than initiating war, or worse, dismantling the newborn church for lack of an agreement. Many issues face new and modern believers, which should be discussed with careful consideration of God's will, versus the desires of psychological comfort or blind tradition.

4 And when they were come to Jerusalem, they were received of the church, and of the apostles and elders, and they declared all things that God had done with them. 5 But there rose up certain of the sect of the Pharisees which believed, saying, That it was needful to circumcise them, and to command them to keep the law of Moses. 6 And the apostles and elders came together for to consider of this matter.

Finally Paul and Barnabas arrive in Jerusalem and Luke notes that they were received (*apodechomai*, **ah-po-DEH-kho-my**) or heartily welcomed by the church and the apostles and elders. They also declare all the things that God had done. The focus is on what God is doing among the Gentiles as this is Paul and Barnabas' unique ministry task.

As much as they are received by the church they also face opposition. This opposition arises from a sect (*hairesis*, **HIGH-ray-sees**) which means a group of people following their own tenets. In this context it refers to a certain group of Pharisees who are given to the same beliefs and practices within the wider group of Pharisees. These men claimed the Gentiles' conversion was not complete. In their opinion, the Gentile Christians needed to be circumcised and to keep the law of Moses.

At the Jerusalem council, the apostles and elders gathered by consent to consider this matter. They came to reason together. They did not give their judgment separately or rashly, but considered the matter rationally and communally. The apostles, although of higher authority than the elders, did not exclude them. Here is an example to the leaders of churches, pastors in particular, when disputes arise (and they will): come together in solemn meeting for mutual advice and encouragement. Bring all together to present their positions so that the church can act in concert and come to the best decision for all involved.

SEARCH THE SCRIPTURES

QUESTION 1
What topic did Paul and Barnabas need to address for new converts?

Circumcision

QUESTION 2
State the two cities that both Paul and Barnabas traveled to share the Gospel.

Phenice and Samaria

LIGHT ON THE WORD

A New Order
Now that some time had passed since Jesus' resurrection, the unique and powerful movement of the Holy Spirit demanded attention and action from those within and outside the established church. Visions experienced by Cornelius (**Acts 10:1–6**) and subsequently Peter (**Acts 10:10–16**) demonstrated God's desire to not only include Gentiles in the Christ movement, but also forge a relationship between those raised under Jewish law

and those not. As with many groups, the Jews grappled with ways to make new believers conform to the older ways. Yet it was clear that any boundaries that had been in place were now demolished by the power of the Holy Spirit.

III. GOD'S WILL REVEALED (vv. 7–12)

As Peter adds his voice to the fervent debate, his words bring a severe but comforting resolution. He uses several words that ring out even in sermons to this day. "God made [a] choice…" While Peter is specifically speaking about his inspiration to proclaim the Gospel to the Gentiles, he is echoing the foundation of both the Jewish and now Christian faith. God's choice was to save His people. This was announced by prophets and by various acts of God all through Scripture. If God has initially chosen who would speak, He has now chosen who may hear and subsequently believe. This is a radical concept considering the Judaizers' lifelong understanding of being "God's chosen" as an elite group, free to discriminate and exclude outsiders.

A chilling summary follows as he declares that God put "no difference between us and them" (**v. 9**) and acknowledges that the rigors of the law were even too much for the Jewish ancestors to bear. Even those who are fully committed to the law are incapable of obeying it completely without fail. To acknowledge this simple human frailty is the first step to embracing the call of God and the power of the Holy Spirit.

Peter's conclusion should motivate anyone attempting to engage in evangelism. The difference between "we" and "they" should never last long in a believer's view of another person. It is simply a matter of timing. Jesus' commission to go, teach, and baptize (**Matthew 28:19–20, Mark 16:15–16**) means that everyone can have an opportunity not only to be called brother and sister, but also be acknowledged as the sons and daughters of God.

7 And when there had been much disputing, Peter rose up, and said unto them, Men and brethren, ye know that a good while ago God made choice among us, that the Gentiles by my mouth should hear the word of the Gospel, and believe. 8 And God, which knoweth the hearts, bare them witness, giving them the Holy Ghost, even as he did unto us; 9 And put no difference between us and them, purifying their hearts by faith. 10 Now therefore why tempt ye God, to put a yoke upon the neck of the disciples, which neither our fathers nor we were able to bear? 11 But we believe that through the grace of the Lord Jesus Christ we shall be saved, even as they. 12 Then all the multitude kept silence and gave audience to Barnabas and Paul, declaring what miracles and wonders God had wrought among the Gentiles by them.

After much disputing (Gk. *suzetesis*, **su-ZAY-tay-sees**) or mutual questioning and discussion on both sides, the Apostle Peter stood to address the group. Peter was the first apostle to preach to a Gentile audience (**Acts 10:34–43**). He reminded them of his experience in preaching the Gospel to the Gentiles. When Peter reported his experience to the Jerusalem church, everyone rejoiced and no one said a word about circumcision (**Acts 11:1–18**).

Peter uses the compound word *kardiognostes* (Gk. **kar-dee-ah-NOS-tays**). This word is used in the Bible only in the book of Acts. In both instances it (there are only two) is in reference to God and His omniscience (**1:24; 15:8**). This is in anticipation of Peter confirming that God gave them the Holy Spirit. He says that God "bare them witness" (Gk. *martureo*, **mar-too-REH-oh**). Peter is letting the council know that God knows people's hearts and therefore knows what He is doing.

Peter went on to say that since God did not differentiate between the Gentiles and the Jews, His followers should not either. The Gentiles were as welcome to the grace of Jesus Christ as the Jews. Their hearts were purified (Gk. *katharizo*, **ka-tha-REED-zo**) by faith. The word for purified is the same word for pronouncing something clean in the Levitical sense. It is used in **Acts 10:15** as God speaks to Peter about clean and unclean food. Now this word is used for the Gentiles. They are no longer "unclean" people because their hearts have been cleansed through faith in Christ. Paul reiterated this point to the church at Galatia: God would not deny anyone who believes in Jesus Christ access to the Holy Spirit. There is no distinction between Christians in Christ (**Galatians 3:28**).

Peter reproved those who wanted to bring the Gentiles under the obligation of the law of Moses. In his indictment against the Jewish leaders, he basically asks why they would want to test God when they can see how powerfully He is moving. In this case, to tempt (Gk. *peirazo*, **pay-ROD-zo**) means to exhibit distrust (**Matthew 16:1**) and it is Peter's way of saying not to go against the movement God has already started to bring the Gentiles to faith. In other words, trust what the Holy Spirit is doing. The Jewish ceremonial law was a heavy yoke (Gk. *zugos*, **zoo-GOHS**) that no one could keep. The yoke was a device that joined two cattle together as they plowed in the field; hence it became used metaphorically for any type of burden or bondage. A yoke could also have a positive connotation of strong support and guidance as in **Lamentations 3:27** or with the yoke of rabbinic instruction. Jesus Christ came to set us free from the yoke of the law, saying, "Take my yoke upon you and learn of me, for I am gentle and humble in heart, and you will find rest for your souls" (**Matthew 11:29, NIV**).

Peter reminds the Jerusalem church leaders that the salvation they received comes by the grace (Gk. *charis*, **KHAH-rees**) or unmerited favor of Jesus Christ. It is not by circumcision or uncircumcision, but by grace through faith in Jesus Christ. They could not obtain salvation by keeping the law. Peter confessed that neither they nor their ancestors could bear up under this weight. Both Jews and Gentiles are now equal in God's eyes and will receive the same salvation because of Christ.

"All the multitude" refers to the believers who were present for the council. These believers kept silent in order to give audience to (Gk. *akouo*, **ah-KOO-oh**) or hear what Paul and Barnabas said. Their accounts are found in **Acts 13 and 14**. During these occasions, their preaching of the Gospel included not only readings from the Law and Prophets and the retelling of God's salvation of Israel, but also signs and wonders were wrought (Gk. *poieo*, **poy-EH-oh**) or worked among the Gentiles. This showed the approval of God on this new work of preaching the Gospel to the Gentiles. To impose the whole Law of Moses now would subvert what God had already begun.

SEARCH THE SCRIPTURES

QUESTION 3
What does multitude refer to in **verse 12**? Share the response of the "multitude" to Peter and Barnabas.

The multitude refers to the believers who were present. After listening to Peter, they were quiet/silent to hear what both men had to say.

LIGHT ON THE WORD

All are Chosen
Many Christian churches today carry on as though they alone are chosen; yet Peter, in agreement with Paul and Barnabas, clarifies that God has chosen to save all who will accept the gift of salvation. Peter goes on to mention that God knows the heart. As the circumcised heart was to be the most authentic indicator

of true belief, Peter forces the divided council to accept that the Gentiles must have the same capacity to believe as anyone else.

BIBLE APPLICATION

AIM: Students will understand why Christians should remember that it is important to know that God gives everyone an equal opportunity.

Many people would not know the first thing about another method of worship outside their own. Even among Christian denominations, there seem to be sharp divisions between the practices of the Baptists, Presbyterians, Episcopalians, Pentecostals, Methodists, Catholics, etc. While there are many styles and even many administrations of worship that are ordained by Scripture (**1 Corinthians 12:5**), there is still only one Lord, one faith, and one baptism (**Ephesians 4:5**). It is the confession of Jesus Christ and faith in Him that unites us all.

STUDENT'S RESPONSES

AIM: Students will learn that Christians understand that it can be difficult to choose between God's laws and society's laws.

God desires unity among all believers in Christ so that we may operate as one body (**1 Corinthians 12:12**). However, the reality is that this desire is often thwarted by believers on numerous levels. One of the ways we can seek out unity is learning how to resolve conflict in a Christlike manner. As a class, construct a model for conflict resolution based on the events in **Acts 15**. Note the different elements that helped the early church to come to a peaceful resolution regarding the circumcision of Gentile believers.

PRAYER

Thank You, Jesus, for choosing us and giving

everyone an opportunity to know You. Like Paul and Barnabas, we want to stand firm on Your word as we speak to others about who You are. In the Name of Jesus, we pray. Amen.

HOW TO SAY IT

Disputation   dis-pyu-**TAY**-shun.

Phenice   fe-**NEES**.

PREPARE FOR NEXT SUNDAY

Read **Acts 16:1–5, 8–15** and "From Derbe to Philippi."

DAILY HOME BIBLE READINGS

MONDAY
Thanking God
(Romans 1:8–15)

TUESDAY
The Forgiving God
(Nehemiah 9:6–12)

WEDNESDAY
Abundant Grace
(Romans 16:25–27)

THURSDAY
Accessible God
(Hebrews 4:12–16)

FRIDAY
God is Making All Things New
(Galatians 3:6–14)

SATURDAY
Grace for Gentiles
(Revelation 21:1–5)

SUNDAY
God Makes No Distinction
(Acts 15:1–12)

Sources:

Carson, D.A., France, R.T., Motyer, J.A., Wenham, J.G. *New Bible Commentary.* Downers Grove, IL: InterVarsity Press, 1993.

Keener, Craig S. *IVP Bible Background Commentary.* Downers Grove, IL: InterVarsity Press, 1993.

Polhill, John B. *Acts. New American Commentary: An Exegetical and Theological Exposition of Holy Scripture.* Nashville: B&H Publishing, 1992.

COMMENTS / NOTES:

_____

_____

_____

_____

_____

_____

_____

_____

_____

_____

_____

_____

_____

_____

_____

_____

_____

_____

_____

_____

_____

_____

_____

_____

_____

_____

_____

_____

_____

_____

FROM DERBE TO PHILIPPI

BIBLE BASIS: ACTS 16:1–5, 8–15

BIBLE TRUTH: Paul's obedience to God and his respect for the elders and apostles gave opportunities for the Gospel to spread to many regions.

MEMORY VERSE: "And after he had seen the vision, immediately we endeavoured to go into Macedonia, assuredly gathering that the Lord had called us for to preach the gospel unto them" (Acts 16:10).

LESSON AIM: By the end of the lesson, we will: RECALL how Paul added Timothy to his missionary team and their labors in spreading the Gospel from Derbe to Philippi; REFLECT on those characteristics needed for members of a successful evangelism team; and SPREAD the Gospel in every aspect of our lives.

TEACHER PREPARATION

MATERIALS NEEDED: Quarterly Commentary/Teacher Manual, Adult Quarterly, Adult resources—charts, worksheets, and other teaching tools, paper, pens, pencils, Bibles (several different versions)

OTHER MATERIALS NEEDED / TEACHER'S NOTES:

_____

_____

LESSON OVERVIEW

LIFE NEED FOR TODAY'S LESSON

Sometimes things that start out small turn out be much larger than expected, and impact the lives of others in surprising ways.

BIBLE LEARNING

Lydia listened to Paul's preaching and then was baptized along with her other family members.

BIBLE APPLICATION

Believers should be sensitive to God's plan for their lives and open to change.

STUDENTS' RESPONSES

Believers can participate in the expansion of the Kingdom of God as they actively and willingly do God's will.

LESSON SCRIPTURE

ACTS 16:1–5, 8–15, KJV

1 Then came he to Derbe and Lystra: and, behold, a certain disciple was there, named Timotheus, the son of a certain woman, which was a Jewess, and believed; but his father was a Greek:

ACTS 16:1–5, 8–15, NIV

1 Paul came to Derbe and then to Lystra, where a disciple named Timothy lived, whose mother was Jewish and a believer but whose father was a Greek.

2 The believers at Lystra and Iconium spoke

2 Which was well reported of by the brethren that were at Lystra and Iconium.

3 Him would Paul have to go forth with him; and took and circumcised him because of the Jews which were in those quarters: for they knew all that his father was a Greek.

4 And as they went through the cities, they delivered them the decrees for to keep, that were ordained of the apostles and elders which were at Jerusalem.

5 And so were the churches established in the faith, and increased in number daily.

8 And they passing by Mysia came down to Troas.

9 And a vision appeared to Paul in the night; There stood a man of Macedonia, and prayed him, saying, Come over into Macedonia, and help us.

10 And after he had seen the vision, immediately we endeavoured to go into Macedonia, assuredly gathering that the Lord had called us for to preach the gospel unto them.

11 Therefore loosing from Troas, we came with a straight course to Samothracia, and the next day to Neapolis;

12 And from thence to Philippi, which is the chief city of that part of Macedonia, and a colony: and we were in that city abiding certain days.

13 And on the sabbath we went out of the city by a river side, where prayer was wont to be made; and we sat down, and spake unto the women which resorted thither.

14 And a certain woman named Lydia, a seller of purple, of the city of Thyatira, which worshipped God, heard us: whose heart the Lord opened, that she attended unto the things which were spoken of Paul.

well of him.

3 Paul wanted to take him along on the journey, so he circumcised him because of the Jews who lived in that area, for they all knew that his father was a Greek. *Sometimes you do things for sake of others*

4 As they traveled from town to town, they delivered the decisions reached by the apostles and elders in Jerusalem for the people to obey.

5 So the churches were strengthened in the faith and grew daily in numbers.

8 So they passed by Mysia and went down to Troas.

9 During the night Paul had a vision of a man of Macedonia standing and begging him, "Come over to Macedonia and help us."

10 After Paul had seen the vision, we got ready at once to leave for Macedonia, concluding that God had called us to preach the gospel to them.

11 From Troas we put out to sea and sailed straight for Samothrace, and the next day we went on to Neapolis.

12 From there we traveled to Philippi, a Roman colony and the leading city of that district of Macedonia. And we stayed there several days.

13 On the Sabbath we went outside the city gate to the river, where we expected to find a place of prayer. We sat down and began to speak to the women who had gathered there.

14 One of those listening was a woman from the city of Thyatira named Lydia, a dealer in purple cloth. She was a worshiper of God. The Lord opened her heart to respond to Paul's message.

15 And when she was baptized, and her household, she besought us, saying, If ye have judged me to be faithful to the Lord, come into my house, and abide there. And she constrained us.

15 When she and the members of her household were baptized, she invited us to her home. "If you consider me a believer in the Lord," she said, "come and stay at my house." And she persuaded us.

LIGHT ON THE WORD

Derbe. Paul is known to have visited Derbe on his first and second missionary journeys. It is likely he passed through during his third missionary journey as well (**Acts 18:23**). Derbe was a small town located near the modern city of Kerti Huyuk, Turkey. This was 20 miles from Lystra, in the southern tip of the Galatia province. The people were poorly educated and had little contact with Roman society. Their language and culture likely reflected Greek influence. Gaius, mentioned in **Acts 20:4** as a fellow minister of Paul's, was originally from Derbe.

Philippi. Philippi was located near the head of the Aegean Sea, in the Roman province of Macedonia. Many Roman soldiers were known to have settled in Philippi due to the many battles that had been waged nearby over the years. During the reign of Caesar August (27 BC–AD 14), it was made a Roman colony, ruled by military officers who reported directly to Rome. It was considered important because of its location on the major commercial highway extending east and west. Only ruins exist on the site of ancient Philippi today.

TEACHING THE BIBLE LESSON

LIFE NEED FOR TODAY'S LESSON

AIM: Students will learn that sometimes things that start out small, turn out much larger than expected, and impact the lives of others in surprising ways.

INTRODUCTION

Differing Cultures

After Paul's first missionary journey (**Acts 13–14**), a debate began raging in the churches at Antioch, Cilicia, and Syria regarding the nature of Christian salvation and how new Gentile believers were to fit into the new Christian church. Regarding salvation, some argued that faith in Christ wasn't enough to be saved, but Jewish Christians must also strictly follow Mosaic Law in order to consider themselves saved (**Acts 15:1**). Additionally, they insisted that Gentile believers must also be circumcised in keeping with the law of Moses.

A meeting was held in Jerusalem to resolve the issue. The Jerusalem council (**Acts 15:1–35**) determined that both Jewish and Gentile believers are saved by grace through faith in Christ alone. Gentile believers were not expected to adhere to Jewish customs. However, they outlined a few directives that would help Gentiles avoid offending fellow Jewish believers. For example, Gentiles didn't have to follow the same dietary laws as Jews, but were directed to abstain from eating "meats offered to idols, and from blood, and from things strangled" (**v. 29, KJV**).

BIBLE LEARNING

AIM: Students will learn that Lydia listened to Paul's preaching and then was baptized

along with her other family members.

I. PAUL RECRUITS TIMOTHY (Acts 16:1–5)

When Paul and Silas met Timothy at Lystra, Timothy had already garnered a good reputation among the believers in Lystra and Iconium. This ecclesial witness of Timothy's suitability as a teacher was why Paul chose him to join them. His father was Greek and his mother was Jewish. It was Greek tradition for a child to follow after his father's religion. However, Jewish tradition held that a child was considered Jewish if his mother was Jewish. Paul knew that in the eyes of the Jewish people they would be ministering to, Timothy would be seen as a Jew and would therefore need to be circumcised to avoid offense. This was not in contradiction with the church's earlier ruling that Gentile converts need not be circumcised for salvation (**Acts 15:10–11, 19**).

Paul's ministry journeys were meant to help establish and maintain new churches as well as communicate the decisions and positions made by the leaders in Jerusalem. This was an important part of cultivating the unity of the early church. The believers' faith and confidence in the Gospel was increased.

Acts 16:1–5, 8–15

16:1 Then came he to Derbe and Lystra: and, behold, a certain disciple was there, named Timotheus, the son of a certain woman, which was a Jewess, and believed; but his father was a Greek: **2** Which was well reported of by the brethren that were at Lystra and Iconium. **3** Him would Paul have to go forth with him; and took and circumcised him because of the Jews which were in those quarters: for they knew all that his father was a Greek. **4** And as they went through the cities, they delivered them the decrees for to keep, that were ordained of the apostles and elders which were at Jerusalem. **5** And so were the churches established in the faith, and increased in number daily.

On their second missionary journey, Paul and Silas traveled north around the eastern end of the Mediterranean and then westward toward the cities of Derbe and Lystra. On this second journey, the order of the cities listed in the Galatian territory is reversed from the first journey. On their first visit to the Galatian territory, Paul and Barnabas traveled from the west rather than the east. On this second journey, Paul revisits the cities that had been evangelized during his first journey two or three years earlier. When Paul and Barnabas began their ministry in Lystra, the people believed they were Greek gods (**14:11–13**). Their short ministry in the Galatian cities ended with Paul being stoned and left for dead outside the walls of Lystra. However, one of the fruits of that short, violent time was a young man named Timothy. Timothy and his mother may have been among the group of disciples that surrounded the apparently lifeless body of the apostle outside the walls of Lystra after Jews from the cities of Iconium and Antioch had stoned Paul (**vv. 19–20**). The young man certainly would have been among those Paul confirmed on his second visit to the city, exhorting them "to continue in the faith" (**v. 22**).

Timothy's mother was a Jewess (Gk. *ioudaias*, eu-DIE-ahs), which is the feminine form of the word for Jew, and also a Christian. The fact that she had married a Greek and had not circumcised her son leads one to question whether she was a practicing Jew before her conversion. Such mixed marriages, though practiced little and disliked by the stricter Jews in Palestine, probably occurred frequently among the Jews of the dispersion, and in such instances if the father was Greek, sons were unlikely to be circumcised because

Judaism was still passed down through the father during the first century AD. Even at a young age, Timothy was well reported of by the brethren who were at Lystra and Iconium. The phrase "well reported of" (Gk. *martureo*, **mar-too-REH-oh**) comes from the Greek word for witness, which in the passive voice means to be witnessed about and is usually used in a positive context.

During the years Paul was away, Timothy had grown in faith, so Paul decided to take the young man under his wing. He asked Timothy to join him and Silas on their journey. Timothy was the first Gentile who became a missionary after his conversion. Later, Titus would join Paul, but he would not be circumcised because he was a true Gentile (**Galatians 2:3**). Mosaic Law commanded that at eight days old, all Hebrew boys were to undergo the rite of circumcision. After God reconfirmed His promise to Abraham for the third and last time, He said of Abraham's descendants, "Any uncircumcised male, who has not been circumcised in the flesh, will be cut off from his people; he has broken my covenant" (**Genesis 17:14**). This meant the uncircumcised Israelite male was not covered by the covenant promise given to Abraham. The rite of circumcision symbolized submission to God and faith in His promise.

Circumcision was not carried over into the church as a requirement for Gentiles. Still, many Jewish Christians tried to impose circumcision and the Mosaic Law on new Gentile believers (**Acts 15:1**). But the Jerusalem council rejected the requirement (**15:1–29**). In mixed marriages, Jewish mothers were not permitted to circumcise their sons against the Gentile father's wishes. Paul had Timothy circumcised because of his parentage. Paul's methodology was to preach the Gospel to the Jew first, then the Gentile. But such a course would have been impossible had Timothy as a Jew not been circumcised; his own people

would have rejected him and dismissed the Gospel message.

The new threesome continued their ministry in Derbe, Lystra, Iconium, other cities in Lycaonia, and in Phrygia and Galatia. They advised the churches in these cities and taught rules of Christian conduct, such as those concerning the Gentiles' abstinence from blood, things strangled, fornication, and from things offered to idols (**Acts 15:20–29**). As a result of these apostolic visits, the churches were established (Gk. *stereoo*, **steh-reh-OH-oh**) or strengthened and the number of believers increased (Gk. *perisseuo*, **peh-rees-SOO-oh**) or multiplied daily. The word for increased or abound is also the word for a flower coming to full bloom. Luke makes it clear that the Jerusalem council's decree was for the church's well-being.

II. A DIVINE CHANGE OF PLANS (vv. 8–12)

Troas was an important Greek port, located near ancient Troy, that sat between the landmasses of Europe and Asia Minor. During their time at Troas, Paul has a vision of a man from Macedonia calling out to him for help. Paul and his group immediately take this vision to mean that they must alter their course and travel to Macedonia. This act of obedience to God's will is historically pivotal in that it eventually results in the Gospel being spread further west into Europe. If Paul and his group had not been sensitive to how God was trying to lead them, they might have missed this important change in their plans. This also underlines why it was important that they choose their ministry partners carefully. These decisions regarding how God was leading them forward were ultimately made as a group.

It is important to note that in **verse 10**, the language changes to "we" rather than "they," which is used earlier in the chapter. This indicates that Luke, the author of Acts, was actually present during this leg of Paul's ministry travels.

8 And they passing by Mysia came down to Troas. 9 And a vision appeared to Paul in the night; There stood a man of Macedonia, and prayed him, saying, Come over into Macedonia, and help us. 10 And after he had seen the vision, immediately we endeavoured to go into Macedonia, assuredly gathering that the Lord had called us for to preach the gospel unto them. 11 Therefore loosing from Troas, we came with a straight course to Samothracia, and the next day to Neapolis; 12 And from thence to Philippi, which is the chief city of that part of Macedonia, and a colony: and we were in that city abiding certain days.

Still traveling over rugged terrain and past unevangelized regions, the apostles passed by another city devoid of ministry and hospitality on the way to their appointed destination. God, through the Holy Spirit, was their travel agent, and the apostles relied solely on God's timing to fulfill His will. Arriving at Mysia, they attempted to enter, but the Holy Ghost prevented them from doing so. Now twice denied access to a people in need of the Gospel message, the apostles no doubt questioned whether they were going in the right direction. Even while waiting for God to open doors, these disciples did not assume a passive posture.

Instead, they participated with active pursuit of God's will—ever going until He said "Stop!" A wide door stood open for them when they came to Troas. The city of Troas was located near the Hellespont, an economically vibrant intersection of race, class, culture, and language. Imagine the cacophony of sounds, smells, philosophies, theologies, dress, and demeanor on display at Troas. It was in this place of diversity that the Holy Spirit released the disciples to minister.

The Greek noun *horama* (**HO-rah-mah**), or "vision," is a sight divinely granted, sometimes while sleeping (**Acts 9:10, 12, 18:9**). It is likely that Paul was asleep when this vision appeared, yet he was fully aware of God's purpose and presence in this vision. The Holy Ghost forbade (**v. 6**) and prevented (**v. 7**) the disciples' movement previously; here the Spirit manifests Himself in a form and function believable to them. The Greek verb *parakaleo* (**pa-ra-ka-LEH-oh**), or "prayed," connotes the image of one begging for consolation, instruction, or teaching. This man from Macedonia showed up in Paul's dream pleading with passion and urgency for the apostles to come to this Roman province to help with some urgent cause that had not been met by all of Rome's prestige, privilege, or military prowess.

After Paul communicated the vision to his companions, they immediately responded to this word from the Lord. Here, companionship in ministry is illuminated as Luke records this first-person plural account that "we endeavoured" (Gk. *zeteo*, **dzay-TEH-oh**), or made a concerted effort, to get to Macedonia. Included in this group were at least Paul, Silas, Timothy, and Luke. This inclusive reference establishes a paradigm of Christian companionship and community that becomes a predominant theme in the rest of Paul's letters to the church. This time, unlike the holy hindrances in **verses 6 and 7**, their collaborative effort to carry the Gospel to the next place of ministry was allowed. Note also that consensus was taken to test whether this vision was from the Lord. Although God spoke through visions, not every vision was unquestionably believed. Upon determining that this was the Holy Spirit's leading ("assuredly gathering"), the apostles acted together with urgency to respond to the vision.

As the disciples were loosing (Gk. *anago*, **ah-NAH-go**) or launching on a boat out from Troas, even the wind was in their favor, providing a straight, smooth course in two days through two ports to their stated destination—Philippi. This Macedonian city was a Roman colony. The inhabitants of such colonies were protected and privileged as full-fledged Roman citizens. Some of the privileges of being a Roman colony were voting rights, preferential legislation, and immunity from taxation.

SEARCH THE SCRIPTURES

QUESTION 1

Timotheus was the son of a Jewish and _____ mother and his father was _____ (**v. 1**).

Christian and Greek.

LIGHT ON THE WORD

Paul's Missionary Journey

The beginning of Acts 16 describes the outset of Paul's second missionary journey. He is visiting churches, like Lystra and Derbe, which were visited on his first mission. This is likely why Paul takes their opinion about Timothy to heart. These are old friends. Paul's second missionary journey would ultimately last three years and cover almost three thousand miles.

III. LYDIA'S HEART IS OPENED (vv. 13–15)

According to Jewish law, ten males were needed for public worship. If there was no established synagogue, worshipers were to gather in an open area, near a body of water. Apparently, Philippi had no synagogue, since Paul and his men went to a nearby riverbank to find people who would be praying. The nearest body of water was likely a tributary

to the Gangites (modern Angitis), which was 1.25 miles from Philippi.

As Paul and his men talked to a gathering of women, they caught the ear of Lydia, a merchant from Thyatira. Thyatira was known for its merchants of dyed cloth, particularly purple material. It has been suggested that purple dyes were created from shellfish or the roots of plants. Lydia "worshipped God" (**v. 14**), which indicates that she was a Gentile who worshiped Yahweh, but was not saved and not part of the Christian church.

13 And on the sabbath we went out of the city by a river side, where prayer was wont to be made; and we sat down, and spake unto the women which resorted thither. 14 And a certain woman named Lydia, a seller of purple, of the city of Thyatira, which worshipped God, heard us: whose heart the Lord opened, that she attended unto the things which were spoken of Paul. 15 And when she was baptized, and her household, she besought us, saying, If ye have judged me to be faithful to the Lord, come into my house, and abide there. And she constrained us.

"Sabbath" (Gk. *sabbaton*, **SAB-ba-ton**) is the seventh day of each week, a sacred day when the Israelites were required to abstain from all work. On the Sabbath, it was customary to gather for worship, prayer, and Scripture reading. Although the apostles could have taken a day off from the work of preaching the Gospel, they were compelled to leave the accommodations in Philippi and journey a mile or two west of the city to a prayer meeting down by the Gangites River. Here, the disciples find women praying to God in a place outside the city where there was no synagogue. No doubt following the leading of the Holy Spirit, the apostles did not bypass or dismiss this gathering of women worshiping God on the Sabbath. Modeling Jesus' radical paradigm of teaching to the outcasts, the disciples were not constrained by gender (**Galatians 3:28**) nor limited by their surroundings when teaching and preaching God's Word. All they required was that hearts were open to hear what the Spirit was saying to the church.

For a synagogue to be established in a city, ten Jewish men had to convene and lead it. With no synagogue in Philippi at this time, the apostles sought out a prayer gathering whose reputation trumped Jewish ritual. This prayer meeting had the structure and leadership of a worship service, including the reading of Jewish prayers and praying to the God of Abraham, Isaac, and Jacob. In the absence of ten male heads of household to found a synagogue, the women were found faithfully worshiping God in spirit and in truth (**John 4:23–24**). Through the apostles, the Holy Spirit of God brought forth the first evangelistic converts in Europe. He did this in this holy place, set up and sanctified by women. It is while attending to the divine act of worship that a certain woman and a gathering of women became the first European converts to our Christian faith. Women's work and women's worship should be heralded in biblical and local church history as integral, not incidental, to the Good News.

Lydia was a woman of Thyatira, the city of commerce, and a seller of purple cloth often used for official Roman garments. She was the first European convert of Paul and his hostess during his first stay at Philippi. Lydia was a businesswoman who was wealthy and well-respected, and who "worshipped" (Gk. *sebomai*, **SEH-bo-my**) God. The relationship she had with God was awe and reverential fear. While leading this prayer gathering, Lydia welcomed the opportunity to hear the apostles preach and teach, and to learn more about the God she worshiped and Christ, His Son. Lydia's enthusiastic and attentive listening was fertile ground for God to open her

heart to understand and accept the Gospel. The "heart" (Gk. *kardia*, **kar-DEE-ah**) represents the soul or mind as the resident place of one's thoughts, passions, desires, appetites, affections, purposes, understanding, intelligence, will, character, and intentions. Lydia's "open heart surgery" was appreciably more than an emotional response to well-crafted rhetoric; as she listened, Lydia engaged her thoughts, affections, and understanding about God to believe in Christ Jesus. While Lydia had been seeking God, God was in the background working His way into her heart and into the city of Philippi.

Lydia's response to accepting the Gospel of Christ Jesus was to be baptized (Gk. *baptizo*, **bap-TEED-zo**), meaning to immerse or submerge in water. Since they were already gathered at the riverside, it was convenient to baptize Lydia and her household immediately following their conversion.

Lydia was not the only person present at the prayer meeting listening to Paul and his companions preach and teach. Her whole household (meaning both family members and servants) heard the Good News, believed, and were baptized. After becoming a baptized member of the church, Lydia extended hospitality to her newfound family—the apostles and by extension the church. She was so emphatic to extend hospitality to these brothers in Christ that she "constrained" (Gk. *parabiazomai*, **pa-ra-bee-AHD-zo-my**), or made a persuasive appeal, for them to stay at her home while in Philippi. Central to this plea for them to accept her hospitality was Lydia's assertion that the apostles found her "faithful" (Gk. *pistos*, **PIS-toce**), meaning trustworthy and reliable. This word also has the connotation of belonging to the faith community.

SEARCH THE SCRIPTURES

QUESTION 2

Lydia was from what city and a seller of what color cloth (v. 14)?

Thyatira and purple.

QUESTION 3

Lydia was the first European convert to Christianity. True or False?

True.

LIGHT ON THE WORD

Lydia's Grateful Heart

At the Lord's prompting, Lydia's heart was opened, and she understood and accepted Paul's message. After she and her household accept salvation and are baptized, Lydia offers to house Paul's entourage at her home. Her home is mentioned again later in Acts 16:40 as a meeting place where believers gathered to hear from Paul and Silas.

BIBLE APPLICATION

AIM: Students will discover that believers should be sensitive to God's plan for their lives and open to change.

Adaptability, agility, flexibility, versatility— these are all words commonly used to describe the ideal business in today's ever-changing global economy. The ability to change course quickly based on new information is a skill that companies are always trying to cultivate or acquire.

This same ability is important in our daily personal and spiritual lives. A healthy, growing relationship with Christ involves being able to adjust to what He is doing in and through us. When we yield ourselves to His plans and purposes, we can be sure that we're where God wants us.

STUDENT'S RESPONSES

AIM: Believers can participate in the expansion of the Kingdom of God as they actively and willingly do God's will.

It can be hard to give up control of our plans for our lives. This can especially be hard after we've begun moving down a path that we believe God has led us down. Review your current goals and plans. Ask God to reveal any areas where you've allowed your personal ideas and ambitions to crowd out what God may be leading you to do instead.

PRAYER

Bless You, O Lord, for providing us with so many opportunities to know You and to Love You. Give us the wisdom to choose You God and to walk in Your faithfulness. In the Name of Jesus, we pray. Amen.

HOW TO SAY IT

Derbe.	der-BAY.
Lystra.	loo-STRAH.
Phrygia.	froo-GEE-ah.

PREPARE FOR NEXT SUNDAY

Read **Acts 17:1–4, 10–12, 22–25, 28** and "Thessalonica, Berea, and Athens."

DAILY HOME BIBLE READINGS

MONDAY
The Way We Should Go
(Jeremiah 26:1–6)

TUESDAY
Boundless Riches of Christ
(Ephesians 3:7–12)

WEDNESDAY
Generosity of God
(Ezekiel 36:22–30)

THURSDAY
The Cost of Following
(Matthew 8:18–22)

FRIDAY
Paul and Silas in Prison
(Acts 16:16–24)

SATURDAY
Paul and Silas Escape
(Acts 16:25–40)

SUNDAY
From Derbe to Philippi
(Acts 16:1–5, 8–15)

Sources:

Barker, Kenneth L. and Kohlenberger III, John R., eds. *The Expositor's Bible Commentary – Abridged Edition: New Testament.* Grand Rapids, MI: Zondervan, 1994. 467-471.

Butler, Trent C., ed. "Derbe." *Holman Bible Dictionary.* Electronic Edition, Quickverse. Nashville, TN: Holman Bible Publishers, 1991.

Butler, Trent C., ed. "Philippi." *Holman Bible Dictionary.* Electronic Edition, Quickverse. Nashville, TN: Holman Bible Publishers, 1991.

Carson, D. A., R. T. France, J. A. Motyer, G. J. Wenham, Eds. *New Bible Commentary.* Downer's Grove, IL: Intervarsity Press, 1994. 1090-1091.

Easton, M. G. "Philippi." *Easton's Bible Dictionary.* 1st ed. Oklahoma City, OK: Ellis Enterprises, 1993.

Elwell, Walter A. and Yarbrough, Robert W. *Encountering the New Testament: A Historical and Theological Survey.* Grand Rapids, MI: Baker Books, 1998. 238-242, 313.

Keener, Craig S. *The IVP Bible Background Commentary: New Testament.* Downers Grove, IL: InterVarsity Press, 1993.366-369.

Thayer, Joseph. "dianoigō." *Thayer's Greek Definitions.* 3rd ed. Electronic Edition, Quickverse. El Cajon, CA: Institute for Creation Research, 1999.

Thayer, Joseph. "stereoō." *Thayer's Greek Definitions.* 3rd ed. Electronic Edition, Quickverse. El Cajon, CA: Institute for Creation Research, 1999.

Walvoord, John F. and Zuck, Roy B., eds. *The Bible Knowledge Commentary: An Exposition of the Scriptures.* Wheaton, IL: Victor Books, 1983. 398-399.

COMMENTS / NOTES:

THESSALONICA, BEREA, AND ATHENS

BIBLE BASIS: Acts 17:1–4, 10–12, 22–25, 28

BIBLE TRUTH: Paul preached the Gospel with strong conviction in spite of opposition.

MEMORY VERSE: "For as I passed by, and beheld your devotions, I found an altar with this inscription, To The Unknown God. Whom therefore ye ignorantly worship, him declare I unto you" (Acts 17:23).

LESSON AIM: By the end of the lesson, we will: LEARN that, although Paul and Silas's message was accepted by some but not all, God received the glory; REFLECT on the effects of rejection in the lives of those who serve God; and SEEK out and use spiritual resources that support perseverance in the midst of rejection.

TEACHER PREPARATION

MATERIALS NEEDED: Quarterly Commentary/Teacher Manual, Adult Quarterly, Adult resources—charts, worksheets, and other teaching tools, paper, pens, pencils, Bibles (several different versions)

OTHER MATERIALS NEEDED / TEACHER'S NOTES:

_____

_____

LESSON OVERVIEW

LIFE NEED FOR TODAY'S LESSON
Some people expect verbal convictions while others reject them.

BIBLE LEARNING
Paul's missionary journey took him to Philippi, Athens, Thessalonica, and Berea.

BIBLE APPLICATION
Believers are to evangelize in humility and faith in the work of the Holy Spirit.

STUDENTS' RESPONSES
Christians learn that the message of the Gospel may be rejected by those they hope will receive it.

LESSON SCRIPTURE

ACTS 17:1–4, 10–12, 22–25, 28, KJV

1 Now when they had passed through Amphipolis and Apollonia, they came to Thessalonica, where was a synagogue of the Jews:

2 And Paul, as his manner was, went in unto them, and three sabbath days reasoned with them out of the scriptures,

ACTS 17:1–4, 10–12, 22–25, 28, NIV

1 When Paul and his companions had passed through Amphipolis and Apollonia, they came to Thessalonica, where there was a Jewish synagogue.

2 As was his custom, Paul went into the synagogue, and on three Sabbath days he reasoned with them from the Scriptures,

3 Opening and alleging, that Christ must needs have suffered, and risen again from the dead; and that this Jesus, whom I preach unto you, is Christ.

4 And some of them believed, and consorted with Paul and Silas; and of the devout Greeks a great multitude, and of the chief women not a few.

10 And the brethren immediately sent away Paul and Silas by night unto Berea: who coming thither went into the synagogue of the Jews.

11 These were more noble than those in Thessalonica, in that they received the word with all readiness of mind, and searched the scriptures daily, whether those things were so.

12 Therefore many of them believed; also of honourable women which were Greeks, and of men, not a few.

22 Then Paul stood in the midst of Mars' hill, and said, Ye men of Athens, I perceive that in all things ye are too superstitious.

23 For as I passed by, and beheld your devotions, I found an altar with this inscription, To The Unknown God. Whom therefore ye ignorantly worship, him declare I unto you.

24 God that made the world and all things therein, seeing that he is Lord of heaven and earth, dwelleth not in temples made with hands;

25 Neither is worshipped with men's hands, as though he needed any thing, seeing he giveth to all life, and breath, and all things;

28 For in him we live, and move, and have our being; as certain also of your own poets have said, For we are also his offspring.

3 explaining and proving that the Messiah had to suffer and rise from the dead. "This Jesus I am proclaiming to you is the Messiah," he said.

4 Some of the Jews were persuaded and joined Paul and Silas, as did a large number of God-fearing Greeks and quite a few prominent women.

10 As soon as it was night, the believers sent Paul and Silas away to Berea. On arriving there, they went to the Jewish synagogue.

11 Now the Berean Jews were of more noble character than those in Thessalonica, for they received the message with great eagerness and examined the Scriptures every day to see if what Paul said was true.

12 As a result, many of them believed, as did also a number of prominent Greek women and many Greek men.

22 Paul then stood up in the meeting of the Areopagus and said: "People of Athens! I see that in every way you are very religious.

23 For as I walked around and looked carefully at your objects of worship, I even found an altar with this inscription: TO AN UNKNOWN GOD. So you are ignorant of the very thing you worship—and this is what I am going to proclaim to you.

24 "The God who made the world and everything in it is the Lord of heaven and earth and does not live in temples built by human hands.

25 And he is not served by human hands, as if he needed anything. Rather, he himself gives everyone life and breath and everything else.

28 'For in him we live and move and have our being.' As some of your own poets have said, 'We are his offspring.'

149

LIGHT ON THE WORD

Thessalonica. This was a city in the Roman province Macedonia, in northern Greece at the head of the Thermaic Gulf. It was named after Thessalonicea, the wife of a general under Alexander the Great. Thessalonica gained the status of a free city within the Roman empire, meaning it was self-governed and issued its own coinage. The city was very wealthy and relatively free from taxation. It also became wealthy from being Macedonia's main port and because of its location on the Via Egnatia, a road which ran through the provinces Illyricum, Macedonia, and Thrace. The people of Thessalonica adhered to a variety of religions, including the worship of traditional Greek deities and the Roman emperor. Jews formed a small minority in the city and became a community which Paul could access in order to preach the Gospel.

Berea. This is actually an alternative spelling of Beroea, a city 45 miles southwest of Thessalonica. The city was located 25 miles inland from the Aegean Sea on a fertile plain. It was one of the most populous cities in Macedonia around the time of Christ. Jews from Thessalonica traveled to Berea in order to oppose Paul's preaching of the Gospel. In spite of this, both Jews and Greeks readily received the message of Christ.

Athens. Paul preached the Gospel in this Greek city named after the goddess Athena. The Parthenon, a world-renowned temple dedicated to Athena, was built on top of the Acropolis in the city's center. Athens was known as a cultural center and the source of Hellenistic philosophy and literature. In the 5th and 6th century BC, Athens was the home of philosophers, authors, poets, sculptors, and architects. During the time of Paul, it had lost its prominence after being conquered by Macedonians and the Roman empire.

TEACHING THE BIBLE LESSON

LIFE NEED FOR TODAY'S LESSON

AIM: Students will learn that some people expect verbal convictions while others reject them.

INTRODUCTION

Paul and Silas in Greece

Paul's second missionary journey took him and his companions Silas and Timothy into Greece. This is the first recorded time the Gospel reached Europe. His first stop was Philippi, a leading city of Macedonia and a Roman colony. There Paul preached to a riverside prayer meeting of women. Lydia, a wealthy woman who was a dealer of purple cloth, led the meeting. As Paul and Silas preached the Good News, the church in Philippi emerged from this all-woman prayer meeting.

Soon Paul and Silas encountered a local fortune teller who followed them through the marketplace. Knowing she was possessed by a demon, Paul commanded the evil spirit to leave her body. She was healed, but the men who gained money from her fortune-telling dragged Paul and Silas before the authorities. Consequently the two missionaries were thrown in jail. During the night while Paul and Silas were singing and praising God, an earthquake shook the jail. In the aftermath, the doors were opened and their bonds were unfastened. The jailer, thinking the prisoners had escaped, feared he would face punishment from the authorities. Instead Paul and Silas assured him they were still inside and preached to him the message of salvation. The jailer accepted. In a wise move, Paul claimed his Roman citizenship upon release in order to protect the church in Philippi from future harassment and persecution. Seeing that their church-planting job was done, Paul and

Silas headed toward another significant city in Macedonia—Thessalonica.

BIBLE LEARNING

AIM: Students will learn that Paul's missionary journey took him to Philippi, Athens, Thessalonica, and Berea.

I. INITIAL RECEPTION (Acts 17:1–4)

Paul and Silas arrived in Thessalonica to proclaim the Gospel. Their usual method was to start off proclaiming the Gospel in the synagogues, because Paul's fellow Jews would be a receptive audience to the message about their long-awaited Messiah. Paul's method included reasoning with them from the Scriptures in order to prove Jesus was the Christ. We can see from Paul's preaching in the synagogue that he used language and concepts familiar to his audience.

1 Now when they had passed through Amphipolis and Apollonia, they came to Thessalonica, where was a synagogue of the Jews: 2 And Paul, as his manner was, went in unto them, and three sabbath days reasoned with them out of the scriptures, 3 Opening and alleging, that Christ must needs have suffered, and risen again from the dead; and that this Jesus, whom I preach unto you, is Christ. 4 And some of them believed, and consorted with Paul and Silas; and of the devout Greeks a great multitude, and of the chief women not a few.

The Apostle Paul usually chose to preach the Gospel in large cities at key transportation hubs, so that the Good News could be spread beyond the places where he preached, a good example of strategizing for the most effective sharing of the Gospel. The Romans had built a road called the Egnatian Way, which stretched from the Adriatic Sea to the Hellespont. This very important road ran right through the city of Thessalonica, so once the message was planted, it could be carried west to the western shore of Greece or east to what is modern-day Turkey. Paul, Silas, and Timothy traveled from Philippi to Amphipolis to Apollonia to Thessalonica, a distance of about 100 miles, no easy stroll. No doubt Paul stopped overnight at both Amphipolis and Apollonia, but when morning came, he hurried on his way.

As always, if there was a synagogue in town, Paul began by preaching there, so that was the first place in Thessalonica that he went. He always had a heart to reach his own people first, even when his people rejected him and the Lord Jesus. Paul showed his listeners from Old Testament Scriptures that it was prophesied that the Messiah had to suffer and die, and then rise from the dead. The Greek word for alleging is *paratithemi* (**pa-ra-TEE-thay-me**) which literally means to place alongside; so we can see Paul setting prophecies alongside their fulfillment in Jesus.

Some of the Jews accepted this message, but there were a large number of Gentiles who had been attending the synagogue who turned to Jesus. Among the new believers were some from a variety of social positions, both men and women.

At first glance it looks like Paul was in Thessalonica for only three weeks, because our verses mention him preaching in the synagogue for only three Sabbaths, but when we look at **Philippians 4:15–16**, we see that the Philippian church sent offerings to Paul in Thessalonica twice, which would imply that Paul was there for a longer period. We also read in **1 Thessalonians 2:9** and **2 Thessalonians 3:7–10** that he supported himself, probably by tent-making (**Acts 18:3**), as he was waiting for the gifts from Philippi. And then we read in **1 Thessalonians 1:9** that most of the converts were steeped in idolatry, so obviously many who turned to Christ were not from the synagogue. Then after three weeks of preaching in the synagogue, Paul began ministering in another part of the city. However, the leaders of the synagogue felt that Paul was stealing their converts, so they ran him out of town.

SEARCH THE SCRIPTURES

QUESTION 1

How many days did Paul speak with the Jews in the synagogue?

Three Sabbath days.

LIGHT ON THE WORD

The Growth of the Church

Some of the Jews of the synagogue, along with their Greek patrons, were persuaded by the claims that Jesus was the Messiah. It is interesting to note that many upper-class women were among the recent followers of Jesus. Due to their status in Thessalonica as free, wealthy women, they were more independent, making it easier for them to decide to follow Jesus without the opposition of their husbands. As a consequence, these upper-class, well-to-do women would be able to share their resources with the new fledgling church.

II. INSPIRING RESEARCH (vv. 10–12)

Paul and Silas left Thessalonica in secret after certain jealous Jews gathered a crowd of wicked men in order to bring them before the authorities. On arriving in Berea, they did not deviate from their usual method but found a local synagogue. This audience was different: nobler, or more open-minded, than the people in Thessalonica. These Jews listened to the Gospel message with eagerness and searched the Scriptures to confirm whether it was true. Rabbis often praised those who listened

attentively and searched the Scriptures. Greek philosophers also valued attentive, scrutinizing listeners.

The methods Paul and Silas used did not change, but they received different results in the two cities because they were preaching to different audiences. The Thessalonicans by and large received their message, despite some opposition. The Bereans eagerly listened and kept a tolerant and open mind. The Gospel challenged those in the synagogue at Berea in a positive way to research whether what Paul said was true. The apostles' rejection in Thessalonica did not discourage them from preaching the same message in Berea, and it produced great results.

10 And the brethren immediately sent away Paul and Silas by night unto Berea: who coming thither went into the synagogue of the Jews. 11 These were more noble than those in Thessalonica, in that they received the word with all readiness of mind, and searched the scriptures daily, whether those things were so. 12 Therefore many of them believed; also of honourable women which were Greeks, and of men, not a few.

After the Jewish leaders of Thessalonica tried to have Paul executed, the believers in Thessalonica slipped Paul out of the city at night. Paul and Silas had a 45-mile hike to their next destination, the city of Berea. This was not such a prominent city, but at least the Jews here were not so prejudiced against the Gospel. The response of the Bereans in the synagogue was quite different from those in the Thessalonian synagogue. When Paul told them that the Messiah did not come the way they expected, they searched the Scriptures he was preaching from. The Greek word for searched is *anakrino* (**ah-na-KREE-no**), which is the word used for judicial investigations; in other words, they investigated, examined, and questioned critically. The Bereans were not content to accept at face value what Paul had to say, but daily checked his words with Old Testament Scripture. The question we can ask ourselves is, when we hear someone preach something we haven't heard before, what is our response? Are we like the Bereans—do we carefully check Scripture to see if this is the truth?

A number of prominent Greek women believed, as did devout Jews. This is probably underscored in both passages—in both Thessalonica and Berea, even wealthy men and women of other ethnicities received Jesus; anyone can receive the Gospel, no matter what socioeconomic class, no matter whether male or female.

III. PROVOKING REFLECTION (vv. 22–25, 28)

The Jews from Thessalonica travel forty-five miles southwest to Berea and manage to incite the crowds. This forced Paul to escape by sea to Athens. While at Athens waiting for Silas and Timothy, Paul notices the city is full of idols. So he goes about his usual custom of proclaiming the Gospel in the synagogues and marketplace. A group of Epicurean and Stoic philosophers, confused by the claims of the Gospel message, invites him to the Areopagus, or Mars Hill, a place where the philosophers and intellectuals gathered to hear the newest and most innovative ideas.

Paul opens his speech with a compliment to the religious sensibilities of the people of Athens. This leads to him pointing out the inscription he noticed on an altar: "To the unknown God." He next uses this inscription and connects it to their ignorance of the God of the Bible. He is the unknown God who Paul will now proclaim to them. Paul goes on to use popular quotes from poets and philosophers of the day in order to convince them

of the resurrection of Christ and their need to repent and believe in Him.

22 Then Paul stood in the midst of Mars' hill, and said, Ye men of Athens, I perceive that in all things ye are too superstitious. 23 For as I passed by, and beheld your devotions, I found an altar with this inscription, To The Unknown God. Whom therefore ye ignorantly worship, him declare I unto you. 24 God that made the world and all things therein, seeing that he is Lord of heaven and earth, dwelleth not in temples made with hands; 25 Neither is worshipped with men's hands, as though he needed any thing, seeing he giveth to all life, and breath, and all things;

The Thessalonian Jewish leaders who had chased Paul out of their city made the trip to Berea and did the same thing there, so the Berean believers escorted Paul out of their city and got him to Athens, presumably by boat, but Silas and Timothy stayed behind to continue teaching the new believers in Berea.

While Paul was waiting for Silas and Timothy to catch up with him in Athens, he was making use of every opportunity to share the Gospel. As was his custom, he used Old Jewish Scripture to convince Jews and Gentiles in the synagogue that Jesus is the Messiah God promised to send. He also hung out in the marketplace to discuss his faith with anyone who was interested. Athens was once the center of its own empire. Now that the Romans ruled, it had lost its political authority, but it was still known for its philosophers, including Plato, Socrates, and Aristotle from prior days. As a Jewish leader and an educated Roman citizen, Paul was a very educated and intelligent man. He was used to a teaching method that emphasized one-on-one debate, as well as the use of public debate.

This was a forum that met to decide matters of morals or religion. Paul began his defense of the Gospel by telling his listeners they were extremely *deisidaimon* (Gk. **day-cee-DIE-mone**), a word which has been translated as either religious or superstitious. This is vague in Greek and could be taken as complimentary (religious) or derogatory (superstitious). In this case, Paul would be complimenting them as being very devout in order to get their attention. As a further bridge into their thinking, he mentions the many altars to the unknown god that were scattered throughout the city. The Athenians had many, many idols, but just in case they missed one, there were a number of altars dedicated to the unknown god. This concept was introduced by a poet, Epiminedes. During a time when Athens was suffering from a plague, he advised the rulers of Athens to sacrifice upon these altars and the plague was subsequently stopped. Because of this, Epiminedes was considered not only a poet but a prophet.

Paul said that he came to introduce them to the God they did not know—the God who created everything, the earth, the heavens, and everything on earth and in heaven. Not only is He the Creator, but also Ruler over everything. This God is too big to be contained in any earthly building. Even King Solomon, the builder of the first temple, acknowledged that God is too big to fit in any temple (**1 Kings 8:27**). And God is the one who sustains us; He does not need anything from us! In fact, our very life and breath are a gift from Him. Here, Paul states that what they have called the Unknown God out of ignorance is the true God. This is not an approval of their idolatry, but an affirmation of the partial truth that was revealed to them. This sets the stage for Paul to introduce them to the God who is the all-powerful, all-knowing, and all-present Creator of everything in existence.

28 For in him we live, and move, and have our being; as certain also of your own poets have said, For we are also his offspring.

In this verse, Paul quotes two Greek poets, both pagans. This surprises many modern Christians, who then wonder why these quotes are in our Bible. From this we can learn some valuable lessons on how to communicate the Gospel to unbelievers. If we can connect to our audience by quoting from sources our listeners are familiar with and that we can agree with, we will get their attention. For instance, if we quote a phrase from a popular rap song that has a kernel of truth in it, teens and young adults may be more willing to listen to us, especially if that quote can lead us to an explanation of the Gospel. In both of these quotes, Paul is showing something of the true nature of the one true God by affirming some truth found in Athenian culture.

Paul's first quote is that "in him we live, and move, and have our being." This quote is believed to be from Epiminedes in regards to Zeus, but Paul attributes it to Israel's God. The Stoic philosophers agreed with Paul on this point, as they believed in divine providence. In contrast, the Epicurean philosophers thought that the gods were too remote to be involved in the lives of human beings, but Paul is about to proclaim that God is as near as the air we breathe. It is only our sin that separates us from Him. Both we and the Greeks can look around at the things that God has made, including our own selves, and see that He is very near!

The second quote from the poet Aratus tells us that we are the offspring of God. The Stoic philosophers believed that there was a divine immanent principle in humanity, but Paul takes it a step further. For Paul, the phrase "we are his offspring" means that God created all humanity and we are ultimately responsible to Him. Later in the speech, Paul elaborates on this concept and concludes with a call to account for our actions and repent.

SEARCH THE SCRIPTURES

QUESTION 2

The men of _____ were thought to _____ (v. 22).

Athens, superstitious

QUESTION 3

The philosophers of Athens had an inscription on their altar that read _____ _____ (v. 23).

"To the Unknown God."

LIGHT ON THE WORD

Paul and the Philosophers

The philosophers took note that Paul was talking in the agora, the marketplace, about ideas that were unfamiliar to them, and so they invited him to speak before the Areopagus (Gk. *Areios pagos*, **AH-ray-ose PAH-gose**), a gathering of philosophers, religious leaders, and learned men who came together regularly just to hear and exchange new thoughts on various matters. This was a forum that met to decide matters of morals or religion.

BIBLE APPLICATION

AIM: Students will see that believers are to evangelize in humility and faith in the work of the Holy Spirit.

Many times Christians are shown in the media as closed-minded and uneducated. Although this portrayal is far from the truth, many have bought into it. This results in many assumptions about those who share their Christian faith and the credibility of the Gospel message. Often our faith is insulted, and we face rejection from those around us. It is disheartening to feel as if the whole world believes the beliefs you hold are outdated and silly. In this lesson, we are encouraged to persevere in spite of rejection, knowing that God is the One who brings people to Him. This is what Paul did in order to see much fruit from his labors in preaching the Gospel.

STUDENT'S RESPONSES

AIM: Students will know that Christians can learn that the message of the Gospel may be rejected by those they hope will receive it.

Paul used the culture of Athens to create a bridge for the Gospel. Have the class create a list of contemporary cultural issues and religions. Next discuss the different ways the Gospel can address each issue. Encourage the class to seek common ground when sharing their faith in order to effectively communicate and minimize rejection for the wrong reasons.

PRAYER

Jesus, we appreciate that we can share Your Word with those who do not know You and those who need to know You more. We rejoice in spreading the Good News of Christ! In the Name of Jesus, we pray. Amen.

HOW TO SAY IT

Agora.	ah-**GOH**-rah.
Amphipolis.	am-**PHI**-po-lis.
Apollonia.	ah-pol-**LON**-ee-ah.
Areopagus.	air-ee-**OP**-a-gus.
Berea.	ber-**EE**-ah.
Egnatian.	eg-**NA**-tian.
Thessalonica.	thes-sa-**LO**-nih-ka.

PREPARE FOR NEXT SUNDAY

Read **Acts 18:1–11, 18–21** and "Teaching God's Word."

DAILY HOME BIBLE READINGS

MONDAY
Creator God
(Deuteronomy 32:1–12)

TUESDAY
Promises of God for All
(Genesis 9:8–17)

WEDNESDAY
Blessing of God for All
(Genesis 12:1–4)

THURSDAY
Majesty of God
(Psalm 8)

FRIDAY
Goodness of God
(Psalm 33:13–22)

SATURDAY
Reign of God
(Psalm 47)

SUNDAY
Thessalonica, Berea, and Athens
(Acts 17:1–4, 10–12, 22–25, 28)

Sources:

Barclay, William. *The Daily Study Bible: The Acts of the Apostles.* Philadelphia: The Westminster Press, 1955.

Bruce, F. F. *Commentary on the Book of the Acts: The New International Commentary on the New Testament.* Grand Rapids, MI: Wm. B. Eerdmans. Reprint, 1983.

Kisau, Paul Mumo. "Acts of the Apostles" from *Africa Bible Commentary.* General Editor: Tokunboh Adeyemo. Grand Rapids, MI: Zondervan, 2006.

Stott, John. *The Spirit of the Church and the World: The Message of Acts.* Downers Grove, IL: InterVarsity Press, 1990.

Toussaint, Stanley D. "Acts" from *The Bible Knowledge Commentary.* Editors: John F. Walvoord and Roy B. Zuck. Wheaton, IL: Victor Books, 1983.

COMMENTS / NOTES:

TEACHING GOD'S WORD

BIBLE BASIS: ACTS 18:1–11, 18–21

BIBLE TRUTH: Luke writes of Paul's mission of proclaiming the Good News to Syria and Ephesus.

MEMORY VERSE: "Then spake the Lord to Paul in the night by a vision, Be not afraid, but speak, and hold not thy peace: For I am with thee, and no man shall set on thee to hurt thee: for I have much people in this city" (Acts 18:9–10).

LESSON AIM: By the end of the lesson, we will: REVIEW Paul's zeal for teaching the Gospel to the Gentiles; EXPLORE feelings after making a transition from a vocation, from rejection to praise; and PRAY for the success of those whom God has placed in a new situation.

TEACHER PREPARATION

MATERIALS NEEDED: Quarterly Commentary/Teacher Manual, Adult Quarterly, Adult resources—charts, worksheets, and other teaching tools, paper, pens, pencils, Bibles (several different versions)

OTHER MATERIALS NEEDED / TEACHER'S NOTES:

_____

_____

LESSON OVERVIEW

LIFE NEED FOR TODAY'S LESSON
People can be persistent when they really believe what they do and say is the real thing.

BIBLE LEARNING
After experiencing a vision, Paul, Timothy, and Silas traveled together to various cities to preach.

BIBLE APPLICATION
God can place us in a situation where our knowledge and skills are embraced so that He is glorified.

STUDENTS' RESPONSES
Believers can pray and praise God for sustaining their work or vocations.

LESSON SCRIPTURE

ACTS 18:1–11, 18–21, KJV

1 After these things Paul departed from Athens, and came to Corinth;

2 And found a certain Jew named Aquila, born in Pontus, lately come from Italy, with his wife Priscilla; (because that Claudius had commanded all Jews to depart from Rome:)

ACTS 18:1–11, 18–21, NIV

1 After this, Paul left Athens and went to Corinth.

2 There he met a Jew named Aquila, a native of Pontus, who had recently come from Italy with his wife Priscilla, because Claudius had ordered all Jews to leave Rome. Paul went to

and came unto them.

3 And because he was of the same craft, he abode with them, and wrought: for by their occupation they were tentmakers.

4 And he reasoned in the synagogue every sabbath, and persuaded the Jews and the Greeks.

5 And when Silas and Timotheus were come from Macedonia, Paul was pressed in the spirit, and testified to the Jews that Jesus was Christ.

6 And when they opposed themselves, and blasphemed, he shook his raiment, and said unto them, Your blood be upon your own heads; I am clean; from henceforth I will go unto the Gentiles.

7 And he departed thence, and entered into a certain man's house, named Justus, one that worshipped God, whose house joined hard to the synagogue.

8 And Crispus, the chief ruler of the synagogue, believed on the Lord with all his house; and many of the Corinthians hearing believed, and were baptized.

9 Then spake the Lord to Paul in the night by a vision, Be not afraid, but speak, and hold not thy peace:

10 For I am with thee, and no man shall set on thee to hurt thee: for I have much people in this city.

11 And he continued there a year and six months, teaching the word of God among them.

18 And Paul after this tarried there yet a good while, and then took his leave of the brethren, and sailed thence into Syria, and with him Priscilla and Aquila; having shorn his head in Cenchrea: for he had a vow.

see them,

3 and because he was a tentmaker as they were, he stayed and worked with them.

4 Every Sabbath he reasoned in the synagogue, trying to persuade Jews and Greeks.

5 When Silas and Timothy came from Macedonia, Paul devoted himself exclusively to preaching, testifying to the Jews that Jesus was the Messiah.

6 But when they opposed Paul and became abusive, he shook out his clothes in protest and said to them, "Your blood be on your own heads! I am innocent of it. From now on I will go to the Gentiles."

7 Then Paul left the synagogue and went next door to the house of Titius Justus, a worshiper of God.

8 Crispus, the synagogue leader, and his entire household believed in the Lord; and many of the Corinthians who heard Paul believed and were baptized.

9 One night the Lord spoke to Paul in a vision: "Do not be afraid; keep on speaking, do not be silent.

10 For I am with you, and no one is going to attack and harm you, because I have many people in this city."

11 So Paul stayed in Corinth for a year and a half, teaching them the word of God.

18 Paul stayed on in Corinth for some time. Then he left the brothers and sisters and sailed for Syria, accompanied by Priscilla and Aquila. Before he sailed, he had his hair cut off at Cenchreae because of a vow he had taken.

19 They arrived at Ephesus, where Paul left Priscilla and Aquila. He himself went into the

19 And he came to Ephesus, and left them there: but he himself entered into the synagogue, and reasoned with the Jews.

20 When they desired him to tarry longer time with them, he consented not;

21 But bade them farewell, saying, I must by all means keep this feast that cometh in Jerusalem: but I will return again unto you, if God will. And he sailed from Ephesus.

synagogue and reasoned with the Jews.

20 When they asked him to spend more time with them, he declined.

21 But as he left, he promised, "I will come back if it is God's will." Then he set sail from Ephesus.

LIGHT ON THE WORD

Priscilla and Aquila. Priscilla and Aquila were a Jewish couple and refugees from Rome. After the Jews were banished by the emperor Claudius, they made their way to Corinth. There they met Paul as fellow tentmakers. It is unclear whether they were already Christians or converted during their stay with Paul at Corinth. Later they made their home in Ephesus, where they helped to mentor and teach the young preacher Apollos. Paul also mentions them in other letters (**Romans 16:3, 1 Corinthians 16:19, 2 Timothy 4:19**). They were his fellow helpers in the Gospel and valuable to him in ministry. Priscilla is usually mentioned before Aquila either to indicate her noble upbringing or her more visible gifting in the church. This is unusual, as throughout Scripture the husband's name is usually mentioned first.

Corinth. This ancient city was the capital of the Roman province Achaea, which included the southern half of modern Greece. It was located around 50 miles southwest of Athens between that city and Sparta. An ancient rival of Athens, by the time of Alexander the Great, Corinth surpassed it in terms of politics and economics. Corinth was also a major religious center and was known for its large temple dedicated to the goddess Aphrodite,

which had a thousand prostitutes dedicated to her service. As such, it was a city synonymous with immorality. Paul stayed in Corinth for eighteen months and left a thriving Christian community. Two letters in the New Testament canon were addressed to the Corinthian church.

TEACHING THE BIBLE LESSON

LIFE NEED FOR TODAY'S LESSON

AIM: Students will appreciate that people can be persistent when they really believe what they are doing and saying is the real thing.

INTRODUCTION

Paul's Vision

In this lesson, we see Paul's focus on the mission and the calling he received from God. This focus has taken him further into the Gentile world and more specifically into the country of Greece. Prior to this, Paul and his companions intended to go into the region of Bithynia in the northernmost part of Asia Minor or modern-day Turkey. While on their way, Paul saw a vision of a man from Macedonia saying "Come over to Macedonia and help us." Taking this as the direction of the Holy Spirit, they set sail for the Grecian province of Macedonia. Immediately Paul and his companions Timothy and Silas began to preach in the cities of Thessalonica, Berea, and Athens. In each of these cities, Paul received a different response to the preaching of the Gospel. In Thessalonica, he was persecuted and run out of town. In Berea, many of his hearers listened and investigated the Scriptures to confirm Paul's message. Finally, in Athens, Paul encountered a mixed response—most of his audience rejected the Gospel, but a few requested him to come back again, while a few others believed.

Paul traveled southwest to the city of Corinth, which was a major commercial center and the leading city of Greece at the time. Although this was an ideal location to preach and plant a church among the Gentiles, Paul was afraid to preach in such a hostile environment (**1 Corinthians 2:3**). With encouragement from God, Paul continued to preach the Gospel and a vibrant church community was formed. Next, Paul would travel to Ephesus. There he would leave his coworkers Priscilla and Aquila and go on to Asia Minor and Syria to teach and encourage the churches he had founded on his first missionary journey with Barnabas. Soon he would return to Ephesus and continue the ministry of the Word.

BIBLE LEARNING

AIM: Students will know that after experiencing a vision, Paul, Timothy, and Silas traveled together to various cities to preach.

I. OCCUPIED WITH THE WORD (Acts 18:1–5)

Paul lands in Corinth, and we get a more in-depth view of his usual ministry methods and lifestyle. He is alone in a new city and meets a Jewish couple, Priscilla and Aquila. They are recent immigrants to Corinth after the emperor Claudius banished all Jews from Rome. Since they shared the common occupation of tentmaking, Paul decided

to stay and work with them. This was very strategic on Paul's part; his character would be on display as he lived in their home and worked in their workshop, presenting many opportunities to preach the Gospel and share his faith. Luke, the writer of Acts, also records that every Sabbath, Paul "reasoned in the synagogue" and attempted to "persuade Jews and Greeks" (**v. 4**). In the same way, our character is always on display no matter what occupation we have, and God has presented opportunities for us to share His Word no matter where we are.

During this time, Timothy and Silas come down from Macedonia to join Paul in preaching the Gospel. It says that as soon as they came, Paul was "pressed in the spirit" (**v. 5**). This phrase means that he was occupied solely with one thing: preaching the Word. The ESV and other contemporary translations read "with the word" rather than "with the spirit" because the oldest Greek manuscripts say word. Either way, the text is telling us that Paul is focused on the Gospel. As he made tents with Priscilla and Aquila, he was also focused on sharing the Gospel and teaching those around him the Word of God. Even without help from his companions, he went to the synagogue every Sabbath to convince those in attendance of the truth about Jesus. The difference between then and after Timothy and Silas arrived in Corinth is he can now devote himself exclusively to the task of preaching. Whether we are in full-time ministry or work in a non-church-related occupation, the Lord wants us to be occupied with His Word and how we can share it with others.

Acts 18:1–4, 18–21, 24–28

1 After these things Paul departed from Athens, and came to Corinth; 2 And found a certain Jew named Aquila, born in Pontus, lately come from Italy, with his wife Priscilla; (because that Claudius had commanded all Jews to depart from Rome:) and came unto them. 3 And because he was of the same

craft, he abode with them, and wrought: for by their occupation they were tentmakers. 4 And he reasoned in the synagogue every sabbath, and persuaded the Jews and the Greeks. 5 And when Silas and Timotheus were come from Macedonia, Paul was pressed in the spirit, and testified to the Jews that Jesus was Christ.

In the beginning of the chapter, we read that Paul left Athens for the city of Corinth (Gk. *Korinthos*, **KOR-een-thoce**), which means was named for a grape that was grown abundantly in the area. Located about 50 miles west of Athens, Corinth was the political and economic bedrock of Greece. Its infamy, however, was its reputation of sexual immorality. There were a dozen temples of worship specializing in lewd and lascivious sexual accommodations. Paul's missionary journey preaching the Gospel seems to have taken him from one challenging place of ministry to another.

When Paul arrived in Corinth, he again sought out Christian community and co-laborers in Christ. While ministering in Athens alone, Paul had no doubt learned the hard way that companionship in ministry affords increased spiritual and physical strength. Paul's first order of business was to find believers. He soon meets Aquila, along with his wife Priscilla. Eventually, this couple became missionary partners with Paul near the end of this two-year journey. Here at their introduction, they are described as residents of Italy, but it is made clear that they were Jewish by birth and religion. The Roman emperor Claudius had issued an edict banishing Jews from the capital. Other historical sources say he did this because Jews were causing unrest at the instigation of Christ. Likely what happened was that the traditional Jews and Jewish Christians came into religious conflict, and not recognizing a different between the religions, Claudius banished all the "Jews" who were causing problems. It was from this edict of religious persecution that the Gospel spread wherever converts and disciples dispersed.

Priscilla and Aquila modeled for believers an egalitarian paradigm for partnership in vocation and ministry. Emphasizing community and companionship rather than gender competitiveness, they complemented each other as tentmakers and teachers. Priscilla and Aquila opened their homes in Ephesus (**1 Corinthians 16:19**) and Rome (**Romans 16:3–5**) to found house churches. Within this partnership of marriage and ministry, Paul found companionship and community among Christians, because he was also a tentmaker (Gk. *skenopoios*, **skay-no-poy-OSE**), or one who fashions tents from leather or goat hair. The term was also used in general for a leatherworker.

Together, the three of them took pride in their craft and enjoyed Christian fellowship as they made tents to house the very Roman soldiers who were their adversaries. This model of bi-vocational ministry is useful even today as it can give someone an avenue to preach the Gospel to those outside the church. It also is helpful as a means of changing the reputation of the clergy as those who are only interested in financial gain.

Paul worked throughout the week, but every Sabbath, he headed to the synagogue. Ever diligent to the cause of the Gospel, he "reasoned" (Gk. *dialegomai*, **dee-ah-LEH-go-my**), or engaged in lively, thoughtful, passionate discussion, continually and repeatedly with the Jews and Greeks regarding the Christ. Paul's goal was to persuade (Gk. *peitho*, **PAY-tho**), that is, to induce others to believe, usually by words or other fair means. Paul taught the Gospel to convert both Jews well-versed in Jewish Scripture and tradition and

God-fearing Greeks well-versed in philosophy but who had not converted to Judaism.

SEARCH THE SCRIPTURES

QUESTION 1

Explain why Paul stayed with Aquila and his wife Priscilla.

Aquila and Priscilla were tentmakers like Paul, so he stayed and worked with them.

LIGHT ON THE WORD

The Holy Spirit and Paul's Ministry

Paul moved as the Spirit led, demonstrating his faithfulness and commitment to spread the Gospel were more important than seeking ease and comfort in ministry. Rather than regarding Corinth as a morally desolate wasteland, Paul seized the opportunity to minister to this city's inhabitants with the very grace and love of God that had compelled him to know and accept Jesus as Lord. In his two letters to the Corinthians, Paul undertakes extensive teaching regarding sexual purity.

II. ENCOURAGED BY THE LORD (vv. 6–11)

The response from the Jews in the synagogue was hostility and opposition. They formed an organized resistance against Paul and insulted him. This caused Paul to shake his clothes and give a disclaimer of responsibility for their souls. They have heard the Word and now will be accountable to it. This is definitely the course of action we need to take when confronted with those who refuse to hear the Gospel. Next, Paul goes to the house of Titius Justus, a Gentile God-fearer and lived next door to the synagogue. The results of Paul's ministry are remarkable in that the synagogue ruler Crispus believed the Gospel along with his entire household. Additionally,

Luke records that many people believed and were baptized.

In spite of this activity, it seems Paul needed some extra encouragement from the Lord. It may have been because of the opposition of the Jews or the immorality that filled Corinth. In any case, he receives a vision at night from the Lord. In the vision, Paul hears the Lord encourage him not to be afraid and to continue to preach the Gospel. God is with him, no one is going to harm him, and the Lord has many people in the city ready to respond to the message of salvation. Sometimes God is working with us in circumstances that may not seem favorable, but it is our job to continue to preach the Word. There are people who need to hear the message, and God has already prepared their hearts.

6 And when they opposed themselves, and blasphemed, he shook his raiment, and said unto them, Your blood be upon your own heads; I am clean; from henceforth I will go unto the Gentiles. 9 Then spake the Lord to Paul in the night by a vision, Be not afraid, but speak, and hold not thy peace: 10 For I am with thee, and no man shall set on thee to hurt thee: for I have much people in this city. 7 And he departed thence, and entered into a certain man's house, named Justus, one that worshipped God, whose house joined hard to the synagogue. 8 And Crispus, the chief ruler of the synagogue, believed on the Lord with all his house; and many of the Corinthians hearing believed, and were baptized. 11 And he continued there a year and six months, teaching the word of God among them.

Paul was making tents and preaching the Gospel whenever he had the opportunity. Once Silas and Timothy arrived, he was "pressed (Gk. *sunecho*, **soon-EK-oh**) in spirit." The word is used for being physically held or confined as a prisoner, and for besieging a city. In this context, it is intended metaphorically to mean the narrowing of Paul's focus. Now he is devoted exclusively to preaching the Gospel and testifying that "Jesus was Christ." The King James Version of the passage states that the Jews' reaction to Paul is that they "opposed themselves." In the active voice, it means to "arrange in battle array face to face." In the middle voice, it is translated "opposed yourself" against someone or to set yourself in opposition against someone. Although the militaristic denotation is still in mind in the middle and passive voice, a better rendering of the text is "resisted" (Gk. *antitasso*, **an-tee-TAHS-so**). Paul's response was to shake out his garment. This act was a disclaimer of any responsibility. Paul took his preaching of the Gospel seriously, in the same vein as the prophet Ezekiel (**Ezekiel 3:18, 33:4, 8**). He was accountable for preaching the message but not whether that message was obeyed. This signals his focus in preaching shifting to the Gentiles of Corinth.

Next Paul finds himself preaching and teaching in the house of Justus. This man is described as a God-fearer whose house was right next to the synagogue. Through Paul's activity during this time, Crispus, the leader of the synagogue, came to believe in the Lord along with his household. Crispus is a Latin name, so he may have been a Roman citizen. Luke might point this out to paint the Christian faith as favorable to the empire. There were also many others in Corinth who believed and became members of the newly emerging church in the city. This is the beginning of the rift between the Jewish and Christian communities. Until now, the disciples have been regarded as a Jewish sect. Soon they will be considered a different religion, with the destruction of Jerusalem in A.D. 70 sealing this separation.

Paul receives a vision at night. The Lord speaks to him and encourages him to stop being

afraid. We know Paul experienced persecution in other Greek cities and from the Jews, especially when preaching in Thessalonica and Berea. He already experienced hostility from the Jews in the synagogue and may have anticipated another even more life-threatening incident. God encourages him to "hold not thy peace." This verb is imperative, which makes God's words to Paul a command to continue habitually doing something. In other words, he must go on speaking.

SEARCH THE SCRIPTURES

QUESTION 2
Who is Crispus?

A synagogue ruler who was baptized with his household.

LIGHT ON THE WORD
God Has a Plan
The Lord assures Paul that He is with the apostle. This echoes Jesus' last words in the Gospel of Matthew: "I am with you always even to the end of the age" (from **Matthew 28:20**). There is also a specific promise God reveals to Paul in the vision: No one is going to harm him because God has a plan. This plan is not just for Paul, but also the salvation of many people in Corinth. Consequently, Paul obeys the vision and continues to minister there for eighteen months. This is his longest stay in a city so far and will become a pattern for his ministry, as seen when he stays for two whole years in Ephesus.

III. COMPELLED TO RETURN (vv. 18–21)

Paul stayed in Corinth for about a year and six months. The opposition of the Jews continued until it finally climaxed with a trial before the Roman proconsul Gallio. Gallio sees the trial as a matter of Jewish customs and admonishes them to take care of it themselves. Luke mentions this trial in order to show Christianity as a non-threat to the Roman Empire; it was a Jewish affair, not a subversive cult.

After this, Paul continues a few days in Corinth after the trial and then heads off for Syria. When they reach Cenchreae, a city on the coast, Paul shaves his head to fulfill a vow. was in fulfillment of the Nazarite vow (**Numbers 6:1–21**), which indicated that Paul had consecrated himself to the Lord for a period of time. The vow included avoiding alcoholic drinks and letting one's hair grow, so shaving his head indicates his period of consecration is complete. Accompanied by Priscilla and Aquila, he stops at Ephesus, where he goes into the synagogue and begins to reason with the Jews. This seems to be a test or experiment to investigate the kind of reception the Gospel would obtain in the city. The Jews in the synagogue at Ephesus seem to be curious and hungry for the Gospel as they ask him to stay for a longer period of time. Paul declines their request; he must go on to encourage and teach the churches he formed in Asia Minor. He lets them know his desire is to return, but it is ultimately up to God. Paul sets sail from Ephesus because he also believes in strengthening the churches he left behind. It is not an either/or thing with Paul. His goal, as well as ours, is to see people built up in Christ and this includes encouraging and teaching God's Word to those who are already followers of Christ. He does this in order for them to mature in the faith.

18 And Paul after this tarried there yet a good while, and then took his leave of the brethren, and sailed thence into Syria, and with him Priscilla and Aquila; having shorn his head in Cenchrea: for he had a vow. 19 And he came to Ephesus, and left them there: but he himself entered into the synagogue, and reasoned with the Jews. 20 When they desired him to tarry longer time with them,

he consented not; 21 But bade them farewell, saying, I must by all means keep this feast that cometh in Jerusalem: but I will return again unto you, if God will.

While teaching many of those gathering in the synagogue weekly, Paul "tarried" (Gk. *prosmeno*, **pros-MEN-oh**), meaning "to continue" or "to remain with" them for an unspecified length of time, but for what is understood to be a considerable number of days. Paul stayed put, preaching and teaching among them, even after a plot to kill him had failed (**18:12–17**). Because the people were receptive, the Word effectively convinced them that Jesus is the Christ. Note that in the previous verse, those gathered were called Jews and Greeks. After Paul's effective and persuasive ministry to them, he now calls them "brethren" (Gk. *adelphos*, **ah-del-FOSE**), which can refer to a brother by birth, national origin, or friendship. However within the Christian context, in its plural form of *adelphoi* (Gk. **ah-del-FOY**), the term became all-inclusive to refer to all who believed, whether Jew or Greek, slave or free.

The "vow" (Gk. *euche*, **ew-KHAY**) that Paul made earlier was most likely a 7-day Nazarite vow when he did not shave or drink wine (cf. **Acts 21:23**). Shaving his head was simply an outward Jewish expression of his inward sincerity when this period of consecration had ended.

The Roman city Ephesus was located on the coast of what is today western Turkey, about 55 miles north from Miletus—the place from which Paul would call the elders of the church (**Acts 20:17**). While in port at Ephesus, Paul left his companions, Priscilla and Aquila, and went directly to the synagogue to again debate with the Jewish religious and philosophical leaders assembled there. Paul was ever ready and seeking to persuade, convince, debate, and prove that Jesus Christ is the

Messiah to all who would listen. The Greek word *sunagoge* (**soo-naw-go-GAY**) is a building and also the formal assembly of Jews who gathered in such a building to pray, read, and discuss Scripture. Synagogue services were held weekly on the Sabbath and on special feast days. The synagogue could also be used for trials. Every town with at least ten Jewish males free to practice their religion could have a synagogue.

Paul's teaching was so efficacious that Jewish religious leaders asked him to tarry (Gk. *meno*, **MEH-no**), or stay with them, a while longer. Even though Paul hastened from the port of Ephesus to meet with those in the synagogue, he was compelled by the Holy Spirit to decline their persistence that he extend his stay. The text says he did not consent (Gk. *epineuo*, **eh-pee-NEW-oh**). The original word means to nod and implies assent. Here, Paul demonstrates that his calling and ministry is to do God's will, not man's desire. The good work to be done among these new believers paled in comparison to the ministry before Paul as he journeyed to Jerusalem for the Feast of the Passover.

SEARCH THE SCRIPTURES

QUESTION 3
Where did Paul journey to after he left Ephesus for what feast?

Paul traveled to Jerusalem for the Feast of the Passover and to talk with Jews in the synagogue.

LIGHT ON THE WORD

Thank You for Your Hospitality
As he sailed from Ephesus, Paul gave the local believers an explanation for resisting their hospitality: he had to go to the place of worship. Paul held fast to his conviction to move on; however, he did leave them with a provision. He promised to come back and continue in ministry and fellowship only if God needed him more there. "God willing" had a shared understanding among Jews and Greeks as a way to express a lack of presumption concerning the future. We must take care to use it, not as doubting God's will for our lives or buffeting a weak promise, but as a faithful declaration to do God's will, in His time, at His appointed place.

BIBLE APPLICATION

AIM: Students will know that God can place us in a situation where our knowledge and skills are embraced so that He is glorified.

Preaching the Gospel is often seen as annoying and offensive, or as someone imposing their beliefs on another. Far from it. As Paul preached and taught, he appealed to the reason of his audience while also acknowledging their freedom of choice and personal responsibility. He was a man with a single-minded focus because he believed God was at work in the hearts of those around him. This ought to encourage us to pray and ask God to give us eyes to see Him at work and assurance that He is with us to equip and protect us. Whether at work or a softball game, we may be presented with opportunities to share our faith. We can also pray for others in new and challenging situations. We can pray for them to keep their eyes open and their hearts focused on the one thing that matters: the Good News of Jesus Christ.

STUDENT'S RESPONSES

AIM: Students will know that believers can pray and praise God for sustaining their work or vocations.

Sometimes opportunities to share our faith can be right under our noses. There may be someone at your work or in your neighborhood whom God may be highlighting to you. One of the best contexts to get to know someone and share our lives is mealtime. Make a plan to sit down in the coming week and eat with at least three people who do not know Christ. Pray for an opportunity to share the Gospel and watch what God does.

PRAYER

Thank you for sending missionaries to spread the Good News of Christ. Thank You for missionaries who share the Good News in the local community and globally. In the Name of Jesus, we pray. Amen.

HOW TO SAY IT

Pontus.	PAHN-tis.
Aquila.	ah-KWI-luh.
Priscilla.	pris-SI-luh.

PREPARE FOR NEXT SUNDAY

Read **Exodus 20:8–11, 31:12–16** and "The Lord's Day."

DAILY HOME BIBLE READINGS

MONDAY
Learning from God
(Psalm 25:8–12, 20–21)

TUESDAY
Living with God
(Psalm 27:4–5, 8–9, 11–14)

WEDNESDAY
Wisdom from God
(Proverbs 16:19–24)

THURSDAY
Commissioned to Teach
(Matthew 28:16–20)

FRIDAY
Teach Me Your Ways
(Exodus 33:12–18)

SATURDAY
Apollos Grows in Ministry
(Acts 18:24–28)

SUNDAY
Teaching God's Word
(Acts 18:1–11, 18–21)

Sources:
Keener, Craig S. *IVP Bible Background Commentary*. Downers Grove, IL: InterVarsity Press, 1993.
Carson, D.A., France, R.T., Motyer, J.A., Wenham, J.G. *New Bible Commentary*. Downers Grove, IL: InteVarsity Press, 1993.
Polhill, John B. Acts. *New American Commentary: An Exegetical and Theological Exposition of Holy Scripture*. Nashville: B&H Publishing, 1992.

COMMENTS / NOTES:

_____
_____
_____
_____
_____
_____
_____
_____
_____
_____
_____
_____
_____
_____
_____
_____
_____
_____
_____
_____
_____
_____
_____

SACRED GIFTS AND HOLY GATHERINGS
by Dr. Rodney Lamar Atkins

This quarter studies religious and family traditions. A close study of the traditions of the Jewish holidays, marriage, and death covers similar aspects of life today. Traditions give us a sense of family as well as belonging to a group of people and not being alone in the world. A thorough investigation of the books of Exodus, Leviticus, Matthew, Genesis, Song of Solomon, Hosea, and John will help us to focus upon and discover the importance of tradition in our lives. In the 1977 book *Tradition and Theology in the Old Testament*, Douglas A. Knight observed "Tradition preserves the memory of the past. It is subject to growth and change at the hands of new generations who face new situations that require a reconsideration of their heritage."

Unit 1: Giving Our Offering

These four lessons will examine worship and the importance of retaining sacred traditions. We should ask ourselves, "How can I commit more of my time to God?"

Christians are not to live today as if all time were their own. Christians should not have the attitude that they can do with time as they please, the God of all time has the right to determine how one's day should be used. To keep the Sabbath day holy is to keep it separate from the other six days. Theologian D. Patrick in his writings, "Old Testament Law," describes the Sabbath day as "a sanctuary of time."

God set aside the Sabbath as a day to remember. "Remembering" is more than a mental act; it is an active observance. Even though our society is changing rapidly, all people must realize that the Sabbath is a divinely given means for all creatures to be in tune with the created order of things by God.

As Christians today, we should wonder, "How should I represent Christ in all my ways?" Pre-exile, the book of Leviticus was the source for regulations on sacrifice and how to properly offer sacrifices to God. Today, Leviticus speaks to us about reverence in worship, purity in lifestyle, and our need for forgiveness. Today the best gift a Christian can give is to obey God's commandments. The main focus of Leviticus is "be holy, for I am holy." God calls for Israel to live a holy life based upon His own holy character.

How can our families serve the Lord? God is the giver of life. The life of the firstborn was consecrated to God in gratitude. God was believed to bring continued life and blessing into the community. Do Christians serve in the church to be seen and heard or to please the Lord? Jesus challenged society's norms. Greatness comes from serving. Jesus exposed the scribes and Pharisees' impure motives. Through their actions, they hoped to gain status, recognition, and respect.

UNIT 2: The Beauty of Marriage and Family

These lessons focus on the sanctity of marriage and family, and also study the death of a loved one. The selection of a lifetime partner is second only to the important decision to trust Christ for salvation. The story of Laban, Jacob, Leah, and Rachel presents a lesson for all to learn from. Even though God's people may experience His blessing on their endeavors, God will effectively discipline them by making them aware of their unresolved sins. Proverbs 3:12 says, "For whom the Lord loves He reproves. Even as a father corrects the son in whom he delights" (NASB). Older saints have always said that "they will reap what they have sown"—even though they seem to be making progress by God's provision. In other words, God may wait patiently before disciplining His people, but discipline He will!

Godly marriages are rooted and grounded in love. No matter how close of a relationship we may have with our parents, only in marriage can we realize our complete union of mind, heart, and body. The book of Hosea is a love story. It tells of God's love for His people and the response of His bride. A covenant has been made. God had been faithful. His love was steadfast, and His commitment unbroken. But Israel, like Gomer was adulterous and unfaithful, spurning God's love and turning instead to false gods.

Then after warning of judgment, God reaffirmed His love and offered reconciliation. God's love and mercy were overflowing, but justice would be served. Hosea in conclusion reminds the Israelites and us that God is a loving God whose loyalty to His covenant people is unwavering.

Should Christians attend some social events, especially for the sake of family members? School events, community events, and church events are always important to the family. In John 2:1–12, Jesus attended the wedding at Cana in Galilee. He proved that even though He was on a mission to save the world, He took time to attend a wedding. Jesus apparently valued attending such an event as wedding festivities.

The last experience of life is death. The reality of death is universal. When a person dies, a family goes through the grieving process. Friends and family members gather to reflect upon the life of a loved one. The ultimate question is always whether a person has made preparation to meet their maker in peace.

UNIT 3: Celebrate His Goodness

These lessons will center upon celebration and how to remember God's goodness.

The understanding of Passover has been important in both Jewish and Christian traditions. The Jewish liturgy for Passover describes that worshipers in every celebration are actual participants in God's saving deed. In other words, God brought us out of Egypt. The Passover serves as important background for the New Testament presentation of the death of Jesus. It also gives the understanding of the Lord's Supper.

Leviticus deals with how to worship God. This book describes the priesthood and the topics of cleanness and holiness. Sacrifices, priests, and the sacred Day of Atonement opened the way for the Israelites to come to God. God's people were able to worship Him with their lives. The final emphasis is celebration. Even though our Christian traditions and holidays are different, they are necessary ingredients of worship. We need special days of worship and celebration to remember God's goodness in our lives!

Dr. Rodney Lamar Atkins
1st Vice President
International Sunday School Department
Church of God in Christ, Inc.

Dr. Rodney Lamar Atkins is the author of five books. He is a writer for the Christian newspaper *The Voice of Texas*. Dr. Atkins is the founder and pastor of Victory Temple Church of God in Christ, Tyler, Texas. He serves as the First Vice President of the International Sunday School Department of the Church of God in Christ.

THE TEACHER TEACHES
Tips for teaching
by Dr. Jeannette H. Donald

The following information is designed to support and aid both the COGIC Commentary series and Sunday School leaders by providing innovative teaching suggestions, proven growth strategies, and thoughtful learning opportunities, thus exciting, benefiting, and enhancing the user.

MATTHEW 28:20 is calling us to be TRANSFORMATIONAL TEACHERS.

"Teaching them to observe all things whatsoever I have commanded you: and, lo, I am with you always, even unto the end of the world" (Matthew 28:20).

JESUS TAUGHT WITH STORIES

Story of a location known to listeners—Luke 10:25–37
Story of people at a familiar event—Matthew 25:1–13
Story using repetition—Matthew 25:14–30

JESUS USED SCRIPTURES

He was so familiar with Scriptures that He knew where to find it in the text—Luke 4:17
He used Scriptures for personal strength—Matthew 4:1–10
Used examples from His own experience as a carpenter—Luke 6:46–49

TEACHER SCRIPTURE TOOL BOX

- Prove all things; hold fast that which is good (*1 Thessalonians 5:21*).

- Every good gift and every perfect gift is from above, and cometh down from the Father of lights, with whom is no variableness, neither shadow of turning (*James 1:17*).

- And he gave some, apostles; and some, prophets; and some, evangelists; and some, pastors and teachers (*Ephesians 4:11*).

As a teacher, we never know how much of an impact we have on others until they open up and tell you something like this: "*Thank you for speaking into my life today, I was troubled in my spirit about how to handle a problem I was going through and now I know what to do.*"

God has chosen to work through us as we teach **HIS WORD**. This is why we should strive to become the most effective **TEACHERS**. To become an effective teacher, it's all about shifting the teaching emphasis from information to transformation. We as teachers should teach biblical truths and principles, but the most effective teachers are always aiming for **TRANSFORMATION**. Every teacher's goal should be interpretation, explanation, application, and transformation. *It is a calling to transform the heart and just not to just inform the mind.*

Scripture: *And be not conformed to this world: but be ye transformed by the renewing of your mind, that ye may prove what is that good, and acceptable, and perfect, will of God (Romans 12:2).*

1. **IF YOU DON'T KNOW IT, THEY WON'T LEARN IT:**

   Know the material before you try to teach your students.

   Study to shew thyself approved unto God, a workman that needeth not to be ashamed, rightly dividing the word of truth (2 Timothy 2:15).

2. **GET YOUR MIND THINKING EARLY:**

   Start early in preparing your lesson, not just because you may already know the lesson from previous lessons taught. If you are starting the night before, you won't think of the perfect activity until it's too late.

3. **TEACH FROM THE BIBLE:**

   Teaching from the **BIBLE** always encourages students to bring their Bible. This way they experience that this was from the **BIBLE**.

4. **KEEP IN TOUCH WITH THE STUDENTS:**

   - . Find out their birthdays.

   - Send a card when they are ill, or to just encourage them.

5. **DEPEND ON GOD:**

   - Pray for your students.

   - Remember that God will support the work, because it is ministry.

   - He will provide the resources, the time, and the talent.

Conclusion: Sometimes people who are going to be a Sunday School teacher are concerned that they don't know enough about the Bible, or that they will make some huge mistake and fail miserably. But there are things a person can do to help:

- **Be Dedicated**—What you are doing is important

- **Be Dependable**—Be on time, ready to teach, or get a substitute teacher

- **Be a Student Yourself**—Learn the lesson first. Understand it yourself.

- **Be Prayerful**—In all things pray first

- **Be an Example**—Apply God's Word to your own life. Be humble, read your Bible, learn the Scripture, and honor God.

Dr. Jeannette H. Donald
Dr. Jeannette H. Donald, Field Representative, serves under the leadership of Bishop Alphonso Denson and Supervisor Dorothy Richardson. She serves as Assistant Dean of W. K. Gordon Institute (Louisiana Eastern First Jurisdiction) and associate professor of Life Christian University (Zachary, Louisiana). She also serves as First Lady and Sunday School teacher of Gospel Temple COGIC. Nationally, she serves in the International Sunday School Department as Director of Education–Leadership Ministry. Her motto is "Each One, Reaching One." She feels it is a tremendous and rewarding opportunity to teach and effect the lives of others through the teaching ministry of Sunday School.

BUILDING THE KINGDOM OF GOD, ONE SOUL AT A TIME
EPHESIANS 4:8, 11–12

by Jurisdictional Superintendent Terence K. Kirk

The following information is designed to support and aid both the COGIC Commentary series and Sunday School leaders by providing innovative teaching suggestions, proven growth strategies, and thoughtful learning opportunities, thus exciting, benefiting, and enhancing the user.

INTRODUCTION:

The aim of this presentation is to encourage and inspire Sunday School leaders and workers to make full proof of their ministries in helping to build the Kingdom of God **numerically, educationally, and spiritually** so that God through them might fulfill His will for His church. John 13:17 says, "If ye know these things, happy are ye if ye do them." Once you know what God wants you to do, the blessings actually come in doing it.

I. **Build the Kingdom Numerically [Win Souls for Christ]**

A. Jesus says go and multiply the numbers of the Kingdom. (**Matthew 28:19–20**) [**Go evangelize, baptize, and educate**] (**Luke 14:22–23**) [**The parable of the Great Supper**]

B. Jesus had a *Must* on the inside of Him when it came to doing the Father's will.

- In **Luke 2:49,** Jesus says to His parents that He "***must*** *be about my Father's business.*"

- In **John 4:4,** the text declares of Jesus that "*He **must** needs go through Samaria.*"

- In **John 9:4,** Jesus declares, "*I **must** work the works of Him who sent me, while it is day.*"

Question: Is there a **Must** *[A strong determination]* on the inside of you, when it comes to doing your part, in helping to build the Kingdom of God?

II. **Build the Kingdom Educationally [Educate Souls for Christ]**

A. Our **Y.P.W.W.** motto says we are to educate Young Willing Workers in scriptural knowledge.

- The Bible declares that the Word of God shall stand for ever. (**Isaiah 40:8**) [Jesus says that "Heaven and earth shall pass away"] (**Matthew 24:35**)

- As leaders and instructors, it's our job to communicate the blessings and benefits of embracing all Scripture. (**2 Timothy 3:16–17**)

B. The **Sunday School Department** has a tremendous responsibility to provide the proper platform whereby members can be educated in scriptural knowledge.

- **The Superintendent**—Responsibility is to provide able (*Capable*) Teachers who are passionate about their purpose and whose #1 goal is to develop disciples for Christ. **(Exodus 18:21a) (1 Corinthians 9:16)**

- **The Teacher**—Responsibility is to skillfully *communicate* and *articulate* *[Clearly Present]* the Word of God. *[Someone who can make the Scriptures come alive]* **(Luke 24:32)**

- **The Student**—Responsibility is to be *receptive* to what's being taught and then go *research* it for yourself. **(Acts 17:11) (2 Timothy 2:15)**

III. **Build the Kingdom Spiritually [*Strengthen Souls for Christ*]**

A. Our goal is to build up believers who are filled with and fully influenced by the Holy Spirit. **(Ephesians 5:18)**

- The Apostle Paul is not suggesting occasional drinking, but rather he's giving an analogy that **whatever you are full of, that's what going to control your *attitude* and *actions*.**

- It's not that we need more of the Holy Spirit, but that the Holy Spirit needs more of us! *[The more we yield to the Spirit, the more we are filled with the Spirit!]*

B. Secondly we need some Spiritual Ambassadors who can speak into the lives of others. *[Spiritual mentors who can give the members a charge about some of the foundational principles of Christianity]* {*Faith, Love, and Stewardship*}

- **Faith** – Having a solid "*Foundation of Faith*" is the essential cornerstone to a successful Christian life. *[How do we obtain faith?]* **(Romans 10:17)** *[Without it, it is impossible to please God] (Hebrews 11:6)*

- **Love** – Although faith is essential for a successful Christian life, but **without love, we are nothing. (1 Corinthians 13:2)** *[The greatest two commandments are about "love"]* **(Matthew 22:37–40)**

- *[New believers need to understand how much God loves them]* **(John 3:16)**

- **Stewardship**—Every believer should be enlightened concerning their need to be *faithful over the four T's.* **(1 Corinthians 4:2)**

- **Time (Ecclesiastes 3:1) (Ephesians 5:15–16)**

- **Talent** (gift) **(1 Peter 4:10)**

- **Treasure** (money) (**Malachi 3:10**) (**Acts 20:35**)

- **Temple** (**1 Corinthians 6:19–20**) (**Romans 12:1**)

CONCLUSION:

We have shared with you a three-step process for *"Building the Kingdom of God, One Soul at a Time"*:

- Winning Souls for Christ

- Educating Souls for Christ

- Strengthening Souls for Christ

Sunday School is where disciples for Christ receive foundational truths and teaching from the Word of God.

Elder Terence K. Kirk
Director of Foundational Sunday School Ministries
Jurisdictional AIM Chairman
Jurisdictional Sunday School Superintendent
Texas Southeast First Ecclesiastical Jurisdiction
Jurisdictional Prelate, Bishop Rufus Kyles Jr.

CALL TO DISCIPLESHIP: EACH ONE TEACH ONE

by Jurisdictional Superintendent Larry L. Polk

The following information is designed to support and aid both the COGIC Commentary series and Sunday School leaders by providing innovative teaching suggestions, proven growth strategies, and thoughtful learning opportunities, thus exciting, benefiting, and enhancing the user.

If Sunday School is the best school in the world, then we must be about teaching our students the knowledge and skills to live a successful and productive life. There is no better place for evangelism to take place than Sunday School. It is here we have the opportunity for training and developing spiritual leaders to effective work to build the Kingdom of God through discipleship.

Discipleship in the New Testament is the rendering of the Greek work, **mathetes**, learner, according to *Unger's Bible Dictionary*. The word *disciple* means a learner, a pupil, a scholar, one who comes to be taught. The idea of teaching and learning is preeminent in the word disciple. The term discipleship is used primarily to describe followers of Jesus or one who teaches others the principles of the teaching of Christ.

Throughout the earthly ministry of Jesus Christ, He was wholly absorbed with the creation of disciples who could and would proclaim the Gospel of God. The word *gospel* or **evangelion** is the term most often used in the New Testament to denote the Christian message. The word means the "the good news." Sometimes it appears as the "gospel of God," meaning not merely Good News about God, but *from* God, who Himself has taken the initiative in making it known to men. At other times the Gospel is spoken of as "the gospel of Christ," which again means not only Good News preached by Christ, but whose content is Christ Himself, beginning with His human ministry. All we know about the ministry of Jesus is found in the four Gospels of the New Testament. It is then to the Gospels that we must look for the written record of the life and teachings of Christ and His perspective on discipleship.

Jesus had a strategy that worked during His life and it works some 2,000 years later. It is a strategy that has its roots in spiritual evangelism: "each one teaching one." One author called it "**spiritual multiplication**." Discipleship encourages those who confess Christ as Lord and Savior to help those "babes" in Christ to develop a solid foundation that they "may be able to stand against the wiles of the devil" (Ephesians 6:11). In 2 Timothy 2:2 ("And the things that thou have heard of me among many witnesses, the same commit thou to faithful men, who shall be able to teach others also"), Paul writes to Timothy, "his son in the faith," to share what he has heard, observed, and learned with others that they may be able to "teach others also." As humans, we are often quick to run and tell someone else what we have heard, believe, and think. To this I say, **if God is as good to you as you say He is, share Him with others.** I suggest you run and tell that! This is the principle of each one teaching one, the principle of true discipleship.

It is in Sunday School that we begin our discipleship program. Each church ought to be about teaching the members of its Sunday School class that they can teach others. For this to happen, we need to have a clear sense of purpose, must first be convicted by the Word of God and have a commitment to share the Gospel of Christ. Being an effective disciple requires an understanding of the difference of being saved and being a disciple. True discipleship is all about dealing with a personal relationship to Jesus Christ as Teacher, Lord, and Master. What better place to develop and strengthen this relationship than in Sunday School?

Pastor Larry L. Polk, Jurisdictional Superintendent
State Sunday School Department
Texas Northeast First Jurisdiction
Bishop J. Neaul Haynes, Prelate
Mother Pia Haynes Williams, Jurisdictional Supervisor

QUARTERLY QUIZ

The questions on this page may be used in several ways: as a pretest at the beginning of the quarter; as a review at the end of the quarter; or as a review after each lesson. The questions are based on the Scripture text of each lesson (King James Version).

LESSON 1

1. The Sabbath is _____ (v. 8) and gives honor to God. Share ways that you treat the Sabbath as holy and honor God.

_____

_____

2. Verse 3 states that the Sabbath is "a sign between me [God] and you throughout genera-tions." Read the following Scripture verses, and then write the other covenant signs for each of the verses: (Genesis 17:10–14) _____ _____ (Genesis 9:8–17) _____ _____ (Matthew 28:19 and John 3:5) _____ _____

_____

_____

LESSON 2

1. Review the memory verse, Romans 12:1. What are the responsibilities Paul states that believers have?

_____

_____

2. Animals with any defect were acceptable for a sacrifice. What types of animals and genders were the sacrificial animals (Leviticus 22:19)?

_____

_____

LESSON 3

1. Verses 11–13 shares a part of God's people leaving Egypt. In verse 12, what does redeem mean?

_____

_____

2. Pharaoh's actions caused what to happen in verse 15?

_____

_____

LESSON 4

1. The Greek for exalt is _____ and the meaning of exalt is _____ _____ (v. 12).

_____

_____

2. Jesus encourages the work of the scribes and the Pharisees regarding the Torah, but con-demns their _____ (vv. 1–3).

_____

_____

LESSON 5

1. Jacob truly _____ Rachel and wanted to marry her. What evidence supports the inten-sity of Jacob's desire to marry her (v. 18)?

_____

_____

QUARTERLY QUIZ

2. Reread the Scripture text and use your notes from the lesson to describe who Laban was and name his two daughters. Review the section "Jacob's Deception" and write the meaning of Jacob's name. Do you think he lived up to his name? Explain.

_____

_____

LESSON 6

1. What two cities does the king use to compare the beauty of his bride (Song of Solomon 6:4)? Why would the king use cities to describe her beauty?

_____

_____

2. Read the Bible Truth and answer the following: What types of beauty is Solomon describing?

_____

_____

LESSON 7

1. What is the ruler's name in **verse 4**?

_____

_____

2. Name two of Hosea and Gomer's children in **verses 8 and 9**.

_____

_____

LESSON 8

1. Name some of the wedding attendees in **verses 1–3**.

_____

_____

2. Jesus' miracle causes what among the disciples (**v. 11**)?

_____

_____

LESSON 9

1. Complete the following Scripture: "And when he thus had _____, he _____ with a _____ _____, Lazarus _____ _____ " (**v. 43**).

_____

_____

2. What does _pisteuo_ mean in **verse 40**?

_____

_____

LESSON 10

1. What types of animals can be offered as a sacrifice (**v. 10**)?

_____

_____

2. Verse 14 states that the feast is a _____ to the _____.

_____

_____

QUARTERLY QUIZ

LESSON 11

1. The Feast of Weeks and Pentecost are the names given for the feast. How many days from the Sabbath should people bring bundled grain to be lifted as a special offering?

_____

_____

2. In verse 20, what is the role of the priest?

_____

_____

LESSON 12

1. Why is the Day of Atonement observed among the Israelites?

_____

_____

2. Aaron is allowed to enter into the _____ of _____ to perform a _____ ceremony. Who else may enter with Aaron?

_____

_____

LESSON 13

1. What was Israel to do on the first day of the Feast of Booths (**v. 35**)?

_____

_____

2. Name the types of boughs (branches) the Israelites were to gather (**v. 40**)?

_____

_____

Answers to Quarterly Quiz can be found on page 508

THE LORD'S DAY

BIBLE BASIS: EXODUS 20:8–11, 31:12–16

BIBLE TRUTH: The Lord gave the Sabbath as a day of rest and to recommit to holy living.

MEMORY VERSE: "Remember the sabbath day, to keep it holy" (Exodus 20:8).

LESSON AIM: By the end of this lesson, we will: EXPLORE the meaning of the Sabbath as expressed in Exodus; RECOGNIZE and appreciate the importance of Sabbath; and DISCOVER ways to practice Sabbath in the twenty-first century.

TEACHER PREPARATION

MATERIALS NEEDED: Quarterly Commentary/Teacher Manual, Adult Quarterly, Adult resources—charts, worksheets, and other teaching tools, paper, pens, pencils, Bibles (several different versions)

OTHER MATERIALS NEEDED / TEACHER'S NOTES:

_____

_____

LESSON OVERVIEW

LIFE NEED FOR TODAY'S LESSON

People sometimes turn away from traditions that give firm foundations and guides for their lives.

BIBLE LEARNING

God gives us provisions to honor Him through the Sabbath.

BIBLE APPLICATION

Christians must remember to honor God even when the issues of life are overwhelming.

STUDENTS' RESPONSES

God revealed the need for all creation to work and rest for its well-being.

LESSON SCRIPTURE

EXODUS 20:8–11, 31:12–16, KJV

8 Remember the sabbath day, to keep it holy.

9 Six days shalt thou labour, and do all thy work:

10 But the seventh day is the sabbath of the LORD thy God: in it thou shalt not do any work, thou, nor thy son, nor thy daughter,

EXODUS 20:8–11, 31:12–16, NIV

8 "Remember the Sabbath day by keeping it holy.

9 Six days you shall labor and do all your work,

10 but the seventh day is a sabbath to the LORD your God. On it you shall not do any work, neither you, nor your son or daughter,

thy manservant, nor thy maidservant, nor thy cattle, nor thy stranger that is within thy gates:

11 For in six days the LORD made heaven and earth, the sea, and all that in them is, and rested the seventh day: wherefore the LORD blessed the sabbath day, and hallowed it.

31:12 And the LORD spake unto Moses, saying,

13 Speak thou also unto the children of Israel, saying, Verily my sabbaths ye shall keep: for it is a sign between me and you throughout your generations; that ye may know that I am the LORD that doth sanctify you.

14 Ye shall keep the sabbath therefore; for it is holy unto you: every one that defileth it shall surely be put to death: for whosoever doeth any work therein, that soul shall be cut off from among his people.

15 Six days may work be done; but in the seventh is the sabbath of rest, holy to the LORD: whosoever doeth any work in the sabbath day, he shall surely be put to death.

16 Wherefore the children of Israel shall keep the sabbath, to observe the sabbath throughout their generations, for a perpetual covenant.

nor your male or female servant, nor your animals, nor any foreigner residing in your towns.

11 For in six days the LORD made the heavens and the earth, the sea, and all that is in them, but he rested on the seventh day. Therefore the LORD blessed the Sabbath day and made it holy.

31:12 Then the LORD said to Moses,

13 "Say to the Israelites, 'You must observe my Sabbaths. This will be a sign between me and you for the generations to come, so you may know that I am the LORD, who makes you holy.

14 "'Observe the Sabbath, because it is holy to you. Anyone who desecrates it is to be put to death; those who do any work on that day must be cut off from their people.

15 For six days work is to be done, but the seventh day is a day of sabbath rest, holy to the LORD. Whoever does any work on the Sabbath day is to be put to death.

16 The Israelites are to observe the Sabbath, celebrating it for the generations to come as a lasting covenant.

LIGHT ON THE WORD

Moses. The account of Moses is a testament to the ebbs and flows of life. Moses, born under a decree that required the murder of all male Hebrew children, should have died as an infant, but through the efforts of his mother and sister, he was raised as a prince in the house of Pharaoh. As an adult, he recognized the Hebrews' plight and followed God to lead them in their liberation. The "man of God" knew both struggle and persecution along the journey through the desert, but remained faithful (**Psalm 90**). He was blessed to stand on holy ground, commune with the burning bush, receive the Ten Commandments, and prepare the next generation for the Promised Land; however, due to his temporary disobedience, Moses was unable to enter the Promised Land (**Numbers 20:12**).

Mount Sinai. God came down to the top of the mountain and instructed Moses to come up (**Exodus 19:20**). Mount Sinai is still considered sacred today because there God spoke to Moses and gave him all of the laws, statutes, and ordinances for the Children of Israel. When the Israelites camped around Mount Sinai, the glory of the Lord settled on the mountain for six days (**Exodus 24:16**). The book of Deuteronomy refers to the site where Moses received the Ten Commandments as Mount Horeb (**Exodus 33:6**); generally Sinai and Horeb are thought to be the same place (**Exodus 34:2**).

TEACHING THE BIBLE LESSON

LIFE NEED FOR TODAY'S LESSON

AIM: Students will learn that people sometimes turn away from traditions that give firm foundations and guides for their lives.

INTRODUCTION

God Commands—Observe the Sabbath

The command to observe the Sabbath was given to Moses in two different contexts. In **Exodus 20**, it is included in a larger body of statutes known as the Ten Commandments. The command to observe the Sabbath is the fourth commandment, following "Thou shalt not take the name of the LORD thy God in vain" (from **v. 7**) and preceding "Honour thy father and thy mother" (from **v. 12**). Scholars debate the significance of the order of the commandments; however, Jesus summarized the first four in His understanding of the greatest commandment (**Matthew 22:34–40**).

The whole of the Ten Commandments shows how we should love God and others.

Moses also received the command to observe the Sabbath in **Exodus 31**. It is important to understand the setting for this text. God used the preceding Scriptures to outline the details for building the tabernacle. He was specific and had made the necessary provisions in terms of skill, labor, and resources. God re-emphasizes the Sabbath statute to make clear that the new assignment does not supersede the Sabbath; there is no justification for working on the Sabbath. If erecting a place to worship the Lord was not a plausible excuse, certainly no excuse would do.

BIBLE LEARNING

AIM: Students will understand that God gives us provisions to honor Him through the Sabbath.

I. A MEMORIAL (Exodus 20:8–10)

When God created humankind, He understood how people would act. Moreover, He understood that humans would be overwhelmed and engrossed in our daily lives and worldly things rather than Him and His precepts. Thus, God not only provided the Sabbath but also instructions to remember it, because He knew there would be an inclination to forget the purpose and benefit.

Sabbath means "rest" in Hebrew. God understood the importance of rest during creation and wants His people to remember not only His commandments but their limitations as creatures and their submission to Him as Creator.

Exodus 20:8–11; 31:12–16

8 Remember the sabbath day, to keep it holy.
9 Six days shalt thou labour, and do all thy

work: 10 But the seventh day is the sabbath of the LORD thy God: in it thou shalt not do any work, thou, nor thy son, nor thy daughter, thy manservant, nor thy maidservant, nor thy cattle, nor thy stranger that is within thy gates:

The fourth commandment has generated endless debate, and this controversy continues today. One of the primary issues involves what exactly constitutes a) remembering and b) not working. Even though this is the longest of the commandments in the Decalogue, or Ten Commandments (**Exodus 34:28; Deuteronomy 4:13**), the struggle to interpret and follow the command in some ways remains unchanged. There would be little controversy over keeping or honoring the Sabbath if the spirit of the command were kept in mind instead of endless fascinations with the letter of the law.

The word "remember" in Hebrew is *zakar* (**zah-KAR**), which is more than just simple recollection, but remembering meaning and history as well. The parallel command in **Deuteronomy 5:12** uses "keep," from the Hebrew *shamar* (**shah-MAR**), which means to guard, protect, or attend. The word sabbath in Hebrew is *shabbath* (**shab-BAHT**), which Strong's defines as "intermission," and is derived from the similar Hebrew verb *shavat* (**sha-VAHT**), which means to rest or stop.

The verse points to the comprehensiveness of the passage, which extends outward from the central figure, presumably a property owner, to his family, servants, animals, and then to strangers (also rendered foreigners, resident aliens, and sojourners in various translations). One's workload cannot simply be transferred to a subordinate—the day of rest applies to all, high and low, rich and poor, master and servant; all are included. Unfortunately, in defining exactly what constituted work, over the centuries, many

completely lost sight of the spirit of the law: holiness. One does not demonstrate keeping something holy by following hair-splitting, bare minimum, or overexacting definitions—to the point where Pharisees, for example, would not even do a "work" of mercy or kindness on the Sabbath (**Luke 14:3–6**), for which Jesus rightly rebuked them. Instead, keeping the Sabbath holy in **v. 8** means setting it apart for God.

II. A BLESSING (v. 11)

The text tells us that the Lord blessed the Sabbath and set it apart. In other words, God distinguished the Sabbath by sanctifying it and making it a holy day. Even in contemporary times, Christians must set apart the Lord's day and ensure it has distinction from every other day. God sanctified the Sabbath, but unless the day is committed to Him, the blessing has no benefits.

God provided a model whereby everything to do was finished in a six-day period. He exhibited organization skills, the advantages of prioritizing, the obligation of completion, and the necessity of rest. Given this example, all believers are challenged to honor God by observing the Sabbath.

Honoring the Sabbath Honors God

11 For in six days the LORD made heaven and earth, the sea, and all that in them is, and rested the seventh day: wherefore the LORD blessed the sabbath day, and hallowed it.

A common misreading is that God was tired from working for six days and needed some time off to recuperate. The reality was that rest was an integral component built into creation—no different from light, plants, animals, or humanity itself; rest is part of nature's rhythm. Violating the Sabbath was to violate nature and introduce man-made chaos into the once-perfect God-made ecology. Today's language would call this the rat race; our common defiance has become our collective cacophony of chaos. On the other hand, aligning with God's intended design has the opposite effect—by letting go of the frenzy, releasing our grip on self-centered pursuits, and embracing the divinely mandated rest, we rejoin the natural rhythm and cosmic harmony, and reap the ordained benefits of the created order's cycle of peace.

SEARCH THE SCRIPTURES

QUESTION 1
In verse 8, the word remember means a recollection and remembering the meaning of _____.

history

LIGHT ON THE WORD
God's Blueprint
Israel's work week is patterned after God's work week; so Israel's day of rest follows God's pattern. God does not ask us to deny ourselves, sacrifice, obey, or take up our cross without first having led the way, without setting the example or giving us footsteps to follow (**1 Peter 2:21**). This pattern was established early on in Israel's history, in commands like this one that form a blueprint that first is created in Heaven, then recreated on earth.

III. A SIGN (31:12–16)

A covenant is a contract or agreement between two parties. In the Old Testament, the Hebrew word *berith* is often translated as covenant. *Berith* is often used with the verb *karat*. This word is derived from a root which means "to cut," and hence a covenant is a "cutting," with reference to the cutting or

dividing of animals into two parts, and the contracting parties passing between them, in making a covenant (**Genesis 15; Jeremiah 34:18–19**).

The observance of the Sabbath signified the covenant between God and the Children of Israel that they were His chosen people. This was not the only sign God had with the Israelites; however, this particular sign symbolized the practical aspect of their relationship. The Children of Israel would rest on the same day their Creator rested. As they sanctified and set apart the Sabbath, God would also sanctify and set them apart.

The Sign of the Mosaic Covenant

31:12 And the LORD spake unto Moses, saying, 13 Speak thou also unto the children of Israel, saying, Verily my sabbaths ye shall keep: for it is a sign between me and you throughout your generations; that ye may know that I am the LORD that doth sanctify you.

The Sabbath as the sign of the Mosaic covenant is parallel to circumcision for the Abrahamic covenant (**Genesis 17:10–14**), the rainbow for the Noahic covenant (**Genesis 9:8–17**), and baptism for the new covenant (**Matthew 28:19; John 3:5**). The practice of resting on a certain day did not set the Children of Israel apart from other nations. The Lord's purpose in the Sabbath was to sanctify (Heb. *qadash*, ka-DASH) or set them apart as His people. It is through His assertion that they are "my sabbaths." Precisely, it is through His covenant and their reverence of Him that they are set apart.

14 Ye shall keep the sabbath therefore; for it is holy unto you: every one that defileth it shall surely be put to death: for whosoever doeth any work therein, that soul shall be cut off from among his people. 15 Six days

may work be done; but in the seventh is the sabbath of rest, holy to the LORD: whosoever doeth any work in the sabbath day, he shall surely be put to death.

Just as other laws were punishable by death (**Exodus 21:12–14, 22–23; Deuteronomy 24:7; Leviticus 20:10–21**), so the Sabbath held equal weight in God's eyes. Ultimately, to desecrate the Sabbath was to turn one's back on God, choose death over life, and ignore the very rhythm of the universe. While the New Testament does not call for capital punishment for such violations, with Christ's fulfillment of the Mosaic Law, He has called all believers to enter into a spiritual Sabbath rest based on our obedience to Him. This often includes resting from physical labor as well as sanctifying the Sabbath unto the Lord by keeping it holy.

Jesus was charged with the crime of violating the Sabbath, one of the reasons the Jewish leaders called for His death (**John 5:16–18**). In all four Gospels, Jesus' response was that the Sabbath had become a burden instead of a blessing (e.g., **Mark 2:23–27**). In response, He reframed the day according to its original intent—re-instituting acts of love, mercy, and necessity as permissible, even on the Sabbath. Moreover, Jesus proclaimed Himself the Lord of the Sabbath (**Mark 2:28**), a claim to deity that became yet another violation in the blind eyes of the Pharisees. He reminded them that the Sabbath was created for man, as a gift and a blessing, and was never intended to become a taskmaster with endless legislative minutia.

16 Wherefore the children of Israel shall keep the sabbath, to observe the sabbath throughout their generations, for a perpetual covenant.

God brought Israel out of bondage in Egypt, a forerunner of Jesus' coming deliverance from the bondage of sin. He established Israel as His people, a forerunner of the bride of Christ. He formalized His presence among them in the tabernacle, a forerunner of the Davidic Temple, and after that the Body of Christ, His church. Finally, He instituted the Sabbath rest, a forerunner of the final exodus leading to His eternal rest and the new creation in which perfect harmony reigns—thus the perpetual covenant aspect of this verse.

Christians have much support for remembering the Sabbath on Sunday. The Old Testament commands that the Sabbath be celebrated on the seventh day of the week, which is the continued practice in Judaism, but in the early church the Sabbath became associated with the day that Christ was resurrected, the first day of the week (**Matt 28:1**). This did not occur until the second century, AD, which is why Acts and other New Testament books still speak of the early church worshiping on the Sabbath with the understanding that this was the last day of the week.

SEARCH THE SCRIPTURES

QUESTION 2
God tells the people of Israel the importance of the Sabbath for them and for who else?

future generations

LIGHT ON THE WORD

Honoring God Every Day
Despite the shift from the seventh to the first day of the week, the Sabbath still has connections with rest and creation for Christians. On the one hand, in the New Testament, all of our time belongs to God, to be holy and used for worship. Just as being angry with someone or mocking was equal to murder in the New Testament (**Matthew 5:21–22**), so being holy was not to be reserved for only one day of the week but rather for every day.

BIBLE APPLICATION

AIM: Students will remember to honor God even when life issues overwhelm them.

God revealed the need to observe a regular rhythm of work and rest for the health and well-being of humans, animals, and plants. Recently this rhythm has been set aside in many places around the globe. Underneath this casting off of the Sabbath is greed. This desire for more has caused corporations to work non-stop, which in turn creates a vicious cycle as the rest of society is swept up in this desire for more. Now we have stores and other businesses open twenty four hours a day, seven days a week. This is contrary to the rhythm God established at the beginning of creation.

It not only is contrary to the Judeo-Christian rhythm, but also traditional African rhythms as well. The observance of the Sabbath can be found throughout Africa. It is observed by many African tribes such as the Yoruba of Nigeria and the Akan (Ashanti) of Ghana. In modern-day Ethiopia, it is observed as an institution of the Ethiopian Orthodox Church and by the Falasha or Ethiopian Jews. This phenomenon of Sabbath observance is a witness to God's truth being spread among all peoples, and African knowledge of the Creator or the Most High God.

STUDENT'S RESPONSES

AIM: Students will learn how God revealed the need for all creation to work and rest for its well-being.

Make a list of everything that comprises a typical Sunday at your house. Circle the activities that can be categorized God-centered, cross out the activities that constitute work or chores, and underline the activities that can be considered rest and relaxation. How can you eliminate the items that were crossed out?

PRAYER

Holy God, You are so Holy and merciful toward us. We worship and honor who You are and who we are in You. We bless You and thank You for all of Your gentleness, mercy, peace, and joy. As we strive to live lives that are holy and pleasing before You, we look to You for direction and guidance. In Jesus' Name we pray. Amen.

HOW TO SAY IT

Hallowed.   HA-load.

Perpetual.   per-PE-choo-ul.

PREPARE FOR NEXT SUNDAY

Read **Leviticus 22:17–25, 31–33** and "Acceptable Offerings."

DAILY HOME BIBLE READINGS

MONDAY
It is Good
(Genesis 1:28–2:3)

TUESDAY
Day of Atonement
(Leviticus 16:29–34)

WEDNESDAY
Silence Before God
(Psalm 62:1–2, 5–9)

THURSDAY
Promised Rest
(Hebrews 4:1–11)

FRIDAY
Eternal Rest
(Revelation 14:12–13, 21:1–5)

SATURDAY
Work then Rest
(Exodus 16:22–26)

SUNDAY
The Lord's Day
(Exodus 20:8–11, 31:12–16)

Sources:

Ahtemeier, Paul J., Boraas, Roger S. Fishburne, Micheal, et al, ed. *Harper Collins Bible Dictionary*. HarperCollins Publishing, 1996. 704-708, 1027-1028.

Bruckner, James K. *Exodus*. Understanding the Bible Commentary Series. Grand Rapids: Baker Books, 2008.

Childs, Brevard S. *The Book of Exodus*. The Old Testament Library. Louisville: The Westminster Press, 1974.

Cole, R. Alan. *Exodus*. Tyndale Old Testament Commentaries. Downers Grove: InterVarsity Press, 1973.

Durham, John I. *Word Biblical Commentary: Exodus*. Waco, TX: World Books Publishers, 1987.

Enns, Peter. *Exodus*. The NIV Application Commentary: From Biblical Text … to Contemporary Life. Grand Rapids: Zondervan, 2000.

Fretheim, Terence E. *Exodus*. Interpretation: A Bible Commentary for Teaching and Preaching. Louisville: John Knox Press, 1991.

Stuart, Douglas K. *Exodus*. The New American Commentary: An Exegetical and Theological Exposition of Holy Scripture, Vol. 2. Nashville: B&H Publishing, 2006. 457-61; 652-53.

COMMENTS / NOTES:

ACCEPTABLE OFFERINGS

BIBLE BASIS: LEVITICUS 22:17–25, 31–33

BIBLE TRUTH: God's people are to give obedience to Him.

MEMORY VERSE: "I beseech you therefore, brethren, by the mercies of God, that ye present your bodies a living sacrifice, holy, acceptable unto God, which is your reasonable service"

(Romans 12:1).

LESSON AIM: By the end of the lesson, we will: REVIEW what Leviticus says about God's requirement for acceptable sacrifices; EXAMINE the connection between obedience to God and sacrificial giving of self and possessions; and PLEDGE to make a self-sacrifice to God.

TEACHER PREPARATION

MATERIALS NEEDED: Quarterly Commentary/Teacher Manual, Adult Quarterly, Adult resources—charts, worksheets, and other teaching tools, paper, pens, pencils, Bibles (several different versions)

OTHER MATERIALS NEEDED / TEACHER'S NOTES:

_____

_____

LESSON OVERVIEW

LIFE NEED FOR TODAY'S LESSON
People believe that material gifts are evidence to show their love towards others.

BIBLE APPLICATION
God knows our heart and expects the best offerings that one has to give.

BIBLE LEARNING
Holiness is a priority for all who worship God.

STUDENTS' RESPONSES
Believers should know that God expects obedient followers in all aspects of their lives.

LESSON SCRIPTURE

LEVITICUS 22:17–25, 31–33, KJV

Leviticus 22:17 And the LORD spake unto Moses, saying,

18 Speak unto Aaron, and to his sons, and unto all the children of Israel, and say unto them, Whatsoever he be of the house of Israel, or of the strangers in Israel, that will

LEVITICUS 22:17–25, 31–33, NIV

Leviticus 22:17 The LORD said to Moses,

18 "Speak to Aaron and his sons and to all the Israelites and say to them: 'If any of you—whether an Israelite or a foreigner residing in Israel—presents a gift for a burnt

offer his oblation for all his vows, and for all his freewill offerings, which they will offer unto the LORD for a burnt offering;

19 Ye shall offer at your own will a male without blemish, of the beeves, of the sheep, or of the goats.

20 But whatsoever hath a blemish, that shall ye not offer: for it shall not be acceptable for you.

21 And whosoever offereth a sacrifice of peace offerings unto the LORD to accomplish his vow, or a freewill offering in beeves or sheep, it shall be perfect to be accepted; there shall be no blemish therein.

22 Blind, or broken, or maimed, or having a wen, or scurvy, or scabbed, ye shall not offer these unto the LORD, nor make an offering by fire of them upon the altar unto the LORD.

23 Either a bullock or a lamb that hath any thing superfluous or lacking in his parts, that mayest thou offer for a freewill offering; but for a vow it shall not be accepted.

24 Ye shall not offer unto the LORD that which is bruised, or crushed, or broken, or cut; neither shall ye make any offering thereof in your land.

25 Neither from a stranger's hand shall ye offer the bread of your God of any of these; because their corruption is in them, and blemishes be in them: they shall not be accepted for you.

31 Therefore shall ye keep my commandments, and do them: I am the LORD.

32 Neither shall ye profane my holy name; but I will be hallowed among the children of Israel: I am the LORD which hallow you,

33 That brought you out of the land of

offering to the LORD, either to fulfill a vow or as a freewill offering,

19 you must present a male without defect from the cattle, sheep or goats in order that it may be accepted on your behalf.

20 Do not bring anything with a defect, because it will not be accepted on your behalf.

21 When anyone brings from the herd or flock a fellowship offering to the LORD to fulfill a special vow or as a freewill offering, it must be without defect or blemish to be acceptable.

22 Do not offer to the LORD the blind, the injured or the maimed, or anything with warts or festering or running sores. Do not place any of these on the altar as a food offering presented to the LORD.

23 You may, however, present as a freewill offering an ox or a sheep that is deformed or stunted, but it will not be accepted in fulfillment of a vow.

24 You must not offer to the LORD an animal whose testicles are bruised, crushed, torn or cut. You must not do this in your own land,

25 and you must not accept such animals from the hand of a foreigner and offer them as the food of your God. They will not be accepted on your behalf, because they are deformed and have defects.'"

31 "Keep my commands and follow them. I am the LORD.

32 Do not profane my holy name, for I must be acknowledged as holy by the Israelites. I am the LORD, who made you holy

33 and who brought you out of Egypt to be your God. I am the LORD."

Egypt, to be your God: I am the LORD.

LIGHT ON THE WORD

Aaron. As Moses and Miriam's brother, Aaron played a significant role in the history of the Israelites during their Exodus from Egypt and time in the wilderness. Because of Moses' speech impediment, God ordained Aaron to be his spokesperson (**Exodus 4:16**). Although he is known for helping to hold up Moses' arms during the battle of Amalek (Exodus 17:12), even most Bible readers fail to recognize that Aaron actually performed many wonders in Egypt prior to the Exodus (**Exodus 7:10, 19, 8:5, 16**). In this text, Aaron is distinguished from the Israelites because he is the high priest. As faithful as Aaron was, like Moses he was not without sin. He made the golden calf (**Exodus 32:2–4**), engaged in agitation and backbiting against Moses (Numbers 12:1–2), and aided him in disobeying God at Kadesh (**Numbers 20:8–12**).

Holiness code. The Holiness code can be found in Leviticus and consists of the laws God gave Israel to have a relationship with Him. These laws and regulations covered all facets of human life and included detailed instructions on preparing and offering sacrifices. This was all done in order to show the distinction between Israel and other nations as well as the perfect holiness of God in light of humanity's sinfulness and imperfection.

TEACHING THE BIBLE LESSON

LIFE NEED FOR TODAY'S LESSON

AIM: Students will see how God's expectations require a different set responsibilities and responses from people.

INTRODUCTION

The Lifestyle for God's People

Leviticus is a written account of the instructions God gave Moses to relay to the Israelites to maintain an intimate relationship with Him. To others the requirements may seem outlandish and far-fetched, but this is because their perspective is skewed. The requirements were given to show the Children of Israel the awesomeness of God and their privilege of having this holy God dwell among them.

Leviticus can be divided into six topics. The first, systems of sacrifices (**1:1–7:38**). The second topic is ordination of priests (**8:1–10:20**). The third, laws concerning what is clean and unclean (**11:1–15:33**). The fourth and fifth are purification from moral uncleanness (**16:1–34**) and laws for living holy (**17:1–26:46**). The final topic concerns the redemption of gifts and tithes (**27:1–34**).

Together, the laws found throughout Leviticus comprise a lifestyle. Consecration was not just an event or act but the sum of their existence. God was informing them how to live in a holy and pure manner because only the righteous could approach Him.

BIBLE LEARNING

AIM: Students will learn that holiness is a priority for all who worship God.

I. ACCEPTABLE OFFERINGS (Leviticus 22:17–18)

Here we see the main requirement given to the Israelites for the offerings they are to give to the Lord. These offering must be without blemish. In addition, these freewill offerings must be male and taken from sheep, cattle, and goats. These are all clean animals, not unclean—the only acceptable freewill or voluntary offering.

These offerings are burnt and given as a sign of total commitment to the Lord and obedience to Him. They are called whole burnt offerings because the whole animal is burned on the altar, implying the total commitment of the worshiper to the God of Israel.

Leviticus 22:17–25, 31–33

17 And the LORD spake unto Moses, saying, 18 Speak unto Aaron, and to his sons, and unto all the children of Israel, and say unto them, Whatsoever he be of the house of Israel, or of the strangers in Israel, that will offer his oblation for all his vows, and for all his freewill offerings, which they will offer unto the LORD for a burnt offering;

One of the realities farmers are well aware of is that animals frequently develop physical problems, such as abscesses, hernias, or lameness. One can easily imagine that farmers in ancient times would want to unload such inferior animals at the Temple for sacrifice—but such sacrifices simply were not acceptable.

This passage is about qualifications for to the Mosaic sacrificial system. Here, the physical qualifications of sacrificed animals are in focus, namely that they were to be unblemished, which meant to be free of serious or visible defects. The book of Leviticus previously stated that the priests have similarly tough qualifications, even more so than for the lay people (cf. **Luke 12:48**). Even a priest's family had to be holy, as their immorality could profane the priest as well. Following this thinking, Paul strove to live an exemplary life so that his priesthood as a believer would not be questioned (**2 Corinthians 6:3–6**).

The passage's focus was for both priests and laity, all of whom were responsible for bringing only the best sacrificial animals to the altar. While the regulations applied to all, enforcement was up to the priests. The common theme throughout is that everyone, from the highest to the lowest, must make holiness their overriding priority—including both Hebrews and strangers (from the Hebrew *ger*, **GAIR**) which is also translated sojourners, aliens, and foreigners, depending on the version. People who were not from the tribes of Israel but who lived with the Israelites were allowed to worship with Israelites as long as they followed Hebrew traditions (**Numbers 15:14–15**); later such people who converted to Judaism were called proselytes (cf. **Matthew 23:15; Acts 6:5, NASB**).

SEARCH THE SCRIPTURES

QUESTION 1
Burnt offerings were given to show total _____ and obedience to the _____.

commitment, Lord

LIGHT ON THE WORD
Burnt Offerings
Burnt offerings in the Bible can be traced back as far as Abel. This offering differs in that the entire sacrifice is burned, not a specific portion. Leviticus 1 outlines the laws for burnt offerings and declares repeatedly it is an aroma pleasing to the Lord.

II. NO BLEMISHES, NO DEFECTS (vv. 19–25)

While people often talk about only giving God their best, this does not usually happen, because some other competing value such as success, wealth, comfort, or pleasure drives their actions. In an agrarian (agricultural) society, like in the ancient Near East, a person's livelihood and wealth are dependent on farm products such as livestock. The same animals that are the largest means of provision are to be used for offering.

It is very easy to see how one might be tempted to offer a defective sheep to God instead of the choice pick of the flock. Therefore, God explicitly forbids anything other than perfection from being offered.

Today, individuals offer unholy sacrifices by giving God their monetary remnants after bills, personal expenses, and leisure activities are paid for. People present defective offerings of their time and talent by prioritizing the things of God after work, children's activities, and entertainment.

Perfect Offerings to the Lord

19 Ye shall offer at your own will a male without blemish, of the beeves, of the sheep, or of the goats. 20 But whatsoever hath a blemish, that shall ye not offer: for it shall not be acceptable for you. 21 And whosoever offereth a sacrifice of peace offerings unto the LORD to accomplish his vow, or a freewill offering in beeves or sheep, it shall be perfect to be accepted; there shall be no blemish therein. 22 Blind, or broken, or maimed, or having a wen, or scurvy, or scabbed, ye shall not offer these unto the LORD, nor make an offering by fire of them upon the altar unto the LORD. 23 Either a bullock or a lamb that hath any thing superfluous or lacking in his parts, that mayest thou offer for a freewill offering; but for a vow it shall not be accepted. 24 Ye shall not offer unto the LORD that which is bruised, or crushed, or broken, or cut; neither shall ye make any offering thereof in your land.

The phrase "without blemish" is translated from the Hebrew *tamim* (**tah-MEEM**), which means complete, full, perfect; thus "without blemish" would refer to all that is less than that definition. The same word is used for Noah (**Genesis 6:9**), who was a "perfect" man ("righteous," NLT), and God told Abram to walk before Him and be "perfect" in **Genesis 17:1** ("blameless," NLT).

The Lord prohibited any animal that was blind, broken, or maimed to be offered as a sacrifice, as well as any animal which had a wen (Heb. *yabbel*, **ya-BAL**), or a running sore, wart, or ulcer, as well as a scurvy (Heb. *garab*, **ga-RAHV**), which is an itch or scab. Animals that were scabbed (Heb. *yallepheth*, **ya-LEF-eth**) or had a skin sore or eruptive disease were also excluded. Animals that were bruised (Heb. *ma'ak*, **ma-AK**), crushed (Heb. *kathath*, **kah-THATH**), broken (**nah-THAK**), or cut (Heb. *karath*, **kah-RATH**) were also excluded from sacrifice, as these were all methods of castration.

A similar, overlapping list in prior chapters applied to priests performing the sacrifices (**Leviticus 21:16–23**). Several of the listed blemishes are the same for priests—blindness, disfigurement, broken bones, sores, or scabs. That list along with the present passage's focus on being without blemish indicate God requires that holiness be a shared quality between priest and sacrifice—which foreshadows Christ, who was both High Priest (**Hebrews 4:14, 7:25**) and sacrificial lamb (**Acts 8:32; 1 Peter 1:19**).

25 Neither from a stranger's hand shall ye offer the bread of your God of any of these; because their corruption is in them, and blemishes be in them: they shall not be accepted for you.

In the NLT, **v. 24** ends with a comma, rather than a period like KJV, which attaches it more directly to **v. 25**. Thus, while it is permissible to purchase animals from foreigners for sacrifices, the same rules about blemishes apply—particularly in the case of castrated animals, a practice forbidden in Israel (**v. 24**). While such animals could be consumed at home, they could not be offered as sacrifices to God (Harris, 621).

III. NO SHAME ON MY NAME (vv. 31–33)

God chose the descendants of Israel as His own people. The Israelites' rescue from the hands of Pharaoh had marked them as God's own possession and He as their God. To disobey the commands of how to worship God would be to "profane" or dishonor His name; instead, they are to hallow or honor Him as holy, because through His presence among them, they are also hallowed or set apart as holy. To offer blemished sacrifices would insult Him and regard Him as not worthy of their best.

The Lord's Name is Holy

31 Therefore shall ye keep my commandments, and do them: I am the LORD. 32 Neither shall ye profane my holy name; but I will be hallowed among the children of Israel: I am the LORD which hallow you, 33 That brought you out of the land of Egypt, to be your God: I am the LORD.

The phrase "I am the Lord" occurs repeatedly throughout the law code. This phrase uniquely underscores the moral imperatives given to the children of Israel. It also proclaims God's authority to create laws. Not only is He the God of Israel through His delivering them from Egypt but He is also the Lord of the universe who makes them holy. This sovereignty is to be recognized in the reading and obeying of these laws.

These verses are a concluding exhortation that both parallels and completes the similar exhortations to the priests in **chapters 18–21**. The word "hallowed" comes from the Hebrew root word *kadash* (**kah-DASH**), which means to consecrate, dedicate, purify, sanctify, or be or keep holy. An overarching theme in Judaism is *kiddush ha-shem*—sanctification of the name of God—which is shown viscerally in **Ezekiel 36:19-23**, which in **verse 23** says, "I will sanctify my great name." Thus God's name is either made holy or profaned, as His people display His public reputation. Then, as now, when His people obey Him, God forgives failures and restores to right relationship with Him—He "hallows" or makes holy those with whom He is pleased—and these holy people in turn and in response "hallow" or set apart God as holy.

The dramatic Exodus narrative provides the pivotal delivering action of God that was Israel's motivation and inspiration to obey His laws. Their rescue from slavery in Egypt was the focal salvation event that defined them as a nation.

SEARCH THE SCRIPTURES

QUESTION 2

True or False: The Israelites could purchase any animal for sacrifice from strangers.

False

QUESTION 3

The Lord reminds the Israelites of what significant event in verse 33? Why is this important?

God's deliverance of the people from Egypt and that this is Israel's motivation and inspiration to obey God.

LIGHT ON THE WORD

Salvation and Freedom in Christ

In the New Testament, much like the priests in the Old Testament, we also are motivated and inspired by our defining salvation event, this time from the slavery of sin (**Romans 12:1-2**), from which Christ's death and resurrection gave us deliverance.

BIBLE APPLICATION

AIM: Students will accept that God knows our heart and expects the best offerings that one has to give.

Sacrifice as a religious ritual is a very ancient tradition. It is practiced throughout the world, including many African cultures. In these African cultures, traditional beliefs dictate that sacrifices given to ancestors or spirits protect one from evil. According to today's text, the best gift one can give to God in worship is obedience. It is important to strive to be acceptable to God in every aspect of life. God wants not only the hearts and souls of believers, but pure minds and bodies as well. **Romans 12:1** says to present your body as a living sacrifice, holy and acceptable. God no longer requires an animal sacrifice for worship and atonement because Jesus shed all the blood that was necessary. However, God still requires our best.

STUDENT'S RESPONSES

AIM: Students will know that God expects obedient followers in all aspects of their lives.

How can you adjust your life to ensure you present your whole self as a living sacrifice to God? Consider the other offerings and sacrifices you make for and on behalf of God—are any of them blemished?

PRAYER

Thank You Lord for the sacrifice of Jesus on the cross and His resurrection for the sins of the world. We thank You Jesus for giving the greatest sacrifice of life and love. In Jesus' Name we pray. Amen.

HOW TO SAY IT

Oblation.	oh-**BLAY**-shun.
Beeves.	BEEVS.
Bullock.	BUL-lok.

PREPARE FOR NEXT SUNDAY

Read **Exodus 13:11–15, Luke 2:22–32** and "Dedication of Firstborn."

DAILY HOME BIBLE READINGS

MONDAY
Living Sacrifice
(Psalm 40:1–8)

TUESDAY
Contrite Sacrifice
(Psalm 51:15–19)

WEDNESDAY
Loving Sacrifice
(Mark 12:28–34a)

THURSDAY
Complete Sacrifice
(Romans 12:1–8)

FRIDAY
Faithful Sacrifice
(Hebrews 11:4–16)

SATURDAY
Perfect Sacrifice
(1 John 4:9–16)

SUNDAY
Acceptable Offerings
(Leviticus 22:17–25, 31–33)

Sources:

Achtemeier, Paul J., Boraas, Roger S. Fishburne, Micheal, et al, ed. *HarperCollins Bible Dictionary.* HarperCollins Publishing, 1996. 2, 603, 1223.

Balentine, Samuel E. *Leviticus.* Interpretation: A Bible Commentary for Teaching and Preaching. Louisville: John Knox Press, 2002. 170-173; 176-179.

Harris, R. Laird. *Genesis, Exodus, Leviticus, Numbers.* The Expositor's Bible Commentary, Vol. 2. Edited by Frank E. Gaebelein. Grand Rapids: Zondervan, 1990. 620-621.

Harrison, R. K. *Leviticus.* Tyndale Old Testament Commentaries. Downers Grove: InterVarsity Press, 1980. 210-217.

Hartley, John E. *Word Biblical Commentary: Leviticus.* Dallas, TX: World Books Publishers., 1992. 362.

Gane, Roy. *Leviticus, Numbers.* The NIV Application Commentary: From Biblical Text ... to Contemporary Life. Grand Rapids: Zondervan, 2004. 382-385.

Rodner, Ephraim. *Leviticus.* Brazos Theological Commentary on the Bible. Grand Rapids: Baker Books, 2008. 228-229; 237-238.

Rooker, Mark F. *Leviticus.* The New American Commentary: An Exegetical and Theological Exposition of Holy Scripture, Vol. 3A. Nashville: B&H Publishing, 2000. 278-281; 286-289.

DEDICATION OF FIRSTBORN

BIBLE BASIS: EXODUS 13:11–15, LUKE 2:22–32

BIBLE TRUTH: Simeon experienced an overflowing joy when he dedicated Jesus.

MEMORY VERSE: "And when the days of her purification according to the Law of Moses were accomplished, they brought him to Jerusalem, to present him to the Lord" (Luke 2:22).

LESSON AIM: By the end of the lesson, we will: EXPLORE the story of Simeon at the presentation of Jesus at the Temple; FEEL the immenseness of joy that Simeon felt; and COMMIT to make Jesus the center of attention during the secular busyness of the season.

TEACHER PREPARATION

MATERIALS NEEDED: Quarterly Commentary/Teacher Manual, Adult Quarterly, Adult resources—charts, worksheets, and other teaching tools, paper, pens, pencils, Bibles (several different versions)

OTHER MATERIALS NEEDED / TEACHER'S NOTES:

_____

_____

LESSON OVERVIEW

LIFE NEED FOR TODAY'S LESSON
People forget the excitement behind holidays and special occasions, and treat them as routine and ordinary.

BIBLE LEARNING
The Holy Ghost revealed to the priest Simeon that he would not die before he saw the Lord's Messiah.

BIBLE APPLICATION
Christians can anticipate in faith what the Lord will do in their lives as they share the Good News of Christ with others.

STUDENTS' RESPONSES
Believers can renew the excitement of celebrating the birth of Christ and their faith through the year.

LESSON SCRIPTURE

EXODUS 13:11–15, LUKE 2:22–32, KJV

Exodus 13:11 And it shall be when the LORD shall bring thee into the land of the Canaanites, as he sware unto thee and to thy fathers, and shall give it thee,

12 That thou shalt set apart unto the LORD all that openeth the matrix, and every

EXODUS 13:11–15, LUKE 2:22–32, NIV

Exodus 13:11 "After the LORD brings you into the land of the Canaanites and gives it to you, as he promised on oath to you and your ancestors,

12 you are to give over to the LORD the first offspring of every womb. All the firstborn

firstling that cometh of a beast which thou hast; the males shall be the LORD's.

13 And every firstling of an ass thou shalt redeem with a lamb; and if thou wilt not redeem it, then thou shalt break his neck: and all the firstborn of man among thy children shalt thou redeem.

14 And it shall be when thy son asketh thee in time to come, saying, What is this? That thou shalt say unto him, By strength of hand the LORD brought us out from Egypt, from the house of bondage:

15 And it came to pass, when Pharaoh would hardly let us go, that the LORD slew all the firstborn in the land of Egypt, both the firstborn of man, and the firstborn of beast: therefore I sacrifice to the LORD all that openeth the matrix, being males; but all the firstborn of my children I redeem.

Luke 2:22 And when the days of her purification according to the law of Moses were accomplished, they brought him to Jerusalem, to present him to the Lord;

23 (As it is written in the law of the LORD, Every male that openeth the womb shall be called holy to the Lord;)

24 And to offer a sacrifice according to that which is said in the law of the Lord, A pair of turtledoves, or two young pigeons.

25 And, behold, there was a man in Jerusalem, whose name was Simeon; and the same man was just and devout, waiting for the consolation of Israel: and the Holy Ghost was upon him.

26 And it was revealed unto him by the Holy Ghost, that he should not see death, before he had seen the Lord's Christ.

27 And he came by the Spirit into the temple: and when the parents brought

males of your livestock belong to the LORD.

13 Redeem with a lamb every firstborn donkey, but if you do not redeem it, break its neck. Redeem every firstborn among your sons.

14 "In days to come, when your son asks you, 'What does this mean?' say to him, 'With a mighty hand the LORD brought us out of Egypt, out of the land of slavery.

15 When Pharaoh stubbornly refused to let us go, the LORD killed the firstborn of both people and animals in Egypt. This is why I sacrifice to the LORD the first male offspring of every womb and redeem each of my firstborn sons.'

Luke 2:22 When the time came for the purification rites required by the Law of Moses, Joseph and Mary took him to Jerusalem to present him to the Lord

23 (as it is written in the Law of the Lord, "Every firstborn male is to be consecrated to the Lord"),

24 and to offer a sacrifice in keeping with what is said in the Law of the Lord: "a pair of doves or two young pigeons."

25 Now there was a man in Jerusalem called Simeon, who was righteous and devout. He was waiting for the consolation of Israel, and the Holy Spirit was on him.

26 It had been revealed to him by the Holy Spirit that he would not die before he had seen the Lord's Messiah.

27 Moved by the Spirit, he went into the temple courts. When the parents brought in the child Jesus to do for him what the custom of the Law required,

28 Simeon took him in his arms and praised God, saying:

in the child Jesus, to do for him after the custom of the law,

28 Then took he him up in his arms, and blessed God, and said,

29 Lord, now lettest thou thy servant depart in peace, according to thy word:

30 For mine eyes have seen thy salvation,

31 Which thou hast prepared before the face of all people;

32 A light to lighten the Gentiles, and the glory of thy people Israel.

29 "Sovereign Lord, as you have promised, you may now dismiss your servant in peace.

30 For my eyes have seen your salvation,

31 which you have prepared in the sight of all nations:

32 a light for revelation to the Gentiles, and the glory of your people Israel."

LIGHT ON THE WORD

Simeon. Simeon (Gk. *Sumeon*, **soo-me-OWN**) was an elderly Jewish man residing in Jerusalem at the time of Jesus' birth, who faithfully observed the Jewish teachings, or Torah. He lived in anticipation of the fulfillment of the arrival of the expectant Messiah, the "anointed one," who would bring comfort and relief to the Jews living under the oppression of the Roman Empire. Luke does not bestow the title "prophet" on Simeon as he does Anna (**Luke 2:36**); however, Simeon does deliver prophetic oracles under the power of the Holy Spirit concerning Jesus' role in God's plan of salvation.

The Temple. The Temple held a significant place in Jewish social, religious, and economic life. It was a place of religious observance including the presentation of tithes and offerings, daily prayers, pilgrimages, and festivals. The Temple referred to in **Luke 2** was not the Temple Solomon had built; the Babylonians destroyed that Temple when they seized Judah and Jerusalem in 586 BC. After King Cyrus of Persia defeated Babylon and allowed the exiles to return to Judah, Zerubbabel, a Jewish leader, led the campaign to restore the Temple of Solomon in 538 BC. This Temple is commonly referred to as the "second temple." Herod the Great began an elaborate reconstruction of the Temple in 20 BC that was completed in eighteen months. This was the Temple in Jerusalem where Jesus was presented. Some scholars refer to it as the Temple of Herod, and many refer to it as the third Temple since Herod made significant developments (those who still call it the second Temple do so because the Temple was not destroyed and rebuilt, simply majorly renovated)

TEACHING THE BIBLE LESSON

LIFE NEED FOR TODAY'S LESSON

AIM: Students will understand how people forget the excitement behind holidays and special occasions, and treat them as routine and ordinary.

INTRODUCTION

Privileges of the Firstborn Son

In ancient Israel, as in many other ancient civilizations, the firstborn son held a privileged place in the family. The firstborn son usually had a legal right to his father's inheritance. According to Exodus, the firstborn son was also dedicated to God. Exodus associates the consecration or setting apart of the firstborn male, both human and animal, with God's saving act of delivering the Israelite firstborn males from death in Egypt (**Exodus 13:14–15**). Moses instructed the Israelites that every male firstling must be set apart for the Lord and redeemed for a price. For example, **verse 13** stipulates that a donkey should be redeemed with a sheep. However, the redemption for a human firstborn is unspecified. By contrast, the book of Numbers specifies that the firstborn should be redeemed for five shekels of silver paid to the priest (**Numbers 3:47–48, 18:15–16**).

Moses commanded the people to teach their children the meaning of the firstborn's consecration. When the children asked why they observed the Passover festival, their parents should tell them that the Lord delivered the Israelites from bondage in Egypt when the king of Egypt refused to release them to worship the Lord. The Lord destroyed the firstborn male of everything and everyone but redeemed the firstborn male of the Israelites. Since the Lord killed the firstborn humans and animals in Egypt, except the firstborn of the Israelites where there was blood on the doorposts, they observe this ritual to commemorate the Lord's salvation.

BIBLE LEARNING

AIM: Students will see how the Holy Ghost revealed to the priest Simeon that he would not die before he saw the Lord's Messiah.

I. JESUS PRESENTED IN THE TEMPLE (Luke 2:22–24)

According to Luke, Mary and Joseph, who were observant Jews, brought Jesus to the Temple to present Him to the Lord as was instructed in the Law of Moses (**Luke 2:22**). Mary also was to give an offering for purification 33 days after giving birth so the priest could declare her clean. Mary's

offering consists of two pigeons or doves, which indicates Mary and Joseph are a poor couple.

Although offering a sacrifice was a requirement of the Law, bringing the child to the Temple was not mandatory, and also not a known practice among first-century Jews. Mary and Joseph come to the Temple to dedicate Jesus similar to how Hannah dedicated Samuel to the Lord (**1 Samuel 1:21–28**). Underneath it all, they know Jesus is more than just an ordinary child. They come to the Temple to show Jesus is the Son of God being given back to His true Father.

Exodus 13:11–15; Luke 2:22–32

11 And it shall be when the LORD shall bring thee into the land of the Canaanites, as he sware unto thee and to thy fathers, and shall give it thee. 12 That thou shalt set apart unto the LORD all that openeth the matrix, and every firstling that cometh of a beast which thou hast; the males shall be the LORD's. 13 And every firstling of an ass thou shalt redeem with a lamb; and if thou wilt not redeem it, then thou shalt break his neck: and all the firstborn of man among thy children shalt thou redeem.

The first set of verses captures just part of the Exodus narrative, in this case, one of Moses' messages to the people at their first stopping place, Succoth, after escaping from the Egyptians (**12:37**). They had not yet entered the Promised Land, "flowing with milk and honey" (**13:5**)—it would be decades before that happened—but when they did, Moses' instructions from God (**13:1**) detailed the way they would commemorate their deliverance from Egypt. By the time the Israelites would finally emerge from the wilderness, ready to overtake the Canaanites per God's sovereign promise to their forefathers, a full forty years would have passed, and by then they would need a way to remember the events that at the time were fresh on their mind.

The second set of verses introduces the ultimate significance of the Old Testament practice when it comes to bear on the life of the infant Jesus.

In this use, "set apart" uses the Hebrew 'abar (ah-VAR), which means to bring over or present as an offering, This is similar to but not the same as setting apart meaning to be or make holy, or to consecrate, from the Hebrew qadash (kah-DASH) (cf. **Exodus 13:2**). The same Hebrew word 'abar is used in **12:12** when God said that He would "pass through" Egypt on the pivotal night for both nations. In **12:13**, God also said that He would "pass over" (Heb. pasakh, **pah-SAKH**) the Israelites' doorposts that had lamb's blood on them. Because both words are used in close proximity, the parallel meaning and wordplay seem to be highlighted and repeated for emphasis. God thus would pass through and bring death to Egyptian firstborns but pass over Israelite homes and spare their firstborn. Here the verb is used in a sacrificial context, as it often is in Mosaic Law, to indicate that the Israelites are to bring their offerings over to God. In the KJV, "all that openeth the matrix" and "firstling" refer to the firstborn, or the first to breach the womb (NKJV "open the womb"; NLT "firstborn").

While donkeys, or asses, were unclean animals by Hebrew law and thus unfit for sacrifice, they also were the most valuable animals in ancient times, both for packing and transportation, so God permitted a substitute sacrifice, a lamb, to be made for them. Commentators agree that the neck breaking was a way to clearly distinguish from an animal that had been killed by a knife and intended for sacrifice. For Israel's firstborn sons, "redeem" comes from the Hebrew padah (pah-DAH), which means "to ransom" or to buy back (cf. **Deuteronomy 9:26**).

14 And it shall be when thy son asketh thee in time to come, saying, What is this? that thou shalt say unto him, By strength of hand the LORD brought us out from Egypt, from the house of bondage: 15 And it came to pass, when Pharaoh would hardly let us go, that the LORD slew all the firstborn in the land of Egypt, both the firstborn of man, and the firstborn of beast: therefore I sacrifice to the LORD all that openeth the matrix, being males; but all the firstborn of my children I redeem.

The passage from Exodus describes the seven-day feast of unleavened bread, which starts with the powerfully metaphorical Passover feast, with unleavened bread representing the haste with which they left Egypt, not being able to bake bread properly. A part of this annual festival, as instituted, included the involvement of children, as a way of saying that God's redemption is perpetual and applies to all future generations. The richness and depth of the symbolism are profound—applying lamb's blood, among the other rituals of the first Passover meal, spared the life of Israel's firstborn (symbolizing all of Israel). To later commemorate their deliverance or rescue from Egypt, the firstborn of each donkey, their most valuable but unclean animal, could be ransomed or redeemed (bought back with a price) with a sacrificed lamb in its place. The sacrifice of their other firstborn animals is analogous to the sacrifice of Egypt's firstborn who were not similarly ransomed or redeemed by a lamb's blood. As well, the annual consecration of Israel's firstborn sons is analogous to the redemption of her firstborn sons from Egypt—cause for perpetual celebration. Just as God passed over them, so they are to pass over to Him their sacrifices in remembrance. Per Cole, "Like all of Israel's religious customs, it is interwoven with the history of salvation" (123).

Luke 2:22 And when the days of her purification according to the law of Moses were accomplished, they brought him to Jerusalem, to present him to the Lord; 23 (As it is written in the law of the Lord, Every male that openeth the womb shall be called holy to the Lord;) 24 And to offer a sacrifice according to that which is said in the law of

the Lord, A pair of turtledoves, or two young pigeons.

The lesson bridges the original Old Testament context of having "set apart" or consecrated (to be or make holy) the sacrificial firstborn to deepen the significance of the event in Jesus' childhood, as He now is to be called holy (Gk. *hagios*, HA-gee-ose—e.g., Holy Ghost, *hagios pneuma*) like all firstborn, but this time the Law applied to the Firstborn of all firstborn.

Had Joseph and Mary been able to afford it, they would have offered a lamb, but because they were poor, they offered the allowed alternative (**Leviticus 12:6–8**). The offering of the turtledoves or pigeons was a purification offering in connection with Mary's giving birth. For the birth of a male child, the woman was unclean for seven days, and on the eighth day the male was circumcised. Following this, she remained in a state of purification for 33 days. For a daughter's birth, she was unclean for 14 days and remained in a state of purification for 66 days. The purification is related to the blood flow that occurs at childbirth, which would make the woman ritually impure at childbirth and in the days following. At the end of the period of purification, the offering was presented as a means of ritually purifying the Temple, something that the woman could not do until she herself was ritually pure again (**Leviticus 12:1–8**). As they had at every point, Jesus' parents had conformed with all Jewish laws (cf. **Luke 2:39**), this time obeying the purification rites after birth (**Leviticus 12:2–4, 6**) as well as setting aside their firstborn to the Lord (**Exodus 13:2, 12, 34:19**).

SEARCH THE SCRIPTURES

QUESTION 1
The Feast of the Unleavened Bread is described in verse 14. How are children involved in the feast?

The son is to ask during the Feast, "What is this?" (meaning why is the Feast celebrated).

QUESTION 2
State the number of days of Mary's purification. Name what offerings and how many that Mary and Joseph presented at the temple.

Seven, and two turtledoves or young pigeons.

LIGHT ON THE WORD
Comfort to the Poor
The reality of Jesus being born into poverty and surrounding Himself with the poor throughout His life should be an encouragement to many, as Ryle states, "it should encourage every poor believer as he approaches the throne of grace in prayer. Let him remember … that his mighty mediator in heaven is used to poverty" (40).

II. SIMEON THE RIGHTEOUS (vv. 25–27)

Simeon, like Mary and Joseph, is presented as a man who faithfully observed the Law of Moses. We know this because he is called "righteous" (**v. 25**), which means to keep God's commands or be just in His sight. Simeon is also called "devout," which means having reverence for God. God rewarded Simeon for his many years of faithfulness and piety by allowing him to see the consolation of Israel.

The Holy Spirit, which was upon him, revealed that he would not die until he had seen the Lord's Messiah (Gk. *Christos*; **v. 26**). Luke explains that the Holy Spirit led Simeon to the Temple at the same time Mary and Joseph were presenting Jesus to the priest.

The Holy Ghost Speaks to Simeon

25 And, behold, there was a man in Jerusalem, whose name was Simeon; and the same man was just and devout, waiting

for the consolation of Israel: and the Holy Ghost was upon him. 26 And it was revealed unto him by the Holy Ghost, that he should not see death, before he had seen the Lord's Christ.

Simeon, a prophet, is one of two witnesses to Christ in the Temple, the other being Anna, a prophetess (**vv. 36–38**). Simeon is mentioned nowhere else in the New Testament. His timely but sole presence at the Temple was only to witness to Christ—similar to his presence in Scripture. God is never without witnesses. Simeon being righteous and devout makes him a credible witness to something so significant as Jesus being presented to God at the Temple. It is no coincidence that Simeon, Joseph, and Mary arrived when they did, confirming the divine appointment, and consoling Simeon, who had waited for Israel's consolation (cf. **Philippians 2:1–2**, KJV).

III. A LIGHT FOR ALL PEOPLE (vv. 28–32)

Upon seeing Jesus, Simeon takes the infant in his arms. He immediately recognizes Jesus' significance and sings praise to the Lord. The song is a confirmation of the Holy Spirit's revelation that Simeon would see the Lord's Messiah. The song proclaims that the time of the salvation of the Lord is now.

Simeon sings a message of fulfillment and peace. The consolation Simeon was expecting was the salvation God had prepared in the presence of all peoples. He could sing of witnessing it with his own eyes: here in his arms was the expected Messiah in the form of a baby. As the prophet Isaiah before him (**Isaiah 49:6**), Simeon proclaims that Jesus would be a light to the Gentiles, bringing them God's salvation and glory for the people of Israel (**v. 32**). Simeon's message is that God's salvation was for all people, both Jews and Gentiles.

Simeon's Joy and Blessing

27 And he came by the Spirit into the temple: and when the parents brought in the child Jesus, to do for him after the custom of the law, 28 Then took he him up in his arms, and blessed God, and said, 29 Lord, now lettest thou thy servant depart in peace, according to thy word: 30 For mine eyes have seen thy salvation, 31 Which thou hast prepared before the face of all people; 32 A light to lighten the Gentiles, and the glory of thy people Israel.

Called Simeon's song or psalm, his words have been loved around the world for centuries. God's work and plan is for all people (**Luke 2:10; cf. Isaiah 52:10; Psalm 98:3**). Now that Simeon has seen this, he is ready to peacefully "depart" (Gk. *apoluo*, **ah-po-LOO-oh**), which can also mean to set free or dismiss, but here figuratively means to die. His words also are curious, because he doesn't say that he has seen the Christ or the Messiah, but rather God's "salvation" (Gk. *soterios*, **so-TAY-ree-ose**, from which we get the English word *soteriology* or the study of salvation), a word used only five times in the New Testament (see also **Luke 3:6; Acts 28:28; Ephesians 6:17; Titus 2:11**). What else has the power to deliver us from the fear of death other than strong faith? It is interesting for an old, devout Jew not only to equate Jesus with salvation but as a light to the Gentiles and the glory of Israel (**Isaiah 45:25, 46:13**, KJV).

SEARCH THE SCRIPTURES

QUESTION 3

What was Simeon's response when he saw Jesus?

"**And he came by the Spirit into the temple: and when the parents brought in the child Jesus, to do for him after the custom of the law, Then took he him up in his arms, and blessed God, and said, Lord, now lettest thou thy servant depart in peace, according to thy** word: For mine eyes have seen thy salvation, Which thou hast prepared before the face of all people; A light to lighten the Gentiles, and the glory of thy people Israel."

LIGHT ON THE WORD

Jesus, the Light of the World

All of Jewish history was great because of God—Israel's entire history was replete with acts of a merciful and forgiving God who loved not only Israel but the entire world. Indeed, the day will come when all Israel, and all the world, will see the glory of the Lord, and that day surely cannot come too soon for any of us who today, like Simeon, also hope to see the "consolation" of Israel, God's people.

BIBLE APPLICATION

AIM: Students will anticipate in faith what the Lord will do in their lives as they share the Good News of Christ with others.

December is a month when many Christians are busy with preparations for the celebration of Jesus' birth and the coming new year. It is also a time when many people spend beyond their means to provide gifts that frequently depreciate in value or interest for the recipient. Jesus was born of humble beginnings. His parents could only afford the substitutionary offering of two pigeons when they presented Him at the Temple. Nevertheless, that did not prevent them from taking several days to faithfully observe the rituals of God. It is important that we take time from the busy holiday season to remember that the celebration of Jesus' birth is not about the material gifts we give, but about His significance in our lives and the world today.

STUDENT'S RESPONSES

AIM: Students will renew their excitement of celebrating the birth of Christ and their faith through the year.

In the United States, Christians tend to focus on December 25, the day Jesus' birth is celebrated, and once the day has passed, we continue with our busy schedules. However, in many Christian communities, the Christmas season actually begins on Christmas Eve and continues another forty days until the Feast of the Presentation of the Lord in February. This holiday season, commit to learning about the different ways Christians celebrate the season, such as the Mexican tradition of Las Posadas, and choose one that you find interesting. Or you could form your own new tradition, such as making a special meal at one of the feast days on the church calendar or volunteering to help someone in need. Whichever you choose, invite family and friends to join you in celebrating a new tradition that will help renew the joy of celebrating Christmas and your faith throughout the year.

PRAYER

Lord, You truly are amazing and awesome. Your gift of Jesus for the world continues to bring excitement, peace, and salvation in our lives. We are thankful for the gift of Christ for all creation! In Jesus' Name we pray. Amen.

HOW TO SAY IT

Matrix.	may-TRIX.
Zerubbabel.	zi-ROO-bu-bel.

PREPARE FOR NEXT SUNDAY

Read Matthew 23:2–12 and Mark 12:38–44 and "A Generous Gift."

DAILY HOME BIBLE READINGS

MONDAY
Separate for a Purpose
(Leviticus 20:7–8, 22–24)

TUESDAY
God's Heart and Dedication
(2 Chronicles 30:5–12)

WEDNESDAY
Dedication of Samson
(Judges 13:2–5, 24–25)

THURSDAY
Dedication of Samuel
(1 Samuel 1:11, 20, 24–28)

FRIDAY
Dedication of David
(1 Samuel 16:10–13)

SATURDAY
Dedication of Saul/Paul
(Acts 9:1–6)

SUNDAY
Dedication of the Firstborn
(Exodus 13:13–15; Luke 2:22–32)

Sources:

Achtemeier, Paul J., Boraas, Roger S., Fishburne, Michael, et al, ed. *HarperCollins Bible Dictionary*. HarperCollins Publishing, 1996. 2, 603, 1223.

Balentine, Samuel E. *Leviticus*. Interpretation: A Bible Commentary for Teaching and Preaching. Louisville: John Knox Press, 2002. 170-173; 176-179.

Harris, R. Laird. *Genesis, Exodus, Leviticus, Numbers*. The Expositor's Bible Commentary, Vol. 2. Edited by Frank E. Gaebelein. Grand Rapids: Zondervan, 1990. 620-621.

Harrison, R. K. *Leviticus*. Tyndale Old Testament Commentaries. Downers Grove: InterVarsity Press, 1980. 210-217.

Hartley, John E. *Word Biblical Commentary: Leviticus*. Dallas, TX: World Books Publishers, 1992. 362.

Gane, Roy. *Leviticus, Numbers*. The NIV Application Commentary: From Biblical Text ... to Contemporary Life. Grand Rapids: Zondervan, 2004. 382-385.

Rodner, Ephraim. *Leviticus*. Brazos Theological Commentary on the Bible. Grand Rapids: Baker Books, 2008. 228-229; 237-238.

Rooker, Mark F. *Leviticus*. The New American Commentary: An Exegetical and Theological Exposition of Holy Scripture, Vol. 3A. Nashville: B&H Publishing, 2000. 278-281; 286-289.

COMMENTS / NOTES:

A GENEROUS GIFT

BIBLE BASIS: MATTHEW 23:2–12; MARK 12:38–44

BIBLE TRUTH: Jesus denounced the Scribes and Pharisees' need for recognition and affirmed the compassion and humility of the poor widow's gift.

MEMORY VERSE: "And whosoever shall exalt himself shall be abased; and he that shall humble himself shall be exalted" (Matthew 23:12).

LESSON AIM: By the end of the lesson, we will: OBSERVE the contrast that Jesus made between the arrogance of the religious leaders and the piety of the humble, poor woman; REFLECT on the tension between wanting recognition and selfless giving that often receives no recognition; and RESOLVE to become more selfless in giving.

TEACHER PREPARATION

MATERIALS NEEDED: Quarterly Commentary/Teacher Manual, Adult Quarterly, Adult resources—charts, worksheets, and other teaching tools, paper, pens, pencils, Bibles (several different versions)

OTHER MATERIALS NEEDED / TEACHER'S NOTES:

_____

_____

LESSON OVERVIEW

LIFE NEED FOR TODAY'S LESSON
People desire to be recognized and held in high esteem by others.

BIBLE LEARNING
God honors those who are humble and selfless in their devotion to Him.

BIBLE APPLICATION
Christians are to give with a good heart and intentions that are right before God.

STUDENTS' RESPONSES
Christians should adopt selfless giving as a way of life.

LESSON SCRIPTURE

MATTHEW 23:2–12; MARK 12:38–44, KJV

2 Saying, The scribes and the Pharisees sit in Moses' seat:

3 All therefore whatsoever they bid you observe, that observe and do; but do not ye after their works: for they say, and do not.

MATTHEW 23:2–12; MARK 12:38–44, NIV

2 "The teachers of the law and the Pharisees sit in Moses' seat.

3 So you must be careful to do everything they tell you. But do not do what they do, for they do not practice what they preach.

4 For they bind heavy burdens and grievous to be borne, and lay them on men's shoulders; but they themselves will not move them with one of their fingers.

5 But all their works they do for to be seen of men: they make broad their phylacteries, and enlarge the borders of their garments,

6 And love the uppermost rooms at feasts, and the chief seats in the synagogues,

7 And greetings in the markets, and to be called of men, Rabbi, Rabbi.

8 But be not ye called Rabbi: for one is your Master, even Christ; and all ye are brethren.

9 And call no man your father upon the earth: for one is your Father, which is in heaven.

10 Neither be ye called masters: for one is your Master, even Christ.

11 But he that is greatest among you shall be your servant.

12 And whosoever shall exalt himself shall be abased; and he that shall humble himself shall be exalted.

Mark 12:38 And he said unto them in his doctrine, Beware of the scribes, which love to go in long clothing, and love salutations in the marketplaces,

39 And the chief seats in the synagogues, and the uppermost rooms at feasts:

40 Which devour widows' houses, and for a pretence make long prayers: these shall receive greater damnation.

41 And Jesus sat over against the treasury, and beheld how the people cast money into the treasury: and many that were rich cast in much.

4 They tie up heavy, cumbersome loads and put them on other people's shoulders, but they themselves are not willing to lift a finger to move them.

5 "Everything they do is done for people to see: They make their phylacteries wide and the tassels on their garments long;

6 they love the place of honor at banquets and the most important seats in the synagogues;

7 they love to be greeted with respect in the marketplaces and to be called 'Rabbi' by others.

8 "But you are not to be called 'Rabbi,' for you have one Teacher, and you are all brothers.

9 And do not call anyone on earth 'father,' for you have one Father, and he is in heaven.

10 Nor are you to be called instructors, for you have one Instructor, the Messiah.

11 The greatest among you will be your servant.

12 For those who exalt themselves will be humbled, and those who humble themselves will be exalted.

Mark 12:38 As he taught, Jesus said, "Watch out for the teachers of the law. They like to walk around in flowing robes and be greeted with respect in the marketplaces,

39 and have the most important seats in the synagogues and the places of honor at banquets.

40 They devour widows' houses and for a show make lengthy prayers. These men will be punished most severely."

41 Jesus sat down opposite the place where the offerings were put and watched the crowd putting their money into the temple

42 And there came a certain poor widow, and she threw in two mites, which make a farthing.

43 And he called unto him his disciples, and saith unto them, Verily I say unto you, That this poor widow hath cast more in, than all they which have cast into the treasury:

44 For all they did cast in of their abundance; but she of her want did cast in all that she had, even all her living.

treasury. Many rich people threw in large amounts.

42 But a poor widow came and put in two very small copper coins, worth only a few cents.

43 Calling his disciples to him, Jesus said, "Truly I tell you, this poor widow has put more into the treasury than all the others.

44 They all gave out of their wealth; but she, out of her poverty, put in everything—all she had to live on."

LIGHT ON THE WORD

Pharisees. A very influential religious group of Jewish men that existed in Judea from second century B.C. through the first century AD. The word Pharisee is ultimately from a word meaning "separated ones" or "set apart" in Hebrew. The group was comprised of laymen who adhered to strict observance of the Sabbath, purity rituals, tithing, and food restrictions based on the Hebrew Scriptures and Jewish traditions. They also believed in the resurrection of the dead.

Scribes. One of several groups in first-century Judaism. The scribes were trained in writing and were very influential as interpreters and teachers of the Law. They also acted as agents of the Roman Empire and the local rulers, preparing legal documents and recording deeds. They could belong to other groups, such as the Pharisees and Sadducees (e.g., "the scribes of the Pharisees" in **Mark 2:16; Acts 23:9**, ESV).

Widows. The Torah contains several injunctions regarding the care for widows to protect them from being taken advantage of because they have lost their husbands. For instance,

Exodus 22:22 states: "You shall not ill-treat any widow or orphan." According to the rabbinical tradition, a widow is disallowed from inheriting her husband's estate. However, she is entitled to receive a settlement on the estate from which she can maintain her livelihood if and when she remarries.

TEACHING THE BIBLE LESSON

LIFE NEED FOR TODAY'S LESSON

AIM: Students will acknowledge that people desire to be recognized and held in high esteem by others.

INTRODUCTION

Jesus Teaches His Disciples

After Jesus makes His entry into Jerusalem and is exalted by the people who shouted hosannas in celebration of the Messiah's coming (**Matthew 21:1–11**), He enters the Temple, the center of Jewish religious and political activity. On seeing this, Jesus cleanses the Temple of exploitative merchant activity (**Matthew 21:12–17**). Jesus then turns His attention to the religious leaders, observing the religious leaders and teachers' abusive practices (**Matthew 21:23–23:36**). He then begins to instruct His disciples and the crowd of people on the ways of the Kingdom of God that are in stark contrast to the personal practices of unrighteous religious leaders.

BIBLE LEARNING

AIM: Students will understand that God honors those who are humble and selfless in their devotion to Him.

I. A LACK OF HUMILITY
(Matthew 23:2–7)

Jesus reveals the Pharisees' and scribes' hypocritical behavior to the crowds and His disciples. To begin with, Jesus encourages the role of the scribes and Pharisees and applauds them for taking on the important task of interpreting and teaching the Torah (or Law) (v. 3). Jesus does not deny the Torah and the importance of the Pharisees' and scribes' role, yet He denounces their hypocritical actions toward their responsibilities. The scribes and Pharisees are making a mockery of the Law by pursuing their own self-interests at the expense of the community. They are abusing their authority as teachers and community leaders, stepping over others to raise themselves up. They are more concerned with appearing as privileged figures (reflected in the clothes they wear and their sitting in the best seats in the synagogue), than loving their neighbor as themselves.

Matthew 23:1–12; Mark 12:38–44

1 Then spake Jesus to the multitude, and to his disciples, 2 Saying, The scribes and the Pharisees sit in Moses' seat: 3 All therefore whatsoever they bid you observe, that observe and do; but do not ye after their works: for they say, and do not.

Many times in the Gospel, Jesus speaks not only to His core group of twelve disciples but also to the multitudes. In this instance, He speaks concerning the practices of the scribes and Pharisees in relation to their status in the Kingdom of God. The scribe (Gk. *grammateus*, **gram-mah-TUSE**) was an expert interpreter and teacher of the Mosaic Law, usually called on to answer difficult questions for the local courts and the Sanhedrin council. Jesus affirms that they sit in Moses' seat (**v. 2**). Although many scholars argue that this was an actual seat in the synagogue used to make authoritative decisions and explanations by the law of Moses, there is no evidence of this; instead, Jesus affirms their authority in interpreting the Law. He says that whatever they tell the people to observe, they should observe (Gk. *tereo*, **teh-REH-oh**); this word means to guard or keep watch. In this context, it means to attend to carefully or take care of; by implication, it means to listen and obey. Jesus says to attend to what they say and do it, but not copy what they do, because "they say and do not."

4 For they bind heavy burdens and grievous to be borne, and lay them on men's shoulders; but they themselves will not move them with one of their fingers. 5 But all their works they do for to be seen of men: they make broad their phylacteries, and enlarge the borders of their garments,

Jesus makes a general statement describing their actions and the way they have twisted the Jewish faith. He describes the burdens (Gk. *phortion*, **for-TEE-on**) of the scribes and Pharisees. These burdens were metaphorically the religious rituals, which the religious leaders derived from the Mosaic Law. They are described as being heavy (Gk. *barus*, **bah-ROOS**), which means weighty and in this context severe and stern. They lay these burdens on other men's shoulders while they do not lift a finger. The shoulders carry weight for the body, which emphasize their strength. The finger is one of the weakest parts of the body. In other words, the Pharisees put people under a life-consuming burden and will not make the smallest effort to help people please God.

Jesus also comments on their motives. All their religion is for the applause of others, as seen in their showing off their phylacteries (Gk. *phulakterion*, **foo-lak-TAY-ree-on**), small cases filled with strips of paper on which were written specific passages from the Torah (**Exodus 13:11–16; Deuteronomy 6:4–9, 11:16–21**). The word for phylactery was first used for a fortified place stationed with a garrison. The word could also more generally mean a preservative or safeguard, which is related to the meaning here, as observant Jews believed the phylacteries could ward off evil spirits and demons. These small cases were worn on the forehead and the left arm against the heart to remind them of their obligation to keep the Mosaic Law in their head and heart (**Deuteronomy 6:8, 11:18**). Instead of serving this purpose, the Pharisees used them to broadcast their religious devotion to others. In addition, they "enlarged the borders of their garments." The borders (Gk. *kraspedon*, **KRAHS-peh-don**) of their garments were the traditional blue and white tassels worn on the edge of their mantles or cloaks (**Numbers 15:38–41**). These also were used to remind the Jews of keeping God's commandments. The Pharisees and scribes elongated these in order to appear more religious.

6 And love the uppermost rooms at feasts, and the chief seats in the synagogues,

Jesus goes further to point out their selfishness and hypocrisy. The Pharisees loved the uppermost rooms (Gk. *protoklisia*, **pro-toh-klee-SEE-ah**) at feasts—this means that they love to sit in prominent places, at the head tables during banquets, and positions of honor. Although there is information on the Greek, Persian, and Roman seating arrangements of the time, it is not known what particular seat

this was for Jews. Ancient evidence contains people's complaints against being seated in low status positions. In another place, Jesus would explain the proper way to handle seating arrangements (**Luke 14:1–11**). For now, He rebukes the Pharisees and scribes for their desire of the first place.

Jesus also says the Pharisees and scribes love the chief seats (Gk. *protokathedria*, **pro-toh-ka-thed-REE-ah**) in the synagogues. Although a simple translation of the word is the "first seat," the seating arrangements in synagogues during the first century varied, so it is hard to pinpoint exactly where this seat would be placed. We can estimate that this seat must have been closest to the *bema*, a precursor of the pulpit, where the Scriptures would be read. There is also the possibility that more honorable guests would have been given chairs while others sat on mats. Both the synagogue and the banquet were public gatherings that presented an opportunity for the religious leaders to call attention to their spiritual importance.

7 And greetings in the markets, and to be called of men, Rabbi, Rabbi. 8 But be not ye called Rabbi: for one is your Master, even Christ; and all ye are brethren. 9 And call no man your father upon the earth: for one is your Father, which is in heaven. 10 Neither be ye called masters: for one is your Master, even Christ.

Greetings in the first century were a very important social component, containing rules on how to address peers, inferiors, and superiors. To not greet a teacher of the Law was a serious offense. Another sign of the Pharisees' self-seeking was their desire to be called Rabbi (Gk. *rhabbi*, **rah-BEE**), meaning "great one." By implication, it also means "master" or "my lord." It was the custom of Jews to refer to their teachers this way, even when not in their presence.

Jesus condemns this practice. He says not to call anyone Rabbi or "great one." There is only one great one—Christ. He continues to proclaim all His followers as "brethren," family and peers not adherent to a hierarchy.

SEARCH THE SCRIPTURES

QUESTION 1

Read verses 7–9 and state who is and who is not to be called Father and Master.

Only God is the Father and the Master. No man is the Father or the Master.

LIGHT ON THE WORD

The Master Teacher

Pupils often called their rabbis father (Gk. *pater*, **pah-TARE**). While Jesus uses the formal designation of father, which in a Jewish context was also used for God, pupils were known to address their rabbis as "Abba" (Aramaic for "our dear father") a way to address them with respect and also signify the type of relationship between student and teacher. The rabbis in turn addressed their pupils as children. Jesus says this is not how it works in the Kingdom of God; there is only one Father, God Himself. He also says there is only one Master (Gk. *kathegetes*, **ka-they-gay-TACE**), which means guide or teacher.

II. INSTRUCTION IN HUMILITY (vv. 8–12)

Jesus' disciples should not desire to be exalted by the people because of their leadership position in the church. Instead, Jesus demands His disciples practice servanthood when He says, "he that is greatest among you shall be your servant" (v. 11). A person's actions will cause others to lift that person up. So, to follow the instructions of the Kingdom, the disciples must do the opposite of the prevailing practice. Jesus says, "And those who exalt

themselves will be humbled, and those who humble themselves will be exalted" (**v. 12**, NLT).

The Status Quo is Reversed

11 But he that is greatest among you shall be your servant. 12 And whosoever shall exalt himself shall be abased; and he that shall humble himself shall be exalted.

Jesus outlines a different path to greatness and significance. He says whoever is the greatest (Gk. *meizon*, **MADE-zone**) or has the highest rank and status must become a servant (Gk. *diakonos*, **dee-AH-ko-noce**). This word means an attendant or waiter, and one who executes another's commands. This is different from the common word for slave (Gk. *doulos*, **DOO-loce**) in the New Testament; *diakonos* emphasizes the activity of the worker, whereas *doulos* denotes the relation between the one serving and the one being served. Jesus further adds that those who exalt (Gk. *hupsoo*, **hoop-SOH-oh**) or lift themselves high will be abased, or brought low and humiliated. The reverse also holds true; those who humble themselves will be exalted. The same Greek verb for humbles is used for abased (*tapeinoo*, **tah-pay-NOH-oh**). The KJV is trying to convey that the verb appears in both the active and the passive voices here. In other words, if you try to make yourself lower (humble yourself), you will be raised up, but if you try to lift yourself up, you will be made lower (abased). The NLT nicely captures Jesus' contrast of the two types of people by translating His words literally.

III. Example of Humility (Mark 12:41–44)

The Temple establishment was supposed to provide social protection and economic assistance to widows (**Deuteronomy 14:29, 26:12–13**); instead, under the scribes' leadership, it had become an institution of oppression. Nevertheless, the widow's offering is an example of an act of humility and generous giving, in spite of her hardship. This act is not depicted in the Matthean version of the story.

The Greedy Scribes

Mark 12:38 And he said unto them in his doctrine, Beware of the scribes, which love to go in long clothing, and love salutations in the marketplaces, 39 And the chief seats in the synagogues, and the uppermost rooms at feasts: 40 Which devour widows' houses, and for a pretence make long prayers: these shall receive greater damnation. 41 And Jesus sat over against the treasury, and beheld how the people cast money into the treasury: and many that were rich cast in much. 42 And there came a certain poor widow, and she threw in two mites, which make a farthing.

Jesus sits across from the treasury (Gk. *gazophulakion*, **god-zo-foo-LA-kee-on**). This is a word used for the different rooms in the Temple, which contained money, public records, and the property of widows and orphans. It is reported in Jewish tradition after the first century that there were ten vessels shaped like trumpets to collect voluntary offerings as well as tax money. The treasury was located in the Temple's Court of Women. This would make it accessible to all Israelites no matter what gender. Jesus watches people give their offerings and sees the rich giving much, but a poor widow stands out from the crowd. She throws in two mites (Gk. *lepton*, **lep-TAHN**), which were the smallest and lightest coins. Together two of them made up a farthing (Gk. *kodrantes*, **kod-RAHN-tays**), which was only worth 3/8 of a cent.

43 And he called unto him his disciples, and saith unto them, Verily I say unto you, That this poor widow hath cast more in, than all they which have cast into the treasury: 44 For all they did cast in of their abundance;

but she of her want did cast in all that she had, even all her living.

The action of the widow prompts Jesus to call His disciples to a true example of greatness in contrast to the Pharisees, scribes, and all the rich people who gave their offerings. They all gave an offering from their abundance (Gk. *perisseuo*, **peh-rees-SUE-oh**), meaning the overflow or what was left over. They gave what they could afford to give. The widow, on the other hand, gave her want (Gk. *husteresis*, **hus-TEH-ray-sees**) or what is lacking. She gave all of her living (Gk. *bios*, **BEE-ose**), the general word for life and by extension the resources, goods, and wealth by which life is sustained. Jesus praises the widow for her absolute trust in God, as opposed to the Pharisees and scribes along with the rich worshipers who trust in themselves.

SEARCH THE SCRIPTURES

QUESTION 2
How does Jesus describe the scribes in verse 38?

The disciples are to beware of the scribes because they like to display who they are by wearing long clothing and giving long salutations in the marketplace.

QUESTION 3
What did Jesus observe in verse 41? How much money did the widow give?

Jesus watched how much people gave to the treasury. The widow gave two mites.

LIGHT ON THE WORD

Humility and Serving Others
In Matthew, Jesus simply explains to His disciples the role of humility in servanthood. In Mark, the widow's act serves as an example of the humility elaborated on in Matthew by illustrating the role of humility and the act of servanthood. By contrast, those who insist on

self-promoting their importance will receive condemnation in the last days.

BIBLE APPLICATION

AIM: Students will understand that Christians are to give with a good heart and intentions that are right before God.

Christians of every circumstance, especially those in leadership positions, tend to yearn for recognition. Everyone wants a title, but not everyone wants to be called a servant. American society, in fact, is established on the basis of privilege and non-privilege. Only by radical departure from the world's values and priorities will Christians be the disciples of the one Teacher and Lord. Only by practicing explicitly selfless acts of humility will Christians be exalted.

STUDENT'S RESPONSES

AIM: Students will accept that Christians should adopt selfless giving as a way of life.

Who are you trusting in for your advancement? Who are you trusting with your reputation? This week, seek to serve others who would be considered lower than you. Offer to serve one of your subordinates at work. Give to a person or organization without them knowing it was you. In this way, you will be seeking to be admired by Jesus and not others.

PRAYER

We bless You Lord for first loving us and giving us Christ. Help us to give and care for those in need even we do not have much. Your kindness and love remind us that we are to are for one another. In Jesus' Name we pray. Amen.

HOW TO SAY IT

Phylacteries.   fi-LAK-tuh-rees.

Synagogue.   si-nuh-GOG.

PREPARE FOR NEXT SUNDAY

Read **Genesis 29:15–30** and "A Bride Worth Waiting For."

DAILY HOME BIBLE READINGS

MONDAY
Modeled Generosity
(John 1:10–18)

TUESDAY
Gracious Generosity
(Ephesians 2:1–10)

WEDNESDAY
Excellent Generosity
(2 Corinthians 8:3–9)

THURSDAY
Wise Generosity
(Colossians 3:12–17)

FRIDAY
Loving Generosity
(Romans 12:6–13)

SATURDAY
Humble Generosity
(Matthew 6:1–6)

SUNDAY
A Generous Gift
(Matthew 23:2–12; Mark 12:38–44)

Sources:
Carson, D.A., France, R.T., Motyer, J.A., Wenham, J.G. *New Bible Commentary.* Downers Grove, IL: InterVarsity Press, 1993.
Keener, Craig S. *IVP Bible Background Commentary.* Downers Grove, IL: InterVarsity Press, 1993.
Polhill, John B. *Acts.* New American Commentary: An Exegetical and Theological Exposition of Holy Scripture. Nashville: B&H Publishing, 1992.

A BRIDE WORTH WAITING FOR

BIBLE BASIS: GENESIS 29:15–30

BIBLE TRUTH: Jacob's love for Rachel was so great, that the additional seven years of labor was not a burden for him.

MEMORY VERSE: "And he went in also unto Rachel, and he loved also Rachel more than Leah, and served with him yet seven other years" (Genesis 29:30).

LESSON AIM: By the end of the lesson, we will: RECALL the story of Jacob's love for and commitment to marry Rachel; REFLECT on marital relationships and the ways unforeseen circumstances affect those relationships; and COMMIT to finding faith-based resolution to difficulties before abandoning relationships.

TEACHER PREPARATION

MATERIALS NEEDED: Quarterly Commentary/Teacher Manual, Adult Quarterly, Adult resources—charts, worksheets, and other teaching tools, paper, pens, pencils, Bibles (several different versions)

OTHER MATERIALS NEEDED / TEACHER'S NOTES:

_____

_____

LESSON OVERVIEW

LIFE NEED FOR TODAY'S LESSON
Relationships can be marred by unforeseen circumstances.

BIBLE APPLICATION
Although people plot and plan against others, God's plans are greater for our lives.

BIBLE LEARNING
Laban planned to deceive Jacob and tricked him into a marriage.

STUDENTS' RESPONSES
Believers know that promises are often broken in relationships.

LESSON SCRIPTURE

GENESIS 29:15–30, KJV

15 And Laban said unto Jacob, Because thou art my brother, shouldest thou therefore serve me for nought? tell me, what shall thy wages be?

16 And Laban had two daughters: the name of the elder was Leah, and the name of the younger was Rachel.

GENESIS 29:15–30, NIV

15 Laban said to him, "Just because you are a relative of mine, should you work for me for nothing? Tell me what your wages should be."

16 Now Laban had two daughters; the name of the older was Leah, and the name of the younger was Rachel.

17 Leah was tender eyed; but Rachel was beautiful and well favoured.

18 And Jacob loved Rachel; and said, I will serve thee seven years for Rachel thy younger daughter.

19 And Laban said, It is better that I give her to thee, than that I should give her to another man: abide with me.

20 And Jacob served seven years for Rachel; and they seemed unto him but a few days, for the love he had to her.

21 And Jacob said unto Laban, Give me my wife, for my days are fulfilled, that I may go in unto her.

22 And Laban gathered together all the men of the place, and made a feast.

23 And it came to pass in the evening, that he took Leah his daughter, and brought her to him; and he went in unto her.

24 And Laban gave unto his daughter Leah Zilpah his maid for an handmaid.

25 And it came to pass, that in the morning, behold, it was Leah: and he said to Laban, What is this thou hast done unto me? did not I serve with thee for Rachel? wherefore then hast thou beguiled me?

26 And Laban said, It must not be so done in our country, to give the younger before the firstborn.

27 Fulfil her week, and we will give thee this also for the service which thou shalt serve with me yet seven other years.

28 And Jacob did so, and fulfilled her week: and he gave him Rachel his daughter to wife also.

29 And Laban gave to Rachel his daughter Bilhah his handmaid to be her maid.

17 Leah had weak eyes, but Rachel had a lovely figure and was beautiful.

18 Jacob was in love with Rachel and said, "I'll work for you seven years in return for your younger daughter Rachel."

19 Laban said, "It's better that I give her to you than to some other man. Stay here with me."

20 So Jacob served seven years to get Rachel, but they seemed like only a few days to him because of his love for her.

21 Then Jacob said to Laban, "Give me my wife. My time is completed, and I want to make love to her."

22 So Laban brought together all the people of the place and gave a feast.

23 But when evening came, he took his daughter Leah and brought her to Jacob, and Jacob made love to her.

24 And Laban gave his servant Zilpah to his daughter as her attendant.

25 When morning came, there was Leah! So Jacob said to Laban, "What is this you have done to me? I served you for Rachel, didn't I? Why have you deceived me?"

26 Laban replied, "It is not our custom here to give the younger daughter in marriage before the older one.

27 Finish this daughter's bridal week; then we will give you the younger one also, in return for another seven years of work."

28 And Jacob did so. He finished the week with Leah, and then Laban gave him his daughter Rachel to be his wife.

29 Laban gave his servant Bilhah to his daughter Rachel as her attendant.

30 And he went in also unto Rachel, and he loved also Rachel more than Leah, and served with him yet seven other years.

30 Jacob made love to Rachel also, and his love for Rachel was greater than his love for Leah. And he worked for Laban another seven years.

LIGHT ON THE WORD

Laban. He was the son of Nahor, who was Abraham's older brother, which means he was Isaac's cousin, but he was also related to Rebekah through her father Bethuel, who was a child of Nahor's. Laban settled on the eastern side of the Euphrates River.

Bridal Week. This was a period of seven days after the initial wedding ceremonies. Although it dates back to the ancient Near East, this tradition continues in many Orthodox Jewish communities. At the beginning of the bridal week, the bride and groom would sexually consummate their marriage. Afterward, the bride would remain in the wedding chamber for six days. During this time, the wedding party and guests would feast and celebrate the marriage of the bride and groom.

TEACHING THE BIBLE LESSON

LIFE NEED FOR TODAY'S LESSON

AIM: Students will understand that relationships can be marred by unforeseen circumstances.

INTRODUCTION

Jacob's Deception

Jacob, whose name means "surplanter" or "heel catcher" (**Genesis 25:26**), was the second son born to Isaac and Rebekah. Jacob and his brother Esau continued Isaac and Ishmael's trend of sibling rivalry with a very adversarial relationship. Jacob outwitted his brother twice. First he tricked

Esau out of his birthright by exploiting his irreverence for his birth position to fulfill his temporary need—a bowl of stew (**Genesis 25:29–34**). The second time, with the help of his mother, who devised the plan, Jacob tricked his father into releasing the firstborn blessing. The deception sent Esau over the edge. Esau pleaded with Isaac to bless him with something, to no avail; he set out to kill Jacob (**Genesis 27**). Now on the run, Jacob has had an unforgettable encounter with the living God where He reveals the promise He has made to his grandfather (Abraham) and father (Isaac) to birth a nation through him (**Genesis 28:10–17**). As Jacob continues his journey, he moves eastward. He meets up with some men tending a flock from Haran, which is 400 miles northeast of Canaan, and learns that they work for his uncle Laban, his father's brother. Jacob's life would forever be changed, as he meets the love of his life Rachel, who was tending sheep with them (**Genesis 29:1–10**).

BIBLE LEARNING

AIM: Students will learn that Laban planned to deceive Jacob and tricked him into a marriage.

I. WILLING TO WORK FOR LOVE (Genesis 29:15–20)

Jacob was sent away from home by his mother not only to escape the threat of murder from his brother Esau, but also to find a wife. Rebekah did not want her son taking a wife among the women of their country but sent him to her homeland (**Genesis 27:46**). In **Genesis 29:9–12**, Jacob and Rachel meet and apparently it is love at first sight. He revealed that they were related through his mother and her father. In hearing the news of Jacob's arrival, Laban immediately travels to greet him warmly and receive him as a relative (**vv. 13–14**).

Laban extends hospitality to Jacob, giving him food and shelter, but he also recognizes the value of Jacob's work. Laban seemingly does not want to take advantage of Jacob and therefore asks him to name his price or wages in exchange for his continued service. Laban had two daughters, Leah, the oldest, and Rachel, the youngest. Leah has been historically portrayed as being the less attractive sister and Rachel the prettier. Jacob seeks compensation, not in money, livestock, or land, but for the beautiful Rachel to be his wife.

Jacob agrees to serve Laban for seven years to marry the younger daughter. In theory, Laban agrees to the terms, desiring to keep Jacob happy and have an extra hired hand. Out of his love for Rachel, he works seven years for Laban, fulfilling his end of the bargain. Jacob was so smitten by love that the seven years of labor seemed but a few days and worth the while to be with her (**v. 20**).

Genesis 29:15–18

15 And Laban said unto Jacob, Because thou art my brother, shouldest thou therefore serve me for nought? tell me, what shall thy wages be?

Jacob is working for his uncle Laban. After running from his brother Esau's wrath, he found a home in Haran. Laban is the brother of Rebekah and soon is discovered to exhibit many of the same deceptive traits that Jacob and Rebekah have shown earlier in the narrative. Laban allows Jacob to negotiate for his wages (Heb. *maskoret*, **mahs-KOH-ret**). This word can also mean reward, but in this context is used as wages exchanged for work. It is also the same word used by Boaz in asking God to reward Ruth for her commitment to Naomi (**Ruth 2:12**).

16 And Laban had two daughters: the name of the elder was Leah, and the name of the younger was Rachel. 17 Leah was tender eyed; but Rachel was beautiful and well favoured. 18 And Jacob loved Rachel; and said, I will serve thee seven years for Rachel thy younger daughter.

Here the narrator begins to describe the daughters of Laban anticipating Jacob's wages. Leah is Laban's older daughter and is described as having weak (Heb. *rak*, **ROCK**) eyes, meaning tender, faint, or delicate. The text could be saying that Leah had weak vision or that she had lovely eyes. In the first instance, Leah struggles not only with being less physically attractive than her younger sister, but also with her vision. In the second instance, she has her own beautiful traits, but she is still not physically attractive enough to gain Jacob's love. In contrast, Rachel is described as beautiful (Heb. *yafeh*, **ya-FEH**) and well favoured (Heb. *mareh*, **ma-REH**). Both phrases use the Hebrew word for beautiful (Heb. *yafeh*, **ya-FEH**). The first phrase states that she is beautiful in form (Heb. *to'ar*, **toe-AR**), and the second says that she is beautiful in appearance (Heb. *mar'eh*, **mar-EH**). In context, both sets of words are used to describe Rachel's loveliness as superior to Leah.

Jacob then offers to serve Laban seven years for Rachel. Being away from home without any family support, Jacob would not be able to pay the dowry or customary bride price. His offer to work for seven years made up for his lack of monetary payment to seal a betrothal. The narrator makes sure to reiterate that Rachel is the younger daughter. This is most likely to draw readers into the deception about to take place and also to point toward Jacob's deception as the younger brother.

II. TRICKED INTO LOVE (vv. 19–28)

The seven years are up and Jacob has completed the terms of his agreement with Laban. He approaches his uncle (soon to be father-in-law) and demands that he upholds his end of the bargain. Laban organizes a wedding feast with the men of his community. Like today, it was custom in Middle Eastern cultures that a banquet would precede the bride and groom coming together. Included in this time of celebration would be plenty of drinking and carousing. Laban threw a party for Jacob, and in the midst of the revelry, gave Leah to Jacob instead of Rachel. When Jacob came to himself, he realized he had been deceived (**v. 25**). The trickster got tricked! He had consummated a marriage to the wrong woman, because once a man engaged in sexual intercourse with a virgin, she was his wife. This turn of events was a low blow on Laban's part, but some speculate that Jacob was getting his just reward for his deception to his brother and father.

Deception runs in the family. Laban gave the perception that he agreed to Jacob's terms but had no intention of ever fulfilling his end of the bargain. Laban says it is not custom in his community to have the younger daughter marry before the older and therefore requires Jacob to fulfill his marital duties of the marriage week to Leah as well as work another seven years for Rachel. Clearly Laban was being blessed by Jacob's presence and not inclined to release him.

The Power of Love

19 And Laban said, It is better that I give her to thee, than that I should give her to another man: abide with me. 20 And Jacob served seven years for Rachel; and they seemed unto him but a few days, for the love he had to her. 21 And Jacob said unto Laban, Give me my wife, for my days are fulfilled, that I may go in unto her.

Laban accepts Jacob's offer, saying how it is favorable to him as well. By giving his daughter to Jacob, he would give her away to a near relative and therefore the wealth that she contributes to her new husband will stay in Laban's family too. He asks Jacob to stay as hired labor. Whatever

work Jacob had to do during his seven years of hired labor watching Laban's flocks seemed to him "but a few days" because of the "love" (Heb. *'ahabah*, **ah-ha-VAH**) he had for Rachel. This word for love encompasses human love for family, God, or objects. In this case it is used for Jacob's desire for Rachel. Although this word has sexual connotations, it is more of an all-encompassing desire of the whole person for another.

Jacob was the one who took the initiative to raise the subject of his wife. This shows his eagerness to consummate the marriage. It also suggests reluctance on Laban's part toward the union, inasmuch as he really did not need to be reminded that Jacob's years of service were fulfilled (Heb. *mala'*, **ma-LA**). The word means to fill or complete, in a physical sense or with regard to intangible things such as desire. Frequently the word is used with respect to time to talk about the completion of a set period or the arrival of a period of time (**Genesis 25:24; Leviticus 8:33**). In the Old Testament, it is used in the temporal sense less often but it is that sense which is used here. Jacob's work was completed and it was time to receive his wages.

22 And Laban gathered together all the men of the place, and made a feast. 23 And it came to pass in the evening, that he took Leah his daughter, and brought her to him; and he went in unto her.

Since no verbal reply from Laban was recorded, it is difficult to know what he was thinking. His silence may indeed suggest his reluctance to give Rachel over at this point. Nevertheless, he invited his neighbors to celebrate the wedding banquet, or marriage feast (Heb. *mishteh*, **mish-TEH**). These feasts commonly lasted seven days, but the length varied according to the circumstances of the bridegroom. In this case, it seems seven days was sufficient (**v. 27**).

During the wedding feast, the bride and groom would consummate the marriage in the wedding chamber or "tent." The phrase "he went in unto her" is a play on words as it describes the entering into the marriage chamber as well as the sexual act. Laban's deception of Jacob was possible because the bride usually entered the marriage chamber veiled, the veil being so long as to conceal not only the face but much of the body as well (cf. **Genesis 24:65**). The text also indicates that Laban brought Leah to Jacob in the evening, when it was dark. On top of all this, a wedding feast usually involved a lot of drinking. So we have three things that possibly contributed to Jacob's deception: Leah's bridal veil, the dark, and alcohol. In addition to tricking Jacob, Laban may very well have brought Leah to Jacob against her will. The Hebrew for "brought her" is a form of the verb "to enter" (*bo'*, **BOE**). In this case, the form of the verb specifically indicates that he made her do it. We do not know how Leah feels about Jacob, but given the language of the verse and the fact that Rachel is described as more physically attractive, at best she would have had mixed feelings, and at worst she would have reviled the entire situation because of what it could do to her relationship with Rachel and/or because she knew the man wanted her sister, not her. She was essentially forced on a man who didn't love her by her father who had also tricked the man.

24 And Laban gave unto his daughter Leah Zilpah his maid for an handmaid.

It was customary at marriages for the bride's father to give her a large present, often a handmaid who became her confidential servant (**Genesis 24:59, 61**). These handmaids were responsible for the women and children of the family and cared for them by attending to personal needs (combing hair, washing) or more general domestic chores. In case of a childless marriage, they also served as concubines (**Genesis 16:1–2, 30:4, 9**). However unpleasant Laban was to Jacob, adhered to custom with regard to his daughters by presenting them each with a handmaid. Even in these handmaids, God would fulfill His purpose in shaping

the nation of Israel, as they gave birth to four of the twelve patriarchs.

25 And it came to pass, that in the morning, behold, it was Leah: and he said to Laban, What is this thou hast done unto me? did not I serve with thee for Rachel? wherefore then hast thou beguiled me?

Seven years he had toiled and worked for Rachel, and now Jacob found he had married her less beautiful sister instead. The question "What is this thou hast done unto me?" expresses Jacob's astonishment. He could not understand why Laban had beguiled (Heb. *ramah*, **rah-MAH**) him. The word for beguile means to throw or cast down. In this context, it means to trick, with the connotation of intentionally tripping someone up. In accusing Laban of deceit, Jacob was in fact condemning himself. The deceiver had been deceived. Jacob argued with Laban, but he could do nothing to alter the situation.

26 And Laban said, It must not be so done in our country, to give the younger before the firstborn.

Laban gave the reason for his action: It is not customary to put the younger sibling before the firstborn. Remember that Jacob, the younger, had put himself before the firstborn Esau, so there was a certain poetic justice in Laban's deception of Jacob. However, Laban's attempt to justify his action was weak. He should have made this known to Jacob much earlier, when they made the agreement in the first place.

27 Fulfil her week, and we will give thee this also for the service which thou shalt serve with me yet seven other years. 28 And Jacob did so, and fulfilled her week: and he gave him Rachel his daughter to wife also.

However unwilling Jacob may have been to continue celebrating his marriage to Leah, he could not opt out: He was isolated and without family support. Laban's only concession was that Jacob could take Rachel immediately as a second wife, and Jacob did want to marry Rachel. Realizing he had Jacob trapped, Laban then added another harsh demand: After marrying Rachel, Jacob had to work for Laban another seven years. Jacob agreed to comply with Laban's terms; Rachel was the focus of his affections and intentions. Although taking a second wife was not Jacob's original intent, his dream of having Rachel was not denied, but deferred.

SEARCH THE SCRIPTURES

QUESTION 1

Jacob was upset when he discovered Laban had tricked him. What questions does he then ask Laban?

"What is this thou hast done unto me? did not I serve with thee for Rachel? wherefore then hast thou beguiled me?"

III. COMMITTED TO FIRST LOVE (vv. 29–30)

Jacob, because of his love for Rachel, once again kept his end of the bargain and fulfilled his marital duties with Leah and worked another seven years for Rachel. Leah was an integral part of building what would be the nation of Israel, as she was the mother of six sons: Reuben, Simeon, Levi, Judah, Issachar, and Zebulun (**Genesis 29:31–35, 30:17–20**). Although Jacob fulfilled his marriage commitment to Leah, he did not love her, so unfortunately her marriage was not a good one. Leah wanted her husband to love her, and although they engaged in marital relations and had children, she was deeply rejected. Laban finally gave Rachel to Jacob along with her handmaid Bilhah. She was truly the love of his life and the Scripture notes that "he loved her more than Leah" (**v. 30**). Rachel was barren for many years, but when she was finally able to bear children, Jacob loved Rachel's children more than the others (**Genesis 45:22, 37:3**). Leah and Rachel are examples of being in relationships for the right and wrong reasons. It was not uncommon for couples in ancient times to have arranged marriages, but marital unions are most fruitful when they start from a place of true love. Jacob and Rachel's relationship was special because together they weathered adversity and separation yet remained in love.

Two Wives and a Husband

29 And Laban gave to Rachel his daughter Bilhah his handmaid to be her maid. 30 And he went in also unto Rachel, and he loved also Rachel more than Leah, and served with him yet seven other years.

The abrupt end of the conversation indicates Jacob's grudging acceptance of Laban's new terms. Both Laban and Jacob did the most honorable thing given the horrible situation they had made for themselves: Jacob completed Leah's bridal week, and Laban gave him Rachel. Rachel, like her sister Leah, was given a maid (**v. 24**). Jacob did indeed serve another seven years, but unlike the first, they are not said to have "seemed unto him but a few days" (**v. 20**). Rather, they were days of sorrow and strife within the new family, as the account of the patriarchs' births would soon make plain.

SEARCH THE SCRIPTURES

QUESTION 2

Name Rachel's handmaid.

Bilhah.

QUESTION 3

Jacob served Laban for _____ years so that he could marry _____.

14, Rachel.

LIGHT ON THE WORD

A Devoted Love

Jacob's intense desire for Rachel far outweighed

the work he had to do. His display of love demonstrates how committed we ought to be to those we love.

BIBLE APPLICATION

AIM: Students will accept that although people plot and plan against others, God's plans are greater for our lives.

The generations of today are least likely to marry and most likely to divorce. The divorce rates of today are alarming, especially among those who profess Christ but do not live a Christian lifestyle. This is because of a multitude of factors including mass incarceration, family dysfunction, and economic disadvantage. It is also due to not understanding the meaning of marriage as God has designed it. It used to be common for couples to be married for fifty or sixty years; now this is not the case, as many are divorced or have never married.

There is life beyond the beautiful day. A couple must have the right foundation in order to last through the ebbs and flows of life. Ideally, two people should be rooted in Jesus Christ in order to build a sure foundation, and it takes working together in the Holy Spirit to make it last. It's important to know your purpose, take the time, ask the right questions, and truly get to know and accept the person before deciding to marry. It is equally important to have godly counsel and the right expectations of marriage and your mate to ensure success. The right one is worth waiting for, so never mind the rush. If you are married, be in it for the long haul and prayerfully seek to understand each other.

STUDENT'S RESPONSES

AIM: Students will know that promises are often broken in relationships.

If you are married, reflect on the ways you and your spouse stay connected. If you are unable to readily pinpoint ways, now is the time to be intentional about staying connected. If you are not married, reflect on how you can use this season to be more in tune with your probable future needs in a marital relationship should you desire to marry. How can your group or church help inform married couples and singles on the realities of marriage no matter the age or life stage?

PRAYER

Lord, Your love for us is so real and true. Your Word reminds us that You are committed to loving and caring for in spite of our not always loving You. We adore You and bless Your Holy Name. In Jesus' Name we pray. Amen.

HOW TO SAY IT

Zilpah.	zil-PA.
Laban.	le-BAHN.

PREPARE FOR NEXT SUNDAY

Read **Song of Solomon 6:4–12** and "The Most Beautiful Bride."

DAILY HOME BIBLE READINGS

MONDAY
Trustworthy Lives
(Proverbs 11:9–13)

TUESDAY
Honesty: the Best Policy
(Proverbs 12:19–26)

WEDNESDAY
Wisdom More than Strength
(Proverbs 24:3–7, 13–14)

THURSDAY
Judged Faithful
(1 Timothy 1:12–17)

FRIDAY
The Lord is Present
(Genesis 28:15–22)

SATURDAY
Welcome Home
(Genesis 29:9–14)

SUNDAY
A Bride Worth Waiting For
(Genesis 29:15–30)

Sources:

Carson, D.A., France, R.T., Motyer, J.A., Wenham, J.G. *New Bible Commentary.* Downers Grove, IL: InterVarsity Press, 1993.

Keener, Craig S. *IVP Bible Background Commentary.* Downers Grove, IL: InterVarsity Press, 1993.

Polhill, John B. *Acts.* New American Commentary: An Exegetical and Theological Exposition of Holy Scripture. Nashville: B&H Publishing, 1992.

COMMENTS / NOTES:

THE MOST BEAUTIFUL BRIDE

BIBLE BASIS: SONG OF SOLOMON 6:4–12

BIBLE TRUTH: Song of Solomon describes mutual adoration for inner and outer beauty.

MEMORY VERSE: "My dove, my undefiled is but one; she is the only one of her mother, she is the choice one of her that bare her. The daughters saw her, and blessed her; yea, the queens and the concubines, and they praised her" (Song of Solomon 6:9).

LESSON AIM: By the end of this lesson, we will: EXPLORE love and adoration as pictured in the Song of Solomon; REFLECT on romantic relationships and the ways to nurture them; and SEEK ways to recognize and express appreciation, in appropriate ways, for inner and physical beauty in others.

TEACHER PREPARATION

MATERIALS NEEDED: Quarterly Commentary/Teacher Manual, Adult Quarterly, Adult resources—charts, worksheets, and other teaching tools, paper, pens, pencils, Bibles (several different versions)

OTHER MATERIALS NEEDED / TEACHER'S NOTES:

_____

_____

LESSON OVERVIEW

LIFE NEED FOR TODAY'S LESSON
Most marriages that are grounded in love allow couples to view each other with adoration.

BIBLE LEARNING
God's love for creation is our example of true love.

BIBLE APPLICATION
Christians should develop true love in relationships that are meaningful and acceptable before the Lord.

STUDENTS' RESPONSES
People learn that true love is unashamed and a precious gift.

LESSON SCRIPTURE

SONG OF SOLOMON 6:4–12, KJV

4 Thou art beautiful, O my love, as Tirzah, comely as Jerusalem, terrible as an army with banners.

5 Turn away thine eyes from me, for they have overcome me: thy hair is as a flock of goats that appear from Gilead.

SONG OF SOLOMON 6:4–12, NIV

4 You are as beautiful as Tirzah, my darling, as lovely as Jerusalem, as majestic as troops with banners.

5 Turn your eyes from me; they overwhelm me. Your hair is like a flock of goats descending from Gilead.

6 Thy teeth are as a flock of sheep which go up from the washing, whereof every one beareth twins, and there is not one barren among them.

7 As a piece of a pomegranate are thy temples within thy locks.

8 There are threescore queens, and fourscore concubines, and virgins without number.

9 My dove, my undefiled is but one; she is the only one of her mother, she is the choice one of her that bare her. The daughters saw her, and blessed her; yea, the queens and the concubines, and they praised her.

10 Who is she that looketh forth as the morning, fair as the moon, clear as the sun, and terrible as an army with banners?

11 I went down into the garden of nuts to see the fruits of the valley, and to see whether the vine flourished and the pomegranates budded.

12 Or ever I was aware, my soul made me like the chariots of Amminadib.

6 Your teeth are like a flock of sheep coming up from the washing. Each has its twin, not one of them is missing.

7 Your temples behind your veil are like the halves of a pomegranate.

8 Sixty queens there may be, and eighty concubines, and virgins beyond number;

9 but my dove, my perfect one, is unique, the only daughter of her mother, the favorite of the one who bore her. The young women saw her and called her blessed; the queens and concubines praised her.

10 Who is this that appears like the dawn, fair as the moon, bright as the sun, majestic as the stars in procession?

11 I went down to the grove of nut trees to look at the new growth in the valley, to see if the vines had budded or the pomegranates were in bloom.

12 Before I realized it, my desire set me among the royal chariots of my people.

LIGHT ON THE WORD

Tirzah. A city located in the northern part of Solomon's kingdom and residence of at least two kings thereafter; its name means "true beauty and delight." This Canaanite city was conquered by Joshua (**Joshua 12:7, 24**) and represented all that was beautiful in royal splendor.

Concubines. A woman who was a secondary wife. A man was legally allowed to have sexual relations with her and bound to materially provide for her and any children conceived from this relationship. The children had no rights of inheritance unless the father declared it so. The custom of women becoming concubines grew out of the ancient Near Eastern desire to produce children, and if a man's first wife could not do this, then he took on a second wife or concubine for this purpose. In time, kings would gather many concubines in a royal harem as a symbol of their manhood and power.

Shulamite Woman. The female lover in the Song of Solomon is known as the Shulamite woman. She describes herself as "black and beautiful" (cf. **Song of Solomon 1:5–6**, NRSV). Some argue that she uses this language to denote her sun-darkened skin; others believe her description points toward her African ancestry. This view can be supported by the way she describes herself as black as the tents of Kedar. This is a reference to tents made from the jet black hair of goats.

TEACHING THE BIBLE LESSON

LIFE NEED FOR TODAY'S LESSON

AIM: Students will know that most marriages that are grounded in love allow couples to view each other with adoration.

INTRODUCTION

A Passionate Love Story

Song of Solomon, also called "Song of Songs," is grouped with the poetic books of the Bible. It is believed to be an exchange between David's son Solomon during his reign and the Shulamite woman who captured his heart, along with a chorus of palace women called "daughters of Jerusalem." It is well documented that Solomon had a harem of more than 1,000 women comprised of 700 wives and 300 concubines at the height of his kingdom (**1 Kings 11:3**), but it is amazing that the Shulamite bride stood out among them to be celebrated in this fashion. This collection of poetry or songs showcases the drama and passion of human love. Jewish and Christian scholars have interpreted the allegorical meanings to God's fierce love for Israel, as well as the Church as the ravishing bride of Christ.

BIBLE LEARNING

AIM: Students will understand that Christians should develop true love in relationships that are meaningful and acceptable before the Lord.

I. COMPLIMENTING BEAUTY
(Song of Solomon 6:4–7)

Earlier (**Song of Solomon 5:10–16**), the bride recalls her love for her king and anticipation of his presence. In response to her love, Solomon uses rich language to express his love for the Shulamite woman as he depicts the uniqueness of her beauty. He uses two cities to capture the splendor of her glory. Tirzah was an ancient Canaanite city captured by Joshua and known for its beautiful location on a hill. Jerusalem, the capital of the Southern Kingdom, was also on a hill and was a treasure of Jewish heritage and significance. The king as a lover sings of the majesty of his bride: she is dignified, worthy of his attention, and he stands in awe of her appearance such that she penetrates his very soul.

Song of Solomon 6:4–7

4 Thou art beautiful, O my love, as Tirzah, comely as Jerusalem, terrible as an army with banners.

The Song of Solomon is a powerful love poem where two lovers, newlyweds by some accounts, sing of their mutual love and unrestrained passion for one another. **Song of Solomon 6:4–7** is the second of two lengthy speeches by the male lover proclaiming his adoration for his beloved. The speaker uses a lyric device characteristic to Arabic poetry known as a *wasf*, which uses imagery from the natural world to praise the lover's human physique, moving from one part of the body to the next (cf. **4:1–5, 6:5–7**). Throughout the speech he likens her beauty to doves, sheep, and pomegranates, to name a few.

In **verse 4,** her loveliness is compared to the beautifully situated city of Tirzah in the tribal territory of Manasseh and the capital city Jerusalem in the Southern Kingdom of Judah. Both were fortified, bustling cities lavished with the ornamental trappings worthy of a royal city. Her beauty is compared in the King James Version to an army with banners (**v. 10**). As stunning as the sight of those banners is, her beauty is comparable in his eyes.

5 Turn away thine eyes from me, for they have overcome me: thy hair is as a flock of goats that appear from Gilead. 6 Thy teeth are as a flock of sheep which go up from the washing, whereof every one beareth twins, and there is not one barren among them.

The writer moves from a general exhortation of her overall beauty to extolling specific parts of her body. Her eyes, which he likened to doves in the first wasf (**4:1**), arouse in him anguish now. He objects that the look of love from her is too overwhelming for him to hold her gaze and he begs her to look away.

The man repeats a compliment first stated in a previous chapter (**4:1**), that her hair is like a flock of goats on Mount Gilead. He is speaking metaphorically here, comparing her hair to the sight of goats descending the rolling hills, which might have appeared as a woman's long, thick, wavy, black hair, the predominant color of goats in Syria-Palestine at that time.

In contrast to the black flock of goats are the white sheep, which the man compares to the woman's teeth. Her teeth are characterized as clean, like the sheep coming up from the water and ready for shearing. Moreover, there is not a tooth missing in her mouth. Dental hygiene being what is was in antiquity, it was unusual to find someone with all his or her teeth. Although today's women might be offended by being compared to sheep and goats, they could appreciate someone complimenting their smile.

7 As a piece of a pomegranate are thy temples within thy locks.

This verse omits the first half of the simile that is part of a couplet in the first wasf: "Thy lips are like a thread of scarlet, and thy speech is comely" (**4:3**). Perhaps the man did not believe that it needed repeating. The second part has proven difficult for many interpreters. The KJV compares her temple, or brow from the Hebrew *raqqah* (**rak-KAH**), to a slice of pomegranate. The Hebrew word is translated temple in its other Old Testament uses (**Judges 4:21, 5:26**). However, in reference to her red lips in **4:3**, her cheeks could just as likely be like halves of red pomegranates. Along with the word *tsammah* (**tsam-MAH**) translated "locks" in the KJV, but as "veil" in modern translations (cf. **4:1, 3; Isaiah 47:2**), **verse 7** should perhaps be translated, "Like a slice of pomegranate are your cheeks behind your veil." **Verse 7** ends this wasf.

SEARCH THE SCRIPTURES

QUESTION 1
Why does Solomon's beloved need to look away from him in verse 5?

Her look arouses anguish in him and is too overwhelming.

LIGHT ON THE WORD

Love for Our Spouses
We should seek to be full of joy and delight over our spouse even as our relationship with them matures over the years. Due to our spouse's uniqueness in our own eyes, our love for them should never fade away but be renewed throughout the different seasons of marriage.

II. CONVINCED BY BEAUTY (vv. 8–10)

Solomon calls his bride his "dove" and "undefiled," or perfect, one and special among her mother's daughters. His bride is honorable in his eyes. Other women cannot help but praise her, because she is precious in his sight. The women in Solomon's harem act as the chorus to this piece of the poetry. The sun and the moon depict her beauty and brightness. She is described as majestic as an army with banners, which echoes the king's language (**v. 4**).

In this loving tribute, the Shulamite woman is the epitome of a virtuous woman worthy of honor from her king, her spouse, and he is uninhibited in his love for her. The language used here shows the Shulamite as unique in the king's eyes. This is an example of how all spouses should be seen in each other's eyes. We need to have eyes for only our spouse and be convinced of their beauty above all others.

Blessed and Highly Favored

8 There are threescore queens, and fourscore concubines, and virgins without number. 9 My dove, my undefiled is but one; she is the only one of her mother, she is the choice one of her that bare her. The daughters saw her, and blessed her; yea, the queens and the concubines, and they praised her. 10 Who is she that looketh forth as the morning, fair as the moon, clear as the sun, and terrible as an army with banners?

In verses 8 and 9, the writer returns to an earlier theme of royal imagery in the poem (cf. **3:6–11**). The man proclaims that his beloved is second to none; not even the royal women of the court, no matter their numbers, can come close to the woman's splendor. In fact, these women of high social status praise this common woman. The man finds the woman so exceptional that he writes that among all her siblings, she is her mother's favorite. Her sisters, like the royal ladies, find favor with her when they look upon and bless her. The man returns to the simile of the banners of the capital cities in **verse 4** to inquire rhetorically, who is this woman who looks as awesome as the dawn, moon, and sun?

III. CAPTIVATED BY BEAUTY (vv. 11–12)

The woman goes to her garden to check on the new spring growth. This is symbolic of how the love she has for him has been renewed. The rich imagery of fruit and grapes from the vine would impact the poem's reader in numerous ways. A garden filled with budding fruit trees would evoke images of lushness, and also remind them of pleasant fragrances.

As the Shulamite's love is renewed, she is overwhelmed. She is transported into the royal chariots. The emotion communicated is excitement and joy. This is descriptive of mature marital love as joy and excitement continue to be renewed.

A Garden of Passion

11 I went down into the garden of nuts to see the fruits of the valley, and to see whether the vine flourished and the pomegranates budded. 12 Or ever I was aware, my soul made me like the chariots of Amminadib.

Scholars agree that **verses 11 and 12** are difficult to translate due to the corruption of the original Hebrew text. However, there is a general consensus that **verse 11** is full of sexual innuendos. In ancient Palestine, walnuts, vines, and pomegranates held certain sexual significance. Having gone to the garden, the speaker, most likely the woman now, is caught unaware by some discovery. The KJV interprets the word *ammi-nadib* (Heb. **am-ME nah-DEEV**) as a proper name, Amminadib. However, *nadib* in Hebrew can mean "noble man" or "prince," and *ammi* could be translated "my people," together making a phrase instead of a name: "my noble people." A better translation then might be that before she knew what was happening, her desire had "taken me to the chariot of a noble man" (NLT) or "had set me in a chariot of a noble man." Perhaps she is so overwhelmed by the many sensual stimuli in the garden that she finds herself metaphorically swept off her feet into her lover's chariot.

SEARCH THE SCRIPTURES

QUESTION 2
What are the forces of nature that Solomon's love, the Shulamite woman, is compared to?

The dawn, moon, and sun.

LIGHT ON THE WORD

The Depth of Your Beauty

Common in poetry of this age in the Eastern tradition, he uses familiar metaphors to paint a picture of the power of her presence. A woman's beauty is to be celebrated and a man does well to shower the woman he loves with words of affirmation.

BIBLE APPLICATION

AIM: Students will learn that Christians should develop true love in relationships that are meaningful and acceptable before the Lord.

We know that God is love, but people often shy away from talking about God's expression of love in a marital relationship via sexual intimacy. The reason sex in the confines of marriage is beautiful is that it is the expression of love, commitment, and connectedness between two people who have gone before Him and pledged to love one another for life.

As Christians, we can provide examples of godly love between a man and a woman. Marital love is symbolic of God's love for His people. We can also impact our culture by supporting Christian media and calling for the end of inappropriate sexual images and song lyrics that demean and objectify the opposite sex. We can also celebrate the unique beauty of our spouse and resist the world's false standard of beauty.

There is nothing wrong with sexual desire, as it is God's design for humanity. He also designed it to be expressed within the boundaries of marriage. This is for His glory, as through marriage we imitate His covenant relationship with His people. It is also for our good, as our greatest joy and fulfillment in romantic relationships can be found in the institution of marriage.

STUDENT'S RESPONSES

AIM: Students will learn that true love is unashamed and a precious gift.

Romance is never out of style between a man and wife. If you are married, take turns in planning a special date night for your mate. Pray and study your mate, seeking to meet their deepest desires, even if it requires coming out of your comfort zone. Dating doesn't end once you're married. Nurture your relationship with one another; most importantly, accept one another and be quick to forgive. If you are single and dating, be sure to have open and honest conversations to ensure the two of you are on the same page in your relationship; be sure to involve others to help you remain accountable. Be sure to have fun and enjoy the journey with planned dates that honor God. If you are single and not dating but would like to at some point, connect with like-minded friends who can help you focus on the things of God and join in prayer with you over discerning God's timing to date.

PRAYER

O Lord, we praise You, and we are thankful for Your wonderful love. As You shower us with new mercies, we pray that we will be merciful, and share Your love with others. May our love for our spouses, family, and friends be enriched by Your love for us. In Jesus' Name we pray. Amen.

HOW TO SAY IT

Amminadib.	aw-min-aw-**DIB**.
Tirzah.	teer-**ZAW**.
Gilead.	**GHIL**-ee-ad.

PREPARE FOR NEXT SUNDAY

Read **Hosea 1** and "Unfaithful Bride."

DAILY HOME BIBLE READINGS

MONDAY
A Perfect Woman
(Proverbs 31:10–11, 20, 25–26)

TUESDAY
The Perfect Shepherd
(John 10:1–6)

WEDNESDAY
The Good Shepherd
(John 10:7–15)

THURSDAY
The Eternal Shepherd
(John 10:22–30)

FRIDAY
The Most Perfect Love
(Song of Solomon 4:9–15)

SATURDAY
The Most Handsome Groom
(Song of Solomon 5:9–16)

SUNDAY
The Most Beautiful Bride
(Song of Solomon 6:4–12)

Sources:
Bergant, Dianne, C.S.A. *The Song of Songs. Berit Olam Studies in Hebrew Narrative & Poetry.* Collegeville, MN: The Liturgical Press, 2001. 42-47, 75-79.
Exum, J. Cheryl. *Song of Songs: A Commentary.* The Old Testament Library. Louisville, KY: Westminster John Knox Press, 2005. 158-164, 214-225.
Garrett, Duane. *Song of Songs.* Word Biblical Commentary Vol. 23B. Nashville, TN: Thomas Nelson, Publishers, 2004, 188-190, 227-230.

COMMENTS / NOTES:

AN UNFAITHFUL BRIDE

BIBLE BASIS: HOSEA 1

BIBLE TRUTH: Israel's alienation from God and His plans for restoration is experienced in the marriage of Hosea and Gomer and their children.

MEMORY VERSE: "The beginning of the word of the LORD by Hosea. And the LORD said to Hosea, Go, take unto thee a wife of whoredoms and children of whoredoms: for the land hath committed great whoredom, departing from the LORD" (Hosea 1:2).

LESSON AIM: By the end of this lesson, we will: LEARN how God commanded Hosea to marry Gomer as a model for His love for Israel, despite their unfaithfulness; REFLECT on the meaning of marriage and unfaithfulness and God's desire for the restoration of broken relationships; and DEMONSTRATE faithfulness to God through a commitment to maintain faithful friendships, relationships, and marriages.

TEACHER PREPARATION

MATERIALS NEEDED: Quarterly Commentary/Teacher Manual, Adult Quarterly, Adult resources—charts, worksheets, and other teaching tools, paper, pens, pencils, Bibles (several different versions)

OTHER MATERIALS NEEDED / TEACHER'S NOTES:

_____

_____

LESSON OVERVIEW

LIFE NEED FOR TODAY'S LESSON
Unfaithfulness in covenant relationships leads to brokenness and alienation.

BIBLE LEARNING
God rebuilds the broken places in our lives as we seek and live in His faithfulness.

BIBLE APPLICATION
Believers accept that God is a God of relationships, who extends a deep love for us to embrace.

STUDENTS' RESPONSES
Believers learn that God is a God of reconciling relationships.

LESSON SCRIPTURE

HOSEA 1, KJV

1 The word of the LORD that came unto Hosea, the son of Beeri, in the days of Uzziah, Jotham, Ahaz, and Hezekiah, kings of Judah, and in the days of Jeroboam the

HOSEA 1, NIV

1 The word of the LORD that came to Hosea son of Beeri during the reigns of Uzziah, Jotham, Ahaz and Hezekiah, kings of Judah, and during the reign of Jeroboam son of

son of Joash, king of Israel.

2 The beginning of the word of the LORD by Hosea. And the LORD said to Hosea, Go, take unto thee a wife of whoredoms and children of whoredoms: for the land hath committed great whoredom, departing from the LORD.

3 So he went and took Gomer the daughter of Diblaim; which conceived, and bare him a son.

4 And the LORD said unto him, Call his name Jezreel; for yet a little while, and I will avenge the blood of Jezreel upon the house of Jehu, and will cause to cease the kingdom of the house of Israel.

5 And it shall come to pass at that day, that I will break the bow of Israel, in the valley of Jezreel.

6 And she conceived again, and bare a daughter. And God said unto him, Call her name Loruhamah: for I will no more have mercy upon the house of Israel; but I will utterly take them away.

7 But I will have mercy upon the house of Judah, and will save them by the LORD their God, and will not save them by bow, nor by sword, nor by battle, by horses, nor by horsemen.

8 Now when she had weaned Loruhamah, she conceived, and bare a son.

9 Then said God, Call his name Loammi: for ye are not my people, and I will not be your God.

10 Yet the number of the children of Israel shall be as the sand of the sea, which cannot be measured nor numbered; and it shall come to pass, that in the place where it was said unto them, Ye are not my people, there it shall be said unto them, Ye are the sons of the living God.

Jehoash king of Israel:

2 When the LORD began to speak through Hosea, the LORD said to him, "Go, marry a promiscuous woman and have children with her, for like an adulterous wife this land is guilty of unfaithfulness to the LORD."

3 So he married Gomer daughter of Diblaim, and she conceived and bore him a son.

4 Then the LORD said to Hosea, "Call him Jezreel, because I will soon punish the house of Jehu for the massacre at Jezreel, and I will put an end to the kingdom of Israel.

5 In that day I will break Israel's bow in the Valley of Jezreel."

6 Gomer conceived again and gave birth to a daughter. Then the LORD said to Hosea, "Call her Lo-Ruhamah (which means "not loved"), for I will no longer show love to Israel, that I should at all forgive them.

7 Yet I will show love to Judah; and I will save them—not by bow, sword or battle, or by horses and horsemen, but I, the LORD their God, will save them."

8 After she had weaned Lo-Ruhamah, Gomer had another son.

9 Then the LORD said, "Call him Lo-Ammi (which means "not my people"), for you are not my people, and I am not your God.

10 "Yet the Israelites will be like the sand on the seashore, which cannot be measured or counted. In the place where it was said to them, 'You are not my people,' they will be called 'children of the living God.'

11 The people of Judah and the people of Israel will come together; they will appoint one leader and will come up out of the land, for great will be the day of Jezreel.

11 Then shall the children of Judah and the children of Israel be gathered together, and appoint themselves one head, and they shall come up out of the land: for great shall be the day of Jezreel.

LIGHT ON THE WORD

Hosea. Hosea, son of Beeri, was likely a native of the Northern Kingdom (Israel). He lived about the middle of the eighth century B.C., and his ministry appears to have begun around the same time as the prophet Amos. Hosea ministered for almost 40 years—prophesying throughout the reigns of Uzziah, Jotham, Ahaz and Hezekiah of Judah and Jereboam II of Israel. Not much is known about Hosea outside of what we learn about him in the book which bears his name.

The Covenant. In ancient times, "cutting" a covenant was essential to life. Parties would covenant together for many reasons: to protect their land or possessions, to show honor or earnestness in a business deal, to seal a marriage arrangement, and so forth. All people in biblical times understood how a covenant worked. It was more than just a contract; it was a pledge of loyalty and the giving of your entire life. God's covenant with Israel, given to Moses on Mt. Sinai, was well-known to the people of Israel. It contained very specific blessings and curses, each tied to a specific point in the Law of Moses. If they disobeyed a specific law, God would curse them with a specific curse. If they obeyed a specific law, God would bless them in a specific way.

TEACHING THE BIBLE LESSON

LIFE NEED FOR TODAY'S LESSON

AIM: Students will know that unfaithfulness in covenant relationships leads to brokenness and alienation.

INTRODUCTION

The Defeat of Israel

The valley of Jezreel was located in an area of central Israel that is today often called Megiddo. During the ministry of the prophet Elijah, Jezreel came to be a significant place. It was the place of Naboth's vineyard, which was coveted by King Ahab (**1 Kings 21**). Naboth refused to sell his vineyard to Ahab, so Ahab's queen Jezebel had Naboth murdered. The prophet Elijah reprimanded Ahab and Jezebel and foretold that their demise would take place on the very same land they had schemed to acquire.

Later, King Jehu did indeed defeat Ahab at Jezreel and began to rid the land of the blatant idolatry brought to the nation by Jezebel. By the time of Hosea, the third generation of Jehu's descendants, Jereboam II, was on the throne. At this time, Israel appeared to be prosperous, vigorous, and strong. They had won back much of the territory previously stolen by their enemies. The house of Jereboam II was in power during the first three chapters of the book of Hosea. After that, we see a sad, quick succession of six kings in 25 years given by God to Israel in anger and punishment.

BIBLE LEARNING

AIM: Students will see how God rebuilds the broken places in our lives as we seek and live in His faithfulness.

I. THE PROPHET'S CHALLENGE (Hosea 1:1)

The prophets would often use demonstrative examples or imagery to convey a message to the people. In the book of Hosea, the life of the prophet himself serves as the example of God's message to the people of Israel and Judah. When God speaks His Word through the prophet Hosea, He gives him a startling command: marry an adulterous woman. Hosea obeys and marries a woman named Gomer. There is some debate over whether Gomer had adulterous tendencies or if she actually practiced prostitution when Hosea married her, but regardless, she was known to be sexually unfaithful.

Hosea 1

1 **The word of the Lord that came unto Hosea, the son of Beeri, in the days of Uzziah, Jotham, Ahaz, and Hezekiah, kings of Judah, and in the days of Jeroboam the son of Joash, king of Israel.**

The superscription in verse 1 opens with the formulaic "The word of the Lord" found in other prophetic books. It introduces the prophet to whom the Lord spoke—in this instance Hosea—and the time the messenger's ministry took place. The introduction looks back to the time of kings Uzziah, Jotham, Ahaz, and Hezekiah of Judah, and the reign of Jeroboam II, king of Israel. This would place Hosea's ministry in the eighth century BC.

II. THE PROPHET'S CHILDREN (vv. 2–9)

Hosea obeys God and marries Gomer. Just as God had once made a binding covenant with the people of Israel, Hosea is now bound by a covenant to Gomer, and just as God loves His people, Hosea loves his wife. She soon bears a son, whom God instructs to be named Jezreel. As noted above, Jezreel was the name of a place of significance

in Israel's history, and means "God scatters." By instructing Hosea to name his son this, God sends a clear message to the Israelites that judgment is coming.

Hosea continues to proclaim God's warning, but the Israelites pay no attention. Soon, Gomer bears a daughter. As instructed by God, Hosea names the little girl "Loruhamah," which means "not loved" or "not pitied." This is a stronger warning than the first, clearly conveying that if Israel continues in their idolatry, God will no longer love nor forgive them. Israel still refuses to listen. Their worship of other gods reveals a flagrant and wanton disregard for God's love, which ultimately leads to their alienation from Him.

After she weans Loruhamah, Gomer gives birth to another son. His God-given name is Loammi, which means "not my people." Sadly, this child's name sums up the break in the covenant relationship between God and His people that He had warned would come. God's heart still longs for His people, but they will not turn back to Him.

Symbols of God's Fate

2 **The beginning of the word of the Lord by Hosea. And the Lord said to Hosea, Go, take unto thee a wife of whoredoms and children of whoredoms: for the land hath committed great whoredom, departing from the Lord. 3 So he went and took Gomer the daughter of Diblaim; which conceived, and bare him a son.**

Hosea 1:2–9 is written as a third person, biographical account of Hosea's marriage and children, which symbolize Israel's fate. It is important for the modern reader to understand that the Old Testament prophets used socially and culturally relevant situations and examples to convey their messages. They were concerned with making real that which is invisible. The marriage metaphor was a way of using a common social institution, such as marriage and the ancient Israelites' views of the roles of husbands and wives, to describe the breach in the covenant relationship between the Lord and Israel. Hosea used demonstrative signs to communicate what was viewed as an act of prostitution committed by Israel against the Lord.

In **verses 2 and 3**, Hosea recalls the Lord's command for him to take a wife of "whoredoms" and children of whoredoms. The Hebrew noun *zenunim* (**zeh-noo-NEEM**) translated whoredoms in the KJV is also translated "promiscuous woman" (NIV) and "harlotry" (NASB). Traditionally, commentators have interpreted this as a command for Hosea to marry a prostitute. However, a more accurate interpretation of *zenunim* would be to marry a woman who is sexually promiscuous or had sexual relations outside of marriage (**Deuteronomy 22:25**). In a culture that placed a high value on women being sexually pure at the time of their marriage, or being faithful in marriage, to the point of threat of death (**Deuteronomy 22:20–21**), all the Israelites would be shocked to be likened to a promiscuous woman.

Hosea shows that by entering into this marriage, he is performing a sign-act symbolizing the state of Israel's relationship with the Lord. The people, personified as the wife of promiscuity, have betrayed the Lord, figured as her husband. Thus, the Lord accuses the nation of Israel of infidelity or apostasy, turning from worshiping the Lord alone to seeking other gods. Hosea does as the Lord commanded and takes a woman named Gomer as his wife.

4 And the Lord said unto him, Call his name Jezreel; for yet a little while, and I will avenge the blood of Jezreel upon the house of Jehu, and will cause to cease the kingdom of the house of Israel. 5 And it shall come to pass at that day, that I will break the bow of Israel, in the valley of Jezreel.

The Lord instructed Hosea a second time, telling him to call his firstborn son Jezreel, which is Hebrew for "God sows." The naming of Hosea's son was a continuation of the sign-act. The idiom "reap what you sow" is applicable in **verse 4**. The Lord will sow or bring upon the dynasty of Jehu what it sowed in spilling the blood of the house of Ahab in Jezreel. Jehu, the grandfather of King Jeroboam son of Joash (cf. **v. 1**), killed Joram, son of King Abab of Israel, along with his mother, Jezebel, and every family member and supporter of the Omride dynasty when he was an army commander, for their idolatry (see **2 Kings 9–10**). Although the Lord had anointed Jehu king of Israel and commanded him to put an end to the house of Ahab, the Lord may have denounced the brutality with which Jehu carried out the assault. Moreover, Jehu himself was guilty of forming political alliances with other nations that were condemned by the Lord. Jehu's dynasty came to an end just as predicted in 747 B.C. with the assassination of King Zechariah.

The parallel pronouncement that the house of Israel would end was more than a prophecy about the end of a particular king's rule—it also declared the fall of Israel to the Assyrians in 722 B.C. The Israelite monarchy was severely weakened following the downfall of Jehu's dynasty, leaving Israel vulnerable to an invasion by Assyria. The idiom "break the bow" meant that the Lord would cause Israel to fall in a military defeat. Ironically, the destruction of Israel would lead to the scattering of the tribes of the Northern Kingdom, perhaps also symbolizing Hosea's son's name.

6 And she conceived again, and bare a daughter. And God said unto him, Call her name Loruhamah: for I will no more have mercy upon the house of Israel; but I will utterly take them away. 7 But I will have mercy upon the house of Judah, and will save them by the Lord their God, and will not save them by bow, nor by sword, nor by battle, by horses, nor by horsemen.

Gomer conceives once more and gives birth to a daughter, whom the Lord instructs Hosea to name Loruhamah (lo-roo-khaw-MAW), Hebrew for "without compassion," "not pitied," or "not loved." She is to be called such because she is a sign of the Lord's Word to Hosea that when Israel fell, the Lord would show no mercy on them. The meaning of the parallel phrase in Hebrew is difficult to interpret; two interpretations are "I will annihilate them completely" or "I will certainly not forgive them."

Some scholars contend that verse 7 is a later addition due to the focus on Judah instead of Israel, and disagree whether it should be attributed to Hosea or a later editor. The message, in contrast to verse 6, is that the Lord would have compassion on Judah and spare it from Assyrian devastation. However, the Lord would deliver Judah from the Assyrians, but not by military might. Instead, the record shows that Judah managed to avoid being overtaken by the Assyrians by paying tribute to King Tiglath-pileser III of Assyria in 732 B.C. (2 Kings 16:5–9; Isaiah 7:1–16; cf. 2 Chronicles 28:5–21), and later King Sennacherib of Assyria stopped short of destroying Judah in 701 B.C.

8 Now when she had weaned Loruhamah, she conceived, and bare a son. 9 Then said God, Call his name Loammi: for ye are not my people, and I will not be your God.

In the ancient world, as well as some places today, children were nursed until around the age of three. Therefore, verse 8 provides the reader with chronological information that is not provided elsewhere. The reader can infer that there were approximately three years between the birth of Loruhamah and her younger brother, whom the Lord told Hosea to name Loammi (lo-am-MEE): "not my people." The marriage metaphor, from the accusation of adultery in verse 2 to the estrangement in verses 4–7, is taken to its final conclusion in verse 9, with the Lord announcing that the relationship between the Lord and Israel is ending in divorce. The declaration "You are not

my people, and I am not yours" is a reversal of the covenant the Lord made with Israel that they would be God's people and He would be their God (Exodus 6:7). It is also thought to be the words written on the bill of divorce required by the Torah (Deuteronomy 24:1).

SEARCH THE SCRIPTURES

QUESTION 1
What did the Lord announce regarding His relationship with Israel?

It would end in divorce.

LIGHT ON THE WORD

Punishment for the Northern Kingdom
God instructed Hosea to prophesy that the strength of the Northern Kingdom would again be defeated at Jezreel, this time by the brutal Assyrians, because of the Israelites' continual desertion of God and turning to idolatry. They took their military victories for granted and worshiped the false gods of Baal, Ashtoreth, and Molech.

III. GOD'S GREAT MERCY (vv. 10–11)

Though the Israelites persist in their wicked ways, God foresees a time when His people would repent and return to Him. In His great mercy and love, God reveals that their punishment would only be for a time. He has a plan for renewal and blessing. God, through Hosea, tells the people of Israel that one day they will be restored to God, and in the very place where He had said, "You are not my people," they would be called the "sons of God." This is in great contrast to verse 2, where the people of Israel are called "children of whoredoms."

God would not only restore His covenant with Israel, but He promises that Israel and Judah will someday be reunited into one nation. Though we are not told the eventual outcome of Hosea and

Gomer's marriage, we can clearly see the promise of blessings and joy that result when reconciliation takes place between God and His chosen people.

When God is Dissatisfied

10 Yet the number of the children of Israel shall be as the sand of the sea, which cannot be measured nor numbered; and it shall come to pass, that in the place where it was said unto them, Ye are not my people, there it shall be said unto them, Ye are the sons of the living God. 11 Then shall the children of Judah and the children of Israel be gathered together, and appoint themselves one head, and they shall come up out of the land: for great shall be the day of Jezreel.

Verses 10 and 11 (Hebrews 2:1–2) conclude this chapter with a series of speeches by the Lord strikingly different from the message above. The use of "yet" as a conjunction here conveys that the Lord's disaffection toward Israel will not last forever. The people's infidelity results in the destruction of the land and their removal from it, yet the Lord promises that the land of Israel will be repopulated with its people, and they will be too numerable to count. This is reminiscent of the promise to Abraham that his descendants would be more numerous than the sand on the shore (Genesis 22:17). Those whom the Lord once declared were children of promiscuity and "not my people" will be called children of the living God.

The reversal of Israel's fate will result in Israel and Judah being united under a single "head" or leader, as in the days of David and Solomon before the kingdom split in two. Moreover, the unification implies the restoration of the covenant and the security and blessings that accompany it. Metaphorically, the people are again in the land of Egypt before the Lord entered into covenant with them; yet, the Lord would symbolically bring them up from Egypt to the wilderness

where they once declared their loyalty to Him. Now Jezreel, which stood for judgment, destruction, and scattering (1:4–5), represents a place where redemption and restoration will occur.

SEARCH THE SCRIPTURES

QUESTION 2
Complete the following sentence in verse 10: "Ye are the _____ of the _____ _____."

sons, living God.

LIGHT ON THE WORD

Hosea's Faithfulness
God asks Hosea to be a living example to vividly point out the unfaithfulness of His people. By their continued and blatant idolatry, God's people had committed adultery, breaking the covenant relationship they had with Him.

BIBLE APPLICATION

AIM: Students will accept that God is a God of relationships, who extends a deep love for us to embrace.

Unfaithfulness in relationships leads to brokenness and alienation. The tragedy of divorce, the ugliness of a breach between lifelong friends, or the pain of separation between siblings or other family members are all too common. Yet God longs to bring reconciliation to those relationships. He also desires for believers to develop empathy and compassion for others who have been hurt in relationships. When we experience restoration and forgiveness in our relationship with God, we can learn to extend that same grace to others.

It can be hard to extend grace when we have unresolved issues in our own lives from past relationships. Many who are unaware of the significance of the hurt and pain they have incurred from these relationships have become toxic in their current interactions with others. This results in more unhappy marriages and families, and ultimately it affects society overall, as the foundation of society—the family—is in need of serious repair.

STUDENT'S RESPONSES

AIM: Students will learn that God is a God of reconciling relationships.

Knowing that God is a God of reconciliation means we can be optimistic and hopeful even during trying circumstances of a difficult or broken relationship. Ask God to show you your part in forgiving or asking for forgiveness. Make a commitment to God that you will do your best to maintain faithfulness in all relationships.

PRAYER

Dear God, Your faithfulness is truly a gift that You give to all of Your creation. You faithfulness is a blessing each and every day. Forgive us of our faithfulness and allow us another chance to direct our desires and work for You and to building Your kingdom. In Jesus' Name we pray. Amen.

HOW TO SAY IT

Beeri.	be-ay-**REE**.
Diblaim.	div-**LIE**-yeem.
Jezreel.	yiz-reh-**EL**.

PREPARE FOR NEXT SUNDAY

Read **John 2:2–12** and "A Wedding in Cana."

DAILY HOME BIBLE READINGS

MONDAY
A Clean and Faithful Heart
(Psalm 51:6–12)

TUESDAY
The Faithful God
(Psalm 89:24–29)

WEDNESDAY
Faithful to Truth
(Psalm 119:25–32)

THURSDAY
Free in the Spirit
(Galatians 4:16–25)

FRIDAY
Unfaithful Israel
(Hosea 4:1–6)

SATURDAY
Faithful God
(Hosea 2:18–23)

SUNDAY
An Unfaithful Bride
(Hosea 1)

Sources:
Dearman, J. Andrew. *The Book of Hosea*. New International Commentary on the Old Testament. Grand Rapids, MI: Eerdmans Press, 2006.
Landy, Francis. *Hosea*. Readings: A New Biblical Commentary. Second Edition. England: Sheffield Phoenix Press, 2011.
Macintosh, A.A. *Hosea*. International Critical Commentary. Edinburgh: T & T Clark, 1997.
Weems, Renita J. *Battered Love: Marriage, Sex, and Violence in the Hebrew Prophets*. Minneapolis, MN: Augsburg Fortress Press, 1995.

COMMENTS / NOTES:

_____
_____
_____
_____
_____
_____
_____
_____
_____
_____
_____

A WEDDING IN CANA

BIBLE BASIS: JOHN 2:1–12

BIBLE TRUTH: Jesus performed His first miracle in Cana and His glory was revealed.

MEMORY VERSE: "And saith unto him, Every man at the beginning doth set forth good wine; and when men have well drunk, then that which is worse: but thou hast kept the good wine until now" (John 2:10).

LESSON AIM: By the end of this lesson, we will: UNDERSTAND that Jesus performed His first miracle when He met an important hospitality need; REFLECT on the meaning and practice of hospitality; and PRACTICE ways in which the learners can demonstrate hospitality.

TEACHER PREPARATION

MATERIALS NEEDED: Quarterly Commentary/Teacher Manual, Adult Quarterly, Adult resources—charts, worksheets, and other teaching tools, paper, pens, pencils, Bibles (several different versions)

OTHER MATERIALS NEEDED / TEACHER'S NOTES:

_____

_____

LESSON OVERVIEW

LIFE NEED FOR TODAY'S LESSON
When guests are invited to particular types of celebrations, they expect the host to have enough food and beverages.

BIBLE LEARNING
John shows how biblical hospitality is modeled by Jesus.

BIBLE APPLICATION
Christians are servants of God, so we are called to serve others.

STUDENTS' RESPONSES
Believers develop ways to build the Kingdom of God by showing hospitality to unbelievers or new believers.

LESSON SCRIPTURE

JOHN 2:1–12, KJV

1 And the third day there was a marriage in Cana of Galilee; and the mother of Jesus was there:

2 And both Jesus was called, and his disciples, to the marriage.

3 And when they wanted wine, the mother

JOHN 2:1–12, NIV

1 On the third day a wedding took place at Cana in Galilee. Jesus' mother was there,

2 and Jesus and his disciples had also been invited to the wedding.

3 When the wine was gone, Jesus' mother said to him, "They have no more wine."

of Jesus saith unto him, They have no wine.

4 Jesus saith unto her, Woman, what have I to do with thee? mine hour is not yet come.

5 His mother saith unto the servants, Whatsoever he saith unto you, do it.

6 And there were set there six waterpots of stone, after the manner of the purifying of the Jews, containing two or three firkins apiece.

7 Jesus saith unto them, Fill the waterpots with water. And they filled them up to the brim.

8 And he saith unto them, Draw out now, and bear unto the governor of the feast. And they bare it.

9 When the ruler of the feast had tasted the water that was made wine, and knew not whence it was: (but the servants which drew the water knew;) the governor of the feast called the bridegroom,

10 And saith unto him, Every man at the beginning doth set forth good wine; and when men have well drunk, then that which is worse: but thou hast kept the good wine until now.

11 This beginning of miracles did Jesus in Cana of Galilee, and manifested forth his glory; and his disciples believed on him.

12 After this he went down to Capernaum, he, and his mother, and his brethren, and his disciples: and they continued there not many days.

4 "Woman, why do you involve me?" Jesus replied. "My hour has not yet come."

5 His mother said to the servants, "Do whatever he tells you."

6 Nearby stood six stone water jars, the kind used by the Jews for ceremonial washing, each holding from twenty to thirty gallons.

7 Jesus said to the servants, "Fill the jars with water"; so they filled them to the brim.

8 Then he told them, "Now draw some out and take it to the master of the banquet." They did so,

9 and the master of the banquet tasted the water that had been turned into wine. He did not realize where it had come from, though the servants who had drawn the water knew. Then he called the bridegroom aside

10 and said, "Everyone brings out the choice wine first and then the cheaper wine after the guests have had too much to drink; but you have saved the best till now."

11 What Jesus did here in Cana of Galilee was the first of the signs through which he revealed his glory; and his disciples believed in him.

12 After this he went down to Capernaum with his mother and brothers and his disciples. There they stayed for a few days.

LIGHT ON THE WORD

Stone jars. In Jesus' time, large stone jars were often used to hold the water used for ceremonial cleansing. Stone jars, as opposed to jars made of other substances, were more easily cleaned and therefore suitable for use as demanded by the strict requirements of Jewish law. The jars would have been used for ritual hand-washing prior to the meal, and the mention of the number and size are an indication of the number of wedding guests. To use these jars for another purpose would temporarily defile them.

Signs. The Apostle John, writer of the Gospel of John, always refers to Jesus' miracles as "signs." This is significant, because John is pointing the reader away from the deed itself to what it accomplished and why. In this story, Jesus performs His first "sign" by turning water into wine. The immediate result of this action is that the wedding guests were happy, but the greater result was that Jesus' glory was revealed and His disciples believed in Him.

TEACHING THE BIBLE LESSON

LIFE NEED FOR TODAY'S LESSON

AIM: Students will learn that when guests are invited to particular types of celebrations, they expect the host to have enough food and beverages.

INTRODUCTION

The Wedding Feast

Weddings were very important social events in biblical times. It is likely that most wedding feasts lasted seven days, and though guests were expected to bring gifts, it was up to the host to provide enough food and drink for the entire feast. People normally drank only water or wine, as not much else was available. However, for a normal beverage, this wine was sometimes watered down with a ratio of two to three parts water and one part wine.

The "master of the banquet" was not necessarily the bridegroom or host, but a person in charge of making sure the wine was properly diluted. This person would also oversee the consumption of wine, to prevent anyone drinking to excess or becoming drunk. Still, the guests' sense of taste would likely be dulled after several days of feasting. Therefore, the best wine was always served first, at the beginning of the celebration, with the cheaper or more watered-down wine being served at the end.

If the supply of wine ran out before the feast was over, the master of the banquet would be held at least partly responsible for this embarrassing social blunder. To fail to offer proper hospitality to guests was a serious offense and would surely be remembered for years to come.

BIBLE LEARNING

AIM: Students will see that John shows how biblical hospitality is modeled by Jesus.

I. JESUS SEES THE NEED (John 2:1–5)

Jesus, His mother, and His disciples were invited to a wedding in Cana, not far from Nazareth. It was customary in those days for people to invite as many guests as possible, especially revered leaders or teachers. After several days of feasting, Jesus' mother Mary came to Jesus to tell him that the host had run out of wine. She seemed to expect Him to do something.

Jesus responded to her, reminding her that His "hour" had not yet come. In the book of John, Jesus' "hour" or "time" refers to His crucifixion (cf. **John 7:6, 8, 30; 8:20**). Jesus knew that once He revealed Himself, His death would be imminent.

Though it seemed as though Jesus brushed off her request, Mary didn't give up. Apparently believing that Jesus would fulfill what she had asked, she told the nearby servants to obey whatever Jesus instructed them to do.

John 2:1–5

1 And the third day there was a marriage in Cana of Galilee; and the mother of Jesus was there: 2 And both Jesus was called, and his disciples, to the marriage.

The story of Jesus turning water into wine at Cana is only told in the Gospel of John. The village of Cana is located northwest of Jesus' hometown of Nazareth. Moreover, the third day foreshadows Jesus' resurrection, the ultimate miracle.

In contrast to the other Gospels, the Gospel of John introduces the mother of Jesus as being present from the beginning of His public ministry. John never refers to Jesus' mother by her name, Mary; she is either referred to as "the mother of Jesus" (**vv. 1, 3, cf. 12; 6:42; 19:25–27**) or "Woman" (**vv. 4; 19:26**). By her introduction in the first verse, the reader can infer that Jesus' mother has a central role in the passage. Jesus is introduced second, with the disciples added as an afterthought.

3 And when they wanted wine, the mother of Jesus saith unto him, They have no wine. 4 Jesus saith unto her, Woman, what have I to do with thee? mine hour is not yet come. 5 His mother saith unto the servants, Whatsoever he saith unto you, do it.

Verse 3 provides a rare instance of direct discourse between Jesus and His mother. John uses Jesus' mother to reveal a problem—the wedding party has run out of wine before the revelers have been sated. Jesus' mother's frank statement implies that she expects Him to do something to resolve the situation. As important as it was to one's family honor in first-century Palestine to make sure that the festivities happened without any mishaps, the potential violation of societal expectations was not the focus here, but rather

what Jesus' response would reveal about Him and His ministry.

Some scholars are surprised at the disrespectful tone Jesus uses with His mother. Jesus appears to place a certain distance between Himself and His mother by calling her "Woman" even in light of the command to honor one's parents (Exodus 20:12). Moreover, the bond between mother and son from ancient times to the present has been understood as usually close. Mothers are held in high esteem. Honoring one's mother and father is one of the Ten Commandments. Jesus' terse response, which amounts to "It's none of our business," is not meant to be interpreted as a disrespectful retort to His mother. In other places in John, this address is used in the context of revelation to a woman (**4:21; 19:26; 20:13–15**). It is more like "Dear woman" like abba is "Dear father." Jesus is understood to be saying that He will not allow even His mother to dictate His divine mandate; only God sets the hour when Jesus' purpose will be revealed to the world.

Rather than respond with, "Boy, don't You use that tone with me," His mother instructs the servants to do whatever He tells them. Several scholars have understood her command to do as Jesus says as her demonstrating what discipleship looks like.

II. JESUS MEETS THE NEED (vv. 6–7)

Though Mary asked Jesus to meet the need of their friends, Jesus chose to do so of His own accord. He instructed the servants to fill up the large stone pots with water. Jesus knew that using these pots for purposes other than ceremonially clean water would defile them, at least temporarily. Apparently, He chose to put His friends' needs over the demands of ritual. He knew that His friends would suffer loss of respect and perhaps even social position if the guests found out that the wine supply was exhausted halfway through the feast. By using the jars for another purpose, Jesus was also pointing out that there was nothing inherently "holy" about them. Moreover, the water in the jars had already been used for the ritual hand washing and the water needed to be replaced before the jars could be used again. Though no doubt wondering to themselves, the servants obeyed Jesus and filled the huge jars.

The Significance of the Waterpots

6 And there were set there six waterpots of stone, after the manner of the purifying of the Jews, containing two or three firkins apiece.

The reader is told that there were six stone water pots. The Greek word for water pot is *hudria* (**hoo-DREE-ah**). The writer specifies that the pots were made of stone because they were intended to hold water for the pools intended for ritual hand-washing prior to a meal. This detail alerts the readers that the Jews, among them Jesus and His mother, attending the wedding ceremony observed the Law of Moses. Jars made of clay were porous and therefore would require much more work to rid them of any impurities. These were not the type of jars that one might associate with women carrying on their shoulders or heads to draw water from a well, but large standing jars that when filled could hold up to 20 to 30 gallons of water each. The Greek word for firkin is *metretes* (**met-ray-TACE**) and means "a measure." Firkin is the English word for the Greek measuring utensil called the *amphora*, which was used to measure around seven gallons.

7 Jesus saith unto them, Fill the waterpots with water. And they filled them up to the brim. 8 And he saith unto them, Draw out now, and bear unto the governor of the feast. And they bare it.

Jesus instructs the servants to fill the jars to the top with water and they do as He commands. He then orders them to draw out some of the contents and take them to the governor. The word translated "governor/ruler of the feast" is *architriklinos* (Gk.

ar-khee-TREE-klee-nos) and means "master of the feast." The master of the feast was responsible for seating arrangements, overseeing the courses, and tasting the food and drink.

III. JESUS GETS THE GLORY (vv. 8–12)

Jesus now instructed the servants to take some liquid from the jars and take it to the master of the banquet. The Scripture points out that the servants knew where this "wine" had come from, but the master did not. The wine's quality so surprised the master that he called the bridegroom aside and asked him why he had kept the best wine until last. Jesus had performed a miracle that saved His friend from social embarrassment. But as Jesus' first "sign," this event had much larger ramifications.

Jesus always kept the end result of any action in mind. Throughout His time on earth, others sometimes asked or urged Jesus to do a specific thing or go to a certain place (**John 7:3-10, 11:1–7**), but because He had the "hour" in mind, He had to move on His own time table. On the occasion of the wedding at Cana, Jesus knew that performing His first miracle would not only show His love for His friends, but reveal His glory and cause His disciples to believe on Him.

The Good Wine

9 When the ruler of the feast had tasted the water that was made wine, and knew not whence it was: (but the servants which drew the water knew;) the governor of the feast called the bridegroom. 10 And saith unto him, Every man at the beginning doth set forth good wine; and when men have well drunk, then that which is worse: but thou hast kept the good wine until now.

The writer informs the reader that the servants share knowledge that the governor of the feast is not privy to—the source of the wine. They know that Jesus is responsible for the wine. The governor tastes it, as was his duty, and is apparently surprised by the taste because he summons the bridegroom. He assumes that the bridegroom has provided the wine, so he never inquires of its origins. The governor compliments the bridegroom for going against custom and saving the best wine until well after the guests have become inebriated from drinking the lesser quality wine. The servants do not disabuse the governor of his misplaced belief.

11 This beginning of miracles did Jesus in Cana of Galilee, and manifested forth his glory; and his disciples believed on him. 12 After this he went down to Capernaum, he, and his mother, and his brethren, and his disciples: and they continued there not many days.

This is the first of many miracles that John refers to as signs that Jesus would perform. *Doxa* (**DOK-sah**) is Greek for "glory" and also means honor, renown, and the manifestation of God. God's power and authority are revealed to humanity in Jesus at Cana. As a result of witnessing His glory, the disciples believe in Jesus. This passage opens and closes with the mention that His mother and disciples were present with Him. The reader is now made aware of the presence of His brothers also. It is ambiguous whether they were always present, since they are not mentioned in **verse 2**. In contrast to the Gospel of Mark that depicts the relationship between Jesus and His followers and His family in Capernaum as divisive (cf. **Mark 3:20–21, 31–35**), John presents a united front, at least briefly.

SEARCH THE SCRIPTURES

QUESTION 1
Which of Jesus' family members also attended the wedding?

Jesus' mother Mary, and His brothers.

LIGHT ON THE WORD
Be a Blessing
True hospitality is rooted in servanthood, opening your heart and home to others, that they might see the love of Jesus working through you. True hospitality is blessing others without expecting anything in return.

BIBLE APPLICATION

AIM: Students will know that because we are God's servants, we are called to serve others.

Virtually all of Africa sees hospitality—a willingness to share one's time and resources—as an essential virtue. This is because in African societies, others are viewed as essential to one's personhood. To treat others like you would treat yourself is to affirm your own humanity (**Matthew 7:12**). The same willingness to share traveled with the slaves brought to America and traces of it can be found especially in the American South. In our culture, hospitality often has the connotation of entertainment—preparing fabulous dinners, making sure the house is spotless. But entertaining guests is very different from the kind of hospitality that Jesus modeled.

STUDENT'S RESPONSES

AIM: Students know that believers develop ways to build the Kingdom of God by showing hospitality to unbelievers or new believers.

Many Scriptures compel us to extend hospitality to others, including unbelievers, orphans, widows, immigrants, foreigners, missionaries, the poor and needy, and even our enemies. Brainstorm ways that you could extend godly hospitality to those in need. Ask God to place someone in your path this week to whom you can show His love and mercy.

PRAYER

Jesus, thank You for caring for us in our times

of need. Your faithfulness and generosity are wonderful blessings that we need to share with others. You give us miracles and mercy in ways that we cannot always explain or imagine. Jesus, we worship You. In Jesus' name we pray. Amen.

HOW TO SAY IT

Cana.	KAY-nuh.
Firkins.	FUR-kins.

PREPARE FOR NEXT SUNDAY

Read **John 11:38–44** and "The Death of a Friend."

DAILY HOME BIBLE READINGS

MONDAY
The Mighty Deeds of God
(Psalm 77:11–15)

TUESDAY
The Resurrected Messiah
(Acts 2:22–28)

WEDNESDAY
The Gift of Sight
(John 9:1–11)

THURSDAY
The Gift of Health
(Matthew 15:29–38)

FRIDAY
The Clean Gift
(Matthew 5:22–26)

SATURDAY
The Healing Mission of Jesus
(Luke 4:16–24)

SUNDAY
A Wedding in Cana
(John 2:1–12)

Sources:
Levine, Amy-Jill, ed., with Marianne Blickenstaff. *A Feminist Companion to John, Vol. 1.* Sheffield, England: Continuum, 2003.
Sloyan, Gerard. *John.* Interpretation: A Bible Commentary for Teaching and Preaching. Atlanta, GA: John Knox Press, 1988. 30-39.
Smith, D. Moody, Jr. *John.* Abingdon New Testament Commentaries. Nashville, TN: Abingdon Press, 1999. 80-82.

COMMENTS / NOTES:

THE DEATH OF A FRIEND

BIBLE BASIS: JOHN 11:38–44

BIBLE TRUTH: Jesus had the power to resurrect Lazarus.

MEMORY VERSE: "And when he thus had spoken, he cried with a loud voice, Lazarus, come forth" (John 11:43).

LESSON AIM: By the end of this lesson, we will: REVIEW the story of Jesus raising Lazarus from the dead; REFLECT on why Lazarus' resurrection may have been both joyous and sobering; and REMEMBER and celebrate the lives of those who have died and affected our faith.

TEACHER PREPARATION

MATERIALS NEEDED: Quarterly Commentary/Teacher Manual, Adult Quarterly, Adult resources—charts, worksheets, and other teaching tools, paper, pens, pencils, Bibles (several different versions)

OTHER MATERIALS NEEDED / TEACHER'S NOTES:

_____

_____

LESSON OVERVIEW

LIFE NEED FOR TODAY'S LESSON
Believers sometimes find it difficult to deal with life and death matters.

BIBLE LEARNING
Jesus has conquered death, so we have hope.

BIBLE APPLICATION
Jesus thanks the Lord for hearing Him before He (Jesus) calls Lazarus from the grave by name.

STUDENTS' RESPONSES
Believers learn that Jesus has the power to raise life in our dead places.

LESSON SCRIPTURE

JOHN 11:38–44, KJV

38 Jesus therefore again groaning in himself cometh to the grave. It was a cave, and a stone lay upon it.

39 Jesus said, Take ye away the stone. Martha, the sister of him that was dead, saith unto him, Lord, by this time he stinketh: for he hath been dead four days.

JOHN 11:38–44, NIV

38 Jesus, once more deeply moved, came to the tomb. It was a cave with a stone laid across the entrance.

39 "Take away the stone," he said. "But, Lord," said Martha, the sister of the dead man, "by this time there is a bad odor, for he has been there four days."

40 Jesus saith unto her, Said I not unto thee, that, if thou wouldest believe, thou shouldest see the glory of God?

41 Then they took away the stone from the place where the dead was laid. And Jesus lifted up his eyes, and said, Father, I thank thee that thou hast heard me.

42 And I knew that thou hearest me always: but because of the people which stand by I said it, that they may believe that thou hast sent me.

43 And when he thus had spoken, he cried with a loud voice, Lazarus, come forth.

44 And he that was dead came forth, bound hand and foot with graveclothes: and his face was bound about with a napkin. Jesus saith unto them, Loose him, and let him go.

40 Then Jesus said, "Did I not tell you that if you believe, you will see the glory of God?"

41 So they took away the stone. Then Jesus looked up and said, "Father, I thank you that you have heard me.

42 I knew that you always hear me, but I said this for the benefit of the people standing here, that they may believe that you sent me."

43 When he had said this, Jesus called in a loud voice, "Lazarus, come out!"

44 The dead man came out, his hands and feet wrapped with strips of linen, and a cloth around his face. Jesus said to them, "Take off the grave clothes and let him go."

LIGHT ON THE WORD

Mary, Martha, and Lazarus. The two sisters, Mary and Martha, along with their brother Lazarus, were close friends of Jesus. The three of them apparently lived as a household in a village called Bethany. The Bible makes it clear in **John 11:1–2** that this Mary was the same Mary who later poured perfume on Jesus' feet and wiped them with her hair (**John 12:1–3**) at a dinner given in His honor.

These sisters were also the same Mary and Martha of the well-known story in **Luke 10:38–42**. Jesus was a guest in their home, and Martha complained that instead of helping her, Mary was sitting and listening to Jesus. Jesus gently rebuked Martha, pointing out that it is better to be concerned about spiritual things than worried about temporal things.

Mourning. Visiting and mourning with those who were bereaved was an essential part of Jewish life and community. Neighbors were expected to help provide the first meal after the funeral. After losing a loved one, the bereaved would spend the first week mourning at home, sitting on the floor surrounded by relatives, friends, and neighbors. This practice, called "sitting shiva," is still practiced in Judaism today. In those days, it was not uncommon for the mourners to weep or wail loudly, and sometimes even "professional" mourners would be hired to come to the home. After the seven days, the bereaved would not wear any kind of adornment for three weeks and would often abstain from normal comforts or pleasure for an entire year after the death.

TEACHING THE BIBLE LESSON

LIFE NEED FOR TODAY'S LESSON

AIM: Students will discover that believers sometimes find it difficult to deal with life and death matters.

INTRODUCTION

An Urgent Plea

According to John 11, Lazarus was very sick and his sisters thought it urgent enough to send word to Jesus that "the one you love is sick" (**v. 4**). Upon receiving this message, Jesus told His disciples that Lazarus' sickness would not end in death, but would instead bring glory to God. Jesus, though He loved Lazarus and Lazarus' sisters, did not immediately begin to journey to Bethany, but waited two days.

Finally, Jesus and His disciples began the long walk to Bethany. Upon their arrival, they learned that Lazarus had already been in the tomb for four days. This is significant, because according to the Talmud, the Jews practiced the ancient custom of shemira, which means to guard the body. They believed that the dead person's spirit stayed near the body for three days after death and that it was possible the person could "come back to life" during that time. By the fourth day, however, there was no hope.

As soon as they saw Jesus, Mary and Martha both expressed what they wholeheartedly believed: If Jesus had arrived while Lazarus was still living, Jesus would have healed him. But now the only hope they had was their belief that their brother would one day rise again in the resurrection of the last day. But Jesus announced to Martha that He is the Resurrection, and that anyone who believed in Him would live (**v. 25**).

Though knowing that He would ultimately raise Lazarus from the dead, Jesus was deeply moved by His friends' grief, and He wept. At this, some of the mourners admired Him for the depth of His love for His friend. Others pointed out that if Jesus was capable of other miracles, He surely should have been capable of keeping Lazarus from death.

BIBLE LEARNING

AIM: Students will accept that Jesus has conquered death, so we have hope.

I. JESUS' INSTRUCTION
(John 11:38–39)

Accompanied by Mary, Martha, and the crowd of mourners, Jesus approached Lazarus' tomb. **Verse 38** says that He again was deeply moved as He came to the tomb.

In biblical times, "graves" were often caves, usually sealed with a large stone to keep out wild animals or intruders. The burial typically took place on the day of death, and the body was wrapped very tightly in strips of cloth. The Jews did not embalm, using only some spices to cover the odor of rotting flesh. The body remained in the tomb for eleven months until it decomposed, then the bones would be in an ossuary and stored on a shelf of the family's tomb.

Martha, though she no doubt wanted to trust Jesus, was horrified at His instruction to remove the stone. She remonstrated with Jesus, reminding Him that Lazarus had already been dead for four days; there was no hope that he was still alive—and surely there would be a terrible smell by now. But Jesus wanted the onlookers to know without a doubt that this truly was the dead man coming back to life, a man who would have to walk through the opening of the tomb back out into the sunlight—not a ghost or figment of their imaginations.

John 11:38–39

38 Jesus therefore again groaning in himself cometh to the grave. It was a cave, and a stone lay upon it.

Jesus is approaching the grave of His friend Lazarus. As He approaches, He begins groaning (Gk. *embrimaomai*, **em-bree-MAH-oh-my**) in Himself. The word for groaning is etymologically related to the word for "to snort in anger." The NLT has translated this as "angry," which could mean that Jesus was angry at the people's unbelief or due to the sorrow death causes in people's lives (**John 11:33**). In this context, anger is not out of the question.

The Greek word used here for grave (*mnemeion*, **mnay-MAY-on**) can also refer to anything visible that recalls the memory of a person or thing. The graves of first-century Palestine were usually caves with a stone disk placed in front. These caves would contain vertical or horizontal vaults constructed out from the main chamber. The stone disk would be placed in front of the main chamber. This would protect the corpse from wild animals, the elements, and the possibility of grave robbers.

39 Jesus said, Take ye away the stone. Martha, the sister of him that was dead, saith unto him, Lord, by this time he stinketh: for he hath been dead four days.

With intentionality, Jesus commands the men around Him to take away the stone. This is the first of three commands associated with this miracle. Martha comments in protest that by this time, the dead body of Lazarus "stinketh" (Gk. *ozo*, **OD-zoh**). This word is used in the New Testament only here in John. It is also used in the Septuagint to describe the stench of the dead frogs from the second plague of Egypt (**Exodus 8:10**). Martha adds that Lazarus has been dead four days. Note that this is one day longer than the time Jesus would spend in the grave.

SEARCH THE SCRIPTURES

QUESTION 1
How many days was Lazarus dead?

Four days.

LIGHT ON THE WORD

The Smell of Death
By the fourth day, the body would begin to decompose, the reason behind the smell mentioned by Martha. Bodies decomposed quickly in Palestine because they were not embalmed. People would anoint the bodies with spices in order to mask the smell.

II. JESUS' PRAYER (vv. 40–44)

Jesus then reminded Martha of what He had already told her earlier (**v. 25**): that if she believed, she would see the glory of God. This glory of God revealed the awesome power of Christ over even the power of death.

The stone was rolled away. Jesus looked up to Heaven and prayed out loud, so that those around Him could hear it. Significantly, His first words thanked God in advance for what God would do through Him. The words of His prayer also bore witness to His personal and powerful relationship with God, and illustrate Jesus' perfect confidence that God always heard His prayers. Lastly, Jesus points out that the miracle about to occur was for the benefit of those watching, that they might believe that Jesus had truly been sent from God.

Belief in Christ

40 Jesus saith unto her, Said I not unto thee, that, if thou wouldest believe, thou shouldest see the glory of God?

In response to Martha's protest, Jesus asks her a question. He points to His statement (**vv. 25–26**) asserting that those who believe (Gk. *pisteuo*, **pis-TOO-oh**) would never die. This word for belief is very familiar in the New Testament. It means to think to be true, to be persuaded, to place confidence in. In effect, He is saying placing one's confidence in Him would allow them to see the glory (Gk. *doxa*, **DOK-sah**) of God. The word "glory" in classical Greek literature has the meaning of what one thinks, an opinion. In the objective sense, it is used favorably as reputation or renown—what one is worth based on reputation. In the New Testament, it takes on a religious meaning connected with the Old Testament concept of glory, which expressed the impressiveness of God in relation to man (cf. **Exodus 33:18, Luke 2:9**). In this verse, Jesus correlates the glory of God with the power of resurrection He spoke of (**vv. 25–26**).

41 Then they took away the stone from the place where the dead was laid. And Jesus lifted up his eyes, and said, Father, I thank thee that thou hast heard me. 42 And I knew that thou hearest me always: but because of the people which stand by I said it, that they may believe that thou hast sent me.

It would have taken several men to roll such a large stone away from the tomb. After they do so, Jesus lifts His eyes to Heaven. This is a traditional Jewish way of praying as opposed to the familiar Western way of bowing the head and closing the eyes. Jesus prays with the knowledge of His Father's will. This is shown in His expression of thanksgiving. He acknowledges that God the Father hears Him always (Gk. *pantote*, **PAN-toe-teh**). Jesus uses this word twice in John in connection with the Father. In **John 8:29**, Jesus declares that He always does those things that please God the Father. This points toward the unique relationship Jesus has with the Father as the only begotten Son.

Jesus wants to give a glimpse of this picture to those standing by (Gk. *peristemi*, **peh-ree-EES-tay-mee**); it is not clear whether they are in mourning or just a crowd gathered to witness Jesus' next action. Jesus wants them to believe that the Father has sent (Gk. *apostello*, **ah-poh-STEL-loh**) Him. In this way, the act of raising Lazarus would mark Jesus as unique and point toward His resurrection as the Son of God.

III. JESUS' TRIUMPH (vv. 43–44)

Jesus could have silently summoned Lazarus from the dead. But once again, He was mindful of the crowd looking on. Since His goal was to reveal God's glory, He called loudly, "Lazarus, come out!" Immediately, the dead man came shuffling out of the grave. There was no delay between Jesus' command and Lazarus' obedience, just like the resurrection of the last day which will be "in a moment, in a twinkling of an eye" (**1 Corinthians 15:52**).

Not only was Lazarus alive again, but he was actually walking. His hands and feet were still bound with strips of cloth, and the burial napkin still covered his face. Those in the crowd knew that it really was Lazarus, not some imposter.

A Loud Cry

43 And when he thus had spoken, he cried with a loud voice, Lazarus, come forth. 44 And he that was dead came forth, bound hand and foot with graveclothes: and his face was bound about with a napkin. Jesus saith unto them, Loose him, and let him go.

Jesus then issues a prayer of command. Unlike a petition, it is an expression of faith in what God has already done. The text says that Jesus cried (Gk. *kraugazo*, **krow-GAHD-zo**) with a loud voice. The word means to cry aloud, not indicating a particular emotion but extreme feeling expressed loudly. The crying out could be connected with great joy or great grief. He calls Lazarus from the grave. His words can also be translated as "Come out!" It gives the appearance that Lazarus may have already been alive and all Jesus had to do was to call him out of the grave.

John records Lazarus coming out of the grave being "bound hand and foot with graveclothes." These would have been long cloth strips used to wrap the body. The head was also wrapped up with a napkin, which was a cloth used for keeping the corpse's mouth shut. The tightness of these clothes made this event even more miraculous, as it would have been hard for anyone to walk in such attire.

SEARCH THE SCRIPTURES

QUESTION 2

Why was Jesus "groaning" or angry when He approached Lazarus' tomb?

Jesus was angry at the people's unbelief or due to the sorrow death causes in people's lives.

QUESTION 3

Why did Jesus call Lazarus' name out loud?

Jesus called Lazarus' name aloud so that the bystanders would believe.

LIGHT ON THE WORD

Lazarus is Alive!

Jesus instructed those around Lazarus to take his grave clothes off and set him free. As they unwound his grave clothes, they would touch him and see him for themselves, thus experiencing tangible proof of Jesus' power and divinity.

BIBLE APPLICATION

AIM: Students will know that Jesus gave thanks to the Lord for hearing Him before He (Jesus) calls Lazarus from the grave by name.

Whether the tragic loss of a friend or family member, through a violent act or a peaceful homegoing, all of us have at least observed the loss and grief that death brings. Thank God that as believers, we can confess with Martha that Jesus is the promised Messiah and Son of God. We can rejoice that, by raising Lazarus, Jesus revealed Himself as "the resurrection and the life." And, even while mourning the loss of loved ones, we confess and believe that for the Christian, death is not final.

STUDENT'S RESPONSES

AIM: Students will learn that Jesus has the power to raise life in the dead places in our places.

We live in a world where death is inevitable. It could be easy to live in hopelessness and fear, but we know that we serve Jesus, who doesn't just perform resurrections—He is resurrection and life. This week, make a conscious effort to thank Him for the gift of eternal life and comfort those who are grieving with the hope found only in Christ.

PRAYER

Dear Jesus, we pray that You continue to help us to love and care for others who are sick and shut-in. Lord, we thank You for Your faithfulness, even when we are unfaithful. Bless You and Praise You. In Jesus' Name we pray. Amen.

HOW TO SAY IT

Lazarus.	LA-zer-us.
Shouldest.	SHUD-ist.

PREPARE FOR NEXT SUNDAY

Read **Exodus 12:1–14** and "The Passover."

DAILY HOME BIBLE READINGS

MONDAY
Trust in Facing Death
(Psalm 56)

TUESDAY
Life Eternal
(Isaiah 25:6–10)

WEDNESDAY
Darkness Dispelled
(Matthew 4:12–17)

THURSDAY
For God's Glory
(John 11:1–6)

FRIDAY
I am Life
(John 11:17–27)

SATURDAY
Jesus Wept
(John 11:28–37)

SUNDAY
The Death of a Friend
(John 11:38–44)

Sources:
Arrington, French L., and Roger Stronstad, eds. *Life in the Spirit New Testament Commentary*. Grand Rapids, MI: Zondervan, 1999. 69-72.
Keener, Craig S. *The IVP Bible Background Commentary: New Testament*. Downers Grove, IL: InterVarsity Press, 1993. 292-293.

COMMENTS / NOTES:

PASSOVER

BIBLE BASIS: EXODUS 12:1–14

BIBLE TRUTH: God gave Moses and the people instructions for the first Passover.

MEMORY VERSE: "And this day shall be unto you for a memorial; and ye shall keep it a feast to the LORD throughout your generations; ye shall keep it a feast by an ordinance for ever"

(Exodus 12:14).

LESSON AIM: By the end of the lesson, we will: RECALL events surrounding the institution of the Feast of Passover; REFLECT on the meaning of Passover and what it says about God; and DEVELOP a festival of praise to God for salvation.

TEACHER PREPARATION

MATERIALS NEEDED: Quarterly Commentary/Teacher Manual, Adult Quarterly, Adult resources—charts, worksheets, and other teaching tools, paper, pens, pencils, Bibles (several different versions)

OTHER MATERIALS NEEDED / TEACHER'S NOTES:

_____

_____

LESSON OVERVIEW

LIFE NEED FOR TODAY'S LESSON
People love to commemorate historic events by celebrating them year after year.

BIBLE LEARNING
The Passover commemorates the Israelites' deliverance from Egyptian bondage.

BIBLE APPLICATION
Believers know that the Children of Israel obey God and that we too should obey the Lord.

STUDENTS' RESPONSES
Christians accept that there is no need in our lives that remains outside of God's care and concern.

LESSON SCRIPTURE

EXODUS 12:1–14, KJV

1 And the LORD spake unto Moses and Aaron in the land of Egypt saying,

2 This month shall be unto you the beginning of months: it shall be the first month of the year to you.

3 Speak ye unto all the congregation of

EXODUS 12:1–14, NIV

1 The LORD said to Moses and Aaron in Egypt,

2 "This month is to be for you the first month, the first month of your year.

3 Tell the whole community of Israel that on the tenth day of this month each man

Israel, saying, In the tenth day of this month they shall take to them every man a lamb, according to the house of their fathers, a lamb for an house:

4 And if the household be too little for the lamb, let him and his neighbour next unto his house take it according to the number of the souls; every man according to his eating shall make your count for the lamb.

5 Your lamb shall be without blemish, a male of the first year: ye shall take it out from the sheep, or from the goats:

6 And ye shall keep it up until the fourteenth day of the same month: and the whole assembly of the congregation of Israel shall kill it in the evening.

7 And they shall take of the blood, and strike it on the two side posts and on the upper door post of the houses, wherein they shall eat it.

8 And they shall eat the flesh in that night, roast with fire, and unleavened bread; and with bitter herbs they shall eat it.

9 Eat not of it raw, nor sodden at all with water, but roast with fire; his head with his legs, and with the purtenance thereof.

10 And ye shall let nothing of it remain until the morning; and that which remaineth of it until the morning ye shall burn with fire.

11 And thus shall ye eat it; with your loins girded, your shoes on your feet, and your staff in your hand; and ye shall eat it in haste: it is the LORD's passover.

12 For I will pass through the land of Egypt this night, and will smite all the firstborn in the land of Egypt, both man and beast; and against all the gods of Egypt I will execute judgment: I am the LORD.

is to take a lamb for his family, one for each household.

4 If any household is too small for a whole lamb, they must share one with their nearest neighbor, having taken into account the number of people there are. You are to determine the amount of lamb needed in accordance with what each person will eat.

5 The animals you choose must be year-old males without defect, and you may take them from the sheep or the goats.

6 Take care of them until the fourteenth day of the month, when all the members of the community of Israel must slaughter them at twilight.

7 Then they are to take some of the blood and put it on the sides and tops of the doorframes of the houses where they eat the lambs.

8 That same night they are to eat the meat roasted over the fire, along with bitter herbs, and bread made without yeast.

9 Do not eat the meat raw or boiled in water, but roast it over a fire—with the head, legs and internal organs.

10 Do not leave any of it till morning; if some is left till morning, you must burn it.

11 This is how you are to eat it: with your cloak tucked into your belt, your sandals on your feet and your staff in your hand. Eat it in haste; it is the LORD's Passover.

12 "On that same night I will pass through Egypt and strike down every firstborn of both people and animals, and I will bring judgment on all the gods of Egypt. I am the LORD.

13 The blood will be a sign for you on the houses where you are, and when I see the

13 And the blood shall be to you for a token upon the houses where ye are: and when I see the blood, I will pass over you, and the plague shall not be upon you to destroy you, when I smite the land of Egypt.

14 And this day shall be unto you for a memorial; and ye shall keep it a feast to the LORD throughout your generations; ye shall keep it a feast by an ordinance for ever.

blood, I will pass over you. No destructive plague will touch you when I strike Egypt.

14 "This is a day you are to commemorate; for the generations to come you shall celebrate it as a festival to the LORD—a lasting ordinance.

LIGHT ON THE WORD

The Firstborn. From the earliest times, the position of firstborn son has been one of honor. Following the father's death, the oldest son or firstborn was expected to become head of the household. Similarly, the firstborn inherited a double portion of the father's property (**Deuteronomy 21:17**). In the Bible, God refers to the entire nation of Israel as His "firstborn" (**Exodus 4:22**). Among the Egyptians, the sun-god Amon-Ra was considered the protector of all firstborns, and firstborn sons were dedicated to him. Following their deliverance from Egyptian bondage, God would mandate that the firstborn Israelites be dedicated to Him (**Exodus 13:2**).

Later, the Law would require that the first-born son be presented to God at the tabernacle or Temple and redeemed by a payment (**Leviticus 12; Numbers 18:15–16**). Similarly, the first-borns of clean animals such as bulls, lambs, or goats were to be presented to God as a sacrifice eight days after their birth. Animals with defects were unacceptable sacrifices and must be eaten at home. The firstborn of unclean animals, such an ass, could not be presented as a sacrifice and were to be redeemed with a clean animal, such as a sheep, in its place.

TEACHING THE BIBLE LESSON

LIFE NEED FOR TODAY'S LESSON

AIM: Students will discover how the followers of Christ understand that people love to commemorate historic events by celebrating them year after year.

INTRODUCTION

God's Deliverance

The Passover commemorates God's deliverance of the Children of Israel from Egyptian slavery. Jacob and his sons had left the land God promised them because of a widespread famine. Over time, Jacob's descendants had become so plentiful that the Egyptian pharaoh became fearful that the Jews would take over his country, so he put them in slavery. This pharaoh went so far as to order the death of all Hebrew baby boys. Moses, a Hebrew boy who was saved from the slaughter through God's intervention, was led by God to bring His people out of bondage. God ordered Moses to lead the Children of Israel into Palestine, the land He had promised to Abraham. However, the pharaoh refused to release the Israelites; even though God sent nine plagues to make the pharaoh change his mind, the ruler's heart was hardened and he steadfastly refused. Now, God would send the tenth and final devastating plague.

BIBLE LEARNING

AIM: Students will accept that the Passover commemorates the Israelites' deliverance from Egyptian bondage.

I. INSTITUTION OF THE PASSOVER (Exodus 12:1–7)

Up until this point in their history, the Children of Israel had been a dismal failure. However, Israel's deliverance from Egyptian slavery will demonstrate God's love for them. God orders Moses to speak to the "entire congregation of Israel" (**v. 3**). By telling Israel to remake their calendar, God is signaling them that through His might, everything in their lives will be changed. This is to be a communal celebration because God delivered the entire people from slavery, something they are to never forget by commemorating their salvation annually.

Now Moses is told to give Israel specific instructions for this new commemoration. The people are told to select an unblemished male sheep or goat that was a year old or younger, and keep it with the household for the four days leading up to the Passover. The young lamb or goat then would have become a part of the household and the family would mourn its eventual sacrifice. Here we see that God requires the sacrifice to be personal. We also see how the Exodus Passover Lamb mirrors Jesus the Passover Lamb. Note also the importance of celebrating the Passover with family members in homes instead of a large community gathering. We want to remember that Jesus, the Son of God, lived with the human family before He was required to sacrifice His life for them. Perhaps more importantly, the sacrifice that Jesus made was personal and must be as relevant to each home as the community or nation.

The people were instructed to slaughter the animals in the evening. This brings to mind that Jesus' crucifixion began at noon on the day of preparation for Passover (**John 19:14**), and that He actually died at the ninth hour (**Matthew 27:45–50**)—the precise time to sacrifice the Passover lambs in the Temple.

After the lamb or goat was slaughtered, God instructed the Israelites to place some of its blood on the doorposts and lintels—the beam forming the upper part of the door's framework—of their houses (**v. 7**). By placing the blood on the doorway, the Israelites would see it every time they entered their homes, reminding them daily of the sacrifice and the fact that God had passed over their homes and spared their first born the night before they left Egypt. Note that only the blood was sacrificed to God—a reminder that only the blood of Jesus could save us from sin.

Exodus 12:1–14

1 And the Lord spake unto Moses and Aaron in the land of Egypt saying, 2 This month shall be unto you the beginning of months: it shall be the first month of the year to you.

Exodus 12 opens with instructions from the Lord to Moses and Aaron on the eve of the Israelites' exodus from Egypt. Three times the Lord spoke to Moses and Aaron about this particular month. The Hebrew word *khodesh* (**KHO-desh**) is "new moon" or "month." It literally means a new moon but also means month since the new moon marked the new month in the lunar calendar. Here God is speaking to Moses and Aaron during the first month of the year. On the Jewish calendar, this month is called Nisan/Abib and corresponds to our March or April (cf. **Deuteronomy 16:1; Esther 3:7**). The narrator prepares the reader to anticipate that the Lord was about to do a new thing in Israel's history—He is preparing the people for the exodus from Egypt by instructing them to commemorate the event with the Passover and Feast of Unleavened Bread.

3 Speak ye unto all the congregation of Israel, saying, In the tenth day of this month they shall take to them every man a lamb, according to the house of their fathers, a lamb for

an house: 4 And if the household be too little for the lamb, let him and his neighbour next unto his house take it according to the number of the souls; every man according to his eating shall make your count for the lamb.

The Lord instructed Moses and Aaron to tell all the people of Israel what they were supposed to do to prepare for their impending departure. The text implies that the people were not present when the Lord spoke with Moses and Aaron. The Lord's instructions were very specific. On the tenth day of the first month, every male head of household should take a lamb for his family for the Passover meal. In ancient Israel, the family was the most basic form of social organization; it provided identity, protection, goods, and resources. Unlike the individualistic faith many observe now, religion in ancient times was communal, beginning at the family level and expanding to include the entire community.

A typical family household in Hebrew, called a *bet 'ab* (**bait av**), "father's house," or "house of the father," consisted of the eldest male, his wife, their adult sons and their spouses and children, their children and unmarried teenagers, unmarried sisters, and maybe another relative. If the patriarch was wealthy, the household might also include secondary wives and concubines, servants, resident aliens, and even people captured in battle. Unlike many contemporary single-family households comprised of nuclear families with a mother, father, and two-and-a-half children, a family household in ancient Israel normally consisted of seven to fifteen people.

5 Your lamb shall be without blemish, a male of the first year: ye shall take it out from the sheep, or from the goats:

In addition to the specific date for selecting the lamb, and who was supposed to partake of it, Moses and Aaron were commanded to tell the people what condition the lamb must be in. First, it must be without any disease or deformities. The Hebrew word for "without blemish" is *tamim*

(tah-MEEM) and means "without defect," "blameless," or "complete." Second, it must be a year-old male lamb or goat. The general understanding in the Hebrew sacrificial system was that clean animals without blemishes were acceptable sacrifices to God. Lambs and goats were generally readily accessible among the acceptable clean animals, and no offering or sacrifice could have any physical defect because it was for God, who deserved the first fruits and the perfect animals.

6 And ye shall keep it up until the fourteenth day of the same month: and the whole assembly of the congregation of Israel shall kill it in the evening. 7 And they shall take of the blood, and strike it on the two side posts and on the upper door post of the houses, wherein they shall eat it.

Moses and Aaron were also instructed to tell the people to slaughter the animals at sunset on the fourteenth day of Nisan, four days after it was selected. The Hebrew word for "evening" is *'ereb* (**EH-rev**). Observant Jews continue to count the new day as beginning at sunset or twilight, not at midnight as Western tradition. This is according to the account of God creating in Genesis 1 (**vv. 5, 8, 13, 19, 23, 31**). They were also told to take the blood of the lamb and splash it on the two side doorposts (Heb. *mezuzah*; **mez-oo-ZAW**) and the lintel (Heb. *mashqoph*; **mash-KOFE**), or horizontal beam holding up the doorposts at the threshold, of the house where the lamb would be eaten.

SEARCH THE SCRIPTURES

QUESTION 1
What instructions were given to Moses and Aaron regarding the blood of the sacrificed animal?

They were to take the blood, and strike it on the two side posts, and on the upper door post of the houses, then the people eat it (the animal).

LIGHT ON THE WORD

Community Religion

There was no concept of individual religious observation in the ancient world. An individual's behavior could have a harmful impact on an entire community, which is why the covenant between Israel and the Lord was with all the people, not a few individuals. This view is similar to the South African principle of Ubuntu: "A person is a person through other people."

II. INSTRUCTIONS FOR THE PASSOVER MEAL (vv. 8–10)

God directed the Israelites to thoroughly roast the rest of the sacrificial animal over a fire and eat it with unleavened bread and bitter herbs. God also told the Israelites to wear their belts and sandals while they ate the meal. The belt and sandals signified that Israel not only believed God would deliver them, they were dressed and ready to go. God's directions reveal His requirement that the Children of Israel place their complete faith in Him, and trust His promise of immediate deliverance. Anything left of the sacrifice was to be burnt. Here we see that God wanted His people to consume all that He had provided for them. This was the usual way to handle an offering or sacrifice in the Old Testament. Because it was holy, dedicated to God, nothing could be wasted or thrown away.

Instruction for No Leftovers

8 And they shall eat the flesh in that night, roast with fire, and unleavened bread; and with bitter herbs they shall eat it. 9 Eat not of it raw, nor sodden at all with water, but roast with fire; his head with his legs, and with the purtenance thereof. 10 And ye shall let nothing of it remain until the morning; and that which remaineth of it until the morning ye shall burn with fire.

Once the people had slaughtered the lamb they were supposed to roast the entire animal—head, legs, and organs included—by fire and serve it with unleavened bread and bitter herbs. The Hebrew word for "unleavened bread" is *matstsah* (**mats-TSAH**). Many might recognize it as the flat, crispy, lightly browned crackers sold in the grocery store during Passover. They are made with water and flour. The Israelites were specifically prohibited from eating the meat raw or boiling it in water. Moreover, all of the meat must be eaten before morning. If any meat is not eaten they are instructed to burn it. The reason for this stipulation is not given but the understanding in the Hebrew sacrificial system was that the offering could only be used for the designated purpose, in this case observing the Passover, so it had to be consumed at that meal.

III. Promise of the Passover (vv. 11–14)

Now, God promises that He will "pass through the land of Egypt" (**v. 12**) and kill the firstborn of every household. For God to spare the Israelites, they had to trust and obey His instructions and mark the doorposts with the blood of the sacrificed animal.

Even if the Israelite family ate the Passover meal but did not mark the doorpost with the blood, they would still be visited by this tenth and final plague—the death angel. To receive the Passover promise, each household had to express obedience to demonstrate their belief. The sole purpose of God instituting the Passover was so He could make a provision of salvation for Israel.

The Lord's Passover

11 And thus shall ye eat it; with your loins girded, your shoes on your feet, and your staff in your hand; and ye shall eat it in haste: it is the Lord's passover. 12 For I will pass through the land of Egypt this night, and will smite all the firstborn in the land of Egypt, both man and beast; and against all the gods of Egypt I will execute judgment: I am the Lord. 13 And the blood shall be to

you for a token upon the houses where ye are: and when I see the blood, I will pass over you, and the plague shall not be upon you to destroy you, when I smite the land of Egypt.

The Lord even specifies how the people are to eat the meal. They are told to eat in with their shoes and clothes on and staff in hand in preparation for a hasty departure. The idiom to "gird your loins" refers to men fastening their lower garments worn between their legs with a cloth or belt. Although this instruction is directed to the adult males in the household, the women and children present were also expected to prepare to leave quickly.

On the night before the Exodus, the Lord would pass through the land of Egypt, bringing the plague of death to the firstborn males, human and animal, that did not have the sign of the blood on the posts at the threshold to their houses. Not even the gods of Egypt would be spared judgment.

The Hebrew word for "Passover" is *pesakh* (**PEH-sakh**). The explanation given for the meaning of the word "passover" is that the Lord would "pass over" (*pesakh*) those households where the Israelites resided indicated by the blood on the posts (**v. 13**). The blood did not have a protective power, but was rather a sign to Israel. The Lord was more than aware which houses contained faithful Israelite families; this was not for the Lord's sake, but for those who were spared to know that He would do what He promised.

14 And this day shall be unto you for a memorial; and ye shall keep it a feast to the Lord throughout your generations; ye shall keep it a feast by an ordinance for ever.

The meal the Israelites would share would not be a time of relaxation and merriment, but rather a solemn occasion. Moses and Aaron were putting their faith in the Lord by going telling the people that the Lord was about to deliver them from slavery in Egypt, when they did not know whether the people would believe them and do as they commanded.

Nonetheless, they were to tell the people that when this happened, they should commemorate the event as the Passover, to be observed on 15 Nisan each year, and they must pass down this tradition to their children for generations. In adherence to this command, the Israelites were to observe the Festival of Unleavened Bread for seven days as a reminder that in their haste to leave Egypt, there was no time to wait for the yeast to rise in the bread. Part of observing the Passover was to abstain from eating anything with leaven during this time or even having any leaven in the house.

SEARCH THE SCRIPTURES

QUESTION 2
How long were the Israelites to observe the Festival of Unleavened Bread?

Seven days.

QUESTION 3
How long are the Israelites to celebrate the feast?

Forever.

LIGHT ON THE WORD
The One True God
Ancient peoples, including the Israelites before the monarchy, acknowledged the existence of multiple gods. However, the Israelites believed that the Lord their God was above all the others. The text does not state what judgment the Lord would execute on the Egyptian gods. Nonetheless, since the Egyptians believed that the pharaoh was divine, some scholars suggest that this statement is directed at the pharaoh.

BIBLE APPLICATION

AIM: Students will want believers to know that the Children of Israel obey God and that we too should obey the Lord.

In the Pentateuch and in Judaism, Passover commemorates God physically delivering the Israelites from slavery and protecting their first born in the process. The passage and the festival serve as a reminder that our God is a God who is involved in people's lives. In a sermon delivered to Dexter Avenue Baptist Church in Montgomery, Alabama, on April 7, 1957, Martin Luther King, Jr., proclaimed, "And I say to you this morning, my friends, rise up and know that as you struggle for justice, you do not struggle alone. But God struggles with you. And He is working every day." Passover serves as an annual reminder of God's willingness and ability to struggle with and for us against oppression. It also serves as an annual opportunity to thank God for all of the continuing work of salvation in our lives.

STUDENT'S RESPONSES

AIM: Students will learn that Christians accept that there is no need in our lives that remains outside of God's care and concern.

In the Passover, we witness a divine liberation enacted under the stern hand of our God. In Christ we share in this liberation, freed from the slavery of our sin.

The Exodus, even though it happened thousands of years ago, called a people into being. More importantly, it demonstrated the extraordinary lengths God will go to to save a people He loved. Sadly, God's people have not always responded to His loving kindness with faithfulness. While God does not require that present-day saints make the physical sacrifice Jesus did, He does require that we demonstrate His extraordinary love. Every day God presents us with an opportunity to love others, especially those who are enduring the oppression of want and poverty.

PRAYER

God, remembering Your deliverance in our lives is a special gift from You. Help us to allow Your goodness to stay at the forefront of our choices. As we travel from bondage to freedom, may we know that You are guiding us along the way. In Jesus' Name we pray. Amen.

HOW TO SAY IT

Sodden.   SOD-in.

Purtenance.   PUHR-tin-ans.

PREPARE FOR NEXT SUNDAY

Read **Leviticus 23:15–22** and "Feast of Weeks."

DAILY HOME BIBLE READINGS

MONDAY
Jesus and the Passover
(Luke 2:41–49)

TUESDAY
The "Last" Passover
(Matthew 26:20–30)

WEDNESDAY
The Fourth Plague
(Exodus 8:20–29)

THURSDAY
The Eighth Plague
(Exodus 10:12–20)

FRIDAY
Detailed Instructions
(Numbers 9:1–4, 13)

SATURDAY
When Your Children Ask
(Joshua 4:1–7)

SUNDAY
Passover
(Exodus 12:1–14)

Sources:

Childs, Brevard S. *Exodus: A Commentary*. London: SCM Press, 1974. 196-199.

Eze, Michael Onyebuchi. *Intellectual History in Contemporary South Africa*. London: Palgrave MacMillan, 2010. 190-191.

Fretheim, Terence. *Exodus*. Interpretation. Louisville, KY: Westminster John Knox Press, 1991. 137-139.

Waldemar, Janzen. *Exodus*. Believers Church Bible Commentary. Waterloo, Ontario: Herald Press, 2000. 154-159.

King, Martin Luther, Jr. "'The Birth of a New Nation': Sermon at Dexter Avenue Baptist Church." Pages 13-42 in A Call to Conscience: The Landmark Speeches of Martin Luther King, Jr. Edited by Clayborne Carson and Kris Shepard. New York: Warner Books, 2001.

COMMENTS / NOTES:

FEAST OF WEEKS = Feast of Pentecost
(50 days after 7th Sabbath)

BIBLE BASIS: LEVITICUS 23:15–22

BIBLE TRUTH: God commanded the Hebrews to offer Him joyful praise and thanksgiving as they share their harvest with the needy.

MEMORY VERSE: "Even unto the morrow after the seventh sabbath shall ye number fifty days; and ye shall offer a new meat offering unto the LORD" (Leviticus 23:16).

LESSON AIM: By the end of the lesson, we will: EXAMINE the Feast of Weeks found in Leviticus; CELEBRATE with joy and thanksgiving times of giving to God what belongs to Him and to the needy; and COMMIT to a life plan of returning to God a portion of what has been received and sharing with those in need.

TEACHER PREPARATION

MATERIALS NEEDED: Quarterly Commentary/Teacher Manual, Adult Quarterly, Adult resources—charts, worksheets, and other teaching tools, paper, pens, pencils, Bibles (several different versions)

OTHER MATERIALS NEEDED / TEACHER'S NOTES:

_____

_____

LESSON OVERVIEW

LIFE NEED FOR TODAY'S LESSON
People share the harvest with thanksgiving and share the fruit with others.

BIBLE LEARNING
Christians learn how the Children of Israel obediently acknowledge the blessings of God.

BIBLE APPLICATION
Believers are to share with those who are in need and celebrate God's bountiful blessing in their lives.

STUDENTS' RESPONSES
Believers learn to commit a portion of what they have received back to the Lord and to help those in need.

LESSON SCRIPTURE

LEVITICUS 23:15–22, KJV

15 And ye shall count unto you from the morrow after the sabbath, from the day that ye brought the sheaf of the wave offering; seven sabbaths shall be complete:

16 Even unto the morrow after the seventh

LEVITICUS 23:15–22, NIV

15 "'From the day after the Sabbath, the day you brought the sheaf of the wave offering, count off seven full weeks.

16 Count off fifty days up to the day after the seventh Sabbath, and then present an

sabbath shall ye number fifty days; and ye shall offer a new meat offering unto the LORD.

17 Ye shall bring out of your habitations two wave loaves of two tenth deals; they shall be of fine flour; they shall be baken with leaven; they are the firstfruits unto the LORD.

18 And ye shall offer with the bread seven lambs without blemish of the first year, and one young bullock, and two rams: they shall be for a burnt offering unto the LORD, with their meat offering, and their drink offerings, even an offering made by fire, of sweet savour unto the LORD.

19 Then ye shall sacrifice one kid of the goats for a sin offering, and two lambs of the first year for a sacrifice of peace offerings.

20 And the priest shall wave them with the bread of the firstfruits for a wave offering before the LORD, with the two lambs: they shall be holy to the LORD for the priest.

21 And ye shall proclaim on the selfsame day, that it may be an holy convocation unto you: ye shall do no servile work therein: it shall be a statute for ever in all your dwellings throughout your generations.

22 And when ye reap the harvest of your land, thou shalt not make clean riddance of the corners of thy field when thou reapest, neither shalt thou gather any gleaning of thy harvest: thou shalt leave them unto the poor, and to the stranger: I am the LORD your God.

offering of new grain to the LORD.

17 From wherever you live, bring two loaves made of two-tenths of an ephah of the finest flour, baked with yeast, as a wave offering of firstfruits to the LORD.

18 Present with this bread seven male lambs, each a year old and without defect, one young bull and two rams. They will be a burnt offering to the LORD, together with their grain offerings and drink offerings—a food offering, an aroma pleasing to the LORD.

19 Then sacrifice one male goat for a sin offering and two lambs, each a year old, for a fellowship offering.

20 The priest is to wave the two lambs before the Lord as a wave offering, together with the bread of the firstfruits. They are a sacred offering to the LORD for the priest.

21 On that same day you are to proclaim a sacred assembly and do no regular work. This is to be a lasting ordinance for the generations to come, wherever you live.

22 "'When you reap the harvest of your land, do not reap to the very edges of your field or gather the gleanings of your harvest. Leave them for the poor and for the foreigner residing among you. I am the LORD your God.'"

LIGHT ON THE WORD

The Sabbath. The Children of Israel worshiped God both at the times He chose and whenever

they sought Him. However, during the leadership of Moses, their worship was assigned mandatory times. Previously, apparently no particular day of rest was assigned to the

Israelites. God blessed and sanctified the seventh day of the week in **Genesis 2:3** when He rested from creating, but God does not command the Israelites to observe the Sabbath until **Exodus 16:23** when the Israelites are in the wilderness. God instructed the people to observe the Sabbath every seven days in honor of His creation work (**Exodus 20:8–11**) and Israel's release from Egyptian slavery (**Deuteronomy 5:12–15**). The Sabbath separated the people from their work and their ordinary activities (**Exodus 35:2–3**). It served as a constant reminder both of their separation from the people around them and of their special covenant relationship with God. Because breaking the Sabbath was akin to breaking Israel's covenant with God, it was punishable by death (**Numbers 15:32–36**).

TEACHING THE BIBLE LESSON

LIFE NEED FOR TODAY'S LESSON

AIM: Students will know that people share the harvest with thanksgiving and share the fruit with others.

INTRODUCTION

The Day of Pentecost

The Feast of Weeks or Pentecost was the second of three appointed feasts given to the Jews to celebrated annually. Because of their solemnity, all able-bodied Jewish males were required to "appear before the LORD" (**Exodus 23:17**), which meant they had to attend the one-day festival and offer sacrifices. The Feast of Weeks celebrated the first fruits of the wheat harvest and usually occurred in late spring. This feast took place exactly fifty days after the second day of Passover when a sheaf of the barley harvest was offered to God. Because of this, it was also known as Pentecost, which in Greek means fifty.

BIBLE LEARNING

AIM: Students will learn how the Children of Israel obediently acknowledge the blessings of God.

I. INSTRUCTIONS FOR THE OFFERING TIME (Leviticus 23:15–16)

When Israel came together to celebrate the Feast of Weeks, they would both commemorate the history of their relationship with God and worship Him. This celebration of thanksgiving was not only for what God had done for them (delivered them from Egyptian bondage), but for what He was doing (giving them a satisfactory harvest) and what He would yet do for them (continue to provide and to guide them as a nation). The Feast of Weeks was essentially a celebration of the harvest. This period of seven weeks falls from the time of the grain harvest to the barley harvest and finally to the wheat harvest. God commanded the people to count a series of seven sevens (49 days) from Passover barley offering (**v. 15**), and then on the "morrow" (i.e., the next day), this feast was to be observed.

Leviticus 23:15–16

From the time of creation when God blessed the seventh day (**Genesis 2:2–3**), everything to do with the Hebrew holy calendar revolves around Sabbath days. Indeed, all of Israel's feasts, convocations, and holy days hold the Sabbath as a core component, which is especially clear in this lesson on the Feast of Weeks, later called Pentecost.

15 And ye shall count unto you from the morrow after the sabbath, from the day that ye brought the sheaf of the wave offering; seven sabbaths shall be complete: 16 Even unto the morrow after the seventh sabbath shall ye number fifty days; and ye shall offer a new meat offering unto the LORD.

Sacred time was measured from Sabbath to Sabbath. In this case, the new one-day festival was to be held after seven Sabbaths, or seven weeks (thus the name Feast of Weeks from **Exodus 34:22**), making forty-nine days, plus the next morning, for fifty days total after Passover. The later name of Pentecost came from the Greek *pentekoste* (**pen-tay-kos-TAY**), meaning "fiftieth" (used three times in the New Testament: **Acts 2:1, 20:16; 1 Corinthians 16:8**). The modern Jewish name for this holiday is Shavuot, which comes from *shavu'ah* (Heb. **shah-voo-AH**), a word related to the Hebrew word for seven, indicating the seven weeks as well as the seven days in each of those weeks. In **Exodus 23:16**, the feast also is called the "Festival of Harvest" (NLT) or "Feast of the Harvest of the first fruits" (NASB).

The concept of first fruits was connected to the idea of continued blessing in the Pentateuch. Paul reinterprets the idea of first fruits in **1 Corinthians 15:20–23** in speaking about Christ's resurrection, which is the first of many for those who believe. Furthermore, Pentecost in the early church is called by the same name in Greek because it occurred at the time of the Feast of Weeks, and it also came to be understood by Luke as the first of many in-dwellings of the Spirit. Jewish celebration of Shavuot celebrates not only the first fruits of the wheat harvest but also God's giving of the Law to Moses, a first in many of God's renewals of His relationship with His people.

II. INSTRUCTIONS FOR THE OFFERINGS (vv. 17–20)

Wow! Explicit rules of O.T.

The Feast of Weeks consisted of four separate sacrificial offerings. The first was the wave offering, when the people were commanded to offer two loaves of baked bread made from finely ground wheat containing leaven (**v. 17**).

During the Passover, the Israelites were commanded to eat unleavened bread as a reminder of the hastily prepared bread they had eaten when they left Egypt. Now, the leaven or yeast was permissible to acknowledge God's continued goodness to them daily. The use of leavening during Pentecost is symbolic of God's ultimate plan to reconcile sinful man back to Himself.

In addition to the wave offering, the people of Israel were also instructed to show their thankfulness to God through burnt offerings. The burnt offering is one of the oldest sacrifices designated by God. Noah offers God one of every clean bird and animal in a burnt sacrifice (**Genesis 8:20**). Significant in the burnt offering is the fact that except for animals' hides and birds' innards (the muscular pouches that are a part of the digestive tract), the entire animal was sacrificed. In this way, we see that the sacrifice to God was to be total and complete.

The Children of Israel were also instructed to make the sin offering of a young goat, or kid. This was required to acknowledge the people's unworthiness and to ask God for forgiveness of their sins against Him and one another. The sin offering only covered sins that were committed unintentionally. Sins that were committed with a defiant attitude or with the express purpose of being disobedient to God were not covered by the sin offering, but had to be addressed in the annual Day of Atonement rituals (**Leviticus 16:11–22**).

The peace offering was an offering of thanksgiving to God for providing the community with all their needs. The word peace (Heb. *shalom*, **shah-LOME**) means well-being and prosperity, so it was fitting that at the time of the harvest the Israelites would thank God with a peace offering for providing them with shalom.

Sacrificial Offerings

17 Ye shall bring out of your habitations two wave loaves of two tenth deals: they shall be of fine flour; they shall be baken with leaven; they are the firstfruits unto the LORD. 18 And ye shall offer with the bread seven lambs without blemish of the first year, and one young bullock, and two rams: they shall be for a burnt offering unto the LORD, with their meat offering, and their drink offerings, even an offering made by fire, of sweet savour unto the LORD. 19 Then ye shall sacrifice one kid of the goats for a sin offering, and two lambs of the first year for a sacrifice of peace offerings. 20 And the priest shall wave them with the bread of the firstfruits for a wave offering before the LORD, with the two lambs: they shall be holy to the LORD for the priest.

The feast dedicated the wheat harvest to God and required a variety of sacrifices, symbolizing that Israel was sanctified and cleansed for a new season of work and celebration of harvest time. The symbolism of bounty was an expression of thanksgiving for God providing food. This leavened bread is prepared with gratitude for God meeting their need for "daily bread" (cf. **Exodus 16:15; Matthew 6:11**), which stands in contrast with the unleavened Passover bread that was baked in memory of the haste with which they left their enslavement in Egypt.

In the New Testament parallel, this was the day the Holy Spirit was poured out, inaugurating a new season of work extending harvest to the Gentiles.

SEARCH THE SCRIPTURES

QUESTION 1

The Lord said not to harvest the edge crops or pick up the dropped crops from the harvesters. Explain.

The crops that were left were for the needy and the foreigners living among them.

QUESTION 2

What animal was sacrificed for the sin offering and the peace offering?

One male goat: sin offering; two one-year old male lambs: peace offering.

LIGHT ON THE WORD

Sin and Peace Offering

Just as we see that the goat was a substitute for the Israelite who had actually committed the sin, we must recognize that the death of our Lord and Savior, Jesus Christ, was the only acceptable substitutionary sacrifice for mankind— only through His death could our sins be forgiven.

III. INSTRUCTIONS TO REMEMBER THE POOR AND FOREIGNERS (vv. 21–22)

These passages emphasize the importance of acknowledging all that God has done for Israel and publicly worshiping and thanking Him. How fitting it is to now see the element of "giving" in the thanksgiving. God instructs the people to be considerate of two marginalized groups: the poor and the non-Israelites living among them. From the time they departed Egypt, the presence of "strangers" or foreigners residing among them was an ever-present reality for the Children of Israel. Here, God commands that when the Israelites harvest their fields, they must leave something behind so that the poor and the foreigners will have something to harvest for their survival.

The Holy Convocation

21 And ye shall proclaim on the selfsame day, that it may be an holy convocation unto

you: ye shall do no servile work therein: it shall be a statute for ever in all your dwellings throughout your generations.

Originally, the feasts or festivals were held at the tabernacle, and later some of them were observed at the Temple and required pilgrimage (Passover, Feast of Weeks and Feast of Booths). These were happy occasions, filled with joy. A total of seven primary feasts were prescribed for Israel. **Leviticus 23** delineates the "appointed festivals" of Israel's holy calendar "holy convocations," which in this case occurred on the same day (**2:2, 21**). A holy convocation served the purpose of solidifying the identity of Israel as a people set apart by God. Other holy convocations occurred on the first and last day of Passover week (**vv. 7–8**), the first day of the seventh month on the Feast of Trumpets (**v. 24**), the day of Atonement (**v. 27**), and the first and last day of the Feast of Booths (**vv. 35–36**). At the end of each list for both the spring and fall festivals, God underscores His self-authorizing statement, "I am the Lord your God" (**vv. 22, 43**), as if to say, "Remember who I am when you follow these instructions."

22 And when ye reap the harvest of your land, thou shalt not make clean riddance of the corners of thy field when thou reapest, neither shalt thou gather any gleaning of thy harvest: thou shalt leave them unto the poor, and to the stranger: I am the LORD your God.

Leaving food for the poor and the strangers (Heb. *ger*, GARE, also translated as a non-israelite who lived among them) during a holy convocation is a reminder even today of the importance of one's horizontal relationships (with others) as well as vertical relationship (with God). This is all part of the many biblical exhortations about doing instead of merely hearing, putting feet to one's faith or practicing what one preaches. Indeed, the church would do well to learn this divine wisdom and compassion (cf. **Leviticus 19:9–10**). In Judaism, the Book of Ruth is read at the Feast of Weeks because of its connections to the grain harvest. In Ruth, Boaz observes this commandment by telling his harvesters not just to leave what they would normally drop (the gleanings), but even to leave a bit extra for this foreigner who lives among them and is in need (**Ruth 2:15–16**). We would do well also to go beyond the Levitical command to just leave our leftovers for those in need, but to give from the "meat" of our plenty as well.

BIBLE APPLICATION

AIM: Students will know that believers are to share with those who are in need and celebrate God's bountiful blessings in their lives.

In much of southern Africa, there is a ceremony of the first fruits of the harvest similar to the Jewish Feast of Weeks. The ritual involves the king eating the food as the head of the tribe and representative of the ancestors. In this way, the crops are imparted with the blessing of the ancestors. As Christians, we acknowledge Jesus as our head. He is the one who blesses the work of our hands and provides for us. Through our giving, we are only returning what already belongs to Him.

STUDENT'S RESPONSES

AIM: Students will know that believers learn to commit a portion of what they have received back to the Lord and to help those in need.

All too often Christians are satisfied with dropping a couple of dollars into the Salvation Army kettle during the holidays, or making a donation to their church's Benevolence Fund once in awhile and feeling as though they have done their "duty." We mistakenly think the ongoing care and support of the poor and needy is the responsibility of others. Throughout the Bible, we are taught that we are our brother's keepers, and this means being committed to helping those in need. Make a commitment to call non-profit organizations, go online and gather information, and choose to donate the "first fruits" of your time, talent, and treasure to those less fortunate.

PRAYER

Jesus, we are to care for others as You have cared for us. As You bless us, we are thankful. We are thankful that we can bless others and rejoice in You. In Jesus' Name we pray. Amen.

HOW TO SAY IT

Morrow.	MAH-row.
Convocation.	kan-vo-KAY-shun.

PREPARE FOR NEXT SUNDAY

Read **Leviticus 16:11–19** and "Day of Atonement."

DAILY HOME BIBLE READINGS

MONDAY
Praise the Lord
(Psalm 147:1–11)

TUESDAY
Thanks be to God
(1 Chronicles 17:16–27)

WEDNESDAY
In All Things, Thanks
(Ephesians 5:15–20)

THURSDAY
In Spite of Everything, Thanks
(Romans 7:14–25)

FRIDAY
Increasing Thanks
(2 Corinthians 4:7–15)

SATURDAY
In the End, Thanks
(Revelation 11:15–19)

SUNDAY
Feast of Weeks
(Leviticus 23:15–22)

Sources:
Balentine, Samuel E. Leviticus. *Interpretation: A Bible Commentary for Teaching and Preaching.* Louisville: John Knox Press, 2002. 177-78.
Gane, Roy. Leviticus, Numbers. *The NIV Application Commentary: From Biblical Text to Contemporary Life.* Grand Rapids: Zondervan, 2004. 390-99.
Harris, R. Laird. Genesis, Exodus, Leviticus, Numbers. *The Expositor's Bible Commentary, Vol. 2.* Edited by Frank E. Gaebelein. Grand Rapids: Zondervan, 1990. 625-26.
Harrison, R. K. Leviticus. *Tyndale Old Testament Commentaries.* Downers Grove: InterVarsity Press, 1980. 216-20.
Packer, James I., and Merrill Tenney. *Nelson's Illustrated Manners and Customs of the Bible.* Thomas Nelson Publishers, Nashville, TN, 1995. 404.
Rooker, Mark F. Leviticus. *The New American Commentary: An Exegetical and Theological Exposition of Holy Scripture, Vol. 3A.* Nashville: B&H Publishing, 2000. 287-88.

COMMENTS / NOTES:

_____
_____
_____
_____
_____
_____
_____
_____
_____
_____
_____
_____
_____
_____
_____
_____
_____
_____
_____

DAY OF ATONEMENT

BIBLE BASIS: LEVITICUS 16:11–19

BIBLE TRUTH: God commanded the Israelites to set aside a day to sacrifice animals for payment of sin debt.

MEMORY VERSE: "And he shall make an atonement for the holy place, because of the uncleanness of the children of Israel, and because of their transgressions in all their sins: and so shall he do for the tabernacle of the congregation, that remaineth among them in the midst of their uncleanness" (Leviticus 16:16).

LESSON AIM: By the end of the lesson, we will: EXPLORE the Day of Atonement rituals found in Leviticus; REFLECT on the meaning of atonement for our sins and its relevance today; and IDENTIFY those things in our lives needing repentance and seek atonement.

TEACHER PREPARATION

MATERIALS NEEDED: Quarterly Commentary/Teacher Manual, Adult Quarterly, Adult resources—charts, worksheets, and other teaching tools, paper, pens, pencils, Bibles (several different versions)

OTHER MATERIALS NEEDED / TEACHER'S NOTES:

_____

_____

LESSON OVERVIEW

LIFE NEED FOR TODAY'S LESSON
People often feel guilty when they hurt others, and sometimes seek to make up for their mistakes.

BIBLE APPLICATION
Believers accept that God wants His people to understand that sin defiles them and separates the from Him.

BIBLE LEARNING
God has provided Jesus as the supreme sacrifice, so animals are no longer needed.

STUDENTS' RESPONSES
Believers acknowledge their sin, and repent, and make atonement.

LESSON SCRIPTURE

LEVITICUS 16:11–19, KJV

11 And Aaron shall bring the bullock of the sin offering, which is for himself, and shall make an atonement for himself, and for his house, and shall kill the bullock of the sin offering which is for himself:

LEVITICUS 16:11–19, NIV

11 "Aaron shall bring the bull for his own sin offering to make atonement for himself and his household, and he is to slaughter the bull for his own sin offering.

12 And he shall take a censer full of burning coals of fire from off the altar before the LORD, and his hands full of sweet incense beaten small, and bring it within the vail:

13 And he shall put the incense upon the fire before the LORD, that the cloud of the incense may cover the mercy seat that is upon the testimony, that he die not:

14 And he shall take of the blood of the bullock, and sprinkle it with his finger upon the mercy seat eastward; and before the mercy seat shall he sprinkle of the blood with his finger seven times.

15 Then shall he kill the goat of the sin offering, that is for the people, and bring his blood within the vail, and do with that blood as he did with the blood of the bullock, and sprinkle it upon the mercy seat, and before the mercy seat:

16 And he shall make an atonement for the holy place, because of the uncleanness of the children of Israel, and because of their transgressions in all their sins: and so shall he do for the tabernacle of the congregation, that remaineth among them in the midst of their uncleanness.

17 And there shall be no man in the tabernacle of the congregation when he goeth in to make an atonement in the holy place, until he come out, and have made an atonement for himself, and for his household, and for all the congregation of Israel.

18 And he shall go out unto the altar that is before the LORD, and make an atonement for it; and shall take of the blood of the bullock, and of the blood of the goat, and put it upon the horns of the altar round about.

19 And he shall sprinkle of the blood upon it with his finger seven times, and cleanse it, and hallow it from the uncleanness of the

12 He is to take a censer full of burning coals from the altar before the LORD and two handfuls of finely ground fragrant incense and take them behind the curtain.

13 He is to put the incense on the fire before the LORD, and the smoke of the incense will conceal the atonement cover above the tablets of the covenant law, so that he will not die.

14 He is to take some of the bull's blood and with his finger sprinkle it on the front of the atonement cover; then he shall sprinkle some of it with his finger seven times before the atonement cover.

15 "He shall then slaughter the goat for the sin offering for the people and take its blood behind the curtain and do with it as he did with the bull's blood: He shall sprinkle it on the atonement cover and in front of it.

16 In this way he will make atonement for the Most Holy Place because of the uncleanness and rebellion of the Israelites, whatever their sins have been. He is to do the same for the tent of meeting, which is among them in the midst of their uncleanness.

17 No one is to be in the tent of meeting from the time Aaron goes in to make atonement in the Most Holy Place until he comes out, having made atonement for himself, his household and the whole community of Israel.

18 "Then he shall come out to the altar that is before the LORD and make atonement for it. He shall take some of the bull's blood and some of the goat's blood and put it on all the horns of the altar.

19 He shall sprinkle some of the blood on it with his finger seven times to cleanse it and to consecrate it from the uncleanness of the Israelites.

children of Israel.

LIGHT ON THE WORD

The Ark of the Covenant. The Ark of the Covenant was a wooden chest that measured approximately 4 x 2.5 x 2.5 feet. It was constructed of acacia, a strong and dense local wood that was resistant to water penetration and decay. The inside and outside were covered with gold and open at the top. The tablets inscribed with the Ten Commandments, a pot of manna, and Aaron's rod—all reminders of God's abiding love for Israel—were kept inside the Ark. The Children of Israel believed that it was the throne of God. The mercy seat is the area of the Ark where they believed God would actually sit.

Tabernacle. The tabernacle was the central place of worship for the Israelites until the Solomonic Temple was built. The tabernacle moved with the Children of Israel through the wilderness. A cloud hovered above it, showing the glory and presence of God among the Israelites. All the tribes were organized around the tabernacle, which was symbolic of God being central to all of life. Although it shared many similarities with the Temple, it was different in that it was a mobile tent. The tabernacle therefore showed that God could not be confined to one place.

TEACHING THE BIBLE LESSON

LIFE NEED FOR TODAY'S LESSON

AIM: Students will understand that people often feel guilty when they hurt others, and sometimes seek to make up for their mistakes.

INTRODUCTION

God's Special Instructions

In Leviticus, the laws of God are given not to the priests or high priest, but directly to His servant, Moses. Moses serves as the mediator between God and His people. In his role as prophet, Moses' position is higher than that of the high priest. Distinctions between clean and unclean, holy and unholy are made clear in Leviticus. When God dwelt on Mt. Sinai, Moses needed a particular reverecnce when he wished to approach the Lord. Now that God dwelled among the Children of Israel, the high priest needed to show this same reverence and requirement of purity. God's specific instructions about exactly how and when the high priest could enter into His presence are emphasized in **Leviticus 16**.

BIBLE LEARNING

AIM: Students will know that God has provided Jesus as the supreme sacrifice, so animals are no longer needed.

I. SIN OFFERING FOR THE HIGH PRIEST (Leviticus 16:11–14)

Now we encounter the greatest expression of God's care and concern for the Children of Israel. God now provides instructions to His people on how to obtain pardon for sins committed against Him and one another, and enter into communion with Him. This should not be surprising since man was created to walk in daily fellowship with God. Through Adam's sin in the Garden, mankind was thrust from the face of God. The sin in our lives not only separates us from God, but its very memory also undermines our confidence to approach until He has cleansed us from all our defilement. In these verses, our attention should immediately be drawn to the fact that only the high priest can perform the atonement sacrifice.

The role of the high priest was special. He was appointed to offer gifts and make sacrifices for sins. That Aaron, or the high priest, is instructed to perform this atoning sacrifice for himself and his own household demonstrates the clear separation between the human priesthood and Jesus. This atoning was necessary for the human priests because they were capable of sinning. Jesus, the perfect High Priest, was incapable of sin. Because the human high priest was susceptible to sin, we read that his first obligation was to offer a sacrifice of a bull for himself and his household. After putting coals and incense inside the veil of the Holy of Holies, the high priest also sprinkles the sacrificed bull's blood on and in front of the mercy seat.

Leviticus 16:11–14

Leviticus 16, which is read on the Day of Atonement among Orthodox and Conservative Jews, immediately follows a section concerning various laws of purification from impurities, many of which are unintentional (out of human control), such as a woman's menstruation and childbirth (chapter 12), skin ailments (13–14), and various bodily discharges (15). The laws in these chapters prescribe ways to atone not for deliberate sins related to morality (i.e., murder, theft, etc.), but for unintentional and even unpreventable impurity that nevertheless makes the Israelites and God's sanctuary unclean. This uncleanness or impurity (Heb. *tum'ah*, **toom-AH**) is not a matter of being dirty or physically infected in the modern medical sense of the word, but instead has a more basic but profound meaning of a broken relationship with God. Chapters 12–15 regard unintentional sins, which are easily eradicated through ritual. However, moral sin could not be permanently eradicated, so it was necessary to purify both the tabernacle (and later the

Temple) and the people once a year on the Day of Atonement (Yom Kippur) by transferring the impurities to a goat that would take those sins into the wilderness, never to return. In addition, the altar was purified by spattering the blood of the bull sacrificed for Aaron and his family and the goat sacrificed for the rest of the Israelites. **Leviticus 16:11–19** provides these instructions for Aaron the high priest to atone for himself and his family, followed by the rest of the people of Israel, so that their relationship with the Lord and the purity of His sanctuary can be restored.

11 And Aaron shall bring the bullock of the sin offering, which is for himself, and shall make an atonement for himself, and for his house, and shall kill the bullock of the sin offering which is for himself:

The bull for the sin offering is distinct both from the kid goats for a sin offering and from the ram for the burnt offering, which are for the Israelite people (**v. 5**). The bull in **v. 11** is the sin offering specifically for Aaron and his family. The high priest must reestablish his own relationship with God before he can atone for the rest of the people. He serves as an intermediary between the Lord and the people, so his own state of purity must be restored to purify the people and the sanctuary.

12 And he shall take a censer full of burning coals of fire from off the altar before the LORD, and his hands full of sweet incense beaten small, and bring it within the vail: 13 And he shall put the incense upon the fire before the LORD, that the cloud of the incense may cover the mercy seat that is upon the testimony, that he die not: 14 And he shall take of the blood of the bullock, and sprinkle it with his finger upon the mercy seat eastward; and before the mercy seat shall he sprinkle of the blood with his finger seven times.

The purpose of the incense is to create a cloud of smoke covering the altar so that Aaron cannot see the Lord's presence. The vail is the curtain that divides the inner part of the sanctuary into two areas. The mercy seat is the cover for the Ark of the Covenant, upon which stand two winged cherubs (**Exodus 25:17–20**). The Hebrew for mercy seat is *kapporet* (**kah-POH-ret**), which belongs to the same root as the verb for atoning, and both words have a sense of covering, whether a physical object such as the Ark or something intangible such as sin. The Ark is referred to here simply as the covenant or testimony (Heb. *'edut*, **eh-DOOT**), indicating that it is a testimony to the Lord's presence in the tabernacle. To be in the presence of God in the Holy of Holies could cause death if the high priest did not properly prepare to prevent himself from seeing God's face, and **vv. 12–13** provide instructions on these matters. In fact, only the high priest was permitted to enter the innermost sanctum, and only once a year to purify the actual sanctuary. Once Aaron has properly entered the Holy of Holies, he is to sprinkle blood from the bull that serves as a sin offering for himself and his family. The blood is to be spattered seven times both over the cover of the Ark and in front of it. Seven times represents completion—in other words, once the high priest has sprinkled the blood seven times, he has done as much as he can to atone. Blood was considered sacred in ancient Israel. The life of any living animal or human was in the blood, so as the essence of life (**Leviticus 17:14**), blood from a sacrifice could purify God's sanctuary.

SEARCH THE SCRIPTURES

QUESTION 1

Aaron was to make atonement for who in verse 11? He had to something sweet in his hands in verse 12. What was it?

Aaron made atonement for himself and his family. His hands were full of sweet incense that was beaten small.

LIGHT ON THE WORD

Keeping Relationship

Both moral sin and physical changes to the body could alter the Israelites' relationship with God, and many of the laws of Leviticus provide a means for reestablishing this relationship.

II. SIN OFFERING FOR THE PEOPLE (vv. 15–16)

The Day of Atonement was for atoning of all the Children of Israel's sins and failures, and allowing for God to dwell among them. Only on this day was the high priest allowed to enter into the veiled Holy of Holies, the holiest of areas, without risking death. While sin separates man from God, His love does not want this separation to remain. In these next verses, the high priest now sacrifices a goat as a sin offering for the people.

This sacrifice of the goat represents the blood sacrifice required to satisfy the righteousness and justice of God on behalf of the people. In Judaism, sacrifices are no longer offered since the Temple no longer exists, but Yom Kippur remains a day of repentance which is coupled with fasting as a way of expressing humility and remorse before God and community. Thus, God no longer requires sacrifices in Judaism, only a humble heart. It is important to understand that God's love cannot be expressed unless His justice is satisfied. That is exactly what Jesus' death on the Cross did; as His son's tortured body hung on the Cross, God poured out all of His wrath against sin on Jesus. Jesus' death freed God to show His love to us. If Jesus had not died, then we would never have known the depth of God's love and His forgiving grace.

Israel's Broken Relationship with God

15 Then shall he kill the goat of the sin offering, that is for the people, and bring his blood within the vail, and do with that

blood as he did with the blood of the bullock, and sprinkle it upon the mercy seat, and before the mercy seat: 16 And he shall make an atonement for the holy place, because of the uncleanness of the children of Israel, and because of their transgressions in all their sins: and so shall he do for the tabernacle of the congregation, that remaineth among them in the midst of their uncleanness.

Two goat sacrifices are involved in the Day of Atonement—one to serve as a slaughter sacrifice for the people's sins and the other as a scapegoat. The decision regarding which goat to slaughter is made by casting lots (**vv. 7–10**). After Aaron atones for himself, he must perform parallel rituals for the people (**v. 15**), which purify God's sanctuary from the sins of the people. Several words for sin are used here in addition to the word for impurity/uncleanness, designating broken relationship with God. Transgressions (Heb. *pesha'*, **PEH-shah**) is a general word for any action that strays from God's commandments, whether intentional or unintentional, though the word often carries the sense of rebellion. Sins (Heb. *chatt'at*, **chaht-TAHT**) are wrong actions that a person does to somebody else or to God, often intentionally. All actions that lead people away from God's commandments by profaning the Lord's name or doing wrong to others harm the people's individual and communal relationship with Him and pollute His sanctuary. The tabernacle of the congregation is the outer room that has become impure due to direct contact with the people, who have sinned. The idea is that everything the Israelites do affects everyone and everything around them, and the commandments in Leviticus serve as a reminder to the people of the gravity of their actions. God has set the regulations in place as not a burden but a guide for how to live a holy life in community with Him and others.

III. ATONEMENT FOR THE HOLY PLACE (vv. 17–19)

One purpose of the Day of Atonement was to cleanse the tabernacle of the uncleanliness introduced into it by the unclean worshipers. The rituals we see here allowed for God's continual presence among His people.

For the second time, the high priest enters the Holy of Holies and sprinkles the blood of the goat on and in front of the mercy seat and over the altar. Now we see that he is atoning not only for the people, but also the place itself. For both Jews and Christians, it is no longer the Old Testament Temple or tabernacle, but our entire beings that are the tabernacles in which God dwells. For Christians, the sacrifice of Jesus atoned for our sins and cleansed our tabernacles—our bodies, souls, and spirits—in the sight of God.

Yom Kippur

17 And there shall be no man in the tabernacle of the congregation when he goeth in to make an atonement in the holy place, until he come out, and have made an atonement for himself, and for his household, and for all the congregation of Israel. 18 And he shall go out unto the altar that is before the LORD, and make an atonement for it; and shall take of the blood of the bullock, and of the blood of the goat, and put it upon the horns of the altar round about. 19 And he shall sprinkle of the blood upon it with his finger seven times, and cleanse it, and hallow it from the uncleanness of the children of Israel.

These verses provide a summary of the rituals outlined in more detail in the previous verses, with the additional proviso that the high priest must be completely alone even in the outer sanctuary when he atones for himself and the people. The following verses provide the remainder of the observances for Yom Kippur, including the transfer of the community's sins to the scapegoat and the fast and Sabbath from work observed by the people. Although the animal sacrifice portions of the holy day were abandoned after the destruction of the Second Temple (70 AD), fasting and refraining from work on Yom Kippur remain central to Jewish tradition as a reminder of human inability to remain completely sinless.

SEARCH THE SCRIPTURES

QUESTION 2
What animal was Aaron to slaughter as a sin offering for himself and his family?

A bull.

QUESTION 3
What animal was Aaron to slaughter as a sin offering on behalf of the people?

A goat.

LIGHT ON THE WORD

God's Holiness
Rather than pointing to a God who requires animal sacrifices, Yom Kippur assures the faithful that despite human transgressions, it is possible to rectify our relationship with God. God is holy, and Yom Kippur serves as a reminder of His holiness in the midst of human sin.

BIBLE APPLICATION

AIM: Students will know that believers accept that God wants His people to understand that sin defiles them and separates the from Him.

All too often Christians struggle with the notion of forgiveness. They say that they know God has forgiven. They insist that they know that God's Word is true and that they understand that Jesus' death on the Cross paid the debt for their sins. However, they struggle under the burden of guilt and shame from what they have done in the past. This sense of shame hampers our praise, inhibits our prayers, and prevents us from being able to worship God in spirit and truth. We must remember that this uncertainty is only a trick of the enemy. Paul called them "the fiery darts of the wicked" (from Ephesians 6:16). Satan wants us to believe that we are unworthy and that God does not fully love and accept us. Nothing could be further from the truth. When the blood of Jesus was shed on Calvary, the punishment for all our sins was paid once and for all. He died so that we might be worthy to stand in the presence of God—forever, and never be separated from His presence again.

STUDENT'S RESPONSES

AIM: Students will know to acknowledge their sin, and repent, and make atonement.

God provided the Day of Atonement so that His flawed and often sinful people could "by the mercies of God, present our bodies as a living sacrifice, holy and acceptable to God, which is our spiritual worship" (from **Romans 12:1**, ESV). Pray and ask God to help you in this area. Commit to believing that not only does God love and accept you the way you are, but more importantly, He is ready to use you without hesitation or exception. Tell God that you are ready for Him to use you, today.

PRAYER

Precious Lord, we are truly grateful that You forgive us of our sins and love us. We thank You for your grace that covers us and allows us to try again. We love You and We adore! In Jesus' Name we pray. Amen.

HOW TO SAY IT

Atonement.	uh-**TONE**-ment.
Yom Kippur.	**YOHM** kip-**POOR**.
Tabernacle.	**TA**-bur-na-kul.
Covenant.	**KUH**-veh-nehnt.

PREPARE FOR NEXT SUNDAY

Read **Leviticus 23:33–43** and "The Feast of Booths."

DAILY HOME BIBLE READINGS

MONDAY
Perfect Atonement
(Hebrews 2:10–17)

TUESDAY
Appointed for Atonement
(Hebrews 3:1–6)

WEDNESDAY
Completed Atonement
(Romans 3:21–26)

THURSDAY
Preparation and Atonement
(Exodus 30:1–10)

FRIDAY
Obedience and Atonement
(Leviticus 8:30–36)

SATURDAY
Sin Offering for Atonement
(Leviticus 16:1–10)

SUNDAY
Day of Atonement
(Leviticus 16:11–19)

Sources:
Balentine, Samuel E. Leviticus. *Interpretation: A Bible Commentary for Teaching and Preaching*. Edited by James Luther Mays. Louisville: John Knox Press, 2002.
Berlin, Adele and Marc Zvi Brettler, eds. *The Jewish Study Bible*. New York: Oxford University Press, 2004.
Eskenazi, Tamara Cohn. "Leviticus." *The Torah: A Women's Commentary*. Edited by Tamara Cohn Eskenazi and Andrea L. Weiss. New York: URJ Press and Women of Reform Judaism, 2008. 567-67.
Eskenazi, Tamara Cohn and Andrea L. Weiss, eds. *The Torah: A Women's Commentary*. New York: URJ Press and Women of Reform Judaism, 2008.
Hartley, John E. Leviticus. *Word Biblical Commentary 4*. Edited by Bruce M. Metzger, David A. Hubbard and Glenn W. Barker. Dallas: Word Books, 1992.
Havrelock, Rachel. "Boundaries of Rituals: The Sanctuary and the Body." *The Torah: A Women's Commentary*. Edited by Tamara Cohn Eskenazi and Andrea L. Weiss. New York: URJ Press and Women of Reform Judaism, 2008. 679.

Kaiser, Walter C. "The Book of Leviticus." *Vol. 1 of New Interpreter's Bible Commentary*. Edited by Leander E. Keck, et al. Nashville: Abingdon Press, 1994. 985-1191.
Sweeney, Marvin A. *Tanak: A Theological and Critical Introduction to the Jewish Bible*. Minneapolis: Fortress Press, 2012.

COMMENTS / NOTES:

_____
_____
_____
_____
_____
_____
_____
_____
_____
_____
_____
_____
_____
_____
_____
_____
_____
_____
_____
_____
_____
_____
_____
_____
_____
_____
_____
_____
_____
_____
_____
_____
_____
_____
_____

THE FEAST OF BOOTHS

BIBLE BASIS: LEVITICUS 23:33–43

BIBLE TRUTH: The Festival of Booths reminded the Israelites in renewing their commitment for God's guidance and protection.

MEMORY VERSE: "Ye shall dwell in booths seven days; all that are Israelites born shall dwell in booths: That your generations may know that I made the children of Israel to dwell in booths, when I brought them out of the land of Egypt: I am the LORD your God" (Leviticus 23:42–43).

LESSON AIM: By the end of the lesson, we will: UNDERSTAND all aspects of the Festival of Booths; APPRECIATE a faith heritage in which God guides and protects the faithful; and DECIDE to pass on to the next generation a legacy of faith.

TEACHER PREPARATION

MATERIALS NEEDED: Quarterly Commentary/Teacher Manual, Adult Quarterly, Adult resources—charts, worksheets, and other teaching tools, paper, pens, pencils, Bibles (several different versions)

OTHER MATERIALS NEEDED / TEACHER'S NOTES:

_____

_____

LESSON OVERVIEW

LIFE NEED FOR TODAY'S LESSON
Families need rituals of celebration to remember their heritage and to pass it on to their children.

BIBLE LEARNING
The book of Leviticus reminds the Israelite parents to pass on their faith.

BIBLE APPLICATION
Christians learn how Israel was to express their gratitude to the Lord.

STUDENTS' RESPONSES
Believers acknowledge that God commanded Israel to celebrate feasts to remember and honor the goodness of the Lord.

LESSON SCRIPTURE

LEVITICUS 23:33–43, KJV

Leviticus 23:33 And the LORD spake unto Moses, saying,

34 Speak unto the children of Israel, saying, The fifteenth day of this seventh month shall be the feast of tabernacles for seven days

LEVITICUS 23:33–43, NIV

33 The LORD said to Moses,

34 "Say to the Israelites: 'On the fifteenth day of the seventh month the LORD's Festival of Tabernacles begins, and it lasts for seven days.

unto the LORD.

35 On the first day shall be an holy convocation: ye shall do no servile work therein.

36 Seven days ye shall offer an offering made by fire unto the LORD: on the eighth day shall be an holy convocation unto you; and ye shall offer an offering made by fire unto the LORD: it is a solemn assembly; and ye shall do no servile work therein

37 These are the feasts of the LORD, which ye shall proclaim to be holy convocations, to offer an offering made by fire unto the LORD, a burnt offering, and a meat offering, a sacrifice, and drink offerings, every thing upon his day:

38 Beside the sabbaths of the LORD, and beside your gifts, and beside all your vows, and beside all your freewill offerings, which ye give unto the LORD.

39 Also in the fifteenth day of the seventh month, when ye have gathered in the fruit of the land, ye shall keep a feast unto the LORD seven days: on the first day shall be a sabbath, and on the eighth day shall be a sabbath.

40 And ye shall take you on the first day the boughs of goodly trees, branches of palm trees, and the boughs of thick trees, and willows of the brook; and ye shall rejoice before the LORD your God seven days.

41 And ye shall keep it a feast unto the LORD seven days in the year. It shall be a statute for ever in your generations: ye shall celebrate it in the seventh month.

42 Ye shall dwell in booths seven days; all that are Israelites born shall dwell in booths:

43 That your generations may know that I made the children of Israel to dwell in booths, when I brought them out of the

35 The first day is a sacred assembly; do no regular work.

36 For seven days present food offerings to the LORD, and on the eighth day hold a sacred assembly and present a food offering to the LORD. It is the closing special assembly; do no regular work.

37 ("'These are the LORD's appointed festivals, which you are to proclaim as sacred assemblies for bringing food offerings to the LORD—the burnt offerings and grain offerings, sacrifices and drink offerings required for each day.

38 These offerings are in addition to those for the LORD's Sabbaths and in addition to your gifts and whatever you have vowed and all the freewill offerings you give to the LORD.)

39 "'So beginning with the fifteenth day of the seventh month, after you have gathered the crops of the land, celebrate the festival to the LORD for seven days; the first day is a day of sabbath rest, and the eighth day also is a day of sabbath rest.

40 On the first day you are to take branches from luxuriant trees—from palms, willows and other leafy trees—and rejoice before the LORD your God for seven days.

41 Celebrate this as a festival to the LORD for seven days each year. This is to be a lasting ordinance for the generations to come; celebrate it in the seventh month.

42 Live in temporary shelters for seven days: All native-born Israelites are to live in such shelters

43 so your descendants will know that I had the Israelites live in temporary shelters when I brought them out of Egypt. I am the LORD your God.'"

land of Egypt: I am the LORD your God.

LIGHT ON THE WORD

The Jewish Feasts and Holidays. The Mosaic Law prescribes nine annual holy days plus weekly Sabbaths. The annual holy days in order are: Passover, Unleavened Bread, First Fruits, Pentecost, Trumpets, the Day of Atonement, Rosh Hashanah (New Year) and Booths (Tabernacles). Not all of the holy days in **Leviticus 23** continue to be observed by all Jews, with the First Fruits being combined with Passover (observed on the second day) and Trumpets not generally observed. Three of these feasts were designated as pilgrimages (**Deuteronomy 16:16**). During these times, the Israelites were supposed to travel to Jerusalem to appear before the Lord in His holy sanctuary for ritual worship, sacrifices and celebration. **Deuteronomy 16:16** indicates only the males are to attend, but **Deuteronomy 16:14** calls for all family members to observe the Festival of Booths. Probably in the earliest days of observance only the males participated, but as time passed, whole families became involved.

Vows. A vow was a pledge or promise to God, made to receive something from Him or as a way of showing thanksgiving to Him for a benefit already received. There was no law demanding that vows be made, although they were regulated to make sure the person offering it understood the seriousness of the pledge.

Freewill offerings. Freewill offerings were made in addition to the required sacrifices. These offerings were spontaneously made as a response to God's goodness. They were usually made with items valuable to the worshiper and were above and beyond the requirements of the Law. Freewill offerings were a demonstration of the worshiper's willing heart to honor God. As such, they are a symbol of the believer's passion and recognition of God and His greatness.

TEACHING THE BIBLE LESSON

LIFE NEED FOR TODAY'S LESSON

AIM: Students will affirm that families need rituals of celebration to remember their heritage and to pass it on to their children.

INTRODUCTION

Seven Day Festival

The Festival of Booths is also known as the Feast of Tabernacles or, in Hebrew, Sukkot. This seven-day feast is last of the mandatory feasts mentioned in **Leviticus 23**, and the last of the three required pilgrimages. A time of rejoicing for Israel, the Feast of Booths celebrated at the end of the harvest season, and was a reminder to Israel that their God had provided them with everything they needed.

BIBLE LEARNING

AIM: Students will accept the importance of the Israelites passing on their faith to their children.

I. INSTITUTION OF THE FEAST (Leviticus 23:33–34)

The Feast of Booths is also known as the Feast of Tabernacles and the Feast of Ingathering. The feast was to be held five days after the Day of Atonement. Unlike the solemnity of the Day of Atonement, the Feast of Booths was quite joyous. This feast also served to remind the Israelites of the "booths," or tent-like shelters, that they lived in during their wilderness experience. During

278

this period in their history, Israel was not yet a nation, but rather a loose confederation of tribes, moving through the desert under the direction and protection of God. In its homeless condition, Israel was totally dependent on God to protect them from enemies.

The Feast of Booths also coincided with the harvesting of the fall harvest. This would probably have included olives and grapes. The people were to give thanks for the productivity of these harvests, recognizing that this too was a blessing from God.

Leviticus 23:33–34

Chapter 23 provides commands concerning the important festivals of the calendar year, beginning with the spring festivals of Passover, the Feast of Unleavened Bread (**vv. 4–8**) and the First Fruits, and the Festival of Weeks (**vv. 9–22**), also known as Pentecost, which celebrates the beginning of the harvest season with the grain harvest. These are followed by the three fall festivals, which fall in the seventh month—Trumpets (**vv. 23–25**), the Day of Atonement or Yom Kippur (**vv. 26–32**), and the Festival of Booths or Tabernacles (**vv. 33–36, 39–43**). Although the ancient Hebrew calendar began with Rosh Hashannah, which is celebrated in late September or early October in the Gregorian calendar, the festival season begins with Passover and Unleavened Bread and concludes with Tabernacles. Both are times of joy, remembering God's deliverance of the Israelites from slavery in Egypt and continued guidance and protection during their time in the wilderness. In **Deuteronomy 31:10–11**, the Israelites are also commanded to read the book of Deuteronomy during the Festival of Booths every seventh year as part of a ceremony renewing their covenant with the Lord.

33 And the LORD spake unto Moses, saying, 34 Speak unto the children of Israel, saying, The fifteenth day of this seventh month shall be the feast of tabernacles for seven days unto the LORD.

The Feast of Tabernacles occurs in the seventh month and is to last for seven days. The seventh month marked the end of the harvest season in Israel, but the number seven also represents completion or perfection in the Old Testament. God created the heavens and the earth in six days, and the Sabbath is the seventh day of the week, marking a celebration of the completion of God's creation. This final celebration of the harvest year is one of feasting, but the Hebrew word for feast (*chag*, **KHAG**) is associated both with celebratory eating as well as pilgrimage. Traditionally, the Israelites were to make a pilgrimage to Jerusalem. Since it lasts for seven days, the Israelites are to erect tents to stay in as a reminder of the time in the wilderness when the Lord guided them and protected them.

SEARCH THE SCRIPTURES

QUESTION 1
The Feast of Tabernacles was to celebrate God's provision and marked the end of what season? How long is the feast to last?

Harvest season, 7 days.

LIGHT ON THE WORD

God's Nourishment
During this time, the people were probably feeling especially grateful to God. The grains had been harvested and stored and now the people were gathering the fruit and hoping for rain to nourish the new crops.

II. REQUIREMENTS OF THE FEAST (vv. 35–39)

As in the other feasts, the celebration of Feast of Booths included sacrifices and offerings to God. Some seventy bulls were sacrificed during the Feast (**Numbers 29:13–34**). Here we see Israel's reminder of its mission to the rest of the world. Many rabbinical scholars believed the seventy bulls symbolized the seventy nations of the world before the confusion of tongues at the Tower of Babel (**Genesis 10–11**). At the covenant instituted on Mount Sinai, Israel had been sanctified, or set apart, as God's special people. They were to be a living witness to the existence of the One True and Holy God before all of the nations on the earth.

We must remember that when the Temple was built in Jerusalem, the non-Jewish were not excluded. Instead, a special court was erected to allow the Gentiles a place in the Temple where they could come and be instructed about the God of Israel. There in the Court of the Gentiles, the non-Jews could pray to the God of Israel. This is a beautiful reminder to us that our worship of God was never intended to be private and celebrated for the benefit only of other Christians. Rather, we are to praise and thank God for His goodness for the benefit of the world—the saved and the unsaved!

Offerings of Fire

35 On the first day shall be an holy convocation: ye shall do no servile work therein. 36 Seven days ye shall offer an offering made by fire unto the LORD: on the eighth day shall be an holy convocation unto you; and ye shall offer an offering made by fire unto the LORD: it is a solemn assembly; and ye shall do no servile work therein.

Both the first day of the Feast and the eighth and final day are days when the Israelites do not work. They are both days of holy assembly, and the entire eight days are marked by offerings of fire. These burnt offerings are outlined in detail in **Numbers 29:13–38**, and the animal sacrifices number many more than the offerings of any other holy festival, indicating the importance of this celebration marking the end of the harvest season. The eighth day is also distinct in that it

is no longer a feast (*chag*) but a solemn assembly (Heb. *'atsarah*, **ah-tsah-RAH**), a word related to the verb to hold back or refrain. This links it with the final day of the Feast of Unleavened Bread, which also closes with a solemn assembly (**Deuteronomy 16:8**). The Hebrew word is associated with communal gathering but also with self-restraint and with closing off. There is a sense of personal and communal sanctity in practicing self-restraint after seven days of feasting, but the word also carries the idea of closing up the festival season in an even more conclusive way than the end of the Feast of Unleavened Bread (Heb. *matsot*, **maht-SOHT**) concludes the eight-day observance of Passover and matsot.

37 These are the feasts of the LORD, which ye shall proclaim to be holy convocations, to offer an offering made by fire unto the LORD, a burnt offering, and a meat offering, a sacrifice, and drink offerings, every thing upon his day: 38 Beside the sabbaths of the LORD, and beside your gifts, and beside all your vows, and beside all your freewill offerings, which ye give unto the LORD.

These verses provide a summary reminder of all of the festivals commanded in this chapter. They are all to be sacred occasions which the Israelites celebrate with feasting and offerings (**v. 37**). These times are distinct from the daily and weekly sabbaths, offerings and vows that the Israelites are to regularly make in celebration to God.

39 Also in the fifteenth day of the seventh month, when ye have gathered in the fruit of the land, ye shall keep a feast unto the LORD seven days: on the first day shall be a sabbath, and on the eighth day shall be a sabbath. 40 And ye shall take you on the first day the boughs of goodly trees, branches of palm trees, and the boughs of thick trees, and willows of the brook; and ye shall rejoice before the LORD your God seven days.

The Feast of Tabernacles is summarized again in **verse 39** after outlining all of the special holy days in **vv. 37–38**. Since this is the final festival of the year, it is important to end with a detailed description of its observance. The four types of branches serve as a reminder of the abundance of the agricultural year, and are used to build the tents (**Nehemiah 8:14–15**). The Israelites are told to rejoice for seven days (**v. 40**), a command that the returning exiles fulfill in **Nehemiah 8:17**. A full week of celebration indicates complete joy concerning God's presence and protection among the Israelites in the wilderness and for each succeeding generation of His people. The connection to creation at the end of the harvest season is crucial, reminding the Israelites that first and foremost the Lord provides through creation itself. Just as God celebrated His creation on the seventh day, so the Israelites should celebrate for seven days at the end of the season.

III. CELEBRATION OF THE FEAST (vv. 40–43)

Just before the beginning of the Feast, the people would collect certain types of tree branches. The "boughs of thick trees" are thought to refer to the myrtle tree branches. The branches of willow, and palm and citron trees were also held in the hands and blessed each day of the festival. These leaves were symbolic of the time Israel had spent wandering in the wilderness. These branches would be used to construct booths that mimicked the Israelites' temporary shelters in the wilderness.

Here we see a powerful analogy to the life of Christians. During that time between accepting the Lord Jesus Christ as our personal Savior and the time we enter into the eternal rest of the Lord, the earth we live in is not our home. Like the Children of Israel, we are just pilgrims, and our bodies are the temporary "booths" that we will have to leave when we finally transition from our reconciliation to God until He calls us to our final reward—everlasting life.

Celebrate God's Protection

41 And ye shall keep it a feast unto the LORD seven days in the year. It shall be a statute for ever in your generations: ye shall celebrate it in the seventh month. 42 Ye shall dwell in booths seven days; all that are Israelites born shall dwell in booths: 43 That your generations may know that I made the children of Israel to dwell in booths, when I brought them out of the land of Egypt: I am the LORD your God.

No matter how the situation changes from one year to the next or one generation to the next, the Feast of Tabernacles is to be celebrated for seven days every year as a reminder of the Israelites' time in the wilderness. All of God's people, no matter who they are or where they are, must make the pilgrimage to live in booths at the end of the harvest season. These temporary dwellings serve as a recollection of the simplicity of the wilderness period, and also a joyful reminder of God's protection in bringing the Israelites out of slavery and oppression and providing for them in the desert.

The Feast of Tabernacles is still celebrated by Jews around the world, though few make the pilgrimage to Jerusalem due to the impracticalities of travel. Instead, they often erect tents outside their synagogues or in other places in their communities. Christianity has not continued this festival observance, but the feast can still serve as a reminder and celebration of God's continuing protection and nourishment through rain, sunshine, and healthy crops, as well as through healthy food, homes, jobs, and education for everyone, regardless of whether we live in rural, suburban, or urban settings. Moreover, the eight-day festival is a time to pause for celebration, especially the first and eighth days, which serve as days of rest from regular work. How often do we allow the day-to-day grind to wear us down physically, emotionally, and spiritually? Though it may not always be possible to take an extended break from work, the Feast of Tabernacles reminds us of the importance of setting aside significant time to celebrate God's protection and abundance in our lives.

SEARCH THE SCRIPTURES

QUESTION 2

In **verse 37**, what were the special gifts to the Lord?

An offering made by fire; a burnt offering; a meat offering; a sacrifice; and drink offerings.

LIGHT ON THE WORD

Celebrate God's Goodness

Since creation, the Lord has continued to provide for His people. The Feast of Tabernacles calls us to rejoice in God's generosity and wisdom that continue to nourish us day after day, year after year, and generation after generation.

BIBLE APPLICATION

AIM: Students will learn how Israel was to express their gratitude to the Lord.

In today's lesson, we see that the Feast of Booths, and in fact all of the Feasts, were instituted by God. He calls them "his own feasts." These days, and the Sabbath, reveal the purpose of mankind's past, present, and future. The feasts also tell us of Jesus' first and second coming. The feasts are relevant to present-day saints because they are a fore-shadowing of God's ultimate plan for us. They also let us communicate the need to set apart special times and days for celebration. African Americans can celebrate how God has carried them through slavery and segregation and gave them freedom. These times and days are important as we give honor to God for His provision and guidance amd also a way for us to connect with friends, family, and fellow believers.

STUDENT'S RESPONSES

AIM: Students will acknowledge that Israel's traditions to honor God encourages Christians to honor the goodness of God.

Not only does the Feast of Booths remind us of the wonderful provisions that God provided to Israel, the feast also sets the stage for the rest and abundance coming to Israel and all the people of God. To those who have loved and obeyed Him and have accepted Jesus Christ as their personal savior, God intends to provide a rest from all pain and suffering. Commit to thanking God for His continual care, protection, and provision, and renew your trust in Him for the wonderful blessings He has in store for believers.

PRAYER

Lord, it is with a joyous heart that we give You praise. We remember how You continue to care for us even we cannot care for ourselves. Help us when we doubt who You are and when we forget to honor You. You give us hope for a brighter today and tomorrow. Thank You Lord. In Jesus' Name we pray. Amen.

HOW TO SAY IT

Convocation. kahn-voh-**KAY**-shun.

Solemn. **SAH**-luhm.

Bough. **BOW**.

PREPARE FOR NEXT SUNDAY

Read **Mark 9:14–29** and "Powerful Faith."

DAILY HOME BIBLE READINGS

MONDAY
God of the Journey
(Psalm 68:5–10)

TUESDAY
The Journey Begins
(Exodus 3:1–6)

WEDNESDAY
The Journey Falters
(Deuteronomy 1:29–33)

THURSDAY
Remember the Journey
(Deuteronomy 8:1–11)

FRIDAY
Jesus and the Journey
(John 3:14–21)

SATURDAY
Stephen and the Journey
(Acts 7:30–42a)

SUNDAY
The Feast of Booths
(Leviticus 23:33–43)

Sources:
Balentine, Samuel E. *Leviticus*. Interpretation: A Bible Commentary for Teaching and Preaching. Edited by James Luther Mays. Louisville: John Knox Press, 2002.

Berlin, Adele and Marc Zvi Brettler, eds. *The Jewish Study Bible*. New York: Oxford University Press, 2004.

Hartley, John E. *Leviticus*. Word Biblical Commentary 4. Edited by Bruce M. Metzger, David A. Hubbard, and Glenn W. Barker. Dallas: Word Books, 1992.

Kaiser, Walter C. "The Book of Leviticus." *Vol. 1 of New Interpreter's Bible Commentary*. Edited by Leander E. Keck, et al. Nashville: Abingdon Press, 1994. 985-1191.

Sweeney, Marvin A. *Tanak: A Theological and Critical Introduction to the Jewish Bible*. Minneapolis: Fortress Press, 2012.

COMMENTS / NOTES:

THE GIFT OF FAITH

By Dr. Jeannette H. Donald

I am not moved by what I see. I am not moved by what I feel. I am moved only by what I believe.

—*Smith Wigglesworth*

"Hast thou not known? hast thou not heard, that the everlasting God, the LORD, the Creator of the ends of the earth, fainteth not, neither is weary? there is no searching of his understanding. He giveth power to the faint; and to them that have no might he increaseth strength. Even the youths shall faint and be weary, and the young men shall utterly fall: But they that wait upon the LORD shall renew their strength; they shall mount up with wings as eagles; they shall run, and not be weary; and they shall walk, and not faint" *(Isaiah 40:28–31).*

God has never asked anyone to believe anything that does not rest upon a foundation. Faith does not mean to be blind in some area and say, "Oh, I am trusting God." Our faith rests upon the historical facts of the death, burial, and resurrection of Jesus Christ. God never asked us to take a leap in the dark. He simply just asks us to believe and trust something which rests upon a firm foundation, and it is the only foundation, *"For other foundation can no man lay than that is laid, which is Jesus Christ"* *(1 Corinthians 3:11).*

Believe completely in Jesus and everything that challenges you will strengthen your faith.

Faith is absolute trust in God and knowing He would never forsake us.

UNIT 1: "TESTS OF FAITH" We get the opportunity to see the noble deeds and admirable character Jesus exemplified through the test of faith. Jesus said, "the words that I speak unto you, they are spirit, and they are life" *(John 6:63)*; "I am the way, the truth, and the life" *(John 14:6)*; and "I am come that they might have life, and that they might have it more abundantly" *(John 10:10)*. Jesus sought to prosper everyone, in every area of their life, and for that everyone needs faith. Jesus demonstrated this when a desperate father tells Him that the disciples were unable to cast out an evil spirit from his son. "Jesus said unto him, if thou canst believe, all things are possible to him that believeth. And straightway the father of the child cried out, and said with tears, Lord, I believe; help thou mine unbelief. Based upon that Father's expressed faith, Jesus cast out the dumb and deaf spirit from the demon-possessed boy" *(Mark 9:23–25).*

There are many tests, as a result of living in a fallen and imperfect world. Therefore, it is imperative that we follow the teaching of Jesus. A test of faith was shown when Jesus showed genuine love for the rich young ruler, because he wanted eternal life but was unable to give up his wealth *(Mark 10:17–31)*. At the Last Supper, Jesus predicted that Peter would deny him three times. "But he spake the more vehemently, If I should die with thee, I will not deny thee in any wise" *(Mark 14:31)*. Peter was tested and denied Jesus three times; when the crock crowed then, he remembered, and he wept. Jesus' family and friends were tested and devastated when He was crucified, but their faith was restored when He was raised from the dead.

UNIT 2: "RESTORATIVE FAITH" One of the most difficult parts of a Christian life is the fact that Christ does not make us immune to life's trials and tribulations. Why would a good and loving God allow us to go through such things as the death of a child, or emotional or physical disorder? Jesus' life was one of blessing, healing, releasing prosperity, compassion, truth, and inner peace, just to name a few. Jesus demonstrated this when the Roman soldier's servant was sick; he believed Jesus was sent from God and his servant would be healed *(Luke 7:1–10)*. God's enabling power can supernaturally bring restoration to any life situation, like that of the sinful woman who anointed Jesus' feet with her tears and hair. Jesus proceeds to tell this woman that her sins, which are many, are forgiven, because her heart was full of love; by the same token, those whose hearts have only a little love will be forgiven only a little *(Luke 7:36–56)*.

Faith allows God to do for us and with us what we could never do alone. Jesus healed a demon-possessed man and urged him to return to his family and tell them what God had done for him *(Luke 8:26–39)*. Jesus uses the parable of a prodigal son to teach us how a lost sinner who lives a very sinful life can and will be accepted by God (represented by the father) through repentance *(Luke 15:11–24)*.

UNIT 3: THE FULLNESS OF FAITH "Now faith is the substance of things hoped for; the evidence of things not seen" *(Hebrews 11:1)*. "When the Son of Man comes, will he find faith on the earth?" *(Luke 18:8b, NIV)*. Faith is not mental delusion or self-deception, but a work of the Holy Spirit and the Word of God. "Consequently, faith comes from hearing the message, and the message is heard through the word about Christ" *(Romans 10:17, NIV)*. Faith is believing in what is true. Faith in God must be from the heart. Faith causes you to know in your heart before you see with your eyes. "For we walk by faith, not by sight" *(2 Corinthians 5:7)*.

Faith in God allows us to have trust and confidence in God and in Christ that leads us to commit our whole soul to Him as our Savior (Justifier, Healer, and Deliverer) and Lord. Being able to forgive a person requires faith. From the beginning of history, God has always been concerned with mankind's heart, thoughts, attitudes and motives. Faith in God helps us through any situation and brings us into maturity to forgive when someone sins against us. *"If your brother or sister sins against you, rebuke them; and if they repent, forgive them" (Luke 17:3, NIV)*. Just like the mustard seed that starts tiny and becomes a great tree, you will become a person of influence for others and will produce fruit when you forgive. What's so amazing is that Jesus said, *"You don't even need a lot of faith."* Jesus said, *"That just a little amount can move mountains."* In other words, just a little faith can do amazing things in our lives and those around us *(Matthew 17:20)*. You water and feed the seed of your faith by giving it nourishment. How do we get nourishment? By reading God's Word, worshiping, and praying. All those things feed the seed of faith in your *life*.

Dr. Jeannette Head Donald is the First Lady of the Gospel Temple Church of God in Christ, Pine Grove, Louisiana under the leadership of her husband, Elder Peter Donald. A graduate of Southeastern Louisiana University, Hammond, Louisiana in Office & Business Administration, Certified & Licensed Belief Therapist (Therapon Institute of New Orleans, Louisiana), IFFC Bible Institute of Baton Rouge, Louisiana (Diploma in Theology) and Life Christian University (Bachelor's Degree in Christian Counseling and Bachelor Degree, Master's Degree & Doctoral Degree in Theology) Zachary, Louisiana. She is a woman of integrity and character called to do a work in the harvest for God; her motto is "Each One Reaching One." Dr. Jeannette serves as Assoc. Professor of Life Christian University (Zachary, Louisiana). She serves in the Louisiana East First Jurisdiction as Asst. Dean of the W. K. Gordon Institute and the Jurisdictional Sunday School Field Representative.

MAKING YOUR TEACHING COUNT
by Jurisdictional Superintendent Dana Watkins

The following information is designed to support and aid both the COGIC Commentary series and Sunday School leaders by providing innovative teaching suggestions, proven growth strategies, and thoughtful learning opportunities, thus exciting, benefiting, and enhancing the user.

INTRODUCTION: The purpose of this presentation is to enhance your ability to make your teaching count in and out of the classroom. It should be the desire of every Bible teacher to enhance and build their teaching ability, skill, and knowledge. It's also important to discover new and effective ways to present material.

Always seek to find helps, aids, classes, seminars, and books to develop your skills in the class room, so your class will be more interesting and the lesson more effective. Make your goal leaving your students with something they can remember and use in their daily walk with Christ, because folk need something they can use today, right now.

So together we will answer two questions:

- Why should my teaching count?

- How can I make my teaching count?

Question #1 - What does "to count" mean in making my teaching count? _____

Definition: to count means to be of value, importance, to matter, worth keeping, worth remembering

Now we can answer our first question:

Why should I make my teaching count? _____

In other words, why should my teaching be of value, important, or worth keeping?

Answer: It is the Word of God.

And the Word of God is valuable, is worth keeping, and will matter. It will make a difference in the student's life and the teacher's life. The Word of God is important and life-changing. It is the living Word. So that's one reason we want to make our teaching count.

Answer: The souls of men and women are at stake. The student is at the center of our purpose. It's an important and sacred task. The teacher may offer the only chance some students will ever have to be led toward righteousness, God, and heaven.

The teacher is not to teach merely to be teaching, give out good information, or display our knowledge. The teacher should have a definite purpose in teaching: to bring Christ into the lives of the student, not just the mere satisfaction of personal ambition. It is not about you! I am an instrument used for the purpose of teaching the Word of God.

Question #2 - How can I make my teaching count?_____

In other words, how can my teaching be effective? How can I teach so that the Holy Spirit transforms people?

First of all, we have to understand our role as a Bible teacher: what is my job, my task, my goal?

I. **UNDERSTANDING THE TEACHER'S ROLE**

   A. The office of teacher is a ministry given by Christ: "And he gave some, apostles; and some, prophets; and some, evangelists; and some, pastors and teachers" (Ephesians 4:11).

   1. Christ gave the teaching ministry to the church. Why did He do that? "For the perfecting of the saints, for the work of the ministry, for the edifying of the body of Christ" (Ephesians 4:12).

   And Christ gave you, who have the calling of teacher, to the church. You are a vital part of the Lord's plan of redemption and it shouldn't be taken lightly. "Let not many of you become teachers, my brethren, knowing that as such we shall incur a stricter judgment" (James 3:1, NASB).

   So we will be judged by what we are telling folks, and how we are telling it. The Lord holds us accountable for what we say and what we teach.

   B. The teacher's personality is the channel which the Gospel must flow through to the student.

   1. *The Rule of Three for Bible Teachers: by C.J. Sharp,* pioneer in teacher training

      a. Three things to be: **True, Thoughtful, Thorough**

      Honest, trustworthy, concerned about student, servant teacher, clear and understandable

      b. Three things to govern: **Time, Temper, Tongue**

      We need to realize that when we teach, we are altering one's mindset, transmitting new knowledge, new information, that may change behavior.

      Keep our channels unclogged, not just from sin, but little quirks and idiosyncrasies that may divert the truth of God's message. With children, we must be especially careful about what we say, how we say it, and how we act.

c. Three things to educate: **Hand, Head, Heart**

> Learning is a continuous process for all of us; "Whatsoever thy hand findeth to do, do it with thy might; for there is no work, nor device, nor knowledge, nor wisdom, in the grave, whither thou goest" (Ecclesiastes 9:10). It's not just about head knowledge.

C. Another point in understanding the teacher's role: we are always teaching inside and outside the classroom.

1. As a teacher in the Body of Christ, we must walk circumspectly, in love, and really understand our true calling as a teacher. Our call doesn't end at the end of the class session. We must watch how we treat people, our attitude, lifestyle, and the company we keep.

2. We should also be an example not only spiritually, but also in our appearance and care of the body, which is the temple of the Holy Spirit.

3. A neat personal appearance helps to command attention from your students.

4. So how you manage and guard your gift as teacher is crucial to fulfilling the Lord's will through His church.

II. **THE TEACHING TASK: EPHESIANS 4:12–13**

A. My job as teacher is a specific task:

1. To equip the saints for the work of the ministry. To prepare God's people for works of service, in and out of the church so that the body of Christ may be built up.

2. How long are we to do this? "Until we all reach unity in the faith and in the knowledge of the Son of God and become mature, attaining to the whole measure of the fullness of Christ" (Ephesians 4:13, NIV). It's ongoing until we are fully built up in Christ, until He comes back.

B. The teachers task is to equip the saints to make disciples of all people, according to the Scriptures. Matthew 28:19–20 commissions us to go and equip the saints to teach others. We did this while serving in the Middle East, so they could in turn teach others. I saw change and growth within 4 months; when my group left, we had no doubt they were ready to continue the church ministry.

The teacher of God's Word has an opportunity heaven-wide not only to the individual student, but to the future of the nation, society of the world, and to the whole future of Christ's cause on Earth. "For you must teach others those things you and many others have heard me speak about. Teach these great truths to trustworthy men who will, in turn, pass them on to others" (2 Timothy 2:2, TLB).

What a child learns in Sunday School is generally the foundation that impacts his or her adulthood choices and decisions when he or she raises his or her family.

How do we equip others? By using effective teaching methods that have the potential for more transformation and growth in the student.

III. TEACHING METHODS THAT CAUSE TRANSFORMATION

1. **Biblical Method:** Always teach from a biblical viewpoint—keep to Scripture and lesson plan (not your opinion or worldview); interject life experiences as the Spirit leads when appropriate

2. **Passive Listening:** Lecturing does not create the best environment for transforming of the whole person; try different learning styles, such as auditory, visual, hands-on

3. **Student Involvement:** Discussion, small groups, role-playing, drama, storytelling

4. **Learning Activities:** Projects, crafts so that students learn from each other and together

5. **Involve the Sense of Sight:** Visual aids, maps, videotapes and DVDs, overhead projection and PowerPoints, charts, hand-outs

Be available to the Holy Spirit: You cannot be a successful teacher in the Body of Christ without the anointing and work of the Holy Ghost through your teaching ministry.

1. So we must be open to the Spirit, not filled up with junk, channels clogged.

2. Have a constant prayer life, and spend time studying and following God's Word (I pray a version of Ephesians 1:17: Open/enlighten the eyes of my heart that I may understand and know the hope which you have called me). Just can't teach the Book; give out good information. The letter kills, but the Spirit of God's Word gives life and transforms.

   We are facing harsh times ahead; the Bible teacher has got to teach the spirit of the Bible, because the true love of God is what will destroy the yoke/bondage of homosexuality, gangbanging, gambling, adultery, lying, stealing, hatred, and suicide. Only Christ's forgiveness of sin can transform/change a life.

3. Know the Spirit of the Bible, character of God, who HE really is. (I pray a version of Ephesians 1:17: "Give me the Spirit of wisdom and revelation that I may know you better.") The only way our teaching can transform is if we are transformed through a close relationship with Jesus.

4. Expect spiritual results, transformation, and growth in the Lord.

5. Praise and worship the Lord for what He is doing, has done, and will do in your ministry and class.

Evangelist Dana L. Watkins is the Jurisdictional Sunday School Superintendent for the First Ecclesiastical Jurisdiction of Western Pennsylvania where Bishop James Miles Foster is her prelate and Mother Wilma Beauford, PhD her state supervisor. She is employed by the 911th Airlift Wing Services Group. She is an Air Force Reserve veteran and has served and ministered in many parts of the United States & abroad

HOW TO LISTEN EFFECTIVELY
by Jurisdictional Superintendent Larry L. Polk

Reading, writing, 'rithmetic! Growing up, learning the 3 R's was not only necessary but mandatory in families across this country, especially among African American families. We were encouraged to not only learn them, but master them as well. These skills were learned in school, but they were augmented in Sunday School—"The Best School in the World."

However, of all the skills we learned and in many ways perfected, the one skill we never developed was the ability to listen. If this then is true, today more than ever before there is a pressing need to call our attention to the art of "listening effectively." With a large number of children facing difficult times at home, school, on the playground, and in church, there is an ever increasing need for Sunday School teachers to have their ears "wide open." As spiritual leaders and examples, it is the Sunday School where youngsters often feel safe and comfortable to share their hurts and frustrations as well as their hopes and dreams. We must be open to not only teach, but learn from our students, regardless of their age and position in life. One of the most important ways to learn is to listen. It isn't by coincidence that God, in His infinite wisdom, gave us two ears and one mouth. Simple logic would indicate we are to listen twice as much as we speak.

When asked, "Are you a good listener?" most people will say, "Yes." Where we would like to think we are, few people have been taught to listen because we think it is "natural." However, effective listening is a learned skill.

Here are some tips for learning to listen effectively.

1. **Learn to listen deeply.** Deep listening requires one to not only hear, but empathetically "walk in the shoes" of the person speaking.

2. When we listen effectively, we always **listen to the satisfaction of the speaker**—not the listener. We often believe we know what the person has said, when we really are clueless.

3. In order to listen to the satisfaction of the speaker, we need to **use simple reflections**. First reword what the speaker said (put his/her thoughts into your words) and wait for them to give you indication that you heard them correctly. Secondly, try to understand the affect (feeling) the speaker may be having. When these two things are combined, we are listening empathetically (listening deeply).

4. We must continue to **interpret the speaker's message (content) and affect (feeling)** until the speaker is satisfied that we have understood.

5. Be aware that you **can't be thinking about a response** at the same time you are listening.

6. **Avoid making judgments and guessing** what you think the speaker is going to say.

7. Finally, **trust what the speaker is saying is "true."** If it is true for them, it need not agree with what you think "their truth is." Help them discover the "truth" as defined by the Word of God, not your opinion.

Remember as leaders, whatever our role is, we have a responsibility to attend to every part of the student that graces our classroom—the physical, spiritual, and emotional. It is difficult, if not impossible, to do this if we have not developed the ability to listen effectively. We must learn **to listen with our eyes, our hearts, and our ears.**

Pastor Larry L. Polk, Jurisdictional Superintendent
State Sunday School Department
Texas Northeast First Jurisdiction
Bishop J. Neaul Haynes, Prelate
Mother Pia Haynes Williams, Jurisdictional Supervisor

EFFECTIVE TIPS FOR SUCCESSFUL TEACHING

by Jurisdictional Field Representative Sandra Daniel

The following information is designed to support and aid both the COGIC Commentary series and Sunday School leaders by providing innovative teaching suggestions, proven growth strategies, and thoughtful learning opportunities, thus exciting, benefiting, and enhancing the user.

1. Prepare each lesson by fresh study.

2. Find in the lesson its analogies to more familiar language.

3. Study the lesson until it takes shape in familiar language.

4. Find the natural order of the steps of the lesson from the simplest to the broadest.

5. Find the relation of the lesson to the lives of the learners.

6. Use freely all legitimate aids.

7. Complete mastery of a few things is better than an ineffective smattering of many.

8. Have a definite time for study of each lesson, in advance of the teaching.

9. Have a plan of study, but don't hesitate to study beyond the plan.

10. Do not deny yourself the help of good books on the subject of your lessons.

11. Read with thinking and comprehension, talk the lesson over with a friend, and write out your own views.

12. Never begin a class exercise until the attention of the class has been secured.

13. Pause whenever the attention is interrupted or lost; wait until it is completely regained.

14. Never wholly exhaust the attention of your students; adapt the length of the class exercise to their ages.

15. Strive to arouse attention, when necessary, by variety in your presentation.

16. Kindle and maintain the highest possible interest in the subject and present those aspects of the lesson that correspond to the ages and attainments of the students.

17. Appeal to the interest of your students and refer to their favorite stories, songs, sports, and subjects.

18. Look for sources of distraction and reduce them.

19. Prepare beforehand thought-provoking questions and make your presentation as attractive as possible.

Jurisdictional Field Representative Sandra Daniel
Evangelist Sandra Daniel serves as the Jurisdictional Field Representative for Southern California First Jurisdiction under the leadership of Bishop Joe L. Ealy and General Assistant Supervisor/ Jurisdictional Supervisor, Mother Barbara McCoo Lewis. She is the Assistant Director of Leadership Ministry for the International Sunday School Department.

QUARTERLY QUIZ

The questions on this page may be used in several ways: as a pretest at the beginning of the quarter; as a review at the end of the quarter; or as a review after each lesson. The questions are based on the Scripture text of each lesson (King James Version).

LESSON 1

1. What did Christ say was the disciples' problem and what was the remedy (**Mark 9:19**)?

_____

_____

2. The scribes and the Pharisees had what type of authority and were considered what in regards to the law?

_____

_____

LESSON 2

1. Complete the following sentence: But _____ who are _____ shall be _____ (**Mark 10:31**).

_____

_____

2. What does Christ say the young man lacks in his quest for eternal life (**v. 21**)?

_____

_____

LESSON 3

1. Describe what activities took place and where after Jesus and the disciples shared their "Last Supper" together (**Mark 14:26**).

_____

_____

2. According to **verse 27**, did Jesus prepare the disciples for all the joy they would experience as they shared God's Word with others?

_____

_____

LESSON 4

1. What did the women bring to the sepulcher (**Mark 16:1**)?

_____

_____

2. What was the women's response (**v. 8**)?

_____

_____

LESSON 5

1. Name the town where the healing took place.

_____

_____

2. Who did the centurion send to speak to Jesus about his sick servant (**Luke 7:3**)?

_____

_____

LESSON 6

1. In **Luke 7:36**, what religious leader decides to eat with Jesus?

_____

_____

QUARTERLY QUIZ

2. During the meal, Jesus forgave whose sin, and what question did the attendees ask about Jesus (**vv. 48–49**)?

_____

_____

LESSON 7

1. Describe the man in **Luke 8:27.**

_____

_____

2. What miracle did people share with others (**v. 36**)?

_____

_____

LESSON 8

1. What does the Prodigal Son decide to do in **Luke 15:15?**

_____

_____

2. The younger son said that he had _____ against _____ and _____ _____(**v. 18**).

_____

_____

LESSON 9

1. And if he trespass against thee _____ times in a day, and _____ times in a day turn again to thee, saying, I repent; _____ _____ _____ _____(**Luke 17:4**).

_____

_____

2. True or False—**verse 9** reminds the reader to thank a servant who does what is commanded because this is an important courtesy to do.

_____

_____

LESSON 10

1. What towns did Jesus pass as He went to Jerusalem (**Luke 17:11**)?

_____

_____

2. Was the man who thanked Jesus Jewish, Samaritan, or Canaanite, and why was this significant (**v. 16**)?

_____

_____

LESSON 11

1. Jesus shared His parable with which types of people (**Luke 18:9**)?

_____

_____

2. What did the publican say in **verse 13?**

_____

_____

LESSON 12

1. What did the disciples do when the people brought babies to Jesus (**Luke 18:15**)?

_____

_____

QUARTERLY QUIZ

2. What did Jesus do with the children (**Mark 10:16**)?

_____

_____

LESSON 13

1. How would the people view Zacchaeus and his occupation as a publican (tax collector), and why (**Luke 19:2**)?

_____

_____

2. The people _____ that Jesus would be the guest of Zacchaeus (**v. 7**).

_____

_____

Answers to Quarterly Quiz can be found on page 509

POWERFUL FAITH

BIBLE BASIS: MARK 9:14–29

BIBLE TRUTH: Jesus encouraged His disciples to believe they could accomplish great things with His help.

MEMORY VERSE: "And he said unto them, This kind can come forth by nothing, but by prayer and fasting" (Mark 9:29).

LESSON AIM: By the end of the lesson, we will: RECALL the disciples' attempt to heal a demon-possessed child and Jesus' later success in doing so; CONTEMPLATE what faith it takes to use the power of Jesus Christ to minister to others; and BELIEVE our prayers have real power.

TEACHER PREPARATION

MATERIALS NEEDED: Quarterly Commentary/Teacher Manual, Adult Quarterly, Adult resources—charts, worksheets, and other teaching tools, paper, pens, pencils, Bibles (several different versions)

OTHER MATERIALS NEEDED / TEACHER'S NOTES:

_____

_____

LESSON OVERVIEW

LIFE NEED FOR TODAY'S LESSON
It is accepted that people are able to accomplish great things by changing self-doubt to believing that they can do all things through Christ.

BIBLE LEARNING
Jesus demonstrated to the disciples that they can do great things by casting out an evil spirit.

BIBLE APPLICATION
Believers struggle with faith when faced with seemingly impossible situations.

STUDENTS' RESPONSES
Believers can see how Jesus helps us during difficult times.

LESSON SCRIPTURE

MARK 9:14–29, KJV

14 And when he came to his disciples, he saw a great multitude about them, and the scribes questioning with them.

15 And straightway all the people, when they beheld him, were greatly amazed, and running to him saluted him.

MARK 9:14–29, NIV

14 When they came to the other disciples, they saw a large crowd around them and the teachers of the law arguing with them.

15 As soon as all the people saw Jesus, they were overwhelmed with wonder and ran to greet him.

16 And he asked the scribes, What question ye with them?

16 "What are you arguing with them about?" he asked.

17 And one of the multitude answered and said, Master, I have brought unto thee my son, which hath a dumb spirit;

17 A man in the crowd answered, "Teacher, I brought you my son, who is possessed by a spirit that has robbed him of speech.

18 And wheresoever he taketh him, he teareth him: and he foameth, and gnasheth with his teeth, and pineth away: and I spake to thy disciples that they should cast him out; and they could not.

18 Whenever it seizes him, it throws him to the ground. He foams at the mouth, gnashes his teeth and becomes rigid. I asked your disciples to drive out the spirit, but they could not."

19 He answereth him, and saith, O faithless generation, how long shall I be with you? how long shall I suffer you? bring him unto me.

19 "You unbelieving generation," Jesus replied, "how long shall I stay with you? How long shall I put up with you? Bring the boy to me."

20 And they brought him unto him: and when he saw him, straightway the spirit tare him; and he fell on the ground, and wallowed foaming.

20 So they brought him. When the spirit saw Jesus, it immediately threw the boy into a convulsion. He fell to the ground and rolled around, foaming at the mouth.

21 And he asked his father, How long is it ago since this came unto him? And he said, Of a child.

21 Jesus asked the boy's father, "How long has he been like this?" "From childhood," he answered.

22 And ofttimes it hath cast him into the fire, and into the waters, to destroy him: but if thou canst do any thing, have compassion on us, and help us.

22 "It has often thrown him into fire or water to kill him. But if you can do anything, take pity on us and help us."

23 Jesus said unto him, If thou canst believe, all things are possible to him that believeth.

23 "'If you can'?" said Jesus. "Everything is possible for one who believes."

24 And straightway the father of the child cried out, and said with tears, Lord, I believe; help thou mine unbelief.

24 Immediately the boy's father exclaimed, "I do believe; help me overcome my unbelief!"

25 When Jesus saw that the people came running together, he rebuked the foul spirit, saying unto him, Thou dumb and deaf spirit, I charge thee, come out of him, and enter no more into him.

25 When Jesus saw that a crowd was running to the scene, he rebuked the impure spirit. "You deaf and mute spirit," he said, "I command you, come out of him and never enter him again."

26 And the spirit cried, and rent him sore, and came out of him: and he was as one dead; insomuch that many said, He is dead.

26 The spirit shrieked, convulsed him violently and came out. The boy looked so much like a corpse that many said, "He's dead."

27 But Jesus took him by the hand, and lifted him up; and he arose.

28 And when he was come into the house, his disciples asked him privately, Why could not we cast him out?

29 And he said unto them, This kind can come forth by nothing, but by prayer and fasting.

27 But Jesus took him by the hand and lifted him to his feet, and he stood up.

28 After Jesus had gone indoors, his disciples asked him privately, "Why couldn't we drive it out?"

29 He replied, "This kind can come out only by prayer."

LIGHT ON THE WORD

Scribes and teachers of religious law. The scribes and teachers of religious law were primarily Pharisees. They were the religious and moral authorities during Jesus' time, considered the experts and protectors of the Law of Moses, and highly regarded by common Jews. In fact, the previous passage (**Mark 9:2–13**) records three of Jesus' disciples asking Him questions about the scribes' teachings on Elijah, indicating that they also viewed these teachers as religious experts. Throughout the Gospels, scribes (lawyers, teachers of the Law) are often Christ's antagonists, questioning Him, challenging His authority, and seeking to discourage His followers. They are often portrayed as arrogant, unbelieving, and hypocritical.

Demon possession. Demon possession means a person is under the influence or power of one or more demons (fallen angels) who reside within him or her, causing disorder. Such possession was a prevalent and grim reality during Christ's times. Mark's Gospel states, "So Jesus healed many people who were sick with various diseases, and he cast out many demons" (from **1:34**, NLT). Several Scriptures record instances of individuals being possessed by demons to the point where the person has no control of his or her actions. Jesus confronts and rebukes these demons, some who caused abnormal mental behavior (such as the man with unusual strength who would cut himself with stones; see **Mark 5:1–20**), others who caused physical illnesses, and others who, as in this case, caused both (deafness, muteness, and seizures).

TEACHING THE BIBLE LESSON

LIFE NEED FOR TODAY'S LESSON

AIM: Students will know that people are able to accomplish great things only by changing self-doubt to believing in themselves.

INTRODUCTION

Deity, Purpose, and Power

The events in this passage occur immediately after the Transfiguration, when Jesus led Peter, James, and John up a mountain, transformed before them, and spoke with Moses and Elijah, who appeared in their presence (**Mark 9:2–4**). The Transfiguration revealed more of Christ's deity, purpose, power, and fulfillment of both the Law and prophecy. Jesus was answering a question related to the scribes' teachings about Elijah when the events in **verses 14–29** begin. The glory, power, and magnificence of the Transfiguration (which left the three disciples speechless in fear) are in direct contrast to the chaotic scene that follows.

Christ is the Son of God, and holds ultimate authority in all things. Mark intentionally reveals this truth by recording several of Christ's miracles. Yet Jesus was constantly (and unsuccessfully) being challenged, as people struggled or refused to believe in Him. The scribes, considered religious experts, likely knew much more about the Law and the prophets than Christ's disciples, who were Jewish commoners from various walks of life. As a result, the disciples would have had no authority over the common man, especially in religious matters. Christ had given them authority, yet the disciples were ineffective and the father's accusation of their inability to demonstrate God's power threatened to undermine their credibility.

BIBLE LEARNING

AIM: Students will learn that Jesus demonstrated to the disciples that they can do great things by casting out an evil spirit.

I. THE PROBLEM (MARK 9:14–18)

Upon returning from the mountain with three disciples, Jesus encounters the remaining nine arguing with some teachers of the Law. While the cause of the argument or why the teachers were involved is not explicitly stated, the father's response suggests it has something to do with the disciples' inability to heal his son. Disciples were supposed to be able to carry out duties (teaching, etc.) in their teacher's absence. The expectation could have been that Christ's disciples would perform miracles like Him; His disciples were commissioned to do so (**Mark 6:7**), and had done it before (**6:12–13**). However, they were rendered powerless in this instance and didn't know why. The unbelieving teachers would have seized such an opportunity to bring shame to Jesus and His followers.

Mark 9:14–29

14 And when he came to his disciples, he saw a great multitude about them, and the scribes questioning with them. 15 And straightway all the people, when they beheld him, were greatly amazed, and running to him saluted him.

Jesus has just come down from the mountain where Peter, James, and John saw Him transfigured and heard God the Father's confirmation of His uniqueness as the Son. As He came down, He saw a great multitude and the scribes were questioning (Gk. *suzeteo*, **sude-zay-TEH-oh**) with them. The word means to debate and discuss vehemently in order to reach a solution or agreement. Jesus comes down to a commotion, and the discussion stops "straightway" or immediately (Gk. *euthus*, **ew-THOUS**). This word comes up in the Gospel of Mark numerous times and gives the whole Gospel a sense of urgency. All the people see Him, are greatly amazed, and salute (Gk. *aspazomai*, **ah-SPAHD-zoe-my**) or greet Him as an honored rabbi.

16 And he asked the scribes, What question ye with them? 17 And one of the multitude answered and said, Master, I have brought unto thee my son, which hath a dumb spirit;

Jesus asks the scribes why they questioned the disciples. These men were educated and well versed in the Mosaic Law, often asked to settle judicial and religious matters. A man from the crowd brought his son to the disciples and by association to Jesus. This man's son was oppressed by a "dumb" (Gk. *alalos*, **AH-lah-los**) spirit, meaning speechless. The spirit was considered mute because those possessed by demons were said to take on the possessor's characteristics. In this case, the demon that could not speak influenced the child to lack speech as well.

18 And wheresoever he taketh him, he teareth him: and he foameth, and gnasheth with his teeth, and pineth away: and I spake

to thy disciples that they should cast him out; and they could not.

Not only does the demon keep the child from speaking, he also controls the boy's body. Mark uses five words to describe the demon's influence over the young man. He takes him, which means possesses or seizes him. He tears him, meaning to distort or convulse. He foams at the mouth. He gnashes (Gk. *trizo*, **TRID-zo**) his teeth, a common feature of epileptic fits. "Gnashing" is usually used for shrill sounds such as the squawking of birds; in this context, it indicates the sound of grating teeth. From this, we can conclude this was a violent seizure that overtook the young man. Lastly, the father adds that he pines away (Gk. *xeraino*, **kseh-RYE-no**), which means the boy would dry up and become rigid. The father expresses his frustration that he brought the boy to the disciples and they couldn't cast the demon out. Mature disciples were expected to know enough of their master's teaching to stand in his stead. Many were called upon to deliver lectures in his absence. This, however, is not a lecture, but an exorcism (casting out of demonic spirits), which is out of their league."

II. THE REBUKES (vv. 19–24)

This passage contains two rebukes. In the first, Jesus addresses the crowd, but especially expresses His disappointment with His disciples. They had been with Him, witnessing many miracles He performed. He commissioned them, and they successfully carried out those missions. However, they still struggled to believe. Lack of faith appears to be a recurring theme in the disciples' lives, as seen in the calming of the storm (**Matthew 8:23–27, Mark 4:35–40**), Peter walking on water (**Matthew 14:25–33**), Christ's warning about the yeast of the Pharisees and Sadducees (**Matthew 16:5–12**), and even after His resurrection (**Mark 16:14**). Jesus rebuked them first, then took action to "fix" where they

failed. The demon then threw the boy into another convulsion, perhaps either to intimidate Jesus or as one final act as it realized it would be cast out.

The second rebuke was directed toward the father who, after watching his son live this way for years with no cure, and his faith shaken by the disciples' inability to help, says, "Do something if you can." Christ reminds him that His ability is unquestioned. The issue is the man's faith. The man expresses the conflict of many believers: "I do believe; help me overcome my unbelief!" (NIV).

Faithlessness and Frustration

19 He answereth him, and saith, O faithless generation, how long shall I be with you? how long shall I suffer you? bring him unto me.

Jesus responds with frustration. He addresses the whole generation, which in this context focuses on all the people living at the current time. Jesus calls them faithless, because they did not believe in Him and His power to cast out devils. Jesus continues in frustration asking a rhetorical question: "How long shall I be with you? How long shall I suffer with you?" In these questions, Jesus points out that He will not always be on earth. One day He will ascend to Heaven and not deal directly with these types of problems. His authority will be delegated to His apostles and church. In other words, if they do not have faith, they better obtain it soon.

20 And they brought him unto him: and when he saw him, straightway the spirit tare him; and he fell on the ground, and wallowed foaming.

Heeding Jesus' request, they brought the boy to Him. The demon saw Him and responded. Immediately the demon caused him to tear (Gk. *susparasso*, **sue-spah-RAH-soh**), or convulse and shake. This verb is the intensified form of the same root word that appears as "rent" in **v. 26**. He fell to the ground and wallowed or rotated his body while foaming at the mouth. This self-destructive behavior is characteristic of demonic possession (**Mark 5:1–5**). Exorcisms are very common in sub saharan Africa as well as in Pentecostal/Charismatic churches in North America. In the African context, demonic possession is often the result of animistic worship. However, the church does not believe that animals have souls. Often when a Christian evangelist or pastor casts the demon out, people are converted.

21 And he asked his father, How long is it ago since this came unto him? And he said, Of a child. 22 And ofttimes it hath cast him into the fire, and into the waters, to destroy him: but if thou canst do any thing, have compassion on us, and help us.

Jesus asks diagnostic questions. It is not quite clear what their purpose was except to reveal the father's desire and measure of faith. The father lets Jesus know that his son who had suffered this was "of a child." The phrase is one word in Greek: *paideothen* (**pie-di-AH-then**), which means since the onset of childhood. The boy had been under this demonic influence for a long time.

The father further adds that this condition endangers the boy; it casts, or throws, him into the fire. The boy clearly is not in control of his body during these episodes. The spirit also throws him into water to destroy or kill him. The father pleads for his son's life when he asks Jesus to have compassion and help them.

23 Jesus said unto him, If thou canst believe, all things are possible to him that believeth. 24 And straightway the father of the child cried out, and said with tears, Lord, I believe; help thou mine unbelief.

Jesus turns the tables on the man's request. He had asked Jesus "If you can do anything"; now Jesus says "If you can believe." It is not about Jesus' ability to heal, but the disciples' and now

the father's ability to put their trust in God. This trust in God, who can do the impossible, is vital and necessary to seeing His wonders.

Immediately the father not only expresses his belief, but calls Jesus Lord. This is no ordinary faith but faith with a definite object: Jesus Christ. After expressing his faith in Jesus as the One who can do the impossible, the father follows up with a seemingly contradictory statement: "Help my unbelief." It may seem contradictory, unless we look at the One asked to help. The father knows he is completely powerless in this situation and even needs Jesus' help to believe. This is the experience of Jesus' followers even now.

III. THE SOLUTION (vv. 25–26)

Jesus' response to the man's request to heal both his son and his wavering faith, was to rebuke the evil spirit. He not only commanded the spirit to come out of the boy, but to never enter him again— complete and permanent healing. Although the term exorcist is not biblical, the concept for casting out demons is. Ungodly efforts did not include the power of the Holy Ghost. Exorcists of the time would have attempted to use various methods to suppress the demon—spells, potions, or pain, for example. Jesus simply used His Word to completely expel demons, further demonstrating His power.

Christ performed this miracle before the crowd grew, presumably to limit being a spectacle, because He knew the people would not believe, indicated by the murmur running through the crowd after the boy was healed. Without waiting, observing, or hoping for the best, they were saying, "He's dead." Such unbelief!

Jesus Rebuked a Foul Spirit

25 When Jesus saw that the people came running together, he rebuked the foul spirit, saying unto him, Thou dumb and deaf spirit, I charge thee, come out of him, and enter no

more into him. 26 And the spirit cried, and rent him sore, and came out of him: and he was as one dead; insomuch that many said, He is dead.

The people began to form a crowd. Jesus notices and doesn't want to create a scene. So He rebuked (Gk. *epitimao*, **eh-pi-ti-MAH-oh**) the spirit, which means to admonish or warn forcefully; in other words, He ordered the spirit. The spirit is described as foul (Gk. *akathartos*, **ah-KAH-thar-tos**), which is to be ceremonially and sometimes morally unclean, in this context referring to the defilement of those supernatural beings hostile to God and His people. These beings' purpose is solely to deface God's creation, and especially man as His representative. Jesus rebukes him by name. He is a "dumb and deaf," referring to the young man's hearing and speaking.

Jesus continues with His rebuke. He charges (Gk. *epitasso*, **eh-pee-TAH-so**), or commands, the demon. Jesus takes authority over the demon as He commands him to come out of the man's son. Here we see that demonic possession is internal; the demon inside the young man's body now must leave, and Jesus commands him to "enter no more into him." This young man's body would no longer be the evil spirit's home.

As soon as Jesus rebuked him, the spirit cried and rent (Gk. *sparasso*, **spa-RAH-so**) the boy sore. The word "rent" means to shake uncontrollably. It seems the demon left but not before putting up a fight. After the demon left, the boy lay there as if dead or comatose.

IV. THE LESSON (vv. 27–29)

27 But Jesus took him by the hand, and lifted him up; and he arose. 28 And when he was come into the house, his disciples asked him privately, Why could not we cast him out? 29 And he said unto them, This kind can come forth by nothing, but by prayer and fasting.

The young man was not left there. Jesus took him by the hand and lifted (*egeiro*, **eh-GAY-ro**) him up. This word, meaning to wake up or rise, is often used in the context of Jesus' resurrection and the resurrection of believers and unbelievers (**Matthew 16:21, Matthew 27:52, John 5:21**). Some scholars say that this suggests the idea of Jesus' resurrection—the boy lay there as dead and was lifted up. This is further confirmed by the use of the verb arose (*anistemi*, **ah-NIH-stay-mee**), which also is often used in the context of Jesus' resurrection (**Matthew 17:9, Mark 8:31, Luke 18:33, John 20:9**). This is different than Lazarus' actual rising from the dead in John 12. Here the language hints at Jesus' resurrection, but the boy did not die, only lay as if dead or comatose (v. 26), so Mark is using the same kind of language to talk about the boy being physically restored after being possessed.

After He came in, the disciples wonder at His spiritual power and ask why they could not cast out the demon. The narrative says privately; from the context, we can assume the disciples were embarrassed by their lack of spiritual power. Jesus' answer is that they were deficient in prayer and fasting. He says "this kind" in reference to the demon. The word kind (*genos*, **geh-NOSS**) means offspring, kindred, or individuals of the same nature; in this context, it refers to the evil spirits of the type who possessed the young man. Jesus is not referring to prayer here in the sense of on-the-spot praying, but a life saturated with prayer. Only one who has a rich and dynamic relationship with God can take authority over evil spirits the way Jesus did. The words "and fasting" are a later addition (which is why they appear in the KJV but not the NLT) but not to be discounted. In most later manuscripts, the words "and fasting" are included, but a couple of significant fourth-century manuscripts and several medieval manuscripts do not include these words. Still, by looking at the testimony of the Old Testament, New Testament, and the early church, we can conclude that prayer was often accompanied by fasting, and served to focus those fasting on the task of prayer. It is probably this frequent connection of prayer and fasting that was the impetus for the addition of fasting to this passage.

Jewish teachers of that day would customarily further explain important subjects in private with their disciples. Once alone, the disciples asked why they were unable to cast out the demon. Christ responded, "This kind can be cast out only by prayer (and fasting)." The disciples had not prayed before attempting to cast out the demon, perhaps because of confidence (or arrogance) because they had done it before, forgetfulness, or the excitement of the moment. Christ's previous rebuke seems to indicate that it was because they lacked faith, and as a result, they neglected to pray. In any regard, Christ pointed out that "this kind" of situation could only be solved by dependency on and faith in God exhibited by prayer and fasting.

SEARCH THE SCRIPTURES

QUESTION 1
What does the father say in verse 22 that indicates he is not sure if Jesus can heal his son?

The father adds the words "if you can" to his request to Jesus to have mercy and help them.

LIGHT ON THE WORD

Trusting God
The father's honesty is refreshing. He does believe; he asked for help, so he believed healing was possible. However, he still doubted; after watching his son struggle for so long, and seeing the disciples' inability to rescue his son, he questioned Christ's ability. Christ put the ownership of the problem in its place— not His power ("Anything is possible..."), but their faith ("...if a person believes"). Faith matters.

BIBLE APPLICATION

AIM: Students will accept that believers struggle with faith when faced with seemingly impossible situations.

We are more like the disciples than we want to admit. They physically walked with Jesus and saw Him perform miracles, but they worried, were ineffective, and lacked faith. We do the same. We have testimonies of God's healing, provision, and power, yet when faced with trials, prayer is often a last resort.

Our culture of self-sufficiency has permeated our churches. We believe if we work hard enough, we can achieve anything and there is little room for dependency on others. Since we believe we have the power, we fail to seek God's power. This lesson reminds us that God is all-powerful, and any ability we have comes from Him.

STUDENT'S RESPONSES

AIM: Students will see how Jesus helps us during difficult times.

What circumstances are you facing that you have not prayed about? Are there people in your life that you have become convinced will never change, or never come to know Jesus? What confessions do you need to make about your view of God, His power, or your faith? Ask God to show you. Confess, repent, have faith, and pray.

PRAYER

Dear Jesus, Your faithfulness is amazing and allows us o believe even with doubt. We are thankful that You care and provide for us and others in spite of not fully trusting You. Love us and keep us. We love You and honor You. In Jesus' Name we pray. Amen.

HOW TO SAY IT

Pineth.   **PIE**-nith.

Tare.   **TER.**

PREPARE FOR NEXT SUNDAY

Read **Mark 10:17–31** and "Simple Faith."

DAILY HOME BIBLE READINGS

MONDAY
Faithful God
(Genesis 15:1–6)

TUESDAY
Saving God
(Genesis 50:15–21)

WEDNESDAY
Powerful God
(Isaiah 43:5–13)

THURSDAY
Healing God
(Matthew 9:27–33)

FRIDAY
Forgiving God
(John 5:19–24)

SATURDAY
Fulfilling God
(John 6:35–40)

SUNDAY
Powerful Faith
(Mark 9:14–29)

Sources:
Barclay, William. *The Gospel of Mark*. The Daily Study Bible. Philadelphia PA: The Westminster Press, 1956.
Evans, Craig A. *Mark*. Word Biblical Commentary. Vol. 34B. Dallas, TX: Word Books, Publisher, 2001.
Keener, Craig S. *The IVP Bible Background Commentary: New Testament*. Downers Grove, IL: Intervarsity Press, 1993.

COMMENTS / NOTES:

SIMPLE FAITH

BIBLE BASIS: MARK 10:17–31

BIBLE TRUTH: Jesus showed that faith in God makes it possible for people to sacrifice their all for the benefit of others.

MEMORY VERSE: "Then Jesus beholding him loved him, and said unto him, One thing thou lackest: go thy way, sell whatsoever thou hast, and give to the poor, and thou shalt have treasure in heaven: and come, take up the cross, and follow me" (Mark 10:21).

LESSON AIM: By the end of the lesson, we will: KNOW the facts of the rich young man's encounter with Jesus; CELEBRATE the direct link between making sacrifices and receiving God's salvation; and COMMIT to making greater sacrifices for others in the name of Jesus Christ.

TEACHER PREPARATION

MATERIALS NEEDED: Quarterly Commentary/Teacher Manual, Adult Quarterly, Adult resources—charts, worksheets, and other teaching tools, paper, pens, pencils, Bibles (several different versions)

OTHER MATERIALS NEEDED / TEACHER'S NOTES:

_____

_____

LESSON OVERVIEW

LIFE NEED FOR TODAY'S LESSON
Christians can find it difficult to give up all their possessions to help others.

BIBLE LEARNING
Believers know that discipleship costs.

BIBLE APPLICATION
Christians accept that some believers are unable to care and sacrifice for others, causing them to turn away from Christ.

STUDENTS' RESPONSES
Believers can make great sacrifices for significant causes.

LESSON SCRIPTURE

MARK 10:17–31, KJV

17 And when he was gone forth into the way, there came one running, and kneeled to him, and asked him, Good Master, what shall I do that I may inherit eternal life?

18 And Jesus said unto him, Why callest thou me good? there is none good but one,

MARK 10:17–31, NIV

17 As Jesus started on his way, a man ran up to him and fell on his knees before him. "Good teacher," he asked, "what must I do to inherit eternal life?"

18 "Why do you call me good?" Jesus answered. "No one is good—except God that is, God.

19 Thou knowest the commandments, Do not commit adultery, Do not kill, Do not steal, Do not bear false witness, Defraud not, Honour thy father and mother.

20 And he answered and said unto him, Master, all these have I observed from my youth.

21 Then Jesus beholding him loved him, and said unto him, One thing thou lackest: go thy way, sell whatsoever thou hast, and give to the poor, and thou shalt have treasure in heaven: and come, take up the cross, and follow me.

22 And he was sad at that saying, and went away grieved: for he had great possessions.

23 And Jesus looked round about, and saith unto his disciples, How hardly shall they that have riches enter into the kingdom of God!

24 And the disciples were astonished at his words. But Jesus answereth again, and saith unto them, Children, how hard is it for them that trust in riches to enter into the kingdom of God!

25 It is easier for a camel to go through the eye of a needle, than for a rich man to enter into the kingdom of God.

26 And they were astonished out of measure, saying among themselves, Who then can be saved?

27 And Jesus looking upon them saith, With men it is impossible, but not with God: for with God all things are possible.

28 Then Peter began to say unto him, Lo, we have left all, and have followed thee.

29 And Jesus answered and said, Verily I say unto you, There is no man that hath left

alone.

19 You know the commandments: 'You shall not murder, you shall not commit adultery, you shall not steal, you shall not give false testimony, you shall not defraud, honor your father and mother.'"

20 "Teacher," he declared, "all these I have kept since I was a boy."

21 Jesus looked at him and loved him. "One thing you lack," he said. "Go, sell everything you have and give to the poor, and you will have treasure in heaven. Then come, follow me."

22 At this the man's face fell. He went away sad, because he had great wealth.

23 Jesus looked around and said to his disciples, "How hard it is for the rich to enter the kingdom of God!"

24 The disciples were amazed at his words. But Jesus said again, "Children, how hard it is to enter the kingdom of God!

25 It is easier for a camel to go through the eye of a needle than for someone who is rich to enter the kingdom of God."

26 The disciples were even more amazed, and said to each other, "Who then can be saved?"

27 Jesus looked at them and said, "With man this is impossible, but not with God; all things are possible with God."

28 Then Peter spoke up, "We have left everything to follow you!"

29 "Truly I tell you," Jesus replied, "no one who has left home or brothers or sisters or mother or father or children or fields for me and the gospel

30 will fail to receive a hundred times as

house, or brethren, or sisters, or father, or mother, or wife, or children, or lands, for my sake, and the gospel's,

30 But he shall receive an hundredfold now in this time, houses, and brethren, and sisters, and mothers, and children, and lands, with persecutions; and in the world to come eternal life.

31 But many that are first shall be last; and the last first.

much in this present age: homes, brothers, sisters, mothers, children and fields—along with persecutions—and in the age to come eternal life.

31 But many who are first will be last, and the last first."

LIGHT ON THE WORD

The rich young man. What little is known about this man is gathered from three different Gospels (**Matthew 19:16–30; Mark 10:17–31; Luke 18:18–30**). All indicate that he was rich. Matthew reveals that he is young (**Matthew 19:20**). **Luke 18:18** says that he was a "ruler," possibly a member of a Jewish council or court. Since he respectfully and genuinely asked a religious question, he presumably is not a scribe or teacher of the Law, as their questions were intended to trap Jesus. He was probably raised in a devoted Jewish home, as Jewish boys were taught they would assume personal responsibility for their own religious lives (following commandments, laws, etc.) at age 13, becoming a "son of the Law/Commandment" (Bar Mitzvah). His belief system is a reflection of the common thought of the day regarding eternal life—self-centered and merit-based.

Eternal life. The terms "eternal life," "saved," and "Kingdom of God" are used interchangeably in this passage. In Scripture, "eternal life" is distinguished from a simple continual existence. All will experience endless existence somewhere after their lives on earth cease. Eternal life connotes a life spent in union and fellowship with God in Heaven,

His Kingdom. The opposite existence is eternal death separated from Him in hell (**Mark 9:43–47**). Those who have trusted in Christ in their natural lives are eternally "saved" or freed from this plight.

TEACHING THE BIBLE LESSON

LIFE NEED FOR TODAY'S LESSON

AIM: Students will learn that Christians can find it difficult to give up all their possessions to help others.

INTRODUCTION

A Childlike Faith

Immediately preceding all three Gospel (Matthew, Mark, and Luke) accounts of this story is a brief interaction Christ has with children. The disciples were attempting to prevent it, but Christ rebuked them, and told them to bring the children to Him. In **Mark 10:15**, He says, "I tell you the truth, anyone who doesn't receive the Kingdom of God like a child will never enter it" (NLT). He then blesses the children. Then comes the rich young ruler.

These two scenes are such a contrast. Christ just taught that people who enter the

Kingdom of God do so because spiritually they come like children—needy, trusting, full of faith, and dependent upon those with more power or authority. While honoring Christ by running to Him, kneeling, and asking questions, the man presented a child-like external stance. However, his allegiance to his riches and refusal to sacrifice them to help the poor betrayed the true stance of his heart.

A recurring theme throughout the Gospels is service and sacrifice. "Take up your cross … follow me … count the cost." In **Mark 10:45**, Christ says, "For even the Son of Man came not to be served but to serve others and to give his life as a ransom for many" (NLT). As for many today, as well as in antiquity, wealth was directly connected to piety. Being rich meant one had God's favor because He rewarded the faithful with material goods, which could then be used for serving others. However, this often did not occur, so in Judaism as well as the rest of the Greco-Roman world, there were groups that believed that piety was not linked to worldly wealth, or even that renouncing worldly wealth was pious.. And as Christ taught, "No one can serve two masters. For you will hate one and love the other; you will be devoted to one and despise the other. You cannot serve both God and money" (**Matthew 6:24**, NLT).

BIBLE LEARNING

AIM: Students will learn that believers know that discipleship costs.

I. RICH RULER'S QUESTIONS (MARK 10:17–22)

When this young man approaches Christ with his question, he is thinking that salvation and righteousness come by works, not grace or gift. He calls Jesus "good," and asks what "good" he must do. No one but God can claim goodness or righteousness. Goodness is not an achievement to merit a reward, it is who God is, and "all good things" and deeds originate with Him. By answering the question, and ending with, "Follow me," Christ claims His deity.

Christ lovingly sees the man's desire, and what prevented his devotion to God—his wealth. So, He tells him to go, sell everything he has, and give to the poor. Then, choose a life of faith in God, "take up the cross" (**10:21**, KJV), which means to prepare to endure suffering for His sake, and follow Christ. Tragically, the man walks away, dejected. His wealth was his god. He chose to put confidence in it over God.

Mark 10:17–31

17 And when he was gone forth into the way, there came one running, and kneeled to him, and asked him, Good Master, what shall I do that I may inherit eternal life? 18 And Jesus said unto him, Why callest thou me good? there is none good but one, that is, God.

We are not told the young man's name, but his purpose in coming to Jesus is clear: he wants to know what to do to inherit eternal life.

His financial situation is quite secure, but he is uncertain about his eternal state. He comes to Jesus expressing what many commentators see as genuine respect for Him: he falls to his knees and addresses Jesus as the "Good Master." Yet his question reveals a problem with his theology. His phrase, "what must I do" (NIV), indicates that the man believes it is within his power to earn his way into the Kingdom of God, something that Jesus' previous statement in **10:15** denies.

Jesus' response, though probably not intending to douse the young man's enthusiasm, challenges his ideas about goodness. The young man did not know that Jesus was God, and therefore he was centering his ideas about goodness not on God but on human achievement.

19 Thou knowest the commandments, Do not commit adultery, Do not kill, Do not steal, Do not bear false witness, Defraud not, Honour thy father and mother. 20 And he answered and said unto him, Master, all these have I observed from my youth.

Jesus pointed the young man to what he knew or understood about the Law of God, as expressed in the Ten Commandments. The Scripture quotes the second half of the Decalogue here (**Exodus 20:12–16**), emphasizing that our response to our neighbors and loved ones demonstrates our reverence for God. Believers are warned against giving false testimony, and told not to "defraud" (Gk. *apostereo*, **ah-po-ste-REH-oh**), meaning not to cheat others, or take advantage of them or their property. The command not to defraud is not in the Decalogue and some scholars believe Jesus added it as an addition to the commands which forbid lying or stealing. It was especially applicable to the rich, who were notorious in first-century Palestine for gaining their wealth through unsavory means. If the young man could keep God's commandments, he would live. Any rabbi of the day would have told him this. Obedience to the Law of God would mean eternal life.

The man's response indicated how superficial his understanding of God's Law really was. The word "observed" in the Greek (*phulasso*, **foo-LAS-so**) means "to keep careful watch or protect." In other words, the young man told Jesus that he vigilantly kept all the commandments from his childhood.

But had he really? We don't know, but nevertheless, the young man was self-assured of his obedience to the Law, which Jesus would lovingly uncover as superficial when

He challenged the man to a deeper level of obedience.

21 Then Jesus beholding him loved him, and said unto him, One thing thou lackest: go thy way, sell whatsoever thou hast, and give to the poor, and thou shalt have treasure in heaven: and come, take up the cross, and follow me.

Jesus' care for this young man's best interests is evident in the first part of this verse, which notes that He looked on this young man with love. The word "beholding" in the Greek (*emblepo*, **em-BLEH-poh**) means "to look at with the mind, to consider." Jesus really wanted to help this young man understand clearly what obtaining eternal life entailed. He responds by calling the man to the one thing that he lacks: a single-minded devotion to God.

What the young man has not done yet is to surrender himself to God, to cast himself fully upon God in child-like dependence. Jesus calls him to discipleship by surrendering himself to God and following Jesus. The King James includes a specific call for the young man to take up his cross and follow Jesus, while the New Living Translation and most twentieth century translations simply tell the man to follow Jesus. The newer translations reflect the oldest manuscripts of Mark, much older than the manuscript available to the King James translators. Probably what happened was that the command that Jesus gave to take up your cross and follow Him was very familiar to the scribes of the later manuscripts, and they included as a basic part of Jesus' exhortation to those who would know God. For the young man, it meant giving all he had to the poor, not as a means of getting in, but as an expression that his surrender was full and true. The point here is not that everyone must sell their goods and give the proceeds to the poor in order to become

Christians. Rather, our commitment involves surrendering ourselves to God in childlike dependence on Him and following Him.

22 And he was sad at that saying, and went away grieved: for he had great possessions.

The man tragically chooses his great wealth over the eternal life that he had been so anxious at first to obtain. For him, the cost was too great, so he opted out and went away grieved (Gk. *lupeo*, **loo-PEH-oh**), which means "deep mental or emotional suffering; painful, sharp regret." In other words, he went away mentally and emotionally disturbed because material riches were more important to him than the wealth of eternal life.

II. DISCIPLES' QUESTION (vv. 23–26)

Christ twice tells His disciples that it is hard for the rich to get into Heaven. His truth surprised them because it disputed the popular "prosperity" teachings of the day. The second time He says it (see **Mark 10:24**, KJV), He specifically says those who "trust in riches," and to further illustrate the impossibility He used the analogy of a large camel trying to squeeze through the eye of a tiny needle. Those who trust in riches (or anything else), problematically, do not trust God. Realizing the impossibility, and revealing their amazement that the rich and highly favored could not enter the Kingdom of God, the disciples asked, "Who then can be saved?"

Placing Trust in Possessions

23 And Jesus looked round about, and saith unto his disciples, How hardly shall they that have riches enter into the kingdom of God!

The man's response gave Jesus an opportunity to speak to His followers about trust in riches and the Kingdom of God. The phrase "Kingdom of God" used throughout Mark means the royal power of Jesus as the triumphant Messiah. His Kingdom will reign forever and ever. The text indicates that Jesus saw riches as a problem for His followers. He knew that many like this rich man put their trust in their material wealth and therefore found it difficult, if not impossible, to surrender themselves fully to God. Riches aren't evil in and of themselves, but Jesus knew that people were prone to put their trust in their possessions.

24 And the disciples were astonished at his words. But Jesus answereth again, and saith unto them, Children, how hard is it for them that trust in riches to enter into the kingdom of God!

The disciples' amazement is not surprising considering the prevailing teachings of the day: that riches were the reward for piety and demonstrated God's favor toward the wealthy. **(Job 1:10; 42:10; Psalm 128:1–2; Isaiah 3:10).** If this is the case, then the disciples would certainly be surprised by Jesus' teaching, which He reiterates at the end of **Mark 10:24.**

25 It is easier for a camel to go through the eye of a needle, than for a rich man to enter into the kingdom of God. 26 And they were astonished out of measure, saying among themselves, Who then can be saved?

Some scholars would like to make Jesus' words here a little easier to swallow by suggesting that "the eye of a needle" referred instead to a small gate in Jerusalem which camels could go through only with great difficulty. This would imply that joining the Kingdom of God was difficult but not impossible. This gate is not what Jesus refers to, as it was built during medieval times, not in the first century. Here Jesus uses hyberbole as He describes the impossibility of a camel going through the literal eye of a needle.

The word "astonished" (Gk. *ekplesso*, ek-PLACE-so) means "they were struck with amazement." The disciples' response clearly suggests that they have misunderstood Jesus' statement. If not even the rich can enter the Kingdom, then who can? The disciples are evidently baffled and need clarification.

III. CHRIST'S PROMISES (vv. 27–31)

Christ then further teaches the truth about salvation—it is based upon God. It is impossible for men and women to save themselves; God does it—all things are possible with Him.

Many of Christ's disciples left their homes and means of living, including fishermen and a tax collector, and they had families. Contrasting the young man's actions, Peter points out that he and the other disciples left those lives behind. In response, Christ promises the disciples that rewards await those who sacrifice for Him and the Gospel. The rewards would be abundant (a hundred-fold), with familial relationships and material provisions. They would be enjoyed in the present (temporal) and future (eternal). Only Mark's account includes "with persecution," perhaps to encourage his original readers (Roman Christians facing persecution). However, it also counteracts the tendency to associate discipleship with temporal rewards, bringing back into focus the truth that a disciple of Christ must "take up your cross." Following Christ has blessings and struggles.

All Things are Possible with God

27 And Jesus looking upon them saith, With men it is impossible, but not with God: for with God all things are possible. 28 Then Peter began to say unto him, Lo, we have left all, and have followed thee. 29 And Jesus answered and said, Verily I say unto you, There is no man that hath left house, or brethren, or sisters, or father, or mother, or wife, or children, or lands, for my sake, and the gospel's, 30 But he shall receive an hundredfold now in this time, houses, and brethren, and sisters, and mothers, and children, and lands, with persecutions; and in the world to come eternal life. 31 But many that are first shall be last; and the last first.

Jesus' point is this: Salvation is not a matter of human achievement. A person cannot enter God's Kingdom via human achievements. The Gospel that Jesus preached declared that salvation is a work of God; only God can provide salvation and open the way to eternal life. This is why we are called to wholehearted surrender to God. Only trust in His power alone will grant us entrance into His Kingdom.

Peter understood the invitation Jesus gave to the rich man and noted that he and the others had done what the rich man had not ("we have left all," **v. 28**). Peter's question, though seemingly problematic since it focuses on rewards, is not rebuked but answered. Yes, Jesus tells him and the other disciples, those who surrender themselves in full reliance upon God are rewarded. And, as Jesus emphasizes, a surrender to God shows itself in our willingness to be last, to be servants.

SEARCH THE SCRIPTURES

QUESTION 1
Jesus states who is good?

Only God.

LIGHT ON THE WORD

A Heart Toward God
The commandments that Christ quotes pertain to the treatment of other people—external actions that are somewhat measurable. The man's response could also be translated as "in all these things I have been careful since my

youth." The man sincerely, but blindly, believes that he had observed all of these commandments since his childhood, and that his actions were good. He still fails to realize that eternal life is based on a heart turned toward God, not following rules.

BIBLE APPLICATION

AIM: Students will accept that some believers are unable to care and sacrifice for others, causing them to turn away from Christ.

Like many of antiquity, we can fall in the trap of following a "prosperity theology" without knowing it. It is subtle, coming in the form of telling people who serve Christ that God will "bless" them, typically meaning financial, material blessings. It shows up in how we expect God to answer our prayers if we are serving Him. It can also come by way of who we tend to elevate. Think of well-known Christian leaders. Now identify people who are known for their sacrifices and service to others. Do these lists overlap? If not, this is not to say that those leaders do not serve or sacrifice, but it perhaps reflects what our culture values and exalts. Those who serve are not looked on highly. This is not Christ-like thinking. Christ says, "But among you it will be different. Those who are the greatest among you should take the lowest rank, and the leader should be like a servant" (**Luke 22:26**, NLT).

STUDENT'S RESPONSES

AIM: Students will see that believers can make great sacrifices that are for significant causes.

This lesson causes us to examine where our allegiance rests. Needs that require sacrifice surround us. Every "cross" is different for each person. Christ challenged the young man who made wealth his god. For some it is their careers or education; for others, it may be ease, security, and comfort. For Paul, it was his status "...of tribe of Benjamin, a Hebrew of Hebrews, a Pharisee..." These things he said he "counted as dung, that I may gain Christ and be found in Him, not having my own righteousness ... but that which is through faith in Christ" (**Philippians 3:5, 8**). What things do you need to "count as dung" that you may gain Christ? What sacrifices have God placed on your heart to make? Who does He want you to serve? How does He want you to serve? Pray. When something comes to mind, pray that God will give you courage and wisdom to obey. Write it down so you will remember and can remind yourself. Then, do it.

PRAYER

Lord, help us to release our things that keep us from loving You and following You. Encourage us to fill our hearts with Your goodness and care for others and not with people and attitudes that are barriers to You. In Jesus' Name we pray. Amen.

HOW TO SAY IT

Bar Mitzvah.   bar **MITS**-va.

Temporal.   **TEM**-por-al.

PREPARE FOR NEXT SUNDAY

Read **Mark 14:26–31, 66–72**, and "Struggling Faith."

DAILY HOME BIBLE READINGS

MONDAY
Faith in Riches?
(Psalm 49:1–6, 16–19)

TUESDAY
Practical Faith
(Proverbs 22:1–4, 23:3–5)

WEDNESDAY
Abundant Faith
(Isaiah 55:1–6a)

THURSDAY
Authoritative Faith
(Matthew 7:24–29)

FRIDAY
Faith and Freedom
(Galatians 5:1–13)

SATURDAY
Priorities of Faith
(Luke 16:10–14)

SUNDAY
Simple Faith
(Mark 10:17–31)

Sources:

Hebrew-Greek Key Word Study Bible, King James Version. Chattanooga, TN: AMG Publishers, Inc., 1991.

Keener, Craig S. *The IVP Bible Background Commentary: New Testament.* Downers Grove, IL: InterVarsity Press, 1993. 162-163.

Walvoord, John F., and Roy B. Zuck, eds. *The Bible Knowledge Commentary: New Testament.* USA: Victor Books, SP Publications, Inc., 1983. 150-152.

COMMENTS / NOTES:

STRUGGLING FAITH

BIBLE BASIS: MARK 14:26–31, 66–72

BIBLE TRUTH: Peter's faith was weakened when he did not stand up publicly as a follower of Jesus Christ.

MEMORY VERSE: "And Jesus saith unto him, Verily I say unto thee, That this day, even in this night, before the cock crow twice, thou shalt deny me thrice" (Mark 14:30).

LESSON AIM: By the end of the lesson, we will: REMEMBER all that happened when Peter denied Jesus as He had foretold; EXPLORE feelings experienced when one fails to meet the expectations of others; and PRACTICE spiritual disciplines to build a stronger relationship with God.

TEACHER PREPARATION

MATERIALS NEEDED: Quarterly Commentary/Teacher Manual, Adult Quarterly, Adult resources—charts, worksheets, and other teaching tools, paper, pens, pencils, Bibles (several different versions)

OTHER MATERIALS NEEDED / TEACHER'S NOTES:

_____

_____

LESSON OVERVIEW

LIFE NEED FOR TODAY'S LESSON
Christians find it challenging to accept at times that they cannot do something they truly believed that could do.

BIBLE APPLICATION
Believers contemplate whether their faith is more important than a particular want or perception.

BIBLE LEARNING
Peter's faith succumbed to the temptation of denial instead speaking the truth.

STUDENTS' RESPONSES
Followers understand that our faith will be challenged in many ways.

LESSON SCRIPTURE

MARK 14:26–31, 66–72, KJV

26 And when they had sung an hymn, they went out into the mount of Olives.

27 And Jesus saith unto them, All ye shall be offended because of me this night: for it is written, I will smite the shepherd, and the sheep shall be scattered.

MARK 14:26–31, 66–72, NIV

26 When they had sung a hymn, they went out to the Mount of Olives.

27 "You will all fall away," Jesus told them, "for it is written: "'I will strike the shepherd, and the sheep will be scattered.'

28 But after that I am risen, I will go before you into Galilee.

29 But Peter said unto him, Although all shall be offended, yet will not I.

30 And Jesus saith unto him, Verily I say unto thee, That this day, even in this night, before the cock crow twice, thou shalt deny me thrice.

31 But he spake the more vehemently, If I should die with thee, I will not deny thee in any wise. Likewise also said they all.

66 And as Peter was beneath in the palace, there cometh one of the maids of the high priest:

67 And when she saw Peter warming himself, she looked upon him, and said, And thou also wast with Jesus of Nazareth.

68 But he denied, saying, I know not, neither understand I what thou sayest. And he went out into the porch; and the cock crew.

69 And a maid saw him again, and began to say to them that stood by, This is one of them.

70 And he denied it again. And a little after, they that stood by said again to Peter, Surely thou art one of them: for thou art a Galilaean, and thy speech agreeth thereto.

71 But he began to curse and to swear, saying, I know not this man of whom ye speak.

72 And the second time the cock crew. And Peter called to mind the word that Jesus said unto him, Before the cock crow twice, thou shalt deny me thrice. And when he thought thereon, he wept.

28 But after I have risen, I will go ahead of you into Galilee."

29 Peter declared, "Even if all fall away, I will not."

30 "Truly I tell you," Jesus answered, "today—yes, tonight—before the rooster crows twice you yourself will disown me three times."

31 But Peter insisted emphatically, "Even if I have to die with you, I will never disown you." And all the others said the same.

66 While Peter was below in the courtyard, one of the servant girls of the high priest came by.

67 When she saw Peter warming himself, she looked closely at him. "You also were with that Nazarene, Jesus," she said.

68 But he denied it. "I don't know or understand what you're talking about," he said, and went out into the entryway.

69 When the servant girl saw him there, she said again to those standing around, "This fellow is one of them."

70 Again he denied it. After a little while, those standing near said to Peter, "Surely you are one of them, for you are a Galilean."

71 He began to call down curses, and he swore to them, "I don't know this man you're talking about."

72 Immediately the rooster crowed the second time. Then Peter remembered the word Jesus had spoken to him: "Before the rooster crows twice you will disown me three times." And he broke down and wept.

LIGHT ON THE WORD

Last Supper. The Passover feast was instituted during the Israelites' exodus from Egypt (**Exodus 12**). One ritual of the feast required the sacrifice of a lamb. During the last of the ten plagues, the Lord set out to kill all of the firstborn males in Egypt. The lamb's blood was to be placed over the doorposts of the Israelites' homes as a sign that He would "pass over" them. In remembrance of their deliverance from death and slavery, they were to celebrate the Passover annually. The last supper Christ shared with His disciples before becoming the sacrificial Lamb for the sins of the world was this Passover feast. It was during this feast that He revealed His betrayal, and betrayer (**14:17–20**), and instituted the Lord's Supper (communion) (**14:22–25**).

Christ's Arrest. The circumstances surrounding Christ's arrest were filled with heartbreak and illegalities. He predicts the disciples' desertion. When He tasks several of them with watching while He prays in the garden of Gethsemane before His arrest, they fall asleep three times. In Gethsemane, His favorite place to meet with His disciples, He is betrayed with a kiss, a symbol of affection and love. He was "tried" by several members of the Sanhedrin, which was made up of 71 men—chief priests, elders, and teachers of the Law—whose roles were to uphold justice. Yet, in Christ's arrest, they used one of His own to betray Him (**14:10–11**), and came with a detachment of armed troops, perhaps as many as 600 (**John 18:3**). They held an illegal trial with false witnesses, in the middle of the night (maybe as late as 3 a.m.), in an unusual location: the home of Caiaphas, the high priest (**Matthew 26:57**).

TEACHING THE BIBLE LESSON

LIFE NEED FOR TODAY'S LESSON

AIM: Christians find it challenging to accept at times that they cannot do something they truly believed that could do.

INTRODUCTION
Christ Rejected

While not explicitly stated in the book, Mark is thought to have written this book for Gentile believers, especially Roman Christians facing horrendous persecution. Throughout the book, Mark chooses not to focus on Jesus' genealogy or Jewish heritage, but His triumphs and tragedies, and His roles as Savior-King and Servant. He vividly shares stories of Christ's miracles, but also His struggles—the hostility of the Jewish leaders, and in this case, the desertion and denial of those closest to Him. Mark wrote with Peter's notes and eyewitness accounts, and likely under his supervision.

Leading up to the events in these passages, Jesus had announced His death to His disciples several times (**8:31, 9:31, 10:33**), and the hour had come. During this final warning about His impending death, and after instituting the Lord's Supper, the disciples sang a hymn. Typically **Psalms 113–118** were sung during the Passover. **Psalm 118:22**—"The stone the builders rejected has become the chief cornerstone"—was used by Peter in his sermon on the day of Pentecost referring to Jesus' betrayal.

BIBLE LEARNING

AIM: Students will learn that our faith can be compromised when, like Peter, we deny the truth.

I. CHRIST PREDICTS PETER'S DENIAL (MARK 14:26–31)

Likely in a very somber mood, Christ and the disciples began the walk to the Mount of Olives, which would have taken at least fifteen minutes. He has reminded them of His impending death and sent His betrayer on his way, but there is more pain to come. Quoting **Zechariah 13:7**, Jesus predicted that when He (the Shepherd) is struck, they (the sheep) would desert him. After three years of living and traveling together, being taught by Him, seeing Him perform miracles and serve others, and coming to a clearer understanding of who He is, they would still lose courage and forsake Him. However, He does not leave them hopeless, reminding them that He will be resurrected and go before them to Galilee. (The angel repeats this to Mary Magdalene and Salome in **16:7**.) With the disappointment of Judas' betrayal looming, Peter found this desertion unfathomable, and confidently proclaims that even if all the others abandoned Christ, he would not.

Mark 14:26–31, 66–72

Mark 14:26 And when they had sung an hymn, they went out into the mount of Olives.

After the Passover meal, in Jewish tradition, Jesus and His disciples sang a hymn. They would have sung **Psalms 113–118**. The Greek word for sing is *humneo* (**hoom-NEH-oh**), which implies a song of praise to God. After this, Jesus and His disciples went to the Mount of Olives for further discussion and prayers, as they often did. The Mount of Olives was outside the walls of Jerusalem, but from there they could look down and see the temple. The Garden of Gethsemane was on the Mount of Olives. Jesus often took His disciples to this quiet and beautiful place.

27 And Jesus saith unto them, All ye shall be offended because of me this night: for it is written, I will smite the shepherd, and the sheep shall be scattered.

Jesus knew that He was soon going to be hung on the Cross—nails hammered in by the Romans at the instigation of His own people.

But perhaps one of the most hurtful things was that His own disciples would desert Him. The word "offended" in Greek is *skandalizo* (**skan-dah-LEED-zoh**) and it means to cause to stumble or in this case to be made to stumble. The English word "scandalize" comes from this same Greek root, and we could say that when Jesus was arrested, His disciples were so scandalized by what had happened to their Master that they ran away in great fear. If this was happening to Him, what would happen to them next? Jesus quoted **Zechariah 13:7**, which predicted that when the Good Shepherd was struck, all of His sheep would be scattered. The sheep were the disciples—the apostles and other followers as well.

28 But after that I am risen, I will go before you into Galilee.

After Jesus had quoted Zechariah's prediction that the sheep would be scattered, He had some words of comfort that seemed to be completely overlooked by the disciples. Jesus said that He would be raised up and once more gather His sheep together and lead them. Peter heard the words that the sheep would fall away, but he did not hear Jesus say that He would rise again. When we look from our view, after it was all over, the disciples were only without their Lord for three short days, but these were the three most amazing days in history.

29 But Peter said unto him, Although all shall be offended, yet will not I. 30 And Jesus saith unto him, Verily I say unto thee, That this day, even in this night, before the cock crow twice, thou shalt deny me thrice.

Peter declared that he would not deny stumble, even if all the others did. But Jesus knew Peter's heart. Peter was too sure of himself. He forgot that it's too easy to slip up in life. Despite this overconfidence, at least Peter had his heart in the right place, and Jesus knew that. Peter could not believe that he would deny the Lord, but Jesus told him that that very night he would deny Him—three times!

Jesus said "verily" or "I tell you the truth" to emphasize the solemnity of His words. This is the same word that we say when we agree with what the preacher says: amen (Gk. *amen*, ah-MAIN), a word that originated in Hebrew.

31 But he spake the more vehemently, If I should die with thee, I will not deny thee in any wise. Likewise also said they all.

"More vehemently" is an adverbial phrase and means Peter kept on speaking. Vehemently in Greek is *perissos* (**per-is-SOS**), which means excessively. Peter insisted that even if it meant his death, he would not deny Jesus; then all the other disciples said the same—they would not deny their Lord. Assuming that our spiritual strength lies in ourselves, rather than in our Lord, is very dangerous. An even greater danger is bragging about our spiritual strength—what we would always do or never do. We can avoid this by humbly asking God for His help in everything we do.

II. PETER'S FIRST DENIALS—THE SERVANT GIRL (vv. 66–69)

In between Christ's prediction of denial and this passage is His prayer in the garden, where three times Peter failed to remain alert and awake. Christ's words to him in the garden were "Watch and pray, lest you enter into temptation. The spirit indeed is willing, but the flesh is weak" (**14:38**, NKJV). This could have served as a warning for what was to come.

After Christ's arrest, the other disciples scattered, but Peter followed at a distance, lingering in the high priest's courtyard by the fire, presumably to see what would happen to Jesus (**14:53–54**). A servant girl, probably a doorkeeper, saw and recognized him: "You also were

with Jesus of Nazareth." He denies, claiming not to understand, a common problem among the disciples, especially in Mark (**4:13; 6:52; 8:17,21; 9:32**). He then moved to a different location, a covered porch, away from light, where he would not be so easily recognized. That is when the rooster crowed the first time. The servant found him again, and pointed him out to those around them. Again, He denied knowing Jesus.

Peter's Identity Revealed

66 And as Peter was beneath in the palace, there cometh one of the maids of the high priest: 67 And when she saw Peter warming himself, she looked upon him, and said, And thou also wast with Jesus of Nazareth. 68 But he denied, saying, I know not, neither understand I what thou sayest. And he went out into the porch; and the cock crew.

In **John 18:15–16**, we read that the Apostle John, known to the high priestly family, interceded with the maid to bring Peter into the lower portion of the palace. So as Peter warmed his hands by the fire, the maid recognized him as the same one she had let in earlier. Peter, who had been so brave, suddenly lost his nerve and denied Jesus, knowing he was under the threat of death if he was identified as one of His followers.

69 And a maid saw him again, and began to say to them that stood by, This is one of them. 70 And he denied it again. And then Peter denied Jesus again. And a little after, they that stood by said again to Peter, Surely thou art one of them: for thou art a Galilaean, and thy speech agreeth thereto. 71 But he began to curse and to swear, saying, I know not this man of whom ye speak.

Evidently Peter entered without trying to hide himself, and the maid (doorkeeper) recognized him as one who was with Jesus.

Not only was he recognized by sight as a disciple, but his dialect gave him away. Those who came from the region of Galilee, as all the disciples but Judas did, had a distinctive dialect. When he opened his mouth to speak, people in Jerusalem could immediately recognize him as a Galilean, and they knew that a famous Galilean (Jesus) was being tried at that unusually early hour.

With his third denial, Peter cursed. The Greek for curse is *anathematizo* (**ah-nah-theh-mah-TEED-zoh**), which means to declare cursed, or to put under a curse. When we read that Peter cursed, we think of taking the Lord's name in vain, but that is not what he did. Jews were very careful not to take the name of God in vain, because this prohibition was one of the Ten Commandments (**Exodus 20:7**). Instead, to verify that they were speaking the truth, they would pronounce an oath upon themselves. This would be similar to saying, "If I am not telling the truth, may lightning strike me dead." Jesus still forbade this, saying that we should let our yes be yes and our no be no (**Matthew 5:37**).

Once again Peter is confronted with potential recognition, and this time he responds with more vehemence, cursing and swearing that he does not know Jesus or His disciples. Peter's adamant promise of unending devotion to Jesus is now contrasted with unending denial of Him, serving as a caution that no matter how devoted we are to God, we always have the potential to abandon Him.

III. PETER'S FINAL DENIAL (vv. 70–72)

About an hour after the first two denials, more bystanders heard him speaking. Judean accents differed from Galilean accents. Noticing his Aramaic dialect was Galilean (and they were in Jerusalem, in Judea), they assumed he must have been a follower of Jesus, from Galilee.

This final denial was more severe than the first. First, he refused to use Jesus' name (calling him "this man"). Then, he swore, not using profanity, but placing himself under God's curse if he was lying to them, which he was. Thus came his third denial in less than two hours, punctuated by the rooster crowing a second time. **Luke 22:61–62** says that Jesus turned to look at Peter, and Peter, remembering Christ's prophecy, wept. It is noted that Mark is the only one to record the rooster would crow twice. As Peter was Mark's informant, Peter would have vividly remembered this detail as he shared the events with Mark.

Peter's Denial Fulfilled

72 And the second time the cock crew. And Peter called to mind the word that Jesus said unto him, Before the cock crow twice, thou shalt deny me thrice. And when he thought thereon, he wept.

As the cock crowed the second time, conviction pierces Peter. The Scripture says that he called to mind Jesus' words to him. These words seal his contrition. The word for call to mind is not just to remember, but to weigh well or consider. Once he thinks on Jesus' words, he begins to weep. Peter is now ashamed of his denial. He realizes his self-confidence has now turned to weakness. His boldness has now turned to fear. Now he sits with the realization that He is not the ideal disciple and is left with the truth of his sinfulness.

SEARCH THE SCRIPTURES

QUESTION 1
How were Jesus' predications about Peter fulfilled?

Peter denied Jesus twice, and then the cock crowed.

LIGHT ON THE WORD

Peter's Painful Denial

Christ solemnly affirmed that Peter's failure would be even greater than desertion: he would refuse to admit or acknowledge that Christ even existed, three times, before the rooster crows twice. Peter still refused to accept this possibility, even promising he would die before denying Him.

BIBLE APPLICATION

AIM: Students will know that believers contemplate whether their faith is more important than a particular want or perception.

In America, we do not face with the same persecution as the disciples or original readers of Mark's Gospel. However, we are often tempted to compromise or abandon what we know to be true. Do we take advantage of that unethical but technically legal financial loophole because we need the money? Do we pursue that relationship—personal or professional—that will cause us to deny Christ in many ways? Do we tell people that we are followers of Christ? Or, do we avoid "spiritual" conversations because we do not want to seem eccentric, "holier than thou," or be associated with "those Christians"? God is calling us to be faithful to Him in all aspects of our lives.

STUDENT'S RESPONSES

AIM: Students will accept that our faith will be challenged in many ways.

The redemptive part of Peter's story is that he was remorseful, repentant, and ultimately restored. Mark records the angel telling the women at the tomb, "Give this message to his disciples, including Peter," indicating Christ's forgiveness (from **16:7**). Peter goes on to become a leader in the early church, courageously and faithfully serving Christ for the rest of his life. So, if you have found that you have denied Christ or abandoned your faith in some areas, know that there is redemption. Pray that God will reveal to you areas of compromise. Confess and repent. Forgive others and ask for forgiveness. Pray for ways to rectify the situations, if possible. Then pray for faith and courage to make different choices when faced with similar circumstances in the future.

PRAYER

Lord, show us how we can guard against temptations that keep us from showing others who Jesus is. As we repent for our sins, may we know that You continue to protect us and show mercy upon us. In Jesus' Name we pray. Amen.

HOW TO SAY IT

Gethsemane.   geth-**SEM**-a-nee.

Galilean.   ga-li-**LEE**-en

PREPARE FOR NEXT SUNDAY

Read **Mark 16:1–8** and "Resurrection Faith."

DAILY HOME BIBLE READINGS

MONDAY
Uniting Faith
(Jeremiah 3:12–18)

TUESDAY
Enlightening Faith
(Isaiah 2:1–6)

WEDNESDAY
Suffering Faith
(1 Peter 4:10–19)

THURSDAY
Restored Faith
(Psalm 85:4–13)

FRIDAY
Overcoming Faith
(Romans 12:14–21)

SATURDAY
Marks of Faith
(Galatians 5:22–26)

SUNDAY
Struggling Faith
(Mark 14:26–31, 66–72)

Sources:

Barclay, William. *The Gospel of Mark.* The Daily Study Bible. Philadelphia PA: The Westminster Press, 1956.

Evans, Craig A. *Mark.* Word Biblical Commentary. Vol. 34B. Dallas, TX: Word Books, Publisher, 2001.

Keener, Craig S. *The IVP Bible Background Commentary: New Testament.* Downers Grove, IL: InterVarsity Press, 1993.

COMMENTS / NOTES:

RESURRECTION FAITH

BIBLE BASIS: MARK 16:1–8

BIBLE TRUTH: Jesus' closest followers were devastated by His crucifixion and validated by His resurrection.

MEMORY VERSE: "And he saith unto them, Be not affrighted: Ye seek Jesus of Nazareth, which was crucified: he is risen; he is not here: behold the place where they laid him" (Mark 16:6).

LESSON AIM: By the end of the lesson, we will: REMEMBER details of the discovery by Jesus' followers of His resurrection and the promise for the future; FEEL the devastating loss experienced by the women as well as the relief that comes from understanding how faith in God helps Christians survive their loss; and TELL one another stories of grief and to encourage and strengthen one another with assurance of good things to come through Jesus Christ.

TEACHER PREPARATION

MATERIALS NEEDED: Quarterly Commentary/Teacher Manual, Adult Quarterly, Adult resources—charts, worksheets, and other teaching tools, paper, pens, pencils, Bibles (several different versions)

OTHER MATERIALS NEEDED / TEACHER'S NOTES:

_____

_____

LESSON OVERVIEW

LIFE NEED FOR TODAY'S LESSON
Believers may find that their strong beliefs may be severely tested.

BIBLE APPLICATION
Christians will accept that Jesus has overcome the world.

BIBLE LEARNING
Jesus' resurrection gave assurance and comfort to the disciples and His followers.

STUDENTS' RESPONSES
Believers know that their victory over sin is in Jesus' resurrection.

LESSON SCRIPTURE

MARK 16:1–8, KJV

1 And when the sabbath was past, Mary Magdalene, and Mary the mother of James, and Salome, had bought sweet spices, that they might come and anoint him.

2 And very early in the morning the first day of the week, they came unto the sepulchre

MARK 16:1–8, NIV

1 When the Sabbath was over, Mary Magdalene, Mary the mother of James, and Salome bought spices so that they might go to anoint Jesus' body.

2 Very early on the first day of the week, just after sunrise, they were on their way to the

at the rising of the sun.

3 And they said among themselves, Who shall roll us away the stone from the door of the sepulchre?

4 And when they looked, they saw that the stone was rolled away: for it was very great.

5 And entering into the sepulchre, they saw a young man sitting on the right side, clothed in a long white garment; and they were affrighted.

6 And he saith unto them, Be not affrighted: Ye seek Jesus of Nazareth, which was crucified: he is risen; he is not here: behold the place where they laid him.

7 But go your way, tell his disciples and Peter that he goeth before you into Galilee: there shall ye see him, as he said unto you.

8 And they went out quickly, and fled from the sepulchre; for they trembled and were amazed: neither said they any thing to any man; for they were afraid.

tomb

3 and they asked each other, "Who will roll the stone away from the entrance of the tomb?"

4 But when they looked up, they saw that the stone, which was very large, had been rolled away.

5 As they entered the tomb, they saw a young man dressed in a white robe sitting on the right side, and they were alarmed.

6 "Don't be alarmed," he said. "You are looking for Jesus the Nazarene, who was crucified. He has risen! He is not here. See the place where they laid him.

7 But go, tell his disciples and Peter, 'He is going ahead of you into Galilee. There you will see him, just as he told you.'"

8 Trembling and bewildered, the women went out and fled from the tomb. They said nothing to anyone, because they were afraid.

LIGHT ON THE WORD

Mary Magdalene. The most widely held explanation for Mary Magdalene's name is that she is from the town of Magdala on the Sea of Galilee coast. Mary is mentioned several times in the Gospels as a faithful follower of Christ, who at some point cast seven demons out of her (**Mark 16:9**). Luke records that she traveled with Jesus and His disciples and that she, along with several other women, supported them out of their own resources (**Luke 8:2–3**). Mary was present at the Crucifixion, watching Jesus on the Cross (**Luke 23:49**), and stayed until His body was removed. Perhaps the most blessed event for her was that she was not only one of the first to see the empty tomb, but the first person to see Jesus after the

Resurrection and received instructions to tell the others (**John 20:17–18**).

Salome. Like Mary Magdalene, Salome was a follower and supporter of Christ who was present at the Crucifixion and Resurrection. She is the mother of Christ's apostles James and John, and made the request of Jesus that her sons sit in places of honor (at Jesus' left and right) when He established His Kingdom. Jesus responded by telling her, James, and John that they did not know what they were asking, as He would be drinking from a "bitter cup of sorrow" in suffering (**Mark 10:38; cf. Matthew 20:20–22**). He then predicted that they would indeed drink from that cup. James was the first apostle martyred and John was eventually exiled to the island of Patmos.

Mary, mother of James. Not much is known about her beyond that she was also a devoted follower and supporter of Christ, was married to Alphaeus, and had two sons, James and Joses. Her son, James, was one of Jesus' apostles, known as James the Lesser to distinguish him from the more prominent apostle James the son of Zebedee. She is referred to in Matthew as the "other Mary" (**28:1**). Some scholars believe she may be the sister of Mary, the mother of Jesus, because of groupings provided in the Gospels, but this is debated.

TEACHING THE BIBLE LESSON

LIFE NEED FOR TODAY'S LESSON

AIM: Student will find that Christians may find their strong beliefs may be severely tested.

INTRODUCTION

Jesus' Predictions

Over the three years the disciples followed Jesus, He revealed His deity and His humanity, unveiling His purpose for coming into the world—"not come to be served, but to serve, and give His life as a ransom for many" (from **Mark 10:45**, NIV).

During His final weeks Jesus taught them about the Holy Spirit, who would come after He departed. While celebrating the Passover with them, He instituted communion, or the Lord's Supper, and informed them of His betrayal and impending death. As they walked toward the garden where He was to be arrested, He predicted that they would all abandon Him as He faced death, but reminded them again that He would be resurrected.

The events that Jesus predicted surrounding His death were fulfilled, yet even His most devoted followers did not believe He would resurrect. They were devastated by His death. Some of them scattered out of fear for their lives. These three women—Mary Magdalene, Salome, and Mary—prepared to anoint His body. Yet, no one at the tomb anticipated that what He said—"Destroy this temple, and I will raise it again in three days" (from **John 2:19**)—would actually be true. In fact, **John 2:22** states only after He rose did the disciples remember His words and believe. Ironically, the chief priests and Pharisees remembered. To safeguard against the disciples stealing Jesus' body and claiming He resurrected, they approached Pilate to request that he secure the tomb, with a seal and guard, telling him "we remember that while he was still alive that deceiver said, 'After three days I will rise again'" (from **Matthew 27:63**). Even Jesus' enemies provided additional witnesses to the truth!

BIBLE LEARNING

AIM: Students will believe that Jesus' resurrection gave assurance and comfort to the disciples and His followers.

I. THE WOMEN'S TASK (MARK 16:1–3)

Mary Magdalene, Salome, and Mary were all Christ-followers and adherents to Jewish custom. As required by the Sabbath, they refrained from working until Saturday evening, when they went to purchase spices to anoint Jesus' body. Instead of embalming, the Jewish custom was to pour spices and oils on dead bodies to express love, loyalty, and devotion, but also to neutralize the odor of decay. With spices in hand, these loyal women leave their homes while it is still dark to anoint Jesus (**v. 2** says they arrived just at sunrise). As they travel, they discuss the practicalities of removing the large stone guarding the tomb, indicating that they may not have been aware of the seal and guard.

Mark 16:1–8

When a pious Jew died, family members anointed the body with perfumed oil and spices, and wrapped strips of cloth around the body (somewhat in the style of a mummy, but there was no embalming). A separate cloth was wrapped around the head. All this had to be done immediately before the body was buried and began to decay. We read in **Mark 15:42–47** that Joseph of Arimathea, a prominent man, buried Jesus in his own tomb. The tomb of a wealthy man such as Joseph would be cut into the side of a rocky hill with a bench carved out of the inside. The body was laid on the bench when it was all prepared. Some tombs meant for family burial sites had more than one bench. After several years, when the body had decayed, the bones were placed in a jar.

1 And when the sabbath was past, Mary Magdalene, and Mary the mother of James, and Salome, had bought sweet spices, that they might come and anoint him. 2 And very early in the morning the first day of the week, they came unto the sepulchre at the rising of the sun. 3 And they said among themselves, Who shall roll us away the stone from the door of the sepulchre?

Jesus was buried late in the day on Friday. The Sabbath (which began at sunset on Friday and continued until sunset on Saturday) interrupted this traditional sign of respect, because Jews were forbidden to buy things or work then. The custom was to anoint the body with spices and oil before the burial cloths were wrapped around the dead body, and because of the Sabbath, Joseph of Arithmathea had no time to finish anointing Jesus' body (**John 19:38–42**). The women probably bought the spices and anointing oil on Saturday evening as soon as the Sabbath was over, after the sun set. Then they got up very early Sunday morning—maybe as early as 3:00 in the morning, because Bethany was about a two-mile walk to Jerusalem. They arrived at the tomb just as the sun was rising. Now they wanted to get into the tomb to do this tardy job, but for one problem: they didn't know who could help them roll away the stone.

II. THE ANGEL'S NEWS (vv. 4–6)

Once they arrive, they see that the stone is already moved, and probably feel a sense of relief that they did not have to orchestrate its removal. Entering the tomb prepared to anoint a dead body, they see an angel and were understandably greatly alarmed! Probably sensing their distress, the young man tells them to not be so surprised. He then goes on to confirm that they were in the right place—"You are looking for Jesus, the Nazarene, who is crucified." Then, he excitedly shares that what Christ predicted has occurred—"He isn't here! He has been raised from the dead!" He shows them the empty tomb as proof.

Surprise! Surprise!

4 And when they looked, they saw that the stone was rolled away: for it was very great.

The women had been very busy discussing their problem, and they were also downcast because of their sorrow. But when they arrived, they were surprised to see that the stone had been rolled away. The tomb was not opened to let Jesus out, but to show His followers that He no longer was inside. Jesus had a resurrection body. He could eat, He could show His disciples His scars, but He could also go through locked doors (**John 20:19, 26**), unlike our earthly bodies. So Jesus did not need the stone rolled away to come forth as Lazarus did (**John 11:38–39**).

5 And entering into the sepulchre, they saw a young man sitting on the right side, clothed in a long white garment; and they were affrighted.

Seeing that the stone was rolled away, the women walked into the tomb, but instead of seeing a dead body, they saw a young man dressed in a long white garment. The Greek for this garment is *stole* (**sto-LAY**), which is a long gown or robe of high quality worn by those in government or religious leadership. The robe seemed to indicate that this was no ordinary human being. Angels are not the chubby little babies that artists love to paint—they often appear as ordinary men (**Genesis 18:1–2, 22, 19:1; Judges 13:3–7**), and they always bring life-changing messages. The Greek for "affrighted" is *ekthambeo* (**ek-tham-BEH-o**), which can be both negative excitement, as in fear, or positive excitement, as in wonder or amazement. The women expected to see a dead body, but instead saw a heavenly messenger.

6 And he saith unto them, Be not affrighted: Ye seek Jesus of Nazareth, which was crucified: he is risen; he is not here: behold the place where they laid him.

The angel knew just what the women were looking for and expecting to do—anoint the crucified body of Jesus—but he showed them that the tomb was empty. The angel gave them an astounding message. Even though Jesus had told His followers that He would rise again, they evidently did not expect Him to! If Jesus had remained dead, we never would have heard of Him; there would be no church and no Christians. You and I are the best proof of the Resurrection. Jesus is more than an historical fact—He is our living Savior. He is alive and with us today. In fact, He lives within our hearts!

III. THE DISCIPLES' MESSAGE (v. 7)

The angel continues with a task for the women: tell a message to Jesus' disciples. In Jewish law, at least two or three witnesses were necessary to make an account reliable (**Deuteronomy 19:15**). Some interpreted this as restricted to males only which makes this account even more significant. Furthermore, the angel gives them credibility, a message from a conversation Jesus had with His disciples right

before He was arrested, which likely was not widely known. However, it still took additional encounters with Jesus to convince all of the disciples that His resurrection was authentic. Jesus mentions not only the disciples but specifically Peter to receive His message. How encouraging it would have been for Peter to know that the Lord specifically mentioned him, letting him know that he was forgiven for denying Jesus the night of His arrest.

The First Witnesses to Jesus' Resurrection

7 But go your way, tell his disciples and Peter that he goeth before you into Galilee: there shall ye see him, as he said unto you.

The first ones to see and tell of the resurrected Christ were women. Women were not considered trustworthy witnesses. However, this is one of the reasons we are so sure of their testimony! If this had just been a made-up story, it would have been Peter and John who would have been the first to discover that Jesus had risen from the dead. But God planned that these three women should be the first witnesses to the Resurrection of our Lord.

The last we heard about Peter was when he denied even knowing the Lord. But as he heard the cock crow, Peter remembered his boast and was so sorry (**Mark 14:66–72**). All the disciples had deserted Jesus, but Peter's betrayal was especially egregious, because he had boasted so confidently that he would never deny Jesus. The angel wanted all the disciples to know that Jesus had risen from the grave, but he mentioned Peter separately to let him know that Jesus never stopped loving him, even when he had failed. Jesus forgave all eleven of His disciples.

IV. THE WOMEN'S RESPONSE (V. 8)

The women are amazed and terrified by what they have just witnessed and heard. In response, they trembled and "fled from the tomb." The magnitude of going to the tomb expecting a dead Jesus, only to encounter an angel who reveals an empty tomb and announces that their beloved Lord and Master is risen from the dead, overwhelms them. God's presence and demonstration of His power leaves them in silent awe. These women solemnly walked to the tomb discussing the logistics of moving a stone to anoint a dead body, but leave in a hurry and speechless, with a far greater responsibility—to announce that He is risen!

8 And they went out quickly, and fled from the sepulchre; for they trembled and were amazed: neither said they any thing to any man; for they were afraid.

The women witnessed the most amazing event in history and acted accordingly. They ran from the tomb and were so excited that their bodies shook. But they were too stunned to tell anyone right away. Thankfully, though, they got over their fear and told the disciples about their experience (**Matthew 28:8; Luke 24:9**).

SEARCH THE SCRIPTURES

QUESTION 1
Describe Mary Magdalene.

She was a follower of Christ and was from Magdala. Jesus cast seven demons out of her. Mary was one of the few people to first tell of Jesus' resurrection.

QUESTION 2
Who did the women see when they entered the tomb?

A young man sitting on the right side in a long white garment.

LIGHT ON THE WORD

The Heavy Stone Tomb
The tomb did not have a door, because people did not go in and out; instead a groove ran parallel to the front of the round entrance to the tomb. A disk-shaped stone, measuring five to six feet in diameter and weighting hundreds of pounds, was placed in this groove. The groove was dug on the down hill, so when the stone was placed in this groove, it rolled down and landed right in front of the tomb opening. Only a group of very strong men could roll the stone away.

BIBLE APPLICATION

AIM: Students will learn that Christians will accept that Jesus has overcome the world.

Like Christ's disciples, we have the tendency to be shortsighted when it comes to His promises. Difficulties weigh us down and we forget that we are followers of a God who has resurrection power. As a result, we continue through life conducting business as usual. When faced with problems, we seek solutions, but often forget to seek God. Christ made a promise, and He kept it. The same God who promised salvation, hope, guidance, and comfort then continues to do so today. Even if we haven't seen our trial's end yet, we have faith that God worked miracles and brought healing in the past, and we can have faith that He will do it again.

STUDENT'S RESPONSES

AIM: Students will know that their is victory over sin in Jesus' resurrection.

If you are a follower of Christ, then you have trusted Him with your eternal life. But what areas of your current life have you not yet surrendered to Him? Is there a loss or hurt that you are still grieving or angry about? Are there prayers you have yet to see answered? Are there people you have been praying will come to follow Christ? Spend a few moments writing out your prayers.

If you are not yet a follower of Christ, what is preventing you from trusting Him for your salvation and eternal life? If you want to discuss this further or have questions, please connect with the teacher or pastor.

PRAYER

Jesus, Jesus, perfect Jesus! We bless You and thank You for dying on the Cross and Your glorious resurrection. You gave Your life, so that our lives could be lived in victory and doing for others. Thank You and thank You. In Jesus' Name we pray. Amen.

HOW TO SAY IT

Arimathea.   air-ih-ma-**THE**-a.

Salome.   sa-**LO**-may.

Sepulchre.   **SEP**-ul-ker.

PREPARE FOR NEXT SUNDAY

Read **Luke 7:1–10** and "Renewed Health."

DAILY HOME BIBLE READINGS

MONDAY
Commandment Living
(Deuteronomy 6:1–9)

TUESDAY
Fear and Serve the Lord
(1 Samuel 12:19–24)

WEDNESDAY
Faithful and Fearless
(Psalm 23)

THURSDAY
Grace-filled Living
(Romans 1:1–7)

FRIDAY
Living Again
(1 Peter 1:21–25)

SATURDAY
Resurrection Living
(1 Peter 3:14b–22)

SUNDAY
Resurrection Faith
(Mark 16:1–8)

Sources:
Evans, Craig A. Mark 8:27-16:20, Vol. 34B. *Word Biblical Commentary*. Dallas, TX: Word Books, 2001. 530-540.
Wuest, Kenneth. C. *Mark in the Greek New Testament for the English Reader*. Grand Rapids, MI: Wm. B. Eerdmans Publishing Company, 1952. 289-291.

COMMENTS / NOTES:

_____

_____

_____

_____

_____

_____

_____

_____

_____

_____

_____

_____

_____

_____

_____

_____

_____

_____

_____

_____

_____

_____

RENEWED HEALTH

BIBLE BASIS: LUKE 7:1–10

BIBLE TRUTH: The centurion's faith in Jesus caused his servant to receive healing from Jesus.

MEMORY VERSE: "When Jesus heard these things, he marvelled at him, and turned him about, and said unto the people that followed him, I say unto you, I have not found so great faith, no, not in Israel" (Luke 7:9).

LESSON AIM: By the end of the lesson, we will: KNOW the story of the centurion's faith and Jesus' healing of the centurion's servant; EXPERIENCE strong faith for deliverance from illness, like the centurion; and COMMIT to regularly visiting the sick to pray with them.

TEACHER PREPARATION

MATERIALS NEEDED: Quarterly Commentary/Teacher Manual, Adult Quarterly, Adult resources—charts, worksheets, and other teaching tools, paper, pens, pencils, Bibles (several different versions)

OTHER MATERIALS NEEDED / TEACHER'S NOTES:

_____

_____

LESSON OVERVIEW

LIFE NEED FOR TODAY'S LESSON
People have desperate needs at times that cause them to wonder if help is available.

BIBLE APPLICATION
Christians learn how faith in God can bring about the healing of our bodies.

BIBLE LEARNING
Mark reminds us that God has the power to heal us of any sickness or disease.

STUDENTS' RESPONSES
Followers of Christ affirm that they can turn to Jesus for help.

LESSON SCRIPTURE

LUKE 7:1–10, KJV

1 Now when he had ended all his sayings in the audience of the people, he entered into Capernaum.

2 And a certain centurion's servant, who was dear unto him, was sick, and ready to die.

3 And when he heard of Jesus, he sent unto him the elders of the Jews, beseeching him

LUKE 7:1–10, NIV

1 When Jesus had finished saying all this to the people who were listening, he entered Capernaum.

2 There a centurion's servant, whom his master valued highly, was sick and about to die.

3 The centurion heard of Jesus and sent

that he would come and heal his servant.

4 And when they came to Jesus, they besought him instantly, saying, That he was worthy for whom he should do this:

5 For he loveth our nation, and he hath built us a synagogue.

6 Then Jesus went with them. And when he was now not far from the house, the centurion sent friends to him, saying unto him, Lord, trouble not thyself: for I am not worthy that thou shouldest enter under my roof:

7 Wherefore neither thought I myself worthy to come unto thee: but say in a word, and my servant shall be healed.

8 For I also am a man set under authority, having under me soldiers, and I say unto one, Go, and he goeth; and to another, Come, and he cometh; and to my servant, Do this, and he doeth it.

9 When Jesus heard these things, he marvelled at him, and turned him about, and said unto the people that followed him, I say unto you, I have not found so great faith, no, not in Israel.

10 And they that were sent, returning to the house, found the servant whole that had been sick.

some elders of the Jews to him, asking him to come and heal his servant.

4 When they came to Jesus, they pleaded earnestly with him, "This man deserves to have you do this,

5 because he loves our nation and has built our synagogue."

6 So Jesus went with them. He was not far from the house when the centurion sent friends to say to him: "Lord, don't trouble yourself, for I do not deserve to have you come under my roof.

7 That is why I did not even consider myself worthy to come to you. But say the word, and my servant will be healed.

8 For I myself am a man under authority, with soldiers under me. I tell this one, 'Go,' and he goes; and that one, 'Come,' and he comes. I say to my servant, 'Do this,' and he does it."

9 When Jesus heard this, he was amazed at him, and turning to the crowd following him, he said, "I tell you, I have not found such great faith even in Israel."

10 Then the men who had been sent returned to the house and found the servant well.

LIGHT ON THE WORD

Capernaum. Capernaum, meaning "a village of comfort," was a city on the western shore of the Sea of Galilee in the region of Gennesaret. The city was on the road from Damascus to Acco and Tyre, in a heavily populated and commercially prosperous district of Galilee. Many important events in the Gospel narrative took place in the city of Capernaum. It was in this city that Jesus healed the nobleman's son (**John 4:46**), Peter's mother-in-law (**Mark 1:31**), and the paralytic (**Matthew 9:6**). Jesus prophesied the downfall of Capernaum due to the people's lack of repentance, even though so many mighty works were done there (**Matthew 11:23, Luke 10:15**).

Synagogue. A synagogue was a building that housed gatherings of Jews for prayers and the worship services. These buildings began to be constructed during the time of the Babylonian exile in the absence of the Temple. Ten Jewish males were required to form a synagogue, as they served as a Jewish meeting place throughout the Diaspora. Since New Testament times, synagogue services were held on feast days and every Sabbath day. As an observing Jew, Jesus frequented the synagogue, which became the site for healing and miracles. Paul also frequented the synagogue in an effort to convince the attendees that Jesus was the Messiah.

TEACHING THE BIBLE LESSON

LIFE NEED FOR TODAY'S LESSON

AIM: Students will see that people have desperate needs at times that cause them to wonder if help is available.

INTRODUCTION

Jesus Breaks Social Taboos

In Luke 6, we see a progression of Jesus' fame growing beyond Galilee. As Jesus broke the social taboos of the Pharisees and scribes, He drew attention to Himself as a Rabbi with a different type of authority. His approval of His disciples eating grain with unwashed hands and healing a man with a withered hand on the Sabbath only aroused the religious leaders' wrath. At the same time, it also increased His fame among the people. After these episodes, Jesus went up to a mountain and prayed to God. Coming down from this all-night prayer session, Jesus selected the twelve as His apostles.

Once He selected the twelve, Jesus taught what scholars call the "Sermon on the Plain" (**Luke 6:17–49**). Jesus' presence in Galilee drew huge crowds waiting to hear the latest teaching or be healed by the Rabbi from Nazareth. Not only did He draw huge crowds from the Jewish population, but people also came from Tyre and Sidon to hear Him and be healed. These crowds came to listen to Jesus as He taught them and redefined what it meant to live life in the Kingdom of God. Once Jesus taught them, He headed into Capernaum, where He would encounter an officer in the Roman army. Now Jesus would demonstrate what it meant to live life in the Kingdom.

BIBLE LEARNING

AIM: Students will remember that God has the power to heal us of any sickness or disease.

I. THE ELDER'S REQUEST (LUKE 7:1–5)

After finishing the Sermon on the Plain, Jesus goes to Capernaum, where He hears about a centurion whose servant is sick. The centurion must have heard of Jesus' fame, because he sends a delegation of synagogue elders to request Jesus' help with his situation. With a sense of urgency, the elders come to Jesus and ask for help. This underscores the desperate condition of the servant: healing needs to happen right away or he will die.

The elders know that as a Gentile, the centurion would have been unclean, because he doesn't follow Jewish kosher laws, so they make the centurion's appeal mentioning his status as a God-fearer, a Gentile who was not a full convert to Judaism but probably lived by the Ten Commandments and believed in Yahweh as the one true God. The centurion built a synagogue for the Jews, and gave this as a reason for Jesus to make an exception in coming to his house.

Luke 7:1–10

This narrative also appears in **Matthew 8:5–13** with alterations. In comparing the two narratives, the reader will be able to gain a broader perspective of the Lukan author's intent.

7:1 Now when he had ended all his sayings in the audience of the people, he entered into Capernaum.

Capernaum is no longer an inhabited town today, but an archaeological site located at the north corner of the Sea of Galilee. Capernaum was the center of Jesus' activities. He taught in the local synagogue there. It was also the town where Peter, James, Andrew, John, and the tax collector Matthew lived. Its citizens were mainly fishermen, farmers, and people who provided services to the Roman road and caravans, including tax collection. Similar to **Luke 7:1, Matthew 8:5** places Jesus in Capernaum.

2 And a certain centurion's servant, who was dear unto him, was sick, and ready to die. 3 And when he heard of Jesus, he sent unto him the elders of the Jews, beseeching him that he would come and heal his servant. 4 And when they came to Jesus, they besought him instantly, saying, That he was worthy for whom he should do this: 5 For he loveth our nation, and he hath built us a synagogue.

A centurion was a Roman army officer who commanded 100 soldiers. The centurion in the Luke narrative appears to be a patron of the Jewish people. During the time of Jesus, the Roman Empire ruled the vast lands that surrounded the Mediterranean Sea, including Palestine. In order to maintain governance over such large territory, the Roman Empire depended on a hierarchical patron-client relationship in which a wealthy and politically powerful person acted as a benefactor to a person or group who needed assistance. This relationship was reciprocal; the clients, who received resources and aid from the patron, were expected to respond to the patron's needs when required. In this verse, the centurion acts as patron to the Jewish population in Capernaum and he sends the Jewish elders, the clients, on a mission to see Jesus on his behalf. The Jewish elders obey their role by pleading the centurion's case for him.

Compare the Luke narrative with **Matthew 8:5–6:** "And when Jesus was entered into Capernaum, there came unto him a centurion, beseeching him, And saying, Lord, my servant lieth at home sick of the palsy, grievously tormented." First, the Lukan verse does not specify the type of illness that ails the centurion's servant, yet Matthew's version does. Second, in Matthew, the centurion himself goes directly to Jesus and pleads with Him to heal his servant from palsy (paralysis). The Jewish elders do not appear in Matthew, so that Gospel does not highlight the existence of a patron-client relationship between the Roman centurion and the Jewish population. That Gospel also does not mention the centurion establishing the Capernaum synagogue, which Luke would have focused on to establish him as a Gentile God-fearer, as Luke wrote for a a majority Gentile audience.

The term "servant" (Gk. *doulos* **DOO-los**) can also be translated "slave." Slavery played an integral part in the Roman Empire of the first century. Besides manual labor, slaves performed many domestic services, and might be employed at highly skilled jobs and professions. Teachers, accountants, and physicians were often slaves. Unskilled slaves, or those condemned to slavery as punishment, worked at farms, mines, and mills. Their living conditions were brutal, and their lives short. Under Roman law, slaves were considered property and had no legal rights of their own. They were subjected to harsh treatment by their masters, sexually exploited, and tortured. In fact, very often a court of law would not accept the testimony of a slave unless the slave was tortured, because they believed slaves would not reveal evidence against their masters unless physically forced to do so.

SEARCH THE SCRIPTURES

QUESTION 1
A Roman centurion had command over who in the army? What was the centurion's relationship to the Jews ?

He commanded 100 soldiers and was a patron of the Jews.

LIGHT ON THE WORD

A Desperate Situation

The centurion is in a crisis. His servant desperately needs help. Some situations are so bad that whatever barriers we face, our faith must go all-out in seeking Jesus.

II. THE CENTURION'S RESPONSE (vv. 6–8)

Jesus decides to go to the centurion's house. Here we see Jesus' compassion for the man and his servant, who is about to die. On the way to the house, the centurion sends a group of friends to Jesus showing that he recognizes Jesus' superiority. The centurion's admission of not being worthy to have Jesus enter into his home shows great humility. Although he is used to being in charge, he realizes that he has no right to ask a miracle. Remarkably, he sees Jesus' higher authority and relies on His mercy and compassion.

The centurion instead asks for Jesus to do a long-distance healing. In the first century, Jewish rabbis commonly performed healings, but a long-distance healing would have been a unique miracle. The centurion bases his faith in Jesus' power to do this on his understanding of authority. He rightly believes Jesus is under a higher authority (God the Father) and has authority over diseases. In the same way he commands his soldiers, Jesus can command diseases; all Jesus has to do is speak, because the power to heal was in the word. The centurion's faith was in the word of Jesus.

Humbled Faith

6 Then Jesus went with them. And when he was now not far from the house, the centurion sent friends to him, saying unto him, Lord, trouble not thyself: for I am not worthy that thou shouldest enter under my roof: 7 Wherefore neither thought I myself worthy to come unto thee: but say in a word, and my servant shall be healed. 8 For I also am a man set under authority, having under me soldiers, and I say unto one, Go, and he goeth; and to another, Come, and he cometh; and to my servant, Do this, and he doeth it.

The second delegation sent to Jesus by the centurion is stated as "friends." Notice that the friends actually speak for the centurion. In the first instance, the centurion, by way of his friends, acknowledges that, as a Gentile, he is unworthy to ask Jesus to enter his house. This is because according to the Mishnah, a compilation of Pharisaic oral tradition, Gentile houses were considered unclean. The second instance is the centurion's sense of unworthiness in relation to his understanding of the authoritative position of Jesus as the Son of God. The centurion's behavior implies that the Kingdom of God is similar to the hierarchical power system of the Roman Empire. The centurion understood the transmission of power in an authority structure and considered that Jesus, by virtue of His relationship to God, would be able to act.

III. THE SERVANT'S RENEWAL (vv. 9–10)

Jesus makes an astonishing remark: He has not found this kind of faith in the nation of Israel. For a Gentile to have this much faith in Him was quite amazing to Jesus. He calls it "great faith" because the centurion believed in the power of Jesus' word and in Jesus' worthiness as opposed to his own. In Matthew's version of this story, the centurion's faith is held up to indicate who will enter into the Kingdom of God and receive the blessings of the covenant. Jesus highlights this faith as what really brings God pleasure and invites His favor.

On hearing this, the servants turn back home. They have received the answer in Jesus' praise of the centurion's faith. Upon entering the house, they find the servant restored back to physical health, all because of Jesus' response to the centurion's faith. Not only did this event bring healing to the centurion's servant, but it showed what God looks at most: faith.

Such Great Faith

9 When Jesus heard these things, he marvelled at him, and turned him about, and said unto the people that followed him, I say unto you, I have not found so great faith, no, not in Israel.

In comparing **Matthew 8:10** with **Luke 7:9**, we see that Matthew has added two more verses after he writes what Jesus said about the centurion having more faith than those in Israel. Matthew goes on to explicitly state that some within Israel will not be part of the Kingdom of God, yet many will come from east and west to eat with Abraham, Isaac, and Jacob in the Kingdom of Heaven (**vv. 11–12**). Matthew states in **verse 12**, "But the children of the kingdom shall be cast out into outer darkness: there shall be weeping and gnashing of teeth." he Lukan narrative does not make such eschatological claims, but instead focuses on praising the Gentile for his great faith.

Overall, when the Lukan story is placed in juxtaposition to the Matthean narrative, distinct differences can be noted. First, Luke writes that two different groups approach Jesus: the Jewish elders, then the centurion's friends. Matthew does not include these groups in his narrative; he has the centurion approach Jesus directly. Luke gives those details because he is writing for a Gentile Roman audience, to engage them with the story. Second, in comparing **Luke 7:6–8** with **Matthew 8:8–9**, we notice that the friends' words on behalf of the centurion in Luke are the same exact words uttered by the centurion himself in Matthew: "Lord, I am not worthy that thou shouldest come under my roof: but speak the word only, and my servant shall be healed. For I am a man under authority, having soldiers under me: and I say to this man, Go, and he goeth; and to another, Come, and he cometh; and to my servant, Do this, and he doeth it." These words give us a grasp of the centurion's faith, the main point of the story.

SEARCH THE SCRIPTURES

QUESTION 2
Jesus found what in verse 9?

No greater faith.

LIGHT ON THE WORD

Tough Reality

Matthew adds a very harsh statement regarding the outcome of those who have no faith in Jesus. Although the eschatological vision in **Matthew 8:11–12** certainly refers to inclusion of the Gentiles in God's promise, it by no means excludes all Jews from the promise. Very recently in **8:14**, Jesus healed a leper and told him to go to the priest an make an offering according to Mosaic law as a testimony, indicating that Jesus continues to witness to both Jews and Gentiles.

BIBLE APPLICATION

AIM: Students will learn how faith in God can bring about the healing of our bodies.

Many in our society are ravaged by sickness and disease. Most of the time we respond to by resorting to natural means. There is nothing wrong with this and we should be encouraged to seek medical care and attention. Many believe the solution is health care and more doctors. Others believe the solution to bad health is a better diet and exercise. In case of terminal illnesses, these things can only do so much. In these times, we are more likely to seek God's intervention. This is when our faith in God is most important. Jesus has authority over all situations, including our bodies. This is why we can approach God with confidence in His power to heal.

STUDENT'S RESPONSES

AIM: Student will affirm that that they can turn to Jesus for help.

Some who are sick do not have faith in God for their healing. They may not even know God. Ask your pastor if there is a ministry to the sick at the church. If not, then ask to start one. Christians can meet the needs of those who are ill by gathering a group of fellow believers and visiting them in hospitals and nursing homes. Be prepared to pray for people's healing and to encourage them to believe God will heal according to His will.

PRAYER

Lord, the commander of our lives, protect us and guide as we follow You. Help us in out times of desperation to learn on, and depend on You. Thank You Lord for Your kindness each and every day. In Jesus' name we pray. Amen.

HOW TO SAY IT

Capernaum.   ka-PER-nee-um.

Centurion.   sen-TUR-ee-an.

PREPARE FOR NEXT SUNDAY

Read **Luke 7:36–50** and "A Reversal of Shame."

DAILY HOME BIBLE READINGS

MONDAY
Rebuilding Health
(Isaiah 58:6–12)

TUESDAY
Healing Wings
(Malachi 3:16–4:2)

WEDNESDAY
Words of Healing
(Proverbs 12:1–2, 13:16–17, 16:22–24)

THURSDAY
Total Health
(Matthew 4:23–25, 5:3–11)

FRIDAY
Emotional Health
(Matthew 6:16–27)

SATURDAY
Eternal Health
(John 5:24–30)

SUNDAY
Renewed Health
(Luke 7:1–10)

Sources:
Barker, Kenneth L. and Kohlenberger III, John R., eds. *The Expositor's Bible Commentary—Abridged Edition: New Testament.* Grand Rapids, MI: Zondervan, 1994. 441.
Burge, Gary M. and Hill, Andrew E. eds. *Baker Illustrated Bible Commentary.* Grand Rapids, MI: Baker Books, 2012. 1187.
Carson, D. A., R. T. France, J. A. Motyer, G. J. Wenham, Eds. *New Bible Commentary.* Downers Grove, IL: InterVarsity Press, 1994. 1082.
Keener, Craig S. *The IVP Bible Background Commentary: New Testament.* Downers Grove, IL: InterVarsity Press, 1993. 647–650, 670–671.

COMMENTS / NOTES:

_____
_____
_____
_____
_____
_____
_____
_____
_____
_____
_____
_____
_____
_____
_____
_____
_____
_____
_____

A REVERSAL OF SHAME

BIBLE BASIS: LUKE 7:36–50

BIBLE TRUTH: Jesus gave forgiveness and peace to a sinful woman, who loved Him very much.

MEMORY VERSE: "Wherefore I say unto thee, Her sins, which are many, are forgiven; for she loved much: but to whom little is forgiven, the same loveth little" (Luke 7:47).

LESSON AIM: By the end of the lesson, we will: KNOW the story of Jesus' tenderness for the repentant woman and His forgiveness of her sins; EXPRESS the great joy that comes from knowing their sins have been forgiven; and FORGIVE others for their failures, shortcomings, and hurtful actions.

TEACHER PREPARATION

MATERIALS NEEDED: Quarterly Commentary/Teacher Manual, Adult Quarterly, Adult resources—charts, worksheets, and other teaching tools, paper, pens, pencils, Bibles (several different versions)

OTHER MATERIALS NEEDED / TEACHER'S NOTES:

_____

_____

LESSON OVERVIEW

LIFE NEED FOR TODAY'S LESSON
People are sometimes remorseful to the point of tears about something they said or did.

BIBLE APPLICATION
Christians find peace in knowing that those who truly know Christ forgives.

BIBLE LEARNING
Jesus cares for those who are rejected by their spiritual and social communities.

STUDENTS' RESPONSES
Christians have joy in learning that Jesus forgives our sins and provides the solutions to our life problems.

LESSON SCRIPTURE

LUKE 7:36–50, KJV

36 And one of the Pharisees desired him that he would eat with him. And he went into the Pharisee's house, and sat down to meat.

37 And, behold, a woman in the city, which was a sinner, when she knew that Jesus sat

LUKE 7:36–50, NIV

36 When one of the Pharisees invited Jesus to have dinner with him, he went to the Pharisee's house and reclined at the table.

37 A woman in that town who lived a sinful life learned that Jesus was eating at the Pharisee's house, so she came there with an

at meat in the Pharisee's house, brought an alabaster box of ointment,

38 And stood at his feet behind him weeping, and began to wash his feet with tears, and did wipe them with the hairs of her head, and kissed his feet, and anointed them with the ointment.

39 Now when the Pharisee which had bidden him saw it, he spake within himself, saying, This man, if he were a prophet, would have known who and what manner of woman this is that toucheth him: for she is a sinner.

40 And Jesus answering said unto him, Simon, I have somewhat to say unto thee. And he saith, Master, say on.

41 There was a certain creditor which had two debtors: the one owed five hundred pence, and the other fifty.

42 And when they had nothing to pay, he frankly forgave them both. Tell me therefore, which of them will love him most?

43 Simon answered and said, I suppose that he, to whom he forgave most. And he said unto him, Thou hast rightly judged.

44 And he turned to the woman, and said unto Simon, Seest thou this woman? I entered into thine house, thou gavest me no water for my feet: but she hath washed my feet with tears, and wiped them with the hairs of her head.

45 Thou gavest me no kiss: but this woman since the time I came in hath not ceased to kiss my feet.

46 My head with oil thou didst not anoint: but this woman hath anointed my feet with ointment.

47 Wherefore I say unto thee, Her sins, which

alabaster jar of perfume.

38 As she stood behind him at his feet weeping, she began to wet his feet with her tears. Then she wiped them with her hair, kissed them and poured perfume on them.

39 When the Pharisee who had invited him saw this, he said to himself, "If this man were a prophet, he would know who is touching him and what kind of woman she is—that she is a sinner."

40 Jesus answered him, "Simon, I have something to tell you." "Tell me, teacher," he said.

41 "Two people owed money to a certain moneylender. One owed him five hundred denarii, and the other fifty.

42 Neither of them had the money to pay him back, so he forgave the debts of both. Now which of them will love him more?"

43 Simon replied, "I suppose the one who had the bigger debt forgiven." "You have judged correctly," Jesus said.

44 Then he turned toward the woman and said to Simon, "Do you see this woman? I came into your house. You did not give me any water for my feet, but she wet my feet with her tears and wiped them with her hair.

45 You did not give me a kiss, but this woman, from the time I entered, has not stopped kissing my feet.

46 You did not put oil on my head, but she has poured perfume on my feet.

47 Therefore, I tell you, her many sins have been forgiven—as her great love has shown. But whoever has been forgiven little loves little."

48 Then Jesus said to her, "Your sins are

are many, are forgiven; for she loved much: but to whom little is forgiven, the same loveth little.

48 And he said unto her, Thy sins are forgiven.

49 And they that sat at meat with him began to say within themselves, Who is this that forgiveth sins also?

50 And he said to the woman, Thy faith hath saved thee; go in peace.

forgiven."

49 The other guests began to say among themselves, "Who is this who even forgives sins?"

50 Jesus said to the woman, "Your faith has saved you; go in peace."

LIGHT ON THE WORD

Sinner. Among first-century Jews in Palestine, many groups were considered ceremonially impure, including shepherds, tax collectors, camel drivers, custom collectors, and tanners. Also included in this group were prostitutes, who were not only ceremonially but also morally impure. The sinners were the social outcasts of first-century Judaism. While most of the religious leaders would affirm that all people sin, these sinners would be those who sinned with a deliberate disregard for the Law or simply those who from were outside of the Jewish people and therefore in no way connected to the Law. This group would have been excluded from the covenant blessings of Israel. Jesus interacted with sinners with no discrimination, which attracted the hostility of the Pharisees.

Alabaster. These were boxes made of a stone found near the town of Alabastron in Egypt. They took their name from the city of their origin. They were often used to make vases or flasks to hold ointment and perfume. The stone they are made from is light, translucent, and resembles marble. In order to obtain the contents of the alabaster vessels, the long and narrow neck must be broken. Eventually this name was given to all containers that contained perfume.

TEACHING THE BIBLE LESSON

LIFE NEED FOR TODAY'S LESSON

AIM: Students will discover that people are sometimes remorseful to the point of tears about something they said or did.

INTRODUCTION

Jesus Accepts the Rejected

The Gospel of Luke is filled with examples of Jesus' acceptance and inclusion of outcasts. In His accepting those rejectedby the religious leaders of Israel, we see the full scope of Jesus' mission. God's redemptive activity will encompass not only the Jews but the Gentiles as well. Luke's Gospel is a global Gospel. God's plan of salvation reaches those far off geographically, culturally, and also morally; no one is outside the reach of His redemptive love. Earlier in chapter 7, the healing of a centurion's servant is highlighted. The centurion was a Gentile official of the Roman Empire. He was a target of Jewish prejudice and hatred, but his being a God-fearer shows that even he can be redeemed. Jesus praises Him as one who has great faith. In this week's passage, the woman who anoints Jesus is a sinner. Luke doesn't tell us what has made her a sinner. She may have committed moral sins, and chances are she was also not Jewish, but Jesus welcomes her efforts to honor Him. This results in the removal of her moral shame. She recognizes who Jesus is and He forgives her of her sins. She is in need of grace and Jesus provides it, showing that His grace is available to all. It is important to note that once Christ has redeemed her, she does not return to her sinful lifestyle. Jesus accepts all sinners and wants them to come completely out of sin.

BIBLE LEARNING

AIM: Students will see how Jesus cares for those who are rejected by their spiritual and social communities.

I. A FEARLESS WOMAN
(LUKE 7:36–39)

Jesus is invited to the home of a Pharisee named Simon. As the guest of honor, Jesus lies beside a table with His feet pointing away from the table. As the banquet is under full swing, a woman appears. She has a bad reputation. Nothing is said about her except that she is a sinner. As an outsider to such a public celebration, she would have been consigned to sitting by the wall, observing the guests, and eating leftover scraps of food. This woman was not here to observe but to act. She goes to Jesus and washes His feet with her tears. She then proceeds to anoint them with expensive perfume from an alabaster jar. Simon the Pharisee reacts in disbelief; Jesus would not have allowed her to touch Him if He really was a prophet.

This woman was fearless. She had to cross two barriers to do what she did. First was a gender barrier; according to the culture then, women were supposed to keep their hair covered. Wiping His feet with her hair would have been considered taboo. Second, she was a sinner and He was a distinguished rabbi. Her place was on the outside with the other sinners and societal rejects. In spite of this, she was bold enough to approach Him. Her desire to honor Jesus was greater than any barriers in her way.

Luke 7:36–50

This narrative also appears in **Matthew 26:6–13, Mark 14:3–9**, and **John 12:1–8** (with major alterations). Notice that both Matthew and Mark place the narrative toward the end of their Gospels—right before Jesus' trial, scourging, and Crucifixion (these portions of text that depict Jesus's trial and suffering are referred to as the "Passion Narrative"), and that both writers relate a very similar version of the story. However, Luke places the narrative of the woman early in his Gospel in chapter 7, which is the section that relates to Jesus' deeds among the people.

36 And one of the Pharisees desired him that he would eat with him. And he went into the Pharisee's house, and sat down to meat.

The Pharisees were an important Jewish sect at the time of Jesus. References to the Pharisees occur throughout Jewish and Christian literature of the first two centuries. Josephus, the Jewish historian who wrote a comprehensive history of the Jewish people at the command in the first century AD, lists the Pharisees as one of the main Jewish parties that emerged during the brief period of Jewish independence at the end of the 1st century B.C. The New Testament portrays the Pharisees as opponents of Jesus and the early Christians (**Mark 3:6, 7:1, 10:2; Matthew 23; John 11:47**). Central to their teaching was the belief in the twofold Law: the written and oral Torah—the recognition of a continuing tradition of interpretation of the Law.

The Gospels present an ongoing conflict between Jesus and the Pharisees, probably due to Jesus being more in favor of many of their theological tenets such as adherence to the Law (**Matthew 5:17–20**) as well as the resurrection of the dead and future rewards and punishments (**Mark 12:18–27, Matthew 25**). Because of their popularity and His frequent contact with them, Jesus gave His sharpest rebukes against the Pharisees.

He also gave them profound teaching moments such as this one (**Matthew 23:1–35, John 3:1–10**).

37 And, behold, a woman in the city, which was a sinner, when she knew that Jesus sat at meat in the Pharisee's house, brought an alabaster box of ointment, 38 And stood at his feet behind him weeping, and began to wash his feet with tears, and did wipe them with the hairs of her head, and kissed his feet, and anointed them with the ointment.

"Alabaster box" should be understood as a flask, the general term translators use to describe vessels. (The word "flask" does not appear in the KJV.) The term refers to a small container of perfumed oil. The flask perhaps had a narrow neck, making it impossible to mend. **Luke 7:37** refers to a small alabaster container as had been used for expensive perfumes for thousands of years.

In the ancient world, one did not sit down in a chair to eat, but rather recline on couches, leaning on their left elbow. Jesus' reclining position with the head toward the table and feet away from the table (the customary position of diners in the ancient world) makes His feet very accessible for the woman's attention. The Israelites, like all other peoples of the ancient Mediterranean world, wore sandals instead of shoes, and as they usually went barefoot in the house, frequent washing of the feet was a necessity.

SEARCH THE SCRIPTURES

QUESTION 1

Jesus was invited by whom to share a _____?

Pharisee, meal.

LIGHT ON THE WORD

Hospitality

The host's first duty was to give his guest water for washing his feet (**Genesis 18:4, 19:2, 24:32, 43:24; Judges 19:21**); omitting this was a sign of marked unfriendliness. It was also customary to wash the feet before meals and before going to bed; abstaining from washing for a long time was a sign of deep mourning (**2 Samuel 19:24**).

II. A FISCAL EXAMPLE (vv. 40–43)

Jesus shows Simon that He really is a prophet. He knows Simon's thoughts and proceeds to tell a short parable about a creditor who forgives two debtors. One debtor owes five hundred denarii and the other owes fifty. A denarius was the standard daily wage for a day laborer. The five hundred denarii would be equivalent to two years' wages, and the fifty denarii to two months' wages. Knowing that neither could pay, the money lender shows grace and forgives both debts. Jesus asks Simon "Which one loved the creditor most?" Simon answered the one who he "forgave most" (**v. 43**).

Jesus commends Simon for judging rightly. Jesus gets Simon to support what He is going to say next. Clearly the one who needed more grace would give more honor to the money lender; his enormous debt was forgiven. The parable provides a stark contrast between the different amounts and parallels the perception of sin in the life of the self-righteous as opposed to the needy sinner. In other words, we all have been forgiven an enormous debt. Only a few realize the greatness of it and respond appropriately to God's grace.

A Debt Forgiven

40 And Jesus answering said unto him, Simon, I have somewhat to say unto thee. And he saith, Master, say on. 41 There was a certain creditor which had two debtors: the one owed five hundred pence, and the other fifty. 42 And when they had nothing to pay, he frankly forgave them both. Tell me therefore, which of them will love him most? 43 Simon answered and said, I suppose that he,

to whom he forgave most. And he said unto him, **Thou hast rightly judged.**

Jesus frequently used parables to illustrate profound, divine truths. Stories like these are easily remembered because the symbolism is rich in meaning. The defining characteristic of the parable is the subtext suggesting how a person should behave or what he or she should believe. Aside from providing guidance and suggestions for proper conduct, parables frequently use metaphorical language that allows people to more easily digest difficult or complex ideas. A feature often involves a character who faces a moral dilemma or makes a bad decision and then suffers the unintended consequences. Although the parable's meaning is often not explicitly stated, it is not intended to be hidden or secret, but straightforward and obvious. Speaking in parables was widely practiced during Jesus' time and the Pharisee himself would have probably used this figure of speech as part of his own teaching style.

III. A FORGIVING CHRIST (vv. 44–50)

Jesus then proceeds to rebuke Simon. He points out that Simon, who should know better, has not offered Him the customary hospitality for a guest of honor. The sinful woman has done even more: she not only washed his feet, but did so with her tears and wiped them with her hair. Jesus was not given the customary greeting of a kiss, but the sinful woman has not stopped kissing His feet. Simon had not anointed Jesus' head with oil, but the woman anointed his feet with expensive perfume. One can only imagine Simon's embarrassment. He was quick to think of how unworthy the woman was, but his actions were more disdainful.

Jesus explains why this woman was so bold in giving honor. She knew her many sins were forgiven so she "loveth much" (v. 47). Jesus then turns to the woman and causes quite a stir with His next words: He declares forgiveness for her sins. Those sitting with Jesus at the banquet were shocked. In traditional Jewish understanding, only God Himself had the right and authority to forgive sins. Although the other guests didn't protest out loud, they questioned this unprecedented act. Jesus responds to their unspoken questions. He turns to the woman and lets her know her faith in Him has saved her. The honor that she gave to Jesus resulted in her shame being taken away. She can now live her life in peace just like all who choose to honor Christ and accept His gift of forgiveness.

Kisses of Gratitude

45 Thou gavest me no kiss: but this woman since the time I came in hath not ceased to kiss my feet. 46 My head with oil thou didst not anoint: but this woman hath anointed my feet with ointment. 47 Wherefore I say unto thee, Her sins, which are many, are forgiven; for she loved much: but to whom little is forgiven, the same loveth little. 48 And he said unto her, Thy sins are forgiven. 49 And they that sat at meat with him began to say within themselves, Who is this that forgiveth sins also? 50 And he said to the woman, Thy faith hath saved thee; go in peace.

These verses represent the climax of the Lukan narrative. This story focused on the sinful woman's faithful actions toward Jesus that led to her salvation. Her actions were juxtaposed with the unfaithfulness of the supposedly pious and righteous Pharisees. The story's meaning is that those from the outside—the unprivileged, the outcast, which includes women—and not necessarily those on the inside—the privileged Pharisees, for example—will enter the Kingdom of God because of their belief in Jesus as the Son of God, the One who can forgive sins. When comparing this Lukan version to the Matthean and Markan narratives which, as stated above, are placed at the end of their Gospels, we gain a better perspective of Luke's intent. In Matthew and Mark, Jesus is in Bethany at Simon the leper's house, not Simon the Pharisee (cf. **Matthew 26:6, Mark 14:2**). The woman who comes to Jesus in these two Gospels is not defined as a "woman of the city" like she is in Luke (cf. **Matthew 26:7; Mark 14:3**). In addition, the disciples are the main characters in the Matthean version (**Matthew 26:8**), while Mark (**Mark 14:4**) is not specific about who questions Jesus about the woman's use of the expensive oil. In both Gospels, we see that these two narratives do not focus on the woman whose sins have been forgiven because of her faith, but rather on a woman who, according to the men, seems to waste valuable resources by pouring the oil on Jesus's head.

In Matthew and Mark, Jesus reprimands those who protest the woman's actions, saying that her deed is good because she has come to "prepare me for my burial" (cf. **Matthew 26:12, Mark 14:8**). The woman's anointing of Jesus is a ritual of burial, so her actions are in relation to Jesus' death on the Cross. However, by Luke placing the story early on in his Gospel, in chapter 7, the section that focuses on Jesus' deeds among the people, the emphasis is on the woman's act as a demonstration of faith and salvation. Luke does not focus on the rite of burial, as the woman does not use the oil on Jesus' head but His feet, the appropriate custom for a dinner guest as a sign of hospitality. Anointing Jesus' head with oil would not have been an appropriate act in the case of the Lukan narrative. Also note that in **John 12:1–8**, Jesus is in the home of Lazarus in Bethany, and Mary, sister of Lazarus and Martha, is who pours the costly perfume upon Jesus' feet and wipes His feet with her hair. In addition, **John 12:4** states that it is Judas Iscariot who questions Mary's misuse of resources. When examining these various stories, it is possible to discern the intent of each author. Each Gospel wrote to suit the particular needs of their specific audiences. When we begin to read the Gospels in this way, by comparing the similarities and differences in each of the different stories, we begin to dip deeper into the well of Scripture.

SEARCH THE SCRIPTURES

QUESTION 2
Jesus tells Simon that He has not any _____ from him, but the woman has _____ his _____ without stopping.

Kisses, kissed, feet.

LIGHT ON THE WORD

Free in Christ
Many seem to feel no shame for their sinful actions. In fact, if you look at reality TV, some have become celebrities by parading their sin in public. While it may seem like most of the world callously acts without a conscience, most feel shame for what they have done. It may not be apparent, but we all experience a desire to hide from others and God because of our sin.

BIBLE APPLICATION

AIM: Students will discover that Christians find peace in knowing that those who truly know Christ forgives.

Jesus shows us that we do not have to hide, but we must be bold in honoring Him as the only One who can offer forgiveness. Christ's acceptance of us is why we no longer have to wear a mask of shame. Those who boldly sin and display their wicked behavior and those who trust in their own righteousness still bear the weight of their sin. Their shameful behvavior cannot be covered no matter how much they try to hide it. Forgiveness and acceptance can only be found in Christ.

STUDENT'S RESPONSES

AIM: Students will know that Christians have joy in learning that Jesus forgives our sins and

provides the solutions to our life problems.

Sometimes it takes a symbolic act to hammer home the spiritual truth we have learned. List all of the ways you believe you do not measure up spiritually. Write them out on a piece of paper, then tear the paper into pieces and dump it into the trash can. This is what God has done for you. He has torn up anything that you have to be ashamed of, and now you are free in Christ.

PRAYER

Lord, You forgive us of sins when we ask You. You allow us to have a fresh start and renew our relationship with You. Keep us forever in Your care and mercy. In Jesus' Name we pray. Amen.

HOW TO SAY IT

Alabaster.   AL-uh-bah-ster.

Creditor.   KRE-di-ter.

PREPARE FOR NEXT SUNDAY

Read **Luke 8:26–36** and "A Sound Mind."

DAILY HOME BIBLE READINGS

MONDAY
Israel's Salvation
(Exodus 14:30–15:3)

TUESDAY
David's Deliverance
(2 Samuel 22:2–7, 17–20)

WEDNESDAY
Prevailing Trust
(Psalm 13)

THURSDAY
Fulfilled Trust
(2 Samuel 7:8–12)

FRIDAY
Triumphant Trust
(Psalm 54)

SATURDAY
Trust Without Shame
(2 Timothy 1:8–14)

SUNDAY
A Reversal of Shame
(Luke 7:36–50)

Sources:
Alexander, David, and Pat Alexander. *Zondervan Handbook to the Bible.* Grand Rapids, MI: Zondervan, 1999.
Barker, Kenneth L. and Kohlenberger III, John R., eds. *The Expositor's Bible Commentary—Abridged Edition: New Testament.* Grand Rapids, MI: Zondervan, 1994.
Burge, Gary M. and Hill, Andrew E. eds. *Baker Illustrated Bible Commentary.* Grand Rapids, MI: Baker Books, 2012.

COMMENTS / NOTES:

_____

_____

_____

_____

_____

_____

_____

_____

_____

_____

_____

_____

_____

_____

_____

_____

_____

_____

_____

_____

A SOUND MIND

BIBLE BASIS: LUKE 8:26–36

BIBLE TRUTH: Jesus healed a man who was demon possessed and told him to share his healing experience with others.

MEMORY VERSE: "Then they went out to see what was done; and came to Jesus, and found the man, out of whom the devils were departed, sitting at the feet of Jesus, clothed, and in his right mind: and they were afraid" (Luke 8:35).

LESSON AIM: By the end of the lesson, we will: KNOW the details of Jesus' healing the Gerasene man from his demons; EMPATHIZE with those who have great troubles and to remember their times of trial; and START, support, promote, or work in a church counseling program.

TEACHER PREPARATION

MATERIALS NEEDED: Quarterly Commentary/Teacher Manual, Adult Quarterly, Adult resources—charts, worksheets, and other teaching tools, paper, pens, pencils, Bibles (several different versions)

OTHER MATERIALS NEEDED / TEACHER'S NOTES:

_____

_____

LESSON OVERVIEW

LIFE NEED FOR TODAY'S LESSON
People can behave abnormally or be a threat to themselves or others when they have suffered emotional or physical disorders.

BIBLE APPLICATION
Believers have joy and can share with others how Jesus has healed them and changed their lives in a healthier and positive way.

BIBLE LEARNING
Believers learn that Jesus faces and heals the fears of a community and the harsh reality of a man who is possessed.

STUDENTS' RESPONSES
Christians discover that Jesus can give direction and clarity to change their troubled minds.

LESSON SCRIPTURE

LUKE 8:26–36, KJV

26 And they arrived at the country of the Gadarenes, which is over against Galilee.

27 And when he went forth to land, there met him out of the city a certain man, which had devils long time, and ware no clothes,

LUKE 8:26–36, NIV

26 They sailed to the region of the Gerasenes, which is across the lake from Galilee.

27 When Jesus stepped ashore, he was met by a demon-possessed man from the

neither abode in any house, but in the tombs.

28 When he saw Jesus, he cried out, and fell down before him, and with a loud voice said, What have I to do with thee, Jesus, thou Son of God most high? I beseech thee, torment me not.

29 (For he had commanded the unclean spirit to come out of the man. For oftentimes it had caught him: and he was kept bound with chains and in fetters; and he brake the bands, and was driven of the devil into the wilderness.)

30 And Jesus asked him, saying, What is thy name? And he said, Legion: because many devils were entered into him.

31 And they besought him that he would not command them to go out into the deep.

32 And there was there an herd of many swine feeding on the mountain: and they besought him that he would suffer them to enter into them. And he suffered them.

33 Then went the devils out of the man, and entered into the swine: and the herd ran violently down a steep place into the lake, and were choked .

34 When they that fed them saw what was done, they fled, and went and told it in the city and in the country.

35 Then they went out to see what was done; and came to Jesus, and found the man, out of whom the devils were departed, sitting at the feet of Jesus, clothed, and in his right mind: and they were afraid.

36 They also which saw it told them by what means he that was possessed of the devils was healed.

town. For a long time this man had not worn clothes or lived in a house, but had lived in the tombs.

28 When he saw Jesus, he cried out and fell at his feet, shouting at the top of his voice, "What do you want with me, Jesus, Son of the Most High God? I beg you, don't torture me!"

29 For Jesus had commanded the impure spirit to come out of the man. Many times it had seized him, and though he was chained hand and foot and kept under guard, he had broken his chains and had been driven by the demon into solitary places.

30 Jesus asked him, "What is your name?" "Legion," he replied, because many demons had gone into him.

31 And they begged Jesus repeatedly not to order them to go into the Abyss.

32 A large herd of pigs was feeding there on the hillside. The demons begged Jesus to let them go into the pigs, and he gave them permission.

33 When the demons came out of the man, they went into the pigs, and the herd rushed down the steep bank into the lake and was drowned.

34 When those tending the pigs saw what had happened, they ran off and reported this in the town and countryside,

35 and the people went out to see what had happened. When they came to Jesus, they found the man from whom the demons had gone out, sitting at Jesus' feet, dressed and in his right mind; and they were afraid.

36 Those who had seen it told the people how the demon-possessed man had been cured.

LIGHT ON THE WORD

Gerasenes. The Gospels vary in identifying this Gentile city. Mark says it is the region of the Gadarenes (**5:1**). In the King James version, Matthew calls the region the Gergesenes (**8:28**). Gadara was eight miles from the lake while Gerasa was thirty miles away. Both were cities in the Decapolis, which means "Ten Towns." We can say it is most likely a Gentile population who lived there, based on the presence of pig herds, which were considered unclean by Jews (**Leviticus 11:7**). There were a few Jewish residents, though.

Demoniac. A demoniac is someone possessed by a devil or demon. Sometimes demon possession causes people to have physical and mental ailments. Evil spirits can also cause some to act and speak in peculiar ways. Jesus made clear that demon possession is real. Every time Jesus encountered a demoniac, He spoke a word, commanding them to leave or release a person. They always obeyed because Jesus is Lord over all, including the natural and spiritual world.

TEACHING THE BIBLE LESSON

LIFE NEED FOR TODAY'S LESSON

AIM: Students will experience that people can behave abnormally or be a threat to themselves or others when they have suffered emotional or physical disorders.

INTRODUCTION

Discipleship Requirements

Many became Jesus' disciples, but out of the group, Jesus chose twelve to become His apostles (**Luke 6:12–16**). Not everybody could go out and represent Jesus to the world. But before Jesus could send the twelve out, they needed preparation. Jesus wanted to make sure they understood their mission and the difficulties ahead. He allowed them to share in experiences like hearing the Beatitudes, calming a storm, delivering a demoniac, healing a woman with an issue of blood, and raising Jairus' daughter from the dead (**Luke 6:17–9:6**).

Each of Jesus' encounters taught His apostles about His ministry and what would be required of them as they went into the world as His representatives. In **Luke 8:22–25**, Jesus and the disciples were alone on a boat crossing the Sea of Galilee. A windstorm came and tossed the boat so much that the disciples thought they would perish, even though Jesus was with them. Jesus was sleeping in the lower part of the boat, so they woke Him up in a panic. Jesus rebuked the winds and sea, which calmed down. Jesus asked them, "Where is your faith?" They had seen Jesus perform miracles but still doubted. Jesus proved He has power and authority over nature. The disciples wondered who Jesus was that the wind and seas obeyed Him. Today in our lesson, the demons will reveal who Jesus is, thus answering the disciples' question.

BIBLE LEARNING

AIM: Students will learn that Jesus faces and heals the fears of a community and the harsh reality of a man who is possessed.

I. THE ENCOUNTER (LUKE 8:26–31)

The disciples and Jesus arrived safely on the other side of the Sea of Galilee in spite of the storm (**Luke 8:22–25**). The place they landed was called Gerasenes (**8:26**). As soon as Jesus stepped out of the boat, a demoniac man approached Him and screamed, "Why are you bothering me, Jesus, Son of the Most High God? Please, I beg you, don't torture me!" (**8:28**). The demons recognized Jesus' power over the spiritual world. The presence of Jesus as Messiah demonstrated the conflict between darkness and light. The demons were disturbed by His presence, as He represented the rule and reign of God, which opposes Satan.

Often we see people who are mentally impaired and try our best to avoid them, fearing what they might do to us. But Jesus did not avoid the man; He commanded the evil spirit to come out (**8:29**). He had compassion because the man had been tormented so long. We, too, need to have compassion on those suffering physical or mental ailments. God will direct us how to best help them.

Luke 8:26–36

26 And they arrived at the country of the Gadarenes, which is over against Galilee. 27 And when he went forth to land, there met him out of the city a certain man, which had devils long time, and ware no clothes, neither abode in any house, but in the tombs. 28 When he saw Jesus, he cried out, and fell down before him, and with a loud voice said, What have I to do with thee, Jesus, thou Son of God most high? I beseech thee, torment me not.

This Scripture describes Jesus' encounter with a demoniac. Jesus reaches land in Gadarenes opposite Galilee. A man comes to him. He "had devils," meaning he was under the complete domination of demons. He has been under their control a "long time"; everyone in the towns by now had known about it. Luke accumulates details of the man's physical and psychological condition to probably point out that his healing will not be easy. He had previously lived in one of towns nearby, but now stays away from all social life. He could not wear clothes or live in a house, instead looking for the solitude of tombs (**v. 27**), in the caves used as burial places. In Judaism, tombs would be unclean due to the proximity of corpses (**Leviticus 22:4; Numbers 5:2**), so it was understandable that the demons would prefer such a location since they were unclean spirits (**Luke 8:29**). The detail description also shows the destructive power of the demons. The demons' influence is not only manifested on the victim's spirit or personality, but also in his body.

The man throws himself at Jesus' feet, calls Him "Son of God most high," and begs Him not to torment him (**v. 28**). The man speaks using the pronoun "I," but expressing the view of demons, shows he is totally under the control of demonic power.

29 (For he had commanded the unclean spirit to come out of the man. For oftentimes it had caught him: and he was kept bound with chains and in fetters; and he brake the bands, and was driven of the devil into the wilderness.) 30 And Jesus asked him, saying, What is thy name? And he said, Legion: because many devils were entered into him. 31 And they besought him that he would not command them to go out into the deep.

Verses **29** through **32** demonstrate the demoniac man's condition. Jesus ordered the demon to come out (**v. 29**). To show the difficulty in healing the man, Luke explains that the man had been possessed for a long time ("had devils long time," **v. 27**), which manifested itself with uncontrollable violence. The expression "oftentimes it had caught him" (**v. 29**) indicates that the sick man has successive seizures with intervals of calm, probably when he was chained.

Jesus cross-examines the demon, wanting to unmask all the demons implicated. The demon claims to be "legion" (Gk. *legeon*, **leh-gee-OWN**) because a plurality of evil spirits is involved (**v. 30**), though the exact number is undetermined. The word "legion" refers to the principal unit of the Roman military in that time period, encompassing 3,000 to 6,000 soldiers. In mentioning that the demons are associated with the Roman military through name, Luke both criticizes the corruption of the empire and proclaims that Jesus' power is greater than that of human might.

The demons themselves now speak, indicated by the use of plural in **verse 31**: "they besought him." They beg Jesus not to send them into the deep, probably where they would be kept and judged (see **Revelation 9:1–2, 11; 11:7; 20:1–3**). This word "deep" (Gk. *abussos*, **ah-BOO-sahs**) means something bottomless, used in the Greek version of the Old Testament for the waters of the deep (**Genesis 1:2, Psalm 24:2, 33:7, 32:7**). The ancients believed that underneath the earth was a subterranean ocean supplying water to the world. In the New Testament, this word is used exclusively for the residence of demons, but not necessarily the place of eternal punishment.

SEARCH THE SCRIPTURES

QUESTION 1

The man was possessed by demons. He was bound with _____ and _____ because the demons in him could not be controlled.

Chains and fetters.

LIGHT ON THE WORD

Demons Ask Jesus for a Favor

The demons ask Jesus to let them enter a herd of pigs feeding nearby. The presence of pigs shows that the majority of people living in the region were non-Jews. The pigs are also representative of unclean animals, so they would be a fitting destination for unclean spirits. Jesus grants their request (**v. 32**). His behavior is part of a continuing theme in the Gospel of Luke. He is not so much concerned with the demons' destruction as much as the deliverance of those under bondage. The present time is for deliverance. The destruction of demons will soon be realized at the end of the age.

II. THE DELIVERANCE (vv. 32–33)

The demons identified themselves as "Legion" (**8:30**). The size of a Roman legion varied over time between 4,500 to nearly 6,000 men. This signified that the man had many demons.

The Demons Plead for Mercy

32 And there was there an herd of many swine feeding on the mountain: and they besought him that he would suffer them to enter into them. And he suffered them. 33 Then went the devils out of the man, and entered into the swine: and the herd ran violently down a steep place into the lake, and were choked.

SEARCH THE SCRIPTURES

QUESTION 2

What do the demons ask of Jesus?

The demons ask Jesus not to kill them and allow them live in the pigs.

LIGHT ON THE WORD

The Herd of Pigs

The demons knew their ultimate fate would be the lake of fire (**Revelation 20:1–3**), so they asked to be cast into the herd of pigs. Maybe they thought they could escape God and their ultimate destiny at least for a while.

Jesus granted the demons' request to leave the man and enter the herd of pigs. However, when the demons entered the pigs, they ran into the lake and died. This massacre revealed the demons' true intentions: to destroy and abuse all life. Demons only have limited power; they cannot stand against the power of God nor Jesus' authority.

III. THE PROCLAMATION (vv. 34–36)

Those who were pig shepherds told everyone in the area what they had witnessed. The crowds came to meet Jesus and see for themselves the man who once was demon-possessed, now sitting with Jesus in his right mind. The people were afraid and begged Him to leave (**8:37**); they feared Jesus' power and were upset about losing a herd of pigs. If Jesus stayed, they feared they would experience greater financial losses. For them, money was much more important than ministering to the people. We cannot allow money and material possessions to take priority over helping people. Jesus always made ministering to the people His top priority.

Before Jesus left, He told the healed man "to go home and tell others all God had done for him" (8:39). The man did not completely obey Jesus' directions; instead of telling all God had done, he went and told everyone what Jesus had done for him.

Healing and Fear

34 When they that fed them saw what was done, they fled, and went and told it in the city and in the country. 35 Then they went out to see what was done; and came to Jesus, and found the man, out of whom the devils were departed, sitting at the feet of Jesus, clothed, and in his right mind: and they were afraid. 36 They also which saw it told them by what means he that was possessed of the devils was healed.

Verses 33 through 36 present the healing and the effect it produces. The demons leave the man and enter into the pigs; the pigs rush into the lake (v. 33). The pig keepers run into "the city and in the country" to tell what had happened (v. 34). People come from all over the area. They hear the testimony of the pig keepers and see for themselves the man healed; they are gripped by fear at the manifestation of divine presence and power (vv. 35–36; cf. 1:12; 2:9; 5:8–10, 26).

The story of the demoniac is a great illustration of what satanic forces can do to a human personality under their control: they bring the destruction of life. They "strive to overpower a man's personality, and ultimately to break down his self-control, and to rob him, as they did the demoniac, of self-respect" (Gooding 144).

SEARCH THE SCRIPTURES

QUESTION 3
The owners of the pigs were _____ because the man was now healed.

Afraid.

LIGHT ON THE WORD

Jesus Has All Power
Thankfully, Jesus came to destroy the work of the devil (1 John 3:8). He has power over satanic forces; Satan and demons recognize Jesus' authority and must obey Him (vv. 29, 32). We may not be necessarily in the same condition as this man, but we or people we live with are often prisoners of bad forces such as destructive habits or thoughts. We can trust Jesus to help fight bad thoughts and bad habits (see Matthew 11:28).

BIBLE APPLICATION

AIM: Students will understand how experiencing healing from Jesus will bring joy and the opportunity to share what He has done with others.

Many people suffer from mental and behavioral disorders. We often may think this is just limited to those we see in the streets talking to themselves and fighting invisible people. But this can include older people with dementia, as well as children with Attention Deficit Disorder. What should we do about these people who are a part of our church congregations? God calls us to show more empathy and devise ways to minister to their needs.

STUDENT'S RESPONSES

AIM: Students will discover that Jesus can give direction and clarity to change their troubled minds.

The most important way to support our friends and family members who have mental illness is to pray and show patience when they struggle with everyday tasks. In church, they may need assistance getting to their seat, finding the bathroom, or finding the Scripture in the Bible. Additionally, we can show support by being a part of those who start or support special counseling groups for those with exceptional needs.

PRAYER

Dear Jesus, You are the inspiration and the motivation that we need to have joy in our lives. In spite of our tears and our messiness, we can share how You bless us and provide us with what we need. Stabilize our minds and our hearts Lord. In Jesus' Name we pray. Amen.

HOW TO SAY IT

Gadarenes.   ga-DAH-ri-nees.

Besought.   bi-SOT.

PREPARE FOR NEXT SUNDAY

Read **Luke 15:11–24** and "A Family Reunion."

DAILY HOME BIBLE READINGS

MONDAY
Completeness in God
(Isaiah 61:1–7)

TUESDAY
Renewed Relationship
(Jeremiah 31:21, 31–35)

WEDNESDAY
Steadfast Love
(Psalm 119:41–48)

THURSDAY
Disciplined Freedom
(1 Corinthians 9:19–27)

FRIDAY
Freedom in the Spirit
(Romans 8:1–11)

SATURDAY
Christian Freedom
(Philippians 2:1–11)

SUNDAY
A Sound Mind
(Luke 8:26–36)

Sources:
Bock, Darrell L. *The NIV Application Commentary: Luke.* Grand Rapids, MI: Zondervan, 1996. 241.
Ellis, E. Earle. *The New Century Bible Commentary: The Gospel of Luke.* Grand Rapids, MI: Eerdmans. Reprint, 1983. 129.
Geldenhuys, Norval. *The New International Commentary on the New Testament: The Gospel of Luke.* Grand Rapids, MI: Eerdmans. Reprint, 1983.

COMMENTS / NOTES:

_____
_____
_____
_____
_____
_____
_____
_____
_____
_____
_____
_____
_____
_____
_____
_____
_____
_____
_____
_____
_____
_____

A FAMILY REUNION

BIBLE BASIS: LUKE 15:11–24

BIBLE TRUTH: Practicing and accepting Godlike love and forgiveness can mend broken relationships and make a difference.

MEMORY VERSE: "For this my son was dead, and is alive again; he was lost, and is found. And they began to be merry" (Luke 15:24).

LESSON AIM: By the end of the lesson, we will: RECOGNIZE God's compassion through the parable of the prodigal son; FEEL the need for reunion in families and connect that to our relation ship with God; and SHARING God's compassion will reconcile with a repentant prodigal.

TEACHER PREPARATION

MATERIALS NEEDED: Quarterly Commentary/Teacher Manual, Adult Quarterly, Adult resources—charts, worksheets, and other teaching tools, paper, pens, pencils, Bibles (several different versions)

OTHER MATERIALS NEEDED / TEACHER'S NOTES:

_____

_____

LESSON OVERVIEW

LIFE NEED FOR TODAY'S LESSON
Family relationships become too easily twisted and broken.

BIBLE LEARNING
Jesus tells a parable of God's compassion toward repentant sinners.

BIBLE APPLICATION
Believers know that we all need to repent and come back to a loving God and rejoice at the prodigal son's return.

STUDENTS' RESPONSES
Believers can see how love and changing attitudes can help bring families and relationships together.

LESSON SCRIPTURE

LUKE 15:11–24, KJV

11 And he said, A certain man had two sons:

12 And the younger of them said to his father, Father, give me the portion of goods that falleth to me. And he divided unto them his living.

LUKE 15:11–24, NIV

11 Jesus continued: "There was a man who had two sons.

12 The younger one said to his father, 'Father, give me my share of the estate.' So he divided his property between them.

13 And not many days after the younger son gathered all together, and took his journey into a far country, and there wasted his substance with riotous living.

14 And when he had spent all, there arose a mighty famine in that land; and he began to be in want.

15 And he went and joined himself to a citizen of that country; and he sent him into his fields to feed swine.

16 And he would fain have filled his belly with the husks that the swine did eat: and no man gave unto him.

17 And when he came to himself, he said, How many hired servants of my father's have bread enough and to spare, and I perish with hunger!

18 I will arise and go to my father, and will say unto him, Father, I have sinned against heaven, and before thee,

19 And am no more worthy to be called thy son: make me as one of thy hired servants.

20 And he arose, and came to his father. But when he was yet a great way off, his father saw him, and had compassion, and ran, and fell on his neck, and kissed him.

21 And the son said unto him, Father, I have sinned against heaven, and in thy sight, and am no more worthy to be called thy son.

22 But the father said to his servants, Bring forth the best robe, and put it on him; and put a ring on his hand, and shoes on his feet:

23 And bring hither the fatted calf, and kill it; and let us eat, and be merry:

24 For this my son was dead, and is alive again; he was lost, and is found. And they began to be merry.

13 "Not long after that, the younger son got together all he had, set off for a distant country and there squandered his wealth in wild living.

14 After he had spent everything, there was a severe famine in that whole country, and he began to be in need.

15 So he went and hired himself out to a citizen of that country, who sent him to his fields to feed pigs.

16 He longed to fill his stomach with the pods that the pigs were eating, but no one gave him anything.

17 "When he came to his senses, he said, 'How many of my father's hired servants have food to spare, and here I am starving to death!

18 I will set out and go back to my father and say to him: Father, I have sinned against heaven and against you.

19 I am no longer worthy to be called your son; make me like one of your hired servants.'

20 So he got up and went to his father. "But while he was still a long way off, his father saw him and was filled with compassion for him; he ran to his son, threw his arms around him and kissed him.

21 "The son said to him, 'Father, I have sinned against heaven and against you. I am no longer worthy to be called your son.'

22 "But the father said to his servants, 'Quick! Bring the best robe and put it on him. Put a ring on his finger and sandals on his feet.

23 Bring the fattened calf and kill it. Let's have a feast and celebrate.

24 For this son of mine was dead and is alive again; he was lost and is found.' So they began to celebrate.

LIGHT ON THE WORD

Father. The father in this parable represents the patient, caring Heavenly Father who has unconditional love for all mankind. This father illustrates how God values people and reveals His heart for the lost. Some scholars believe embracing his son was to protect him from the shame and humiliation of the community.

Younger brother. The Jews in Jesus' audience would have wanted to identify with the younger brother at first since Jacob, the father of Israel, was the younger of Isaac and Rebekah's sons. However, the parable upsets that close connection, challenging everyone in the audience to consider whether they are more like the older or younger brother. Since Luke's audience was probably a combination of Jews and Gentiles, the parable would have challenged everyone to reflect on their own behavior with regard to straying from family, community and responsibility.

Older brother. Despite remaining faithful to his father and his responsibilities as the oldest son, the older brother faces a situation similar to Esau other older bothers in Genesis, being left with the responsibility but seemingly little of the recognition from God or their parents. Some have proposed that the older brother represents any Jewish leaders who showed no grace with regard to sinners, but the parable is about more than just religious leadership. It is about love, tolerance and grace when anyone in the family or community messes up.

TEACHING THE BIBLE LESSON

LIFE NEED FOR TODAY'S LESSON

AIM: Students will know that family relationships become too easily twisted and broken.

INTRODUCTION

Family Dynamics

According to the Mosaic Law, after the father died, the older son inherited two thirds of his father's land, flocks, and wealth and the younger sibling one third (**Deuteronomy 21:17**). The parable is framed with regard to inheritance, with the younger son squandering his and ending up destitute. However, for both Jesus' original audience and for Luke's community, the economic matters in the story are important but not ultimate. While the older son certainly provides a better model for how to live responsibly with your future and your family in mind, the father's love of both sons regardless of their actions is the real essence of the parable. Parents should love children regardless of their successes and failures. Neither son is perfect. The younger is irresponsible and neglectful, while the older is strident and unforgiving. Yet, through everything, the father remains balanced, loving both and acknowledging their value as members of his family.

BIBLE LEARNING

AIM: Students will understand Jesus' parable of God's compassion toward repentant sinners.

I. THE OPENLY REBELLIOUS SON (LUKE 15:11–16)

The younger son stood tall in the family as a bold, outspoken rebel. He got into his father's face and demanded his inheritance. If the father, died the elder brother would be in charge; obviously the younger son didn't want to wait for any of this to occur. He wanted to be his own master and move out from under his father's protective wing. He wanted freedom, arrogantly believing he could manage his money and take care of himself. This request broke the father's heart, yet he refused to argue.

Once the father's property reached the younger son, he no doubt quickly converted the inheritance of flocks and grains into spendable funds. These kinds of transactions ordinarily took several days of bargaining and negotiation. However, the careless son probably sold to the first bidder, at bargain prices. The son traveled a long way from home, intentionally breaking all family ties. He wasted his inheritance on extravagant, reckless living. He operated from an unsound mind and quickly depleted his funds.

Soon a famine hit the area. The son ended up impoverished, begging for a job. He ended up slopping pigs to feed himself, a despicable job for a Jew who labeled swine as unclean (**Leviticus 11:7**). His meals consisted of pods from a carob tree, food for poverty-stricken people and pigs.

Luke 15:11–24

11 And he said, A certain man had two sons: 12 And the younger of them said to his father, Father, give me the portion of goods that falleth to me. And he divided unto them his living. 13 And not many days after the younger son gathered all together, and took his journey into a far country, and there wasted his substance with riotous living.

As if the two previous parables (vv. **3–10**) are not enough to fully illustrate His point, Jesus proceeds to tell a story which has become one of the greatest illustrations of man's relationship with God the Father. Here Christ illustrates people's sinful nature, how we wander away from God by our acts, and how God, through His loving compassion, seeks to save us from our sin, as well as God's attitude to repentant sinners who come to Him. It also illustrates the difference between God's concern and the attitude of the murmuring religious people over the salvation of a lost soul.

The story's setting is a typical Jewish household where the children can live off their family's inheritance during their father's lifetime, while the estate remains under his control until his death. According to Jewish custom, and consistent with that of many countries (especially in Africa), at the death of the father, the children would share his inheritance among themselves. For example, among the Igbo of Nigeria, the eldest child would inherit one-half of the property, with the other half shared among the rest of the children. If there are only two children, the eldest receives two-thirds of the inheritance. However, in ancient Israel people, the eldest received the double portion of the inheritance (**Deuteronomy 21:17**), while the rest shared the remaining portion among them. Although most often the eldest son probably received the double portion since it was a patrilineal society, there is evidence that daughters also received an inheritance and may have been treated equally in some families.

This knowledge will help us understand the implication of the younger child's request of the father, and the gravity of his sin. Asking his father, "Give me the portion of goods that falleth to me," is irregular in the Jewish custom. It shows disrespect for the father and, by implication, amounts to treating the father as if he were already dead. Neither Jewish nor Roman law permitted the father to arbitrarily dispose of his estate.

The young man asks his father to give him his own portion of his father's estate. His father complies, dividing his estate between his two sons. The younger son takes off after a few days to "a far country" with his inheritance. There he "wasted his substance with riotous living." The word here translated "wasted" is *diaskorpizo* (Gk. **dee-ah-skor-PEED-zoh**) which means to disperse or scatter abroad; used in the context of money, it means to squander. Therefore, the young man squanders his possession with "riotous" (Gk. *asotos*, **ah-SO-toce**) or loose lifestyle. The word *asotos* is found only here in the New Testament. Its noun form, asotia, is found three times and translated as "excess" (**Ephesians 5:18**) and "riot" (**Titus 1:6; 1 Peter 4:4**). Jesus' parable therefore gives a picture of a young man overwhelmed with so much wealth who does not know how to control himself. He lives extravagantly.

14 And when he had spent all, there arose a mighty famine in that land; and he began to be in want. 15 And he went and joined himself to a citizen of that country; and he sent him into his fields to feed swine. 16 And he would fain have filled his belly with the husks that the swine did eat: and no man gave unto him.

After he has "spent all" (*dapanao*, **dah-pah-NAH-o**), which means to incur expense in a good sense or to waste or squander in a negative sense, he finds himself starving. He becomes destitute in a foreign land. His situation is made worse because of "a mighty famine" that fell on that land. He is left without help, including those who helped him waste his riches. No one seems to care about him. The situation becomes so desperate that he accepts the most humiliating and repulsive type of work: taking care of swine. To this Jewish audience and many other nations, tending to swine is repugnant and degrading employment, because to them, pigs are unclean animals. Among the Egyptians, swine tenders were cut off from society—they were not allowed

to marry even from the lowest class in society, and they could not worship the gods.

His deplorable situation is heightened by the fact that not only does he accept this most humiliating job, but he also hungers after the pigs' food. The word "fain" is from *epithumeo* (Gk. **eh-pee-thoo-MEH-oh**), which can have a positive or negative meaning for strongly desiring something, including good deeds (**1 Timothy 3:1**), material goods (**Acts 20:33**) or a person (**Matthew 5:28**). This word and the clause "and no man gave unto him" suggest that he is in the field as a slave, feeding swine without food or pay. It also implies he is not even allowed to eat of the swine's food, just as slaves on sugar planations were forbidden to eat any sugar cane on penalty of beating. How much lower could he go?

II. THE FLIGHT HOME (vv. 17–20A)

The rebellious son, in his demoralized state, began to change his mind about his father and repent. The father used to be the barrier between his money and a good time, but now, the son thinks of him as a fair and generous man. The son admitted he had messed up; he thought real living was doing anything and everything he pleased. He confessed that home with his father was better than living on his own. The son did not merely dwell on pleasant memories; he decided to return to his father. He rehearsed a confession, "I sinned against heaven," which revealed a heartfelt brokenness before God. He admitted, "I don't deserve anything." He'd ask his father to make him a hired servant, feeling he no longer deserved sonship.

Home is Where I Belong

17 And when he came to himself, he said, How many hired servants of my father's have bread enough and to spare, and I perish with hunger! 18 I will arise and go to my father, and will say unto him, Father, I have sinned against heaven, and before thee, 19 And am

no more worthy to be called thy son: make me as one of thy hired servants.

The turning point of the story comes when his condition brings him to his senses, and he realizes that if he continues, it would be his end. Disillusioned by his desperate condition, he acknowledges how foolishly he acted by deserting his family, and plans a way to return home. "And when he came to himself" is a figurative way of saying that he came to his senses. Talking to himself out of frustration and disgusted with himself, he compares his present unpleasant and shameful condition to the condition of his father's "hired servants," or *misthios* (Gk. MEESE-thee-ose). They are paid servants, and they have "enough and to spare" while he is not even allowed to eat from the pigs' pen. The phrase "enough and to spare" is a translation of the Greek word *perisseuo* (peh-rees-SU-oh), which means superfluous, to have excess. They have more than enough while he suffers in poverty.

The thought of this spurs him to a decision. Instead of continuing in this despicable situation, he decides to return home and plead for the lowest place in his father's household. He rehearses how he is going to plead with his father. From this plea, we see a sense of remorse, repentance, faith, and action working together. He feels sorry for his action and repents. He has faith that his father would not reject his confession nor his plea. Hence, he says that he would go to his father and would confess to him saying, "I have sinned against heaven, and before thee." He realizes that his sin is both vertical (against heaven) and horizontal (against his father) in nature.

He doesn't say he sinned only against his father. He first says, "I have sinned against heaven." This reference to heaven is a substitute for God. God's residence is heaven, so to sin against heaven is to sin against Him (**Psalm 51:4**). This is the proper perspective on sin. All sin, no matter to whom it is against, is sin against God, for all sin is disobedience of God's law. Next the son acknowledges

that what he did offended his father as well. The son's sadness over his sin is seen in the abdication of his rights as a son. He believes he is no longer "worthy" (Gk. *axios*, **AK-see-ose**), which conveys weight or value; it also has the secondary sense of what is congruous or befitting. The son is saying he is not fit to be a son because of his past sin.

20 And he arose, and came to his father. But when he was yet a great way off, his father saw him, and had compassion, and ran, and fell on his neck, and kissed him.

After his resolve to return home and rehearsing how he would approach his father, the prodigal son acts. He begins his journey home. As he gets near, his father sees him while he is still afar off, runs to him, embraces, and kisses him. The word "fell" translates the Greek verb *epipipto* (eh-pee-PIP-tow), which means to seize, embrace, to press or fall upon someone. Used metaphorically, it means to take possession of someone. It is used, for example, for the Holy Spirit in His inspiration and impulse. The word translated "kissed" here is *kataphileo* (kah-tah-fi-LEH-oh), which literally means to kiss in greeting or farewell.

SEARCH THE SCRIPTURES

QUESTION 1
The young man knows that he done wrong and wants his father to accept him back as a

_____.

Hired servant.

LIGHT ON THE WORD

A Grand Welcome Back Home
A few important facts should be noted here about the father. Although his son deserted the home, the father's love for him never wavered. He never stopped hoping and looking out for the return of his lost son, which is why he is able to recognize him afar off. He is driven by loving "compassion"

(Gk. *splagchnizomai*, **splankh-NEED-oh-meye**), which literally means to be moved to one's bowels, seen as the seat of love and emotion. He runs immediately to meet him, affectionately hugging and kissing him. This clearly demonstrates God's extravagant love for the repentant sinner. He always yearns, and lovingly awaits, for the return of the wayward.

III. THE FORGIVING FATHER (vv. 20b–24)

The father saw his son coming home and ran toward him; he refused to wait. The son admitted his guilt, but the forgiving father interrupted; his return home said enough. The father ordered the servants to bring one of his best robes, a ring, and shoes, all symbolizing restored sonship. He insisted on a kingly feast, serving a prime calf, one the father may have been saving, in hopes of his son's return.

The son returned to the father's loving arms instead of the shame and guilt that he thought would await him. Instead of condemnation, there was a celebration. The community which would have humiliated him now celebrates him. This would have been a shocking surprise to the earlier hearers of this story, and it is shocking even now. To know that we have a Heavenly Father who embraces us and removes our shame is an amazing reality that we ought to treasure. It also should motivate us to embrace others who may feel shame and guilt over wrongs they have done.

A Son Begs for Forgiveness

21 And the son said unto him, Father, I have sinned against heaven, and in thy sight, and am no more worthy to be called thy son. 22 But the father said to his servants, Bring forth the best robe, and put it on him; and put a ring on his hand, and shoes on his feet: 23 And bring hither the fatted calf, and kill it; and let us eat, and be merry:

The son repeats his rehearsed speech before his father and throws himself at his mercy. The father's response is more than expected; he says to bring forth the best robe (Gk. *stole*, **sto-LAY**). This word can refer to a garment worn by kings, priests, and people of rank. This would have been the father's robe since it was the best robe in the house. He receives a ring, which more than likely was a family signet ring. This ring symbolizes his reinstatement as a son. He puts shoes on his feet. Only servants walked around without shoes. By putting shoes on his feet, the father receives his son back as true family, not a hired hand.

Next the father calls for a fatted calf for them to kill and eat. For the father, it is time to be merry (*euphraino*, **ew-FRAI-no**). This word connotes being joyful and is often used for the merriment of a feast. This feast would include not just the immediate family; a fatted calf would have been enough to feed the whole village. The context shows that this family is well off and so this party would have included family, servants, neighbors, and friends.

24 For this my son was dead, and is alive again; he was lost, and is found. And they began to be merry.

The father gives the reason for the occasion: the reunion with his son. He was dead (Gk. *nekros*, **nek-ROCE**)—this word can mean dead in a physical or spiritual sense—but now his son is alive again (Gk. *anazao*, **ah-NAD-zah-oh**). This word, found only in the New Testament, means to live again but also can mean being restored to a correct life. This is what happened to the prodigal son and what happens to all those who reunite with their heavenly Father. They are lost (Gk. *apollumi*, **ah-POE-loo-me**)—not in location, but destroyed or made of no use. Those without Christ are damaged and lack hope of being restored. Only God can restore them. The son was lost and was now found (Gk. *heurisko*, **hew-REES-koe**), which carries the usual meaning of discover or find; here it signifies how the lost person who is destroyed gets restored. They are found by God and put in right relationship with Him.

SEARCH THE SCRIPTURES

QUESTION 2

The young man lived below the poverty level. What was his source of food (v. 16)?

He ate the husks that were food for the swine.

LIGHT ON THE WORD

The Misery of Arrogance and Selfishness

In Jewish society, swine tenders would be treated as lepers. Jesus made use of this fact to show how desperate the young man was, to what depths of misery his riotous living had brought him. This illustrates the depravity and misery of sinners in their wrongdoing and sin.

BIBLE APPLICATION

AIM: Students will affirm that we all need to repent and return to a loving God, we can all rejoice at the prodigal son's return.

It is easy to discard someone and treat them as an outcast. We often do it to celebrities who get into trouble with the law, or when one of the clergy has fallen into sin. This matter hits close to home when a relative is addicted to drugs or a child has gotten pregnant out of wedlock. God does not make light of our wrongs, but has nailed them all to the Cross. He can show compassion on us, so we can have compassion on those in our lives who society would treat as outcasts.

STUDENT'S RESPONSES

AIM: Students will see how love and changing attitudes can help bring families and relationships together.

Ask God to bring to mind any family member, friend, church member, or co-worker you might be holding something against. Read the Scriptures below, one each day this week, and make the verses a prayer for help with forgiveness:

Matthew 6:14–15

Colossians 3:13

Ephesians 4:31–32

Matthew 18:21–22

2 Corinthians 2:5–8

PRAYER

Lord, our families need extra love and care from You and from us. Give us Your peace, prosperity, and guidance on what to do and how to do. Holy Spirit, we need Your presence in each of us. Letting go of attitudes, accepting forgiveness, and learning ways to show love for one another, is crucial to building and restoring broken families. In Jesus' Name we pray. Amen.

HOW TO SAY IT

Riotous.   RY-uh-tus.

Fain.   FAYN.

PREPARE FOR NEXT SUNDAY

Read **Luke 17:1–10** and "Increased Faith."

DAILY HOME BIBLE READINGS

MONDAY
The Father's Gift
(Matthew 7:7–12)

TUESDAY
Called into Family
(2 Timothy 1:3–10)

WEDNESDAY
The Generosity of God
(2 Corinthians 9:6–11)

THURSDAY
Eternal Family
(Romans 5:12–21)

FRIDAY
Journeying from Family
(Acts 20:17–24)

SATURDAY
The Lost Brought Home
(Luke 15:1–7)

SUNDAY
A Family Reunion
(Luke 15:11–24)

Sources:
Bock, Darrell L. *The NIV Application Commentary: Luke.* Grand Rapids, MI: Zondervan, 1996. 241.
Ellis, E. Earle. *The New Century Bible Commentary: The Gospel of Luke.* Grand Rapids, MI: Eerdmans. Reprint, 1983. 129.
Geldenhuys, Norval. *The New International Commentary on the New Testament: The Gospel of Luke.* Grand Rapids, MI: Eerdmans. Reprint, 1983.

COMMENTS / NOTES:

INCREASED FAITH

BIBLE BASIS: LUKE 17:1–10

BIBLE TRUTH: Jesus teaches His followers that even the smallest amount of genuine faith can rebuke sin.

MEMORY VERSE: "Take heed to yourselves: If thy brother trespass against thee, rebuke him; and if he repent, forgive him" (Luke 17:3).

LESSON AIM: By the end of the lesson, we will: REVIEW what Jesus said about causing another to stumble; APPRECIATE the importance of giving and receiving correction; and IMPROVE our methods and style of godly correcting of others when necessary.

TEACHER PREPARATION

MATERIALS NEEDED: Quarterly Commentary/Teacher Manual, Adult Quarterly, Adult resources—charts, worksheets, and other teaching tools, paper, pens, pencils, Bibles (several different versions)

OTHER MATERIALS NEEDED / TEACHER'S NOTES:

_____

_____

LESSON OVERVIEW

LIFE NEED FOR TODAY'S LESSON
Christians often do their best, but may need helpful correction when they fail.

BIBLE LEARNING
Jesus wants us to increase our faith and forgive others and ourselves.

BIBLE APPLICATION
Christians are to show how genuine faith is an important aspect of people rebuking sin and repent.

STUDENTS' RESPONSES
Believers are to develop a loving attitude to receive and give ways to help one another.

LESSON SCRIPTURE

LUKE 17:1–10, KJV

1 Then said he unto the disciples, It is impossible but that offences will come: but woe unto him, through whom they come!

2 It were better for him that a millstone were hanged about his neck, and he cast into the sea, than that he should offend one of these little ones.

LUKE 17:1–10, NIV

1 Jesus said to his disciples: "Things that cause people to stumble are bound to come, but woe to anyone through whom they come.

2 It would be better for them to be thrown into the sea with a millstone tied around their neck than to cause one of these little

3 Take heed to yourselves: If thy brother trespass against thee, rebuke him; and if he repent, forgive him.

4 And if he trespass against thee seven times in a day, and seven times in a day turn again to thee, saying, I repent; thou shalt forgive him.

5 And the apostles said unto the Lord, Increase our faith.

6 And the Lord said, If ye had faith as a grain of mustard seed, ye might say unto this sycamine tree, Be thou plucked up by the root, and be thou planted in the sea; and it should obey you.

7 But which of you, having a servant plowing or feeding cattle , will say unto him by and by, when he is come from the field, Go and sit down to meat ?

8 And will not rather say unto him, Make ready wherewith I may sup , and gird thyself, and serve me, till I have eaten and drunken ; and afterward thou shalt eat and drink ?

9 Doth he thank that servant because he did the things that were commanded him? I trow not.

10 So likewise ye, when ye shall have done all those things which are commanded you, say, We are unprofitable servants: we have done that which was our duty to do.

ones to stumble.

3 So watch yourselves. "If your brother or sister sins against you, rebuke them; and if they repent, forgive them.

4 Even if they sin against you seven times in a day and seven times come back to you saying 'I repent,' you must forgive them."

5 The apostles said to the Lord, "Increase our faith!"

6 He replied, "If you have faith as small as a mustard seed, you can say to this mulberry tree, 'Be uprooted and planted in the sea,' and it will obey you.

7 "Suppose one of you has a servant plowing or looking after the sheep. Will he say to the servant when he comes in from the field, 'Come along now and sit down to eat'?

8 Won't he rather say, 'Prepare my supper, get yourself ready and wait on me while I eat and drink; after that you may eat and drink'?

9 Will he thank the servant because he did what he was told to do?

10 So you also, when you have done everything you were told to do, should say, 'We are unworthy servants; we have only done our duty.'"

LIGHT ON THE WORD

Sycamore/Mulberry tree. The sycamore or sycamine tree was a black mulberry tree. These trees produce a dark edible berry and possess long leaf stalks. In his battles with the Philistines, David was instructed to listen for the sound of rushing wind at the top of the mulberry trees (2 Samuel 5:23–24), due to the trees' long leaves, which tremble at the slightest gust of wind and the reason the trees have also been called "trembling poplars." These trees populate the rivers and streams of Lebanon and the ravines of southern Palestine.

Millstone. These stones were used for grinding grain. One stone was placed on top of the other and provided pressure in the process of grinding the whole kernels into flour. Large community mills were comprised of even larger stones and produced grain for the whole community. Millstones were usually made from basalt rock, as this was more porous and provided sharp edges for cutting. These stones were large and heavy enough to kill a man if dropped on his head.

Mustard Seed. The mustard plant was a plant that could grow to about ten feet in height. These were ground to produce a powder for seasoning or into oil. The type of mustard Jesus was referring to is unclear, but evidence indicates that the mustard seed would have been the smallest seed the people of Palestine knew at the time.

TEACHING THE BIBLE LESSON

LIFE NEED FOR TODAY'S LESSON

AIM: Students will know that they often do their best, but may need helpful correction when they fail.

INTRODUCTION

Treating Others Correctly

As Jesus traveled toward Jerusalem, He used many opportunities to teach the people, including His disciples. He was always concerned about righteous living and proper treatment of others, since these contribute to harmonious living in our communities. Jesus has showed us the way, but we sometimes fail to follow it. Many communities are fragmented by selfishness and deceit. The root of the problems begins with sin and the need for forgiveness.

We are all going to face God on the Day of Judgment, so we must repent of our sins before we die (**Luke 13:1–5**). And salvation is open to all who believe, not a select group of people. We have to be humble in all that we do (**14:7–11**).

BIBLE LEARNING

AIM: Students will know that Jesus wants us to increase our faith and forgive others and ourselves.

I. FORGIVE OTHERS (LUKE 17:1–4)

Jesus turns His attention to teaching the disciples about offending others and forgiveness. His caution is the same as in **Matthew 18:6–7**. His concern was to warn them about causing weaker believers or new converts to sin (**Luke 17:1–2**). Those who cause others to sin, especially the young and immature believers, are doomed to severe punishment. Jesus said, "It would be better to be thrown into the sea with a millstone hung around your neck than to cause one of these little ones to fall into sin." A millstone is a heavy stone used for grinding grain. If a person falls into the sea with one around their neck, death would be imminent, but far less severe than to have to face punishment from God.

However, Jesus wants us to learn to forgive and show love toward those who have offended us (**vv. 3–4**). It is proper to go to the person who has offended us and confront them in private (**Matthew 18:15–17**). We have to lovingly explain what the offense was and how it affected us. If the person is truly sorry and acknowledges the sin, we should forgive them. How many times they sin against us does not matter; if they confess and change their ways, we must forgive them (cf. **Matthew 18:21–22**). We should pray for God's grace and mercy to be extended toward them. We can remind them that God forgives them and let go of all our resentment and anger. Our actions allow reconciliation in our relationships.

Luke 17:1–10

1 Then said he unto the disciples, It is impossible but that offences will come: but woe unto him, through whom they come!

The disciples are the immediate recipients of this message. In the preceding chapter, Jesus spoke to an audience of Pharisees (16:14–31).

By this time on their mission with Jesus, the disciples had seen Him perform miracles and knew they were called. As they prepared to do Jesus' works and spread His Word, some possibly worried they would become isolated from human concerns and failings. Here Jesus reminds them of their human condition, and the situations that await as they continue in ministry with Him and after His departure. They needed to defend against anything that distracted them from justice and compassion for the poor and needy.

A stumbling block is any hostility or opposition to hinder the plan and purpose of God. These are synonymous to criminal offenses directly against God, and consequences face those who cause such wrongdoings. The threats causing temptation are also noted by Gospel writers in **Matthew 18:6–7** and **Mark 9:42**.

2 It were better for him that a millstone were hanged about his neck, and he cast into the sea, than that he should offend one of these little ones.

A millstone was a heavy upper stone used for grinding flour in a large rotary mill driven by a mule or donkey. Death by millstone was favored over not showing compassion to the poor who deserved justice.

In **verses 1–2**, Jesus draws from the story of the wealthy man and Lazarus, found in **Luke 16:19–31**.

3 Take heed to yourselves: If thy brother trespass against thee, rebuke him; and if he repent, forgive him.

The warning issued here to disciples reflects the warning issued earlier in **12:1** regarding not being like hypocritical Pharisees. Here Jesus references concrete practices identified with the

Pharisees talked about in Luke, who would have had little regard for "the little ones" and sinners while preoccupied with status. A similar saying regarding forgiveness is also found in **Matthew 18:5, 21–22**.

4 And if he trespass against thee seven times in a day, and seven times in a day turn again to thee, saying, I repent; thou shalt forgive him.

The act of forgiveness would have no limits, and be considered a daily way of life. In order to continually forgive, the one offended must remain in communion with their offender. Thus, followers of Jesus must not keep sinners at a distance, but seek their restoration and stand ready to forgive.

SEARCH THE SCRIPTURES

QUESTION 1
What did Jesus say you should do if someone trespasses against you?

Rebuke him.

LIGHT ON THE WORD

Compassion—The Missing Ingredient
Jesus wants us to be loving and kind toward others, including the poor, crippled, lame, and blind (14:13–14). They cannot repay us, but God will. We have to seek after the lost because they are valued by God, just like in the parables of the lost sheep (15:3–7), the lost coin (15:8–10), and the lost son (15:11–32).

II. HAVE GENUINE FAITH (vv. 5–6)

The disciples felt incapable of measuring up to Jesus' standards. They asked of Him, "Increase our faith" (v. 5). The disciples wanted a greater outpouring of God's power that they could ultimately be able to forgive others, and not offend others nor be offended. Forgiving people who have offended us is not always easy, and only by God's grace and mercy can we do so.

Jesus acknowledged the little faith they possessed. The mustard seed represented their small faith. If their faith was genuine, they could do the impossible. God's power is unlimited, symbolized by being able to pull up a sycamine (mulberry, NLT) tree and put it into the sea (**v. 6**). God gives us the power to live out our faith. We have to rely on Him to help us. We will grow in faith and spiritual wisdom as we obey God and treat others with kindness and love according to His demands.

A Little Faith is Strong Faith

5 And the apostles said unto the Lord, Increase our faith.

As they followed Jesus and encountered people in need, especially those they tried to send away when they could not heal or help them, the disciples realized they fell short in many ways. They request faith so they can meet the tasks and mandates Jesus now issues. For the disciples, faith would be needed to truly forgive, and would lead to faithful behavior. By asking for their faith to be increased, they showed their understanding that faith was a gift that could not be obtained outside of God. Similar sayings regarding faith are also found in **Matthew 17:19–21** and **Mark 9:28–29**. For Luke, faith is manifested in faithfulness.

6 And the Lord said, If ye had faith as a grain of mustard seed, ye might say unto this sycamine tree, Be thou plucked up by the root, and be thou planted in the sea; and it should obey you.

Jesus knows that difficult times are ahead, and replies to the disciples' request for more faith. For faith to have its perfect work, Jesus tells them to have faith as a mustard seed, and that even a small faith can accomplish great deeds.

In the natural world, commanding a tree to be uprooted through word alone sounds like an impossible task; however, Jesus reminds the disciples that all things are possible with full dependence on God. The size of the mustard seed is explained in **Mark 4:31**.

Considered one of the smallest seeds, Jesus is telling them that even just a smidgen of faith can initiate the impossible. Even a little faith can move or dismantle what appears to be deeply rooted and strong.

In other translations, the tree may be identified as a sycamore, which is also deeply rooted but this was a different variety of tree than either the eastern Mediterranean or the American sycamores.

III. OBEY GOD (vv. 7–10)

Jesus used a parable to teach about obeying God. He uses the slave-master relationship to communicate His message to the disciples about performance of duty. Jesus shared that the slave's duty is to work both in the field and the house. The slave has to serve the master because it is his duty; his time and labor are controlled by the master.

The master is not obliged to the slave. He does not have to say "thank you" to the slave, because it is his duty to serve (**v. 9**). Jesus "came to serve and not be served." We must not look for others to serve us. Our duty is to serve Christ and others. Jesus presumably used this parable to remind the disciples that their leadership position did not give them the right to special treatment (**v. 10**). We are all servants who need to thank God for the opportunity to be of service in His kingdom work. In the end, we will be rewarded with the gift of eternal life with Jesus Christ.

Obligation and Obedience to God

7 But which of you, having a servant plowing or feeding cattle, will say unto him by and by, when he is come from the field, Go

and sit down to meat? 8 And will not rather say unto him, Make ready wherewith I may sup, and gird thyself, and serve me, till I have eaten and drunken; and afterward thou shalt eat and drink? 9 Doth he thank that servant because he did the things that were commanded him? I trow not.

These three verses deal with the obligation of obedience to God, which is more duty than effort for a reward. This kind of obedience to service can be found earlier in **Luke 12:35–36**.

There is a quick shift from the discussion about faith to this parable of the worthless slaves. In some translations, the word "slave" is used instead of "servant." In the Roman Empire, there were hired workers (*misthios*, **MIS-thee-os**; see **Luke 15:17**) and servants/slaves (*doulos*, **DOO-los; Luke 17:10**). Hired workers were free persons who were hired for daily, seasonal or yearly terms, whereas servants worked for their masters with no monetary compensation, only accomodations and food. Servants could become part of a household through war or debt, and they could be lifelong servants or servants who were free after working off a debt. Jesus is saying that the disciples should not expect to be regarded or rewarded for their service to others. Just as they should forgive anyone who sins against them (vv. 3–4), so they should serve others without expectation of anything in return. Jesus is not suggesting that the master-servant relationship is an ideal one, upholding the difference in power and treatment. Instead, He is speaking in language the disciples' would have understood in order to make His point that in this world, people are not always treated properly, but people of faith should continue to serve out of faith rather than expectations of reward.

10 So likewise ye, when ye shall have done all those things which are commanded you, say, We are unprofitable servants: we have done that which was our duty to do.

The Greek word for "duty" is *opheilo* (oh-FAY-lo), which means here "we owe (out) to do." esus continues with the servant metaphor, using language of debt, suggesting that perhaps the disciples should think of themselves like indentured servants. They owe a debt, and they do the things they are commanded to do as part of paying back that debt. He is not saying that they actually have a debt to pay, but that this is the type of attitude people of faith should have. Grateful to God for what God has given and done, they follow God's commandments and do for others (**6:31**) because this is what God has asked of them.

SEARCH THE SCRIPTURES

QUESTION 2
Complete the following "...when he is come from the field, ____ and sit ____ to _____?"

Go, down, meat

LIGHT ON THE WORD

Use What We Have
Being loving and considerate of others also flows into our management of the resources God has given us. This issue is addressed in the parable of the shrewd manager (**16:1–18**) and the rich man and beggar (**vv. 19–31**). We have to be willing to use and share what God has given us to bless others. Moreover, if God has given us His love and forgiveness, we must also extend it to others.

BIBLE APPLICATION

AIM: Students will see how genuine faith is an important aspect of people rebuking sin and repent.

God wants us to treat one another like we want to be treated. We do not like it when others offend us and never say, "I'm sorry." So when we offend others, we need to repent and ask for forgiveness. The failure to apologize after offending someone has caused much strife in our churches, families, and communities. This is part of the reason violence has increased in our society. We can only have peace in the world when we each acknowledge our sins, repent, and seek forgiveness.

STUDENT'S RESPONSES

AIM: Students will learn that believers are to develop a loving attitude to receive and give ways to help one another.

Sometimes it is not easy to forgive others. If we do not forgive those who sin against us, God will not forgive us (**Matthew 6:15**). Therefore it is vital we pray and ask God to help us forgive others, no matter how many times they sin. This week, think about those who have committed offenses against you. Ask God to help you to have the strength to find a way to forgive them. And if you have offended anyone, confess and seek forgiveness from God and the person.

PRAYER

God, thank You for forgiving us. Help us to have an open heart and mind to forgive others. Let us not harbor thoughts and actions that hurt others when we have been hurt. Grant us calmness and peace to choose You and not our desires. In Jesus' Name we pray. Amen.

HOW TO SAY IT

Sycamine.   si-ka-MINE.

Trow.   TROH.

PREPARE FOR NEXT SUNDAY

Read **Luke 17:11–19** and "Saying Thanks."

DAILY HOME BIBLE READINGS

MONDAY
Kept by God's Faithfulness
(Genesis 28:13–17)

TUESDAY
Fed by God's Faithfulness
(Deuteronomy 2:4–8)

WEDNESDAY
Helped by God's Faithfulness
(Psalm 121)

THURSDAY
Saved by God's Faithfulness
(Jeremiah 23:33–24:6)

FRIDAY
Living with Integrity
(Psalm 101:1–4, 6–7)

SATURDAY
Strength for Faithful Living
(Luke 21:33–38)

SUNDAY
Increased Faith
(Luke 17:1–10)

Sources:
Green, Joel B. *The New International Commentary on the New Testament: The Gospel of Luke.* Grand Rapids, MI: William B. Eerdmans, 1997.
Hogan, L.L. "Eighteenth Sunday After Pentecost." New Proclamation Year C, 2004: 221-222.

COMMENTS / NOTES:

_____

_____

_____

_____

_____

_____

_____

_____

_____

_____

_____

_____

SAYING THANKS

BIBLE BASIS: LUKE 17:11–19

BIBLE TRUTH: Luke tells us that one of the men who had leprosy returned to thank Jesus.

MEMORY VERSE: "And one of them, when he saw that he was healed, turned back, and with a loud voice glorified God" (Luke 17:15).

LESSON AIM: By the end of the lesson, we will: REVIEW the story of the ten healed lepers; EXPRESS gratitude for all blessings including healing we have received; and CELEBRATE how the expression of gratitude for personal healing becomes beneficial in the healing of others.

TEACHER PREPARATION

MATERIALS NEEDED: Quarterly Commentary/Teacher Manual, Adult Quarterly, Adult resources—charts, worksheets, and other teaching tools, paper, pens, pencils, Bibles (several different versions)

OTHER MATERIALS NEEDED / TEACHER'S NOTES:

_____

_____

LESSON OVERVIEW

LIFE NEED FOR TODAY'S LESSON
Some people are able to express their gratitude with sincerity and others with difficulty, and some are ungrateful for what is done for them.

BIBLE LEARNING
Faith and a sincere spirit helped the healed man express his thanks and praise to Jesus.

BIBLE APPLICATION
We have to forgive those who commit wrongdoings against us.

STUDENTS' RESPONSES
Believers will learn that Jesus wants us to have genuine faith and do as He has called us to do: forgive.

LESSON SCRIPTURE

LUKE 17:11–19, KJV

11 And it came to pass, as he went to Jerusalem, that he passed through the midst of Samaria and Galilee.

12 And as he entered into a certain village, there met him ten men that were lepers, which stood afar off:

13 And they lifted up their voices, and said,

LUKE 17:11–19, NIV

11 Now on his way to Jerusalem, Jesus traveled along the border between Samaria and Galilee.

12 As he was going into a village, ten men who had leprosy met him. They stood at a distance

13 and called out in a loud voice, "Jesus,

Jesus, Master, have mercy on us.

14 And when he saw them, he said unto them, Go shew yourselves unto the priests. And it came to pass, that, as they went, they were cleansed.

15 And one of them, when he saw that he was healed, turned back, and with a loud voice glorified God,

16 And fell down on his face at his feet, giving him thanks: and he was a Samaritan.

17 And Jesus answering said, Were there not ten cleansed? but where are the nine?

18 There are not found that returned to give glory to God, save this stranger.

19 And he said unto him, Arise, go thy way: thy faith hath made thee whole.

Master, have pity on us!"

14 When he saw them, he said, "Go, show yourselves to the priests." And as they went, they were cleansed.

15 One of them, when he saw he was healed, came back, praising God in a loud voice.

16 He threw himself at Jesus' feet and thanked him—and he was a Samaritan.

17 Jesus asked, "Were not all ten cleansed? Where are the other nine?

18 Has no one returned to give praise to God except this foreigner?"

19 Then he said to him, "Rise and go; your faith has made you well."

LIGHT ON THE WORD

Priest. Descendants from the tribe of Levi, a priest's duties included representing the people before God, caring for the Temple, and administering the Jewish sacrifices and services outlined in the Mosaic Law. Only they could declare a diseased person clean (**Leviticus 13–14**).

Leper. Someone who contracted the disease of leprosy. "Leprosy" in the Bible could refer to any number of contagious skin diseases. The diseased person was quarantined and cut off from the rest of society. The leper was considered unclean according to Jewish law (**Leviticus 13:44–46**). Whenever they approached a person, the leper was required to yell, "Unclean! Unclean!" As a result, they were isolated socially and spiritually and treated as outcasts.

TEACHING THE BIBLE LESSON

LIFE NEED FOR TODAY'S LESSON

AIM: Students will learn that some people are able to express their gratitude with sincerity and others with difficulty, and some are ungrateful for what is done for them.

INTRODUCTION

The 10 Lepers

In this lesson, Jesus is on His way to Jerusalem and finds Himself on the border between Galilee and Samaria. It is significant that as He reaches this border, He encounters ten lepers; the borders are geographical margins and the lepers exist on the social margins of society. The lepers in this Scripture are not the same as in Jesus' previous encounter with a leper (**Luke 5:12–15**). In **Luke 5**, the leper is in the city amidst many other people,

Read this

indicating that he was not treated in the same way as most lepers, though Luke does not tell us why he's treated differently. Lepers were the outcasts of society, as they could not be near others nor participate in the religious rites of the Jewish community. Jesus not only talks to lepers but touches and heals them.

This healing was different than Jesus' previous healing of lepers; it did not require His touch. He only commanded them to show themselves to the priests. This type of healing can be classified as a word of command and is very common in the Gospel narratives. When Jesus touched the leper in Luke, His compassion was more of the focus or theme; here as He speaks this word of command, absent physical touch, His power is on display, though only one leper recognizes and acknowledges it.

BIBLE LEARNING

AIM: Students will know that faith and a sincere spirit helped the healed man express his thanks and praise to Jesus.

I. TEN LEPERS ASK FOR HEALING (LUKE 17:11–13)

Jesus encounters ten lepers who observe Him entering a village. They keep their distance because leprosy was known to be contagious. One of the ten lepers, a Samaritan, lived among the group. Ordinary Jews refused to settle in the same area inhabited by Samaritans. However, the lepers, isolated from the general population, bonded and ignored ethnicity. They cry out to Jesus, addressing Him as Master. This title indicates He had authority as a chief commander, rabbi, and teacher. They ask Him to have mercy, desiring for Him to extend compassion and alleviate their misery. They acknowledge Jesus as a worker of miracles, one who had a history of healing incurable diseases (**Luke 5:15**).

Luke 17:11–19

Jewish, digried social norms

11 And it came to pass, as he went to Jerusalem, that he passed through the midst of Samaria and Galilee.

This pericope (a self-contained section of the Gospel narrative) is a continuation of the travel narrative found in Luke, which has limited direct reference to Jesus' travel and begins in **9:51** and ends in **19:27–48**. The narrative's focus is not on the travel specifics, but Jesus' interactions with followers, crowds, Pharisees, and others interpreting the Law. His final destination is Jerusalem, the Holy City. Joel B. Green asserts the ambiguity of the location does not directly inform us what kind of people He will encounter; however, the verse suggests he could interact with Samaritans. Previously in Luke's Gospel, Samaria was a site of divisiveness, as found in **9:51–56**.

12 And as he entered into a certain village, there met him ten men that were lepers, which stood afar off.

This verse presents socio-cultural boundaries that are important to note. The ten men are identified by their physical condition which requires physical boundaries. We learn about the geographic limitations of lepers in **Numbers 5:2**, and lepers are also found gathering near the city entrance in **2 Kings 7:3–5**. Leprosy was a disorder with physical, emotional, and spiritual consequences, as those identified as lepers were dislocated from their communities and unable to worship.

Luke first presents an account of leprosy in **5:12–14**. As with parables, the identification of a specific number indicates a large group. Francois Brown contends we should not seek symbolic significance from the number referenced.

13 And they lifted up their voices, and said, Jesus, Master, have mercy on us

Even if they are on the outskirts of the city because of their condition, the lepers know who has entered the city. They call out to Jesus, whom they have heard about and believe can respond to their situation. Those who are sick are often thought to be weak, but these men had the strength to cry out. They do not whimper or whine, but lift their collective voices to get Jesus' attention.

The title of "Master" used by the lepers is peculiar in the New Testament and is often heard from the disciples. The Greek word used here is *epistates* (eh-pee-STA-tase), a word used to identify someone as a "boss" or "chief" with the focus on their power. When Jesus' disciples used the honorary title, it demonstrates their weak faith and limited understanding. "In the development of the story, these ten men suffering from 'leprosy' were, with one exception, to reveal the limits of their appropriate initial confidence" (Brown).

II. JESUS HEALS THE TEN LEPERS (v. 14)

Jesus instructs the lepers to go to the priest, the only authority able to pronounce them clean and permit them to re-enter their communities (**Leviticus 13:13**). After being observed by the priest and declared cured, the examiner would perform a ceremonial cleansing called the Law of the Leper (**Leviticus 14**).

All ten men start toward the Temple to find the priest, demonstrating extreme faith. Previously, Jesus healed a leper immediately by touching him (**Luke 5:12–13**); these lepers did not receive instant healing but acted exclusively on Jesus' word. They were told to report to the priest, spots still covered their bodies. As they make their way down the road, they realize their flesh is healthy.

A Ritual of Healing

14 And when he saw them, he said unto them, Go shew yourselves unto the priests. And it came to pass, that, as they went, they were cleansed.

To heal them, Jesus tells the lepers to go show themselves to the priests. Lepers were prohibited from entering the Temple and approaching the priests. If the Jews' place of worship was in Jerusalem, then the Samaritans must determine which priests to show themselves to because of the division between the Jews and the Samaritans. Here we begin to see how Jesus becomes the mediator between both groups. The inspection they will undergo by the priests is explained in the Old Testament in **Leviticus 14:1–32**. Although there was a ritual to identify and ban them from their communities, there was also a ritual if a leper was healed. After being examined by the priest, a leper could be designated "clean."

III. ONE LEPER RETURNS TO THANK JESUS (vv. 15–19)

One leper sees the recovery of his body, stops, and goes back. After finding Jesus, he loudly proclaims God's greatness. Prostrated at Jesus' feet, he expresses gratitude. His posture testifies that Jesus deserved the same honor as God (**Psalm 95:6, Revelation 4:10**). Jesus asks the one returning leper, "Where are the nine?" (**v. 17**). The others, after being declared clean by the priest, went on their way, living their lives, perhaps taking their healing for granted. Jesus instructs the Samaritan to get up and go his way. The healed leper obtains more than physical healing: Jesus also says he was made "whole," indicating the leper's salvation (**Luke 7:50**). For Luke, genuine faith made you not only physically but also spiritually well.

Glorifying God

15 And one of them, when he saw that he was healed, turned back, and with a loud voice glorified God.

En route to the priests, the lepers realize they were healed; however, one leper does not continue on to the Temple to receive clearance from the priests. Instead, he returns to the one who restored him. The Samaritan's healing is not only an account of physical healing, but also redirecting his life, which is representative of what occurs with the salvific work of Christ. The voice once joining in the collective cry is now a solo voice with a shout. As a leper, he shouted from afar, but as a cleansed and restored man, he can come directly into Jesus' presence.

16 And fell down on his face at his feet, giving him thanks: and he was a Samaritan.

The act of worship exhibited by the Samaritan went beyond just calling Jesus "master"; he has physically shown his submission by falling at Jesus' feet, showing that the one who has healed is worthy to be praised. By indicating that the man is a Samaritan, Luke indicates that God's mercy extends beyond boundaries as will the message of the Gospel. The Greek term for the Samaritan's thanksgiving is *eucharisteo* (ew-khah-rees-TEH-oh), from which we get the word eucharist to refer to Communion. The word means to show gratitude, at times specifically through prayer.. While a reader could become fixated on this man's identification as an outsider, the main point is this man's desire to praise God for the gift of restoration, both physical and spiritual.

17 And Jesus answering said, Were there not ten cleansed? but where are the nine? 18 There are not found that returned to give glory to God, save this stranger.

Though some translations render the Greek *katharizo* (ka-tha-REED-zo) here as "healed," the KJV renders the word "cleansed," which better captures the word's possible religious connotations. Although Jesus adheres to the purity standards of the culture and sends the lepers to the priests for clearance, one man could not go on without giving honor to God for the healing no other could grant.

This story is told not to isolate the one leper as the one who did the right thing, but rather focus on

the proper response to God's grace. "It is right to give our thanks and praise," suggests The Great Thanksgiving, which is included in the liturgies of churches of many traditions (Book of Common Prayer). Thanksgiving is given to Jesus, but glory is given to God because His work is done publicly through Jesus.

The Greek word for foreigner is *allogenes* (al-lo-ghen-ACE; from another tribe or family), and occurs numerous times in the Greek Old Testament but only here in the New Testament, probably because tribal affiliations were not as central during the Roman Empire and other terms became more widely used, such as the word *ethnos* (ETH-nos, a people who associate themselves due to geography, ethnicity, religion and/or political affiliation), which is usually translated as Gentile. Samaritans identified themselves as descendants of Abraham, but historically a rift occurred that caused Samaritans to worship at Mt. Gerizim, while Israelites and later Jews worshiped in Jerusalem. Jesus is emphasizing that, like the Gentiles (7:9), those who are considered outsiders among His Jewish audience sometimes exhibit exemplary faith.

In the books of Luke and Acts, Luke shows us that Samaritans and Gentiles often respond with more faith and gratitude than the Jews who are God's chosen people. Luke consistently shows these reversals where the one expected to give praise or thanks does not respond accordingly. Thus, Jews and insiders aren't the only ones privileged to receive divine mercy.

19 And he said unto him, Arise, go thy way: thy faith hath made thee whole.

Jesus offers words to the leper echoed in other healing narratives. Previously in **Luke 8:46–48**, healing associated with faith was received by the woman in the crowd who touched Jesus' garment.

SEARCH THE SCRIPTURES

QUESTION 1

What did Jesus ask about the nine lepers?

Jesus wanted to know what happened to them since only one of the 10 returned to thank Him.

QUESTION 2

The man who returned to thank Jesus was from where?

Samaria.

LIGHT ON THE WORD

Jesus Healed the Samaritan

Whether it is the restoration of vision or body parts, the one healed or cleansed, in this instance, will rise and walk into their new reality. The healed Samaritan man is now a part of the people of God. He has not only been physically but also spiritually made whole.

BIBLE APPLICATION

AIM: Students will accept that believers are forgive those who commit wrongdoings against us.

We daily see how much easier it is to complain than give thanks. Mental disorders, busy schedules, aggravation, loneliness, anger, and stress all cause us to whine and complain instead of be grateful. The media stirs up an attitude of wanting more and being discontent. The negative attitudes are a result of ignoring God, and not acknowledging Him as the source of all our possessions and well-being.

STUDENT'S RESPONSES

AIM: Students will learn that Jesus wants us to have genuine faith and do as He has called us to do: forgive.

Read **Psalm 100:4–5**. Sometime this week make up a prayer, song, poem, praise dance, or something creative based on these verses and the lesson. Share it with a member of your family, friend, or co-worker and ask them to be an accountability person. When you start complaining, tell them to remind you of your creative piece and your desire to be more grateful.

PRAYER

God, thank You for healing us and helping us. When we feel rejected or are rejected, we know that You care for us. Let us show love to others. In Jesus' name we pray. Amen.

HOW TO SAY IT

Foreigner.	FOR-in-er.
Leprosy.	LEH-pruh-see.
Pericope.	peh-RI-co-pee.

PREPARE FOR NEXT SUNDAY

Read **Luke 18:9–14** and "Humble Faith."

DAILY HOME BIBLE READINGS

MONDAY
God Cares for All
(Deuteronomy 11:12–21)

TUESDAY
A Psalm of Thanksgiving
(Jonah 2:2–9)

WEDNESDAY
Powerful God
(Psalm 9:1–4, 7–10)

THURSDAY
Thankful Reverence for God
(Hebrews 12:25–28)

FRIDAY
Living Gratefully
(Colossians 2:6–12)

SATURDAY
Giving Thanks
(Luke 22:14–20)

SUNDAY
Grateful Faith
(Luke 17:11–19)

Sources:

Brown, Francois. *A Commentary of the Gospel of Luke 9:51-19:27.* Fortress Press: Minneapolis, MN. 2013.

Carroll, John T. Luke 17:11-19, *Interpretation: A Journal of Bible and Theology.* Oct. 1, 1999, Vol 53 Issue 4. 405-408.

Green, Joel B. *The Gospel of Luke.* W.B. Eerdmans Publishing; Grand Rapids, Michigan. 1997.

The Holy Eucharist: Rite Two. http://www.bcponline.org/HE/he2.htm. Accessed December 4, 2014.

COMMENTS / NOTES:

HUMBLE FAITH

BIBLE BASIS: LUKE 18:9–14

BIBLE TRUTH: Jesus taught that prayer spoken in humility has power over a prayer spoken self-righteousness.

MEMORY VERSE: "And the publican, standing afar off, would not lift up so much as his eyes unto heaven, but smote upon his breast, saying, God be merciful to me a sinner" (Luke 18:13).

LESSON AIM: By the end of the lesson, we will: KNOW why the Pharisee's words were wrong and the tax collector's words were right; APPRECIATE God's mercy and grace; and INSPECT, and if necessary correct, our motivation for our own piety.

TEACHER PREPARATION

MATERIALS NEEDED: Quarterly Commentary/Teacher Manual, Adult Quarterly, Adult resources—charts, worksheets, and other teaching tools, paper, pens, pencils, Bibles (several different versions)

OTHER MATERIALS NEEDED / TEACHER'S NOTES:

_____

_____

LESSON OVERVIEW

LIFE NEED FOR TODAY'S LESSON
The faithful wonder whether their words, which are sometimes spoken out of desperation, will make a difference.

BIBLE LEARNING
Humble faith allows the power and presence of God to prevail.

BIBLE APPLICATION
Humility is marked by the person who credits God and others for their success.

STUDENTS' RESPONSES
Christians come to accept that Jesus hears our prayers.

LESSON SCRIPTURE

LUKE 18:9–14, KJV

9 And he spake this parable unto certain which trusted in themselves that they were righteous, and despised others:

10 Two men went up into the temple to pray; the one a Pharisee, and the other a publican.

LUKE 18:9–14, NIV

9 To some who were confident of their own righteousness and looked down on everyone else, Jesus told this parable:

10 "Two men went up to the temple to pray, one a Pharisee and the other a tax collector.

11 The Pharisee stood and prayed thus with himself, God, I thank thee, that I am not as other men are, extortioners, unjust, adulterers, or even as this publican.

11 The Pharisee stood by himself and prayed: 'God, I thank you that I am not like other people—robbers, evildoers, adulterers—or even like this tax collector.

12 I fast twice in the week, I give tithes of all that I possess.

12 I fast twice a week and give a tenth of all I get.'

13 And the publican, standing afar off, would not lift up so much as his eyes unto heaven, but smote upon his breast, saying, God be merciful to me a sinner.

13 "But the tax collector stood at a distance. He would not even look up to heaven, but beat his breast and said, 'God, have mercy on me, a sinner.'

14 I tell you, this man went down to his house justified rather than the other: for every one that exalteth himself shall be abased; and he that humbleth himself shall be exalted.

14 "I tell you that this man, rather than the other, went home justified before God. For all those who exalt themselves will be humbled, and those who humble themselves will be exalted."

LIGHT ON THE WORD

Pharisees. A religious group very popular in first-century Palestine. The name Pharisee means "separatists." This name may have come from their tendency to stress the importance of ritual purity and eating exclusively with righteous Jews. They also stressed the importance of following the oral tradition in order to keep the Law handed down by Moses. As a result, they often came into conflict with Jesus, who summed up the Law as loving God with your whole being and loving your neighbor as yourself.

Publicans. Publicans were tax collectors and custom officers. They worked for Rome and collected taxes in various provinces. The tax system was open to abuse, and many publicans were extortioners who created taxes in order to profit. As most Jewish tax collectors would tax and extort their own people, they were considered traitors. To work for Rome was to be not only an outcast but a sinner in the eyes of the average Jew. The Gospel accounts record Jesus having two significant encounters with tax collectors: one with Matthew, who became one of the twelve disciples (**Matthew 9:9**), and the other with Zacchaeus, who repented of his extortion and paid back four times what he stole (**Luke 19:1–9**).

TEACHING THE BIBLE LESSON

LIFE NEED FOR TODAY'S LESSON

AIM: Students will understand how the faithful wonder whether their words, which are sometimes spoken out of desperation, will make a difference.

INTRODUCTION

Two Approaches to Prayer

Luke was a physician (**Colossians 4:14**), a ministry partner to the Apostle Paul (**2 Timothy 4:11; Philemon 23–24**), and the author both of the Gospel of Luke and of Acts. To pen his Gospel, Luke relied on extensive investigative research believed to have been gleaned from the apostles, including Paul, and other eyewitnesses (**Luke 1:1–3**). Throughout his account, Luke hones in on Jesus' core teaching that salvation and redemption are available to anyone who believes—Jew or Gentile, rich or poor, Pharisee or tax collector.

The parable in today's lesson reveals how Pharisees and tax collectors—societal polar opposites—approach prayer. The Pharisee prayed from an attitude of arrogance and self-righteousness, detailing his good character and works in contemplative prayer to himself. The tax collector drew near to God, praying from a repentant heart that acknowledged sin and begged for His mercy.

Examining the dual prayers, we can appreciate the difference between self-righteous platitudes and true gratitude for God's mercy and grace. Jesus commended the tax collector, saying, "This sinner, not the Pharisee, returned home justified before God" (from **v. 14**, NLT). The parable's message to Christians is clear: humble faith encompasses every area of life, including our prayers.

BIBLE LEARNING

AIM: Students will accept that a humble faith allows the power and presence of God to prevail.

I. HAUGHTY FAITH (LUKE 18:9–12)

Jesus told parables to illustrate real-life issues. In the parable of the Pharisee and tax collector, He highlighted the differences in the content and manner of their public prayer; these, in turn, demonstrated what was so wrong about what the Pharisee said and right about what the tax collector said. From their prayers, we learn that prayer mirrors the heart. We also learn that prayer is the ideal vehicle for expressing gratitude for all God has done for us and brought us through. Unfortunately, the Pharisee's prayer fell short of true thanksgiving because it exclusively focused on self-exaltation, exposing his prideful heart. **Luke 6:45** lets us know the importance of the heart as the source of good or evil.

Answered prayer can spark arrogance. How do we share answered prayers? Some give God all glory, humbly admitting His role in our provision, protection, or other answered prayer. Others give a testimony peppered with sentences and phrases that begin with "I." If we are not careful, like the Pharisee, we can become haughty, attributing answered prayers to our righteousness, eloquent or anguished words, acts of service, or financial stewardship (tithes, offerings, "love gifts," etc.). The Pharisee's prayer made mention of things he considered noteworthy; the tax collector's prayer was devoid of such items.

Luke 18:9–14

The parable of the Pharisee and the publican is found only in the Gospel of Luke. It focuses on the type of person God approves of, and contrasts pride and humility.

9 And he spake this parable unto certain which trusted in themselves that they were righteous, and despised others: 10 Two men went up into the temple to pray; the one a Pharisee, and the other a publican. 11 The Pharisee stood and prayed thus with himself, God, I thank thee, that I am not as other men are, extortioners, unjust, adulterers, or even as this publican. 12 I fast twice in the week, I give tithes of all that I possess.

Jesus proposes a parable to certain people who consider themselves righteous and despise others; it may be a reference to the Pharisees or the legalistic Jews (cf. **Romans 10:2–3**). The Pharisees regarded themselves as the pillars of righteousness and maintainers of a higher standard for obeying Israel's covenant stipulations. As such they became guardians and enforcers in matters of the Law, especially ritual purity, Sabbath keeping, and tithing. The concern for ritual purity expanded into a concern for table fellowship and keeping proper company. Excluded from table fellowship were those sinners who broke the Law, such as publicans and tax collectors. This explains the Pharisee's later distancing of himself from the tax collector.

A Pharisee and a publican went up to the Temple to pray (v. 10). Private prayer in the Temple was possible any time, and public prayers took place twice daily (Luke 1:9–10; Acts 3:1). The first hour of prayer was 9 a.m., the second at 3 p.m. These two times coincided with the morning and evening sacrifice (Exodus 29:39). Prayer also came to be viewed as equal to a sacrifice to God (Psalm 141:2, Proverbs 15:8). The two men may have gone to the Temple at a spontaneous time or during these specific hours designated for prayer.

The Pharisee "stood and prayed." Standing was one of the many acceptable positions for prayer in Judaism, but in Matthew 6:5, Jesus points out the hypocrisy behind that posture. The Pharisee, with self-confidence, thanks God, first for all the bad things he does not do, then for all the good he does (vv. 11–12). He went up into the Temple to pray, but not to God; he "prayed thus with himself." He shows his righteousness by holding himself against not the Law of God but "other men" and even "this publican" (v. 11). The good people are known by their religious practice such as fasting twice a week and tithing from their possessions. The Pharisee, in his pride and self-righteousness, was guilty of the sin of self-sufficiency, which recognizes no need of God's power.

II. HUMBLE FAITH (v. 13)

The tax collector prayed to exhibit humility. He stood at a distance, considering himself unworthy to be near the Temple grounds. In contrast, the Pharisee believed he was entitled to God's presence. The tax collector's avoidance of looking at Heaven shows that he was aware of his sin and his unworthiness to stand before a holy God. His posture shows he wants to experience mercy versus one who has no need for mercy.

Instead of congratulating himself, he beats his chest in sorrow. This was not a happy or self-righteous prayer, but one of sorrow. The tax collector was sorry for his sins. He has no religious resume. The only thing he remembers is that his sins make him desperately in need of God. He has nothing to bring to God but his need. This is the correct posture for prayer; it is not about what we have done or can do, but about our desire for God and His mercy in our lives.

In church, believers may look at how a person prays and assume that he or she is praying from a heart of arrogance or humility. All too often, we make snap judgments based on such attributes as volume (Is he/she "praying the house down" with loud, forceful words, or quietly asking for God's help?) or posture (Prostrate or standing? Hands lifted or not?). However, as the parable shows, our words are the true harbingers of haughty or humble faith.

Praying for Mercy

13 And the publican, standing afar off, would not lift up so much as his eyes unto heaven, but smote upon his breast, saying, God be merciful to me a sinner.

The publican's attitude and words show his humility and his profound repentance from his sins. First he is "standing afar off," at a distance from the sanctuary and others. Second, he "would not lift up so much as his eyes unto heaven" as a sign of his unworthiness before God. Third, he "smote upon his breast" as a sign of profound grief, a common expression of mourning in the cultures of the ancient Near East. Here the publican shows intense sorrow for his sin.

Finally, he speaks simple words: "God be merciful to me a sinner." The words "be merciful" translate the Greek verb *hilaskomai* (**hi-LAS-ko-my**), meaning to wipe away or show mercy (also Hebrews 2:17). The word conveys the idea of God's mercy giving a total pardon. The publican prays for God's mercy so that his sins may be forgiven. He does not use a lot of words; his prayer is a cry from his soul.

III. HUMILITY'S REWARDS (v. 14)

In the parable, Jesus identifies two key rewards of humility: first, God exalts those who are humble. According to this world's way of thinking, we must exalt ourselves, but in the Kingdom of God, those who humble themselves receive God's exaltation. To go down in the Kingdom is to go up. A second reward is that God justifies the person who prays humbly.

As maturing Christians, we want our prayers to be received and answered by God. That only happens when we walk before Him in humble faith, as evidenced by our daily Christian walk—including our prayers.

Humble and Exalted

14 I tell you, this man went down to his house justified rather than the other: for every one that exalteth himself shall be abased; and he that humbleth himself shall be exalted.

Jesus declares that the publican goes back forgiven, unlike the Pharisee. The Pharisee goes home unaccepted, unjustified, and still under God's displeasure because he counts on his own merit. The publican is justified by faith without work (cf. **Ephesians 2:8–9; Genesis 15:6**). Through His parable, Jesus teaches that justification is by faith, not works.

Jesus concludes the parable by saying "he that humbleth himself shall be exalted" (cf. **Matthew 23:12; 1 Peter 5:5–6**). He here warns the disciples against the consequences of pride. Whoever exalts himself before men will be lowered. We cannot approach God on the basis of our own justice. Self-confidence and proud judgment toward others close the door of Heaven, even if we are zealous and religious as the Pharisee.

SEARCH THE SCRIPTURES

QUESTION 1

Standing to prayer was the way that many persons prayed. The publican prayed standing up and did what during his time of prayer?

He stood away from people and the sanctuary; did not lift up his eyes; and hit his chest.

QUESTION 2

If you exalt yourself, then you will be _____.

Abased.

LIGHT ON THE WORD

True Humility

True humility and repentance open the door of Heaven and get answers to prayer. When we pray, we must see God's holiness and our own miserable state as a repentant sinner. Then prayer becomes genuine.

BIBLE APPLICATION

AIM: Students will explore how humility is marked by the person who credits God and others for their success.

Public prayer offers a forum for people to be drawn humbly into God's presence. At times, however, public prayer can be a platform for individuals to showcase eloquence, educational training, or new attire. All prayer is not created equal. When given the opportunity, let us model humble faith via prayer that 1) seeks God's mercy; and 2) extends an invitation for us to model humility in every area of Christian service, including prayer.

STUDENT'S RESPONSES

AIM: Students will accept that Jesus hears our prayers.

Ask God to help you identify and eliminate self-exaltation in your own prayers. Try this: write down one of your recent public prayers (i.e., at a meal, at church, with a friend). Now, in light of today's parable, ask God's forgiveness for any pride that you exhibited. Then rewrite the prayer based on information you learned from today's lesson.

PRAYER

Thank You God for giving us opportunities to know that You are greater than us. As we rest in You, may our humble spirits that are pleasing before You, be acceptable in all that we do and say. In Jesus' name we pray. Amen.

HOW TO SAY IT

Pharisee.   FAIR-ih-see.

Publican.   PUH-bli-kin.

Extortioner.   ek-STOR-shi-ner.

PREPARE FOR NEXT SUNDAY

Read **Luke 18:15–17, Mark 10:16** and "Childlike Faith."

DAILY HOME BIBLE READINGS

MONDAY
Faith in a Merciful God
(Deuteronomy 4:32–40)

TUESDAY
Faith in a Trustworthy God
(Daniel 9:15–19)

WEDNESDAY
Living Humbly
(Micah 6:6–8; 7:18–19)

THURSDAY
Living a Blessed Life
(Matthew 5:1–10)

FRIDAY
Living a Peaceful Life
(1 Peter 2:9–16)

SATURDAY
Living a Fulfilled Life
(Luke 1:68–80)

SUNDAY
Humble Faith
(Luke 18:9–14)

Sources:

Bock, Darrell L. *The NIV Application Commentary: Luke*. Grand Rapids, MI: Zondervan, 1996. 241.

Ellis, E. Earle. *The New Century Bible Commentary: The Gospel of Luke*. Grand Rapids, MI: Eerdmans. Reprint, 1983. 129.

Geldenhuys, Norval. *The New International Commentary on the New Testament: The Gospel of Luke*. Grand Rapids, MI: Eerdmans. Reprint, 1983.

Gooding, David. *According to Luke*. Leiscester, England: InterVarsity Press, 1987.

Morris, Leon. *Tyndale New Testament Commentaries: The Gospel According to Saint Luke: An Introduction and Commentary*. Grand Rapids, MI: Wm. B. Eerdmans Publishing Co., 1974.

COMMENTS / NOTES:

_____

_____

_____

_____

_____

_____

_____

_____

_____

_____

_____

_____

_____

_____

_____

_____

_____

_____

CHILDLIKE FAITH

BIBLE BASIS: LUKE 18:15–17; MARK 10:16

BIBLE TRUTH: Jesus taught that to receive the gift of the Kingdom of God, the faithful must become as children.

MEMORY VERSE: "Verily I say unto you, Whosoever shall not receive the kingdom of God as a little child shall in no wise enter therein" (Luke 18:17).

LESSON AIM: By the end of the lesson, we will: KNOW Jesus valued children and that they were models for His Kingdom; BELIEVE that we should seek to cultivate in ourselves the qualities of children; and COMMIT to self-examinations and improvements with childlike faith.

TEACHER PREPARATION

MATERIALS NEEDED: Quarterly Commentary/Teacher Manual, Adult Quarterly, Adult resources—charts, worksheets, and other teaching tools, paper, pens, pencils, Bibles (several different versions)

OTHER MATERIALS NEEDED / TEACHER'S NOTES:

_____

_____

LESSON OVERVIEW

LIFE NEED FOR TODAY'S LESSON
Children's openness to life is a worthy model for everyone.

BIBLE LEARNING
Jesus placed a high value on children and their ability to show openness and trust.

BIBLE APPLICATION
Believers should develop a childlike faith that cultivates a deeper trust, respects, and honors God.

STUDENTS' RESPONSES
Believers can develop a better sense of how to develop a stronger with God through by having a childlike faith.

LESSON SCRIPTURE

LUKE 18:15–17; MARK 10:16, KJV

15 And they brought unto him also infants, that he would touch them: but when his disciples saw it, they rebuked them.

16 But Jesus called them unto him, and said, Suffer little children to come unto me, and

LUKE 18:15–17; MARK 10:16, NIV

15 People were also bringing babies to Jesus for him to place his hands on them. When the disciples saw this, they rebuked them.

16 But Jesus called the children to him and said, "Let the little children come to me, and forbid them not: for of such is the kingdom of God.

17 Verily I say unto you, Whosoever shall not receive the kingdom of God as a little child shall in no wise enter therein.

Mark 10:16 And he took them up in his arms, put his hands upon them, and blessed them.

do not hinder them, for the kingdom of God belongs to such as these.

17 Truly I tell you, anyone who will not receive the kingdom of God like a little child will never enter it."

Mark 10:16 And he took the children in his arms, placed his hands on them and blessed them.

LIGHT ON THE WORD

Infants and children. Jewish people highly valued children, the instruments through which their legacy as a people and as individual families would continue (**Genesis 1:28**). As a result, children were viewed as a blessing (**Psalm 127:3–5**). Even still, children had no social status and were considered unimportant in society. Not so with Jesus, who welcomed children, thwarting the disciples' attempt to block the children's access to Him.

Laying on of hands. An act of blessings and/or healing. In the Old Testament, laying on of hands is used to bless children (**Genesis 48:13–20**) or appoint someone to a position (**Numbers 27:15–23**). This practice continues in the New Testament. The teachers and prophets at Antioch laid their hands on Paul and Barnabas in order to bless their ministry and confirm their new positions as apostles (**Acts 13:1–3**). Jesus healed many by laying on hands—a leper (**Matthew 8:2–3**), Peter's mother-in-law (**Matthew 8:14–15**), Jairus' daughter (**Luke 8:54**), a man who was deaf and mute (**Mark 7:31–35**), and others. Paul warns Timothy against hastily laying hands on others because it also indicates a responsbility or sharing in their actions (**1 Timothy 5:22**).

TEACHING THE BIBLE LESSON

LIFE NEED FOR TODAY'S LESSON

AIM: Students will learn that a child's

openness to life is a worthy model to follow.

INTRODUCTION

Jesus Loves and Respects Children

In Luke 18, Jesus taught two parables about prayer: one with an emphasis on persistent prayer that revealed God as just, the other concerning humility in prayer. Sometime after these teachings, parents brought their children to Jesus "that he would touch them" (**18:15**).

The parents' actions mirrored the lessons in Jesus' parables. They persisted in bringing their children despite social norms that dictated otherwise, and they exemplified humility, believing Jesus had the power to heal. The disciples missed the similarities and an ideal opportunity to demonstrate that they understood Jesus' teaching that God is just and rewards the humble. More troubling, they rebuked the parents, proving they did not have the heart of their leader.

According to Mark, "[Jesus] was much displeased" (**Mark 10:14**, KJV) when the disciples did this. Therefore, He rebuked the disciples, informing them that the Kingdom of God is made up of believers who approach Him and His Kingdom with childlike faith. Jesus then "took [the children] up in his arms, put his hands upon them and blessed them" (from **Mark 10:16**, KJV). By doing so, Jesus reinforced that He valued children, as well as believers who embodied childlike faith.

BIBLE LEARNING

AIM: Students will understand that Jesus placed a high value on children and their ability to show openness and trust.

I. ALL GOD'S CHILDREN
(LUKE 18:15; MARK 10:16)

Throughout the Old and New Testament, covenant believers have been dubbed "children" to denote their relationship as people of God and beneficiaries of covenant access and blessings. The term first referred to the Israelites but now also applies to born-again believers. The Apostle Paul explains, "The Spirit of God, who raised Jesus from the dead, lives in [us]" (**Romans 8:11**), and that we "received God's Spirit when he adopted [us] as his own children. Now we call him, 'Abba, Father.' For his Spirit joins with our spirit to affirm that we are God's children. And since we are his children, we are his heirs" (from **vv. 15–17**). Jesus' touching the children reaffirms that God welcomes all who come to Him.

Luke 18:15–17; Mark 10:16

The Gospel of Luke sharing stories with Mark deserves some attention, as they had different motives in their writing. In **Mark 10:1–12**, for instance, Mark writes about marriage and divorce—a subject which connects well with subject of blessing children. Luke's avoiding this section and placing this story among others talking about discipleship and the Kingdom of God suggests a different emphasis. Most of the material in **Mark 10:1–12** is paralleled in various places in Luke's Gospel, so he may have left it out intentionally.

Luke builds up his story of Jesus' progress toward Jerusalem, preparing the reader for the crescendo coming in **Luke 19:28–46**—with Jesus' arrival in Jerusalem. As Luke comes toward the end of this travel section, the theme of the Kingdom of God becomes prominent. In this chapter, he dedicates these three verses to this story of parents bringing even infants to be touched by Jesus following the two parables—one about the desperate woman and the unjust judge and the other about a Pharisee and a publican in prayer at the Temple—which, taken together, are about the vindication of God for God's people living in humility and with penitent faith.

15 People were bringing even infants to him that he might touch them; and when the disciples saw it, they sternly ordered them not to do it.

While Matthew and Mark say little children (Gk. *paidia*, **pie-DEE-ah**), were brought to Jesus, Luke says they were infants (Gk. *brephe*, **BREH-phay**). He makes his emphasis by adding "even" to the statement, suggesting that the children were among other people being brought to Jesus. Possibly some brought toddlers or diseased elders to be healed, but the disciples found bringing infants problematic. Luke says that the parents brought the children to Jesus so He might touch them. Matthew says for Jesus to "put His hands on them and pray," or invoke a "blessing" on them (**Matthew 19:13**), while Mark adds that Jesus "laid his hands on them, and blessed them" (**Mark 10:16**).

Bringing children to the elderly for blessing is a custom that we find in the Old Testament (**Genesis 48:14–15**). As a longstanding tradition, people brought their children to the elders, scribes, or rabbis for a prayer of blessing on the evening of the Day of Atonement, believing that the blessings of a respected religious figure would be beneficial. Jewish children were brought to the rabbi for a blessing on their first birthday. Some cultures still do this today, such as in most parts of Africa and the Middle East where respectable elders pronounce blessings upon children. These blessings are believed to be able to influence someone's future.

When the disciples saw the infants brought to Jesus, they rebuked "them," probably both the parents and the children. Jesus may have been busy and the disciples felt it necessary to protect His time and priorities. They probably thought it would waste Jesus' time and abuse His kindness. Children can wait, after all, or come another day. Matthew precedes this story with Jesus agreeing with the disciples that, "It is better not to marry" (**Matthew 19:10**, NIV), suggesting that the solitary life, like eunuchs with no family ties to claim attention, are better for the work of the Kingdom. Was this teaching still on their minds? Would Jesus giving attention to these children be a waste of precious time?

II. A FATHER'S REBUKE (vv. 15–16)

Jesus, the consummate mentor, fulfilled Isaiah's prophecy: "And the Spirit of the Lord will rest on him—the Spirit of wisdom and understanding, the Spirit of counsel and might, the Spirit of knowledge and the fear of the Lord. He will delight in obeying the Lord" (**Isaiah 11:2–3**). As such, He trained the disciples in accurate doctrine and taught them God's ways. As any good mentor, He also corrected the disciples as necessary. Today we benefit from the same rebuke that turns our heart to Father God. And each mature believer who has childlike faith will believe God and gladly follow His spiritual guidance.

Jesus' Special Children's Invitation

16 But Jesus called for them and said, "Let the little children come to me, and do not stop them; for it is to such as these that the kingdom of God belongs.

However, when Jesus saw this, Mark tells us that He was greatly displeased. He called the children to Himself and said to the disciples, "Let the little children come to me, and do not forbid them" (**v. 16**, NKJV). "Let" (NLT) or "suffer" (KJV) is from the Greek verb aphiemi (**ah-FEE-ay-mee**) which means to physically release or set free, or in a figurative sense to permit or to forgive with regard to sin. Jesus is telling the adults not

to hold the children back, suggesting that their instinct draws them to Him. No one is too small to be brought to Jesus; He has time to attend to even the least of us. He will attend to those who can do nothing for Him—even infants. What a difference it would make for the church if many Christians followed this example. The measure of a person is how they treat those who cannot reciprocate. This Gospel is needed especially now, when Christian communities are not sure what to do with the poor in their societies.

Jesus added that the Kingdom of God belongs to those who are like these children. Of course, it is not simply these children, but all who are spiritually like children. He makes children models of what it takes to be a citizen of the Kingdom of God. He says they most truly show us what it means to accept and enter God's Kingdom. Nolland writes, "Is it their openness, willingness to trust, freedom from hypocrisy or pretention, conscious weakness and readiness for dependence?" The helplessness of children, and their complete trust of those who love and care for them, perfectly demonstrate the humble trust Jesus has been speaking of all along. Plummer adds, "It is not these children, nor all children, but those who are childlike in character, especially in humility and trustfulness, who are best suited for the Kingdom." These qualities are essential for entry into the Kingdom of God.

III. AWAKENING THE INNER FAITH-CHILD (v. 17)

Jesus taught that to receive the gift of the Kingdom of God, the faithful must become as children: open, attentive, and receptive to what God has freely given. Children's openness often manifests as curiosity; they are able to make new friends and experience new things simply because they are willing to trade the familiar for something new and different. At the time adults doubted whether Jesus was the Messiah, children chanted "hosanna" (**Matthew 21:15–16**).

Then, too, as natural children undergo growth and development, so do we as God's spiritual children. We grow through Bible study, fellowship with other believers, church attendance, and other spiritual disciplines. We flourish as we choose God's choice spiritual fare: "milk" representing the Word of God, and "meat" representing His will (**1 Peter 2:2, John 4:34**).

Many adults look down on children, despising their noise, naivete, and rambunctiousness. But their very best qualities are ones worth emulating and cultivating as we grow in Christ. That can only happen if we examine ourselves. Are we too exclusive, not allowing others to join our fellowships or learn from our spiritual experiences? Do we exhibit fear, refusing to step out in faith as God directs us in relationships, careers, or ministry opportunities? Do we hold tightly to the familiar ways of doing things, shutting down our younger believers whose ideas could enhance our churches, families, or workplaces? Honestly answering these questions will help us shed practices that inhibit our childlike faith.

Faith and Trust

17 Truly I tell you, whoever does not receive the kingdom of God as a little child will never enter it."

Luke brings his lesson to its climax: childlike humility is the gateway to the Kingdom. Jesus makes an earnest statement: "Truly, I tell you." He continues, away from the great displeasure that Mark mentioned earlier, to a teachable moment. He delivers a profound lesson that must change the disciples' lives—pride which may have led them to send the children away must give way to humility—and is modeled by the children themselves. Jesus declares that living in the Kingdom of God is only possible through childlike faith in a God who cares for us as His own children. However, this trust is not easy; it is a constant work in progress, for pride always looks to take us away from God's presence.

Mark 10:16 And he took them up in his arms, laid his hands on them, and blessed them.

Luke's account finishes with the lesson that whoever does not receive the Kingdom of God as a little child will never enter it. After this, Luke begins to talk about the rich young ruler—another story that teaches humility and self-denunciation as the key to the Kingdom of God. However, Mark finishes the story with Jesus actually taking the children up in His arms, laying His hands on them, and blessing them. Jesus does more than what was asked of Him: He embraces them, lifting them in His arms. Not only that, He blesses them (Gk. *eulogeo*, **ew-lo-GEH-oh**), meaning that He praises them and even shows them special favor. This continues the lesson that Jesus is teaching His disciples, not just by what He says but also by what He does: not just humility toward God, but also humility toward even "the least of these" (**Matthew 25:45**). If they sent the children away to protect His time, He showsthem that even these children deserve His time. True Kingdom humility cares for those who, like children, are sometimes marginalized.

SEARCH THE SCRIPTURES

QUESTION 1

Jesus responds to the presence of the children in **Mark 10:16** by doing what?

He takes them in His arms, puts His hands on them, and blesses them.

QUESTION 2

Jesus declared that you can only enter into the kingdom of God if you do what?

Receive the Kingdom of God as a little child.

LIGHT ON THE WORD

Children's Attitude and the Kingdom

The children represent the attitude that a person must have if they are to receive the Kingdom of God. In addition, Jesus is saying that children are welcome in God's Kingdom. God is available to them; His kingdom is not only for adults.

BIBLE APPLICATION

AIM: Students will know that believers should develop a childlike faith that cultivates a deeper trust, respects, and honors God.

It's so important to train children in godly instruction (**Proverbs 22:6**) and allow them to make decisions for Christ when young. Turning them away only leaves one alternative—the world. As we model Christ-like faith and behavior for children, we whet their appetites for God, His Word, and His Kingdom. When we show them that we can also learn from their examples of open, childlike faith, we also demonstrate to them their importance as current or future believers. Finally, God has no favorites (**Acts 10:34–35**), and He welcomes a close, satisfying relationship with each of His children—at the expense of none.

STUDENT'S RESPONSES

AIM: Students will appreciate that believers can develop a better sense of how to develop a stronger with God through by having a childlike faith.

What area of your faith has most suffered from your inability to exercise childlike faith? Have you drawn back from mission trips, financial giving, or praying for the sick and shut in? This week, ask God to help you return to your childlike faith in at least one of those areas. Then look for opportunities to exercise that faith this week.

PRAYER

God, our faith is sometimes not as strong as it should be. We waiver in our faith and have doubt because we cannot see or know what You are doing. Bless us to have and keep a childlike faith in our lives. In Jesus' name we pray. Amen.

HOW TO SAY IT

Disciple.   di-SAI-pul.

Consummate.   KAHN-su-mit.

PREPARE FOR NEXT SUNDAY

Read **Luke 19:1–10** and "Joyous Faith."

DAILY HOME BIBLE READINGS

MONDAY
Peaceful Faith
(Isaiah 11:1–9)

TUESDAY
Children of Light
(1 Thessalonians 5:1–11)

WEDNESDAY
Children of Freedom
(Galatians 3:23–29)

THURSDAY
Children of God
(Romans 8:12–17)

FRIDAY
Innocent Faith
(Matthew 18:1–5)

SATURDAY
Certain Faith
(Luke 1:46–56)

SUNDAY
Childlike Faith
(Luke 18:15–17; Mark 10:16)

Sources:
Dunn, James D. G., and J. W. Rogerson. *Eerdmans Commentary on the Bible.* Grand Rapids, MI: W.B. Eerdmans, 2003.
Marshall, I. Howard. *The Gospel of Luke: A Commentary on the Greek Text.* The New International Greek Testament Commentary. Exeter Eng.: Paternoster Press, 1978.
Nolland, John L. *Word Biblical Commentary.* Vol. 35b, Luke 9:21-18:34. edited by David A. Hubbard and Glenn W. Barker. Dallas, TX: Word Books, 1993.
Plummer, Alfred. *A Critical and Exegetical Commentary on the Gospel According to St. Luke.* The International Critical Commentary. 5th ed. Edinburgh: T & T Clark, 1902.

JOYOUS FAITH

BIBLE BASIS: LUKE 19:1–10

BIBLE TRUTH: Zacchaeus welcomed Jesus with great faith and repentance.

MEMORY VERSE: "For the Son of man is come to seek and to save that which was lost" (Luke 19:10).

LESSON AIM: By the end of the lesson, we will: REMEMBER the details of the encounter of Zacchaeus with Jesus; BELIEVE that they can make necessary dramatic changes in their lives with God's help; and REPENT of their shortcomings and then to commit to living godly lives.

TEACHER PREPARATION

MATERIALS NEEDED: Quarterly Commentary/Teacher Manual, Adult Quarterly, Adult resources—charts, worksheets, and other teaching tools, paper, pens, pencils, Bibles (several different versions)

OTHER MATERIALS NEEDED / TEACHER'S NOTES:

_____

_____

LESSON OVERVIEW

LIFE NEED FOR TODAY'S LESSON
All people have experienced a loss of direction in their lives and an inability to make necessary changes and new plans.

BIBLE APPLICATION
Believers must learn that repentance and making changes to follow the Lord create new opportunities and possibilities.

BIBLE LEARNING
Jesus declared that His own work was to seek and save the lost.

STUDENTS' RESPONSES
Believers can trust Jesus for direction and guidance in their lives.

LESSON SCRIPTURE

LUKE 19:1–10, KJV

1 And Jesus entered and passed through Jericho.

2 And, behold, there was a man named Zacchaeus, which was the chief among the publicans, and he was rich.

3 And he sought to see Jesus who he was; and could not for the press, because he was

LUKE 19:1–10, NIV

1 Jesus entered Jericho and was passing through.

2 A man was there by the name of Zacchaeus; he was a chief tax collector and was wealthy.

3 He wanted to see who Jesus was, but because he was short he could not see over

little of stature.

the crowd.

4 And he ran before, and climbed up into a sycomore tree to see him: for he was to pass that way.

4 So he ran ahead and climbed a sycamore-fig tree to see him, since Jesus was coming that way.

5 And when Jesus came to the place, he looked up, and saw him, and said unto him, Zacchaeus, make haste, and come down; for to day I must abide at thy house.

5 When Jesus reached the spot, he looked up and said to him, "Zacchaeus, come down immediately. I must stay at your house today."

6 And he made haste, and came down, and received him joyfully.

6 So he came down at once and welcomed him gladly.

7 And when they saw it, they all murmured, saying, That he was gone to be guest with a man that is a sinner.

7 All the people saw this and began to mutter, "He has gone to be the guest of a sinner."

8 And Zacchaeus stood, and said unto the Lord: Behold, Lord, the half of my goods I give to the poor; and if I have taken any thing from any man by false accusation, I restore him fourfold.

8 But Zacchaeus stood up and said to the Lord, "Look, Lord! Here and now I give half of my possessions to the poor, and if I have cheated anybody out of anything, I will pay back four times the amount."

9 And Jesus said unto him, This day is salvation come to this house, forsomuch as he also is a son of Abraham.

9 Jesus said to him, "Today salvation has come to this house, because this man, too, is a son of Abraham.

10 For the Son of man is come to seek and to save that which was lost.

10 For the Son of Man came to seek and to save the lost."

LIGHT ON THE WORD

Sycamore tree. A type of fig tree, this variety of tree was known for its distinctive branches, leaves, and fruit. Plentiful in both Old Testament and New Testament times, it boasted branches strong enough for a person to climb and broad leaves that provided ample shade along the many roads where it was planted. Yielding fruit a few times a year, the tree provided a reliable source of food for the poor and offered a cheaper source of wood than other tree varieties, such as cedar.

Zacchaeus. Zacchaeus was a rich Jew who worked as a high-level tax collector, or publican. Because of his position, he could extort excessive taxes from other Jews. The source of his wealth may have been money collected from the poor. He proved meeting Jesus was a life-changing event by volunteering to give half of his goods to the poor and restore the fortunes of people he may have falsely accused. "Jesus responded, 'Salvation has come to this home today, for this man has shown himself to be a true son of Abraham'" (**Luke 19:9**, NLT).

TEACHING THE BIBLE LESSON

LIFE NEED FOR TODAY'S LESSON

AIM: Students will accept that all people have experienced a loss of direction in their lives and an inability to make necessary changes and new plans.

INTRODUCTION
Jesus Invites Himself to Dinner

The Israelites and Jews were expected to love their neighbors and strangers as they loved themselves (**Leviticus 19:18, Matthew 5:43; Luke 10:25–37**). Thus, in both Old and New Testament times, hospitality was a way of life, practiced and extended to friends and family. However, in the broadest interpretation of the term, it also conveyed showing hospitality to strangers, treating them as guests of honor, and meeting their basic needs for a meal, foot bath, place to rest or sleep, or protection from hostile residents (Genesis 19:1–11). Entertainment could also be provided, but varied based on the host's financial resources. Under normal circumstances, the homeowner extended invitations.

During Jesus' earthly ministry, He accepted hospitality from His disciples (e.g., **Matthew 8:14**), Pharisees (**Luke 7:36**), and known "sinners" (i.e., **Matthew 9:9–11**). In today's lesson, however, Jesus invited Himself to Zacchaeus' home. Given hospitality mores then, refusal was not an option. Furthermore, as a rich man, Zacchaeus would have had the resources to host Jesus at a moment's notice.

On the other hand, as a wealthy person and sinner, Zacchaeus may have had wiggle room for refusing to host Jesus. None of these factors appear to have influenced him. Rather, from his joyous response, Zacchaeus was clearly delighted to be called and chosen to host Jesus. That acceptance paved the way for Zacchaeus to accept a greater invitation—salvation—and sparked his public declaration to make restitution for past sins.

BIBLE LEARNING

AIM: Students will understand that Jesus declared that His own work was to seek and save the lost.

I. AGAINST ALL ODDS (LUKE 19:1–4)

Anyone can change, and getting back on track after a loss of direction is possible—with God's help. Those encouraging facts undergird the story of Zacchaeus' conversion. Zacchaeus was rich yet despised because of his occupation and the way he conducted business affairs. Nonetheless, something within him prompted a desire to "see Jesus who he was" (**v. 3**, KJV).

Zacchaeus' spiritual interest would have to overcome three major obstacles: 1) a reputation as a sinner; 2) the crowd; and 3) his height. Against these odds, he found a way to satisfy his curiosity and was rewarded with a personal meeting with Jesus.

Opposition abounds for everyone seeking a change of spiritual direction. Multiple obstacles stand in the path of righteousness. Zacchaeus was determined to overcome every obstacle that thwarts converting to Christianity and growing in Christ. Zacchaeus was not satisfied with a mere glimpse of Jesus, and no one seeking to make necessary life changes should be either.

Luke 19:1–10

This story of the rich, short Zacchaeus is unique to Luke; it does not occur in any of the other Gospels. It serves Luke's purposes well to have it in his Gospel, which often takes sides with the poor against the rich. In the previous chapter, Jesus had an encounter with a rich young ruler who, when told to sell everything he has to follow Jesus, walked away sad (**18:18–27**). Jesus concluded that brief dialogue saying, "How hard it is for the rich to enter the Kingdom of God!" (**18:24**, NLT). As if to qualify that episode, Luke now talks about a rich man who actually received salvation. Luke thus shows that despite his critique of wealth, rich people who help people are among the outcasts whom Jesus came to save. Tradition has it that Zacchaeus—saved on this day—went on to become the first bishop of Caesarea in Palestine.

The story takes place toward the end of Jesus' life on earth—at the end of Luke's travel narratives. Jesus was on His final trip to Jerusalem, reaching the city by the end of this chapter, where He would be crucified in the following few days. At the close of the preceding chapter, as He drew near Jericho, Jesus had healed the blind Bartimaeus (**18:35–43**; cf. **Matthew 20:29–34, Mark 10:46–52**). He passed through Jericho, even though there were many other ways—probably just to meet Zacchaeus, as this is the only incident recorded in the city. Jericho itself was a rich city located about seventeen miles from Jerusalem and six miles from the Jordan River. It was known for its palms and balsam, but it was also located on a significant trade route from Peraea to Judaea and Egypt. The balm that came from Gilead on the other side of the Jordan was transported through Jericho into all parts of the world. Thus, Jericho was an important center of trade. It had an important toll-house and Zacchaeus was at the head of Jericho's customs department. We come to this story understanding two important facts: (1) Jesus is a friend of tax collectors and sinners (**Luke 5:30, 7:34**), even having a former publican among His disciples (**Matthew 9:9; Luke 5:27–32**) and (2) it is very hard for rich people to enter the Kingdom of God (**Luke 18:24–25**).

1 He entered Jericho and was passing through it. 2 A man was there named Zacchaeus; he was a chief tax collector and was rich. 3 He was trying to see who Jesus was, but on account of the crowd he could not, because **he was short in stature. 4 So he ran ahead and climbed a sycamore tree to see him, because he was going to pass that way.**

The first verse serves as a connector, providing the context of Zacchaeus' story and linking it with what happened in the preceding chapter where Jesus healed the blind man, Bartimaeus, just outside Jericho. Now He has gone into the city and is passing through. He is still surrounded by the entourage of His disciples and the large crowds who have been following Him, as well as those who had sought to prevent Bartimaeus from seeing Jesus (**18:39**). In the city lived a wealthy tax collector named Zacchaeus, the Greek form of a Hebrew name Zakkay (or Zaccai—an abbreviation of Zacharia), which means in the abbreviated form "pure" or "innocent." The full form means "The Lord has remembered." At the beginning of the story, Zacchaeus is anything but pure and innocent. As a Jewish tax collector, he was a betrayer of his own people. Tax collectors were hated and marginalized by their people, not only because taxes are generally uncomfortable, but also because the tax collectors served the Roman government that colonized them. In addition, tax collectors made their profit through extortion, as they were permitted to collect more than the Romans exacted and keep the surplus. That may explain John the Baptist's admonition to the tax collectors who asked how they could get right with God. He told them to collect no more than what is appointed for them (**Luke 3:13**). Thus, generally, if you were a rich tax collector, you were a thief. Zacchaeus is a chief tax collector, and he is unscrupulous just like other tax collectors.

But Zacchaeus sought to see Jesus—who He was. We do not know how Zacchaeus came to know about Jesus. Maybe he had heard the news about the miracles, or just wondered who this crowd-pulling Rabbi was. Had he heard that a publican like himself was among the chosen disciples of the Teacher whom the people were receiving as the Son of David? Had someone told him of the parable of the Pharisee and the publican? Had the fame of the miracle at the entrance into Jericho made him eager to see the Miracle Worker? Further, we are not told why Zacchaeus made the effort to see who Jesus was. Possibly he was really looking to change his life. Maybe he was tired of being marginalized and was trying to make things right by giving away half of his possessions to the poor and restoring fourfold to anyone he had cheated. Or was he trying to get his life in right order, and found it hard to imagine how he could maintain his style of living if he did that? Whatever his condition, because he was a thieving tax collector, Jesus had come to seek the lost like him.

Zacchaeus was unable to see Jesus over the crowd because he was too short. Despite his wealth and political power, he could not penetrate the crowd. Just like in the preceding chapter, the crowd became a barrier to someone who wanted to see Jesus. Part of the problem was that as a tax collector, he was a social outcast. He would not freely mingle with the multitudes, especially where he was known. In the eyes of his community, Zacchaeus' smallness was not just physical, but moral as well. He sought to gain some elevation to help him see Jesus. Thus, he ran before the crowd, and in spite of the dignity that went with his prestigious position in society, he dismissed the shame and, in a childlike manner, climbed a sycamore fig. Only mentioned here in the Scriptures, it was a large oak-like evergreen tree that was easy to climb. It is not mentioned whether this was Zacchaeus' way of hiding as well. Was he hoping not to be noticed by Jesus or the crowd? Of course, a man of his status would not have wanted to be seen in a tree.

II. CALL AND RESPONSE (vv. 5–6)

Does God know where we are any given moment? Can He reach us, even when others can't due to sin, irreconcilable differences, or distance? Will God notice our effort to change, as Jesus noticed

Zacchaeus (and as the father did his son's in the parable of the prodigal son, **Luke 15:11–32**)? Today's passage answers each of these questions with a resounding yes.

Rather than simply walk under the tree and continue His journey, Jesus looked up (**v. 5**). His was a divine call to a sinner, inviting Zacchaeus on a faith journey. In response, "Zacchaeus quickly climbed down and took Jesus to his house in great excitement and joy" (**v. 6**, NLT).

The Grumblers and the Naysayers

5 When Jesus came to the place, he looked up and said to him, "Zacchaeus, hurry and come down; for I must stay at your house today." 6 So he hurried down and was happy to welcome him. 7 All who saw it began to grumble and said, "He has gone to be the guest of one who is a sinner."

The good thing is that Jesus knew he was in the tree, knew his name. We are not told how He knew; it may have been supernatural knowledge (as in the case of Nathanael, **John 1:47**), but He may also have heard it from the people around. There is no reason to assume that the other people did not see Zacchaeus in the tree. Jesus called him to "hurry and come down." There was no need to waste time. He had been seeking to see Jesus, but here, it was Jesus looking at him and calling him down. Jesus takes the greater initiative to befriend another tax collector here when He invites Himself to Zacchaeus' house, "for today, I must stay at your house." Here, the story changes. The one who was seeking becomes the one sought, even though he is also shunned by society. As seen in the parable of the Good Samaritan, Jericho was among the cities devoted to the priests in Jesus' time (it wasn't one originally given to the Levites in Moses' time but later during the Greco-Roman period, **Luke 10:30–31**). Therefore, there may have been many priests' houses in the city where Jesus could have stayed, but instead, He chose to stay with a tax collector loathed by the Jews. Zacchaeus did as he was told, and he welcomed Jesus to his house joyfully. Having Jesus in his house was significant as it symbolized forgiveness. The whole incident turns out to be an honor that Zacchaeus could not have expected. John Nolland adds that "The language of welcome evokes that of the mission charges (**10:8–9**) and its import is underlined in the language of joy for the kingdom of God has come to this man, and he has embraced it. [Thus] he is no longer the outsider he was in **vv. 3–4**."

At this point, the crowd begins to grumble that Jesus is again making Himself the guest of "sinners." In Luke's words, "all the people who saw this began to murmur." "All" here might suggest that not only the Pharisees murmured, but even some of the other Jews and Gentiles who were present. In addition, this was a priestly city, which may have made it religiously segmented. Whatever the case, this murmuring may be expected, because in their minds, the tax collector was a sinner (and Zacchaeus chief among them) who should be shunned by the moral majority; to stay in such a sinner's house was tantamount to sharing in his sin. In general, it was believed that to accept hospitality from someone whose wealth was acquired in dubious ways is to become a partner in their crimes. In being the Good Shepherd, Jesus put Himself in questionable circumstances.

III. PUBLIC DECLARATIONS
(vv. 7–10)

Zacchaeus repented of his sin and volunteered to make amends. His character and attitude contrast with those of the Pharisee and the tax collector in the parable Jesus told in **Luke 18:9–14**. The Pharisee's self-righteousness prevented him from seeing his need to get back on track spiritually. The tax collector humbled himself before God, admitting his faults, and was justified. Conversely, Zacchaeus' public declaration revealed his gratitude for Jesus' intervention in

his life and also his joy of salvation. These, in turn, provided a forum for Jesus to declare His own mission—to seek and save the lost (**v. 10**). As Christians, we showcase Jesus' mission by our joyous faith.

Sin separates us from God. Knowing this, many people delay making a faith decision because they want to "clean up" their lives first, but this misunderstands the Scriptures. According to **1 John 4:19**, "We love him, because he first loved us." Because He loves us, we can pray, "Create in me a clean heart, O God; and renew a right spirit within me" (**Psalm 51:10**, KJV). We then can get back on track, publicly declaring our joyous faith (**Romans 10:10**).

Jesus Declares His Ministry

8 Zacchaeus stood there and said to the Lord, "Look, half of my possessions, Lord, I will give to the poor; and if I have defrauded anyone of anything, I will pay back four times as much." 9 Then Jesus said to him, "Today salvation has come to this house, because he too is a son of Abraham. 10 For the Son of Man came to seek out and to save the lost."

Zacchaeus is here speaking to Jesus, but he seems to be responding to the grumbling crowd. (Jesus, then, in turn addresses the crowd in the following verse.) He goes on to state, "Look, half of my possessions, Lord, I will give to the poor; and if I have defrauded anyone of anything, I will pay back four times as much." His statement suggests that he was publicly repenting of his bad past. This was his grateful response to the initiative that Jesus took to see him. However, it is also Zacchaeus' declaration to assure the crowd that he is now a changed person. He was not a sinner anymore, and therefore, the accusations against Jesus lodging with a sinner were not valid.

Roman law required fourfold restitution only under certain circumstances, like in a wrongful accusation in court. However, Zacchaeus was so touched by the events of the day that he promises a degree of restitution far beyond normal. While some may read the promises in a futuristic sense, that he will give away his property, others read it in the present tense—suggesting that Zacchaeus is already giving away his property to the poor. Such a reading, however, downplays the central theme of the story, that salvation is available even to the outcast who responds to God's call (**v. 9**). Instead of being a salvation story, it becomes a vindication story, which does not sit well with the rest of the story.

Jesus responds to Zacchaeus, "Today, salvation has come to this house." However, the following statement sounds like Jesus was addressing the crowd about Zacchaeus: "For he too is a son of Abraham." The mention of Zacchaeus' house— or household—is in line with Luke's motif of the salvation of households in Acts (**10:2, 11:14, 16:15, 31, 18:8**). With that motif, Luke implies that the members of the household were saved too. The wider significance of this saying is that this house which was shunned as a sinner's house has now been transformed. Further, this transformation will not happen in the future—it has already happened, because Zacchaeus was a Jew and a son of Abraham, even though he was a tax collector. More than that, Jesus' words seem to say that since Zacchaeus has embraced the Kingdom of God, he has become a spiritual son of Abraham who belongs among His followers.

The final statement in this story is uttered by Jesus. By "Son of Man," Jesus is talking about Himself (**v. 10**). He uses similar language to what He said at **5:32**: "I came not to call the righteous, but sinners to repentance" (KJV). However, the image is similar to the language of **Ezekiel 34**, where God and David gather the scattered sheep back to the fold. In a nutshell, Jesus is explaining why He was friends with sinners and tax collectors like Zacchaeus—to seek and save the lost. The church today ought to follow in Jesus' footsteps to extend the Kingdom to those rejected in

society. This applies even to those Christians who backslide and lose direction. Jesus came to seek them too, and the church must join Him in this search.

SEARCH THE SCRIPTURES

QUESTION 1
Why did the people grumble?

Zacchaeus was a tax collector and had taken their money.

QUESTION 2
Zacchaeus promised to give to who and repay how many times back to people he defrauded?

He promised to give to the poor and repay four times what he defrauded from others.

LIGHT ON THE WORD

The Big Payback
Zacchaeus' promise to give away half his riches and pay back fourfold to all he defrauded is amazing. The Law did not require the repentant sinner to give half his property to the poor, nor restore fourfold, except in the case of theft. Where a person voluntarily confessed, the law required restitution of only a fifth above the principle.

BIBLE APPLICATION

AIM: Students will learn that repentance and making changes to follow the Lord, creates new opportunities and possibilities.

Ascertaining whether someone is interested in the Gospel is not always easy. However, their actions may speak louder than their words. If someone is taking a risk to speak with us regarding our faith, then it indicates they are curious about our Savior—even if they won't come to church with us. Zacchaeus was in a tree—not in the Temple. That fact provides ample support for openly sharing our faith wherever we find spiritual seekers.

STUDENT'S RESPONSES

AIM: Students will affirm that believers trust Jesus for direction and guidance in their lives.

The inability to make necessary changes and new plans plagues sinners and Christians alike. Ask God for the courage and help to make a dramatic change in a specific area. Then take a specific step—apologize to a loved one, make arrangements to repay a debt, enroll in an addiction recovery program, return to Bible study, etc.

PRAYER

Dear Creative Lord. we are blessed by Your spirit that humbles us, and rejoices with us. We are excited to welcome You into our homes and hearts. Allow us to declare like Zacchaeus that we are changed to follow what is right before the Lord. Thank You Jesus. In Jesus' name we pray. Amen.

HOW TO SAY IT

Publican.   PUH-bli-kin.

Sycomore.   SIH-ko-mor.

Mores.   MORE-aze.

PREPARE FOR NEXT SUNDAY

Read **Zephaniah 1:4–6, 14–16, 2:3** and "The Day of the Lord."

DAILY HOME BIBLE READINGS

MONDAY
Singing Faith
(Isaiah 44:23-26)

TUESDAY
Dancing Faith
(Jeremiah 31:11–14)

WEDNESDAY
Proclaimed Faith
(Psalm 19:1–4, 14)

THURSDAY
Fruitful Faith
(Galatians 5:19–26)

FRIDAY
Sending Faith
(3 John 2–8)

SATURDAY
Connected Faith
(John 15:1–11)

SUNDAY
Joyous Faith
(Luke 19:1–10)

Sources:
Dunn, James D. G., and J. W. Rogerson. *Eerdmans Commentary on the Bible.* Grand Rapids, MI: W.B. Eerdmans, 2003.
Marshall, I. Howard. *The Gospel of Luke: A Commentary on the Greek Text.* The New International Greek Testament Commentary. Exeter Eng.: Paternoster Press, 1978.
Nolland, John L. *Word Biblical Commentary.* Vol. 35c, Luke 18:53-24:53. edited by David A. Hubbard and Glenn W. Barker. Dallas, TX: Word Books, 1993.

COMMENTS / NOTES:

_____

_____

_____

_____

_____

_____

_____

_____

_____

_____

_____

TOWARD A NEW CREATION
by Elder Oscar Owens, Jr.

Father God's promise in Jesus Christ is that He is making everyone who believes in Jesus a new creation (2 Corinthians 5:17). Therefore, God is re-creating in Jesus by the power of the Holy Spirit a new humanity, or the church of God which is in Christ (2 Thessalonians 2:14). This humanity is united with our heavenly Father by faith in the sacrificial death of Jesus (John 1:12–13), it has been born again by the Holy Spirit (John 3:5–16), and it has been sanctified by the precious blood of Christ (Hebrews 10:10, 13:12). Now, this new humanity, as a new creation in Christ, is in the process of transforming into the likeness of Jesus by the power of the Holy Spirit (2 Corinthians 3:18).

This quarter's study helps us to focus on human beings' desperate need for God's transforming power in Jesus. Since we are broken by sin and unable to repair ourselves, we need the Father, Son, and Holy Spirit to re-create us. We must believe in Jesus Christ as our Lord and Savior and be reborn to new life in Him. We begin our journey in the small, but mighty book of the prophet Zephaniah. He is the son of Cushi, possibly of some African ancestry in Israel, and has royal heritage descending from the faithful Judean King Hezekiah (Zephaniah 1:1). Zephaniah, a contemporary of Jeremiah, prophesied early during the reign of King Josiah, who later brings an idolatrous Judah back to obedience to Yahweh (2 Chronicles 34:1–33).

The major theme of Zephaniah's prophecies are his visions of the coming "day of the Lord" (Zephaniah 1:14–16), when God will being destruction on those in Judah who rebel against Him by worshiping idol gods. However, times of distressing judgment will also come for surrounding nations that reject Yahweh (Zephaniah 2:4–15), as well as a final future day of destruction to judge all the sinful nations of earth (Zephaniah 3:8). The conclusion we may draw from this lesson is that human beings are hopeless sinners, incapable of changing ourselves toward true righteousness and obedience to God.

Our study continues in the Apostle Paul's greatest theological writing, the glorious letter to the Romans. In this book, the Lord reveals through Paul the true answer to humanity's sin problem. The solution is revealed in the Gospel, or Good News of Jesus Christ, which is God's power of salvation to all humans who believe (Romans 1:16–17). In this book, we will examine the most important information on planet earth! By the Holy Spirit, Paul will unveil the sad state of sin all humanity is willingly bound with, and sadly sickened by (Romans 3:21–26). However, God has revealed His remedy for our sin problem, in the wonderful work of justification and salvation achieved by Jesus and received by believing in Him, as Lord and Savior (Romans 10:9–10).

Paul picturesquely unfolds the beauty of this new life in Christ. It is the "new creation life" (2 Corinthians 5:17) of Jesus within us that helps us, by the power of the Holy Spirit, to overcome and conquer our sin problems (Romans chapters 5–7). We actually experience the realities of our "new creation life" in Jesus as we agree with, yield to, and constantly receive by faith and obedience the transforming power of the Holy Spirit (Romans 8:1–39). In the concluding chapters 12–16 of Romans, Paul challenges believers to respond with appropriate action toward God with gratitude, love, and obedience for mercifully giving us the solution to our sin problem. In light of what Jesus has done for us, we are to be "transformed by the renewing of our minds" (Romans 12:2), to live in our "new creation life" no longer constantly "conformed to this world" (Romans 12:2) or the old life of sinful humanity. We are now a new humanity in Jesus Christ, empowered by the Holy Spirit to increasingly grow in practical behavior, toward the likeness of Jesus as we trust, obey, and believe Him. We are not perfectly like Jesus or sinless in this life, but we can continuously overcome our sinful behaviors and experience the reality of our "new creation life" in Jesus as we "grow in grace and the knowledge" (2 Peter 3:18) of Him. Let us continue to say, "Yes, Lord, I agree with Your new creation life, will, and way for me!"

Elder Oscar O. Owens Jr. is a member of the West Angeles Church Of God In Christ, where Presiding Bishop Charles E. Blake is his pastor. For 23 years he has served within the Christian Education Department. He currently serves as President of the West Angeles Bible College and Christian Education Director. Elder Owens holds a B.A. in English Literature from UCLA, M.Div. from the Union Theological Seminary in New York City, and he is currently pursuing a Doctor of Ministry degree at the Azusa Pacific Seminary.

DON'T DWELL ON THE PROCESS, JUST FOCUS ON MY PLAN

In Everything Give Thanks

by Evangelist Betty J. Byrd

The following information is designed to support and aid both the COGIC Commentary series and Sunday School leaders by providing innovative teaching suggestions, proven growth strategies, and thoughtful learning opportunities, thus exciting, benefiting, and enhancing the user.

SCRIPTURAL REFERENCE FOR THIS LESSON:

- 1 Thessalonians 5:18: "In every thing give thanks: for this is the will of God in Christ Jesus concerning you."

- James 1:2–3: "My brethren, count it all joy when ye fall into divers temptations; Knowing this, that the trying of your faith worketh patience."

- Jeremiah 29:11: "For I know the thoughts that I think toward you, saith the LORD, thoughts of peace, and not of evil, to give you an expected end."

- Jonah chapters 1 and 2

IN EVERYTHING GIVE THANKS.

In our teaching process, it is essential for us to address the needs and issues of our students through the Word of God. Before we can continue to teach, we need to help them understand why things happen in our lives and that giving thanks to God in everything is His will. Where so much is happening in the lives of people, we must teach our students to understand to give thanks IN everything. The Scripture in 1 Thessalonians 5:18 does not say FOR, but IN. Now we must teach and help our students understand the difference in IN and FOR. For example, we do not thank God necessarily for losing a job, but in the midst of trouble, we can still give Him thanks.

In a popular comedy TV show *Hee-Haw* (1969-1992), Buck Owens and Roy Clark would sing a song entitled "Gloom, Despair, and Agony on Me." A verse from the song says:

> Gloom, despair, and agony on me.
>
> Deep, dark depression, excessive misery.
>
> If it weren't for bad luck, I'd have no luck at all.
>
> Gloom, despair, and agony on me.

We think we are in a bad situation, but someone else may be going through something worse than you are. So be grateful for where you are.

GOD HAS A PLAN FOR OUR LIVES.

"Now these are the words of the letter that Jeremiah the prophet sent from Jerusalem unto the residue of the elders which were carried away captives, and to the priests, and to the prophets, and to all the people whom Nebuchadnezzar had carried away captive from Jerusalem to Babylon" (Jeremiah 29:1).

Sometimes bad things will happen to good people. Israel had to go into captivity to learn their lesson. God said He would answer them when they call to Him out of a sincere heart, but they still had to go the way of captivity.

DON'T DWELL ON THE PROCESS, JUST FOCUS ON MY PLAN

Look at Joseph in Genesis 45:1–8. You've heard of the 12 tribes of Israel; they derived from the 12 sons of Jacob, later called Israel. But this would not have happened if Joseph was not sold into slavery by his brothers, and imprisoned in Egypt. Can you imagine Joseph wondering why this was happening to him? But through the process of events and time, Joseph interprets the king's dreams and eventually becomes governor of Egypt in charge of grain in the time of famine. Again through time, Joseph's family encounters famine in Canaan and comes to him for help. Pharaoh moves Joseph's family to Goshen in Egypt.

Joseph says to his brothers who sold him into slavery in Genesis 50:20, "But as for you, ye thought evil against me; but God meant it unto good, to bring to pass, as it is this day, to save much people alive." Joseph's family multiplied in that land, and when they left Egypt with Moses, they were a nation. God had a plan for Israel, but they had to go through the process.

GOD DOES HAVE A PLAN FOR MY LIFE.

Our students must know that God has a plan for our lives, if we do not faint in the midst of the process. "For I know the thoughts that I think toward you, saith the LORD, thoughts of peace, and not of evil, to give you an expected end" (Jeremiah 29:11).

God may have to allow havoc in our lives to bring about the necessary changes He has set for you. Just continue to give God thanks.

Conclusion – Read Jonah chapters 1–2:

- *1:4 – ...**the LORD sent** out a great wind...*
- *1:17 – Now **the LORD had prepared a great fish** to swallow up Jonah.*
- *2:1 – Then Jonah prayed unto the LORD his God out of the fish's belly.*

- *2:4 – Then I said, I am cast out of thy sight; yet I will look again toward thy holy temple.*

- *2:7 – When my soul fainted within me **I remembered the LORD**...*

- *2:9 – But I will sacrifice unto thee with the voice of **thanksgiving**:...*

- *2:10 – And **the LORD spake unto the fish**, and it vomited out Jonah upon the day land.*

As teachers, we must make it plain how Jonah had to suffer for his disobedience to God. But we see that God had a plan for his life, and through the process of events, He worked His plan. When Jonah gave God thanks in Jonah 2:9, God released him on dry land (out of harm's way).

When we give God thanks, He will release us into a blessing. Remember God has a plan for our lives, and don't focus or faint in the process, but give Him thanks, because this is the will of God concerning you.

Evangelist Betty J. Byrd
Adult Sunday School Teacher
Fairfield First COGIC, Elder James Brinkley Jr., Pastor
Alabama First Jurisdiction
Jurisdictional Young Women's Christian Council (YWCC) President
Mother Mattie B. Taylor, Jurisdictional Supervisor
Bishop O. L. Meadows, Jurisdictional Prelate

"LET'S LIVE IT!
OBEYING GOD WITH A DO GOOD PLAN"
Nehemiah 10:28–39

by Jurisdictional Field Representative Sandra Daniel

The following information is designed to support and aid both the COGIC Commentary series and Sunday School leaders by providing innovative teaching suggestions, proven growth strategies, and thoughtful learning opportunities, thus exciting, benefiting, and enhancing the user.

In the ninth chapter of Nehemiah, the people of Judah confessed their sins. They promised God they would do better. They put their promises in writing (Nehemiah 9:38). Read Nehemiah 10:28–39.

Repentance is necessary when we sin. Once repentance has taken place, we need a "*do good in the future*" plan. You can plan ahead to please God; this takes planning and commitment.

Activity:

- Get a journal, notebook or binder, and paper.

- Look at how the people in Nehemiah began to write their commitment to obey God.

- Divide your paper into three columns.

- Every day write a promise to God.

- Then write how you plan to go through the day to obey Him, keeping your promise.

- Remember that it is important to pray at the beginning of the day and at the end of the day.

- Before going to bed, write a summary of how your day went and if and how your promise was kept.

Do Good Plan Journal Page

Date	Promise	Do Good Plan

Summary: (can be written as a letter to God)

_____
_____
_____
_____
_____
_____
_____
_____

Jurisdictional Field Representative Sandra Daniel
Evangelist Sandra Daniel serves as the Jurisdictional Field Representative for Southern California First Jurisdiction under the leadership of Bishop Joe L. Ealy and General Assistant Supervisor/ Jurisdictional Supervisor, Mother Barbara McCoo Lewis. She is the Assistant Director of Leadership Ministry for the International Sunday School Department

TEACHING TIPS FOR SUNDAY SCHOOL TEACHERS
by Jurisdictional Superintendent Jean Gardner

The following information is designed to support and aid both the COGIC Commentary series and Sunday School leaders by providing innovative teaching suggestions, proven growth strategies, and thoughtful learning opportunities, thus exciting, benefiting, and enhancing the user.

"Study to show thyself approved unto God, a workman that needeth not be ashamed, rightly dividing the Word of truth" (2 Timothy 2:15).

As a teacher, one should personally ask, "Am I teaching and reaching students? Are students engaged in the class? Are their spiritual needs being met?" A teacher should be passionate about teaching students.

1. Food for Thought

To keep your students engaged and to organize structure, the following tips are offered:

- Keep your class spiritual and remember laughter is good for the soul.

- Don't allow your class to be a debating, judgmental classroom. Students are there to learn the Word of God, not to be judged, argued at, or condemned for their lack of biblical knowledge. New converts/visitors may become lost if the class room becomes a battleground.

- Always study the lessons and use reference Scriptures and other helps to teach.

- Teachers should attend workshops, training, and forums to be equipped with knowledge to empower students with spiritual growth and development.

- Create a mission statement and place it on the classroom bulletin board.

2. Class Officers

- Appoint class officers; students like responsibility. It helps them to feel like they are a part of the team. Appoint a person to call absent students. It makes the absent student feel special to receive a call. Please don't scold the student for being absent and don't pry for answers, just simply say, "We missed you at Sunday School, and is there anything we can do to assure your attendance next Sunday?"

3. Activities/Incentives

Motivate students to achieve excellence by rewarding them. Some suggestions are:

- Certificate of Attendance at the end of the quarter.

- Certificate for Student of the Quarter. This person should be an achiever who has good attendance, class participation, class offering, punctuality, etc.

- Certificates for each student who verbally memorizes and recites the books of the Bible. If there's space, frame certificates on the class room wall and name it the Bible Hall of Fame (or something similar).

- Outreach Certificate for the student who invites the most visitors to class at end of quarter.

- Occasionally, give the entire class an "I appreciate you" gift, especially at Christmas, Valentine's Day, etc.

- Recognition of students' birthdays. Engage a birthday club where students pay a very small monthly amount in the fund. A small gift is given on their birthday. Allow a student to coordinate this project.

- Occasionally change the scene of Sunday School. You may want to have class at a McDonald's, or another local restaurant. This can be momentous, as well as an outreach/recruitment to get new members.

Evangelist Jean Gardner serves as the Eastern Missouri Western Illinois Jurisdictional Sunday School Superintendent under the leadership of Bishop Lawrence M. Wooten, General Board Member, and Mother Rosetta Watts, Supervisor of Women. She is an International Executive Board member of the International Sunday School Department and Task Force Chairperson for Sunday School at the Holy Convocation. She is a member of Victory Temple COGIC serving under Pastor R. Lloyd Gardner, St. Louis, MO.

QUARTERLY QUIZ

The questions on this page may be used in several ways: as a pretest at the beginning of the quarter; as a review at the end of the quarter; or as a review after each lesson. The questions are based on the Scripture text of each lesson (King James Version).

LESSON 1

1. Describe the prophet Zephaniah based on the information in Light on the Word (**Zephaniah 1:4–6, 14–16, and 2:3**).

_____

_____

2. Circle one of the following phrases to complete the sentence: Zephaniah pronounced that the Day of the Lord is a day of joy and tears of happiness or a day of trouble and distress (**v. 5**).

_____

_____

LESSON 2

1. Although Judah persisted in rebelling against God, who would be left to honor and worship the Lord (**Zephaniah 3:6–8**)?

_____

_____

2. God's _____ in **verse 8** will consume all who are not obedient and have turned from the Lord.

_____

_____

LESSON 3

1. Complete verse 14: "Sing, O daughter of Zion; shout O Israel; be glad and rejoice with all heart, O daughter of Jerusalem. Sing, _____; shout O Israel; _____ with all heart, O daughter of _____" (**Zephaniah 3:9–14, 20**).

_____

_____

2. What four things does God promise to Jerusalem in **verse 20**?

_____

_____

LESSON 4

1. Paul states how some people "knew God, but they wouldn't worship him as God" (**Romans 1:21**). What are the effects of those who hold this posture toward God (**vv. 18–23, 28–32**)?

_____

_____

2. How does Paul describe the extreme sinfulness of the Gentiles in **verse 32**?

_____

_____

QUARTERLY QUIZ

LESSON 5

1. The Jewish ceremony of circumcision has value only if you do what (**Romans 2:25**)?

_____

_____

2. A person is a Jew if the parents are Jewish and the ceremony circumcision has happened (**v. 28**). True, False, or Partially True?

_____

_____

LESSON 6

1. Paul makes reference to what Scripture when he states that "No one is righteous" (**Romans 3:10**)?

_____

_____

2. What animal and its deadly poison does Paul use in writing "...drips from their lips" (**v. 13**)?

_____

_____

LESSON 7

1. Complete the following: "Even the _____ of God which is by faith of Jesus Christ unto _____ and upon all them that _____: for there is no _____" (**Romans 3:22**).

_____

_____

2. We are justified by Christ through what (**v. 24**)?

_____

LESSON 8

1. Paul writes that when God's people are without strength, what happens (**Romans 5:6**)?

_____

2. We have been made right by _____ _____, then, we will be saved from _____ _____ (**v. 9**).

_____

_____

LESSON 9

1. Read the section on "Baptism" and "Slavery" under The People, Places, and Times. Describe baptism and what it was based upon.

_____

_____

2. List ways that slaves were acquired in the Greco-Roman world.

_____

_____

QUARTERLY QUIZ

LESSON 10

1. Can anything "separate us from the love" God has for us in Christ Jesus **(Romans 8:35)**? Name two things that Paul lists in this verse that may cause some people to separate themselves from Christ.

_____

_____

2. We have the victory over all things in _____ and Jesus _____ loved _____ **(v. 37)**.

_____

_____

LESSON 11

1. Why is it impossible to obtain salvation by thinking or working as hard as one can **(Romans 9:16)**?

_____

_____

2. How did Pharaoh showcase God's power to the rest of the world **(v. 17)**?

_____

_____

LESSON 12

1. According to Paul, why did salvation come to the Gentiles after Israel's disobedience **(Romans 11:11)**?

_____

_____

2. What does Paul compare the Gentiles to **(v. 17)**?

_____

_____

LESSON 13

1. How does Paul instruct the Romans to be transformed **(Romans 12:2)**?

_____

_____

2. State the commandment that sums up the commandments regarding harm or destruction to others **(v. 9)**.

_____

_____

Answers to Quarterly Quiz can be found on page 510

THE DAY OF THE LORD

BIBLE BASIS: ZEPHANIAH 1:4–6, 14–16, 2:3

BIBLE TRUTH: The Lord promised punishment to the Israelites because of their unfaithfulness and an opportunity for them to seek righteousness and save their relationship with Him.

MEMORY VERSE: "Seek ye the LORD, all ye meek of the earth, which have wrought his judgment; seek righteousness, seek meekness: it may be ye shall be hid in the day of the LORD's anger" (Zephaniah 2:3).

LESSON AIM: By the end of the lesson, we will: LEARN that on the Day of the Lord, God will punish those who have not repented; RECOGNIZE the relationship between righteous living and one's responsibility to maintain "the good" found in God's created order; and REPENT and reaffirm our faithfulness to God.

TEACHER PREPARATION

MATERIALS NEEDED: Quarterly Commentary/Teacher Manual, Adult Quarterly, Adult resources—charts, worksheets, and other teaching tools, paper, pens, pencils, Bibles (several different versions)

OTHER MATERIALS NEEDED / TEACHER'S NOTES:

_____

_____

LESSON OVERVIEW

LIFE NEED FOR TODAY'S LESSON
People sometimes greatly damage relationships.

BIBLE LEARNING
Zephaniah describes the Israelites marring creation as sinning against God.

BIBLE APPLICATION
The Lord will judge the world, so all people must be mindful of what they say, do, and think.

STUDENTS' RESPONSES
Christians must seek the Lord wholeheartedly and walk in His ways.

LESSON SCRIPTURE

ZEPHANIAH 1:4–6, 14–16, 2:3, KJV

4 I will also stretch out mine hand upon Judah, and upon all the inhabitants of Jerusalem; and I will cut off the remnant of Baal from this place, and the name of the Chemarims with the priests;

ZEPHANIAH 1:4–6, 14–16, 2:3, NIV

4 "I will stretch out my hand against Judah and against all who live in Jerusalem. I will destroy every remnant of Baal worship in this place, the very names of the idolatrous priests—

5 And them that worship the host of heaven upon the housetops; and them that worship and that swear by the LORD, and that swear by Malcham;

6 And them that are turned back from the LORD; and those that have not sought the LORD, nor enquired for him.

14 The great day of the LORD is near, it is near, and hasteth greatly, even the voice of the day of the LORD: the mighty man shall cry there bitterly.

15 That day is a day of wrath, a day of trouble and distress, a day of wasteness and desolation, a day of darkness and gloominess, a day of clouds and thick darkness,

16 A day of the trumpet and alarm against the fenced cities, and against the high towers.

2:3 Seek ye the LORD, all ye meek of the earth, which have wrought his judgment; seek righteousness, seek meekness: it may be ye shall be hid in the day of the LORD's anger.

5 those who bow down on the roofs to worship the starry host, those who bow down and swear by the LORD and who also swear by Molek,

6 those who turn back from following the LORD and neither seek the LORD nor inquire of him."

14 The great day of the LORD is near—near and coming quickly. The cry on the day of the LORD is bitter; the Mighty Warrior shouts his battle cry.

15 That day will be a day of wrath—a day of distress and anguish, a day of trouble and ruin, a day of darkness and gloom, a day of clouds and blackness—

16 a day of trumpet and battle cry against the fortified cities and against the corner towers.

2:3 Seek the LORD, all you humble of the land, you who do what he commands. Seek righteousness, seek humility; perhaps you will be sheltered on the day of the LORD's anger.

LIGHT ON THE WORD

Zephaniah. Zephaniah was born during the long reign of Manasseh, an evil king who reigned for fifty-five years. His ministry, however, took place mostly during the reign of Josiah, the grandson of Manasseh. Josiah was a godly king who instituted sweeping reforms and commanded that idols be destroyed.

Zephaniah prophesied after Israel had been taken captive by Assyria. His was the last prophecy given to Judah before being carried into exile in Babylon. Before him, Amos, Isaiah, Jeremiah, and Ezekiel had all prophesied about the coming Day of the Lord.

Host of Heaven. The term "host of heaven" refers to the celestial bodies. Ancient people believed that the stars and heavenly bodies in the sky formed an army. This army guided the fate of nations and controlled the destiny of individuals. This is the reason the sun, moon, and stars were some of the first objects of idolatry and continued to be a temptation for the

Israelites. God condemns this type of worship (**Deuteronomy 17:2–5**).

TEACHING THE BIBLE LESSON

LIFE NEED FOR TODAY'S LESSON

AIM: Students will learn that people sometimes greatly damage relationships.

INTRODUCTION

Judgment and Repentance

In the beginning of the book of the same name, Zephaniah prophesied of God's coming judgment because of the idolatry that had filled Judah and Jerusalem. Zephaniah dealt with this particular aspect of the unfaithfulness of God's people in major detail. Many of the practices condemned by the prophet anticipate the reforms of King Josiah in 622 BC.

Zephaniah started off giving a sweeping vision of what will happen on the Day of the Lord, a day when everything would be consumed. This picturesque description of God's wrath will serve as a bookend to chapter two, which is more encouraging and offers hope. Here, in the midst of judgment, God's people were encouraged to repent and seek Him.

BIBLE LEARNING

AIM: Students will examine how Zephaniah describes the Israelites marring creation as sinning against God.

I. JUDGMENT IS COMING (ZEPHANIAH 1:4–6)

Judgment is coming for the people of God. Even the City of God, where the Temple stands, will feel His wrath. This first section of Zephaniah's prophecy indicates that mankind is responsible for the condition of the earth. In **verses 1–3**, the Lord promises to send judgment on the whole world. His judgment will include everything, even animal life and the land.

This judgment will also fall on those with divided loyalties. In Zephaniah's day, the people of Judah were swearing allegiance to both God and Molech. Not only is the Lord displeased by their half-worship, He will impose the same punishment on Judah as on idolaters. The very names of the Chemarims, the priests of Baal, will be erased from memory. Those who worship the heavenly bodies would also be destroyed. Those who worship the Lord and Molech will be judged for their unfaithfulness.

Verse 6 speaks of those who used to worship the Lord but no longer do. Zephaniah proclaims that these, too, will be destroyed. Judgment will come on all classes of people, and all who worship the sun, moon, stars, and other gods will be consumed.

Zephaniah 1:4–6, 14-16, 2:3

4 I will also stretch out mine hand upon Judah, and upon all the inhabitants of Jerusalem; and I will cut off the remnant of Baal from this place, and the name of the Chemarims with the priests; 5 And them that worship the host of heaven upon the housetops; and them that worship and that swear by the LORD, and that swear by Malcham; 6 And them that are turned back from the LORD; and those that have not sought the LORD, nor enquired for him.

In the previous verses, Zephaniah begins with a thunderous pronouncement speaking in proxy for God: "I will utterly consume all things from off the land, saith the LORD" (**v. 2**). This sweeping away includes all of creation. Judah and Jerusalem would not be safe as God declares that He will "stretch out" His hand. The word to stretch out (Heb. *natah*, **nah-TA**) is often used in the context of God's hand in judgment. This stretching out of judgment is focused on cleansing, as the

Lord says that He will "cut off the remnant of Baal from this place and the name of the Chemarims with the priests." The word "remnant" (Heb. *shear*, **she-AR**) is often used to describe whatever is left whether in reference to people, animals, or inanimate objects. It is a general term for "the rest," and in this context, anticipates when the Lord would judge Judah and Jerusalem and eradicate Baal worship with finality.

Zephaniah prophesied during the reign of King Josiah, which was characterized by religious reform. The book of the Law was found and the Temple was restored. Josiah proceeded to eliminate the worship of idols in the nation of Judah. The people of Judah had worshiped not only Baal, a principal Canaanite deity, but wicked kings had installed "Chemarims," or priests of foreign gods. These priests would worship other false gods to supplement the worship of Yahweh (**2 Kings 23:5**). They also worshiped the host of Heaven, another term for the sun, moon, stars and other celestial bodies. This type of idolatrous worship was prevalent in the ancient Near East and originates in Mesopotamia. God's people were tempted by this even in the days of Moses (**Deuteronomy 4:19**). The cleansing of the nation from idol worship would not just cover those who proactively and brazenly sought after false gods, but also include those whose loyalties were divided as they swore by the Lord and also Malcham (Heb. *malcham*, **mal-KAM**), which means "their king" and could refer to the Ammonite deity Milcom or to the Israelite name Molech, which probably also refers to Milcom (see **1 Kings 11:5; Leviticus 18:21**). This statement makes clear that the Lord would not tolerate a half-hearted commitment and loyalty but wanted full covenant devotion. The Lord would judge all those who have turned back (Heb. *sug*, **SOOG**). This word is commonly used to refer to backsliding. This was not a passive drifting away but an intentional avoidance and refusal to follow the Lord, the attitude and lifestyle of all those who have not sought (Heb. *baqash*, **bah-KHASH**) after the Lord. In this context, "sought" is to seek in order to find. This is also the attitude of those who have not inquired (Heb. *darash*, **da-RHASH**) of Him. The word means to frequent or consult. Those who turn back from God avoid His counsel.

II. THE DAY OF THE LORD IS NEAR (vv. 14–16)

The Day of the Lord is described as being a terrible day when the Lord's wrath will be poured out. Even mighty men will cry like children.

Zephaniah describes the Day of the Lord as a day of gloom, darkness, and distress, as well as trumpets and battle cries. This indicates military invasion and alludes to Babylonia's invasion of Judah in 597 B.C. The attack will be directed at Judah's defenses, which will fail on that day.

Zephaniah prophesies the Day of the Lord; the ultimate judgment of the earth. He also refers to the immediate judgment of Judah, called the "voice of the day of the Lord," which will come before the Day itself. It will be a terrible day when even the strongest will be in distress and anguish. Judah will experience the Lord's judgment, and the full impact will be released on all creation at the last judgment.

It will be a day of trouble and distress for all sinners, and a day of ruin and desolation for all creation. The animals and the land will be wiped away. In **verse 17**, Zephaniah describes how the people will grope like the blind. Their blood will be poured out, and their bodies will rot on the ground. Rich and poor alike will suffer the same fate (**v. 18**).

God's Judgment

14 The great day of the Lord is near, it is near, and hasteth greatly, even the voice of the day of the Lord: the mighty man shall cry there bitterly. 15 That day is a day of wrath, a day of trouble and distress, a day

of wasteness and desolation, a day of darkness and gloominess, a day of clouds and thick darkness, 16 A day of the trumpet and alarm against the fenced cities, and against the high towers.

Zephaniah goes on to announce that the great Day of the Lord is near (Heb. *qarov*, **ka-ROVE**). This word can be used for nearness of place or time; in this context, time. He adds "it is near and hasteth greatly." The word "hasteth" (Heb. *maher*, **mah-HER**) which means hurrying or speeding is not a verb in the Hebrew but an adjective describing the day of the Lord. The Day of the Lord is not a far off concept but a very near reality. Zephaniah then goes on to describe voice (Heb. *qowl*, **KOL**) or sound of the Day of the Lord. It will be a day when a mighty man will cry bitterly (Heb. *tsarach*, **tsah-RAHK**). This word for cry means to suddenly cry aloud with a penetrating and high pitched sound. Strong men cry out in pain and agony as they experience God's judgment.

This day will be filled with wrath (Heb. *'ebrah*, **ev-RAH**) or outpoured anger. It will be a day of trouble (Heb. *tsarah*, **tsah-RAH**) which is extreme anguish of body or mind. It will be a day of distress (Heb. *metsuqah*, **met-su-KAH**) or extreme psychological suffering. Zephaniah adds that it will be a day of wasteness (Heb. *sho'ah*, **sho-AH**) and desolation (Heb. *mesho'ah*, **me-show-AH**). The word for wasteness means damaging something beyond repair and desolation is from the same root as wasteness, also indicating total annihilation. The Day of the Lord would be filled with total devastation. Desolation means something that is decayed or destroyed. Zephaniah goes on to describe the day as one where there would be no light or happiness. It would be a day of the trumpet (Heb. *shofar*, **sho-FAR**) and alarm (Heb. *teruah*, **te-roo-AH**). The trumpet was used as not only an instrument of merriment, but also war. It gave the call to arms. The alarm was the sound it made; a more specific definition would be "battle cry." This "battle cry" was sounded throughout an entire battle. From

this, we can see that the Day of the Lord would be a day of war and destruction.

III. REPENT AND SEEK THE LORD (2:3)

Zephaniah urges the people of Judah to gather together and repent while there is still time (**v. 1**). The fierce fury of the Lord is set to descend on them but they have the opportunity to repent and turn from their wickedness. Judah needs to collectively humble themselves and seek the Lord earnestly. Refusing to seek the Lord is one of the causes for judgment (**1:6**). Now, Judah must seek the Lord once again, pursuing righteousness and doing what is right by following the Lord's commands.

Seek Righteousness and Meekness

2:3 Seek ye the Lord, all ye meek of the earth, which have wrought his judgment; seek righteousness, seek meekness: it may be ye shall be hid in the day of the Lord's anger.

Zephaniah calls those who want to be saved from the devastation of the Day of the Lord to seek Him. The prophet particularly announces this to the meek (Heb. *'anaw*, **ah-NAHV**) of the earth— the poor, afflicted, and humble. Zephaniah further adds that they are to seek righteousness and meekness (Heb. *anawah*, **ah-naw-AH**). Righteousness is what is right, normal, and just. Meekness is lowliness of mind and status. It is having the attitude of proper self-estimation in relation to God as one who is poor and humble.

SEARCH THE SCRIPTURES

QUESTION 1
What instrument is described in the Day of the Lord?

The trumpet sounds the "battle cry" which denotes that Day of the Lord would be a war and destruction.

QUESTION 2

How can Judah demonstrate their repentance (**2:3**)?

Zephaniah tells Judah to seek righteousness and meekness.

LIGHT ON THE WORD

Submitting to the Lord

Judah must live humbly, submitting to the Lord in everything. In order to be saved, Judah must show humility, or meekness. Humbly seeking the Lord would cause Him to spare them.

BIBLE APPLICATION

AIM: Students will accept that the Lord will judge the world, so all people must be mindful of what they say, do and think.

Sin is destructive. Not only does it affect the individual and his or her relationship with God, it affects others, sometimes on a large scale. On the prophesied Day of the Lord, all creation will suffer judgment. Like the Lord's prophets and disciples, we are called to preach the Gospel of God's grace. We should call people to repent, turn from their wicked ways, and seek the Lord. We should boldly proclaim the message of God: both His punishment of sin and His abundance of grace.

As in the past, the Lord has promised judgment for sin. He will not let sin go unpunished. The Good News is that Jesus took the punishment for every believer. We are to warn people of the consequences of sin and proclaim salvation in Christ.

STUDENT'S RESPONSES

AIM: Students will know that Christians must seek the Lord wholeheartedly and walk in His ways.

Spiritual complacency is very common in our society. Many say they are Christians, but their lifestyle and worldview do not reflect Christian beliefs. Many also take elements of various religions and mix them with Christianity. God's Word states that Jesus Christ is the way, the truth, and the life. Believers must be careful not to add other false religions, teachings, or practices (e.g., Islam, Buddhism, New Age, numerology, etc.) to the Gospel.

As believers, we must take seriously the teachings of the Lord and endeavor to please Him in all we do. We must turn away from sin and follow God wholeheartedly. Spend some time reading the Bible and praying. Seek the Lord with all your heart. Seek His guidance and meditate on His goodness.

PRAYER

Dear Lord, help us to stay focused on You, and not our desires. Your righteousness and love are amazing toward us in spite of our sinful ways. Lord, as we strive look toward Jesus, and follow Him, we learn to love You, more and more. In Jesus' Name we pray. Amen.

HOW TO SAY IT

Chemarims.   ki-mah-**REEMS**

Malcham.   mal-**KAM**.

PREPARE FOR NEXT SUNDAY

Read **Zephaniah 3:6–8** and "The Consequences of Disobedience."

DAILY HOME BIBLE READINGS

MONDAY
A Day of Celebration
(Exodus 23:14–19)

TUESDAY
A Day of Rest
(Exodus 16:25–30)

WEDNESDAY
A Day of Agreement
(Deuteronomy 26:14b–19)

THURSDAY
A Day without Tears
(Isaiah 65:13–19)

FRIDAY
A Day to Finish
(2 Timothy 4:1–8)

SATURDAY
A Day for Faithfulness
(Matthew 24:42–47)

SUNDAY
The Day of the Lord
(Zephaniah 1:4–6, 14–16, 2:3)

Sources:
Carson, D. A., R. T. France, J. A. Motyer, J. G. Wenham. *New Bible Commentary*. Downers Grove, IL: InterVarsity Press, 1993.
Polhill, John B. Acts. *New American Commentary: An Exegetical and Theological Exposition of Holy Scripture*. Nashville: B&H Publishing, 1992.

COMMENTS / NOTES:

THE CONSEQUENCES OF DISOBEDIENCE

BIBLE BASIS: ZEPHANIAH 3:6–8

BIBLE TRUTH: Zephaniah recounts how God punished the people for their disobedience, and wanted them to correct their behavior.

MEMORY VERSE: "Therefore wait ye upon me, saith the LORD, until the day that I rise up to the prey: for my determination is to gather the nations, that I may assemble the kingdoms, to pour upon them mine indignation, even all my fierce anger: for all the earth shall be devoured with the fire of my jealousy" (Zephaniah 3:8).

LESSON AIM: By the end of the lesson, we will: EXAMINE Zephaniah's prophecy that God would want to save His people and the people's intransigent rebellion; HELP adults realize that God loves us, wants our obedience, and will give us a second chance to repent; and COMMIT to asking God to give another opportunity for redemption and salvation.

TEACHER PREPARATION

MATERIALS NEEDED: Quarterly Commentary/Teacher Manual, Adult Quarterly, Adult resources—charts, worksheets, and other teaching tools, paper, pens, pencils, Bibles (several different versions)

OTHER MATERIALS NEEDED / TEACHER'S NOTES:

_____

_____

LESSON OVERVIEW

LIFE NEED FOR TODAY'S LESSON
People sometimes destroy something beautiful even when they know the consequences.

BIBLE LEARNING
Believers know that there are consequences to their sinful behavior.

BIBLE APPLICATION
God offers hope for change and wants to save people from their disobedience.

STUDENTS' RESPONSES
Christians affirm that God provides opportunities for people to repent and seek God's ways.

LESSON SCRIPTURE

ZEPHANIAH 3:6–8, KJV

6 I have cut off the nations: their towers are desolate; I made their streets waste, that none passeth by: their cities are destroyed, so that there is no man, that there is none inhabitant.

ZEPHANIAH 3:6–8, NIV

6 "I have destroyed nations; their strongholds are demolished. I have left their streets deserted, with no one passing through. Their cities are laid waste; they are deserted and empty.

7 I said, Surely thou wilt fear me, thou wilt receive instruction; so their dwelling should not be cut off, howsoever I punished them: but they rose early, and corrupted all their doings.

8 Therefore wait ye upon me, saith the LORD, until the day that I rise up to the prey: for my determination is to gather the nations, that I may assemble the kingdoms, to pour upon them mine indignation, even all my fierce anger: for all the earth shall be devoured with the fire of my jealousy.

7 Of Jerusalem I thought, 'Surely you will fear me and accept correction!' Then her place of refuge would not be destroyed, nor all my punishments come uponher. But they were still eager to act corruptly in all they did.

8 Therefore wait for me," declares the LORD, "for the day I will stand up to testify. I have decided to assemble the nations, to gather the kingdoms and to pour out my wrath on them—all my fierce anger. The whole world will be consumed by the fire of my jealous anger.

LIGHT ON THE WORD

Jerusalem. Jerusalem was the capital city of the Southern Kingdom, Judah. It was known as the Holy City. The Temple, central to Jewish worship, was located in Jerusalem. Because Judah persisted in her sinful ways, the Lord promised judgment. True to Zephaniah's prophecy, the city was captured by Babylonia's king, Nebuchadnezzar, in 597 BC and destroyed in 587 after a decade of occupation.

TEACHING THE BIBLE LESSON

LIFE NEED FOR TODAY'S LESSON

AIM: Students will explore how people sometimes destroy something beautiful even when they know the consequences.

INTRODUCTION

God's Restoration Refused

Beginning in **Zephaniah 2**, the prophet describes God's coming judgment on the nations. First, the Lord started with Philistia. He promised to make the coastlands that the people inhabited a pasture for flocks. Next He judged Moab and Ammon, the descendants of Lot, who had

mistreated God's people. He promised that He would humble them, and did so. The Lord then turned to Egypt and promised to punish the Egyptians through war, killing their youths. Next, He promised the Ethiopians death by the sword. Finally, the Lord addressed Assyria and promised that the great city of Nineveh would become a wilderness.

Here in **Zephaniah 3** is a prophecy directed at Jerusalem. **Verses 1 through 6** give a detailed picture of Jerusalem. The City of God had deteriorated into a polluted city filled with violence and crime (**v. 1**). The people of Jerusalem resisted all attempts at correction. Though Josiah had instituted religious reforms and nearly eradicated Baal worship, the people of Judah remained rebellious. They had no faith in the Lord and would not seek Him (**v. 2**). The leaders preyed on the people. Even their worship was tainted. The priests defiled the Temple and the prophets were seeking only personal gain. The Lord had attempted to restore Jerusalem, but they refused. At this point, the Lord's wrath will come upon the people of Jerusalem for their sinful ways.

BIBLE LEARNING

AIM: Students will know that believers know that there are consequences to their sinful behavior.

I. OTHER NATIONS ARE DESTROYED (ZEPHANIAH 3:6)

The Lord describes how He executed judgment on other nations. **Zephaniah 2:4–15** describe the Lord's judgment on surrounding nations. He pronounces judgment on Philistia, Moab, Ammon, Ethiopia, and Assyria. He uses their destruction as an example of judgment for sin. Their foundations and their towers had been destroyed. These other nations had been "cut off." There were no survivors. These nations had become extinct.

Zephaniah 3:6–8

6 I have cut off the nations: their towers are desolate; I made their streets waste, that none passeth by: their cities are destroyed, so that there is no man, that there is none inhabitant.

In the previous verses, God has indicted Jerusalem. He describes the wrongs of the officials and leaders. He contrasts their injustice with His justice as a righteous judge. Next the Lord, through Zephaniah, declares His track record and the foolishness of Jerusalem's rebellion. He declares, "I have cut off the nations: their towers are desolate." The word for tower (Heb. *pinnah*, **pee-NAH**) refers to the corners of a building, usually where a tower of a citadel or fortress would be positioned. These towers would be key points in the defense of the city. Once these towers fell, the whole city would be open and vulnerable to attack. These towers were now desolate (Heb. *shaman*, shah-**MAHM**), which means destroyed to the point of being empty. The Lord is saying that the strength

of the nations—their armies—is no more. The streets are made waste (Heb. *charab*, **khah-RAHV**), which means here to be in ruins. The picture is that the streets would have no one walking on them. After God's judgment, no one would be left.

II. JUDAH REFUSES TO REPENT (v. 7)

While Judah was aware of the destruction and judgment of surrounding nations, they were certain that it would not happen to them. They believed that the Lord would do nothing to them (**1:12**). As a result, Judah was unaffected by the destruction of other nations.

The Lord had hoped that after seeing the destruction that had come to the surrounding nations, Judah would repent and turn to Him. He did not want to strike Judah and bring destruction. Judah, however, remained deeply entrenched in its sin—so much so that the inhabitants of Judah rose early in the morning to engage in their sin (**v. 6**).

By making examples of surrounding nations, God was giving Judah a chance to repent. He gave them a chance to choose wholeness rather than desolation. Judah had an opportunity to receive the Lord's instruction and correction, and avoid judgment. Instead, Judah chose to continue in their sin.

No Fear of God

7 I said, Surely thou wilt fear me, thou wilt receive instruction; so their dwelling should not be cut off, howsoever I punished them: but they rose early, and corrupted all their doings.

Zephaniah gives us a glimpse into the divine mind and heart. After all that God has done to the nations, He expects His own people to fear (Heb. *yara*, **yah-RAH**) Him. This fear is a theological term with reverential awe as the dominant aspect, which would drive those who possess it to a life of piety and obedience and a willingness to receive instruction (Heb. *musar*, **moo-SAHR**). This word also refers to discipline, correction, and chastisement. In this context, Zephaniah specifically has in mind discipline and chastisement with a view to a change of behavior. The purpose of the discipline is to keep Israel from being cut off (Heb. *karat*, **kah-ROT**), a euphemism for ceasing to exist in the sense that God would find a way to end the person's family line (cf. **Leviticus 7:20–21; Jeremiah 11:19**). The Lord desires His people to continue on in spite of the fact that He needs to punish them. This punishment was something that could not be averted, but if they repented of their sins, it would be remedial and not result in total destruction.

III. THE LORD PROMISES UTTER DESTRUCTION AND OFFERS HOPE (v. 8)

Because Judah did not heed the Lord's warning and refused to repent, the Lord promised utter destruction for the unrepentant. Still, a message of hope remained for the faithful. The Lord also spoke to the small remnant that served Him. He commanded them to wait on Him. He promised that He would judge the sinners and restore the righteous. The faithful were instructed to await the redemption of the Lord. He urged them to wait on Him and depend on Him alone.

The prophecy describes the final Day of the Lord when the nations will be judged. This time of extreme tribulation will be unlike anything that has ever been seen before (**Matthew 24:21**). The Lord will pour out His fury against the nations for their rebellion against Him.

The Lord promises a tragic end: the whole earth will be devoured by the fire of His jealousy. This is particularly unfortunate because He is destroying the very creation He delighted in making and declared good. The fire of His jealousy would consume all.

The Fire of God's Jealousy

8 Therefore wait ye upon me, saith the LORD, until the day that I rise up to the prey: for my determination is to gather the nations, that I may assemble the kingdoms, to pour upon them mine indignation, even all my fierce anger: for all the earth shall be devoured with the fire of my jealousy.

As a result of Jerusalem's continuous rebellion, the Lord says to wait (Heb. *chakah*, **kha-KAH**) for Him—the day when God's judgment comes, when He rises up to seize the prey. The word for rise up (Heb. *qum*, **KOOM**) means to rise up, but also to physically stand up or to arise with power over somebody or something-in this case the deserved punishment of the people of Jerusalem is the consequence of God assuming His full power. The Lord says His decision is to gather (Heb. *asaph*, **ah-SAHF**) or bring in the nations into the court of justice. He will assemble (Heb. *qabats*, **kah-VATS**) the kingdoms. The Hebrew word for assemble means to collect in the sense of grasping by the hand as with grain during the harvest, but most of the time means a gathering of people. This gathering of the nations would be according to the Lord's sovereign plan and He would be intimately involved. The purpose is that He will pour out His indignation (Heb. *za'am*, **ZAH-am**), which is related to the idea of foaming. This indignation will be unleashed on the nations, and Judah will be a recipient as well. Zephaniah adds that in the fire of the Lord's jealousy, the whole earth will be consumed. Here jealousy (Heb. *qin'ah*, **kee-NAH**) means the appropriate desire for what someone has a right to—in this case, the jealousy of God who is Lord over the whole earth and His people in particular.

SEARCH THE SCRIPTURES

QUESTION 1

God's jealousy is intense against Jerusalem only. True or False?

False.

QUESTION 2

Which nations will remain after God's fury is poured because of their rebellion?

None.

LIGHT ON THE WORD

Repent, Judah, Repent!

The Lord reminded Judah of the destruction of these other nations as an appeal for Judah to repent. He had judged sinners. Would He not judge His own people who had lost faith in Him, the ones who had chosen not to walk in His ways, even more so?

BIBLE APPLICATION

AIM: Students will know that God offers hope for change and wants to save people from their disobedience.

So many in our society believe, like the people of Judah, that the Lord will do nothing to them. Many lose sight of the fact that we will one day stand before God (**Romans 14:12**). Each person will have to give an account. So many carry on as if there were no punishment for sin and no need for a savior.

Zephaniah prophesies the judgment of the whole earth. God does indeed punish for sin, but He is also rich in mercy and seeks repentance and reconciliation. Spend some time with the Lord to confess any sin and let Him speak to you about how you can please Him more.

STUDENT'S RESPONSES

AIM: Students will affirm that God provides opportunities for people to repent and seek His ways.

Proverbs 15:32 says, "If you reject discipline, you only harm yourself; but if you listen to correction, you grow in understanding." The Holy Spirit is constantly speaking to us. We must be attentive and responsive to the Lord's leading and correction. Regularly spend time reading the Bible and praying. Seek the Lord and let Him instruct you.

PRAYER

God, hear our prayers of needing and wanting You in our lives. Help us and guide us to know that You give us love, forgiveness, and opportunities in so may ways to seek You, love You, and honor You. Thank You for forgiving us and blessing us. In Jesus' Name we pray. Amen.

HOW TO SAY IT

Inhabitant.   in-ha-bi-**TENT**.

Indignation.   in-dig-**NAY**-shun.

PREPARE FOR NEXT SUNDAY

Read **Zephaniah 3:9–14, 20** and "Assurances and Joy for the Faithful."

DAILY HOME BIBLE READINGS

MONDAY
Remember the Commandments
(Deuteronomy 4:9–14)

TUESDAY
Godly Planning
(Proverbs 16:1–9)

WEDNESDAY
Ungodly Planning
(Ezekiel 33:27–33)

THURSDAY
Promised Rest
(Matthew 11:25–30)

FRIDAY
Humble Planning
(1 Peter 5:1–6)

SATURDAY
Faithful Planning
(1 Peter 5:7–11)

SUNDAY
Consequences of Disobedience
(Zephaniah 3:6–8)

Sources:
Carson, D. A., R. T. France, J. A. Motyer, J. G. Wenham.. *New Bible Commentary.* Downers Grove, IL: InterVarsity Press, 1993.
Keener, Craig S. *IVP Bible Background Commentary.* Downers Grove, IL: InterVarsity Press, 1993.

COMMENTS / NOTES:

ASSURANCES AND JOY
FOR THE FAITHFUL

BIBLE BASIS: ZEPHANIAH 3:9–14, 20

BIBLE TRUTH: God's intervention was required to stop the people from rebelling and to return to the Lord with singing.

MEMORY VERSE: "Sing, O daughter of Zion; shout aloud, O Israel! Be glad and rejoice with all your heart, O daughter of Jerusalem!"

(Zephaniah 3:14).

LESSON AIM: By the end of the lesson, we will: TELL of God's proclamation through Zephaniah that He would bring the people to obedience; BE ASSURED God will help us through our times of trouble and disobedience; and PRAY for one another and ourselves for God's presence and involvement in our lives.

TEACHER PREPARATION

MATERIALS NEEDED: Quarterly Commentary/Teacher Manual, Adult Quarterly, Adult resources—charts, worksheets, and other teaching tools, paper, pens, pencils, Bibles (several different versions)

OTHER MATERIALS NEEDED / TEACHER'S NOTES:

_____

_____

LESSON OVERVIEW

LIFE NEED FOR TODAY'S LESSON
People will sometimes repent of their harmful, destructive ways, and seek to restore what has been ruined.

BIBLE LEARNING
God is faithful and is worthy of all praise.

BIBLE APPLICATION
God desires people to seek after the Lord.

STUDENTS' RESPONSES
Believers know that God deserves honor, glory, and reverence.

LESSON SCRIPTURE

ZEPHANIAH 3:9–14, 20, KJV

9 For then will I turn to the people a pure language, that they may all call upon the name of the LORD, to serve him with one consent.

10 From beyond the rivers of Ethiopia my suppliants, even the daughter of my dispersed, shall bring mine offering.

ZEPHANIAH 3:9–14, 20, NIV

9 "Then I will purify the lips of the peoples, that all of them may call on the name of the LORD and serve him shoulder to shoulder.

10 From beyond the rivers of Cush my worshipers, my scattered people, will bring me offerings.

11 On that day you, Jerusalem, will not be

11 In that day shalt thou not be ashamed for all thy doings, wherein thou hast transgressed against me: for then I will take away out of the midst of thee them that rejoice in thy pride, and thou shalt no more be haughty because of my holy mountain.

12 I will also leave in the midst of thee an afflicted and poor people, and they shall trust in the name of the LORD.

13 The remnant of Israel shall not do iniquity, nor speak lies; neither shall a deceitful tongue be found in their mouth: for they shall feed and lie down, and none shall make them afraid.

14 Sing, O daughter of Zion; shout, O Israel; be glad and rejoice with all the heart, O daughter of Jerusalem.

20 At that time will I bring you again, even in the time that I gather you: for I will make you a name and a praise among all people of the earth, when I turn back your captivity before your eyes, saith the LORD.

put to shame for all the wrongs you have done to me, because I will remove from you your arrogant boasters. Never again will you be haughty on my holy hill.

12 But I will leave within you the meek and humble. The remnant of Israel will trust in the name of the LORD.

13 They will do no wrong; they will tell no lies. A deceitful tongue will not be found in their mouths. They will eat and lie down and no one will make them afraid."

14 Sing, Daughter Zion; shout aloud, Israel! Be glad and rejoice with all your heart, Daughter Jerusalem!

20 At that time I will gather you; at that time I will bring you home. I will give you honor and praise among all the peoples of the earth when I restore your fortunes before your very eyes," says the LORD.

LIGHT ON THE WORD

Ethiopia. In the time of Zephaniah, the land around the southern parts of the Nile was called Ethiopia or the land of Cush. This land is named after the grandson of Ham, the son of Noah. It is not to be confused with modern-day Ethiopia, but more accurately located in the region of the modern-day nation of Sudan. The term Ethiopia is also used in the Bible to refer to the whole African continent. In ancient times, Ethiopia was often connected with Egypt and gave birth to many powerful rulers such as Tirhakah and Queen Candace (**2 Kings 19:9; Acts 8:27**).

The Remnant. The remnant is the group of people that survive the judgment of the Lord. When Israel and Judah escaped capture, the survivors were called a remnant. The word also refers to other groups throughout the Old Testament: a remnant of Israel entered the Promised Land; those who remain faithful when others fall away from the faith can also be called a remnant. The remnant survives divine judgment and remains faithful as God destroys those who are unfaithful to Him. The remnant is therefore a purified group, and described in **Zephaniah 3:9–13**.

TEACHING THE BIBLE LESSON

LIFE NEED FOR TODAY'S LESSON

AIM: Students will understand how people will sometimes repent of their harmful,

destructive ways, and seek to restore what has been ruined.

INTRODUCTION

God's Remnant

The book of Zephaniah was written in the seventh century BC during the reign of Josiah. When Josiah ascended to the throne, Judah was filled with idol worship. Their rituals were so deeply ingrained that some practices still remained after Josiah had instituted religious reform. The Lord promised to bring judgment that would destroy everything in the land of Judah. However, even amid the judgment, the Lord promised that He would preserve a remnant that would worship Him.

BIBLE LEARNING

AIM: Students will know that God is faithful and is worthy of all praise.

I. PURIFICATION OF THE REMNANT (ZEPHANIAH 3:9–10)

After the Babylonian captivity, the language of Judah had been mingled with that of pagans (**Nehemiah 13:24**). The Lord said He would make for Himself a people of "pure speech." Once their speech was purified, they would call on the name of the Lord (**v. 9**). Purified speech is tied to separation from temptation and evil. Not only is it a sign of loyalty the Lord, but also a behavior that demonstrates commitment to God. The people whom the Lord purifies will "shall not...speak lies" (**v. 13**) and do no injustice. This people will show their devotion to God by following in His ways. Even now, our speech also demonstrates our loyalty to God. **Romans 10:10** says "with the mouth confession is made unto salvation."

The purification would not be limited to the faithful in Jerusalem. The Lord would gather those who have been scattered and number them among the faithful.

Zephaniah 3:9–14, 20

9 For then will I turn to the people a pure language, that they may all call upon the name of the Lord, to serve him with one consent.

Zephaniah prophesies that hope will come after Jerusalem's destruction. The Lord will turn (Heb. *haphak*, **ha-FAK**), which can mean overturn or change, the people's language. It will be a pure (Heb. *barar*, **ba-RAR**) language, purged of defilement. Zephaniah concludes that this is so the people would call on the Lord and serve Him with one consent (Heb. *shekem*, **she-KEHM**). This word literally means shoulder, but metaphorically the place where a burden or responsibility is carried. In this context the image is that the Lord's people will, as one, shoulder the weight of serving Him.

10 From beyond the rivers of Ethiopia my suppliants, even the daughter of my dispersed, shall bring mine offering.

The mention of rivers of Ethiopia here does not refer to the modern nation of Ethiopia, but the area of ancient Nubia or modern Sudan. "Beyond the rivers of Ethiopia" would refer to all of Africa, including sub-Saharan Africa. The word for suppliants (Heb. *atar*, **ah-TAR**) can refer to the people who worship a deity, or the incense the people of this time and place would commonly use in their worship especially in supplication for help. This worship will include the daughter of God's dispersed (Heb. *putz*, **POOTZ**), that is, pushed out and scattered. This is likely a reference to the coming exile This would have resonated with Judahites who knew of the Assyrian and Babylonian empire's tactics of war and conquest. The Assyrians were known for removing people from their land and distributing their population throughout the many provinces of their empire in order to weaken their physcial unity and political will. The Babylonians continued this tactic when they took over the Ancient Near East This makes clear that not even exile would keep God from realizing His plans for His people.

II. BLESSINGS FOR JERUSALEM (vv. 11–13)

When the Lord restores Judah, He will remove their shame. As children who have been punished are often ashamed, those disciplined by the Lord often feel shame for their actions. However, the Lord promises to cleanse Judah from guilt and shame. Likewise, the Lord removes any sense of condemnation from those who are in Christ (**Romans 8:1**).

The Lord would purify for Himself a people of humility and faith. Their faith will not be in themselves, but the Lord alone. They will have pure speech, pure hearts, and pure actions (**v. 13**). The Lord Himself will be their protection, and they will have no reason to fear as they go about their daily activities (**3:13**).

The Fall of Pride and Arrogance

11 In that day shalt thou not be ashamed for all thy doings, wherein thou hast transgressed against me: for then I will take away out of the midst of thee them that rejoice in thy pride, and thou shalt no more be haughty because of my holy mountain.

The phrase "in that day" refers to do the Day of the Lord and the rebuke and chastisement that will take place when God gets rid of those who are proud and arrogant. God declares that Judah will not be ashamed (Heb. *bush*, **BOOSH**), which means that they will not experience disgrace for their deeds. God's people would no longer have to fear and be astonished at His judgment. They had transgressed (Heb. *pasha'*, **pa-SHAH**), meaning sinned or rebelled, against Him, but He had a remedy. The Lord would take away from them those who rejoice (Heb. *'alliz*, **ah-LEEZ**) or are jubilant and exultant. This word is often used for those who rejoice in a bad sense (**Isaiah 13:3,**

22:2). They are rejoicing insolently in their pride. One of the few other times this word is used is in **Zephaniah 2:15**, when the prophet describes Jerusalem as the "rejoicing city." The city was full of proud people who thought they were safe because of Jerusalem's strategic military position on a mountain. The Lord says they will no longer be haughty (Heb. *gavah*, **ga-VAH**), which means to be high or lifted up, and can be used positively (like for God) or negatively (like here). This could be a play on words as Jerusalem is high up on a mountain. In other words, the people had been proud and haughty because of God's holy mountain. They are rejoicing in being God's covenant people while at the same time not adhering to His covenant stipulations.

12 I will also leave in the midst of thee an afflicted and poor people, and they shall trust in the name of the Lord. 13 The remnant of Israel shall not do iniquity, nor speak lies; neither shall a deceitful tongue be found in their mouth: for they shall feed and lie down, and none shall make them afraid.

The Lord will leave an afflicted (Heb. *'ani*, ah-NEE) and poor (Heb. *dal*, **DAHL**) people in Judah. These words have different connotations for people's condition. *'Ani* means to be without property and marked by meekness or modesty. This would refer to people's internal disposition as a result of their external circumstances. *Dal* refers to the actual condition of people as weak, powerless, and insignificant. These are people who would have no alternative but to trust (Heb. *chasah*, kha-SAH) in the name of the Lord. The word for trust has an underlying meaning of flee or take refuge. Where once the people took refuge in their own pride at being God's chosen people, this time they would humbly seek Him for their refuge. This same remnant would do no iniquity (Heb. *'awlah* av-LAH). This word can be defined as sin but often refers specifically to violent deeds of injustice. The phrase "they shall feed and lie down" metaphorically speaks of them as sheep in the care of a shepherd and shows their safety and security is in God. Because of this restoration and hope, Israel is exhorted to sing (Heb. *ranan*, **rah-NAN**), which has the connotation of shouting for joy. This is no ordinary liturgical singing, but the singing of people overwhelmed with hope. They are told to be glad and rejoice, because God's favor would shine on His people again.

III. REJOICING FOR THE REMNANT (v. 14)

The messages in this section of the prophecy are very different from those of punishment and destruction. The Lord promises that Judah will once again rejoice. They will sing and shout aloud (**v. 14**). The fear of punishment will be removed and the Lord Himself will live among them (**v. 15**). Judah will be fully forgiven and would have the very presence of God and once again would be filled with rejoicing.

Rejoice, Jerusalem, Rejoice!

14 Sing, O daughter of Zion; shout, O Israel; be glad and rejoice with all the heart, O daughter of Jerusalem.

Zephaniah's prophecy would be fulfilled after seventy years of Babylonian captivity. However, the prophecy also refers to the Second Coming of Christ, when there will be no more sorrow and the whole earth will be filled with the knowledge and glory of the Lord (**Revelation 21:4; Habakkuk 2:14**). Like the people of Judah, we can rejoice because we have been forgiven of our sins. We have the Spirit of God living within us. Ultimately, Jesus will return and we will be with Him forever. We will rejoice in the glory of the Lord.

The terms of endearment God uses for His people are significant for believers in Christ. He calls them the "daughter of Zion," which is an affectionate name for the faithful and a reference to God's holy mountain. He calls them "Israel," the

name for God's chosen people, not just the inhabitants of the Northern Kingdom. Finally, the Lord calls His people the "daughter of Jerusalem." The earthly city of Jerusalem is a foreshadowing of the new Jerusalem, where all those who profess faith in Christ will live with Him forever.

IV. RESTORATION OF THE REMNANT (v. 20)

The Lord promises to gather the faithful together and bring them honor and blessing. He promises them a homeland, an esteemed name among the nations, and the restoration of their fortunes. He fulfilled these promises when Judah returned from bondage.

However, a gathering and restoration of Israel will come when its name will be a praise to the whole world (**v. 20**). When Jesus returns, He will gather His people, and Israel will shine. This will be the ultimate fulfillment of the Lord's promises and a time of great rejoicing, of total redemption, free from all suffering.

Restoration is Promised

20 At that time will I bring you again, even in the time that I gather you: for I will make you a name and a praise among all people of the earth, when I turn back your captivity before your eyes, saith the LORD.

In this verse, God promises restoration. The people will return from exile. The Lord says that He Himself will gather them and return them to the land, as well as He will make them a name and a praise. To make them a name (Heb. *shem*, **SHEM**) is to give them a good reputation, as the name is more than just a title or label, but a person's character and reputation. The word for praise (Heb. *tehillah*, **te-hee-LAH**) is a word that is often used for singing hymns to God. His people would receive praise due to their association with Him and His blessings.

God's people would receive a good reputation and be praised by all the people of the earth. The language here is reminiscent of God's promise to Abram in **Genesis 12:1–3**. The Lord would restore them and they would receive the blessings He promised to Abraham and his descendants. This would all happen when He turned back (Heb. *shub*, **SHOOV**) or restored the fortunes of those who had been in captivity.

SEARCH THE SCRIPTURES

QUESTION 1
Who is the remnant that God leave and what will they do?

The poor and the afflicted will be left. They will trust in the name of of the Lord.

QUESTION 2
What is the term of endearment that God uses in verse 14?

Daughter of Zion.

LIGHT ON THE WORD

International Community
As in centuries past, the Lord will gather His people from all corners of the world. Many are unaware of their Christian brothers and sisters laboring, teaching, and suffering for the name of Christ. Make it a point to pray for the persecuted church around the world.

BIBLE APPLICATION

AIM: Students will learn that God desires people to seek after the Lord.

The Lord promises to restore the nation of Judah. Even His judgment is executed with transformation in view. He does this to purify a people for Himself.

Not only will He preserve a remnant from Judah, He will unite the faithful who have been scattered abroad. As Christians in the United States, we hear few reports about the church worldwide. We hear little of the Christians who are persecuted for their faith and meet in secret. When Jesus returns, He will gather all His people from around the world and we will praise Him forever.

STUDENT'S RESPONSES

AIM: Students will know that God deserves honor, glory, and reverence.

Similar to the people of Zephaniah's day, many in our society don't follow the Lord wholeheartedly. They value some of the Lord's instructions but ignore others. Some mix other elements into their Christian faith. We must follow the Lord and put our faith in Him alone. The Lord still seeks to purify a people wholly devoted to Him. Jesus gave us the greatest commandment: to love the Lord your God with all your heart and with all your soul and with all your mind (**Matthew 22:37–38**). Let this be the focus of our lives.

PRAYER

Lord, restore and renew our passion for You. We are blessed to have Your gracious love and correction in our lives. Allow us to remain Your servants and bless others so that You receive the glory and the honor. Forgive us of our sins as we press toward remaining faithful servants of Christ. In Jesus' Name we pray. Amen.

HOW TO SAY IT

Suppliants. SUP-plea-ents.

Haughty. HAW-tee.

PREPARE FOR NEXT SUNDAY

Read **Romans 1:18–23, 28–32** and "Ignoring God's Plain Truth."

DAILY HOME BIBLE READINGS

MONDAY
Encouraging Others
(Hebrews 10:19–25)

TUESDAY
Pleasing God
(Hebrews 11:1–6)

WEDNESDAY
Trusting God
(Hebrews 11:7–12)

THURSDAY
Testing God
(Hebrews 11:13–22)

FRIDAY
Serving God
(Hebrews 11:23–28)

SATURDAY
Commendable Faith
(Hebrews 11:29–39)

SUNDAY
Assurances and Joy for the Faithful
(Zephaniah 3:9–14, 20)

Sources:
Bentley, Michael. *Opening Up Zephaniah*. Opening Up Commentary. Leominster, United Kingdom: Day One Publications, 2008.
Myers, Allen C. *The Eerdmans Bible Dictionary*. Grand Rapids, MI: Eerdmans, 1987.
Smith, James E. *The Minor Prophets*. Old Testament Survey Series. Joplin, MO: College Press, 1994.

COMMENTS / NOTES:

IGNORING GOD'S PLAIN TRUTH

BIBLE BASIS: ROMANS 1:18–23, 28–32

BIBLE TRUTH: Paul recounts how people will disobey God and take pride in filling their lives with actions that oppose Him.

MEMORY VERSE: "For the invisible things of him from the creation of the world are clearly seen, being understood by the things that are made, even his eternal power and Godhead; so that they are without excuse" (Romans 1:20).

LESSON AIM: By the end of the lesson, we will: KNOW Paul's plaintive story of God's magnificent creation choosing to wreck itself with sin; FEEL that humans really do have the freedom to be disobedient but will suffer God's punishment; and DO God's will instead of sinning.

TEACHER PREPARATION

MATERIALS NEEDED: Quarterly Commentary/Teacher Manual, Adult Quarterly, Adult resources—charts, worksheets, and other teaching tools, paper, pens, pencils, Bibles (several different versions)

OTHER MATERIALS NEEDED / TEACHER'S NOTES:

_____

_____

LESSON OVERVIEW

LIFE NEED FOR TODAY'S LESSON
Some people do what they believe is right, while others constantly do what is wrong.

BIBLE LEARNING
Paul notes how some people know God, but choose to live their lives opposite of His love, mercy, and justice.

BIBLE APPLICATION
Christians must decide to follow God and not to choose wickedness or teachings that lead people away from Him.

STUDENTS' RESPONSES
Believers will commit to accepting and follow after God's decrees for their lives.

LESSON SCRIPTURE

ROMANS 1:18–23, 28–32, KJV

18 For the wrath of God is revealed from heaven against all ungodliness and unrighteousness of men, who hold the truth in unrighteousness;

19 Because that which may be known of God is manifest in them; for God hath

ROMANS 1:18–23, 28–32, NIV

18 The wrath of God is being revealed from heaven against all the godlessness and wickedness of people, who suppress the truth by their wickedness,

19 since what may be known about God is plain to them, because God has made it

shewed it unto them.

plain to them.

20 For the invisible things of him from the creation of the world are clearly seen, being understood by the things that are made, even his eternal power and Godhead; so that they are without excuse:

20 For since the creation of the world God's invisible qualities—his eternal power and divine nature—have been clearly seen, being understood from what has been made, so that people are without excuse.

21 Because that, when they knew God, they glorified him not as God, neither were thankful; but became vain in their imaginations, and their foolish heart was darkened.

21 For although they knew God, they neither glorified him as God nor gave thanks to him, but their thinking became futile and their foolish hearts were darkened.

22 Professing themselves to be wise, they became fools,

22 Although they claimed to be wise, they became fools

23 And changed the glory of the uncorruptible God into an image made like to corruptible man, and to birds, and fourfooted beasts, and creeping things.

23 and exchanged the glory of the immortal God for images made to look like a mortal human being and birds and animals and reptiles.

28 And even as they did not like to retain God in their knowledge, God gave them over to a reprobate mind, to do those things which are not convenient;

28 Furthermore, just as they did not think it worthwhile to retain the knowledge of God, so God gave them over to a depraved mind, so that they do what ought not to be done.

29 Being filled with all unrighteousness, fornication, wickedness, covetousness, maliciousness; full of envy, murder, debate, deceit, malignity; whisperers,

29 They have become filled with every kind of wickedness, evil, greed and depravity. They are full of envy, murder, strife, deceit and malice. They are gossips,

30 Backbiters, haters of God, despiteful, proud, boasters, inventors of evil things, disobedient to parents,

30 slanderers, God-haters, insolent, arrogant and boastful; they invent ways of doing evil; they disobey their parents;

31 Without understanding, covenantbreakers, without natural affection, implacable, unmerciful:

31 they have no understanding, no fidelity, no love, no mercy.

32 Who knowing the judgment of God, that they which commit such things are worthy of death, not only do the same, but have pleasure in them that do them.

32 Although they know God's righteous decree that those who do such things deserve death, they not only continue to do these very things but also approve of those who practice them.

LIGHT ON THE WORD

Idolatry. Idolatry was widespread when Paul was writing to the Romans. The primary focus of worship for most people in the Roman empire was the Roman state and its rulers. "Emperor worship" was common. For example, Caligula, emperor from A.D. 37–41, declared himself a god and commanded the Romans to worship him. Although Paul probably wrote to Rome in a time of relative peace toward the beginning of Nero's reign, under Claudius (41-54 A.D.), some of the members of the church at Rome had been forced to leave due to persecution of the Jews and had only recently returned (**Acts 18:1–3; Romans 16:3–4**).

Roman degradation. The Roman world evidenced the kind of godless characteristics that Paul listed in **verses 28–32**. The Roman Empire was known for its brutality against the powerless, and persecution of Jews, as well as anyone in the churches since churches consisted of Jews and Gentiles, became more and more common in the second half of the first century AD. In addition, wealthy and powerful Roman men were known for sexual licentiousness both with women prostitutes and with their male servants and other males in relatively powerless positions. The Romans also enjoyed their arena conquests, men fighting to the death against each other or wild animals. This love of spectacle and cruelty grew to the point that defenseless people, including children, were thrown to wild animals as an attempt to purge the Christians during the great persecutions. Although there were many philosophical and religious groups who supported morality and the common good in the Roman Empire, as with many empires, often those in power abused their authority, and frequently the powerless and the synagogues and churches were victims of such abuse.

TEACHING THE BIBLE LESSON

LIFE NEED FOR TODAY'S LESSON

AIM: Students will know that some people do what they believe is right, while others constantly do what is wrong.

INTRODUCTION

The Sinfulness of Humanity

In the introduction of Romans, Paul starts with the purpose of his writing and essentially the purpose of his life: the Gospel. He lets the Romans know that he longs to come to them and build them up spiritually, for the Gospel's sake. He is a debtor to the Jews and Gentiles to deliver this message, the two ethnic groups that made up the Roman church.

As Paul lays the foundation for the whole book, he addresses the sinfulness of humanity in general and the Gentiles in particular. The first thing he talks about is idolatry, a sin particularly repugnant to the monotheistic Jews. By addressing idolatry first, the Jews in the Roman church would have assumed Paul was going to attack the Gentiles. This passage is a setup for a wider argument that not only the Gentiles but also the Jews were in sinful rebellion against God.

BIBLE LEARNING

AIM: Students will understand that some people know God, but choose to live their lives opposite of His love, mercy, and justice.

I. PEOPLE RESIST MANIFEST TRUTH (ROMANS 1:18–20)

Paul said that God is wrathful toward ungodliness and unrighteousness. His wrath is against those who reject the truth of His existence. God's wrath, unlike ours, is not capricious or selfish but holy in His desire to see us living rightly. Paul said that the existence of God is clearly manifested, or obvious, to those who will look at creation.

These verses are part of the answer to the age-old question, "What about those people who have never heard?" Paul said that they are without excuse. Creation in its beauty, power, complexity, and harmony shows clear evidence of the Creator. More than just His existence is evident—Paul said creation reveals His character as well.

Romans 1:18–23, 28-32

In this letter to the saints in Rome, Paul expounds for his largely Gentile audience the core of the epistle's message—that all have sinned and need saving, but this saving is only possible by grace through faith. All here really does mean all, including both the Gentiles (exemplified in this letter by the Greeks) and the Jews. He states that Gentiles have sinned and are worthy of punishment. Then, Paul goes on to explain how the Gentiles have sinned when they have not had access to the Law for them to understand their condition. Thus, while Paul in this letter focuses on the righteousness of God, he has to show that where that righteousness is not practiced, God's wrath is unleashed.

The wrath of God is commonly spoken of in today's modern society. It is said that some cultures believe life is being shaped by a very active spirit-world—and these spirits (both good and evil) are closely involved in human life. Some believe that reigning over the spirits and all creation is a god who, through the spirits, controls the affairs of this world. They further believe that occasionally the spirits become displeased with the undertakings of human beings, and unleash their wrath on the human world. This misunderstood view regarding spirits is the enemy's attempt at negating the power and authority of the Lord. Jesus Himself gives the born again believer power over all the power of the enemy confirming that "nothing shall by any means hurt you (**Luke 10:19**)." When cultures violate the Word of God

to appease the wrath of the deity, they endanger themselves to the wrath and punishment of God the Creator. For Malawians, for instance, when the spirits (generally of their ancestors) get angry—*mizimu yakwiya*—people must do everything in their power to appease them. God's wrath is not an impersonal process, but a deliberate judgment. It is not some irrational passion on the part of God, but rather of His righteous and wholly justified indignation against sinful belief and sinful behavior. It is the inevitable retributive response of the eternally holy God against anything that violates His own being.

18 For the wrath of God is revealed from heaven against all ungodliness and unrighteousness of men, who hold the truth in unrighteousness.

After **verse 17**, where Paul writes about the righteousness of God revealed in the Gospel, he suddenly drops his readers into the fearsome pit of God's wrath. The connection between **verses 18 and 17** is obvious. While God's righteousness is revealed in the Gospel to humankind, His wrath is revealed from heaven against ungodliness and wickedness. Thus Paul diverts from this theme of God's righteousness and dedicates the remainder of the chapter and the two subsequent chapters to the need to understand the only way to get right with God—by grace through repentance and faith. Here, he begins to explain what God's righteousness amounts to for those who have exchanged the truth about Him for a lie—His wrath. Paul is straight to the point: The Gentiles, just like all law-breakers who deserve a penalty, are under the wrath of God. Central to Paul's argument here is that even though the Gentiles have not received the Gospel yet, they have had a chance to know God's truth, but chose to ignore and suppress it. Therefore, they are equally deserving of judgment. Paul believes that sinful humanity universally represses the knowledge of God available to them and so is held accountable; thus, no one is condemned for not knowing God, but rather for suppressing and ignoring the knowledge of God available to them. The Gentiles are at fault.

The wrath of God is being revealed from heaven, not in the Gospel but in the facts of human experience—in the reality of punitive events of history. Thus, Paul is not talking about the wrath of God that will be revealed at the end of time (cf. **Revelation 19:15**). Paul is talking about God's wrath revealed in the punishments imposed by human governments, the accusations of conscience, the pain of childbirth, the necessity of toil as a result of a sin-cursed environment, and the inescapable penalty of death itself. Most significantly, the most obvious revelation of God's wrath is His "giving over" the Gentiles to the consequences their sinful desires and depraved lifestyles (**vv. 24, 26, 28**). This wrath—the consuming fire of God—is His settled and perfectly righteous antagonism toward evil.

This wrath, says Paul, is directed against those who "suppress (Gk. *katecho*, **ka-te-KOH** to hold down, even though the KJV translates it "hold") the truth by their wickedness." One would ask, "What truth?" And this is the question that Paul wrestles with in the verses that follow, coming to a crescendo in **verse 25** where he reveals it to be God's truth. In saying that the Gentiles suppress the truth, Paul implies that the Gentiles already have the truth and know it is true. This is why the Gentiles are not exempt from God's wrath, and must need grace to be saved. They have no excuse at all. Their ignorance of the truth is not real; it is a false ignorance. It is only pretense intended to cover their neglect of the truth—the very act of suppressing the truth.

19 Because that which may be known of God is manifest in them; for God hath shewed it unto them. 20 For the invisible things of him from the creation of the world are clearly seen, being understood by the things that are made, even his eternal power and Godhead; so that they are without excuse: 21 Because that, when they knew God, they glorified him not as God, neither were thankful; but became vain in their imaginations, and their foolish heart was darkened.

This group of verses is a continuation—and explanation—of what was said in the preceding verse. The wrath of God is being revealed because all people know God and His truth since He has shown or made it plain to them, but they have chosen to reject God and the truth that He reveals. In a nutshell, Paul is arguing that the Gentiles know the truth because God has revealed it to them through the created universe. What the Gentiles can know about God is plain for them to see. Paul's use of the word *phaneros* (Gk. *phaneros*, **fah-neh-ROS**, evident or clearly visible) suggests that it cannot be missed at all. This act of God's deliberate self-disclosure to humankind, even today, grants people who have not heard the Gospel access to God's truth, communicated in and through the created universe.

Verse 20 continues to explain Paul's argument that the Gentiles have access to the truth of God even though they have not heard the Gospel yet. How is this possible? The answer is simple: since the creation of the world, certain invisible attributes of God—like His eternal (Gk. *aidios*, **EYE-dee-oss**, everlasting) power and divine nature—have been clearly seen through the created universe. In other words, the creation is the visible disclosure of the invisible God. Looking at the vastness of the universe draws us to ponder the Creator of this universe. When we see the cycles of the seasons and how every animal is suited to its habitat, we can see the wisdom of this Creator. As we even take note of our own human qualities of kindness and love for our loved ones and especially children, we see the love and care of the Creator for His creation. This is how the visible creation testifies to the existence of an invisible Creator and our accountability to Him. This is what scholars have called general revelation—the type of revelation that is made to everyone everywhere. The Gentiles are left without an excuse as there can be no pretense of ignorance. Creation's general revelation in itself gives sufficient knowledge to all human beings whereby every person can be judged.

Paul explains that the Gentiles had enough knowledge about God to offer Him their due thanks and praise, but did not. They neither glorified God nor gave thanks, instead directing their "natural instinct" for praise and honor to false gods like the sun, the moon, and other created animals, and in so doing, they were taken over by falsehood. This unwillingness to honor the true God with praise and gratitude led to further corruption and idolatry. These Gentiles became vain in their imaginations, or "futile in their thoughts" (from **v. 21**, NKJV). They became foolish and useless in their thoughts and reasonings. They darkened their hearts so they would not perceive or comprehend the truth.

II. PEOPLE TURN TO FALSE GODS (vv. 21–23)

Paul is speaking of idolatry when he speaks of turning the image of God into the image of creatures (**v. 23**). However, this same accusation is directed toward those today who worship anything other than God. Science, wealth, social standing, our children—nothing can replace God as the object of our worship.

Paul began this section by saying that these people knew God before turning away from Him. Humankind is glad enough to receive God's gifts, but not willing to recognize God or thank Him for those gifts, so their foolishness results in blindness (**vv. 21–22**). Since they cannot see God, they replace Him with something they can see. Idols become their corrupted substitution.

The Foolishness of the Gentiles

22 Professing themselves to be wise, they became fools, 23 And changed the glory of the uncorruptible God into an image made like to corruptible man, and to birds, and fourfooted beasts, and creeping things.

These Gentiles believed themselves to be wise. Some boasted to be the *sophi*—wise men—but their rejecting God is evidence of their lack of wisdom. The fool says in his heart, "There is no God" (**Psalm 14:1**). They called themselves "philosophers" (translated "lovers of wisdom"), always thinking themselves wiser than believers. Of course, it is not unusual for people to confuse wisdom for foolishness, and vice versa (**1 Corinthians 1:18–2:8**).

The Gentiles "became fools" (Gk. *moraino*, **moe-RYE-no**, to be foolish or silly). Some Bibles say, "they made fools of themselves" (**v. 22**, CEB and NIRV), and became insipid in their imaginations, opinions, and conduct. They exchanged the glory of the immortal God for images made to look like mortal man and birds and animals and reptiles. They forsook the God of whom they had knowledge and offered the honor due to Him to idols. Trading the true God for impotent idols only demonstrates how foolish these people were. Paul, here, may have had in mind the forms of Greek worship he had seen on Mars Hill, which involved exquisite carvings and sculptures of the human form.

Paul has already made his case, that the Gentiles know truth about God but have suppressed and rejected it and have freely chosen to serve idols instead. Thus God is completely justified in pouring out His wrath upon them.

III. PEOPLE THEN ARE CONSIGNED TO DEPRAVITY (vv. 28–32)

A moral decision is required to follow God. The people in the text did not like to remember God, and, "did not see fit to acknowledge God" (**v. 28**, NASB). Paul does not intend the list of depraved behavior that follows to be exhaustive, but illustrates how this mind works.

Possibly the saddest part in this passage is that these people know they are doing wrong, continue to do so, and encourage others who do the same (**v. 32**). This had become a concert of sin: they practiced, performed, and then applauded.

The Gentiles Had Forsaken God

28 And even as they did not like to retain God in their knowledge, God gave them over to a reprobate mind, to do those things which are not convenient; 29 Being filled with all unrighteousness, fornication, wickedness, covetousness, maliciousness; full of envy, murder, debate, deceit, malignity; whisperers, 30 Backbiters, haters of God, despiteful, proud, boasters, inventors of evil things, disobedient to parents, 31 Without understanding, covenantbreakers, without natural affection, implacable, unmerciful.

Paul is still talking about the Gentiles here. He has come to the root of their problem: they did not choose to acknowledge God. As he has argued before, the Gentiles had the knowledge of God but chose to forsake His glory to follow their own passions and lusts. They did not find it wise to follow God. They chose not to think of, nor serve or adore God. This is where they went wrong. They forsook God, so He gave them up to a reprobate mind—a mind destitute of judgment, an incompetent understanding. The Greek word for reprobate is *adokimos* (Gk. **ah-doe-KEE-mos**, useless, failing the test, unsatisfactory, or disreputable), which may be taken passively, for a mind disapproved by God, or actively, for a mind which disapproves of all good. As we read the text, it is important to note that God did not compel them nor refuse them knowledge; He did not abandon them at all. They chose to forsake God. And God gave them to their own worthless speculations. In the face of stubborn and obstinate refusal to honor God, people are left to their own twisted ways.

These Gentiles were left to have corrupt judgment, or none at all. Any mind that thinks of God as worthless is itself worthless. Furthermore, this reprobate mind not only led to sexual immorality as seen in the previous verses, but also to a list of twenty-one problematic practices that Paul says "ought not to be done" (**v. 28**, ESV and NIV). Some translators have "which are not convenient" (e.g., KJV). These practices are not fit or proper for human society, but disgraceful and shameful.

Paul finishes this part of his argument on the moral deprivation of the Gentiles with the list of sins characteristic of those who choose to forsake God. Taken in the context of Paul's other lists elsewhere in his epistles, this list is not exhaustive. Some of the vices are listed in very general terms like wickedness, while others are quite specific like murder. Such lists were common even in secular literature at the time. Several such lists appear elsewhere in the New Testament, even though none of them are nearly as extensive as this one. Put together, these sins signify a societal meltdown, although this is not to say that all humanity or Gentiles are evil all the time. He goes on to further explain that general revelation revealed in nature and the conscience has been obeyed by some Gentiles as Paul later explains in **chapter 2**.

32 Who knowing the judgment of God, that they which commit such things are worthy of death, not only do the same, but have pleasure in them that do them.

They know God's decree-that those who practice such things deserve to die—yet they not only do them but even applaud others who practice them.

In this final verse of the chapter, Paul draws his argument to a conclusion—that the Gentiles had enough knowledge of God and His truth to be judged. However, here, Paul adds a new dimension to the argument, saying that the Gentiles also had knowledge of God's judgment. They know that to practice the sins he had just outlined in the previous verses deserves death. Thus, they not only know the right thing to do in their consience, they also know the penalty for not obeying that conscience. Paul will go into further detail regarding this knowledge of God being implanted in the conscience in **chapter 2**. Sadly, these Gentiles not only commit these sins, but take pleasure in those that do them. Committing these sins is in itself bad and worthy of judgment. However, Paul adds here that to applaud and celebrate those who commit these sins is just as bad, if not worse, than doing them.

SEARCH THE SCRIPTURES

QUESTION 1

Verse 18 states that God's anger is shown against all who suppress the _____ by their _____.

Truth, wickedness.

QUESTION 2

Paul declares that those who claim to be wise are _____ _____.

Utter fools.

LIGHT ON THE WORD

The Price of Idolatry

The worship of false gods—idolatry—only leads to further deception. Ingratitude toward God will always harden hearts and make them unresponsive to His self-revelation.

BIBLE APPLICATION

AIM: Students will learn that Christians must decide to follow God and not to choose wickedness or teachings that lead people away from Him.

Most of us who attend Bible study have chosen God and His revelation. However, sometimes we act like we are functional atheists. We go through our days not giving God the thought and devotion He expects.

He told us that He would take care of us; do we wonder if He will come through? He told us not to worry about food and clothing, but how often do we? He told us everything we had lost for His sake would be restored; do we try to get even?

We might not show the litany of traits listed in **verses 29–31**, but sometimes we also do not glorify Him as God or are ungrateful **(v. 21)**. How differently will we live and act when we believe everything God has promised?

STUDENT'S RESPONSES

AIM: Students will commit to accepting and following after God's decrees for our lives.

So many today choose to willfully ignore God and His revelation of Himself. Many also want to aggressively prevent others from believing, too. Our challenge is to continue our hopeful work, expecting and planning for opposition and unbelief. We should prepare ourselves to stand strong in our faith, and especially for the dark days when "no one can work" **(John 9:4**, NLT).

PRAYER

Jesus, thank You for dying for us, and forgiving us, and allowing us to rejoice in Your resurrection. The world is indebted to Your sacrifice for our sins. We bless You and honor You as we do Your will. In Jesus' Name we pray. Amen.

HOW TO SAY IT

Reprobate.	**RE**-pro-bayt.
Maliciousness.	muh-**LI**-shus-nis.
Malignity.	muh-**LIG**-ni-tee.

PREPARE FOR NEXT SUNDAY

Read **Romans 2:17–29** and "Ignoring God's Truth Within Us."

DAILY HOME BIBLE READINGS

MONDAY
A Person of God
(1 Kings 17:17–24)

TUESDAY
Judging Deceit
(Psalm 52)

WEDNESDAY
Liars and Truth Speakers
(Psalm 63:1–5, 11)

THURSDAY
God Hates Injustice
(Isaiah 59:12–16)

FRIDAY
Utter Contempt for Truth
(Jeremiah 5:1–5)

SATURDAY
Seek Good and Truth
(Amos 5:10–15)

SUNDAY
Ignoring God's Plain Truth
(Romans 1:18–23, 28–32)

Sources:

Cottrell, Jack. Romans. *College Press NIV Commentary.* 2 vols. Joplin, MO: College Press, 1996.

Stott, John R. W. *The Message of Romans: God's Good News for the World.* The Bible Speaks Today. Leicester, England: InterVarsity Press, 2001.

Stuhlmacher, Peter. *Paul's Letter to the Romans: A Commentary.* 1st ed. Louisville, KY.: Westminster, 1994.

Witherington, Ben, and Darlene Hyatt. *Paul's Letter to the Romans: A Socio-Rhetorical Commentary.* Grand Rapids, MI: Eerdmans, 2004.

COMMENTS / NOTES:

IGNORING GOD'S TRUTH WITHIN US

BIBLE BASIS: ROMANS 2:17–29

BIBLE TRUTH: Paul declares that some people teach others to follow the Law, but do not follow the Law themselves.

MEMORY VERSE: "For not the hearers of the law are just before God, but the doers of the law shall be justified" (Romans 2:13).

LESSON AIM: By the end of the lesson, we will: TELL what Paul reveals about the people who claim to follow God's Law while failing to keep it; RECOGNIZE the hypocrisy of claiming to belong to God while breaking God's Law; and IDENTIFY the hypocrisy in our beliefs and daily actions and ways to comply with God's Law.

TEACHER PREPARATION

MATERIALS NEEDED: Quarterly Commentary/Teacher Manual, Adult Quarterly, Adult resources—charts, worksheets, and other teaching tools, paper, pens, pencils, Bibles (several different versions)

OTHER MATERIALS NEEDED / TEACHER'S NOTES:

_____

_____

LESSON OVERVIEW

LIFE NEED FOR TODAY'S LESSON
Many people talk about appreciating the world around them, but do not demonstrate it.

BIBLE LEARNING
God's judgment and rule was against all the nations and included Israel's punishment.

BIBLE APPLICATION
The Lord will judge the world, so believers need to be mindful of all that they think, do, and say.

STUDENTS' RESPONSES
Christians should seek the Lord wholeheartedly and walk in God's ways.

LESSON SCRIPTURE

ROMANS 2:17–29, KJV

17 Behold, thou art called a Jew, and restest in the law, and makest thy boast of God,

18 And knowest his will, and approvest the things that are more excellent, being instructed out of the law;

19 And art confident that thou thyself art a

ROMANS 2:17–29, NIV

17 Now you, if you call yourself a Jew; if you rely on the law and boast in God;

18 if you know his will and approve of what is superior because you are instructed by the law;

19 if you are convinced that you are a guide

guide of the blind, a light of them which are in darkness,

20 An instructor of the foolish, a teacher of babes, which hast the form of knowledge and of the truth in the law.

21 Thou therefore which teachest another, teachest thou not thyself? thou that preachest a man should not steal, dost thou steal?

22 Thou that sayest a man should not commit adultery, dost thou commit adultery? thou that abhorrest idols, dost thou commit sacrilege?

23 Thou that makest thy boast of the law, through breaking the law dishonourest thou God?

24 For the name of God is blasphemed among the Gentiles through you, as it is written.

25 For circumcision verily profiteth, if thou keep the law: but if thou be a breaker of the law, thy circumcision is made uncircumcision.

26 Therefore if the uncircumcision keep the righteousness of the law, shall not his uncircumcision be counted for circumcision?

27 And shall not uncircumcision which is by nature, if it fulfil the law, judge thee, who by the letter and circumcision dost transgress the law?

28 For he is not a Jew, which is one outwardly; neither is that circumcision, which is outward in the flesh:

29 But he is a Jew, which is one inwardly; and circumcision is that of the heart, in the spirit, and not in the letter; whose praise is not of men, but of God.

for the blind, a light for those who are in the dark,

20 an instructor of the foolish, a teacher of little children, because you have in the law the embodiment of knowledge and truth—

21 you, then, who teach others, do you not teach yourself? You who preach against stealing, do you steal?

22 You who say that people should not commit adultery, do you commit adultery? You who abhor idols, do you rob temples?

23 You who boast in the law, do you dishonor God by breaking the law?

24 As it is written: "God's name is blasphemed among the Gentiles because of you."

25 Circumcision has value if you observe the law, but if you break the law, you have become as though you had not been circumcised.

26 So then, if those who are not circumcised keep the law's requirements, will they not be regarded as though they were circumcised?

27 The one who is not circumcised physically and yet obeys the law will condemn you who, even though you have the written code and circumcision, are a lawbreaker.

28 A person is not a Jew who is one only outwardly, nor is circumcision merely outward and physical.

29 No, a person is a Jew who is one inwardly; and circumcision is circumcision of the heart, by the Spirit, not by the written code. Such a person's praise is not from other people, but from God.

LIGHT ON THE WORD

Jews. This word originally referred specifically to a member of the tribe of Judah named for Jacob's fourth son. The word first occurs in **2 Kings 16:6**, when the ten northern tribes called Israel joined with the king of Syria to fight against Judah. In the New Testament, the word "Jew" is used to describe members of the Jewish faith and their leaders. In modern times, the word is used to describe ethnic birth but not necessarily religion.

Gentiles. This was the term Jews used to describe those outside the people of Israel. The Jews believed that God was ruler of the whole world, including the Gentile nations. Gentiles were able to be saved by converting to the Jewish faith. At the same time, they were forbidden to mix with unconverted Gentiles. This meant that dining and intermarriage with Gentiles were forbidden. Ultimately the Jews regarded the Gentiles as impious, as most worshiped idols.

TEACHING THE BIBLE LESSON

LIFE NEED FOR TODAY'S LESSON

AIM: Students will learn that many people talk about appreciating the world around them, but do not demonstrate it.

INTRODUCTION

Paul's Accusation Against False Teachers

Paul opposed the Jewish Christians who believed in the value of circumcision. Paul was not against the circumcision itself, if practiced as part of obeying God's whole Law, but the Jews wanted to impose circumcision on the Gentile Christians. Paul accuses them of being poor teachers: proud and doing whatever they want. If their hearts were changed at salvation, Paul argues, why do they need an outward show to validate this change?

BIBLE LEARNING

AIM: Students will learn how God's judgment and rule was against all the nations and included Israel's punishment.

I. FRIEND OR FOE?
(ROMANS 2:17–24)

God gave the Mosaic law to His people. He chose them to be an example to the nations that they might know who He really is. Instead of this resulting in humble gratitude and reverent service, it actually turned into boasting. They thought of themselves as better than the Gentiles. However, in **verses 19–20**, Paul says they are confident (assured, boastful) in being a guide of the blind and a light for those in darkness. Paul is almost quoting **Isaiah 42:6–7**, where God calls Israel to be a "light of the Gentiles" and to "open the blind eyes." Paul argues that even though the Jews possessed the Law and were God's chosen people, they had no right to think of themselves as better than the Gentiles. They had commited the same sins , and Moses had given them the written law. The Gentiles only had general revelation, but the Jews had specific revelation of how to live before God. This would make them even more guilty before God.

Verse 24 speaks to the issue of ignoring God's truth within you and mocking what you say you believe. This was the case with some of the Jews of Paul's day.

Romans 2:17–29

The reader should engage **Romans 2:17–29** understanding the wider context of the conversation that started at **Romans 1:18** and will continue until **Romans 3:20**. At **1:18**, Paul started a discourse to prove that both the Jews and the Gentiles have sinned before God, so both equally deserve to be punished.

This argument reaches its climax at **3:23**, where Paul concludes, "For all have sinned, and come short of the glory of God." To get there, Paul addresses the Gentiles outside Christ first (**Romans 1:18–32**). He dismisses the excuse that the Gentiles did not have the knowledge of God or His truth and therefore could not be judged. He says that the Gentiles did have the knowledge of the truth but chose to ignore it, and therefore deserve their punishment.

After that, in **2:1–16**, Paul changes his rhetorical style and engages an interlocutor (person with whom he is speaking) whom he addresses only as "O man." Scholars are divided whether this person is a Gentile or a Jew. The dialogue with this person is focused on God's judgment being inescapable, righteous, and impartial—a conversation that could be more directed toward a Gentile, even though Paul possibly had a Jewish audience in mind. When we come to **verse 17**, Paul's attention shifts toward the Jews outside Christ. And here again, Paul engages an interlocutor who calls himself a Jew.

17 Behold, thou art called a Jew, and restest in the law, and makest thy boast of God, 18 And knowest his will, and approvest the things that are more excellent, being instructed out of the law; 19 And art confident that thou thyself art a guide of the blind, a light of them which are in darkness, 20 An instructor of the foolish, a teacher of babes, which hast the form of knowledge and of the truth in the law.

Here in **verse 17**, Paul begins his diatribe against the Jews who felt secure in their heritage by engaging an imagined interlocutor: a confident Jew who takes pride in his "privileged position" with the Law and circumcision. This Jew calls himself a Jew, thus taking pride in his identity—and the monopoly on

God that he thinks it gives him. Paul observes that this Jew relies on the Law. He boasts in God. He knows God's will. He approves of what is superior. He is instructed in the Law. He is convinced that he is a guide for the blind and a light for those in the dark. He does all this because he has the "form" (Gk. *morphosis*, **MOR-fo-sees**), or embodiment, of knowledge and truth in the Law.

Several important points should be noted here. First, this Jew (whom Paul uses to address the wider attitudes of some of the Jews toward the law and the Gentiles) fancied himself to be a teacher of the Law both for those who are spiritually blind or in the dark, and those who are foolish or very young (Gk. *nepios*, **NAY-pee-ose**; infant, figuratively meaning those who are childish or immature). He may have been like Paul himself, a teacher to the God-fearers or Gentiles (**v. 24**). Of course, the Jews were supposed to be guides to the blind and light to those in darkness (**Isaiah 42:6–7, 49:6**). The Bible often uses blindness and darkness to portray ignorance of spiritual things, and the light of the Word of God dispels them both.

Paul is not saying that what the Jew does is wrong. If anything, only the first one may be problematic—he relies on the Law—and everything else he does is only skewed because of this. Relying on the Law to attain righteousness was the main problem of the non-Christian Jews. For many Jews, having the Law was a sign of favor. In their estimation, they were better taught than those without the Law. Many believed that simply the bestowal of the Law proved them to be favored by God above all others, so just having the Law, even without following it, was a ground of safety. Thus, the Jews boasted and bragged about their relationship with God, which is acceptable when done in the right spirit (see **Jeremiah 9:23–24**), and Paul does not condemn it here. It just shows the confidence that some of the Jews had in themselves. This particular Jew also approved of what is superior. This could mean simply discerning right from wrong, or more specifically discerning the essential superior elements of God's will. Both the knowing of God's will and the discerning of the essentials are possible because this Jew was instructed by the Law.

21 Thou therefore which teachest another, teachest thou not thyself? thou that preachest a man should not steal, dost thou steal? 22 Thou that sayest a man should not commit adultery, dost thou commit adultery? thou that abhorrest idols, dost thou commit sacrilege? 23 Thou that makest thy boast of the law, through breaking the law dishonourest thou God? 24 For the name of God is blasphemed among the Gentiles through you, as it is written.

Many translations introduce the previous four verses with an "if" in **v. 17**. The "then" in those translations finally comes up here in **v. 21**. In essence, Paul is saying, "If you bear the honorable name of a Jew, then why don't you act as a real Jew should?" Paul is turning the tables on this Jew who does not live up to his knowledge or practice what he preaches.

Following this, Paul asks five rhetorical questions that testify to the Jew's inconsistency: (1) you who teach, do you not teach yourself? (2) you who preach against stealing, do you steal? (3) you who say people should not commit adultery, do you commit adultery? (4) you who abhor idols, do you rob temples? and (5) you who boast in the Law, do you dishonor God by breaking the Law? These questions sound accusatory, but it would be wrong to assume that all Jews are guilty of these all the time. Paul is trying to get the Jews of the church in Rome to examine themselves. As his argument goes, these questions drive home the fact that every Jew has broken the

Law at some point, so they also deserve punishment like the Gentiles.

Paul cites several of the Ten Commandments here (stealing, adultery and idolatry), which is both the beginning and the heart of the Mosaic Law. In essence, Paul is suggesting that any Jews who cannot even keep the Ten Commandments yet who also teach those commandments to others are in fact blaspheming God's name (the second of the commandments after idolatry). In teaching the Law but not practicing it, these so-called teachers are in a far worse condition than those do not know the Law at all because they are blaspheming God's very name by leading others astray through their actions as leaders..

The Jews boasted in the Law as much as they boasted in God (**Romans 2:17**). This too is not to be frowned upon, because the Jews were to honor the Law and take pride in it, rejoicing in its truth and guidance. Several Scriptures of the Old Testament, especially the Psalms, talk about rejoicing in the Law. For instance, **Psalm 119:97** testifies, "Oh, how I love your law! I meditate on it all day long" (NIV). Even though these Jews bragged in the Law, their transgression made their boasting of little consequence. Paul then implies that as a result of their transgressions, God's name was blasphemed among the nations. The breaking of the Law did not only disgrace the Law but also the Lawgiver. Paul may have **Isaiah 52:5** and **Ezekiel 36:20–23** in mind here. In both texts, God's name is mocked because His people had been defeated and enslaved. However, the defeat does not cause the blaspheming that Paul is talking about here, but their misconduct. The sins committed not only cause the sinner to offend God, but also cause others to blaspheme against Him. Even in our society today, the sins of the Christians bring dishonor to God's name.

II. REAL CIRCUMCISION (vv. 25–29)

Paul argues that circumcision had no profit if unaccompanied by a righteous life. Circumcision circumcision doesn't matter if one doesn't keep the Law of God. In the same way we can say our church attendance or tithing means nothing if we are committing sin. None of our religious rituals means anything if we do not live righteously and obey God's commands. The real circumcision was the circumcision of the heart. Circumcision was a sign of the covenant the Jews had with God as His chosen people. Paul here says the heart must be changed to show true loyalty to God.

Paul goes on to explain who is a true Jew. Circumcision was considered the mark of a Jew; every Jewish male had to be circumcised. Here Paul says that circumciion does not make one a true Jew. A true Jew is one who follows the Law of God. One sign was external and could be praised by others; the other was inward and could only be seen by God.

The Controversy Over Circumcision

25 For circumcision verily profiteth, if thou keep the law: but if thou be a breaker of the law, thy circumcision is made uncircumcision. 26 Therefore if the uncircumcision keep the righteousness of the law, shall not his uncircumcision be counted for circumcision? 27 And shall not uncircumcision which is by nature, if it fulfil the law, judge thee, who by the letter and circumcision dost transgress the law?

In this group of verses, Paul focuses his argument toward what the Jews considered their last line of defense—the circumcision. In a nutshell, Paul says if possession (and knowledge) of the Law could not exempt the Jews from the judgment, neither could circumcision. It was not a surefire insurance against the wrath of God, which many of the people of the time believed. Several Rabbinic epigrams expressed that common belief: "Circumcised men do not descend into Gehenna [i.e., hell]," and "Circumcision will deliver Israel from Gehenna."

To prove his point about circumcision, Paul does the same thing he has done with the Law in the preceding verses. He demolishes any confidence in circumcision to show that it has no basis for the salvation of the Jews from judgment, just like adherence to the Law. The very first statement in this section throws down the gauntlet: circumcision has value— if they observe the Law. Thus, Paul does not deny the significance of circumcision, only shifts the emphasis to where it should be— obedience. Circumcision does not replace the need for observing the whole Law. In fact, for circumcision to be effective, it requires obedience to the entire Law. Consequently, the Law and circumcision work together, and one without the other is useless for salvation. The primary requirement for the covenant is neither the possession of the Law nor circumcision; it is obedience which both the Law and circumcision require. Thus, Paul can conclude that breaking the Law even once negates the circumcision. He says circumcision without obedience is the same as no circumcision at all. On the other hand, uncircumcision with obedience is just as good as circumcision.

28 For he is not a Jew, which is one outwardly; neither is that circumcision, which is outward in the flesh: 29 But he is a Jew, which is one inwardly; and circumcision is that of the heart, in the spirit, and not in the letter; whose praise is not of men, but of God.

Paul goes a step further to redefine what it means to be a true Jew in contrast to the self-righteous Jew of vv. 17–21. At first, he states what a true Jew is not—one who is only outwardly Jewish. True Jewishness is not based on external circumstances, like circumcision of the flesh. In fact, circumcision is not merely outward and physical. Thus, true Jewishness depends on things of the inside where only God can see. The real circumcision that matters is that of the heart. Paul says a man is a Jew if he is one inwardly (Gk. *en to krypto*, **en toe kroop-TOE**, in secret), and true circumcision is of the heart by the Spirit, not of the Law. Paul is adopting a concept of the Old Testament. Several times, God talks about uncircumcised hearts, pleads with His people to circumcise their hearts, and then says that He will circumcise them (**Leviticus 26:41; Deuteronomy 10:16, 30:6**). Paul sums this concept well when he says, "For we are the circumcision, which worship God in the spirit, and rejoice in Christ Jesus, and have no confidence in the flesh. Though I might also have confidence in the flesh" (from **Philippians 3:3–4**). In the context of **Romans 2**, Paul is saying that not all Jews are real Jews, because the real Jews are those who are circumcised in the heart by the Spirit (Gk. *pneuma*, **puh-NEW-ma**, either a person's spirit or the Holy Spirit) and not in the "letter" (Gk. *gramma*, **GRAH-mah**, writing; here, particularly sacred writing). With this idea, Paul begins to establish the difference between the old covenant (of the external Law) and the new covenant (the gift of the Spirit).

SEARCH THE SCRIPTURES

QUESTION 1
Paul challenges the teachers in **verse 21** about their teaching the truth when he asks if they teach against stealing or "do they _____?"

Steal.

QUESTION 2
Paul states in **verse 25** that "circumcision has has value only if you _____ God's _____.

Obey, law.

LIGHT ON THE WORD

What's On the Inside
A true Jew's praise is not from other people but from God, because only He sees the heart, where the real circumcision is evident. People only see the outside and thus cannot praise with truth, sometimes praising those who do not deserve praise and other times withholding praise where it is due. Thus Paul again asserts true Jews are those who are God's children by the Spirit and not those who boast to be Israel's descendants by the flesh.

BIBLE APPLICATION

AIM: Students will know that Jesus expects truth and authentic behaviors and actions from believers.

Corporate America makes demands of many workers. Companies sometimes uphold rules that encourage employees to neglect their Christian duties. However, at the end of the day, Christ will ask His believers, "Did you try to fit your Christian lifestyle onto your job, or did you let your Christianity lead you in work decisions?" Will the job run your life or will you allow Christ to lead you?

STUDENT'S RESPONSES

AIM: Students will understand that Christians should seek the Lord wholeheartedly and walk in His ways.

The world encourages us to center our thoughts on anything but God's truth. From the media to our legal system, there are examples of God's truth being distorted and ignored as something repressive or primitive. This week, write down all the times that you notice the media upholding ideas opposite to God's truth.

PRAYER

God, we are thankful for Your protection, and Your care. We fear and respect Your judgment and mercy. Thank You for allowing us to witness who You are in our lives and the world. In Jesus' name we pray. Amen.

HOW TO SAY IT

Blasphemy.   BLAS-fi-mee.

Gentiles.   JIN-tiles.

PREPARE FOR NEXT SUNDAY

Read **Romans 3:9–20** and "We Were All Under Sin's Power."

DAILY HOME BIBLE READINGS

MONDAY
Dark vs. Light
(John 1:1–9)

TUESDAY
Hate vs. Love
(John 15:18–27)

WEDNESDAY
Doubt vs. Faith
(2 Corinthians 4:1–6)

THURSDAY
Grace vs. Law
(Galatians 2:11–21)

FRIDAY
Lies vs. Truth
(Ephesians 4:25–32)

SATURDAY
Wicked vs. Righteous
(Isaiah 26:1–12)

SUNDAY
Ignoring God's Truth Within Us
(Romans 2:17–29)

Sources:

Cottrell, Jack. Romans. *College Press NIV Commentary.* 2 vols. Joplin, MO: College Press, 1996.

Dunn, James D. G., and J. W. Rogerson. *Eerdmans Commentary on the Bible.* Grand Rapids, MI: W.B. Eerdmans, 2003.

Stott, John R. W. *The Message of Romans: God's Good News for the World.* The Bible Speaks Today. Leicester, England: InterVarsity Press, 2001.

COMMENTS / NOTES:

WE WERE ALL UNDER SIN'S POWER

BIBLE BASIS: ROMANS 3:9–20

BIBLE TRUTH: Humans are God's creation. Paul laments that we have corrupted ourselves from the beginning and that all unrepentant sinners will be held accountable by God.

MEMORY VERSE: "Therefore by the deeds of the law there shall no flesh be justified in his sight: for by the law is the knowledge of sin" (Romans 3:20).

LESSON AIM: By the end of the lesson, we will: KNOW that humankind began corrupting creation from the start and God's retribution to sinners will surely come; ACCEPT our personal roles toward our own corruption; and BE ATTENTIVE to the biblical prophets and accept accountability with God by repenting and being redeemed back to God.

TEACHER PREPARATION

MATERIALS NEEDED: Quarterly Commentary/Teacher Manual, Adult Quarterly, Adult resources—charts, worksheets, and other teaching tools, paper, pens, pencils, Bibles (several different versions)

OTHER MATERIALS NEEDED / TEACHER'S NOTES:

_____

_____

LESSON OVERVIEW

LIFE NEED FOR TODAY'S LESSON
Many people are grateful for all they have in life, but others take every opportunity to abuse their privileges.

BIBLE LEARNING
Although the Word of God reveals how sinful man is, God can restore and redeem us from the control of sin's grip.

BIBLE APPLICATION
Sinners should take personal responsibility for their role in sin and turn to God for repentance.

STUDENTS' RESPONSES
Christians are excited to know that if they sin, God is faithful and just to forgive them and cleanse them from all unrighteousness (1 John 1:9).

LESSON SCRIPTURE

ROMANS 3:9–20, KJV

9 What then? are we better than they? No, in no wise: for we have before proved both Jews and Gentiles, that they are all under sin;

10 As it is written, There is none righteous, no, not one:

ROMANS 3:9–20, NIV

9 What shall we conclude then? Do we have any advantage? Not at all! For we have already made the charge that Jews and Gentiles alike are all under the power of sin.

10 As it is written: "There is no one righteous,

11 There is none that understandeth, there is none that seeketh after God.

12 They are all gone out of the way, they are together become unprofitable; there is none that doeth good, no, not one.

13 Their throat is an open sepulchre; with their tongues they have used deceit; the poison of asps is under their lips:

14 Whose mouth is full of cursing and bitterness:

15 Their feet are swift to shed blood:

16 Destruction and misery are in their ways:

17 And the way of peace have they not known:

18 There is no fear of God before their eyes.

19 Now we know that what things soever the law saith, it saith to them who are under the law: that every mouth may be stopped, and all the world may become guilty before God.

20 Therefore by the deeds of the law there shall no flesh be justified in his sight: for by the law is the knowledge of sin.

not even one;

11 there is no one who understands; there is no one who seeks God.

12 All have turned away, they have together become worthless; there is no one who does good, not even one."

13 "Their throats are open graves; their tongues practice deceit." "The poison of vipers is on their lips."

14 "Their mouths are full of cursing and bitterness."

15 "Their feet are swift to shed blood;

16 ruin and misery mark their ways,

17 and the way of peace they do not know."

18 "There is no fear of God before their eyes."

19 Now we know that whatever the law says, it says to those who are under the law, so that every mouth may be silenced and the whole world held accountable to God.

20 Therefore no one will be declared righteous in God's sight by the works of the law; rather, through the law we become conscious of our sin.

LIGHT ON THE WORD

Saul/Apostle Paul. A well-educated Roman citizen, Saul was a Pharisee who persecuted Christians as proof of his zeal for the Jewish faith and way of life (**Philippians 3:4–6; Acts 26:4–5**). On such a mission on the road to Damascus, he had a remarkable encounter with Jesus. Shortly after, he learned of his call from God to take "[God's] message to the Gentiles and to kings, as well as to the people of Israel" (**Acts 9:15**, NLT). As an apostle, Paul's life exemplified one of great sacrifice and persecution. He wrote about his experiences in hopes of drawing people to Christ, and to strengthen and mature believers.

Roman believers. Scripture does not record who founded the church at Rome, but it boasted members of both Gentile and Jewish backgrounds. The congregation struggled with various problems, including disunity based on the differences between their Jewish and Gentile members and because of conflicting ideology about sin, repentance, and judgment.

TEACHING THE BIBLE LESSON

LIFE NEED FOR TODAY'S LESSON

AIM: Students will affirm that many people are grateful for all they have in life, but others take every opportunity to abuse their privileges.

INTRODUCTION

Repentance, Faith, and Salvation

In the book of Romans, Paul helped believers understand the importance of salvation by faith, not works. Because of their need for a solid, faith-based spiritual foundation, Paul provided clarification of Christian doctrine. He offered glimpses into the Jewish way of life by the law, but stressed the importance of service to Christ by faith, rather than through legalistic activities.

Further, he emphasized the importance of repentance, salvation, and unity among believers. In underscoring that all believers—Jews and Gentiles—are equal in God's eyes, he also confirmed that God's promise to the Jews remains intact (**Romans 9–11**).

In today's lesson, Paul addresses the fact that all human beings are inherently sinful. He reminds us: "all people, whether Jews or Gentiles, are under the power of sin" (**Romans 3:9**, NLT). Thus, we equally were guilty and deserved God's judgment. However we also all need God's grace and need continual reminders that: 1) sin is universal—meaning that the tempter will try anyone; 2) we all were guilty at some point; and 3) only God can restore us to fellowship with Him as we accept accountability and repent for our words and deeds.

BIBLE LEARNING

AIM: Students will understand that the Word of God shows how sinful man is and reassures that God can restore any repentant heart.

I. SIN IS UNIVERSAL (ROMANS 3:9–12)

Some Jews (especially the Pharisees and their followers) believed following the letter of the Law made them righteous in man's and God's eyes. Upon converting to Christianity, they needed to be reminded that justification is based on faith, not works. Paul facilitated their understanding by exploring the notion of sin in two contexts. First, he defined it as a presence that is ever presented to all people. Second, he defined it as the unrighteous deeds to which under its power yields and those redeemed by God resists.

And, he made it clear that sin is universal, meaning that temptation is all around us and none is exempt from the deceiver's attempts at trying to get you to turn away from God. Paul reminded Roman believers, "As it is written, There is none righteous, no, not one" (**v. 10**, KJV). He was referring to **Psalm 14:2–3** (NLT), which states: "The LORD looks down from heaven on the entire human race; he looks to see if anyone is truly wise, if anyone seeks God. But no, all have turned away; all have become corrupt. No one does good, not a single one!" This makes it clear that every single person was once marked by sin. We were all unworthy of God's grace. No one was innocent, which confirms the Scripture stating that while we were yet sinners, Christ died for us (**Romans 5:8**).

Romans 3:9–20

9 What then? are we better than they? No, in no wise: for we have before proved both Jews and Gentiles, that they are all under sin.

In this passage, Paul sets out to show how whether Jew or Gentile, all are under sin. He refers to the argument in **Romans 2** (especially **vv. 11–12**) which proved (Gk. *proaitiaomai*, pro-eye-tee-AH-oh-my), or brought a charge against previously, that all are under sin. The phrase "under sin" means to be in the sphere of sin's power and recipients of God's judgment of sin. This is very similar to non-Western cultures of today who consider that the world is ruled by various "powers." For Paul, sin is one of those powers which holds sway over every human on the planet. It is not just that people sin as an action. They are trapped and imprisoned by sin and are in need of a rescue. The fact that Jews were also under sin made them worthy of judgment just like the Gentiles.

10 As it is written, There is none righteous, no, not one: 11 There is none that understandeth, there is none that seeketh after God.

Paul then goes through a list of Old Testament quotations that describe humanity's fallen condition. The method of stringing together verses, or "pearl stringing," was very common in first-century Judaism. This method was often used in synagogue exhortations and can be seen in some Dead Sea Scroll writings, which were written before and around the time of Christ. Now Paul uses this technique of pearl stringing to deal with an anticipated objection: Although Jews are not perfectly righteous, they are better in God's sight than Gentiles.

By introducing them with the phrase "As it is written," Paul points toward the Word of God as his objective support for the claim of humanity's sinfulness and not his own subjective speculation.

He quotes **Psalm 14:3**, which states there is none righteous (Gk. *dikaios*, **DEE-keye-ose**). This word means to be right with God and to act justly. It holds the idea of being in alignment with or conformed to His will in thinking, feeling, and acting. This lack of righteousness is expressed in that no one "understandeth" (Gk. *suniemi*, **soon-EE-ay-me**), meaning "to understand," with the image of someone bringing together their perception with the thing perceived. They see the creation, they see good and evil, but cannot understand that they owe their loyalty and allegiance to a Creator. Not only this, but there is none who

"seeketh" (Gk. *ekzeteo*, **ek-zay-TEH-oh**), or searches out and craves, for God.

12 They are all gone out of the way, they are together become unprofitable; there is none that doeth good, no, not one.

Paul continues to describe the human race and states that we have all "gone out of the way." This is actually one compound word in Greek, *ekklino* (**eh-KLEE-no**), and means to turn aside or deviate from a path. In other words, the Lord has given people the right path and they have intentionally chosen to follow another path. Paul further adds that they are unprofitable (Gk. *achreioo*, **ah-kray-OH-oh**), which also means useless or unserviceable. This leads into the next phrase which states conclusively: "There is none that doeth good, no, not one."

II. SINFUL DEEDS (vv. 13–18)

No one is born a Christian. Rather, everyone is born in iniquity. In fact, Paul contended, nearly from the beginning of God's creation, humankind began corrupting creation and that God's retribution will surely come (**Romans 1:20–23**). Now Paul shows from the Jewish scriptures how this inclination to sin applies to not only the Gentile world but also to the Jewish people.

Verses 13–18 cite specific verbal and physical deeds for which we will be held accountable. These include deceit, cursing, shedding blood, and other acts of destruction. The problem lies in the fact that sinful acts reveal that people do not truly fear God (**v. 18**), and thus fail to honor Him by committing such deeds. This adds on to Paul's case that the Jews are no better than the Gentiles in the sight of God.

Deceit, Lies, and Bloodshed

13 Their throat is an open sepulchre; with their tongues they have used deceit; the poison of asps is under their lips: 14 Whose

mouth is full of cursing and bitterness: 15 Their feet are swift to shed blood.

This list of proof texts is based on "gezerah shavah," a rabbinical principle which linked Old Testament texts by key words. The key words here are the parts of the body. Paul lists Scriptures that mention the throat, tongue, lips, mouth, and feet. In other words, when one yields to the control of sin, the whole body from head to toe is subject to the power or influence of sins.

16 Destruction and misery are in their ways: 17 And the way of peace have they not known: 18 There is no fear of God before their eyes.

To further demonstrate his point Paul quotes **Isaiah 59:7–8** to show that their sins are not only restricted to their body but extend in violence toward others. The passage in Isaiah actually points toward the need for a mediator and how God's own arm brought salvation (**vv. 17–20**). While the Isaiah passage shows God the Father coming with salvation, Paul would use these quotations as his argument in Romans to show how God brought salvation through Christ. This is because Christ is God Himself according to the orthodox belief in the Trinity (**John 1:1–3**).

Paul wraps up this list of quotations with a literary device called inclusion. The "there is no" here in **verse 18** echoes the "there is none" refrain in **vv. 10–11**. This is done purposefully to show the finality of the reality of sin in the unbeliever. Ungodly people are both destructive and will be punished with destruction. It is the final nail that drives home the point that all are deserving of God's judgment under sin. All sinners and unbelievers will face this judgement if they do not forsake sin and turn to God.

III. SIN EXPOSED (vv. 19–20)

While the Jews rejoiced in their relationship to the Law, Paul pointed out that the Law had one purpose: to expose sin. The "knowledge of sin" becomes clear under the Law's requirements, as does the truth that no one can live up to them. Neither Jews nor Gentiles are righteous before God, hence our need for a Savior.

This points to later in the passage where Paul presents Jesus as the solution to sinful mankind's dilemma (**vv. 23–24**). Although we cannot be justified through the Law, we are shown our need for the only one who can justify us—Jesus. Thanks to Jesus, our sins are judged by God on the Cross and His blood gives us forgiveness of sins.

Consistent Grace

19 Now we know that what things soever the law saith, it saith to them who are under the law: that every mouth may be stopped, and all the world may become guilty before God.

Those under the Law are Jews and their knowledge of sin is given so "that every mouth may be stopped." This illustration was taken from the law courts; those who were silenced had no reasonable defense. Paul points toward the Jewish understanding that all people sinned and were therefore in need of grace. The Jewish religion of Jesus' day theoretically knew of the need for God's grace; this was not the issue Paul was contending for. His main point is for the Jews to be consistent.

If grace was needed for the Jews to be saved, then it will also save the Gentiles. Both groups would be saved by grace, not works of the Law. The picture of a law court continues as Paul states that the whole world would be guilty (Gk. *hupodikos*, **hoo-PO-dee-koce**) before God. The compound parts of the Greek word mean to be "under judgment," the logical result for a world that is "under sin." The word often refers to someone who lost their suit or became a debtor. This is an adequate picture of those under sin without Christ.

451

20 Therefore by the deeds of the law there shall no flesh be justified in his sight: for by the law is the knowledge of sin.

The implications of Paul's argument for humanity's guilt before God are seen in **verse 20**. Through the deeds of the Law, no one can be justified (Gk. *dikaioo*, **de-keye-OH-oh**), which means to be rendered and pronounced righteous. On the contrary, through the Law comes the knowledge (Gk. *epignosis*, **eh-PEEG-no-sees**), the precise and accurate acknowledgement, of sin. His point is that while those who do not have the Law know sin only in their conscience, those under the Law know exactly what wrong they have done. They have experienced the full meaning of sin: transgression of the Law.

SEARCH THE SCRIPTURES

QUESTION 1
What is Paul's response to his rhetorical question, "we Jews are better than" others **(Gentiles)?**

His response to this question is "no" and "all under the power of sin."

QUESTION 2
Who are the people that are good, according to Paul in **verse 12**?

No one is good.

LIGHT ON THE WORD

An Ideal Missionary
As a Roman citizen and former Pharisee, the Apostle Paul was an ideal choice of missionary to teach on such issues as sin, salvation, and grace. While doing so, he refuted potential arguments, providing keys to a victorious, faith-based Christian life.

BIBLE APPLICATION

AIM: Students will accept that Christians should take personal responsibility for their role in sin and turn to God for repentance.

Some people believe their good deeds will get them to heaven. Thus, they often cite their charitable giving, volunteerism, or fulfillment of local laws as reasons they are "good people." On the other hand, some people always seem to blow it and feel unworthy of God's love, and thus delay making a decision for Christ. How does **Romans 3:9–20** address both types of people? What would you say to either if they said, "I don't need to be saved"?

STUDENT'S RESPONSES

AIM: Students will affirm that Christians are excited to know that if they sin, God is faithful and just to forgive them and cleanse them from all unrighteousness (1 John 1:9).

Verbal abuse has received more attention in recent years than ever before. Yet many individuals still don't view it as a "big" sin. Paul underscored the fact that sin is sin, and that everyone sins. Ask God to show you ways your words could be more Christ-like.

PRAYER

Dear God in Heaven, we know that we are sinners saved by Your precious grace. What a joy divine that You love us have given us Jesus Christ. Forgive us and keep us each and every day. In Jesus' Name we pray. Amen.

HOW TO SAY IT

Justified.	JUS-ti-fide.
Sepulchre.	SE-pool-ker.

PREPARE FOR NEXT SUNDAY

Read **Romans 3:21–31** and "God Sets Things Right."

DAILY HOME BIBLE READINGS

MONDAY
No One without Sin
(John 8:2–11)

TUESDAY
Forgiveness of Sin
(Acts 13:36–41)

WEDNESDAY
Confess Our Sins
(Psalm 38:17–22)

THURSDAY
Open Your Eyes
(Acts 26:12–18)

FRIDAY
Freedom from Temptation
(James 1:12–18)

SATURDAY
Walk Free of Sin
(1 John 2:1–6)

SUNDAY
We're All Under Sin's Power
(Romans 3:9–20)

Sources:
Adeyemo, Tokunboh, ed. *Africa Bible Commentary.* Grand Rapids, MI: Zondervan, 2010. .

COMMENTS / NOTES:

GOD SETS THINGS RIGHT

BIBLE BASIS: ROMANS 3:21–31

BIBLE TRUTH: There is hope that faith in Jesus Christ can save those who continue in sin.

MEMORY VERSE: "Even the righteousness of God which is by faith of Jesus Christ unto all and upon all them that believe: for there is no difference: For all have sinned, and come short of the glory of God; being justified freely by his grace through the redemption that is in Christ Jesus" (Romans 3:22–24).

LESSON AIM: By the end of the lesson, we will: RECALL Paul's Good News of God providing Jesus Christ as a way for humankind to reestablish its loving, obedient relationship with God; HOPE for getting right with God by believing in Christ Jesus; CONFIRM our belief in Jesus Christ as Savior and pledge anew to follow Him.

TEACHER PREPARATION

MATERIALS NEEDED: Quarterly Commentary/Teacher Manual, Adult Quarterly, Adult resources—charts, worksheets, and other teaching tools, paper, pens, pencils, Bibles (several different versions)

OTHER MATERIALS NEEDED / TEACHER'S NOTES:

_____

_____

LESSON OVERVIEW

LIFE NEED FOR TODAY'S LESSON
Some people give thanks for all that is good in life, while others have no hope.

BIBLE APPLICATION
God offers a way for all to restore and build relationships through Jesus Christ.

BIBLE LEARNING
Christ offers hope for all who want to develop a relationship with Him.

STUDENTS' RESPONSES
Christians have hope in Christ and make commitments to renew their relationship with Christ through faith, prayer, and love.

LESSON SCRIPTURE

ROMANS 3:21–31, KJV

21 But now the righteousness of God without the law is manifested, being witnessed by the law and the prophets;

22 Even the righteousness of God which is by faith of Jesus Christ unto all and upon all

ROMANS 3:21–31, NIV

21 But now apart from the law the righteousness of God has been made known, to which the Law and the Prophets testify.

22 This righteousness is given through faith in Jesus Christ to all who believe. There is no

them that believe: for there is no difference:

23 For all have sinned, and come short of the glory of God;

24 Being justified freely by his grace through the redemption that is in Christ Jesus:

25 Whom God hath set forth to be a propitiation through faith in his blood, to declare his righteousness for the remission of sins that are past, through the forbearance of God;

26 To declare, I say, at this time his righteousness: that he might be just, and the justifier of him which believeth in Jesus.

27 Where is boasting then? It is excluded. By what law? of works? Nay: but by the law of faith.

28 Therefore we conclude that a man is justified by faith without the deeds of the law.

29 Is he the God of the Jews only? is he not also of the Gentiles? Yes, of the Gentiles also:

30 Seeing it is one God, which shall justify the circumcision by faith, and uncircumcision through faith.

31 Do we then make void the law through faith? God forbid: yea, we establish the law.

difference between Jew and Gentile,

23 for all have sinned and fall short of the glory of God,

24 and all are justified freely by his grace through the redemption that came by Christ Jesus.

25 God presented Christ as a sacrifice of atonement, through the shedding of his blood—to be received by faith. He did this to demonstrate his righteousness, because in his forbearance he had left the sins committed beforehand unpunished—

26 he did it to demonstrate his righteousness at the present time, so as to be just and the one who justifies those who have faith in Jesus.

27 Where, then, is boasting? It is excluded. Because of what law? The law that requires works? No, because of the law that requires faith.

28 For we maintain that a person is justified by faith apart from the works of the law.

29 Or is God the God of Jews only? Is he not the God of Gentiles too? Yes, of Gentiles too,

30 since there is only one God, who will justify the circumcised by faith and the uncircumcised through that same faith.

31 Do we, then, nullify the law by this faith? Not at all! Rather, we uphold the law.

LIGHT ON THE WORD

Sacrificial System. This was the system God gave to Israel in order to maintain their holiness as a people and reconcile them to Him when they sinned. The sacrificial system was instituted once the Israelites were in the wilderness and built the tabernacle. It consisted of various animal and grain offerings. These were all to be given for different offenses and on different occasions for different groups of people. Now God's people have one sacrifice that makes us holy and reconciles us to God: Jesus Christ.

The Law. This was the civil, moral, and ceremonial laws given to Israel at Mount Sinai. It consists of over 413 commands. The Law was given on tablets of stone to Moses. These laws were taught by the priests and also were to be discussed by parents with their children. Adherence to the Law was one of the main things that made an Israelite an Israelite.

TEACHING THE BIBLE LESSON

LIFE NEED FOR TODAY'S LESSON

AIM: Students will experience that some people give thanks for all that is good in life, while others have no hope.

INTRODUCTION

Sin is No Respecter of Persons

Paul writes to the church at Rome and shows them how being an ethnic Jew is no better than being a Gentile when it comes to the righteousness of God. His aim is to present all people as being under sin and worthy of God's judgment. Paul does this by showing how a Gentile who doesn't know God can still obey His Law in his heart and be righteous while a Jew who is supposed to know God and has the Law can disobey the Law and not be right with God.

He then goes on to show how sin is a reality for the whole human race by quoting the Psalms which state that there is no one who is righteous. This is all a setup to show how God is righteous in His judgment and has provided a way for us to escape it through faith in the righteousness of Christ. In **Romans 3:21–31**, Paul discusses further how Jesus makes those who believe in Him right with God.

BIBLE LEARNING

AIM: Students will know that Christ offers hope for all who want to develop a relationship with Him.

I. THE ANNOUNCEMENT (ROMANS 3:21–22)

Here, Paul boldly announces a change that has taken place in the law courts of the universe. Before, all men were judged according to the Law, and all were condemned. Now there is a righteousness apart or separate from the Law. This righteousness comes from Jesus Christ and is available to all.

Now Paul announces that righteousness is achieved through a person who was once sentenced and executed by religious and secular authorities. Jesus is now presented as the fulfillment of the Law. This initial transformation in thought and understanding is key to helping not only the ancient Roman church, but contemporary seekers and believers as well.

Romans 3:21–31

21 But now the righteousness of God without the law is manifested, being witnessed by the law and the prophets.

When Paul began his argument proving that all humanity was guilty before God, he used the phrase "for the wrath of God is revealed from heaven against all" (**1:18**). Humanity is indeed worthy of God's wrath. "But now" is a favorite expression of Paul (cf. **Ephesians 2:11–13; 1 Corinthians 15:16–20**); he uses this phrase when making a transition from a dire, seemingly hopeless situation to something divinely wonderful.

Here, Paul's transition "but now" opens to the manifestation of "the righteousness of God" in contrast to the wrath of God on humanity's sinfulness. As used here, God's righteousness is not a reference to His character. (Paul deals with that aspect of righteousness later in **verse 26**.) In **verse 21**, righteousness refers to God's gift of righteousness to all those who enter the Kingdom of God (**Romans 5:17**). By faith in Christ and His work of atonement, unrighteous sinners receive God's righteousness. This means that God forgives all their sins and provides a new "right" standing with Him. God's gift of righteousness includes victory over our sinful nature (**Romans 6:12–14**), separation from evil (**2 Corinthians 6:14**), and new eternal life under the rule of God (**Ephesians 4:22–24**).

God's gift of righteousness is "without," or apart from, the Law. At the same time, although it is apart from the Law, Paul further states that this righteousness is witnessed to by both the Law and the Prophets. The Law, in this case, refers to the Mosaic sacrificial system. When the Jews took their sin offering to the Temple, laid their hands on the bullock's head, confessed their sins, and killed the animal, they attested to their belief in a righteousness not their own (cf. **Leviticus 4:1–4**).

22 Even the righteousness of God which is by faith of Jesus Christ unto all and upon all them that believe: for there is no difference: 23 For all have sinned, and come short of the glory of God.

God freely offers His righteousness to all who have faith in Jesus Christ. One must have faith in the incarnation, death, resurrection, and ascension of Jesus Christ. He is the only way (**John 14:6**). Paul states that God's gift of righteousness is "unto all and upon all them that believe." The apostle appears to repeat himself here, but in fact he uses very precise language to say that God's gift of righteousness is not universal. It does not save everyone. God's righteousness is available to, or "unto," all. However His righteousness only comes to, or is "upon," those who believe. The condition for receiving God's gift is faith in Christ.

Faith in Christ is the only condition for the gift, and there is no difference between people accepting His gift. The word "difference" is a translation of the Greek word *diastole* (**dee-ah-sto-LAY**), which also means "distinction." In other words, God makes no distinction between Jews and Gentiles; He treats both exactly the same. The latter part of **verse 22** (beginning with "for") and all of **verse 23** form a parenthetical statement. Just as there is no difference between Jew and Gentile, there is no difference between the liar and the murderer in regard to their righteousness with God. Both are equally lost and in need of God's gift of righteousness.

To drive home his point that all the world is under sin and condemnation, Paul again employs two similar words to paint the full picture. In the phrase, "For all have sinned," the verb "sinned" (Gk. *hamartano*, **ha-mar-TAH-no**) means that we erred or missed our goal. "Come short" (Gk. *hustereo*, **hoos-teh-REH-oh**) can mean to come after, lack, or lag behind. The point is that through missing our path and coming up short, humanity fails to achieve its ultimate goal: partaking in the glory of God. The verb "sinned" is used in the aorist tense to indicate God's view of sin. The Creator looks back on all sin as an accomplished fact. He simply says, "All have sinned." In contrast, "come short" is present tense and could be read "all continuously come short." This clause refers to our practical everyday living. We all sin continuously.

The meaning of the phrase "glory of God" (Gk. *doxes tou theou*, **DOKE-sees too theh-OO**) is hotly debated. The term "glory" is generally used to describe the aggregate of God's divine attributes and His revelation of Himself (cf. **Exodus 34:6–7**). This cannot be what Paul means, because humanity is not condemned because of falling short of God's attributes. Another interpretation is that in this case, the glory of God means divine approval or praise. Others believe the glory of God refers to an idea similar to that from **John 1:14**: ("And we beheld his glory, the glory as the only begotten of the Father,) full of grace and truth." Jesus' glory here was not the out-shining of His divine attributes, because He did not have that divine glory then (cf. **Philippians 2:7**, where He "emptied" Himself). Rather, it was His moral and spiritual glory. Jesus was sinless and that was His glory on earth. In this view, when we "come short of the glory of God," it means that we come up short in following Christ's example of sinlessness.

II. THE SACRIFICE (vv. 23–26)

God is not only an exemplar of righteousness, He IS righteousness. As such, Paul is setting forth all humanity under the singular umbrella of sin. He explains in **Romans 3:23** that even the pious Jews who attempted to obey the law were just as subject to sin as the worst Gentile. Despite being unclean for worship or unwelcome within the Temple, the Gentile is now welcome to worship God through Christ, who has become a "propitiation" for everyone.

Jesus needed no salvation or Savior for Himself, as He was without sin. Yet in order for God to absolve humankind of sin, there had to be both an innocent sacrifice, and one that would be worthy of the task. Although in His flesh He was a man and able to be tempted, He was also God and resisted the temptation to sin, remaining holy and innocent. In other words, Jesus Himself is righteousness as He is one with the Father; making it possible for Him—and only Him—to justify us.

Redemption through Jesus Christ

24 Being justified freely by his grace through the redemption that is in Christ Jesus.

This final view would explain why humanity needs to be justified. We cannot live according to the standard set by God and modeled by Christ. Because it is impossible to live righteous lives, how can humanity ever hope to gain a right standing with God? The answer is: by being justified. The words "righteousness" and "justified" are spiritually linked in this epistle. Notice how the apostle clusters these words in these few verses: "righteousness" (**vv. 21, 22, 25, 26**; Gk. *dikaiosune*, **dee-keye-oh-SOO-nay**); "justify" (**vv. 24, 30**; Gk. *dikaioo*, **dee-keye-OH-oh**); "just" (**v. 26**; Gk. *dikaios*, **DEE-keye-ose**); and "justifier" (**v. 26**; Gk. *dikaion*, **dee-keye-OWN**). All the words share the same root *dike* (Gk. **DEE-kay**), which means an order, pumishment, or justice.

To justify means to declare and treat as righteous or to make right. In other words, God says that we are righteous, then treats us as if we had never sinned. Our sins are not merely forgiven or pardoned; they are wiped away! God declares us as righteous as Jesus Christ Himself. Our justification is accomplished through the redemption that is in Christ Jesus. The word "redemption" is from the Greek word *apolutrosis* (**ah-poe-LOO-troe-sees**), which specifically refers to a release on payment of a ransom. The word could possibly conjure up a slave auction where people are held in bondage and are incapable of freeing themselves. Christ is portrayed as One who sees our hopeless state and pays the ransom for our freedom. The ransom not only is sufficient to purchase our freedom, it also had to satisfy the wrath of a just and holy God. The only thing Christ had to offer to cover this great price was His blood.

25 Whom God hath set forth to be a propitiation through faith in his blood, to declare his righteousness for the remission

of sins that are past, through the forbearance of God; 26 To declare, I say, at this time his righteousness: that he might be just, and the justifier of him which believeth in Jesus.

Sometimes when the Bible refers to "the blood," it symbolically refers to a life laid down in sacrifice (e.g., **Hebrews 9:7**). In this case, "his blood" signifies the death of Christ by the shedding of His blood on the Cross. Since the life of the flesh is in the blood (**Leviticus 17:11**) and death is the cost of sinfulness (**Romans 6:23**), then only the shedding of the blood of a sinless Savior could cover the cost of everyone's redemption.

God demonstrated His love for us through the death of His only begotten Son (**John 3:16**). However, that was not the only purpose of Christ's sacrifice on Calvary. The other reason was to declare God's righteousness in the remission of sins. Why was it necessary for God to declare His righteousness? The word "remission" (Gk. *paresis*, **PAH-reh-sees**) is better translated "overlooking" or "disregard." This explains how God dealt with sin before the sacrifice of Christ. God patiently tolerated the sins of the generations before Christ. As a result, His holiness was called into question. In order for God to show that He is righteous, He sent Christ to the Cross where He punished every sin—past, present, and future. This does not mean that God ignored sin in the Old Testament, but that He did not deal with it fully and completely until Calvary. Christ's death on the Cross satisfied God's justice and executed the punishment for sin which humanity so richly deserved.

Christ thus became our propitiation. The actual Greek word for "propitiation" is *hilasterion* (**hee-las-TAY-ree-on**). In classical and ancient Greek, *hilasterion* referred to sacrifices offered to pagan deities to appease their anger. However, this is not how Paul

uses the word. In the Septuagint, the Greek translation of the Old Testament, *hilasterion* is used to translate the Hebrew term for the mercy seat which has the sense of atonement connected with sin offerings in the Levitical laws (e.g., **Exodus 25:18; Leviticus 16:2**). The writer of Hebrews also uses this Greek word for mercy seat (**9:5**).

On the Day of Atonement, the high priest appeared before the Ark of the Covenant and poured blood from a sacrifice on the golden lid of the ark called the "mercy seat." This symbolic act showed that sin, which separated God from His people, was judged through the shedding of blood. So the place of judgment—the mercy seat—became the place of mercy and reconciliation. For Paul and the early church the ritual pointed to Christ's sacrificial death, where God's legitimate demands for justice against sinful humanity were fully met. Therefore, He is free to show mercy to those who formally were only worthy of judgment. Christ as our propitiation (mercy seat) allows God to righteously punish sin and at the same time show mercy and treat repentant sinners as if they had never sinned. Christ allows God to be both just and the justifier.

III. THE ONE GOD FOR ALL (vv. 27–31)

Next, Paul asks a question in order to prove his point. Here he shows that no boasting is allowed in the righteousness given by faith. Believers cannot measure up to God's holiness through the Law or good works, but through the law of faith we are justified, apart from the "deeds of the law" (**v. 28**). It is through faith in the finished work of Christ.

Paul next asks questions about God and His domain and territory. He is a global God. He is not just the God of a certain people. The Jews had the Law and this was seen as the marker of the people of God. Those who lived without the Law were Gentiles and therefore not God's people. Paul says this is not the case, due to the righteousness that comes through faith in Christ. He is the God of the Jews and the Gentiles—the God of all peoples.

No Bragging Rights

27 Where is boasting then? It is excluded. By what law? of works? Nay: but by the law of faith. 28 Therefore we conclude that a man is justified by faith without the deeds of the law. 29 Is he the God of the Jews only? is he not also of the Gentiles? Yes, of the Gentiles also: 30 Seeing it is one God, which shall justify the circumcision by faith, and uncircumcision through faith. 31 Do we then make void the law through faith? God forbid: yea, we establish the law.

Paul now asks, what did we do to earn our salvation that we can brag about? He answers with three short words: "It is excluded." Anyone who wants to be reconciled to God has two options. The first is justification by works. With this option, people earn their righteousness by living according to the Law. The problem comes in that when one aspect of the Law is violated, then the entire Law is violated (**James 2:10**). So one would have to live an absolutely perfect life in order to enjoy God's fellowship. The other option is to achieve righteousness apart from the deeds of the Law. Here people are justified by faith in the life and work of Jesus Christ.

Paul then asks the question that flows from this explanation: Does this void or nullify the Law? The answer: By no means; rather it establishes the Law in the sense of strengthening its foundation so that the Law is made firm. In this way, faith in Christ causes the Law to stand as a guide for human behavior.

SEARCH THE SCRIPTURES

QUESTION 1
What makes us right with God?

Faith.

QUESTION 2
Why is Jesus the true sacrifice for Jew and Gentile in **verse 23**?

We all have sinned and fallen short of God's glory.

LIGHT ON THE WORD

Christ and God's Law
As Paul declares revisions to the way God will be accessed and understood through Christ, he concludes this chapter rather simply. While the Law and faith to this point have functioned somewhat differently, he does not seek to replace one with the other. He essentially clarifies that in order to exercise faith in God through Christ, one must accept that all God's Law is as valid as it ever was. However, the main difference is to understand that faith in Christ now fulfills all that the Law had set out to accomplish.

BIBLE APPLICATION

AIM: Students will understand that God offers a way for all to restore and build relationships through Jesus Christ.

Many believe that all roads lead to God, and that the different religions are just different in the details, and one day we will all be surprised to worship the same God. In this lesson, we see that the Christian faith is different from all others in that it requires faith in the sacrifice of Jesus. Through Him, we can see how we all are under the judgment of the same God and how we all can be right with Him through Jesus Christ.

STUDENT'S RESPONSES

AIM: Students will know that Christians have hope in Christ and make commitments to renew their relationship with Christ through faith, prayer, and love.

Our righteousness in Christ is secured by faith in Him. At the top of a piece of paper, write down "How to be right with God." Next draw two columns. In one column, write down "faith in Christ." In the other column, write down all the good things you can do to try and earn your way to Heaven. Ask a friend or neighbor to pick which side will make them righteous in God's sight.

A DOCTRINAL ATTACHMENT

We believe that man was created holy by God, composed of body, soul, and spirit. We believe that man, by nature, is sinful and unholy. Being born in sin, he needs to be born again, sanctified and cleansed from all sins by the blood of Jesus. We believe that man is saved by confessing and forsaking his sins, and believing on the Lord Jesus Christ. Salvation deals with the application of the work of redemption to the sinner and with his restoration to divine favor and communion with God. This redemptive operation of the Holy Ghost is brought about by repentance, faith, justification, regeneration, sanctification, and the baptism of the Holy Ghost by which He delivers the justified sinner from the pollution of sin, renews his whole nature in the image of God, and enables him to perform good works (Romans 6:4, 5:6; Colossians 2:12, 3:1).

For further reading, please refer to the back of this book in the section on COGIC doctrine under the headings of Man, Sin, and Salvation.

PRAYER

Dear Jesus, we can not earn or buy our way into Heaven or for our salvation. Thank You for paying the price and redeeming us with your blood. Our faith and righteousness is because of You. In Jesus' name we pray. Amen.

HOW TO SAY IT

Propitiation.   pro-pi-she-AY-shun.

Forbearance.   for-BARE-ins.

PREPARE FOR NEXT SUNDAY

Read **Romans 5:1–11** and "Not Without Hope."

DAILY HOME BIBLE READINGS

MONDAY
Free in Christ
(Galatians 4:28–5:1)

TUESDAY
One in Christ
(1 Corinthians 1:10–17)

WEDNESDAY
Rich in Christ
(Romans 11:30–36)

THURSDAY
United in Christ
(1 Corinthians 12:12–20)

FRIDAY
Dwelling in Christ
(Ephesians 2:15–22)

SATURDAY
Believing in Christ
(John 12:40–50)

SUNDAY
God Set Things Right
(Romans 3:21–31)

Sources:
Greathouse William M., and George Lyons. *Romans 9–16: A Commentary in the Wesleyan Tradition.* New Beacon Bible Commentary. Kansas City, MO: Beacon Hill Press of Kansas City, 2008.
Moo, Douglas, Romans. *New International Commentary on the New Testament.* Grand Rapids, MI: Wm. B. Eerdmans. 1996.

NOT WITHOUT HOPE

BIBLE BASIS: ROMANS 5:1–11

BIBLE TRUTH: There is faith in Christ with the presence of the Holy Spirit; God has given reconciliation and hope.

MEMORY VERSE: "And hope maketh not ashamed; because the love of God is shed abroad in our hearts by the Holy Ghost which is given unto us" (Romans 5:5).

LESSON AIM: By the end of the lesson, we will: KNOW Paul's encouraging words about peace, endurance, character, hope, and love as gifts God gave through the death of Jesus; FEEL that God's provision of the Savior is His continuing commitment to His creation; and TAKE hope through Jesus Christ into the difficult times in life.

TEACHER PREPARATION

MATERIALS NEEDED: Quarterly Commentary/Teacher Manual, Adult Quarterly, Adult resources—charts, worksheets, and other teaching tools, paper, pens, pencils, Bibles (several different versions)

OTHER MATERIALS NEEDED / TEACHER'S NOTES:

_____

_____

LESSON OVERVIEW

LIFE NEED FOR TODAY'S LESSON
People are weak, endure suffering of different kinds, do wrong, and face various enemies all around them.

BIBLE LEARNING
In Christ, there is hope for us all.

BIBLE APPLICATION
Christians experience that having hope in difficult times is the right choice.

STUDENTS' RESPONSES
Believers are encouraged through God's love, hope, mercy, and endurance.

LESSON SCRIPTURE

ROMANS 5:1–11, KJV

1 Therefore being justified by faith, we have peace with God through our Lord Jesus Christ:

2 By whom also we have access by faith into this grace wherein we stand, and rejoice in hope of the glory of God.

3 And not only so, but we glory in

ROMANS 5:1–11, NIV

1 Therefore, since we have been justified through faith, we have peace with God through our Lord Jesus Christ,

2 through whom we have gained access by faith into this grace in which we now stand. And we boast in the hope of the glory of God.

tribulations also: knowing that tribulation worketh patience;

4 And patience, experience; and experience, hope:

5 And hope maketh not ashamed; because the love of God is shed abroad in our hearts by the Holy Ghost which is given unto us.

6 For when we were yet without strength, in due time Christ died for the ungodly.

7 For scarcely for a righteous man will one die: yet peradventure for a good man some would even dare to die.

8 But God commendeth his love toward us, in that, while we were yet sinners, Christ died for us.

9 Much more then, being now justified by his blood, we shall be saved from wrath through him.

10 For if, when we were enemies, we were reconciled to God by the death of his Son, much more, being reconciled, we shall be saved by his life.

11 And not only so, but we also joy in God through our Lord Jesus Christ, by whom we have now received the atonement.

3 Not only so, but we also glory in our sufferings, because we know that suffering produces perseverance;

4 perseverance, character; and character, hope.

5 And hope does not put us to shame, because God's love has been poured out into our hearts through the Holy Spirit, who has been given to us.

6 You see, at just the right time, when we were still powerless, Christ died for the ungodly.

7 Very rarely will anyone die for a righteous person, though for a good person someone might possibly dare to die.

8 But God demonstrates his own love for us in this: While we were still sinners, Christ died for us.

9 Since we have now been justified by his blood, how much more shall we be saved from God's wrath through him!

10 For if, while we were God's enemies, we were reconciled to him through the death of his Son, how much more, having been reconciled, shall we be saved through his life!

11 Not only is this so, but we also boast in God through our Lord Jesus Christ, through whom we have now received reconciliation.

LIGHT ON THE WORD

The Apostle. Apostles were literally "the sent out ones." God called them, equipped them, and then sent them to establish His Word among His people. The Apostle Paul was, as he said, an apostle "born out of due time" (**1 Corinthians 15:8**) meaning he was late to be called one of the apostles. He was, in fact, an enemy to the early church until God plucked him out from among his Pharisaical brothers.

However, Paul showed the same zeal in serving Christ that he had shown in persecuting Him and His people. In our focal verses today, we see several characteristics of Paul that are important to our study. 1) He was radically changed, completely taken with his Master. His loyalty to Jesus was unimpeachable, and he was driven to get others to follow with the same zeal. 2) He was completely convinced of salvation by grace. In these verses, he showed that this salvation gives a new perspective, one that carries us through even the toughest times.

Redemptive Tribulations. Few themes are more distinctive of our faith than that of tribulations resulting in positive net values (**Matthew 5:10; Romans 8:35–37; 2 Corinthians 12:9–10; James 1:2–3**). We find thinking like this outside of Christian thought, but not to the same extent. Our faith can mirror what Jesus did on the Cross: what appears to be complete failure can be, in fact, great victory.

TEACHING THE BIBLE LESSON

LIFE NEED FOR TODAY'S LESSON

AIM: Students will know see how people are weak, endure suffering of different kinds, do wrong, and face various enemies all around them.

INTRODUCTION

Hope in Tribulation

Paul is in the middle of his argument about justification by faith in Romans 4. He points to Abraham and his righteousness being imputed by God before the Law was given. He illustrates that God imputed righteousness to Abraham because of his faith in God's promise that he would be the father of many nations. The example of Abraham is given to the Romans to show the kind of faith in Jesus that justifies one before God. This faith can sustain us in the midst of difficulties.

The Christians in Rome had to deal with a cruel, militaristic, and threatening government. They certainly felt the weight of this kingdom and its displeasure. Jesus' death had been ordered by

Roman officials (with the help of some of the Jews), and He had told His followers, "If the world hate you, ye know that it hated me before it hated you" (**John 15:18**).

It is hard for us to understand how greatly tribulation was a part the lives of these believers, but it was extensive. Paul spoke to people who had every natural right to be fearful, but he reminded them to base their courage on the supernatural event of the resurrection of Jesus Christ. The King of kings had the final word even over mighty Rome. Paul encouraged them to let this fuel their hope in tribulation.

BIBLE LEARNING

AIM: Students will learn that Christians experience that having hope in difficult times is the right choice.

I. JUSTIFICATION OFFERS HOPE IN TRIBULATION (ROMANS 5:1–5)

Paul indicates in these verses that this justification (the opposite of condemnation) gives us hope, even by way of tribulation. It is clear, especially in **verses 1 and 2**, that our part is faith.

Paul explains that tribulation leads through several steps to hope, but what produces this hope is the establishment of character. Character is established not by our suffering, but by our patience in suffering. Paul concludes this section by showing that through this process the Holy Spirit communicates God's love to us (**v. 5**). His love enables us to endure tribulations and hard times.

Romans 5:1–11

1 Therefore being justified by faith, we have peace with God through our Lord Jesus Christ.

With the close of the fourth chapter, Paul completes his teaching on how God justifies a person. Justification is the initial blessing of salvation, but it carries with it all the other blessings of Christian life. In **chapter 5**, Paul launches into an explanation of eight attendant blessings of justification by faith. Because we are justified by faith, we have "peace with God" (**v. 1**); "access" to God's presence and a standing in grace, joy, and "hope" (**v. 2**); "the love of God" and "the Holy Ghost" (**v. 5**); we are "saved from wrath" (**v. 9**), and "saved by his life" (**v. 10**).

Another literal translation of verse 1 is "Since we have been justified by faith, we continually have peace with God." In the Greek, "justified" is in the aorist aspect, which points to an accomplished fact. This illustrates that justification is not a process, but rather an instantaneous act that takes place at the moment a sinner accepts Christ as Lord.

The phrase "we have peace with God" could also be translated "we continually have peace with God." The verb "to have" is from the Greek present tense verb *echomen* (Gk. EH-koh-men), which means to keep on having or enjoying our peace with God. Those who are justified are privileged to "have peace with God," and Paul is encouraging believers to both realize this privilege and enjoy it.

This peace is first a change in God's relationship to us. Then, as the natural consequence of His changed relationship to us, we change in our relationship toward Him. Because of our fallen nature, humanity is in a state of hostility with God as His enemies (**v. 10**). When we are justified, that hostility is removed and we have peace with Him. Awareness of our peace with God brings a sense of peace to our souls.

2 By whom also we have access by faith into this grace wherein we stand, and rejoice in hope of the glory of God. 3 And not only so, but we glory in tribulations also: knowing that tribulation worketh patience; 4 And patience, experience; and experience, hope.

Not only does Christ remove the hostility that existed between God and sinners, He also gives us "access" (Gk. *prosagoge*, **pro-sah-go-GAY**, a bringing to) into His very presence. In the Hebrew Temple, the presence of God was in a room called the Holy of Holies. A thick veil separated this room from the rest of the Temple, and only the high priest was allowed past the veil once a year to purify the altar which has been made unclean by the sins of the people (**Leviticus 16:16**). This curtain represented the separation of sinful humanity from God. When Christ died on the Cross, the veil that led to the Holy of Holies ripped down the middle (**Matthew 27:51**). Ripping the veil represented the elimination of the separation so that all believers now have access to God. Christ's eternal sacrifice in our behalf brings us into the presence of God and allows us to have continuous access to Him.

Being justified by faith also brings us into a new permanent standing with God where we enjoy His divine favor. The basis of our new standing is obtained by grace. We can't stand before God by our own deeds, character, or righteousness. Our new standing is totally the result of God's undeserved favor.

Therefore, we rejoice "in hope of the glory of God." The glory spoken of here is twofold. First, we hope to experience the Divine Presence in Heaven. Second and more immediate, we hope to bring glory to God through and in our tribulations. Paul says we glory, or rejoice, in tribulation because we realize it is Heaven's way of teaching us patience or longsuffering. Patience is the confident endurance of things hoped for or difficulties we wish removed. The spiritual fruit of patience (cf. **Galatians 5:22**) is seen in the humble endurance of ill because of the realization that nothing comes against us that has not been allowed by God.

This patience then brings about "experience" (Gk. *dokime*, **doe-kee-MAY**), a word also translated as "proof" (**2 Corinthians 2:9, 13:3; Philippians 2:22**). Proof is the experimental evidence that we have believed through grace. Believers enter periods of tribulation and patiently endure. Our patient endurance is rewarded with eventual victory over our circumstance, and our victorious experience proves the faithfulness to God to deliver us from future trials. Another meaning for *dokime* is "character." Testings prove or establish our character because it is made evident through patient endurance. Then, experience brings us back to "hope."

We have hope in two distinct ways and at two successive stages of the Christian life. First, immediately upon believing, along with the sense of peace and abiding access to God, we have hope in our new relationship. Next, hope grows after the reality of our faith has been proven by the patient endurance of trials sent to test it. Our hope comes from looking away from ourselves to the Cross of Christ, then looking into ourselves as being transformed into the image of Christ. In the first case, our hope is based on faith and in the second by experience.

5 And hope maketh not ashamed; because the love of God is shed abroad in our hearts by the Holy Ghost which is given unto us.

Our hope of Heaven, which presupposes faith, is the confident expectation of future good. Our faith assures us that Heaven will be ours, and our hope expectantly anticipates it. This hope in the glory of God will never make us ashamed (like empty hopes do) because it is based on "the love of God"—not our love of God, but His love of us which is "shed abroad"

(Gk. *ekkheo*, ek-KHE-oh, "poured forth," used literally of blood or wine, and figuratively of love or the Holy Spirit itself). God's love for us is seen in the indwelling presence of the Holy Spirit.

II. HELP FOR THE HELPLESS (vv. 6–8)

Several versions of the Bible translate the word in **verse 6** as "helpless" (e.g. NASB and NLT). The KJV has "without strength." Paul states that when it comes to our spiritual state, we are helpless without the person and work of Christ.

We see that the word "die" or "died" appears frequently in these verses, four times in three verses. Three of the references are pointing to Christ's death rather than our own. His death is the crucial pivot where our helplessness becomes strength. Paul says in **verse 8** that Christ died for us while we were still sinners. He did not expect us to be self-sufficient before He helped us, nor did He disdain our sinfulness—His death for us is the proof and substance of His love.

God's Appointed Time for Christ

6 For when we were yet without strength, in due time Christ died for the ungodly.

At the appointed time, Christ offered Himself as our eternal sacrifice "when we were yet without strength"—that is, when we were powerless to deliver ourselves and therefore ready to perish. Christ's death reveals three properties of God's love. First, "the ungodly" are those whose character and sinful nature are repulsive in God's eyes. Second, He did this when they were "without strength"— nothing stood between humanity and damnation but divine compassion. Third, He did this "in due time" when it was most appropriate that it should take place.

7 For scarcely for a righteous man will one die: yet peradventure for a good man some

would even dare to die. 8 But God commendeth his love toward us, in that, while we were yet sinners, Christ died for us.

The apostle now proceeded to illustrate God's compassion. Few, if any people, would be willing to sacrifice their lives for a "righteous man" of exceptional character. A few more might be willing to die for a man who, besides being exceptional, is also distinguished for goodness or a benefactor to society. But God, in glorious contrast to what men might do for each other, displayed His love, "while we were yet sinners"—that is, in a state in of absolute rebellion—"Christ died for us."

III. THE RECONCILIATION OF GOD LEADS TO OUR JOY (VV. 9–11)

In these final verses of our text, Paul continues to expound on the benefits of our justification. We are justified and therefore saved from wrath. We have atonement with God which gives us joy. We have been reconciled to God and therefore saved by the life of Christ. In **verse 9**, Paul uses the phrase "much more," and again in **verse 10**. Then in **verse 11** he adds, "And not only so…" He piles one benefit upon another. He is overcome with the positive nature of our standing in Christ! Our justification through Jesus' blood has moved us from helplessness to being reconciled, no longer under His wrath but now sharing His life, which leads to our joy.

Here Paul makes an extraordinary statement: God's love reconciled us through Christ. In contrast to the heresies that state that the Father was vengeful and appeased by Jesus who alone loves, God's love brought about our salvation through His Son.

Christ's Sacrifice for Humanity

9 Much more then, being now justified by his blood, we shall be saved from wrath through him. 10 For if, when we were enemies, we were reconciled to God by the death of his Son, much more, being reconciled, we shall be saved by his life.

Having been "justified by his blood," we shall be saved from wrath through the sacrifice of Christ. Christ's death restored our relationship with God while we were in open rebellion against Him. Since we are now reconciled, "we shall be saved by His life." If Christ's sacrifice was offered for people incapable of the least appreciation for God's love or Christ's labors on their behalf, how much more will He do all that remains to be done? "For since our friendship with God was restored by the death of his Son while we were still his enemies, we will certainly be saved through the life of his Son" (**v. 10**, NLT). To be "saved from wrath through him," refers to the entire work of salvation—from the moment of justification to the great white throne judgment (**Revelation 20:11–15**), when the wrath of God shall be revealed to all who ignore the Gospel of Jesus. The Apostle Jude best described Christ's continuing work of salvation when he said that He "is able to keep you from falling, and to present you faultless before the presence of his glory with exceeding joy" (**Jude 24**).

11 And not only so, but we also joy in God through our Lord Jesus Christ, by whom we have now received the atonement.

"And not only so" refers back to the blessing Paul mentioned previously. We not only find joy in our newfound peace, access, standing, hope, love, indwelling, and salvation, but we rejoice in God Himself. We find joy in our God for what He has done and for who He is. Our joy proceeds from our union with Christ who brought about our atonement.

"Atonement" (Gk. *katallage*, **kah-tah-lah-GAY**) is the noun form of the verb for reconciling in **v. 10**. It indicates a shift from a negative relationship to a positive one, or from a broken relationship to a healthy one. Paul moves beyond the sacrificial language here to focus on the restored relationship that Christ's atoning death provides. This restored relationship with God brings about joy, or more literally boasting (see **v. 2**).

Atonement is the gracious act by which God restores a relationship of harmony and unity between Himself and believers. The word contains parts that express this great truth in simple but profound terms: "at-one." Through God's atoning grace and forgiveness, we are reinstated to a relationship of being "at one" with God.

SEARCH THE SCRIPTURES

QUESTION 1
Verse 2 states because of our _____, Christ has bought us into a place privilege that we do not deserve (NLT).

Faith.

QUESTION 2
Our _____ with God was restored by the death of Christ even when we were still _____ (NLT, **v. 10**).

Friendship, enemies.

LIGHT ON THE WORD

Faith Carries Us
Faith introduced us to the grace that justifies us and keeps us in the hope that it offers. Therefore, faith carries us through any tribulation so that we might have the hope that is the promise of salvation.

BIBLE APPLICATION

AIM: Students will know that Christians experience having hope in Jesus in difficult times is the right choice.

It is interesting that the Scripture never presents living in faith and being hopeful as requests but as commands. We should keep in mind that the Lord is aware of our weaknesses even more than we are. He also knows our enemies and challenges but still requires our victorious outlook. When we are fearful and unsettled, then it shows we are not focused on His assurances.

Our believing brothers and sisters need to see our hope in the Lord. Our hopeless world needs to see our hope as well. When we correct our relationship with Christ—when our daily walk is firm— we will grow in the ability to share this hope.

STUDENT'S RESPONSES

AIM: Students will learn that believers are encouraged through God's love, hope, mercy, and endurance.

We choose first to believe the Lord. When we say with Joshua, "As for me and my house, we will serve the LORD" (**Joshua 2:15**), we have chosen to trust Him with our lives. When we choose to act this way, then we follow with actions and thoughts that reflect that.

Today, commit your life anew to God's truth. Consider all thoughts that dishonor Christ as enemies, and choose not to allow them a place in your life.

PRAYER

Dear God, we rest and have hope in You. We are reassured of Your amazing grace and comfort through Jesus. It is in faith and hope that we have our confidence that You provide and care for the world. In Jesus' Name we pray. Amen.

HOW TO SAY IT

Commendeth.   kuh-MEN-dith.

Peradventure.   pur-ad-VIN-ture.

PREPARE FOR NEXT SUNDAY

Read **Romans 6:1–4, 12–14, 17–23** and "Death Becomes Life."

DAILY HOME BIBLE READINGS

MONDAY
Hope in God
(Isaiah 40:27–31)

TUESDAY
Redeemed in God
(Isaiah 52:7–12)

WEDNESDAY
Safe in God
(Isaiah 54:9–14)

THURSDAY
Restored in God
(Jeremiah 29:10–14)

FRIDAY
Help in God
(Psalm 42)

SATURDAY
Fulfilled in God
(Matthew 12:15–21)

SUNDAY
Not Without Hope
(Romans 5:1–11)

Sources:
Carson, D. A., R. T. France, J. A. Motyer, J. G. Wenham.. *New Bible Commentary.* Downers Grove, IL: InterVarsity Press, 1993.
Keener, Craig S. *IVP Bible Background Commentary.* Downers Grove, IL: InterVarsity Press, 1993.

COMMENTS / NOTES:

DEATH BECOMES LIFE

BIBLE BASIS: ROMANS 6:1–4, 12–14, 17–23

BIBLE TRUTH: Christ provides freedom from sin and believers can be slaves of righteousness, and thus receive sanctification and eternal life.

MEMORY VERSE: "Therefore we are buried with him by baptism into death: that like as Christ was raised up from the dead by the glory of the Father, even so we also should walk in newness of life" (Romans 6:4).

LESSON AIM: By the end of the lesson, we will: RECALL Paul's explanation that accepting Jesus frees one from sin while it enslaves them to righteousness and gains them eternity; CONNECT being baptized into Christ with giving up sin and renewing creation; and RENEW our baptismal commitments.

TEACHER PREPARATION

MATERIALS NEEDED: Quarterly Commentary/Teacher Manual, Adult Quarterly, Adult resources—charts, worksheets, and other teaching tools, paper, pens, pencils, Bibles (several different versions)

OTHER MATERIALS NEEDED / TEACHER'S NOTES:

_____

_____

LESSON OVERVIEW

LIFE NEED FOR TODAY'S LESSON
People often give in to do wrong.

BIBLE LEARNING
In Christ, people can overcome temptation.

BIBLE APPLICATION
Renewing our commitment to Christ gives us an opportunity to reconnect and strengthen our relationship with Him.

STUDENTS' RESPONSES
Believers can rejoice in knowing that their baptism in Christ is a way to acknowledge that Jesus frees us from sin.

LESSON SCRIPTURE

ROMANS 6:1–4, 12–14, 17–23, KJV

1 What shall we say then? Shall we continue in sin, that grace may abound?

2 God forbid. How shall we, that are dead to sin, live any longer therein?

ROMANS 6:1–4, 12–14, 17–23, NIV

1 What shall we say, then? Shall we go on sinning so that grace may increase?

2 By no means! We are those who have died to sin; how can we live in it any longer?

3 Know ye not, that so many of us as were baptized into Jesus Christ were baptized into his death?

4 Therefore we are buried with him by baptism into death: that like as Christ was raised up from the dead by the glory of the Father, even so we also should walk in newness of life.

12 Let not sin therefore reign in your mortal body, that ye should obey it in the lusts thereof.

13 Neither yield ye your members as instruments of unrighteousness unto sin: but yield yourselves unto God, as those that are alive from the dead, and your members as instruments of righteousness unto God.

14 For sin shall not have dominion over you: for ye are not under the law, but under grace.

17 But God be thanked, that ye were the servants of sin, but ye have obeyed from the heart that form of doctrine which was delivered you.

18 Being then made free from sin, ye became the servants of righteousness.

19 I speak after the manner of men because of the infirmity of your flesh: for as ye have yielded your members servants to uncleanness and to iniquity unto iniquity; even so now yield your members servants to righteousness unto holiness.

20 For when ye were the servants of sin, ye were free from righteousness.

21 What fruit had ye then in those things whereof ye are now ashamed? for the end of those things is death.

22 But now being made free from sin, and become servants to God, ye have your fruit

3 Or don't you know that all of us who were baptized into Christ Jesus were baptized into his death?

4 We were therefore buried with him through baptism into death in order that, just as Christ was raised from the dead through the glory of the Father, we too may live a new life.

12 Therefore do not let sin reign in your mortal body so that you obey its evil desires.

13 Do not offer any part of yourself to sin as an instrument of wickedness, but rather offer yourselves to God as those who have been brought from death to life; and offer every part of yourself to him as an instrument of righteousness.

14 For sin shall no longer be your master, because you are not under the law, but under grace.

17 But thanks be to God that, though you used to be slaves to sin, you have come to obey from your heart the pattern of teaching that has now claimed your allegiance.

18 You have been set free from sin and have become slaves to righteousness.

19 I am using an example from everyday life because of your human limitations. Just as you used to offer yourselves as slaves to impurity and to ever-increasing wickedness, so now offer yourselves as slaves to righteousness leading to holiness.

20 When you were slaves to sin, you were free from the control of righteousness.

21 What benefit did you reap at that time from the things you are now ashamed of? Those things result in death!

22 But now that you have been set free from sin and have become slaves of God, the

unto holiness, and the end everlasting life.

23 For the wages of sin is death; but the gift of God is eternal life through Jesus Christ our Lord.

benefit you reap leads to holiness, and the result is eternal life.

23 For the wages of sin is death, but the gift of God is eternal life in Christ Jesus our Lord.

LIGHT ON THE WORD

Baptism. Baptism is cleansing through water immersion. It was the ritual for non-Jews to convert to Judaism. It initiated their life in God by symbolically washing away their Gentile ways and turning their life toward His commandments. This ritual is related to Levitical law, which required cleansing from impurities. John espoused a similar ritual as he preached a baptism of repentance and renewal, and later Jesus did as well, as a command for all those who would become initiated into the Christian faith.

Slavery. In the Greco-Roman world, slavery was quite common. As much as one-third of the urban population of the Roman empire is thought to have been made up of slaves. Slaves could be acquired through warfare, piracy, kidnapping, seizing infants, and criminal sentencing. Unlike slavery in the antebellum American South, this type of slavery was not based on race. Slaves could buy themselves out of slavery and also be freed through their master's own free will. Nevertheless, while enslaved, the slave was the master's property and was forced to do the master's bidding. It is this picture of slavery that permeates many of Paul's writings, where he refers to himself and other believers as slaves to Jesus Christ.

TEACHING THE BIBLE LESSON

LIFE NEED FOR TODAY'S LESSON

AIM: Students will accept how people often give in to do wrong.

INTRODUCTION

Faith, Peace, and Joy!

In Romans, Paul outlines the Gospel that he preached throughout the Roman empire. He clearly shows the need for the Gospel by painting a picture of the sinful Gentile world as well as the equally sinful and hypocritical Jewish world. This picture shows that all are under sin and in need of God's grace. This grace has come to us in Jesus Christ. Paul explains that the Good News is that Christ died for all and everyone can be justified in God's sight through Him.

He also explains how the Gospel is for all and must be received by faith. He then shows the effects of the Gospel in the believer's life. As we believe in the person and work of Christ, we have access to God and experience peace and joy, because we are now in Christ and have been freed from the condemnation that came through the sin of Adam. This is all because of grace, not works. Paul now demonstrates that although our salvation is based on grace, the believer must still honor the grace given through Christ by yielding to God and His righteousness, not sin.

BIBLE LEARNING

AIM: Students will affirm that in Christ, people can overcome temptation.

I. BAPTIZED AND RAISED TO NEW LIFE (ROMANS 6:1–4)

Paul wants the believers to know that grace does not exempt them from righteous living. He anticipated that some would think continuing to sin would just further the effects of grace. He counters with the truth: if one has experienced the genuine grace of God, they could not do things that displease Him. He further supports this claim by asking a rhetorical question concerning the believer's union with Christ in baptism. This union with Christ in baptism is given as the foundation for the following passage concerning living righteously.

Baptism is symbolic of the believer's union with Christ and His work; just as Christ was buried, the believers are also "buried" in the water of baptism, and the power of sin is buried with them. Those who are baptized is raised from the water to "walk in the newness of life" (v. 4), They are called to live and walk in a different way than before, outside the influence of sin.

Romans 6:1–4, 12–14, 17–23

1 What shall we say then? Shall we continue in sin, that grace may abound? 2 God forbid. How shall we, that are dead to sin, live any longer therein?

Here Paul enlists rhetorical questions to lead into the next section of his argument. In Romans 6, he outlines the different position the believer is placed in as a result of God's grace. In the previous chapter, Paul showed how sin magnifies grace, saying that this could be taken as a license to sin. Here he shows that grace—far from being an encouragement to sin—is actually an impediment to sin.

3 Know ye not, that so many of us as were baptized into Jesus Christ were baptized into his death?

Christ's death and resurrection in the Gospel are much more than historical facts and the basis for Christian doctrine; they are the personal experiences of all true Christian believers. What does it mean to be baptized into Christ? Many commentators believe that the phrase "baptized into Christ" implies that union with Christ is a direct result of baptism. In **Romans 3–5**, Paul argues that justification is by faith alone. It is inconceivable that the apostle would now make the work of baptism the means of justification. The context clearly indicates that Paul is evoking the symbolism of baptism rather than the physical act. In this case, the word "into" speaks to the effect, not the cause, of our union with Christ.

Baptism is a physical act that symbolizes the spiritual reality appropriated by faith. All believers are inwardly (by faith) and outwardly (symbolized by baptism) placed into personal union with Christ, meaning we are united to Christ in both His death and His resurrection. Christ's died once for all to cover all sin (see **v. 2**). The phrase "dead/died to sin" occurs three times in **Romans 6**; two times referring to believers (**vv. 2, 11**), and one time to Christ (**v. 10**). Because of our union with Christ, we died to sin in the same way that Christ died to sin. Since Christ did not have a sinful nature, He was never sensitive to sin in the first place; therefore, He could not become insensitive to it. So how did Christ die to sin? Christ died to sin in the sense that He bore the penalty for our sins. Paul soon says that the "wages of sin is death" (**v. 23**). Jesus paid the penalty for all of our sins. Death has no claims or demands on Christ or our union with Him. The wage has been paid; the account has been settled once and for all.

We are dead to sin. We generally misunderstand death; it is often equated with the physical effects of death, where the senses cease to operate and the dead person cannot respond to physical stimuli. This concept leads to the false notion that those who are dead to sin are no longer sensitive to temptation and therefore cannot respond to sin. In this view, our "old nature" was somehow actually supernaturally crucified with Christ on the Cross. However, careful observation of the text points out the flaws of this view. When a person dies, the spirit separates from the body. In fact, when the New Testament speaks of death, it generally refers to separation. The spiritually dead are those people separated from God. To be "dead to sin" in this case means to be separated from the penalty of sin.

4 Therefore we are buried with him by baptism into death: that like as Christ was raised up from the dead by the glory of the Father, even so we also should walk in newness of life.

The rite of baptism has changed over the centuries and varies for different Christian traditions, but the symbolism remains the same. When the convert enters the water, it symbolizes that the person is "in Christ." The immersion shows that the person is "buried with him," and his or her emergence from the water demonstrates understanding of being raised up from the dead and walking " newness of life."

"Newness of life" means that believers are to live their present lives as resurrected creatures. The verb for walk (Heb. *peripateo*, **peh-ree-pah-TEH-oh**) is in the subjunctive mood, which implies that our living out the resurrection life is a potentiality and possibility, not an accomplished fact. This is something that the believer must choose to do based on the new reality of being planted in Christ's death and resurrection.

II. FREED FROM SIN'S POWER (vv. 12–14)

Followers of Christ were once under the reign or control of sin, unable to break free from the lusts that sin produced in their hearts and under the sway of a different master. Sin ruled over their lives, and they could do nothing about it. Now sin no longer reigns over the believers' lives; they do not have to obey its desires. So Paul exhorts them to take this truth and make it reality.

This is coupled with another exhortation to take our body parts and make them instruments or weapons of righteousness instead of unrighteousness. We are to present our bodies to God, which is the same language of **Romans 12:1**, in which Paul exhorts believers to present their bodies as living sacrifices. Those who believe in Christ are alive, and the old life of sin no longer has sway over their actions.

Disobey Sin

12 Let not sin therefore reign in your mortal body, that ye should obey it in the lusts thereof.

Paul exhorts the believer to not let sin reign (Gk. *basileuo*, **ba-see-LEW-oh**) or to control completely as king. Bodies are described as mortal (Gk. *thnetos*, **thnay-TOSE**), or subject to death. This is indicative of Paul's understanding of the role of the body. It is subject to death and is temporary, the site of sin or righteousness. To let sin control us as king is to obey its lusts (Gk. *epithumia*, **eh-pee-thoo-ME-uh**), inordinate, self-indulgent cravings. These lusts compete with the proper affection for God.

13 Neither yield ye your members as instruments of unrighteousness unto sin: but yield yourselves unto God, as those that are alive from the dead, and your members as instruments of righteousness unto God.

The government analogy is then changed to a warfare analogy. Our "members" refers to our collective body parts. These are to be yielded

(Gk. *paristemi*, **pah-REESE-tay-mee**) or presented as instruments (Gk. *hoplon*, **HOP-lon**) of righteousness. "Instruments" is the word used for any tool, but especially a weapon. The picture is of soldiers presenting arms and ready for battle, but this battle is not physical but spiritual. We are to present ourselves to God as those spiritually alive from the dead.

14 For sin shall not have dominion over you: for ye are not under the law, but under grace.

Sin is not supposed to have dominion (Gk. *kurieuo*, **koo-ree-EW-oh**) or exercise control over the believer as a master. This signals a change in Paul's analogies to that of the servant/master relationship. The basis for this statement lies in the fact that the believer is "not under the law," which refers to the Mosaic Law and all its stipulations. Believers no longer function under the realm of the law which brought condemnation. Now they live within the realm of grace (Gk. *charis*, **KHAH-reese**). This is the unmerited favor of God, and the vehicle for true righteousness through Jesus Christ.

III. MADE A SERVANT OF RIGHTEOUSNESS (vv. 17–23)

Now Paul points us toward the past. Believers can thank God that they "were servants of sin" (**v. 17**). The key word is "were," past tense; that occupation is no more because they have obeyed the entire doctrine that was delivered to them, and have become servants of righteousness. In the earlier verses, the picture is one of soldiers presenting themselves for battle as they present their bodies as weapons of righteousness. The current picture is one of slaves presenting themselves as ready for service. They are freed from sin, not to be their own masters, but for their new master: Jesus Christ.

By contrasting their former lives of being "servants to uncleanness and to iniquity," Paul presses further into the example of a servant and puts the argument in terms that they can understand. He states that just as they were servants to sin, now their loyalty and allegiance are to righteousness toward a growing holiness. Serving sin made them free from the obligation to do right, but they did not profit from their sin. Now they look on those things as shameful because the end was death. Because they serve God through righteousness, holiness and eternal life are the fruit of their service. Paul concludes with contrasting the two different lifestyles: The lifestyle of sin only brings about death, while God's gift is eternal life. The old creation life brings us nothing but death and decay, while God's gift of eternal life motivates us to live according to the righteousness of the new creation.

Servants of Righteousness

17 But God be thanked, that ye were the servants of sin, but ye have obeyed from the heart that form of doctrine which was delivered you. 18 Being then made free from sin, ye became the servants of righteousness.

An exclamation of thanksgiving interrupts the flow of thought in these verses. Paul thanks God that the Roman Christians, who were once servants (Gk. *doulos*, **DOO-lohs**) of sin, are no longer obeying sin as their master. The word *doulos* can also be translated "slave," which would bring to the Romans' minds the slavery of those days, where someone was owned by someone else and his or her livelihood and purpose was determined by their owner. To be a slave of sin was to be owned by it and do its bidding. Now the Roman believers are obeying the form (Gk. *tupos*, **TOO-pohs**) of doctrine delivered to them. The word "form" is a pattern to imitate. The teaching, or doctrine, was delivered to them, and now they obey it from the heart (Gk. *kardia*, **kar-DEE-ah**), which is the center and seat of their intellect, emotions, and will. This resulted in being free from sin's power and becoming servants of righteousness.

19 I speak after the manner of men because of the infirmity of your flesh: for as ye have yielded your members servants to uncleanness and to iniquity unto iniquity; even so now yield your members servants to righteousness unto holiness.

Paul has used so many different analogies for salvation, he explains, because of the weakness of the Romans' flesh. Their natural limitations caused him to use word illustrations they could understand, and in **verse 19**, he continues to drive the point home. He continues and urges them to present themselves as slaves to "righteousness unto holiness." The word "unto" (Gk. *eis*, **ACE**) indicates that presenting themselves as servants of righteousness will lead *toward* holiness (Gk. *hagiasmos*, **ha-gee-oss-MOSE**), or sanctification. This is quite the opposite of presenting themselves as servants of uncleanness (Gk. *akatharsia*, **ah-ka-thar-SEE-uh**), which can describe any kind of sexual or moral impurity, but especially sexual sins in the New Testament. Another synonym for the word is "filth."

20 For when ye were the servants of sin, ye were free from righteousness. 21 What fruit had ye then in those things whereof ye are now ashamed? for the end of those things is death. 22 But now being made free from sin, and become servants to God, ye have your fruit unto holiness, and the end everlasting life. 23 For the wages of sin is death; but the gift of God is eternal life through Jesus Christ our Lord.

The things that were done as servants of sin made the Roman Christians ashamed (Gk. *epaischunomai*, **eh-pies-KHOO-no-my**). This is a strengthened form of the normal verb "to be ashamed" and indicates the utter shame the Christians would feel over their past sin. These things produced no fruit (Gk. *karpos*, **kar-POCE**), which metaphorically stands for any benefit or advantage.

The fruit that comes from being a servant of God leads to holiness and everlasting life. In contrast, the wages (Gk. *opsonion*, **ope-SO-nee-on**) or reward for sin is death. The gift (Gk. *charisma*, **KHAH-reese-ma**), or gracious act, of God is to bestow eternal life on the believer.

SEARCH THE SCRIPTURES

QUESTION 1
What does Paul ask the Roman believers regarding "abounding in sin"?

Paul asks if the Romans should keep sinning so that God's grace can be shown more.

QUESTION 2
Sin should not control our _____.

Bodies or lives.

LIGHT ON THE WORD
New Life
Baptism is a symbol of the new creation and life in the Kingdom of God, which is devoid of the effects and influence of sin and radically different from the fallen, old creation.

BIBLE APPLICATION

AIM: Students will understand that renewing our commitment to Christ gives us an opportunity to reconnect and strengthen our relationship with Him.

God is often seen as a stern judge sitting on a throne in Heaven. Many imagine Him as looking down on us to see if we have done something wrong so He can zap us. This is far from the truth. Jesus died and rose from the dead so we can have a better picture of God. We are no longer under the expectations of the Law, but called to grace, God's unmerited favor. For the believer, this motivates all of the good that we do for God. We do not need to practice righteousness in order to escape hell and judgment, but because we have already escaped hell and judgment. We yield ourselves to God because Jesus' sacrifice means so much for us.

STUDENT'S RESPONSES

AIM: Students will seek ways to rejoice in knowing that their baptism in Christ is way to acknowledge that Jesus frees us from sin.

Righteousness is more than just about avoiding bad things; it is also about doing good things. There are not only sins of commission but also omission. On a sheet of paper, write "Slave of Sin" and "Slave of Righteousness" at the top. Next draw a vertical line between them all the way down the middle of the paper. On the side under "Slave of Sin," write sins that you will avoid, and on the "Slave of Righteousness" side, write down positive actions you will do this week to live a righteous life.

PRAYER

Thank You God for freeing us from sin. Your righteousness allows us to choose freedom in You and serving Jesus. Your love and faith are evidence of your kindness for all of Your creation. In Jesus' Name we pray. Amen.

HOW TO SAY IT

Dominion.   doe-MIN-yon.

Infirmity.   in-FUR-mi-tee.

PREPARE FOR NEXT SUNDAY

Read **Romans 8:28–39** and "Safe in God's Love."

DAILY HOME BIBLE READINGS

MONDAY
Kept in Christ
(John 17:1–6, 12–15)

TUESDAY
Raised in Christ
(1 Corinthians 15:12–19)

WEDNESDAY
Alive in Christ
(1 Corinthians 15:51–57)

THURSDAY
Ambassadors in Christ
(2 Corinthians 5:17–21)

FRIDAY
In Christ for Others
(Philippians 1:20–26)

SATURDAY
Pressing On in Christ
(Philippians 3:7–14)

SUNDAY
Death Becomes Life
(Romans 6:1–4, 12–14, 17–23)

Sources:
Carson, D. A., R. T. France, J. A. Motyer, J. G. Wenham. *New Bible Commentary*. Downers Grove, IL: InterVarsity Press, 1993.
Keener, Craig S. *IVP Bible Background Commentary*. Downers Grove, IL: InterVarsity Press, 1993.

SAFE IN GOD'S LOVE

BIBLE BASIS: ROMANS 8:28–39

BIBLE TRUTH: Believers can never be separated from the love of Christ for humanity.

MEMORY VERSE: "What shall we then say to these things? If God be for us, who can be against us?" (Romans 8:31).

LESSON AIM: By the end of the lesson, we will: REVIEW the principal points of Paul's teaching on Jesus, from whose love we can never be separated by any turmoil or hardship; BELIEVE that Christ Jesus was God's plan for humankind from the beginning of creation; and COMMUNICATE the joy and love of Christ with others.

TEACHER PREPARATION

MATERIALS NEEDED: Quarterly Commentary/Teacher Manual, Adult Quarterly, Adult resources—charts, worksheets, and other teaching tools, paper, pens, pencils, Bibles (several different versions)

OTHER MATERIALS NEEDED / TEACHER'S NOTES:

_____

_____

LESSON OVERVIEW

LIFE NEED FOR TODAY'S LESSON
People are constantly tossed about by the trials and tribulations of life.

BIBLE APPLICATION
Christians can discover ways that they can find safety and peace in Jesus.

BIBLE LEARNING
Paul states that in Christ Jesus there are safety and provisions during times of tribulations.

STUDENTS' RESPONSES
As Christians study biblical doctrines of God's Word, they can learn more about God's plan for their lives.

LESSON SCRIPTURE

ROMANS 8:28–39, KJV

28 And we know that all things work together for good to them that love God, to them who are the called according to his purpose.

29 For whom he did foreknow, he also did predestinate to be conformed to the image of his Son, that he might be the firstborn

ROMANS 8:28–39, NIV

28 And we know that in all things God works for the good of those who love him, who have been called according to his purpose.

29 For those God foreknew he also predestined to be conformed to the image of his Son, that he might be the firstborn among many brothers and sisters.

among many brethren.

30 Moreover whom he did predestinate, them he also called: and whom he called, them he also justified: and whom he justified, them he also glorified.

31 What shall we then say to these things? If God be for us, who can be against us?

32 He that spared not his own Son, but delivered him up for us all, how shall he not with him also freely give us all things?

33 Who shall lay anything to the charge of God's elect? It is God that justifieth.

34 Who is he that condemneth? It is Christ that died, yea rather, that is risen again, who is even at the right hand of God, who also maketh intercession for us.

35 Who shall separate us from the love of Christ? shall tribulation, or distress, or persecution, or famine, or nakedness, or peril, or sword?

36 As it is written, For thy sake we are killed all the day long; we are accounted as sheep for the slaughter.

37 Nay, in all these things we are more than conquerors through him that loved us.

38 For I am persuaded, that neither death, nor life, nor angels, nor principalities, nor powers, nor things present, nor things to come,

39 Nor height, nor depth, nor any other creature, shall be able to separate us from the love of God, which is in Christ Jesus our Lord.

30 And those he predestined, he also called; those he called, he also justified; those he justified, he also glorified.

31 What, then, shall we say in response to these things? If God is for us, who can be against us?

32 He who did not spare his own Son, but gave him up for us all—how will he not also, along with him, graciously give us all things?

33 Who will bring any charge against those whom God has chosen? It is God who justifies.

34 Who then is the one who condemns? No one. Christ Jesus who died—more than that, who was raised to life—is at the right hand of God and is also interceding for us.

35 Who shall separate us from the love of Christ? Shall trouble or hardship or persecution or famine or nakedness or danger or sword?

36 As it is written: "For your sake we face death all day long; we are considered as sheep to be slaughtered."

37 No, in all these things we are more than conquerors through him who loved us.

38 For I am convinced that neither death nor life, neither angels nor demons, neither the present nor the future, nor any powers,

39 neither height nor depth, nor anything else in all creation, will be able to separate us from the love of God that is in Christ Jesus our Lord.

LIGHT ON THE WORD

Firstborn. In this passage, Paul refers to Jesus as the firstborn from the dead—first to die but rise up from the dead and never die again. Jesus as forerunner made the pathway for believers to pass from earth to heaven after death (**John 6:39, 44, 14:4–6**). The firstborn is considered extremely valuable and given specific responsibilities, but also special privileges, as God gave to Jesus (**John 5:20, 30**).

God's elect. All the redeemed whom God by His sovereign initiative has predetermined to set His love and establish an intimate relationship with according to His good pleasure. The term is used in the Old Testament for Israel, and in the New Testament for those whom Christ will gather together at the end of the age to be with Him. Election is based on God's love and initiative, not on the virtues of the elected; it is purely based on God's choice.

TEACHING THE BIBLE LESSON

LIFE NEED FOR TODAY'S LESSON

AIM: Students will explore ways that people are constantly tossed about by the trials and tribulations of life.

INTRODUCTION

The Truth About Heaven

The terms foreknowledge and predestination cause a great amount of controversy among Christians. When Paul penned these words, he was not attempting to win a theological argument. Christians during Paul's time faced extreme opposition. The letter may have been written before the extreme violence to Christians under Nero's reign (AD 54–68).

Paul wanted to lay out truth, without deviation. He wanted the Christian congregation in Rome to know of the certainty of their future state in heaven. Any one of them at any time might face death. The apostle wanted to plant in their mind that those who love God are appointed from on high with a purpose. God has recognized and determined to harmoniously place them in the body of Christ (**Ephesians 4:15–16**).

Paul simply breaks down the progression that leads to the ultimate honor of the saints. He magnifies God's supreme gift, His Son, to which all other gifts pale in comparison. He notes that none can condemn them for anything because Christ gave His life and He is their eternal security.

BIBLE LEARNING

AIM: Students will learn that Paul states in Christ Jesus there are safety and provisions during times of tribulations.

I. GOD WORKING IT OUT (ROMANS 8:28–30)

God is at work behind the scenes. He always used the Christians' experiences (even negative ones) to draw His children nearer to Him, build godly character, and fulfill His plans and purposes (**Romans 5:3–5**).

God knows absolutely everything about all individuals. Before creation, He knew each person's past, present, and future. His desire and goal is for each person to come to Him and be like Christ (**Philippians 3:21**). Those who trust Christ for their salvation become His brothers and sisters. Christ made it possible for Christians to be clean and pure in God's eyes and made ready for heaven. This group is showered with special advantages. They are given the title "God's elect," His called ones.

Romans 8:28–39

28 And we know that all things work together for good to them that love God, to them who are the called according to his purpose.

Paul has been explaining how the Spirit of God helps and aids the believer in prayer. Now he transitions into the ultimate goal of the believer's life. This ultimate goal is the result of all things working together (Gk. *sunergeo*, **su-ner-GEH-oh**) which means to partner together in labor on a common enterprise or project. The partners in this common enterprise are all things. This encompasses the whole of life whether negative or positive. The whole of life works together for good (Gk. *agathos*, **ah-gah-THOS**) which means to have positive or desirable qualities for the thing specified. In this case the thing specified is God's purpose (Gk. *prothesis*, **prah-thay-SEES**). This word means to set forth and is also used for the shewbread of the tabernacle which was set forth on a dedicated table. The main sense is of planning a future course of action.

29 For whom he did foreknow, he also did predestinate to be conformed to the image of his Son, that he might be the firstborn among many brethren.

Here Paul goes further in explaining and elaborating on the purpose of God in the believer's life. God foreknew (Gk. *proginosko*, **prah-gi-NAH-skoh**). and predestined (Gk. *proorizo*, **prah-ah-REE-zoh**) the believers for this specific purpose. The two words are in conjunction with the purpose God had in mind for believers. To foreknow is be acquainted with beforehand relative to those excluded from the choice. To be predestined is to be determined or arranged ahead of time. The believer's destiny is already known, ordered, and arranged ahead of time for the specific purpose of being conformed to the image of God's son. The word conform (Gk. *summorphos*, **su-MOR-phos**) is to be made into similar essence or representative nature as something else. The end goal of the believer's existence is to be made like Christ (**1 John 3:2**). This will result in Christ being firstborn

(Gk. *prototokos*, **pro-tah-TAH-kahs**) or preeminent among the believers and He will relate to them as brothers as they will share the same image (Gk. *eikon*, **AYE-kon**) or likeness.

30 Moreover whom he did predestinate, them he also called: and whom he called, them he also justified: and whom he justified, them he also glorified.

These verses continue the foundation Paul lays for the believers' assurance of God's working all things together for their good. After he lays out the purpose and shows the end result of the foreknowledge and predestination of the Christian, he goes into the process God takes to get them there. They are predestined, as Paul talks about in **verse 29**. They are also called (Gk. *kaleo*, **kah-LEH-oh**) or divinely summoned. This call is not the same as the general invitation to obey the Gospel, but it is a divine command that will not fail to be put into effect. This sense of the word *call* can be seen in **Romans 4:17**. If this were only a general command the argument of Paul concerning God's sovereign care in fulfilling His purpose in the life of the follower of Christ breaks down. It is the certainty of God's action that supports such a claim. Those who are called are also justified, and those who are justified are also glorified (Gk. *doxazo*, **dok-SAHD-zoh**) which means to be recognized and acknowledged for one's nature or attributes. The purpose of God the Father is to have the believer share in the glory of God the Son.

II. GOD SIDES WITH BELIEVERS (vv. 31–34)

Paul here attempts to explain God's loving intentions concerning salvation, growth, and final destinations. God's children should respond by knowing nothing will come up against them that they will not be able to handle because God is powerful and He surrounds and carries them. Believers can go through this life with confidence.

What is our assurance of this? Jesus is the guarantee. God is not deciding whether things will work out for His children based on how well they kept the law or were good, but He declared all believers righteous when Christ died on the Cross. God provides everything needed to live the Christian life (**2 Peter 1:3–4**). Only Jesus was given the privilege to sit on the right hand of God (**Romans 8:34**). He constantly speaks on the believer's behalf, because He faced earthly temptations (**Hebrews 2:18**). He pleads before the Father concerning His brothers and sisters. The conversation is always free of judgment. He will never point an accusing finger. He assists believers as we stand in a world that opposes God.

God's Sovereignty

31 What shall we then say to these things? If God be for us, who can be against us? 32 He that spared not his own Son, but delivered him up for us all, how shall he not with him also freely give us all things?

As a result of this knowledge of divine sovereignty, Paul exults in the comfort of knowing God is for His people. He asks and answers his own question, "If God be for us, who can be against us?" The concept of God being for His people runs throughout the Old Testament (**Psalm 56:9, 105:12–15; Isaiah 54:17**). The uniqueness of Paul's words are that now through the lens of Christ even the hard times are seen as under the sovereign hand of God. Even trials and opposition are placed in our lives to conform us to the image of Christ. God is for us in all things whether good or bad. With that in mind Paul could say nothing and no one is a formidable foe.

Not only that, but God did not spare (Gk. *pheidomai*, **FAY-doh-my**) His own Son when it came to our good. The word *spare* means

to refrain or keep from harm. The sense in this verse is that God did not hold Him back as a treasure. The same word is used in the Septuagint when Joseph tells his family to "regard not your stuff" or not to take their treasured belongings to Egypt (**Genesis 45:20**). God delivered (Gk. *paradidomi*, **pah-rah-di-DOH-mee**) Him, which means to hand over or to give up. The word is often used for betrayal as in the betrayal of Jesus by Judas (**Mark 14:10**). It is also used for the Sanhedrin's giving Jesus over to Pilate (**Mark 15:1**) and for Pilate's giving of Jesus to the will of the Jews in Jerusalem (**Luke 23:25**) and to the Roman soldiers for crucifixion. In this sense, Paul is showing God was sovereignly superintending the whole of Jesus' death on the Cross. It was God who ordained that Jesus would be crucified for our good since before the creation of the world (**Revelation 13:8**).

This understanding of God's gracious act in giving Jesus "for us all" is the ground by which Paul asks rhetorically, "How shall he not with him also freely give us all things?" The two words "freely give" (Gk. *charizomai*, **kah-REE-zoh-mye**) are actually one word in Greek. It means to give as a sign of one's goodwill toward another. Paul emphatically states that when we see what God has done in Christ, we can be assured that God has goodwill towards us.

33 Who shall lay any thing to the charge of God's elect? It is God that justifieth. 34 Who is he that condemneth? It is Christ that died, yea rather, that is risen again, who is even at the right hand of God, who also maketh intercession for us.

The argument continues as Paul lays out the reasons one may disbelieve God's goodwill towards His people. He proceeds with legal terminology and asks "Who shall lay anything to the charge of God's elect?" The phrase "lay anything to the charge" (Gk.

enkaleo, **en-KAH-lay-oh**) means to accuse or file a formal legal complaint against someone. The answer for Paul is obviously no. It is God who "justifieth" (Gk. *dikaioo*, **di-KAI-ya-oh**) or who makes or pronounces one as righteous.

There is no one to condemn (Gk. *katakrino*, **kah-tah-KREE-no**) the believer. The word condemn means to pronounce guilt for a crime and punishment for the crime in a legal context. Paul's answer to the question of "Who is he that condemneth?" is the work of Christ. This work is not limited to Jesus' death and resurrection but also continues as Jesus is at the right hand of God making intercession (Gk. *entynchano*, **en-tin-KAH-no**) for us. To make intercession or intercede is to petition an authority on behalf of someone else. It is Christ who speaks to God on behalf of the Christian. The believer's confidence that God hears him and he is no longer condemned is assured by the righteousness of Christ.

III. GOD'S LOVE IS INSEPARABLE (vv. 35–39)

The New Testament church suffered and withstood horrible persecution. Paul painted a vivid image of the love of God. He wanted all to know that absolutely nothing can pull them apart from His love. Jews were persecuted by the empire, and both Jewish and Christian church members were attacked by the empire and some of the Jews. Many times they went without food and the necessities of life. Some faced torture and death. In spite of this, Paul declared believers to be winners; because of God's upholding power and love, they overcame (**1 John 4:4**).

The apostle offered confident comfort to frail human beings. No earthly or heavenly power can pull them away from God's compassion and grace–not even the final moments before death, one's daily irritations and problems, spiritual beings, supreme rulers, a mighty work or miracle,

anything on this present earth, or anything that will have to be faced in the future, no present earthly philosophy or profound mystery or anything in creation.

The Power of God's Love

35 Who shall separate us from the love of Christ? shall tribulation, or distress, or persecution, or famine, or nakedness, or peril, or sword? 36 As it is written, For thy sake we are killed all the day long; we are accounted as sheep for the slaughter. 37 Nay, in all these things we are more than conquerors through him that loved us.

Next the question is asked of possible separation from the love of Christ. The different earthly woes of God's people are listed. Tribulation (Gk. *thlipsis*, **THLEEP-sees**) is the first of the problems listed. This word comes from *thlibo*, which means to press or sqaush and metaphorically has the sense of oppression or affliction. The next word is distress (Gk. *stenochoria*, **ste-no-ko-REE-ah**) which has the sense of being in constricted conditions. In some languages it can be expressed as the world falling down on someone. The third problem is persecution (Gk. *diogmos*, **dee-og-MAHS**) which is the systematic hunting down of believers for torture and execution in the effort to destroy the religion. This would be a real threat especially as Paul faced much persecution in his lifetime. Famine is the shortage of food resulting in acute hunger and death. The word for nakedness is *gum-notes* (Gk. **goom-NO-tess**) which in this context means insufficient clothing and not total exposure. Peril (Gk. *kindunos*, **keen-DOO-noss**) is to be in danger from any circumstance. Paul used this word in reference to his being in danger as an apostle (**2 Corinthians 11:26**). The believer also faces the reality of the sword (Gk. *machaira*, **mah-KHIE-rah**), which is the word for the small sword as opposed to a large one. This designation has caused some to question whether Paul has in mind the official "sword" of the state. However, this word is also used in **Romans 13:4** in connection with the authority of the state to punish. Here Paul may have been drawing up the image of official state execution. The general sense is that the believers face death at any moment.

Paul then quotes from **Psalm 44:22**. This psalm was often quoted by second-century rabbis with martyrdom in view and Paul may have had this in view here. In contrast to this dismal fate, there is triumph and hope in **verse 37**. Although the Christian's life is similar to being a sheep prepared for the slaughter, Paul says this is not the whole of the story. Believers are more than conquerors through Christ. The KJV translates the Greek as "we are more than conquerors." The Greek is a single word, with the basic verb for conquering intensified by a prefix (*huper*, **hoo-PAIR**) that tells the church this will be no normal victory. It will be the ultimate victory (*hupernikao*, **hoo-per-ni-KAH-oh**). To think of ultimate victory as persecuted subjects only magnifies the power of God to reward the faithful.

38 For I am persuaded, that neither death, nor life, nor angels, nor principalities, nor powers, nor things present, nor things to come, 39 Nor height, nor depth, nor any other creature, shall be able to separate us from the love of God, which is in Christ Jesus our Lord.

Paul is totally convinced. Nothing physical, social, or spiritual can separate us from the love of God in Christ Jesus. Paul speaks of items in the three categories which would have the capacity for separating us from God's love. Paul summarizes these, noting the opposites: life nor death, heights nor depths, things present or things to come with all of their abilities to frighten, paralyze, or make us turn away. None of these can separate us from the love of God.

SEARCH THE SCRIPTURES

QUESTION 1
How do all things, good and bad events in life, work together for the good of believers (v. 28)?

They **"work together for the good to them that love God and are called according to his purpose."**

QUESTION 2
Although things work against us at times in life, who stands for us all the time?

God, as Paul states in v. 31, "If God be for us, who can be against us?"

LIGHT ON THE WORD

Inseparable Love
At the beginning of the church age, the riches of God's glory laid a sure foundation. Paul leaves no stone unturned to express the inseparable love of God toward those in Christ.

BIBLE APPLICATION

AIM: Students will discover ways that they can find safety and peace in Jesus.

You've probably heard the phrase "looking for love in all the wrong places." People often get tangled up in sexual activities because they are seeking deep friendships and companionship. They hope their relationships will last. However, the end result is often sexually transmitted diseases, broken hearts, or children growing up in homes without two parents. Some of them eventually find God and realize His love is what they were looking for all along.

STUDENT'S RESPONSES

AIM: Students will note that as Christians study biblical doctrines of God's Word, they can learn more about His plan for their lives.

God rains His love down on each one of us—not just a gentle sprinkle but buckets full, a heavy shower. But some of us have sheltered ourselves from these drops of love under an umbrella. Read **1 John 4:7–16** this week and ask God to help you take down your umbrella.

PRAYER

Gracious God, Your magnificent mercy, love, kindness, peace, joy, and great grace, are wonderful blessings that we appreciate and need in our lives. We share our gifts from You with others. In Jesus' Name we pray. Amen.

HOW TO SAY IT

Predestinate.   pree-**DES**-ti-net.

Principality.   prin-si-**PAL**-i-tee.

PREPARE FOR NEXT SUNDAY

Read **Romans 9:6–18** and "Living Under God's Mercy."

DAILY HOME BIBLE READINGS

MONDAY
Safe in Evil Times
(Psalm 12)

TUESDAY
God's Safety and Care
(Ezekiel 39:25–29)

WEDNESDAY
Living Safely
(Proverbs 28:18–20, 26–27)

THURSDAY
Living Steadfastly
(2 Thessalonians 3:1–5)

FRIDAY
God Is Truth
(1 John 5:13, 18–21)

SATURDAY
God Is Love
(1 John 4:7–16)

SUNDAY
Safe in God's Love
(Romans 8:28–39)

Sources:
Carson, D.A., France, R.T., Motyer, J.A., Wenham, J.G. *New Bible Commentary.* Downers Grove, IL: InterVarsity Press, 1993.Keener, Craig S. *IVP Bible Background Commentary.* Downers Grove, IL: InterVarsity Press, 1993.

COMMENTS / NOTES:

_____

_____

_____

_____

_____

_____

_____

_____

_____

_____

_____

_____

_____

_____

_____

_____

_____

_____

_____

_____

LIVING UNDER GOD'S MERCY

BIBLE BASIS: ROMANS 9:6–18

BIBLE TRUTH: Trust in God and belief in what Jesus has done for all through God's mercy provides an unbounding love and opportunities for believers.

MEMORY VERSE: "Therefore hath he mercy on whom he will have mercy, and whom he will he hardeneth" (Romans 9:18).

LESSON AIM: By the end of the lesson, we will: KNOW the details of Paul's teaching about who are the true descendants and inheritors of God's promise; FEEL a strong familial connection to the people of God as inheritors of the promise God intended from creation; and PROCLAIM God as the author and reason for all the good we do in order that God may be glorified.

TEACHER PREPARATION

MATERIALS NEEDED: Quarterly Commentary/Teacher Manual, Adult Quarterly, Adult resources—charts, worksheets, and other teaching tools, paper, pens, pencils, Bibles (several different versions)

OTHER MATERIALS NEEDED / TEACHER'S NOTES:

_____

_____

LESSON OVERVIEW

LIFE NEED FOR TODAY'S LESSON
People's need for healthy self-worth and self-esteem creates a longing to know who they are and where they came from.

BIBLE LEARNING
Paul states believers will become new creatures in Christ Jesus.

BIBLE APPLICATION
Believers learn that it is God decides who should receive mercy.

STUDENTS' RESPONSES
Believers will come to know that by studying biblical doctrines of God's Word, they can learn more about God's plan for our lives.

LESSON SCRIPTURE

ROMANS 9:6–18, KJV

6 Not as though the word of God hath taken none effect. For they are not all Israel, which are of Israel:

7 Neither, because they are the seed of Abraham, are they all children: but, In Isaac shall thy seed be called.

ROMANS 9:6–18, NIV

6 It is not as though God's word had failed. For not all who are descended from Israel are Israel.

7 Nor because they are his descendants are they all Abraham's children. On the contrary, "It is through Isaac that your offspring will

8 That is, They which are the children of the flesh, these are not the children of God: but the children of the promise are counted for the seed.

9 For this is the word of promise, At this time will I come, and Sarah shall have a son.

10 And not only this; but when Rebecca also had conceived by one, even by our father Isaac;

11 (For the children being not yet born, neither having done any good or evil, that the purpose of God according to election might stand, not of works, but of him that calleth;)

12 It was said unto her, The elder shall serve the younger.

13 As it is written, Jacob have I loved, but Esau have I hated.

14 What shall we say then? Is there unrighteousness with God? God forbid.

15 For he saith to Moses, I will have mercy on whom I will have mercy, and I will have compassion on whom I will have compassion.

16 So then it is not of him that willeth, nor of him that runneth, but of God that sheweth mercy.

17 For the scripture saith unto Pharaoh, Even for this same purpose have I raised thee up, that I might shew my power in thee, and that my name might be declared throughout all the earth.

18 Therefore hath he mercy on whom he will have mercy, and whom he will he hardeneth.

be reckoned."

8 In other words, it is not the children by physical descent who are God's children, but it is the children of the promise who are regarded as Abraham's offspring.

9 For this was how the promise was stated: "At the appointed time I will return, and Sarah will have a son."

10 Not only that, but Rebekah's children were conceived at the same time by our father Isaac.

11 Yet, before the twins were born or had done anything good or bad—in order that God's purpose in election might stand:

12 not by works but by him who calls—she was told, "The older will serve the younger."

13 Just as it is written: "Jacob I loved, but Esau I hated."

14 What then shall we say? Is God unjust? Not at all!

15 For he says to Moses, "I will have mercy on whom I have mercy, and I will have compassion on whom I have compassion."

16 It does not, therefore, depend on human desire or effort, but on God's mercy.

17 For Scripture says to Pharaoh: "I raised you up for this very purpose, that I might display my power in you and that my name might be proclaimed in all the earth."

18 Therefore God has mercy on whom he wants to have mercy, and he hardens whom he wants to harden.

LIGHT ON THE WORD

wow!

Him that wills. A person who wants to be saved. This person thinks he can choose eternal life based merely on a willingness to be saved. He believes the salvation process leans heavily on man's free will and choices, but God does not give salvation based on desire.

Him that runs. A person who is working toward salvation. This person thinks, "I can be good, I've done all these good things, I've got my list and I'm getting into heaven, my good is going to outweigh my bad," but God does not give salvation based on good works.

Pharaoh. The common reference to rulers in Egypt. The word means "the sun." Several pharaohs are mentioned throughout the Scriptures. The Pharaoh during the time of Abraham (**Genesis 12:15**), about 2081 BC, was Salatis. The Pharaoh who appointed Joseph second in command to oversee the famine crisis in Egypt, was Apepi, 1876–1850 BC (**Genesis 41:1**). The Pharaoh 400 years later who claimed to have no knowledge of Joseph and the promises given to the Hebrews, therefore enslaving the growing Israelite population, was Amois (or Ahmes) or some identify him as Ramses II, 1340 BC (**Exodus 1:8**).

TEACHING THE BIBLE LESSON

LIFE NEED FOR TODAY'S LESSON

AIM: Students will learn that people's need for healthy self-worth and self-esteem creates a longing to know who they are and where they came from.

INTRODUCTION

Jesus is God's Blessing for the World

Although many believe the book of Romans to be a Gospel tract, it is so much more. Essentially a missionary book, it outlines the mission of God to bless all the peoples of the world through Christ. It explains how God's promise to Abraham has been fulfilled in Christ's death and resurrection. Here in Romans, Paul lays out the plan of God and how it encompasses not only the Jewish people but also the Gentiles who believe in the Good News of Jesus.

Through Abraham and his line, God blesses the world. This blessing of Abraham did not come through his own effort or ability, but God and His mercy.

Amen!

BIBLE LEARNING

AIM: Students will understand why Paul states believers will become new creatures in Christ Jesus.

I. GOD'S MERCY, NOT HUMAN ETHNICITY (ROMANS 9:6–9)

Because the Gentile believers in Rome were struggling both with acceptance from their fellow Jewish believers and with thinking they had somehow supplanted the Jews as God's people, Paul reminds everyone in the Roman church that all are God's people due to God's mercy alone. On the one hand, some of the Gentiles thought that they had replaced the Jews as God's people since not all Jews believed in Jesus. On the other hand, some of the Jews thought that it was necessary to be born into God's people to be a part of the promise.

Paul strongly rejects both these claims. He goes on to state that Abraham had more than one son, but only one was an heir of the promise of God—Isaac. His birth was a miracle because Abraham and Sarah were past ninety years old. He was born through the promise of God. The other sons of Abraham were connected to him biologically, but God had given Isaac through supernatural means. The children of Isaac would be counted as the heirs of Abraham and thus the chosen people of God.

Paul concludes that it was God's mercy and not physical ancestry that makes one a child of Abraham. It is this understanding that enables us to praise God, as we do not deserve His salvation. It is only because of His mercy that we are counted as His children. Those who believe in Christ are children of promise just like Isaac.

Romans 9:6–18

In **Romans 9:1–5**, Paul addresses his fellow Jews who resist joining his evangelization of the Gospel to the Gentiles. Paul constantly faced criticism and rejection from some of his fellow Jews, and Paul himself had persecuted those who believed in Christ until his vision on the road to Damascus. Once he answered his call to be an apostle to the Gentiles, he struggled with those Jews who thought that Gentile believers had to conform to the whole Mosaic Law (see especially Galatians). Here in Romans he addresses those Jewish believers in Christ who are unwilling to do what God has ultimately called the Jews to do through Christ–bring God's promise to the Gentiles. Here in **vv. 6–18** Paul reminds both the Gentiles and the Jews that all are a part of God's people because of God's promise and mercy alone, retelling the story of Jacob and Esau as a reminder that heritage is not the assurance for being God's people. Instead, God's mercy and faith in God's mercy are what make both Jews and Gentiles members of God's people.

6 Not as though the word of God hath taken none effect. For they are not all Israel, which are of Israel: 7 Neither, because they are the seed of Abraham, are they all children: but, In Isaac shall thy seed be called. 8 That is, They which are the children of the flesh, these are not the children of God: but the children of the promise are counted for the seed. 9 For this is the word of promise, At this time will I come, and Sarah shall have a son.

Beginning from verse 6, Paul contends that God had not abandoned His purpose in electing the nation Israel, strongly denying that God's Word—His promise to bless Israel as the descendants of Abraham (**Genesis 12:1-2**)—had failed. Paul then makes a distinction between the physical descendants of Abraham and the children of promise, arguing that their identities must not be confused. In other words, not everyone descended from the patriarch Israel (i.e., Jacob) belonged to Israel, the people of God, nor because they have descended from Abraham are they necessarily his children (cf. **Romans 2:28-29**). On the contrary, "It is through Isaac that offspring shall be named for [Abraham]" (**Genesis 21:12**, NRSV), meaning that the children born in fulfillment of the promise will be regarded as Abraham's true descendants. The promise to Abraham was that Sarah would have a son (**Genesis 18:10, 14**)—Isaac, not Ishmael, was the child of promise. As God chose Isaac over Ishmael, so also does He now choose to bless anyone who place their faith in Christ and become the true children of Abraham.

Thus, according to Paul, spiritual kinship, not ethnic origin, determined who was a true Israelite. Similarly, today the blessings of salvation extend only to those who are right with God through genuine faith in Jesus Christ. The visible church includes many who belong to "Ishmael," but salvation belongs only to "Israelites" who belong to the "line" of Isaac. God has not turned His back on the nation Israel; He has simply clarified what it means to be a true child of Abraham.

II. GOD'S MERCY, NOT HUMAN EFFORT (vv. 10–13)

Paul continues his argument with the example of Jacob and Esau. Although Esau was the oldest, God favored Jacob. God's favor was given to Jacob before either of the children were born, before he could do anything good or bad. Jacob's life is full of sin and failure. It wasn't his human effort that made him a recipient of God's favor, but God's mercy.

A further reference is given to Jacob being loved by God and Esau being hated. This statement is shocking at face value. Not only did God choose Jacob over Esau, but He loved Jacob and hated Esau. Esau had done nothing in the womb to merit this hatred, nor Jacob to merit this favor. It strongly supports Paul's argument that God's mercy is not about our works, but God's purpose as He is free to choose whomever He wants to receive His favor.

God's Plans, Not Ours

10 And not only this; but when Rebecca also had conceived by one, even by our father Isaac; 11 (For the children being not yet born, neither having done any good or evil, that the purpose of God according to election might stand, not of works, but of him that calleth;) 12 It was said unto her, The elder shall serve the younger. 13 As it is written, Jacob have I loved, but Esau have I hated.

At this point, a Jewish antagonist might have questioned Paul's argument, saying Ishmael was not a true son of Abraham; his mother was Hagar, Sarah's maidservant. So Paul strengthens his case by bringing in the account of the two sons of Rebekah. In this case, legitimacy was not questioned; Jacob and Esau had the same parents and were in fact twins. Even before they were born, Rebekah was told that the older would serve the younger (**Genesis 25:23**). In His sovereignty, God determined that was how it would be. This story confirms that our path depends not on what we do, but God's calling. Neither national heritage nor personal merit has anything to do with the sovereign freedom of God in assigning priority. This accords with the testimony of Scripture: "I loved Jacob, and I hated Esau" (from **Malachi 1:2–3**). This should not be interpreted to mean that God actually hated Esau; the strong contrast is a Jewish idiom that heightens the comparison by stating it in absolute terms.

Many try to use these verses to say that salvation does not involve personal consent or action. Paul was not arguing for salvation that disregards consent, nor double predestination. Rather he was arguing that those Jews who thought that they were superior to Gentiles due to heritage needed to rethink their relationship to God and the Law. It is the spirit of the Law that matters to God, and that spirit is based on a promise on the part of God and faith on the part of Abraham.

III. GOD'S MERCY, NOT HUMAN UNDERSTANDING (vv. 14–18)

God's mercy on some and judgment on others may lead one to believe that He is unfair. Paul responds to this by saying "God forbid." God is not beholden to our standards of righteousness; we are not His judges. He will distribute His mercy and compassion as He wills, not by our choice or efforts.

As an example Paul sets up Pharaoh as a case study. God kept Pharaoh alive and well to accomplish His purpose, which was to showcase His mighty hand. The Scripture clearly testifies to God being superior over Pharaoh. The news about the greatness of Israel's God was reported throughout the entire world; every kingdom marveled and trembled at Him (**Joshua 2:9–11; 1 Samuel 4:8**). He used Pharaoh's hardened heart to extend compassion toward Israel and display His power, now extended to all those whom God had chosen, including the Gentiles.

God's Plan of Mercy

14 What shall we say then? Is there unrighteousness with God? God forbid. 15 For he saith to Moses, I will have mercy on whom I will have mercy, and I will have compassion on whom I will have compassion. 16 So then it is not of him that willeth, nor of him that runneth, but of God that sheweth mercy. 17 For the scripture saith unto Pharaoh, Even for this same purpose have I raised thee up, that I might shew my power in thee, and that my name might be declared throughout all the earth. 18 Therefore hath he mercy on whom he will have mercy, and whom he will he hardeneth.

Paul then anticipated another objection: If God chose with sovereign freedom, then wasn't He guilty of injustice? Could we think God was unfair to Esau in choosing Jacob? The Greek text makes clear that Paul expected a negative response: "God forbid" God is not unjust in His actions. The point is that His favors are not determined by anyone or anything but Himself.

Although God elects with sovereign freedom, that does not mean that humans do not play a role in their acceptance or rejection. Later in the chapter Paul argues that through Christ the Gentiles can now be a part of the promise through faith, while Jews who live by works of the Law without faith risk stumbling because it is faith, not works, and God's mercy that make both Jews and Gentiles a part of the promise (**vv. 30–32**). Thus, God calls for faith on our part.

Paul uses the case of pharaoh to demonstrate that God withholds mercy and hardens hearts however He chooses (cf. **Exodus 7:3, 14:17**). Pharaoh, who opposed God's people, was raised to the position of king of Egypt so that God might display in him the evidence of His power (cf. **Exodus 9:13–16**). Although Pharaoh's rise to a position of authority undoubtedly had a secular interpretation, God was at work in his career to display His power by bringing Pharaoh to his knees so that God's character in delivering the Children of Israel might be known throughout the world. God shows mercy or hardens people's hearts as He chooses. He is sovereign in all that He does.

God's freedom to do with His will can conflict with a modern philosophy of relativism and personal autonomy. The Christian, however, must build their theology not on personal perceptions but on the biblical revelation of God's character and purpose. The modern reader can have a hard time understanding God's unalterable nature and the absolute justice of His actions, but many resources are available for us to study Scripture in its historical context. Scripture's meaning will never change, but applying it correctly depends on the reader's understanding. We can't fault God for showing mercy to some while hardening others, because He does not conform to our fallible and arbitrary concept of justice.

SEARCH THE SCRIPTURES

QUESTION 1
Only the children of _____ are counted as Abraham's seed in **verse 8**.

Promise.

QUESTION 2
God's plans for creation is not dependent or created on our individual or group plans. In fact, the Word tells us that God has plans for those who are not yet _____.

Born.

LIGHT ON THE WORD

God Chooses

God's plan to bless the world is dependent on His mercy to save those He chooses. It is not dependent on our ethnic status or good works. Here in **Romans 9**, Paul addresses those Jews who do not want to accept believing Gentiles and what it means to be the elect of God—to be a recipient of His immeasurable mercy.

BIBLE APPLICATION

AIM: Students will learn that it is God who decides who should receive mercy.

Many people believe that they are God's chosen people based on their wealth or status in society. Others believe that their good works and charitable donations make them targets of God's blessings. Contrary to these opinions, it is God who chooses to distribute His mercy on those whom He wills. If this is the case, then we cannot dismiss the unbelievers in our lives as outside of the scope of God's mercy. It is God who decides and not us.

STUDENT'S RESPONSES

AIM: Students will come to know that studying biblical doctrines of God's Word, they can learn more about His plan for our lives.

A hard heart can slowly form in our lives without even realizing it. Consider how open you are to believing God's Word, which can indicate whether our hearts are hardened to God (**Hebrews 3:8–12**). You could be beginning to develop a hard heart toward God and His mercy. Pray that the Lord would develop in you a soft heart for His mercy in your life.

PRAYER

Lord, have mercy on us. Encourage our hearts and minds to turn toward You. For only You are worthy of the praise and honor that we offer. Keep us in Your perfect peace and bring us back when we wonder from Your plans for our lives. In Jesus' Name we pray. Amen.

HOW TO SAY IT

Hardeneth.   har-DI-nith.

Sovereignty.   SOV-rin-tee.

PREPARE FOR NEXT SUNDAY

Read **Romans 11:11–24** and "God Prunes and Grafts."

DAILY HOME BIBLE READINGS

MONDAY
Reproach and Mercy
(Deuteronomy 3:22–29)

TUESDAY
Sovereign Mercy
(2 Samuel 7:20b–29)

WEDNESDAY
Awesome Mercy
(Psalm 68:20, 24–26, 32–35)

THURSDAY
Hopeful Mercy
(1 Peter 1:3–9)

FRIDAY
Wise Mercy
(James 3:13–18)

SATURDAY
Patient Mercy
(James 5:7–12)

SUNDAY
Living Under God's Mercy
(Romans 9:6–18)

Sources:
Achtemeier, Paul. *Romans. Interpretation: A Bible Commentary for Teaching and Preaching.* Louisville, KY: John Knox Press, 1985.
Bryne, Brendan S.J. *Romans.* Sacra Pagina. Collegeville, MN.: Liturgical Press, 1996.
Moo, Douglas, *Romans. New International Commentary on the New Testament.* Grand Rapids, MI: Wm. B. Eerdmans, 1996.

GOD PRUNES AND GRAFTS

BIBLE BASIS: ROMANS 11:11–24

BIBLE TRUTH: Belief in Jesus Christ is the core belief that Jews and Gentiles can be united.

MEMORY VERSE: "Behold therefore the goodness and severity of God: on them which fell, severity; but toward thee, goodness, if thou continue in his goodness: otherwise thou also shalt be cut off" (Romans 11:22).

LESSON AIM: By the end of the lesson, we will: KNOW the details of Paul's teaching about who are the true inheritors of God's promise; AFFIRM that God has not rejected the Jews and that Gentiles believers have not superseded the Jews, but believing in Jesus is the fulfillment of creation; and DEVELOP an ecumenical ministry to encourage unity among God's people.

TEACHER PREPARATION

MATERIALS NEEDED: Quarterly Commentary/Teacher Manual, Adult Quarterly, Adult resources—charts, worksheets, and other teaching tools, paper, pens, pencils, Bibles (several different versions)

OTHER MATERIALS NEEDED / TEACHER'S NOTES:

_____

_____

LESSON OVERVIEW

LIFE NEED FOR TODAY'S LESSON
Sometimes, people find themselves living, relating, or working with others with whom they feel antagonism or no connection.

BIBLE APPLICATION
Believers of Christ know and respond accordingly to the truth that one group of believers is not superior to others.

BIBLE LEARNING
Paul teaches that regardless of our differences, God's promises are for all believers.

STUDENTS' RESPONSES
Christians can rejoice in believing that we have the promises of God as testimonies to God's faithfulness and love for us.

LESSON SCRIPTURE

ROMANS 11:11–24, KJV

11 I say then, Have they stumbled that they should fall? God forbid: but rather through their fall salvation is come unto the Gentiles, for to provoke them to jealousy.

12 Now if the fall of them be the riches of

ROMANS 11:11–24, NIV

11 Again I ask: Did they stumble so as to fall beyond recovery? Not at all! Rather, because of their transgression, salvation has come to the Gentiles to make Israel envious.

12 But if their transgression means riches for

the world, and the diminishing of them the riches of the Gentiles; how much more their fulness?

13 For I speak to you Gentiles, inasmuch as I am the apostle of the Gentiles, I magnify mine office:

14 If by any means I may provoke to emulation them which are my flesh, and might save some of them.

15 For if the casting away of them be the reconciling of the world, what shall the receiving of them be, but life from the dead?

16 For if the firstfruit be holy, the lump is also holy: and if the root be holy, so are the branches.

17 And if some of the branches be broken off, and thou, being a wild olive tree, wert graffed in among them, and with them partakest of the root and fatness of the olive tree;

18 Boast not against the branches. But if thou boast, thou bearest not the root, but the root thee.

19 Thou wilt say then, The branches were broken off, that I might be graffed in.

20 Well; because of unbelief they were broken off, and thou standest by faith. Be not highminded, but fear:

21 For if God spared not the natural branches, take heed lest he also spare not thee.

22 Behold therefore the goodness and severity of God: on them which fell, severity; but toward thee, goodness, if thou continue in his goodness: otherwise thou also shalt be cut off.

23 And they also, if they abide not still in

the world, and their loss means riches for the Gentiles, how much greater riches will their full inclusion bring!

13 I am talking to you Gentiles. Inasmuch as I am the apostle to the Gentiles, I take pride in my ministry

14 in the hope that I may somehow arouse my own people to envy and save some of them.

15 For if their rejection brought reconciliation to the world, what will their acceptance be but life from the dead?

16 If the part of the dough offered as firstfruits is holy, then the whole batch is holy; if the root is holy, so are the branches.

17 If some of the branches have been broken off, and you, though a wild olive shoot, have been grafted in among the others and now share in the nourishing sap from the olive root,

18 do not consider yourself to be superior to those other branches. If you do, consider this: You do not support the root, but the root supports you.

19 You will say then, "Branches were broken off so that I could be grafted in."

20 Granted. But they were broken off because of unbelief, and you stand by faith. Do not be arrogant, but tremble.

21 For if God did not spare the natural branches, he will not spare you either.

22 Consider therefore the kindness and sternness of God: sternness to those who fell, but kindness to you, provided that you continue in his kindness. Otherwise, you also will be cut off.

23 And if they do not persist in unbelief,

unbelief, shall be grafted in: for God is able to graff them in again.

24 For if thou wert cut out of the olive tree which is wild by nature, and wert graffed contrary to nature into a good olive tree: how much more shall these, which be the natural branches, be grafted into their own olive tree?

they will be grafted in, for God is able to graft them in again.

24 After all, if you were cut out of an olive tree that is wild by nature, and contrary to nature were grafted into a cultivated olive tree, how much more readily will these, the natural branches, be grafted into their own olive tree!

LIGHT ON THE WORD

Natural branches. Natural branches on a tree are the original branches, and in this passage, they symbolize the Jewish people or the Israelites. The Israelites/Jews were the first people assigned by God to be holy, a people separate from all others, representing Him. They were to revere God and encourage others to do the same. God intended for them to lead the way for the Messiah (**Genesis 3:15, 12:1–3**).

Roots. The Jews, especially the patriarchs, are also considered the root of the tree in Paul's illustration, recognizing them as the originators of the olive tree, giving nourishment. Everything springs from the root. God chose the patriarchs and separated them from the other nations exclusively for His use. God called Abraham out of his native land of Haran, and Abraham went to Canaan as God commanded (**Genesis 12:1–6**). Therefore, the generations after Abraham are blessed and entitled to God's promises, despite their disobedience.

Grafted in branches. Paul uses branches grafted in to symbolize the Gentiles, which can refer to nations or peoples generally, but in the Bible generally refers to peoples other than the Israelites/Jews. These peoples are now attached to God's people through faith in Christ, although they were not originally included in the promise. Paul warns that the root, the Jews, could be cut off if they do not accept the Gentiles into God's

people, but in Paul's vision of the eschaton, God will find a way for all the Jews and for the believing Gentiles to be a part of the olive tree.

TEACHING THE BIBLE LESSON

LIFE NEED FOR TODAY'S LESSON

AIM: Students will note that sometimes people find themselves living, relating, or working with others with whom they feel antagonism or no connection.

INTRODUCTION

The Unity of Humanity

God intended for mankind from all walks of life to come together in unity (**Matthew 8:11; Romans 11:25**). His plan for this grand family reunion spanned all human history. First, everyone who ever lived on the earth proceeded from one man, Adam (**Acts 17:26**). All races were reproduced through the sons of Noah (**Genesis 10**), and God promised all people would be blessed through Abraham (**Genesis 12:3**).

God initially worked through the Jewish race. Some inaccurately concluded that since the Jews were His chosen people, He was set against the other races. Not so. Throughout history are hints of this mystery of God's goodness toward the Gentile nations (**Romans 11:25**). God miraculously worked through His servants to perform miracles for Gentiles (Elijah and the widow,

1 **Kings 17:13–24**; Jesus and the centurion, **Matthew 8:5–13**). God appointed Gentile rulers, calling them His servants (**Jeremiah 43:10**) and using them to divinely preserve and give provisions to His chosen people (King Cyrus, **Ezra 1:1–4**; King Darius, **Ezra 6:1–12**; King Ahasuerus, **Esther 8:3–14**, Nebuchadnezzar, **Daniel 3:28–30**).

These examples from Scripture indicate God had no displeasure with races coming together. The problem arose when the some of hte Israelites/Jews came under the influence of the ungodly Gentile nations. The Jews began to mix the worship of the true God with other gods.

In the end, God's saints will gather from everywhere, and all nationalities will come around God's throne, in the presence of the Lamb, praising Him (**Revelation 7:9**).

BIBLE LEARNING

AIM: Students will acknowledge that Paul teaches that regardless of our differences, God's promises are for all believers.

I. THE FALL RESULTED IN FORTUNE (ROMANS 11:11–12)

In the beginning of this chapter, Paul addresses the restoration of Israel and the inclusion of the Gentiles in God's promise. Paul whole-heartedly believes that even the Jews who do not accept Jesus as the Messiah continue to be a part of God's plan, but for a time their hearts are hardened. He uses himself as an example–an Israelite from the tribe of Benjamin (**v. 1**), reminding the Jews and Gentiles in the church that more than once God's own people have fought against Him, but each time He has responded with grace (**vv. 3–5**). So too at this time, the hearts of some of the Jews are turned against God's plan through Christ, but God has not rejected them completely.

Paul continues in **vv. 11–12** by asking if the Jews have stumbled and fallen, concluding that their stumbling has not caused them to fall but instead has brought salvation to the Gentiles as well. This inclusion has made some of the Jews jealous, but God will use this for the greater good as well.

Romans 11:11–24

In **Romans 9:30–10:21**, Paul showed that although some of the Jews lost their right relationship with God because of their unbelief, still God had not rejected them entirely. He used two examples to prove that God always preserves a faithful remnant, even when the situation seems hopeless (**11:1–5**). He then describes the way God does His work in the world—by choosing some and rejecting others—so that in the end, all nations may receive His blessing (**vv. 6–10**).

11 I say then, Have they stumbled that they should fall? God forbid: but rather through their fall salvation is come unto the Gentiles, for to provoke them to jealousy. 12 Now if the fall of them be the riches of the world, and the diminishing of them the riches of the Gentiles; how much more their fulness?

In **verse 11**, Paul began his explanation of how God planned to extend His salvation plan beyond Israel to the whole world, and then, in the end, restore Israel as well. Although Israel had stumbled (**9:32**) because some did not recognize Jesus as Messiah, they had not stumbled irrevocably. God had a definite purpose in allowing them to stumble; because of their rejection of the Gospel, salvation went out to the other nations (Gk. *ethnos*, ETH-noce, a multitude or people; Gentiles, non-Jews, especially Greek Christians in the New Testament). Israel's unbelief opened the door of opportunity for the nations, so God's purpose in history would be accomplished. Israel in turn would be stirred up to envy when they saw the nations enjoying the blessings they could have had. Although Israel had stumbled, the God who makes "all things work together for good to them that love" Him (from **8:28**) purposed that the result would ultimately provide the incentive for their return. Paul now argues that if Israel's misstep had brought enrichment to the world and their defeat had proved to be such a benefit for the Gentiles, the greatness of their restoration would be unimaginable.

II. THE DEAD BROUGHT BACK TO LIFE (vv. 13-15)

Paul addresses the Roman Gentile Christians, identifying himself as their apostle, having the privilege to bring the Gospel to the non-Jewish world (**Acts 9:15**). However, Paul's heart continued to be filled with compassion for his own people, greatly desiring for the Jewish people to come to Christ. He wanted his relationship with the heavenly Father, through Christ, to look so attractive that Paul's people would long for the same kind of experience.

The Jews' stubborn rebellion against Christ opened the door of salvation to everyone else in the world. However, Paul remained hopeful; if God can reject His own people, He can also receive them back to Himself. God's covenant people died a spiritual death when they denied Christ as Messiah. However, God will totally restore their spiritual life and privileges when they accept the truth about Jesus (**Romans 11:24-25; Ezekiel 37:1-14**).

God's Salvation for All

13 For I speak to you Gentiles, inasmuch as I am the apostle of the Gentiles, I magnify mine office: 14 If by any means I may provoke to emulation them which are my flesh, and might save some of them. 15 For if the casting away of them be the reconciling of the world, what shall the receiving of them be, but life from the dead? 16

For if the firstfruit be holy, the lump is also holy: and if the root be holy, so are the branches.

Verses 13-14 constitute a parenthesis. Paul will resume his argument in **verse 15**. In **verse 13**, Paul tells his Gentile audience that they were his primary concern by reminding them that he was their apostle and, therefore, should not assume that what he was saying had nothing to do with them, but rather, makes him even more zealous in his work for them. In laying stress on his ministry as "the apostle to the Gentiles," Paul hopes he might stir his countrymen to envy so that "some of them" might be saved (**v. 14**).

Paul returns to the idea of **verse 12** in **verse 15**. If Israel's rejection led to reconciliation for the world, what would "the receiving of them" mean but "life from the dead"? Paul reasons that if such a benefit flowed from their rejection, a greater benefit may be expected when those who have been rejected are now accepted. The final resurrection is an expression for all the events accompanying the end times, which will come only when God's purposes for humanity have been fully achieved. Paul takes for granted that Israel plays a decisive role in these purposes. The inclusion of that part of Israel as yet unresponsive to the Gospel is an indispensable element in the events of the end.

In **verse 16**, Paul mixes metaphors to make his point. He alludes to **Numbers 15:17-21**, which required Israel to offer to God the first portion of its grain or dough as an offering made from the first grain harvested and ground. The cake presented to the Lord consecrated the rest of the batch. Paul wrote that if the dough offered as firstfruits was holy, then the entire batch was holy. The holiness of the first fruits (Gk. *aparche*, **op-ar-KHAY**) ensured that the entire batch would be holy. In this metaphor, the dough represents the Jewish believers who had accepted Christ (the remnant of **Romans 11:5**), and the whole batch those who would come to believe. The metaphor changes to a tree with its branches. If the root is holy, so are the branches. In this case, the "root" represents the patriarchs (especially Abraham), and the "branches," the tribes and people that follow. The point is that if the patriarchs were holy (and they were), so were the Jewish people. God's rejection of some of the Jews was neither complete (**Romans 11:1–10**) nor final (**11:11–24**).

III. THE CULTIVATED AND THE WILD OLIVE TREE (vv. 16–17)

Paul built a strong case that God is not finished with the Jewish people, but regards them as the life-giving tree. Paul pointed to Abraham and other patriarchs like Isaac, Jacob, and Joseph. God set them apart for His special plans and purposes, so the remaining members of the patriarchal family and their future descendants are also considered sacred, designated to live by God's agenda.

The firstfruit offering illustrates Israel as God's possession. When one small part of a lump of dough is presented to God as an offering, it represents the rest. The tiny dough piece for the offering and the entire lump all belong to God (**Numbers 15:20–21**).

God broke off some of the branches of the cultivated olive tree in order to keep the tree holy. On the other hand, the wild olive shoot represented the Gentiles, some of whom wholeheartedly embraced Christ. After His crucifixion and the coming of the Holy Spirit, many Gentiles accepted Christ. This group is no longer considered unholy, but now part of the sacred tree.

All Believers are Dependent on God

17 And if some of the branches be broken off, and thou, being a wild olive tree, wert grafted in among them, and with them partakest of the root and fatness of the olive tree; 18 Boast not against the branches. But if thou boast, thou bearest not the root, but the root thee. 19 Thou wilt say then, The branches were broken off, that I might be grafted in. 20 Well; because of unbelief they were broken off, and thou standest by faith. Be not highminded, but fear: 21 For if God spared not the natural branches, take heed lest he also spare not thee.

Building on **v. 16**, Paul presumes that both Jewish and Gentile believers mutually share in (Gk. *synkoinonos*, **soon-koy-no-NOS**) being nourished by Israel's graced heritage. Both partake in the holiness of the patriarchs, the one historical root of the people of God, and in the blessings attached to it. In **verses 17–24**, Paul uses the figure of grafting olive trees to illustrate how the Gentiles came to share the spiritual blessings of Israel. He warns Gentiles that arrogance would lead to being cut off, and reminding them of God's ability to later graft in the natural branches once again.

Paul's Gentile readers should not view themselves as superior to the established branches. They owed their spiritual existence to Israel; the tree's Jewish roots supported them. Gentile believers were correct in their understanding that unbelieving Jews were broken off so they could be grafted in. This metaphor should not be taken too literally, as it is not about making more room on the tree. The central point is that now the Gentiles have the opportunity to become a part of God's people. Paul essentially said: "Well, it is true. But do not forget that they were broken off because of unbelief and your permanence depends upon your continuing faith." Therefore, Gentile believers were to be on guard and eschew arrogance. After all, if God did not spare the natural branches (Israel), why would He spare grafted branches (the Gentiles)? Paul's point is that the church is not entirely new, nor a replacement of Israel, but the continuation of God's ancient people. Thus, he insists that the church is no place for competition but for community and continuity. Believers—both Jews and Gentiles—live by dependence on God and the ancient traditions of His people. The purpose of the olive tree illustration is to prevent any false sense of security on the Gentiles' part.

IV. THE PRIDEFUL AND THE HUMBLE (vv. 18–24)

Paul knows the Gentiles, at this time, the majority in the Roman church, might take God's goodness for granted. As a precaution, he attempted to eliminate any kind of arrogance or superior attitude. They needed to understand and appreciate Christianity's Jewish heritage (**Genesis 12:3; Galatians 3:29**). He wanted them to continue to walk in faith and humility, not on personal merit.

Some of the Jews have not accepted Christ as Messiah yet, so their branches have been removed for a time and the Gentiles' wild branches grafted in, but the Jews still belong to the tree. Paul reminded the Gentiles to be thankful because God graciously planted them into the holy olive tree. In His appointed time, He will also restore the Jewish people.

The Olive Tree, A Sign of Hope

22 Behold therefore the goodness and severity of God: on them which fell, severity; but toward thee, goodness, if thou continue in his goodness: otherwise thou also shalt be cut off. 23 And they also, if they abide not still in unbelief, shall be grafted in: for God is able to graft them in again. 24 For if thou wert cut out of the olive tree which is wild by nature, and wert grafted contrary to nature into a good olive tree: how much more shall these, which be the natural branches, be grafted into their own olive tree?

The Gentile believers ought to consider that God is both good and severe. "Goodness," or that which is beneficial (Gk. *chrestotes*, **krays-to-TAYS**) and "severity" (Gk. *apotomia*, **ah-po-to-MEE-uh**) are aspects of divine nature. The word for kindness means useful and good, and Jesus used it when He said "my yoke is easy" (**Matthew 11:30**). Paul's use of the word "severity" may be a possible play on words, as the root word in Greek means "sharply cut." This mention of severity could possibly be related to his olive tree metaphor; a proper understanding of the doctrine of God must include both His kindness and His sternness. While on the one hand some emphasize God's kindness and neglect His sternness, on the other hand others focus on sternness and exclude His kindness. To the former, God comes across as a well-intentioned but doting father, and to the latter, a ruthless despot. However, goodness does not rule out strict justice, and sternness does not rule out grace. The two qualities must be maintained in balance. God's sternness is seen in His cutting off unbelieving Israel. His kindness is seen in including into His family those who at one time were "foreigners to the covenants of the promise, without hope and without God in the world" (from **Ephesians 2:12**, NIV). His kindness to Gentile believers is, of course, contingent on their continuing response to that kindness. Failing this responsibility will lead to their being cut off, too. Those who do not demonstrate real faith will have no security.

Paul said if Israel did not persist in unbelief, they would be grafted back into their own olive tree (**v. 23**). God certainly had the power to graft them in again. The only thing that stood in Israel's way was their continuing unbelief. God would never overpower their unwillingness to believe and force them back into His family. The logic of **verse 24** is clear. The fact that God has grafted in the wild olive tree holds out good hope of success in the easier case—the grafting in of the branches that belonged "by nature" to their own olive tree. If God can take a wild olive shoot and graft it into a cultivated olive tree (as He did with the nations), grafting the natural branches (Israel) back into their parent tree would be easy. The strength of Paul's argument is that the process he describes is contrary to nature. It is a process unexpected in horticulture. Paul disarms his critics by acknowledging the unnaturalness of this particular kind of grafting. It goes beyond normal grafting practice, as a cut branch would've died and would not have the chance to be grafted back on. However, this is what God has done (and will do), contrary to nature or not. Ethnicity or national identity has no bearing on membership of the people of God. God has grafted wild olive branches into His cultivated tree, and He certainly can graft the natural branches in again.

Paul does not envision the church as a replacement for Israel, nor of separate Jewish and Gentile churches, but rather a church made up of Jews and Gentiles.

SEARCH THE SCRIPTURES

QUESTION 1
Paul is Jewish and he is an apostle to who?

The Gentiles.

QUESTION 2
Paul wants to make the Jews _____ of what the Gentiles have in **verse 14.**

Jealous.

LIGHT ON THE WORD
Bringing People Together
The God who was able to bring Gentiles to faith is able to restore unbelieving Israel into His one people. If the incorporation of Gentiles into Israel is possible, how much possible is the restoration of unbelieving Israel to the people of God? God is able!

BIBLE APPLICATION

AIM: Students will accept that that one group of believers is not superior to others.

Racial tension is universal. Groups commonly degrade and look down on one another. However, the body of Christ should be different. Following Jesus' example and depending on the Holy Spirit's wisdom and power, Christians must not put down other races and cultures. Getting to know someone who looks, thinks, and talks unlike you may be a perfect way to learn to respect others' differences.

STUDENT'S RESPONSES

AIM: Students will explore how Christians can rejoice in believing that we have the promises of God as testimonies to His faithfulness and love for us.

Research people or groups in your community who have come from different backgrounds but are now Christians (converted Jews, Muslims, or any other groups who are now believers). Start with prayer. Ask God's guidance and see how you can assist them in helping others come to know Christ.

PRAYER

Jesus, Your sacrifice on the Cross, Your shed blood, and the forgiveness of our sins brings us in awe, respect, fear, and gratitude for who You are. We are humbled by Your love and continual mercy on all of creation. Bless us and allows us to share in a mighty way Your love with others and our salvation. In Jesus' Name we pray. Amen.

HOW TO SAY IT

Consummation. kon-su-MAY-shun.

Severity.   se-VER-i-tee.

PREPARE FOR NEXT SUNDAY

Read **Romans 12:1–2, 13:8–10** and "Love Fulfills the Law."

DAILY HOME BIBLE READINGS

MONDAY
Restoration after Repentance
(Isaiah 49:8–13)

TUESDAY
Repent and Return
(Hosea 14:1–7)

WEDNESDAY
Repent and Repair
(Ezra 9:5–9)

THURSDAY
Repent and Live
(Zechariah 8:9–17)

FRIDAY
Repent and Grow Strong
(Zechariah 9:16–17, 10:6–12)

SATURDAY
Repent and Bear Fruit
(John 15:1–8)

SUNDAY
God Prunes and Grafts
(Romans 11:11–24)

Sources:
Greathouse William M. and George Lyons. *Romans 9–16: A Commentary in the Wesleyan Tradition.* New Beacon Bible Commentary. Kansas City, MO: Beacon Hill Press of Kansas City, 2008.
Moo, Douglas. *Romans.* New International Commentary on the New Testament. Grand Rapids, MI: Wm. B. Eerdmans, 1996.

COMMENTS / NOTES:

LOVE FULFILLS THE LAW

BIBLE BASIS: ROMANS 12:1–2, 13:8–10

BIBLE TRUTH: Paul encourages believers to allow the love of Christ to transform their minds so that we can love others and ourselves as Christ does.

MEMORY VERSE: "Owe no man any thing, but to love one another: for he that loveth another hath fulfilled the law" (Romans 13:8).

LESSON AIM: By the end of the lesson, we will: RECALL Paul's exhortation to be transformed in order to discern the will of God so we can love others effectively; ACCEPT God's will to love one another unconditionally; and COMMIT to a new beginning in which they actively carry God's love into the world.

TEACHER PREPARATION

MATERIALS NEEDED: Quarterly Commentary/Teacher Manual, Adult Quarterly, Adult resources—charts, worksheets, and other teaching tools, paper, pens, pencils, Bibles (several different versions)

OTHER MATERIALS NEEDED / TEACHER'S NOTES:

_____

_____

LESSON OVERVIEW

LIFE NEED FOR TODAY'S LESSON
People want to know how to live in a manner that transcends the selfish and corrupt ways of the world.

BIBLE LEARNING
Jesus allows believers to fill the law of love in their lives.

BIBLE APPLICATION
Christians can show their love for God in their attitude and actions toward others.

STUDENTS' RESPONSES
Believers can create additional ways and opportunities to show the love of Christ to all of creation.

LESSON SCRIPTURE

ROMANS 12:1–2, 13:8–10, KJV

1 I beseech you therefore, brethren, by the mercies of God, that ye present your bodies a living sacrifice, holy, acceptable unto God, which is your reasonable service.

2 And be not conformed to this world: but be ye transformed by the renewing of your

ROMANS 12:1–2, 13:8–10, NIV

1 Therefore, I urge you, brothers and sisters, in view of God's mercy, to offer your bodies as a living sacrifice, holy and pleasing to God—this is your true and proper worship.

2 Do not conform to the pattern of this world, but be transformed by the renewing

mind, that ye may prove what is that good, and acceptable, and perfect, will of God.

13:8 Owe no man any thing, but to love one another: for he that loveth another hath fulfilled the law.

9 For this, Thou shalt not commit adultery, Thou shalt not kill, Thou shalt not steal, Thou shalt not bear false witness, Thou shalt not covet; and if there be any other commandment, it is briefly comprehended in this saying, namely, Thou shalt love thy neighbour as thyself.

10 Love worketh no ill to his neighbour: therefore love is the fulfilling of the law.

of your mind. Then you will be able to test and approve what God's will is—his good, pleasing and perfect will.

13:8 Let no debt remain outstanding, except the continuing debt to love one another, for whoever loves others has fulfilled the law.

9 The commandments, "You shall not commit adultery," "You shall not murder," "You shall not steal," "You shall not covet," and whatever other command there may be, are summed up in this one command: "Love your neighbor as yourself."

10 Love does no harm to a neighbor. Therefore love is the fulfillment of the law.

LIGHT ON THE WORD

Sacrifice. This was any object offered to God. The act of sacrifice was central to Israel's religious life. Some sacrifices were animal offerings of lambs, goats, or cows. Sacrifices were prepared with attention to the finest detail. The most pure and healthy animals were offered as they represented something valuable to the worshiper. Other types of sacrifices were given, such as grain and wine, often given in thanksgiving and worship, while the sacrifices of animals were usually intended to atone for sin.

Fulfilling the Law. In the first century, many rabbis encouraged Jews to fulfill or obey the Law. Paul reminds us of how to fulfill God's Law: the best way was to be mindful of our interactions. Jesus answered that to love God and to love our neighbors as ourselves is the greatest commandment. Our responsibility is to love one another unconditionally like Christ loves us. We need Christ in order to accomplish this, and by doing so, we will fulfill the Law.

TEACHING THE BIBLE LESSON

LIFE NEED FOR TODAY'S LESSON

AIM: Students will discover ways to live in a manner that transcends the selfish and corrupt ways of the world.

INTRODUCTION

Transformation and God's Perfect Will

Paul's letters not only explain the theoretical but are also very practical. **Romans 12** begins his shift, turning the theoretical into practical. He goes from the doctrinal to the pragmatic. These practical commands are based on the foundation Paul laid out in **Romans 1–11.** He demonstrated God's mercies and described what Christ has done in the believer's life. Through Christ, the believer has been justified, redeemed, freed from the Law, freed from sin, and made righteous before God. These mercies are aspects of God's grace based not on our experience but the facts of Jesus' work on the Cross.

Because of this work, Paul says we should not only appreciate God's mercy, but apply this in our daily lives by offering ourselves to Him. He presents a metaphor taken directly from Jewish Temple worship of one who commits themselves to a life of love. This life of love expresses itself in the spiritual gifts that God has given us, hospitality and loving our enemies, as well as our obedience to the laws of the land. Paul shows that this Gospel is beautiful in both theory and practice.

BIBLE LEARNING

AIM: Students will discover that Jesus allows believers to fill the law of love in their lives.

I. THE BELIEVER AND GOD (ROMANS 12:1–2)

A Christian's body is the temple of the Holy Spirit (**1 Corinthians 6:19**). We must surrender our bodies, our whole selves, to God. In the Old Testament, animals were killed and presented to God as sacrifices. Here, our entire bodies must be presented as sacrifices, living bodies calling for a total commitment to God. This presentation is not only a responsibility, but also a privilege. The sacrifice is holy and pleasing because of Jesus' blood.

A negative command is given here, "do not conform," along with a positive one, "be ye transformed." Christians should not pattern themselves after the world but diligently allow their minds to be changed and renewed through the Word of God, prayer, and Christian fellowship. This transformation is a process that grows with consistent fellowship with the Holy Spirit. The transformation happens as we renew our minds, causing our bodies to totally commit to God based on our actions. After being transformed, we gain access to God's will, which is perfect because it is His.

Romans 12:1–2, 13:8–10

1 I beseech you therefore, brethren, by the mercies of God, that ye present your bodies a living sacrifice, holy, acceptable unto God, which is your reasonable service.

Paul beseeches (Gk. *parakaleo*, **pah-rah-kah-LEH-oh**) or urges that the body be presented as a living sacrifice. Some choose to become organ donors to help others; however, this sacrifice is not just organs or certain body parts but all of the body.

This sacrifice is different from those made in the Old Testament that were killed; this sacrifice requires life. This indicates that it is a continual, daily, ongoing sacrifice. The entire body is presented to God, our Heavenly Father. This presentation is not only a responsibility but also a privilege; it is holy and pleasing because of Jesus' blood. We have given up sin and been set apart to God; when presented to Him in this manner, it is acceptable to Him.

Furthermore, this commitment is for all. Both church leaders and lay people must all present in the same manner for it to be acceptable (Gk. *euarestos*, **ew-AH-res-tos**) to God. We must do away with sin and make love the center of our lives.

Paul says this is our reasonable (*logikos*, **lo-ghi-KOS**) service (Gk. *latreia*, **lah-TRAY-ah**). The word for service is also used for the service of priests. Now instead of the Temple, the Christian's daily life becomes the arena of worship to God. Paul believes this to be reasonable and proportionate to the "mercies of God," the benefits outlined in previous chapters, as a result of Christ's sacrifice for us.

2 And be not conformed to this world: but be ye transformed by the renewing of your mind, that ye may prove what is that good,

and acceptable, and perfect, will of God.

Two commands are given here. One is negative: be not conformed (Gk. *suschematizo*, **soo-skay-mah-TEED-zoh**) to this world (Gk. *aion*, **eye-OWN**). Here Paul refers not to the actual earth or globe, but the time period we live in. This age is characterized by the Fall and runs according to the pattern of sin and Satan. The word for conform means to be shaped by something external and transitory and does not refer to an inward transformation. We must not live our lives according to the world's ways, which are contrary to the coming age when God's rule will be established and clearly made visible.

The other command is positive: be transformed (Gk. *metamorphoo*, **me-tah-mor-FOH-oh**) by the renewing of the mind. The Greek word means to be changed into another form, the opposite of conforming. It is clear how the transformation will take place, i.e. "by the renewing of your mind." The word for renewing (Gk. *anakainos*, **ah-nah-KEYE-noh-sees**) has the sense of rebuilding and improving something. The Holy Spirit will guide this transformation. As we submit ourselves, the Holy Spirit transforms us by gradually renewing our minds. Daily, we submit ourselves to be transformed and commit ourselves to not conform—the two sides of committing to the Christian life.

The purpose of having a true commitment is so we can test and prove (Gk. *dokimazo*, **do-kee-MOD-zoh**) what God's will is. The word for prove means to judge as worthy or genuine and was often used for testing metals. Additionally, this true commitment also helps us develop the confidence of knowing and trying to realize God's expectations.

II. THE BELIEVER AND HIS FELLOW CITIZENS (ROMANS 13:8–10)

As Christians, we must constantly pay back the debt of love that Christ gave to us, but we will always "owe" more love. We should pay every person in our lives love. Paul says this is what is expected of us from God. God has loved us so much that we owe not only Him but everyone around us the debt of love.

Love has been the core of God's law since the beginning. Jesus says, "Love the Lord your God with all your heart and with all your soul and with all your mind.' This is the first and greatest commandment. And the second is like it: 'Love your neighbor as yourself" (**Matthew 22:36–38**, NIV; cf. **Deuteronomy 6:4–5** and **Leviticus 19:18**). When we love the Lord and all others, we fulfill the law. Paul gives us some examples of what not to do: adultery, murder, steal, or covet. However, we will love God and love our neighbors as ourselves. In sum, Paul repeats, love does not harm its neighbor. When we completely love God and others, the Law is fulfilled.

Indebted to Love Everyone

13:8 Owe no man any thing, but to love one another: for he that loveth another hath fulfilled the law.

As Paul outlines the behaviors of someone who grasps and obeys God's will, he addresses life in the church and obeying the government. Here, the transition from vv. 1–7 goes from what we should pay our rulers to what we should pay everyone. Paul contrasts his earlier words about monetary debts with a commandment to love. He says we are not to owe anyone anything, but we are indebted to love everyone. This is the gift that keeps on giving—we love now and continue to owe love, today and tomorrow and continually, like the living sacrifice mentioned in **12:1**. We don't owe one another another but love.

Through love, you fulfill (Gk. *pleroo,* **play-ROH-oh**) the law. This word means to carry into effect or realization. It is no coincidence that Jesus also said that He came to fulfill the law (**Matthew 5:17**). This is because Jesus is God incarnate and God is love (**1 John 4:8**). Thus, to love is to be aligned with the character and nature of the God of the universe.

9 For this, Thou shalt not commit adultery, Thou shalt not kill, Thou shalt not steal, Thou shalt not bear false witness, Thou shalt not covet; and if there be any other commandment, it is briefly comprehended in this saying, namely, Thou shalt love thy neighbour as thyself. 10 Love worketh no ill to his neighbour: therefore love is the fulfilling of the law.

Paul explains his point in verse 8 about "the law" by here listing examples of that Law. He focuses on five of the Ten Commandments related to loving our neighbor. Paul's examples point out what love looks like: it does not commit adultery, kill, steal, bear false witness, nor covet. These actions would not display love toward a neighbor, and are not Christian characteristics. A Christian may be guilty of doing these actions, but they should be not be daily pursuits in their life. When we love our neighbors, we refrain from breaking thee=se relational commands. The love we have for our neighbor demonstrates our relationship with God. We cannot see God, and our relationship with Him is by faith, but we can see people and interact with them in tangible ways. We can use our words and try to convince others we love God, but our actions prove our true love for Him.

SEARCH THE SCRIPTURES

QUESTION 1
In **Romans 13:8**, Paul declares what debt should we always owe and always pay?

Love.

QUESTION 2
What is the result of love (**13:10**)?

Love does not do any wrong.

LIGHT ON THE WORD
Love Humanity
To display love to God, we must display love to people. We are sorely mistaken if we think we can love God without loving humanity. God is love, and His characteristics should show up in us, His creation. We cannot possibly love God and not love humanity; this is the fulfillment of the Law.

BIBLE APPLICATION

AIM: Students will accept that Christians can show their love for God in their attitude and actions toward others.

Today many in our communities are loaded down with debt and absent of God's love. From payday loans to student loans, the African American community is saddled with obligations to lenders. This greatly hinders our life and witness. **Proverbs 22:7** states that "the rich rule over the poor, and the borrower is servant to the lender" (NIV). While the writer of the time was speaking of actual physical slavery, today we are under financial and psychological slavery as we struggle to make ends meet. Before you take on debt, have a reliable plan for paying it off as soon as you can and read the fine print. You could be taking on more than you bargained for, hindering opportunities to practically love people as Paul exhorted the Romans. Debt hinders our ability to give to Kingdom work or obey God in proclaiming the Gospel, due to working long hours or not having enough money at the end of the month. God wants to free us up to love, and being chained by debt is a sure way to hinder that mandate.

STUDENT'S RESPONSES

AIM: Students will find that believers can create additional ways and opportunities to show the love of Christ to all of creation.

Examine yourself and ask the question, "How do I present my body as a living sacrifice? Do I sincerely make an effort to renew my mind? How? When?" When you come in contact with another person, is your first response to love them? Start today!

PRAYER

Gracious Holy Spirit, each and every day, grant us a renewal of our spirit, our minds, and our hearts. Sustain us as we make sacrifices that are pleasing before God, and fill us with those things that satisfy our thirst, knowledge, and desire for Jesus. In Jesus' Name we pray. Amen.

HOW TO SAY IT

Beseech.   bi-SEECH.

Epoch.   EH-pok.

PREPARE FOR NEXT SUNDAY

Read **Isaiah 11:1-9** and "The Peaceful Kingdom."

DAILY HOME BIBLE READINGS

MONDAY
Diligence and Law
(1 Timothy 4:11–16)

TUESDAY
Obedience and Law
(Deuteronomy 11:1–9)

WEDNESDAY
Choose the Law and Life
(Deuteronomy 11:13–21)

THURSDAY
Take Care and Live
(Joshua 22:1–6)

FRIDAY
Love and the Law
(1 John 3:4–11)

SATURDAY
Prayer and Love
(Ephesians 3:14–21)

SUNDAY
Love Fulfills the Law
(Romans 12:1–2; 13:8–10)

Sources:
Greathouse William M. and George Lyons. *Romans 9–16: A Commentary in the Wesleyan Tradition.* New Beacon Bible Commentary. Kansas City, MO: Beacon Hill Press of Kansas City, 2008.
Moo, Douglas. *Romans.* New International Commentary on the New Testament. Grand Rapids, MI: Wm. B. Eerdmans, 1996.

COMMENTS / NOTES:

_____

_____

_____

_____

_____

_____

_____

_____

_____

_____

_____

_____

_____

_____

ANSWERS TO QUARTERLY QUIZZES

SEPTEMBER • OCTOBER • NOVEMBER 2015

LESSON 1 1. They wanted to serve God with boldness and spread the Word of God because of the opposition they faced; 2. The Lord shook the entire place.

LESSON 2 1. Lacked: To be in need, destitute. Consolation: Help that is near, comfort, encouragement; 2. Selfishness or not believing they have enough to share.

LESSON 3 1. Peter and the other apostles said that they are to obey God rather than men; 2. Theudas and Judas of Galilee.

LESSON 4 1. Hellenist Jew; 2. Solomon built God a temple.

LESSON 5 1. The people of Samaria had accepted God's message; 2. Philip

LESSON 6 1. Doubted; 2. Damascus.

LESSON 7 1. God had revealed to Peter than no one is unclean; 2. Simon, a tanner; Peter.

LESSON 8 1. Three represents something established by God; 2. They were his witnesses to what would happen and could testify to God's faithfulness.

LESSON 9 1. Four squads of four soldiers; 2. Praying without ceasing.

LESSON 10 1. Hearts, difference, faith; 2. The Gentiles were converted.

LESSON 11 1. The riverside in Philippi; 2. Lydia encouraged them to stay so that she and her household could learn more.

LESSON 12 1. God-fearing Greek men and quite a few prominent women; 2. The Bereans were more open-minded than the Thessalonians. They listened and searched the Scriptures every day to see if Paul and Silas were speaking the truth.

LESSON 13 1. To be held by, closely occupied with any business; 2. Paul shaved his head according to Jewish custom to mark the end of a vow.

DECEMBER 2015 • JANUARY • FEBRUARY 2016

LESSON 1 1. holy; 2. circumcision, Abrahamic Covenant; rainbow, Noahic Covenant; baptism, new covenant

LESSON 2 1. Believers are to "present their bodies as living sacrifices, holy, and acceptable unto God"; 2. Male animals—a bull, a ram, and a male goat.

LESSON 3   1. Redeem means to ransom or buy back; 2. The death of every firstborn child and animal that was not under the protective covering of the blood on the doorpost.

LESSON 4   1. Hupsoo; to raise on high, lift up; 2. Hypocrisy.

LESSON 5   1. Loved; he agreed to work for Laban for seven more years; 2. Laban is Jacob's uncle, as well as a planner, shrewd negotiator, trickster, and father of two daughters, Leah and Rachel. Jacob means "supplanter" or "heel catcher."

LESSON 6   1. Tizrah and Jerusalem; 2. Inner and outer beauty

LESSON 7   1. King Jehu; 2. Lo-ruhamah and Lo-ammi.

LESSON 8   1. Jesus, the disciples, and Jesus' mother Mary; 2. They believed in Him.

LESSON 9   1. Spoken, cried, loud, voice, come, forth; 2. Believe

LESSON 10   1. A year-old male lamb or goat; 2. Memorial, Lord.

LESSON 11   1. 50 days; 2. The priest will lift up the bread and the two lambs as a special offering to the Lord that is holy to Him, and belongs to the priest.

LESSON 12   1. It was observed because Israel needed to atone for their sins and failures on a yearly basis so God could dwell among them; 2. Holy of Holies, purification; no one.

LESSON 13   1. Declare an official day for no one to do ordinary work; 2. Palm trees (good trees), leafy trees (thick trees), willows that grow by the stream.

MARCH • APRIL • MAY 2016

LESSON 1   1. Lack of faith; prayer and fasting; 2. Moral authority.

LESSON 2   1. Many, last, first; 2. He needs to sell everything he has and give to the poor.

LESSON 3   1. They sang a hymn and left to go into the Mount of Olives; 2. He did not.

LESSON 4   1. They bought sweet spices (to anoint Jesus' body); 2. The women left quickly and ran from the sepulcher; they trembled and were amazed, and did not say anything to anyone because of their fear.

LESSON 5   1. Capernaum; 2. The elders of the Jews.

LESSON 6	1. A Pharisee; 2. The woman who anointed his feet with oil, and "Who is this that forgiveth sins also?"
LESSON 7	1. He lived outside of the city in a cemetery, he wore no clothes, and he did not live in a house; 2. The man who was possessed was healed from the demons.
LESSON 8	1. He became a citizen of another country and had a job feeding pigs/swine; 2. Sinned, heaven, his, father.
LESSON 9	1. Seven; seven; thou shalt forgive him; 2. False.
LESSON 10	1. Samaria and Galilee; 2. Samaritan; the Jews hated Samaritans.
LESSON 11	1. Those who trusted in themselves, who were righteous and despised others; 2. "God be merciful to me a sinner."
LESSON 12	1. They rebuked the parents; 2. He took them in His arms, placed His hands on them, and blessed them.
LESSON 13	1. Negatively. As a tax collector, he worked for the Roman government and often cheated people; 2. Murmured.

JUNE • JULY • AUGUST 2016

LESSON 1	1. Zephaniah was born during the reign of Manasseh and prophesied during the reign of Josiah; 2. A day of trouble and distress.
LESSON 2	1. A remnant; 2. Jealousy
LESSON 3	1. O daughter of Zion; be glad and rejoice, Jerusalem; 2. To gather the people together; bring them home; a good name; and their fortune will be restored.
LESSON 4	1. They become futile in their thinking and their foolish hearts become darkened; 2. They not only do sinful practices but approve of those who practice them.
LESSON 5	1. Obey God's law; 2. False
LESSON 6	1. Psalm 14:2–3; 2. Snake venom.
LESSON 7	1. Righteousness, all, believe, difference; 2. His grace.
LESSON 8	1. Jesus came and died for the ungodly at the right time; 2. Jesus' blood, God's condemnation.
LESSON 9	1. Baptism was the ritual for non-Jews to convert to Judaism based on Levitical law; 2. One-third of the Roman Empire were slaves who could be acquired through war, piracy, kidnapping, seizing infants, and criminal sentencing.

LESSON 10 1. nothing; famine (hunger) or peril (danger); 2. Jesus, first, us

LESSON 11 1. God is the one who chooses to show mercy and not us; 2. God chose Pharaoh to display God's power through him and share God's fame throughout the world.

LESSON 12 1. God wanted the Israelites to become jealous and claim salvation for themselves; 2. A wild olive tree

LESSON 13 1. The renewing of their minds; 2. "Thou shalt love thy neighbor as thyself."

GLOSSARY

A

Abomination: A foul and detestable thing

Affliction: Anguish, burden, persecution, tribulation, or trouble

Angel: A messenger of God, not eternal or all-knowing; specific types include cherubim and seraphim

Ascension: Raising up in authority or physical place. Can especially refer to the event forty days after Jesus' death, burial, and Resurrection, when He went returned to heaven to sit at the right hand of the Father (Acts 1:9–11)

Atone: To propitiate, satisfy the demands of an offended holy God; or reconcile to a holy God after sin

B

Baptize: To dip, immerse, or submerge

Blameless: Irreproachable, faultless, flawless

Blessedness: Happiness, joy, or prosperity, to be well spoken of by God or others

Bless the Lord: To bend the knee in praise to God

Blood of the Lamb: The blood that Jesus shed on the Cross that redeems humanity

Bowels: To ancient Middle Easterners, the place of emotion, distress, or love

C

Called by God: Appointed or commissioned to fulfill a task

Charge: Admonish, order, command

Chosen: To be approved and selected by God

Christ: The Anointed One, The expected Messiah the Jews hoped for and whom Christians believe came as Jesus of Nazareth

Commandments: God's mandates; the entire body of Laws issued by God through Moses for Israel

Conduct: Manner of living

Confess: To acknowledge or fully agree

Consider: To determine or make out

Covenant: An agreement or promise between God and humanity based on God's character, strength, and grace

Crucifixion: A method of Roman execution in which a criminals was hung on a cross

D

Decalogue: From "ten words" in Greek; the Ten Commandments

Desolation: The state of being deserted or uninhabited

Disciples: Learners, students, followers

Dominion: Rule or reign

Dwelling place: A person's refuge or home

E

El: The Hebrew word for "god" or "mighty one"

Evil: Bad, unpleasant, or displeasing things

Evil doer: A malefactor, wrongdoer, criminal, troublemaker

Evil spirits: Messengers and ministers of the devil

Exalt: To raise up to the highest degree possible

Exhortation: Giving someone motivation to change his or her behavior either by rebuke or encouragement

F

Faithfulness: Steadfastness, steadiness

Fear of the Lord: Reverence or awe of who God is resulting in obedience to Him and abstaining from evil

G

Glory: Splendor, unparalleled honor, dignity, or distinction; praise, and worship

God's Bride: The church

God's own hand: God's strength, power

Gospel: The Good News of Jesus the Messiah's arrival and founding of His kingdom

Graven image: An idol cut (often from stone, wood, or metal) and worshiped as a god

Great Tribulation: A time of great suffering that has not been experienced since the world began (Matthew

24:21, Revelation 7:14)

H
Hallowed: Consecrated, dedicated, or set apart

Hear: Listen to, yield to, or obey

Hearken: Pay attention to, give attention to

Heart: The figurative place of emotion and passion

Heathens: The Gentiles, all those who are not a part of the people of God

Holy: Anything consecrated and set aside for sacred use; set apart from sin

Honor: To revere or value

Host: An army or vast number

I
Idolatry: The worship of anything other than God

Infidel: One who is unfaithful, unbelieving, and not to be trusted

Iniquity: Perversity, depravity, guilt, sin

J
Just: Righteous, that which is right and fair

Justice: Righteousness in government

K
Kingdom of Christ: The rule and reign of Christ as king both now and in the age to come

L
Law: Either the Mosiac Law or any human law; synonyms include commandments, ordinances, statutes, legal regulations, authoritative instructions, and teachings

Logos (LOW-gos): (Gk.) Word; the Word of God, either the Bible or Jesus

M
Manna: Food from heaven baked into a kind of bread, which God miraculously gave to the Israelites in the wilderness

Messiah: The Anointed One

Minister: A servant, an attendant, one who executes the commands of another

Mosiac Law: The law passed down by Moses from God to the Hebrew people at Mt. Sinai

O
Omnipotent: All powerful

Omnipresent: All present, being everywhere

Omniscient: All knowing

Ordained: Established and founded by God; founded, fixed, or appointed

P
Parousia (par-oo-SEE-ah): (Gk.) presence; Christ's Second Coming

Peace: Wholeness, quietness, contentment, health, prosperity; more than an absence of conflict or problems, but every part of life being blessed.

Pentateuch: The first five books of the Old Testament

Power: Boldness, might, or strength, especially God's

Prophets: People filled with the Spirit of God and under the authority and command of God, who pleaded His cause and urged humanity to be saved

Profit: To gain or benefit

Prosper: To succeed, especially in spiritual things; to move forward or succeed in one's efforts

Proved: Examined, tested, tried

Psalm: A piece of music or a melody, especially one dedicated to God or a god

Purity: Sinlessness, without blemish spiritually

R
Ransom: To buy back or pay a price for a person, buying their freedom

Redeem: To ransom or purchase

Refuge: A shelter from rain, storm, or danger; stronghold or fortress; a place to run to and be secure when the enemy threatens

Repent: To turn back from sin and turn to God in faith

Righteous: To be declared not guilty

Righteousness: Justness, rightness, especially God's, which He works as a gift in His people; the right way to live as opposed to a lifestyle that treats others unfairly or unjustly

S

Sabbath: From "ceasing (from work)" in Hebrew; the day set aside to worship God

Sanctuary: The holy place, either in the tabernacle or the temple

Salvation: Rescue, safety, or deliverance, especially from eternal punishment

Satan: A fallen angel who is opposed to God and His people

Savior: A defender, rescuer, or deliverer, A term applied to Christ as the rescuer of those who are in bondage to sin and death

Scribes: Secretaries, recorders, men skilled in the Law during Jesus' day

Selah (SEE-lah): (Heb.) A pause in singing to allow for an instrumental musical interlude or silent meditation.

Septuagint: "Seventy" in Latin; the Greek translation of the Hebrew Old Testament made by 70 Jewish scholars beginning in the third century BC.

Servant: A slave, subject, or worshiper

Shalom (sha-LOME): (Heb.) Peace, prosperity, blessing

Shekinah Glory: The awesome presence of the Lord; His honor, fame, and reputation

Shofar (sho-FAR): (Heb.) A ram's horn; commonly used in celebration, as well as in signaling armies or large groups of people in civil assembly

Soul: The immaterial part of a person (what leaves the body after death), or to the whole being, the self, one's life

Stiffnecked: Obstinate and difficult

Strengthen: To secure, make firm

Strive: To struggle, to exert oneself

Supplication: Seeking, asking, entreating, pleading, imploring, or petitioning

T

Tabernacle: A tent; the name of the portable temple constructed by Moses and the people of Israel

Tetragrammaton: YHWH; the four consonants of God's name, as the Jews would often write it

Torah: (Heb.) Law, instrument, or direction; the first five books of the Old Testament

Transfiguration: A change or transformation. Often refers to Jesus' transformation while on the Mount of Olives with His disciples Peter, James, and John, when His face shone like the sun and His clothing was white as snow (Matthew 17:2; Mark 9:2; Luke 9:29).

Transgression: Sin, rebellion, breaking God's Law

Try: In the sense of a test: refined or purified

Trumpet: A ram's horn or simple metal tube used in celebration as well as in signaling armies or large groups of people in civil assembly

V

Vanity (vain): A waste, a worthless thing, or simply emptiness

W

Wisdom: Prudence, an understanding of ethics

Woe: Grief or sorrow

Worship: Bow down deeply, show obedience and reverence

Wrath: Burning anger, rage

Y

Yahweh: God's name, often spelled with consonants only (see Tetragrammaton)

OUR AFFIRMATION OF FAITH

is a reminder of the basic beliefs of the Church Of God In Christ. It witnesses to the reality that God has been active in creation, history, and our lives. Being Trinitarian, our affirmation focuses on the work of the Father, Son, and Holy Spirit, while proclaiming the Gospel holistically. God tells us through Scripture that salvation is available to all through Jesus Christ.

Our Affirmation of Faith is woven throughout the testifying, singing, praying, preaching, and teaching of the Church. Hence, one can hear the cardinal beliefs through these events.

The affirmation makes no pretense of being exhaustive, or being a complete statement of all our beliefs. It presents a set of key beliefs that are grounded in Scripture.

The affirmation echoes the classic testimony: "Giving honor to God in the highest and to the Lord Jesus Christ, I thank God that I'm saved, sanctified, and filled with the Holy Ghost." Our theology begins with God; the doctrine of God shapes all other doctrines for the Church Of God In Christ.

The Church Of God In Christ — Affirmation of Faith

We Believe the Bible to be the inspired and only infallible written Word of God,

We Believe that there is One God, eternally existent in three Persons; God the Father,

God the Son, and God the Holy Spirit.

We Believe in the Blessed Hope, which is the rapture of the Church of God, which is in

Christ at His return.

We Believe that the only means of being cleansed from sin, is through

repentance and faith in the precious Blood of Jesus Christ.

We Believe that regeneration by the Holy Ghost is absolutely essential

for personal salvation.

We Believe that the redemptive work of Christ on the Cross provides

healing for the human body in answer to believing prayer.

We Believe that the Baptism in the Holy Ghost, according to Acts 2:4,

is given to believers who ask for it.

We Believe in the sanctifying power of the Holy Spirit, by whose indwelling,

the Christian is enabled to live a Holy and separated life in this present world.

Amen.

THE SYMBOL OF THE CHURCH OF GOD IN CHRIST

The Symbol of the Church Of God In Christ is an outgrowth of the Presiding Bishop's Coat of Arms, which has become quite familiar to the Church. The design of the Official Seal of the Church was created in 1973 and adopted in the General Assembly in 1981 (July Session).

The obvious GARNERED WHEAT in the center of the seal represents all of the people of the Church Of God In Christ, Inc. The ROPE of wheat that holds the shaft together represents the Founding Father of the Church, Bishop Charles Harrison Mason, who, at the call of the Lord, banded us together as a Brotherhood of Churches in the First Pentecostal General Assembly of the Church, in 1907.

The date in the seal has a two-fold purpose: first, to tell us that Bishop Mason received the baptism of the Holy Ghost in March 1907 and, second, to tell us that it was because of this outpouring that Bishop Mason was compelled to call us together in February of 1907 to organize the Church Of God In Christ.

The RAIN in the background represents the Latter Rain, or the End-time Revivals, which brought about the emergence of our Church along with other Pentecostal Holiness Bodies in the same era. The rain also serves as a challenge to the Church to keep Christ in the center of our worship and service, so that He may continue to use the Church Of God In Christ as one of the vehicles of Pentecostal Revival before the return of the Lord.

This information was reprinted from the book *So You Want to KNOW YOUR CHURCH* by Alferd Z. Hall, Jr.

COGIC AFFIRMATION OF FAITH

We believe the Bible to be the inspired and only infallible written Word of God.

We believe that there is One God, eternally existent in three Persons: God the Father, God the Son, and God the Holy Spirit.

We believe in the Blessed Hope, which is the rapture of the Church of God, which is in Christ at His return.

We believe that the only means of being cleansed from sin is through repentance and faith in the precious Blood of Jesus Christ.

We believe that regeneration by the Holy Ghost is absolutely essential for personal salvation.

We believe that the redemptive work of Christ on the Cross provides healing for the human body in answer to believing in prayer.

We believe that the baptism in the Holy Ghost, according to Acts 2:4, is given to believers who ask for it.

We believe in the sanctifying power of the Holy Spirit, by whose indwelling the Christian is enabled to live a Holy and separated life in this present world. Amen.

The Doctrines of the Church Of God In Christ

THE BIBLE

We believe that the Bible is the Word of God and contains one harmonious and sufficiently complete system of doctrine. We believe in the full inspiration of the Word of God. We hold the Word of God to be the only authority in all matters and assert that no doctrine can be true or essential if it does not find a place in this Word.

THE FATHER

We believe in God, the Father Almighty, the Author and Creator of all things. The Old Testament reveals God in diverse manners, by manifesting His nature, character, and dominions. The Gospels in the New Testament give us knowledge of God the "Father" or "My Father," showing the relationship of God to Jesus as Father, or representing Him as the Father in the Godhead, and Jesus himself that Son (St. John 15:8, 14:20). Jesus also gives God the distinction of "Fatherhood" to all believers when He explains God in the light of "Your Father in Heaven" (St. Matthew 6:8).

THE SON

We believe that Jesus Christ is the Son of God, the second person in the Godhead of the Trinity or Triune Godhead. We believe that Jesus was and is eternal in His person and nature as the Son of God who was with God in the beginning of creation (St. John 1:1). We believe that Jesus Christ was born of a virgin called Mary according to the Scripture (St. Matthew 1:18), thus giving rise to our fundamental belief in the Virgin Birth and to all of the miraculous events surrounding the phenomenon (St. Matthew 1:18–25). We believe that Jesus Christ became the "suffering servant" to man; this suffering servant came seeking to redeem man from sin and to reconcile him to God, His Father (Romans 5:10). We believe that Jesus Christ is standing now as mediator between God and man (I Timothy 2:5).

THE HOLY GHOST

We believe the Holy Ghost or Holy Spirit is the third person of the Trinity; proceeds from the Father and the Son; is of the same substance, equal to power and glory; and is together with the Father and the Son, to be believed in, obeyed, and worshiped. The Holy Ghost is a gift bestowed upon the believer for the purpose of equipping and empowering the believer, making him or her a more effective witness for service in the world. He teaches and guides one into all truth (John 16:13; Acts 1:8, 8:39).

THE BAPTISM OF THE HOLY GHOST

We believe that the Baptism of the Holy Ghost is an experience subsequent to conversion and sanctification and that tongue-speaking is the consequence of the baptism in the Holy Ghost with the manifestations of the fruit of the Spirit (Galatians 5:22–23; Acts 10:46, 19:1–6). We believe that we are not baptized with the Holy Ghost in order to be saved (Acts 19:1–6; John 3:5). When one receives a baptismal Holy Ghost experience, we believe one will speak with a tongue unknown to oneself according to the sovereign will of Christ. To be filled with the Spirit means to be Spirit controlled as expressed by Paul in Ephesians 5:18,19. Since the charismatic demonstrations were necessary to help the early church to be successful in implementing the command of Christ, we, therefore, believe that a Holy Ghost experience is mandatory for all believers today.

MAN

We believe that humankind was created holy by God, composed of body, soul, and spirit. We believe that humankind, by nature, is sinful and unholy. Being born in sin, a person needs to be born again, sanctified and cleansed from all sins by the blood of Jesus. We believe that one is saved by confessing and forsaking one's sins, and believing on the Lord Jesus Christ, and that having become a child of God, by being born again and adopted into the family of God, one may, and should, claim the inheritance of the sons of God, namely the baptism of the Holy Ghost.

SIN

Sin, the Bible teaches, began in the angelic world (Ezekiel 28:11–19; Isaiah 14:12–20) and is transmitted into the blood of the human race through disobedience and deception motivated by unbelief (I Timothy 2:14). Adam's sin, committed by eating of the forbidden fruit from the tree of knowledge of good and evil, carried with it permanent pollution or depraved human nature to all his descendants. This is called "original sin." Sin can now be defined as a volitional transgression against God and a lack of conformity to the will of God. We, therefore, conclude that humankind by nature is sinful and has fallen from a glorious and righteous state from which we were created, and has become unrighteous and unholy. We therefore, must be restored to the state of holiness from which we have fallen by being born again (St. John 3:7).

SALVATION

Salvation deals with the application of the work of redemption to the sinner with restoration to divine favor and communion with God. This redemptive operation of the Holy Ghost upon sinners is brought about by repentance toward God and faith toward our Lord Jesus Christ which brings conversion, faith, justification, regeneration, sanctification, and the baptism of the Holy Ghost. Repentance is the work of God, which results in a change of mind in respect to a person's relationship to God

(St. Matthew 3:1–2, 4:17; Acts 20:21). Faith is a certain conviction wrought in the heart by the Holy Spirit, as to the truth of the Gospel and a heart trust in the promises of God in Christ (Romans 1:17, 3:28; St. Matthew 9:22; Acts 26:18). Conversion is that act of God whereby He causes the regenerated sinner, in one's conscious life, to turn to Him in repentance and faith (II Kings 5:15; II Chronicles 33:12,13; St. Luke 19:8,9; Acts 8:30). Regeneration is the act of God by which the principle of the new life is implanted in humankind, the governing disposition of soul is made holy, and the first holy exercise of this new disposition is secured. Sanctification is that gracious and continuous operation of the Holy Ghost, by which He delivers the justified sinner from the pollution of sin, renews a person's whole nature in the image of God, and enables one to perform good works (Romans 6:4, 5:6; Colossians 2:12, 3:1).

ANGELS

The Bible uses the term "angel" (a heavenly body) clearly and primarily to denote messengers or ambassadors of God with such Scripture references as Revelations 4:5, which indicates their duty in Heaven to praise God (Psalm 103:20), to do God's will (St. Matthew 18:10), and to behold His face. But since Heaven must come down to earth, they also have a mission to earth. The Bible indicates that they accompanied God in the Creation, and also that they will accompany Christ in His return in Glory.

DEMONS

Demons denote unclean or evil spirits; they are sometimes called devils or demonic beings. They are evil spirits, belonging to the unseen or spiritual realm, embodied in human beings. The Old Testament refers to the prince of demons, sometimes called Satan (adversary) or Devil, as having power and wisdom, taking the habitation of other forms such as the serpent (Genesis 3:1). The New Testament speaks of the Devil as Tempter (St. Matthew 4:3), and it goes on to tell the works of Satan, the Devil, and demons as combating righteousness and good in any form, proving to be an adversary to the saints. Their chief power is exercised to destroy the mission of Jesus Christ. It can well be said that the Christian Church believes in demons, Satan, and devils. We believe in their power and purpose. We believe they can be subdued and conquered as in the commandment to the believer by Jesus. "In my name they shall cast out Satan and the work of the Devil and to resist him and then he will flee (WITHDRAW) from you" (St. Mark 16:17).

THE CHURCH

The Church forms a spiritual unity of which Christ is the divine head. It is animated by one Spirit, the Spirit of Christ. It professes one faith, shares one hope, and serves one King. It is the citadel of the truth and God's agency for communicating to believers all spiritual blessings. The Church then is the object of our faith rather than of knowledge. The name of our Church, "CHURCH OF GOD IN CHRIST," is supported by I Thessalonians 2:14 and other passages in the Pauline Epistles. The word "CHURCH" or "EKKLESIA" was first applied to the Christian society by Jesus Christ in St. Matthew 16:18, the occasion being that of His benediction of Peter at Caesarea Philippi.

THE SECOND COMING OF CHRIST

We believe in the second coming of Christ; that He shall come from Heaven to earth, personally, bodily, visibly (Acts 1:11; Titus 2:11–13; St. Matthew 16:27, 24:30, 25:30; Luke 21:27; John 1:14, 17; Titus 2:11); and that the Church, the bride, will be caught up to meet Him in the air (I Thessalonians 4:16–17). We admonish all

who have this hope to purify themselves as He is pure.

DIVINE HEALING

The Church Of God In Christ believes in and practices Divine Healing. It is a commandment of Jesus to the Apostles (St. Mark 16:18). Jesus affirms His teachings on healing by explaining to His disciples, who were to be Apostles, that healing the afflicted is by faith (St. Luke 9:40–41). Therefore, we believe that healing by faith in God has scriptural support and ordained authority. St. James's writings in his epistle encourage Elders to pray for the sick, lay hands upon them and to anoint them with oil, and state that prayers with faith shall heal the sick and the Lord shall raise them up. Healing is still practiced widely and frequently in the Church Of God In Christ, and testimonies of healing in our Church testify to this fact.

MIRACLES

The Church Of God In Christ believes that miracles occur to convince people that the Bible is God's Word. A miracle can be defined as an extraordinary visible act of divine power, wrought by the efficient agency of the will of God, which has as its final cause the vindication of the righteousness of God's Word. We believe that the works of God, which were performed during the beginnings of Christianity, do and will occur even today where God is preached, faith in Christ is exercised, the Holy Ghost is active, and the Gospel is promulgated in the truth (Acts 5:15, 6:8, 9:40; Luke 4:36, 7:14, 15, 5:5, 6; St. Mark 14:15).

THE ORDINANCES OF THE CHURCH

It is generally admitted that for an ordinance to be valid, it must have been instituted by Christ. When we speak of ordinances of the church, we are speaking of those instituted by Christ, in which by sensible signs the grace of God in Christ and the benefits of the covenant of grace are represented, sealed, and applied to believers, and these in turn give expression to their faith and allegiance to God. The Church Of God In Christ recognizes three ordinances as having been instituted by Christ himself and, therefore, are binding upon the church practice.

THE LORD'S SUPPER (HOLY COMMUNION)

The Lord's Supper symbolizes the Lord's death and suffering for the benefit and in the place of His people. It also symbolizes the believer's participation in the crucified Christ. It represents not only the death of Christ as the object of faith, which unites the believers to Christ, but also the effect of this act as the giving of life, strength, and joy to the soul. The communicant by faith enters into a special spiritual union of one's soul with the glorified Christ.

FOOT WASHING

Foot washing is practiced and recognized as an ordinance in our Church because Christ, by His example, showed that humility characterized greatness in the Kingdom of God, and that service rendered to others gave evidence that humility, motivated by love, exists. These services are held subsequent to the Lord's Supper; however, its regularity is left to the discretion of the pastor in charge.

WATER BAPTISM

We believe that Water Baptism is necessary as instructed by Christ in St. John 3:5, "UNLESS MAN BE BORN AGAIN OF WATER AND OF THE SPIRIT..."

However, we do not believe that water baptism alone is a means of salvation, but is an outward demonstration that one has already had a conversion experience and has accepted Christ as his personal Savior. As Pentecostals, we practice immersion in preference to sprinkling because immersion corresponds more closely to the death, burial, and Resurrection of our Lord (Colossians 2:12). It also symbolizes regeneration and purification more than any other mode. Therefore, we practice immersion as our mode of baptism. We believe that we should use the Baptismal Formula given to us by Christ for all "...IN THE NAME OF THE FATHER, AND OF THE SON, AND OF THE HOLY GHOST..." (Matthew 28:19).

NOTES

NOTES

NOTES

NOTES

NOTES

Suggested Order of Service

1. Call to order.

2. Singing.

3. Prayer.

4. Responsive reading:

Supt.: Behold, how good and how pleasant it is for brethren to dwell together in unity!

Psalm 133:1

School: And let the peace of God rule in your hearts, to the which also ye are called in one body; and be ye thankful.

Colossians 3:15

Supt.: Blessed are they that dwell in thy house: they will be still praising thee.

Psalm 84:4

School: Praise ye the LORD. I will praise the LORD with my whole heart, in the assembly of the upright, and in the congregation.

Psalm 111:1

Supt.: And the LORD said unto him, I have heard thy prayer and thy supplication, that thou hast made before me: I have hallowed this house, which thou hast built, to put my name there for ever; and mine eyes and mine heart shall be there perpetually.

1 Kings 9:3

School: Ye shall keep my sabbaths, and reverence my sanctuary: I am the LORD.

Leviticus 19:30

Supt.: And I say also unto thee, That thou art Peter, and upon this rock I will build my church; and the gates of hell shall not prevail against it.

Matthew 16:18

School: My soul longeth, yea, even fainteth for the courts of the LORD: my heart and my flesh crieth out for the living God.

Psalm 84:2

Supt.: And other sheep I have, which are not of this fold: them also I must bring, and they shall hear my voice; and there shall be one fold, and one shepherd.

John 10:16

School: But if I tarry long, that thou mayest know how thou oughtest to behave thyself in the house of God, which is the church of the living God, the pillar and ground of the truth.

1 Timothy 3:15

All: Lift up your hands in the sanctuary, and bless the LORD.

Psalm 134:2

5. Singing.

6. Reading lesson by school and superintendent.

7. Classes assemble for lesson study.

8. Sunday School offering.

9. Five-minute warning bell.

10. Closing bell.

11. Brief lesson review by pastor or superintendent.

12. Secretary's report.

13. Announcements.

14. Dismissal.